# Children's
# Literature
# Review

# Guide to Gale Literary Criticism Series

**When you need to review criticism of literary works, these are the Gale series to use:**

**If the author's death date is:**

      **You should turn to:**

After Dec. 31, 1959
(or author is still living)

**CONTEMPORARY LITERARY CRITICISM**

for example: Jorge Luis Borges, Anthony Burgess,
William Faulkner, Mary Gordon,
Ernest Hemingway, Iris Murdoch

1900 through 1959

**TWENTIETH-CENTURY LITERARY CRITICISM**

for example: Willa Cather, F. Scott Fitzgerald,
Henry James, Mark Twain, Virginia Woolf

1800 through 1899

**NINETEENTH-CENTURY LITERATURE CRITICISM**

for example: Fedor Dostoevski, George Sand,
Gerard Manley Hopkins, Emily Dickinson

1400 through 1799

**LITERATURE CRITICISM FROM 1400 TO 1800**
**(excluding Shakespeare)**

for example: Anne Bradstreet, Pierre Corneille,
Daniel Defoe, Alexander Pope,
Jonathan Swift, Phillis Wheatley

**SHAKESPEAREAN CRITICISM**

Shakespeare's plays and poetry

---

**Gale also publishes related criticism series:**

**CONTEMPORARY ISSUES CRITICISM**

Presents criticism on contemporary authors writing
on current issues. Topics covered include the social
sciences, philosophy, economics, natural science, law,
and related areas.

**CHILDREN'S LITERATURE REVIEW**

Covers authors of all eras. Presents criticism on
authors and author/illustrators who write for the
preschool to junior-high audience.

ISSN 0362-4145

volume 8

# Children's Literature Review

Excerpts from Reviews,
Criticism, and Commentary
on Books for Children

Guest Essay, "Children's Books about Blacks:
A Mid-Eighties Status Report,"
by Rudine Sims

**Gerard J. Senick**
Editor

Gale Research Company
Book Tower
Detroit, Michigan 48226

## STAFF

Gerard J. Senick, *Editor*

Susan Miller Harig, Melissa Reiff Hug, *Senior Assistant Editors*

Jeanne A. Gough, Motoko Fujishiro Huthwaite, *Assistant Editors*

Sharon R. Gunton, *Contributing Editor*

Lizbeth A. Purdy, *Production Supervisor*
Denise Michlewicz Broderick, *Production Coordinator*
Eric Berger, *Assistant Production Coordinator*
Robin L. DuBlanc, Kelly King Howes, *Editorial Assistants*

Victoria B. Cariappa, *Research Coordinator*
Jeannine Schiffman Davidson, *Assistant Research Coordinator*
Kevin John Campbell, Rebecca Nicholaides, Leslie Kyle Schell, Valerie J. Webster, *Research Assistants*

Linda M. Pugliese, *Manuscript Coordinator*
Donna D. Craft, *Assistant Manuscript Coordinator*
Colleen M. Crane, Maureen A. Puhl, Rosetta Irene Simms, *Manuscript Assistants*

L. Elizabeth Hardin, *Permissions Supervisor*
Janice M. Mach, *Permissions Coordinator*
Patricia A. Seefelt, *Assistant Permissions Coordinator, Illustrations*
Margaret A. Chamberlain, Mary M. Matuz, Susan D. Nobles, *Senior Permissions Assistants*
Sandra C. Davis, Kathy Grell, Josephine M. Keene, *Permissions Assistants*
H. Diane Cooper, Dorothy J. Fowler, Yolanda Parker, Mabel E. Schoening, *Permissions Clerks*

Arthur Chartow, *Art Director*

Frederick G. Ruffner, *Publisher*
James M. Ethridge, *Executive Vice-President/Editorial*
Dedria Bryfonski, *Editorial Director*
Christine Nasso, *Director, Literature Division*
Laurie Lanzen Harris, *Senior Editor, Literary Criticism Series*

Since this page cannot legibly accommodate all the copyright notices,
the Appendix constitutes an extension of the copyright notice.

Copyright © 1985 by Gale Research Company

Library of Congress Catalog Card Number 75-34953
ISBN 0-8103-0333-7
ISSN 0362-4145

Computerized photocomposition by
Typographics, Incorporated
Kansas City, Missouri

Printed in the United States

R
628.5
C536
v.8

# CONTENTS

40740

# PREFACE

As children's literature has evolved into both a respected branch of creative writing and a successful industry, literary criticism has documented and influenced each stage of its growth. Critics have recorded the literary development of individual authors as well as the trends and controversies that resulted from changes in values and attitudes, especially as they concerned children. While defining a philosophy of children's literature, critics developed a scholarship that balances an appreciation of children and an awareness of their needs with standards for literary quality much like those required by critics of adult literature. *Children's Literature Review* (*CLR*) is designed to provide a permanent, accessible record of this ongoing scholarship. Those responsible for bringing children and books together can now make informed choices when selecting reading materials for the young.

## Scope of the Series

Each biannual volume contains excerpts from published criticism on the literary works of authors and author/illustrators who create books for children from preschool to junior high age. The author list for each volume is international in scope and represents the variety of genres covered by children's literature—picture books, fiction, folklore, nonfiction, poetry, and drama. The works of approximately fifteen to forty authors of all eras are represented in each volume. Although earlier volumes of *CLR* emphasized critical material published after 1960, recent volumes have expanded their coverage to encompass criticism written before 1960. Since many of the authors included in *CLR* are living and continue to write, it is necessary to update their entries periodically. Thus, future volumes will supplement the entries of selected authors covered in earlier volumes as well as present criticism on the works of authors new to the series.

## Organization of the Book

An author section consists of the following elements: author heading, author portrait, author introduction, excerpts of criticism (each followed by a bibliographical citation), and illustrations, when available.

- The **author heading** consists of the author's full name followed by birth and death dates. The portion of the name outside the parentheses denotes the form under which the author is most frequently published. If the majority of the author's works for children were written under a pseudonym, the pseudonym will be listed in the author heading and the real name given on the first line of the author introduction. Also located at the beginning of the introduction are any other pseudonyms used by the author in writing for children and any name variations, including transliterated forms for authors whose languages use nonroman alphabets. Uncertainty as to a birth or death date is indicated by a question mark.

- An **author portrait** is included when available.

- The **author introduction** contains information designed to introduce an author to *CLR* users by presenting an overview of the author's themes and styles, biographical facts that relate to his or her literary career, a summary of critical response to the author's works, and information about major awards and prizes the author has received. Where applicable, introductions conclude with references to additional entries in biographical and critical reference series published by Gale Research Company. These sources include past volumes of *CLR* as well as *Contemporary Authors, Something about the Author, Yesterday's Authors of Books for Children, Contemporary Literary Criticism, Twentieth-Century Literary Criticism, Nineteenth-Century Literature Criticism, Dictionary of Literary Biography,* and *Authors in the News.*

- **Criticism** is located in three sections: **author's commentary** and **general commentary** (when available) and within individual **title entries,** which are preceded by **title entry headings.** Criticism is arranged chronologically within each section. Titles by authors being profiled are highlighted in boldface type within the text for easier access by readers.

The **author's commentary** presents background material written by the author or by an interviewer. This commentary may cover a specific work or several works. Author's commentary on more than one work appears after the author introduction, while commentary on an individual book follows the title entry heading.

The **general commentary** consists of critical excerpts that consider more than one work by the author being profiled. General commentary is preceded by the critic's name in boldface type or, in the cases of unsigned criticism, by the title of the journal.

**Title entry headings** precede the criticism on a title and cite publication information on the work being reviewed. Title headings list the work's title as it appeared in its country of origin; titles in languages using nonroman alphabets are transliterated. If the original title is in a language other than English, the title of the first English-language translation follows in brackets. The work's first publication date is listed in parentheses following the title. Differing U.S. and British titles of works originally published in English follow the publication date within the parentheses.

**Title entries** consist of critical excerpts on the author's individual works, arranged chronologically by publication date. The entries generally contain two to six reviews per title, depending on the stature of the book and the amount of criticism it has generated. The editors select titles that reflect the entire scope of the author's literary contribution, covering each genre and subject. An effort is made to reprint criticism that represents the full range of each title's reception —from the year of its intitial publication to current assessments. Thus, the reader is provided with a record of the author's critical history.

• Selected excerpts are preceded by **explanatory notes,** which provide information on the critic or work of criticism to enhance the reader's understanding of the excerpt.

• **A complete bibliographical citation** designed to facilitate the location of the original book or article follows each piece of criticism. An asterisk (*) at the end of a citation indicates that the essay or book is on more than one author.

• Numerous **illustrations** are featured in *CLR.* For entries on author/illustrators, an effort has been made to include illustrations that reflect the author's style as represented in the criticism. Entries on major authors who do not illustrate their own works may also include photographs and other illustrative material pertinent to the authors' careers.

## Other Features

• A list of **authors to appear in future volumes** follows the preface.

• A **guest essay** appears before the first author entry. These essays are written specifically for *CLR* by prominent critics on subjects of their choice. Past volumes have included essays by John Rowe Townsend, Zena Sutherland, and Sheila A. Egoff. Volume 8 contains Rudine Sims's "Children's Books about Blacks: A Mid-Eighties Status Report." The editors are honored to feature Dr. Sims in this volume.

• An **appendix** lists the sources from which material has been reprinted in the volume. It does not, however, list every book or periodical consulted for the volume.

• *CLR* volumes contain **cumulative indexes** to authors, nationalities, and titles.

The **cumulative index to authors** lists authors who have appeared in *CLR* and includes cross-references to *Contemporary Authors, Something about the Author, Yesterday's Authors of Books for Children, Contemporary Literary Criticism, Twentieth-Century Literary Criticism, Nineteenth-Century Literature Criticism, Dictionary of Literary Biography,* and *Authors in the News.*

The **cumulative nationality index** lists authors alphabetically under their respective nationalities. Author names are followed by the volume number(s) in which they appear. Authors who have changed citizenship or whose current citizenship is not reflected in biographical sources appear under both their original nationality and that of their current residence.

The **cumulative title index** lists titles covered in *CLR* followed by the volume and page number where criticism can be found.

## New Features

Among the most popular stories for children are those tales of traditional literature and folklore that have delighted young readers for generations. Due to suggestions from *CLR* users, the series now includes retellers of traditional literature as well as those who have been the first to record oral tales and other folklore.

Another new feature in this volume is an increased number of photographs. In addition to author portraits, entries on important writers who do not illustrate their own works now contain other illustrative materials, when available, such as holographs of manuscript pages and photographs of people and places pertinent to the authors' careers.

## Acknowledgments

No work of this scope can be accomplished without the cooperation of many people. The editors especially wish to thank the copyright holders of the criticism included in this volume, the permissions managers of many book and magazine publishing companies for assisting us in securing reprint rights, and the staffs of the Kresge Library at Wayne State University, the University of Michigan Library, the Detroit Public Library, and the Wayne Oakland Library Federation (WOLF) for making their resources available to us. We are also grateful to Carole McCollough, Coordinator of Children's and Young Adults' Services for WOLF, and to Jeri Yaryan for her assistance with copyright research.

## Suggestions Are Welcome

Readers are cordially invited to write the editor with comments and suggestions for enhancing the usefulness of the *CLR* series.

# AUTHORS TO APPEAR IN FUTURE VOLUMES

Aardema, Verna 1911-
Adams, Adrienne 1906-
Adams, Harriet S(tratemeyer)
    1893?-1982
Adams, Richard 1920-
Adler, Irving 1913-
Aesop 620?BC-564?BC
Aliki 1929-
Anderson, C(larence) W(illiam)
    1891-1971
Arnosky, Jim 1946-
Asbjörnsen, Peter Christen 1812-1885
    and Jörgen Moe 1813?-1882
Asch, Frank 1946-
Asimov, Isaac 1920-
Avery, Gillian 1926-
Avi 1937-
Aymé, Marcel 1902-1967
Bailey, Carolyn Sherwin 1875-1961
Ballantyne, R(obert) M(ichael)
    1825-1894
Banner, Angela 1923-
Bannerman, Helen 1863-1946
Barrett, Judi(th) 1941-
Barrie, J(ames) M(atthew) 1860-1937
Baum, L(yman) Frank 1856-1919
Baumann, Hans 1914-
BB 1905-
Beatty, Patricia 1922- and John
    1922-1975
Behn, Harry 1898-1973
Belloc, Hilaire 1870-1953
Benary-Isbert, Margot 1889-1979
Benchley, Nathaniel 1915-1981
Berenstain, Stan(ley) 1923- and
    Jan(ice) 1923-
Berger, Melvin 1927-
Berna, Paul 1910-
Beskow, Elsa 1874-1953
Bianco, Margery Williams 1881-1944
Bishop, Claire Huchet
Blades, Ann 1947-
Blake, Quentin 1932-
Blos, Joan W(insor) 1928-
Blyton, Enid 1897-1968
Bodecker, N(iels) M(ogens) 1922-
Bond, Nancy 1945-
Bonham, Frank 1914-
Branley, Franklyn M(ansfield) 1915-
Brazil, Angela 1869-1947
Breinburg, Petronella 1927-
Briggs, Raymond 1934-
Bright, Robert 1902-
Brink, Carol Ryrie 1895-1981
Brooke, L(eonard) Leslie 1862-1940

Brown, Marc 1946-
Brown, Marcia 1918-
Brown, Margaret Wise 1910-1952
Buff, Mary 1890-1970 and Conrad
    1886-1975
Bulla, Clyde Robert 1914-
Burch, Robert 1925-
Burchard, Peter 1921-
Burgess, Gelett 1866-1951
Burgess, Thornton W(aldo) 1874-1965
Burnett, Frances Hodgson 1849-1924
Burningham, John 1936-
Burton, Virginia Lee 1909-1968
Butterworth, Oliver 1915-
Caines, Jeannette
Carle, Eric 1929-
Carlson, Natalie Savage 1906-
Carrick, Donald 1929- and Carol 1935-
Chönz, Selina
Christopher, Matt(hew) 1917-
Ciardi, John 1916-
Clapp, Patricia 1912-
Clark, Ann Nolan 1896-
Clarke, Pauline 1921-
Cleaver, Elizabeth 1939-
Cohen, Barbara 1932-
Colby, C(arroll) B(urleigh) 1904-1977
Colman, Hila
Colum Padraic 1881-1972
Cone, Molly 1918-
Conford, Ellen 1942-
Coolidge, Olivia 1908-
Coolidge, Susan 1835-1905
Cooney, Barbara 1917-
Courlander, Harold 1908-
Cox, Palmer 1840-1924
Cresswell, Helen 1934-
Crompton, Richmal 1890-1969
Cunningham, Julia 1916-
Curry, Jane L(ouise) 1932-
Dalgliesh, Alice 1893-1979
Daugherty, James 1889-1974
d'Aulaire, Ingri 1904-1980 and Edgar
    Parin 1898-
de la Mare, Walter 1873-1956
de Regniers, Beatrice Schenk 1914-
Dillon, Eilís 1920-
Dodge, Mary Mapes 1831-1905
Domanska, Janina
Duvoisin, Roger 1904-1980
Eager, Edward 1911-1964
Edgeworth, Maria 1767-1849
Edmonds, Walter D(umaux) 1903-
Epstein, Sam(uel) 1909- and Beryl 1910-
Ets, Marie Hall 1893-

Ewing, Juliana Horatia 1841-1885
Farber, Norma 1909-
Farjeon, Eleanor 1881-1965
Field, Eugene 1850-1895
Field, Rachel 1894-1942
Fisher, Dorothy Canfield 1879-1958
Fisher, Leonard Everett 1924-
Flack, Marjorie 1897-1958
Forbes, Esther 1891-1967
Forest, Antonia
Freeman, Don 1908-1978
Fujikawa, Gyo
Fyleman, Rose 1877-1957
Galdone, Paul 1914-
Gardam, Jane 1928-
Garfield, Leon 1921-
Garis, Howard R(oger) 1873-1962
Garner, Alan 1935-
Gates, Doris 1901-
Gerrard, Roy
Giblin, James Cross 1933-
Giff, Patricia Reilly 1935-
Ginsburg, Mirra 1919-
Goble, Paul 1933-
Godden, Rumer 1907-
Goodrich, Samuel G(riswold) 1793-1860
Gorey, Edward 1925-
Goudge, Elizabeth (de Beauchamp)
    1900-
Graham, Lorenz B(ell) 1902-
Gramatky, Hardie 1907-1979
Greene, Constance C(larke) 1924-
Grimm, Jacob 1785-1863 and Wilhelm
    1786-1859
Gruelle, Johnny 1880-1938
Guillot, René 1900-1969
Hader, Elmer 1889-1973 and Berta
    1891?-1976
Hale, Lucretia Peabody 1820-1900
Harnett, Cynthia 1893-1981
Harris, Christie 1907-
Harris, Joel Chandler 1848-1908
Haywood, Carolyn 1898-
Heide, Florence Parry 1919-
Hill, Eric
Hoberman, Mary Ann 1930-
Hoff, Syd(ney) 1912-
Hoffman, Heinrich 1809-1894
Holling, Holling C(lancy) 1900-1973
Howe, James 1946-
Hughes, Langston 1902-1967
Hughes, Monica 1925-
Hughes, Shirley 1929-
Hunter, Mollie 1922-
Ipcar, Dahlov 1917-

Iwasaki, Chihiro 1918-
Jackson, Jesse 1908-1983
Jacobs, Joseph 1854-1916
Janosch 1931-
Jeschke, Susan 1942-
Johnson, Crockett 1906-1975
Johnson, James Weldon 1871-1938
Jonas, Ann
Jones, Diana Wynne 1934-
Jordan, June 1936-
Judson, Clara Ingram 1879-1960
Juster, Norton 1929-
Keith, Harold 1903-
Kelly, Eric P(hilbrook) 1884-1960
Kennedy, Richard 1932-
Kent, Jack 1920-
Kerr, Judith 1923-
Kettelkamp, Larry 1933-
King, Clive 1924-
Kipling, Rudyard 1865-1936
Kjelgaard, Jim 1910-1959
Kraus, Robert 1925-
Krauss, Ruth 1911-
Krumgold, Joseph 1908-1980
Krüss, James 1926-
La Farge, Oliver 1901-1963
La Fontaine, Jean de 1621-1695
Lang, Andrew 1844-1912
Langton, Jane 1922-
Lasky, Kathryn 1944-
Latham, Jean Lee 1902-
Lauber, Patricia 1924-
Lavine, Sigmund A(rnold) 1908-
Leaf, Munro 1905-1976
Lenski, Lois 1893-1974
Levy, Elizabeth 1942-
Lewin, Hugh (Francis) 1939-
Lewis, Elizabeth Foreman 1892-1958
Lightner, A(lice) M. 1904-
Linklater, Eric 1899-1974
Lofting, Hugh 1866-1947
Lunn, Janet 1928-
MacDonald, George 1824-1905
MacGregor, Ellen 1906-1954
Mann, Peggy
Marshall, James 1942-
Martin, Patricia Miles 1899-
Masefield, John 1878-1967
Mayer, Mercer 1943- and Marianna
    1945-
Mayne, William 1928-
McClung, Robert M(arshall) 1916-
McCord, David 1897-
McDermott, Gerald 1941-
McGovern, Ann
McNeer, May 1902- and Lynd Ward
    1905-

Meader, Stephen W(arren) 1892-1977
Means, Florence Crannell 1891-1980
Meigs, Cornelia 1884-1973
Merriam, Eve 1916-
Merrill, Jean 1923-
Miles, Betty 1928-
Milne, Lorus 1912- and Margery 1915-
Minarik, Else Holmelund 1920-
Mizumura, Kazue
Molesworth, Mary Louisa 1842-1921
Morey, Walt(er) 1907-
Mukerji, Dhan Gopal 1890-1936
Munari, Bruno 1907-
Naylor, Phyllis Reynolds 1933-
Neville, Emily Cheney 1919-
Nic Leodhas, Sorche 1898-1969
Nichols, Ruth 1948-
North, Sterling 1906-1974
Nöstlinger, Christine 1936-
Olney, Ross R(obert) 1929-
Ormondroyd, Edward 1925-
Ottley, Reginald
Oxenbury, Helen 1938-
Parish, Peggy 1927-
Pearce, A(nn) Philippa 1920-
Peck, Robert Newton 1928-
Peet, Bill 1915-
Perl, Lila
Perrault, Charles 1628-1703
Petersham, Maud 1890-1971 and Miska
    1888-1960
Petry, Ann (Lane) 1908-
Pfeffer, Susan Beth 1948-
Picard, Barbara Leonie 1917-
Politi, Leo 1908-
Prelutsky, Jack
Price, Christine 1928-1980
Provensen, Alice 1918- and Martin
    1916-
Pyle, Howard 1853-1911
Reeves, James 1909-1978
Richards, Laura E(lizabeth) 1850-1943
Richler, Mordecai 1931-
Robertson, Keith 1914-
Rockwell, Anne 1934- and Harlow
Rodgers, Mary 1931-
Rollins, Charlemae Hill 1897-1979
Ross, Tony 1938-
Rounds, Glen 1906-
Saint-Exupéry, Antoine de 1900-1944
Sandburg, Carl 1878-1967
Sandoz, Mari 1896-1966
Sawyer, Ruth 1880-1970
Scarry, Huck
Scott, Jack Denton 1915-
Seredy, Kate 1899-1975
Seton, Ernest Thompson 1860-1946

Sharmat, Marjorie Weinman 1928-
Sharp, Margery 1905-
Shotwell, Louisa R(ossiter) 1902-
Sidney, Margaret 1844-1924
Silverstein, Alvin 1933- and Virginia
    1937-
Simon, Seymour 1931-
Sinclair, Catherine 1880-1864
Skurzynski, Gloria 1930-
Sleator, William 1945-
Slobodkin, Louis 1903-1975
Smith, Doris Buchanan 1934-
Smucker, Barbara (Claassen) 1915-
Snyder, Zilpha Keatley 1927-
Spence, Eleanor 1928-
Sperry, Armstrong W. 1897-1976
Spykman, E(lizabeth) C. 1896-1965
Spyri, Johanna 1827-1901
Steele, William O(wen) 1917-1979
Stevenson, James 1929-
Stevenson, Robert Louis 1850-1894
Stolz, Mary 1920-
Stratemeyer, Edward L. 1862-1930
Streatfeild, Noel 1897-
Taylor, Mildred D(elois)
Taylor, Sydney 1904?-1978
Taylor, Theodore 1924-
Ter Haar, Jaap 1922-
Titus, Eve 1922-
Tolkien, J(ohn) R(onald) R(euel)
    1892-1973
Treadgold, Mary 1910-
Trease, Geoffrey 1909-
Tresselt, Alvin 1916-
Treviño, Elizabeth Borton de 1904-
Tudor, Tasha 1915-
Turkle, Brinton 1915-
Udry, Janice May 1928-
Unnerstad, Edith 1900-
Uttley, Alison 1884-1976
Ventura, Piero 1937-
Vincent, Gabrielle
Vining, Elizabeth Gray 1902-
Waber, Bernard 1924-
Wahl, Jan 1933-
Walter, Mildred Pitts
Wells, Rosemary 1943-
Wiese, Kurt 1887-1974
Wilkinson, Brenda 1946-
Williams, Barbara 1925-
Williams, Vera B. 1927-
Yates, Elizabeth 1905-
Yonge, Charlotte M(ary) 1823-1901
Zemach, Harve 1933-1974 and Margot
    1931-
Zion, Gene 1913-1975

Readers are cordially invited to suggest additional authors to the editors.

# GUEST ESSAY

## Children's Books about Blacks:
## A Mid-Eighties Status Report
### by Rudine Sims

The heyday of publishing children's books about blacks is past. Since the mid-seventies, the number of available children's books dealing with black life has declined steadily. *The Black Experience in Children's Books,* a comprehensive bibliography published about every five years that lists in-print children's books about blacks, reflects some dramatic statistics: the 1974 edition listed approximately 950 titles, but the 1984 edition cites only about 450 books. Approximately 100 of the books in this latest edition are titles newly published between 1979 and 1984, and only 80 of the new books published between 1980 and 1983—an average of 20 per year—focus on American blacks. If publishers release approximately 2,000 new children's books each year, as the bibliography's compiler, Barbara Rollock, notes, only about 1 percent of the children's books published in the first half of the eighties focused on black experience in the United States.

As would be expected, this diminution of children's books about blacks reflects the social, economic, and political climate of the times. The bounty of the seventies resulted from the social ferment of the late fifties and sixties; during the eighties, however, a vastly different cultural climate has emerged. The national conscience is no longer being pricked by nightly newscasts of racial clashes in Birmingham and riotous burnings in Watts. In fact, the national government is busy trying to turn back the clock on civil rights. Censors from the "New Right" often include books by and about blacks among their prime targets for removal from library shelves. In the past few years, many publishing houses have either merged or been taken over by large corporations whose major business is not publishing. This leads many to suggest that the pressure for profits has resulted in a strong reluctance on the part of publishers to take risks with new authors or with books they perceive to have a limited market, such as books about blacks. It is not at all surprising, then, that the number of available books by and about blacks has decreased. The situation is distressing, since it means black children may once more be moving towards invisibility in literature, and white children may continue to be given a distorted picture of the world and their place in it.

With so few books about blacks being published, it becomes even more important to raise questions about the quality of the books, their themes, their perspective on the black experience, and the issues and controversies surrounding them. My *Shadow and Substance: Afro-American Experience in Contemporary Children's Fiction* (Urbana: National Council of Teachers of English, 1982) raises some of these questions in relation to books published from 1965 to 1979. This essay briefly examines what has happened to children's books about blacks—contemporary fiction, historical fiction, folklore, and nonfiction—since 1980.

By 1979, it was possible to identify five major "image-makers," black authors who can be credited with creating whatever self-determined images of blacks could be gained from realistic fiction in the seventies—Lucille Clifton, Eloise Greenfield, Virginia Hamilton, Sharon Bell Mathis, and Walter Dean Myers. As we arrive at the midpoint of the eighties, it is well to ask if they are still writing, if their themes and emphases have changed, and if they have been joined by new authors. The answers to these questions will provide an overview of the current state of children's books that focus on blacks.

Virginia Hamilton, a Newbery Medalist, is by far the most prolific of the group. Since 1980 she has produced four novels—*Sweet Whispers, Brother Rush* (1982), *The Magical Adventures of Pretty Pearl* (1983), *Willie Bea and the Time the Martians Landed* (1983), and *A Little Love* (1984). *Willie Bea* is probably her most easily accessible book since *Zeely* (1967). It is a straightforward account of the experience of Willie Bea and her family on the Halloween of Orson Welles's Martian hoax in 1938, when he terrified America with the realism of his radio broadcast of H. G. Wells's *The War of the Worlds.* Hamilton calls *A Little Love* her first young adult novel. A love story, it also depicts main character Sheema's search for her father and, ultimately, for herself. The fantasy *The Magical Adventures of*

*Pretty Pearl* is an experimental blend of African and Afro-American folklore and African history. It features Pretty Pearl, a young goddess who disguises herself as a human and travels from Mt. Kenya to Georgia with her older brother, High John the Conqueror, to help the Africans taken to America as slaves. *Sweet Whispers, Brother Rush,* a Newbery Honor Book, focuses on Sweet Tree (Teresa), who discovers her family's history and learns about some of life's realities with the help of the ghost of her youngest uncle. While Hamilton often experiments with form and language, she has always concentrated on a small set of themes—home and community, family, heritage, continuity, survival—and these newer books are no exception.

Like Hamilton, Lucille Clifton has stayed very close to her original sources and emphases. She has, for example, added one more "Everett Anderson" book to the series of picture books in verse about this irrepressible young boy and his family. In *Everett Anderson's Goodbye* (1983), Everett must learn to cope with the death of his father and moves through the five stages of grief listed in the front of the book. As in many of Clifton's works, the strength that comes from love finally enables Everett Anderson to transcend his despair. Following the pattern of *The Boy Who Didn't Believe in Spring* (1973), Clifton has written another story about a black boy and his white friend, *My Friend Jacob* (1980). In this case, Jacob, the white friend, is mentally retarded. In a stark departure from her usual work, Clifton has also created a book with exclusively white characters, *Sonora Beautiful* (1981). Sonora has to learn to cope with being a member of an unorthodox family; her father, like Clifton, is a poet.

Eloise Greenfield has published four books since 1979: *Grandmama's Joy* (1980), *Darlene* (1980), *Alesia* (1981), and *Daydreamers* (1981), an extended poem. *Grandmama's Joy* is about the special relationship between a girl and her grandmother and expresses the theme of family love prevalent in Greenfield's work. Her next books incorporate a new focus—the disabled. *Darlene,* a picture book, portrays a girl who is confined to a wheelchair but is otherwise like most children her age—fun-loving and daring to "change my mind when I want to." *Alesia* is the biography of an accident victim who learns to walk again. As in much of Greenfield's work, the characters' race is not an issue. For example, were it not for George Ford's pictures, one would not know that Darlene is black. Instead, Greenfield focuses on personal problems or concerns, such as sibling relationships and family issues, while reflecting some aspect of Afro-American experience in the characters' speech, behavior, or values.

Walter Dean Myers has both continued and departed from writing the urban stories for which he was best known in the late seventies. *Won't Know Till I Get There* (1982) adds to his work in this genre. Steve, his friends, and his new foster brother are sentenced to two months of service in a senior citizens' home for vandalizing a train. As a result, they come to understand some of the problems and joys of being old in this society, and also do a little maturing themselves. Written in the form of a diary, this book reasserts Myers's optimistic perspective on growing up black in an urban environment. Three of his other works move into new genres and settings. Myers ventures into fantasy in *The Legend of Tarik* (1981), which is set in medieval northern Africa. Tarik, a young black knight, uses his magic sword and extraordinary horse to do battle with the evil El Muerte. *The Golden Serpent* (1980), illustrated by Alice and Martin Proensen, is a picture book set in an unnamed Asian country. It relates the search for an elusive golden serpent and allows readers to solve the mystery on their own. *The Nicholas Factor* (1983) is a mystery-thriller involving a college student, Gerald McQuillan, who joins an elitist society at the request of a black government agent and finds himself involved in intrigue in the Amazon jungle.

Thus the seventies' "image-makers," with the exception of Sharon Bell Mathis (who has been absent from the field for personal reasons), have continued to make literary contributions in the eighties. For the most part they have not changed their general themes and emphases, yet each has done something a bit different—Clifton's creation of a book about exclusively white characters, Hamilton's venture into young adult literature as well as Afro-American folklore and fantasy, Greenfield's focus on the disabled, and Myers's experiments with mystery-adventure and fantasy. In all likelihood, the fact that they are well-established authors has permitted them the freedom to explore new genres and topics while continuing to reflect the Afro-American experience from an insider's perspective.

A few other black authors who were writing in the seventies continue to be published, though most have produced just one or two books since 1979. These authors include Ashley Bryan, Jeannette Caines, Alice Childress, Rosa Guy, June Jordan, Julius Lester, Mildred Taylor, Ianthe Thomas, and Brenda Wilkinson. Most of them, like the "image-makers," have retained the themes and focuses of their earlier work. Taylor and Wilkinson created sequels to previous books, Lester produced a book of short stories about slaves and ex-slaves who experience both freedom and love, and Bryan published additional collections of folk tales and spirituals. Caines, Jordan, and Thomas created picture books—Caines's on family relationships, Jordan's about a little girl's exploration of her neighborhood, and Thomas's a story of a small boy's devotion to his jazz-musician father. Childress introduced her second young adult novel, while Guy translated an African folk story, illustrated by John Steptoe.

Steptoe himself produced another picture book about life with his family, *Daddy Is a Monster. . .Sometimes* (1980). In a major departure from his past works, he also adapted and illustrated a Native American legend, *The Story of Jumping Mouse* (1984). Cited as a Caldecott Honor Book, it is Steptoe's first venture into black-and-white art. It also marks Steptoe's departure from profiling the black experience in his works. As with the "image-makers," Steptoe was one of the better-established black author/illustrators of children's books when he was inspired to try something new.

Mildred Pitts Walter is one author who has joined the five "image-makers" because of the quantity of her works in the eighties; hers is a talent to watch. She has published four books since 1979. Two are picture books: *My Mama Needs Me* (1983), a new-baby-in-the-family story, and *Ty's One-Man Band* (1980), the story of a peg-legged drifter who livens up Ty's neighborhood by creating a one-man band with spoons and other household items. Walter's other two works are novels. *The Girl on the Outside* (1982) is a fictionalized account of the desegregation of Little Rock's Central High School, told from the alternating points of view of two girls, one white and one black. *Because We Are* (1983) features a black high school senior coming to grips with her membership in a black community. With the exception of *The Girl on the Outside,* with its focus on school desegregation, Walter's books generally resemble those of the "image-makers" in their themes and emphases.

Given the decline in the publication of books about blacks, it is not surprising that only a few new black authors have emerged in the eighties: Barbara Campbell, Joyce Hansen, Emily Moore, Eleanora Tate, and Joyce Carol Thomas. Each of them has published one or two books since the beginning of the decade. Possibly the most visible is Joyce Carol Thomas, a poet, who was the co-winner of an American Book Award for her novel *Marked by Fire* (1982). It was followed by a sequel, *Bright Shadow* (1983). Both are set in a rural Oklahoma black community earlier in this century and chronicle the development of Abyssinia Jackson, "daughter of patience and strength."

By and large, black authors of contemporary fiction have continued to examine the same topics that concerned them in the seventies: Afro-American heritage and history, pride in being black, a sense of community among blacks, warm and loving human relationships, a sense of continuity, and the will and strength to cope and survive—both physically and psychologically. Most of the works written by black authors of children's fiction in the eighties are set in black communities and have to do with black families, though many include white characters. There is very little focus on racial conflict. As in the past, many of these books concentrate on concerns or experiences common to children and adults everywhere—family relationships, friendships, the search for identity, the problems of growing up, humorous episodes, etc. Such emphases permit readers to acknowledge the universality of all human experience. At the same time, the insider's view of the black experience assures that this universality is grounded in the authenticity of growing up black in the United States. The black experience takes place within a range of economic, geographic, philosophic, and linguistic realities, and those, too, are reflected in the books published within the last five years.

In the past, however, much of the literature about the black experience has been created by authors who are not themselves black. This situation has frequently led to criticism and questions, if not open controversy, over the authenticity and accuracy of their work as well as their need to portray the black experience from an outsider's perspective. On the other hand, the contributions of some white authors, particularly such picture book creators as the late Ezra Jack Keats, have been widely appreciated.

In the eighties, a few white authors still write about blacks, some continuing the kind of writing they were doing in the seventies. Bette Greene, for instance, published another of her "Philip Hall" books, *Get On Out of Here, Philip Hall* (1981). Milton Meltzer recently published *The Black Americans* (1984), a history told through the writings of blacks. This is a one-volume revision of his earlier three-volume series, *In Their Own Words* (1964, 1966, 1967). Molly Bang contributed *Ten, Nine, Eight* (1983), a charming counting book featuring a black father and daughter that was a Caldecott Honor Book. For the most part, these works have been of good quality, and the absence of controversy over their authenticity and accuracy is a good sign.

Historical fiction is one area in which a few white authors and artists have felt comfortable treating the black experience. James Lincoln Collier and Christopher Collier have created a set of books about Northern slaves and free blacks in the late eighteenth century; Christopher Collier, a historian specializing in the American Revolution, brings a special knowledge and a contemporary historian's perspective to the materials. Their works *Jump Ship to Freedom* (1981), *War Comes to Willy Freeman* (1983), and *Who is Carrie?* (1984) are all based on historical fact and portray strong young black men and women participating in the struggle for freedom.

Not all authors, however, are as successful as the Colliers in creating historical fiction about the slave era. Belinda Hurmence has produced two books set in the South, using as her source material the narratives collected from ex-slaves during the 1930s WPA Project. Hurmence is much less convincing in presenting the thinking and behavior of her slaves than when she focuses on their undying loyalty to their good masters and their ambivalence about freedom. Both *A Girl Called Boy* (1982) and *Tancy* (1984) suffer from these problems. Such books keep alive the controversy over the ability of nonblack authors to "get inside" the black experience and present it authentically from a fictional viewpoint.

In the past half decade, perhaps the most controversy among concerned children's literature professionals has been prompted not by realistic fiction but by two "black folk tales." The first, *Jake and Honeybunch Go to Heaven* (1982), is an adaptation of several elements of black folklore by prizewinning illustrator Margot Zemach. Jake and his mule, Honeybunch, are hit by a freight train when the ornery animal refuses to move off the railroad tracks. After Jake squeezes into heaven through the Pearly Gates, he takes two left wings from a clothesline and proceeds to fly about recklessly. After being banned from heaven by St. Peter, Jake earns his own wings when God calls on him to control the rambunctious Honeybunch. When the San Francisco library system refused to buy the book, Zemach's editor fired off an angry letter to the librarians. The controversy grew, and charges of racism and censorship flew back and forth across the country. At issue was the authenticity and appropriateness of the book's images and actions—a heavenly environment featuring a fish fry and barbecue, heavenly music played by a jazz band, a God so powerless as to be unable to handle a mule, angels dressed in decidedly earthly attire, etc. It seemed a throwback to Marc Connelly's *The Green Pastures* (1929), another nonblack interpretation of black religious traditions. In addition to the stereotyped religious imagery in *Jake and Honeybunch,* there was the important question of the misinterpretation or misunderstanding of the original folk tales. In this version, the irony of the original is omitted and one is left with only the humor. The risk is that the characters look merely ridiculous.

The other "black folk tale" to cause a stir was Mary Calhoun's *Big Sixteen* (1983), illustrated by Trina Schart Hyman. Big Sixteen, named for his shoe size, was such a big, strong slave that his master sent him to fetch the devil. He violently killed the devil and dutifully delivered the body to his master. Later, when Big Sixteen died, a black St. Peter denied him entrance into heaven because he was too strong to handle; since he had killed the devil, he was also denied admission to hell. Thus Big Sixteen was left to wander the earth, "a-lookin' for a place to go." The illustrations depict the devil's wife and his naked children as gross caricatures of black people—complete with bulging eyes and Afros as well as horns and tails. The wife is dressed like a typical movie streetwalker with a great deal of "African" jewelry. Making St. Peter black and underplaying the master/slave relationship obscures the subtle points about black/white relationships in the original folk tale. Elizabeth Fitzgerald Howard's review in *The Horn Book Magazine* (February, 1984, pp. 41-42) probably best summarizes the negative view of the book, calling it "an unbelievable combination of stereotyping, violence, and blasphemy. The black-and-white illustrations are unfunny, crude, ugly, and offensive."

I have discussed these books at length because the issues of stereotyping, lack of authenticity, and cultural imperialism are still being raised in the eighties. With the publication of *Jake and Honeybunch Go to Heaven* and *Big Sixteen,* black folklore became the new battleground. Perhaps partly as a result of the controversies, Virginia Hamilton has produced a new book of Afro-American folklore, *The People Could Fly,* to be published in 1985. Interestingly, one of the upcoming Mildred Pitts Walter books is an Afro-American fantasy about a boy who learns to fly (both authors' works will be illustrated by Leo and Diane Dillon). Clearly, Hamilton and Walter have delved into the same sources. The folk tale about a slave who gains the ability to fly is also a major motif in Toni Morrison's *Song of Solomon* (1977). It may be that the rest of the decade will see more books derived from the rich soil of Afro-American folklore by authors who know it intimately.

Outside of realistic fiction, only biography has provided a fairly substantial number of new titles on black subjects. The 1984 edition of *Black Experience* lists 23 new biographies. Of those, 12 are of sports figures, and 4 are of entertainers. While biographies of sports and entertainment figures are not in themselves objectionable, their preponderance tends to suggest, incorrectly, that other fields lack worthy black subjects. In terms of themes, choice of subject, and literary quality, biography about blacks is an area ripe for study. One author, James Haskins, is probably the most prolific creator of children's nonfiction about blacks. He has created a large number of biographies on individuals ranging from Barbara Jordan to Magic Johnson. He also wrote *Black Theater in America* (1982) as well as *The Cotton Club* (1977), an adult book which became the basis for the Francis Ford Coppola film.

Books about blacks in other genres are scarce indeed. Not surprisingly, the two other categories in the *Black Experience* bibliography with the largest numbers of new entries after fiction and biography are "poetry and verse" and "music and the arts," with 6 books listed in each. Half the titles in the poetry category are from the prolific pen of Arnold Adoff, the poet and anthologist who is married to Virginia Hamilton. None of the other categories in the bibliography—history, science, reference, folklore—have enough new titles to average even one a year.

It is clear, then, that the heyday of publishing children's books about blacks is over. Still, there are some hopeful signs.

A few new writers are being published, and most of the well-established ones continue to be productive. There is a possibility that appropriate Afro-American folklore may become more widely available for children. While there are still many books that deal exclusively with white characters, there is a tendency in illustrations to include more black faces in the crowd in such appropriate settings as classrooms and public places as well as in illustrations for nonfiction books; blacks probably will not revert to a state of near-total invisibility again. Also, books about blacks seem to be listed somewhat more often among those chosen for awards and citations—the American Book Awards, the Newbery and Caldecott Honor Books, the American Library Association Notable Books. Although some past award-winning books about blacks were severely criticized, the optimistic view is that there may be an increase in quality books about blacks.

On the other hand, the dearth of children's books about blacks and other people of color is appalling in this pluralistic society. Children's books mirror our values, our priorities, our beliefs. Publishers, teachers, and librarians need to decide what kind of society we want to mirror for our children and then look to see if we are doing our best. I think we are not.

## Bibliography

Bang, Molly. *Ten, Nine, Eight.* New York: Greenwillow, 1983.

Calhoun, Mary. *Big Sixteen.* Illustrated by Trina Schart Hyman. New York: Morrow, 1983.

Childress, Alice. *Rainbow Jordan.* New York: Coward, 1981.

Clifton, Lucille. *The Boy Who Didn't Believe in Spring.* Illustrated by Brinton Turkle. New York: Dutton, 1973.

Clifton, Lucille. *Everett Anderson's Goodbye.* Illustrated by Ann Grifalconi. New York: Holt, 1983.

Clifton, Lucille. *My Friend Jacob.* Illustrated by Thomas Di Grazia. New York: Dutton, 1980.

Clifton, Lucille. *Sonora Beautiful.* New York: Dutton, 1981.

Collier, James Lincoln, and Christopher Collier. *Jump Ship to Freedom.* New York: Delacorte, 1981.

Collier, James Lincoln, and Christopher Collier. *War Comes to Willy.* New York: Delacorte, 1983.

Collier, James Lincoln, and Christopher Collier. *Who Is Carrie?* New York: Delacorte, 1984.

Connelly, Marc. *The Green Pastures: A Fable.* New York: Farrar, 1929.

Greene, Bette. *Get On Out of Here, Philip Hall.* New York: Dial, 1981.

Greenfield, Eloise, and Alesia Revis. *Alesia.* Illustrated by George Ford. New York: Philomel, 1981.

Greenfield, Eloise. *Darlene.* Illustrated by George Ford. New York: Methuen, 1980.

Greenfield, Eloise. *Daydreamers.* Illustrated by Tom Feelings. New York: Dial, 1981.

Greenfield, Eloise. *Grandmama's Joy.* Illustrated by Carole Byard. New York: Philomel, 1980.

Hamilton, Virginia. *A Little Love.* New York: Philomel, 1984.

Hamilton, Virginia. *The Magical Adventures of Pretty Pearl.* New York: Harper, 1983.

Hamilton, Virginia. *The People Could Fly.* (in press)

Hamilton, Virginia. *Sweet Whispers, Brother Rush.* New York: Philomel, 1982.

Hamilton, Virginia. *Willie Bea and the Time the Martians Landed.* New York: Greenwillow, 1983.

Hamilton, Virginia. *Zeely.* New York: Macmillan, 1967.

Haskins, James. *Black Theater in America.* New York: Harper, 1982.

Haskins, Jim. *The Cotton Club.* New York: Random, 1977.

Howard, Elizabeth Fitzgerald. Review of *Big Sixteen,* by Mary Calhoun. *The Horn Book Magazine* 60, no. 1 (February 1984): 41-42.

Hurmence, Belinda. *A Girl Called Boy.* New York: Clarion, 1982.

Hurmence, Belinda. *Tancy.* New York: Clarion, 1984.

Meltzer, Milton. *The Black Americans: A History in Their Own Words.* New York: Crowell, 1984.

Meltzer, Milton. *In Their Own Words: A History of the American Negro, 1619-1865.* New York: Crowell, 1964.

Meltzer, Milton. *In Their Own Words: A History of the American Negro, 1865-1916.* New York: Crowell, 1965.

Meltzer, Milton. *In Their Own Words: A History of the American Negro, 1916-1966.* New York: Crowell, 1967.

Morrison, Toni. *Song of Solomon.* New York: Knopf, 1977.

Myers, Walter Dean. *The Golden Serpent.* Illustrated by Alice and Martin Provensen. New York: Viking, 1980.

Myers, Walter Dean. *The Legend of Tarik.* New York: Viking, 1981.

Myers, Walter Dean. *The Nicholas Factor.* New York: Viking, 1983.

Myers, Walter Dean. *Won't Know Till I Get There.* New York: Viking, 1982.

Rollock, Barbara. *The Black Experience in Children's Books.* New York: The New York Public Library, 1974.

Rollock, Barbara. *The Black Experience in Children's Books.* New York: The New York Public Library, 1984.

Sims, Rudine. *Shadow and Substance: Afro-American Experience in Contemporary Children's Fiction.* Urbana: National Council of Teachers of English, 1982.

Steptoe, John. *Daddy Is a Monster . . . Sometimes.* Philadelphia: Lippincott, 1980.

Steptoe, John. *The Story of Jumping Mouse.* New York: Lothrop, 1984.

Thomas, Joyce Carol. *Bright Shadow.* New York: Avon, 1983.

Thomas, Joyce Carol. *Marked by Fire.* New York: Avon, 1982.

Walter, Mildred Pitts. *Because We Are.* New York: Lothrop, 1983.

Walter, Mildred Pitts. *The Girl on the Outside.* New York: Lothrop, 1982.

Walter, Mildred Pitts. *My Mama Needs Me.* Illustrated by Pat Cummings. New York: Lothrop, 1983.

Walter, Mildred Pitts. *Ty's One-Man Band.* Illustrated by Margot Tomes. New York: Scholastic, 1980.

Wells, H.G. *The War of the Worlds.* London: Heinemann, 1898.

Zemach, Margot. *Jake and Honeybunch Go to Heaven.* New York: Farrar, 1982.

---

Rudine Sims is a black American author, critic, educator, and lecturer. She is currently Professor of Education at the University of Massachusetts, Amherst. Dr. Sims is the author of *Shadow and Substance: Afro-American Experience in Contemporary Children's Fiction* (1982) and has published numerous articles and reviews in scholarly journals. She is Chairperson of the Elementary Section Committee of the National Council of Teachers of English (NCTE) and a member of the Editorial Advisory Board for their periodical, *Live Wire.* She is also President of the Center for Expansion of Language and Thinking (CELT), a national organization of educators dedicated to the improvement of language arts instruction in the schools. Dr. Sims has recently been nominated for the Vice-Presidency of the National Council of Teachers of English.

# Children's Literature Review

# Molly (Garrett) Bang

## 1943-

(Also writes as Garrett Bang) American author/illustrator and illustrator of picture books, reteller, editor, journalist, and translator.

Bang's works reflect her belief in the power and beauty of ethnic legends. Best known for her folklore retellings, she has also written an intriguing wordless book, *The Grey Lady and the Strawberry Snatcher,* and the well-received counting book, *Ten, Nine, Eight,* which is likened to Margaret Wise Brown's *Goodnight Moon.* Bang has gathered her folktales mainly from Japan, China, India, Africa, and the southern United States, and features them in three collections as well as in works which spotlight single tales. The most distinguishing characteristic of Bang's texts and illustrations is her emphasis on horror and mystery, elements which she tempers with humor. She displays them particularly in *The Goblins Giggle and Other Stories,* five international tales which place the human and the supernatural in opposition; *Wiley and the Hairy Man,* a black American folktale set in the South in which a boy and his mother cleverly outwit a monster; and *The Grey Lady,* an original tale with multinational motifs in which a strange creature pursues an elderly shopper.

Bang has said that she was inspired as a child to become an illustrator when she saw the illustrations by Arthur Rackham in her parents' books. Bang's formal education and exposure to differing cultures greatly influenced her work. In addition to a degree in French, she holds two advance degrees in Oriental Studies and has lived in Japan, India, and Mali. While overseas, she designed pictures for village health manuals, often using folktales to reinforce her points. When Bang tried to interest American publishers in her illustrations, she was told that they were uncomfortably scary and had too much Japanese style to be of use with current writing. She then set about finding stories to reflect her illustrative concerns, which she compiled to produce her first book, *The Goblins Giggle.* Bang created *Ten, Nine, Eight* for her adopted Bengali daughter, Monika, after realizing that there were few stories which offered a positive image of brown children. She has also illustrated several Bengali tales adapted by Betsy Bang, her mother.

Bang gives her own variations to many of the stories she retells. For instance, she presents two versions of the Japanese tale "The Crane Wife." The first occurs in a traditional rendering, "The Cloth of a Thousand Feathers," in *Men from the Village Deep in the Mountains and Other Japanese Folk Tales.* A considerably more dramatic variant appears in *Dawn;* here Bang devises a nineteenth-century New England setting and a significant role for the daughter. *Wiley* and *Tye May and the Magic Paintbrush,* a Chinese tale in which an orphan girl outwits a wicked Emperor, are retellings written in the easy reader format. Bang's illustrations often express her admiration for Oriental style and her fascination with fearsome monsters. She conveys the setting or mood of each story by employing various illustrative techniques. These include watercolor and tempera paintings as well as brush and line drawings which are sometimes framed with intricately patterned borders. In *The Grey Lady,* she suggests an eerie feeling by

*Courtesy of William Morrow & Company, Inc.*

coloring the escaping woman in grey, while the frightening humanoid snatcher is painted in wild, garish hues. A succession of ethnic subsidiary characters adds interest to the story. Critics consider Bang a skillful writer and versatile illustrator whose dramatic texts and pictures faithfully depict a geographical area or culture. They admire her ability to demonstrate a range of emotion, including the terror generated by the hairy man, the haunting beauty of *Dawn,* and the reassuring love of the father for his sleepy child in *Ten, Nine, Eight.* Some reviewers feel that Bang is too grotesque at times in both her stories and illustrations. They agree, however, that her authentic portrayals of universal emotions and accurate delineations of specific cultures have earned Bang a respected place in the field of retellers. Her awards include Caldecott Honor Book designations for *The Grey Lady and the Strawberry Snatcher* in 1981 and *Ten, Nine, Eight* in 1984.

(See also *Something about the Author,* Vol. 24 and *Contemporary Authors,* Vol. 102.)

---

### THE GOBLINS GIGGLE AND OTHER STORIES (1973)

Another selection of horror stories from many lands, these are remarkably hackle-raising, particularly **"Mary Culhane and the Dead Man"** from Ireland. They are recommended only for children with steely nerves, especially since the illustrations are equally terrifying.

> *A review of "The Goblins Giggle and Other Stories,"* in Publishers Weekly, *Vol. 204, No. 16, October 15, 1973, p. 61.*

Bang retells five variously "scary" folktales from as many countries (sources not provided) and illustrates them in black and white with a broadly gruesome band of naked Halloween hobgoblins. The first story—about the old man with a disfiguring wen who finally loses it when goblins take it as insurance that he will return to their dance—is the most awkwardly told, with the old man making superfluous comments such as "Oh! I fell asleep!" and "What a terrible song!" (and then inexplicably wanting to dance and sing himself though there is no indication that the goblins' song has become any less terrible). Other selections, about the dullwitted **Boy Who Wanted to Learn to Shudder**" or the Chinese son who retrieves his long lost father from fish-monsters who had kept him to play "Soccer on the Lake," are adequate versions of well known tales, and one, about the old Japanese woman, aided by a nun, who crosses an abacus bridge to rescue her daughter from a goblins' castle, has a climax reminiscent of Mosel's more skillfully developed *Funny Little Woman . . .* , but with a twist: when the goblins drink up the river to stop the women's escape by boat, the giggles that send the water back out of their mouths are brought about when the nun, the old woman and the daughter "lean right over and show (their) bare white bottom(s)!" That should be good for a startled laugh, but only the grisly Irish tale of a dead man who eats blood and tries to pull young Mary Culhane into the grave with him will make you shudder. (pp. 1262-63)

> *A review of "The Goblins Giggle: And Other Stories,"* in Kirkus Reviews, *Vol. XVI, No. 22, November 15, 1973, pp. 1262-63.*

The assorted goblins brought together here are just gruesome enough to whet the appetites of fascinated goblin fanciers. . . . Each story projects an earthiness that at times verges on the grotesque but is rescued by the humor or wit displayed by the protagonist. Bang's haunting illustrations in grey, black, and starkly illuminating white bestow a scarey luminescence over the whole.

> *A review of "The Goblins Giggle and Other Stories,"* in The Booklist, *Vol. 70, No. 7, December 1, 1973, p. 384.*

Five spooky folk tales—two Japanese, two European, one Chinese—are smoothly told and greatly enhanced by full- or double-page black-and-white illustrations. Young readers are likely to find only one of the tales familiar—**"The Boy Who Wanted to Learn to Shudder."** In the title story, three women escape the horrifying goblins by flashing their "bare bottoms". . . . (Children will be delighted with this turn of events, though it might offend uptight library patrons.) Otherwise, this is a charming collection in which humans triumph over supernatural adversaries after a few suitably chilling thrills.

> *Margaret A. Dorsey, in a review of "The Goblins Giggle and Other Stories,"* in School Library Journal, *an appendix to* Library Journal, *Vol. 20, No. 1, January, 1974, p. 45.*

Taken with one dark and stormy night, this collection of ghost stories should satisfy any phantophile. . . . [The] tone is the same throughout, dispassionate, almost cold, which is always the best way with ghost stories. Molly Bang has a splendid feeling for general chill, and her choices are all scary but end comfortably so as not to keep anyone awake for long. Her illustrations are unique and intriguing.

> *A review of "The Goblins Giggle and Other Stories,"* in The New York Times Book Review, *January 13, 1974, p. 8.*

---

## MEN FROM THE VILLAGE DEEP IN THE MOUNTAINS AND OTHER JAPANESE FOLK TALES (1973)

It would be hard to match Bang's village deep in the mountains for its colorful population including the crafty, the dim-witted and the stingy. . . . And keeping with Bang's fluent, sure retelling are her richly patterned, finely finished black ink pictures, elegantly Japanese in design and spirit and framed in what appears to be a reproduction of a tapestry-like fabric.

> *A review of "Men from the Village Deep in the Mountains: And Other Japanese Folk Tales,"* in Kirkus Reviews, *Vol. XLI, No. 21, November 1, 1973, p. 1203.*

Twelve Japanese folk tales are effectively told and illustrated in this useful collection. . . . Only two of the tales are readily

*From* The Goblins Giggle and Other Stories, *selected and illustrated by Molly Bang. Charles Scribner's Sons, 1973. Copyright © 1973 Molly Garrett Bang. All rights reserved. Reprinted with permission of Charles Scribner's Sons.*

available in similar form: **"Raw Monkey Liver"** . . . and **"The Cloth of a Thousand Feathers,"** a version of "The Crane Maiden." Full-page black-and-white drawings, placed within a gray brocade border, precede each story and help make this an attractively designed package for browsers.

> *Margaret A. Dorsey, in a review of "Men from the Village Deep in the Mountains and Other Japanese Folk Tales," in* School Library Journal, *an appendix to* Library Journal, *Vol. 20, No. 1, January, 1974, p. 45.*

There are a varied assortment of characters here . . . who once again demonstrate the universality of folk motifs. **"Raw monkey liver"** is reminiscent of the African tale of a monkey that outwitted a crocodile by saying he left his liver back home, and **"Picking mountain pears"** echoes the quest motif with the youngest son finally succeeding in rescuing his brothers. Many of the selections are suitable for telling, and the author's black-and-white drawings framed by oriental tapestry enhance the Eastern flavor of the tales.

> *A review of "Men from the Village Deep in the Mountains and Other Japanese Folk Tales," in* The Booklist, *Vol. 70, No. 12, February 15, 1974, p. 653.*

Most delightful of all [the tales], **"The Strange Folding Screen"** contains an element familiar to our time: Frogs persuade a landowner not to sell his land to one who would cut down the trees and cause the river valley to dry. The strong Japanese-style, brush-and-line illustrations are each unnecessarily bordered with a reproduction of finely woven brocade. (pp. 143-44)

> *Virginia Haviland, in a review of "Men from the Village Deep in the Mountains and Other Japanese Folk Tales," in* The Horn Book Magazine, *Vol. L, No. 2, April, 1974, pp. 143-44.*

A story-telling style, very swift and laconic, characterises the Japanese folk tales assembled in *Men from the village deep in the mountains.* There are some animal fables here, with animals often in human guise, prominent among them the wily badger who is such an important symbol of a human type in Japanese folk lore. Here, too, is that touching tale of the princess transformed into a crane and the humble couple who cherish the bird and receive their due reward for their piety. Though the sub-title defines these elegant, simple tales as "fairy tales", many of them are less concerned with magic than in the celebration of virtues by tradition to be inculcated in a peasant community—for instance, loyalty, kindness and a hard-working acceptance of a humble station in life.

> *Margery Fisher, in a review of "Men from the Village Deep in the Mountains," in her* Growing Point, *Vol. 14, No. 4, October, 1975, p. 2720.*

---

**WILEY AND THE HAIRY MAN: ADAPTED FROM AN AMERICAN FOLKTALE** (1976)

In outline, skinny black Wiley in Alabama and the scary "hairy man" he has to fool three times to be rid of can't help reminding you of Mayer's Liza Lou . . . and the separate swamp monsters she tricks, but Bang's glowing gray-and-white pictures are far more subdued and there's a touch of humor in her monster even though he's as ferocious a creature as you'd want to see. That the hairy man keeps coming back makes for a better story, and though the three-times-and-out condition, introduced toward the end, does seem to be stacking the cards for the hero,

you will admire Wiley's mother and her resourceful final routing of the bogey.

> *A review of "Wiley and the Hairy Man," in* Kirkus Reviews, *Vol. XLIV, No. 8, April 15, 1976, p. 466.*

Ms. Bang has created through the text and her magnificent illustrations a book that should be noted by all who work with the older reluctant reader because it does not have the "baby" look of so many series books. If only the series name ["Ready-to-Read"] was not marked everywhere. This tends to label the book as an educational reader, when in reality it is just a fun black folktale.

> *Ann L. Kalkhoff, in a review of "Wiley and the Hairy Man: An American Folktale," in* Children's Book Review Service, *Vol. 4, No. 11, June, 1976, p. 92.*

The tale has all the best elements of entertainment—humor, suspense, action, and ethnic color—with the stylistic simplicity befitting an easy reader. Flourishes are accomplished via illustrations in moss-grey, black, and white. Among the indigenous southern flora, Bang's grotesque Hairy Man looks quite at home. Though scariest of all when grinning hideously down from his conjured giraffe shape (a delicious mixture of grace and evil), the Hairy Man is still memorably frightening in everyday goatfooted form. A skinny Wiley is the perfect fall-guy-turned-boy-hero; his mother, the wise beauty of the backwoods. It is hard to imagine a reader unaffected by this book's punch.

> *Judith Goldberger, in a review of "Wiley and the Hairy Man, Adapted from an American Folk Tale," in* The Booklist, *Vol. 72, No. 22, July 15, 1976, p. 1601.*

Realistic brush and line sketches in grey-green shades on white, picturing area wildlife and homey details of long-ago country living, set off the super-natural and humorous aspects of the story. Monster-loving second and third graders could read the inviting text with no trouble, and the format and subject matter would attract older slow readers.

> *Ruth M. McConnell, in a review of "Wiley and the Hairy Man," in* School Library Journal, *Vol. 23, No. 1, September, 1976, p. 95.*

Molly Garrett Bang's subdued, repetitive style and clipped sentences are dictated by the Ready-to-Read format, but she overcomes these limitations. . . .

Bang uses Wiley's fear to build suspense. Indicating that his escape is no sure thing, she emphasizes his courage in facing real danger. The mother looks strong as a tree. Wiley is a gangly youth wearing a rope belt and shoes too large.

Bang's book is less slick than Mayer's ["Liza Lou"] and therefore seems more authentic. Her dramatic illustrations, drawn in black and white on a gray ground surrounded by white space, are tender. The effect is not amusement, but fear and relief.

> *Jane Resh Thomas, in a review of "Wiley and the Hairy Man: Adapted from an American Folk Tale," in* The New York Times Book Review, *September 19, 1976, p. 18.*

---

**THE BURIED MOON AND OTHER STORIES** (1977)

[Bang retells five stories from four different cultures.] The title story from England, in which "the folk" free the moon from tangled branches, resembles others which have been told with more humor, and another English tale, about heedless William who marries the princess and his brother Jack who saves William's life and takes an enchanted milk-white deer for his own wife, is a similarly unexciting combination of familiar elements. . . . With redundantly literal illustrations and no unifying theme, it's as unexceptional as it is inoffensive.

> *A review of "The Buried Moon and Other Stories,"* in Kirkus Reviews, *Vol. XLV, No. 10, May 15, 1977, p. 541.*

Bang's sure touch with word and image, which recently graced **Wiley and the Hairy Man** . . . , is extended here. . . . The illustrations, predominantly painted with India ink and white tempera on coarse gray paper, are unusually composed and textured (there is a stunning horse stable in the second story), adding a deeper dimension to the folklore that Bang so clearly respects in her clean, rhythmic retelling. A sequel to **The Goblins Giggle and Other Stories** . . . , this selection is not so much scary as mysterious. For reading alone or aloud.

> *Betsy Hearne, in a review of "The Buried Moon and Other Stories,"* in Booklist, *Vol. 73, No. 21, July 1, 1977, p. 1650.*

Five tales of magic are told in high style, with a good sense of the oral tradition, and in one case, **"The Wolf in Disguise,"**

*From* The Buried Moon and Other Stories, *selected and illustrated by Molly Bang. Charles Scribner's Sons, 1977. Copyright © 1977 Molly Bang. All rights reserved. Reprinted with permission of Charles Scribner's Sons.*

adroitly blending the Grimm Brothers' "The Wolf and the Seven Kids" and a Japanese version of the story. . . . There's nice variety of source and style, and the dramatic black and white illustrations are softened by grey tones, strong in use of light and shadow and in the contrast between delicate details and textural masses.

> *Zena Sutherland, in a review of "The Buried Moon and Other Stories,"* in Bulletin of the Center for Children's Books, *Vol. 31, No. 2, October, 1977, p. 26.*

The author avoids a deadly sameness of style through differences of length, mode, and theme, supported by luminous mixed-media paintings ranging through all of the shades of white and black.

> *Ruth M. Stein, in a review of "The Buried Moon and Other Stories,"* in Language Arts, *Vol. 55, No. 2, February, 1978, p. 214.*

It is claimed in the preface to this collection of five stories that they "depict the progress of human life, from birth, or 'rebirth,' through adventure away from home, adult responsibility and dedication, to retirement from society for a spiritual life alone in nature"—a large order for a book for young readers. In fact, the selection seems haphazard. . . . [**"The Wolf in Disguise"**] is "an amalgam of Grimm and a Japanese version," but no further information about the source is given. **"William and Jack . . ."** a variation on the theme of look-alike brothers, and the title story, which the author pompously says is about **"The Buried Moon"** in all of us, are folk tales from England, but the source is only given for the former. Then there is one story from the Indian epic *The Mahabharata*, attractively retold. A brief Chinese story in which a **". . . Mad Priest"** invokes magic to humiliate a puffed up courtier is taken almost word for word from the standard English translation by H. A. Giles, but its original satirical intent would be difficult for readers to grasp. (The one small piece of biographical information in the preface about the Chinese author is inaccurate.) The ink-and-brush illustrations are striking, but are not sufficient to hold together this miscellaneous sampling of lore. (pp. 53-4)

> *Dorothea Scott, in a review of "The Buried Moon and Other Stories,"* in School Library Journal, *Vol. 24, No. 6, February, 1978, pp. 53-4.*

---

## THE GREY LADY AND THE STRAWBERRY SNATCHER  (1980)

[**"The Grey Lady and the Strawberry Snatcher"**] is a sumptuously executed paranoid-druggy eye-feast that is guaranteed to frighten and bewilder any kids sensitive enough to follow its story about an old black lady fleeing a grotesque humanoid thief.

> *Harold K. Rice, in a review of "The Grey Lady and the Strawberry Snatcher,"* in The New York Times Book Review, *April 27, 1980, p. 58.*

A wordless picture book depends on eerie art and high drama for holding its scrutinizers, and they will be held. . . . Bang's art is a sum of disparate colors, patterns, and spreads of gray that unexpectedly blend. None of her figures is conventional; the tropical-type setting is peopled by warm brown faces and hot colors. Backgrounds point to a variety of ethnic motifs— a Persian rug, an Indian woman on a skateboard, a Buddha-like figure smiling out of a shop window, a banjo-picking grandfather at the gray lady's house. It's a visual jigsaw that somehow balances and holds beyond the story line. (pp. 1673-74)

> *Denise M. Wilms, in a review of "The Grey Lady and the Strawberry Snatcher," in* Booklist, *Vol. 76, No. 22, July 15, 1980, pp. 1673-74.*

The old woman of the title is not so much grey as colorless: only her hands and face are painted in, and although she is Black, *they* are purple. In this wordless book, the grey lady is pursued, at first covertly then openly, by a repulsive electric-blue nightmare creature in a chartreuse cloak, whose bony arms end in red-tipped fingers and whose enormous skeletal feet leave fungi springing up in their tread. The chase is played out against a series of "photo-surrealist" settings. A Martian monster looks out a distant window; a Chinese goddess glides by on a skateboard; the snakes she has been carrying in a basket are released by her collision with the Strawberry Snatcher and twist in gruesome closeup against the foreground of the page. Most of the pursuit occurs in an eerie swamp and a cheerless forest, where the grey lady effects a timely Tarzan-type escape via a swinging vine and her creepy humanoid pursuer is diverted by a discovery: wild blackberries. (In an earlier frame, he has inexplicably passed by a bush of ripe blueberries.) The details and design are wasted on a comic-book color scheme zinged with Day-Glo. The "story" is so thin and weird, and the sophisticated technique so obvious, that the ideal audience would appear to be non-literate 20 year olds rather than pre-literate 4 year olds.

> *Patricia Dooley, in a review of "The Grey Lady and the Strawberry Snatcher," in* School Library Journal, *Vol. 27, No. 1, September, 1980, p. 56.*

[The story] is strange, eerie, but the luminous images of evasion and pursuit are so beautiful that a sense of happy peacefulness emanates from these pages. (p. 136)

The reader is drawn back to the book again and again, each time to discover new surprises. The author is interested in Zen Buddhism, and the images resonate with symbolic meaning. In one extraordinary pair of pictures, we see first the lady stepping from the bus on a curved road, and on the facing page she walks away as the thief approaches her from behind on the skateboard—but the image is reversed so that the two curves of the road make a circle and the two events take place at the same time. The oneness of nature is a reiterated theme: the lady's house is full of patterns of birds, shells, flowers, ferns; the snatcher reveals a thatch of yellow hair like the blossom of a blackberry bush as he wades further into the scratchy branches. An entrancing, fascinating work well worth the attention of older teens. (p. 137)

> *Patty Campbell, in a review of "The Grey Lady and the Strawberry Snatcher," in* Wilson Library Bulletin, *Vol. 55, No. 2, October, 1980, pp. 136-37.*

[This allegory] is filled with surprises, lively humor, and suspense. Its unusual colors and its characters are ethnically indeterminate, but the whole is strongly suggestive of a folktale from India. The skillfully executed, impressionistic illustrations, so full of meticulous, often startling details, offer an exciting visual treat to the readers of this wordless book.

> *Patricia Jean Cianciolo, "The Imaginative World: 'The Grey Lady and the Strawberry Snatcher'," in her* Picture Books for Children, *revised edition, American Library Association, 1981, p. 151.*

Bang incorporates the suspense of this totally wordless book into the unique juxtaposition of colors, as well as into the foreboding expressionism of the trees of the swamp. The red-lined, chartreuse cape of the Snatcher, he of cobalt skin, and the violet hat possess an iridescence against the grey backgrounds and shapes. Negative areas become important shapes in the compositions as they envelop the Grey Lady and mask her from the Snatcher's view. Only face, hands, and strawberries are discernible at times, giving a hint to the whereabouts of the woman, and at one point only her reflection in the swamp serves as an indication of her presence.

As the pursuance proceeds, the figures progress across the full-page spreads, and the continual movement of the characters from left to right recreates the sequence and necessity of escape, as well as the dimension of passing time. Bang's innovative techniques will no doubt encourage the extension of these principles by other picturebook artists; the effectiveness of the work depends solely on the absence of text. The book stimulates an internal, silent dialogue with the viewer, and, unlike many wordless books, the spoken word disrupts the spell of the story—its silent fear and suspense. (p. 375)

> *Linda Kauffman Peterson and Marilyn Leathers Solt, "The Caldecott Medal and Honor Books, 1938-1981: 'The Grey Lady and the Strawberry Snatcher'," in their* Newbery and Caldecott Medal and Honor Books: An Annotated Bibliography, *G. K. Hall & Co., 1982, pp. 374-75.*

---

### TYE MAY AND THE MAGIC BRUSH (1981)

This adaptation of a dramatic Chinese tale of magic puts a girl in the role of heroine. Bang's account of a poor orphan whose magic paintbrush enables her to do battle with an evil emperor is both colorful and carefully engineered for the beginning reader. In addition, her delicate pencil drawings, accented with bits of red, borrow tastefully from oriental art without being formal and make use of empty white areas to suggest broad spaces or blank walls. Neither action nor irony is lost in this satisfying, simply told rendering.

> *Judith Goldberger, in a review of "Tye May and the Magic Brush," in* Booklist, *Vol. 77, No. 14, March 15, 1981, p. 1036.*

A story from China that might be told there today, lightly illustrated with some style and charm and more than a touch of Chinese flavor. . . . As told, it's not one of the more resonant folk tales available, but for a read-it-yourself cultural sampling it beats out the recent Demi version [*Liang and the Magic Paintbrush*].

> *A review of "Tye and the Magic Brush," in* Kirkus Reviews, *Vol. XLIX, No. 6, March 15, 1981, p. 354.*

The adventure flows easily; the six chapters provide stopping places. The soft charcoal drawings depict the Chinese folklore elements appropriately, and the subtle touches of Tye May's red jacket and the pink accents in some illustrations seem just right. A superb book.

> *Sharron McElmeel, in a review of "Tye May and the Magic Brush," in* School Library Journal, *Vol. 27, No. 9, May, 1981, p. 79.*

*From* The Grey Lady and the Strawberry Snatcher, *written and illustrated by Molly Bang. Four Winds Press, 1980. Copyright © 1980 by Molly Bang. All rights reserved. Reprinted with permission of Macmillan Publishing Company.*

### TEN, NINE, EIGHT  (1983)

No tricks, nothing fancy—just (in a welcome departure for Bang) a simple, reverberating bedtime count-down. The full-color, flatly-painted illustrations have in fact something of a primitivist *Goodnight Moon* feel (and somewhat the same coloration). ''10 small toes all washed and warm,'' we begin; ''9 soft friends in a quiet room.'' The feet are brown (with pink-rimmed toes against a red ground); the ''soft friends'' are stuffed animals and dolls, and a Siamese cat; the one unobtrusive pictorial device is the repetition of motifs from one illustration to the next—the toes poke into the stuffed animal picture, the cat does various cat-like things further on. But there is also of course a natural progression, not only numerically but in-point-of-time. At ''5 round buttons on a yellow gown,'' we narrow in on the father-and-child we saw at the outset—and then proceed, via ''3 sleepy kisses,'' to ''1 big girl all ready for bed.'' Counting-down, from counting toes, is an inspired approach to bedtime. The pictures don't exhaust themselves, and neither does the experience.

*A review of ''Ten, Nine, Eight,'' in* Kirkus Reviews, *Vol. LI, No. 6, March 15, 1983, p. 303.*

A counting lesson and bedtime story deftly unite in this spare but rich and tender picture book. . . . The pictures are luxurious paintings, thick with color but simply composed and spiced with judicious use of pattern and unexpected brightness. The yellow of the child's nightgown, for instance, is echoed in the outline of her rocking chair, the form of daddy's head, and a patch on her bed cover. Intimate details of her room—a doll, a row of shoes with one of a pair missing, a shell mobile—create a warm, familiar mood that enhances the clear pleasure this father and daughter find in each other. A loving book, perfect for sharing with the youngest lap-sitters.

*Denise M. Wilms, in a review of ''Ten, Nine, Eight,'' in* Booklist, *Vol. 79, No. 15, April 1, 1983, p. 1026.*

The simplicity of the illustrations enhance and extend the meaning of each phrase. The clear brilliant colors and the simple broad lines further distinguish the illustrations: small brown toes almost wiggle against the vibrant orange background; a black girl sleeps soundly under a patchwork comforter with her large, snowy white, fuzzy bear. Gentle happenings and warm pictures make a delightfully satisfying book for the younger set. These rhythmic verses are sure to be enjoyed over and over again.

*Sharron McElmeel, in a review of ''Ten, Nine, Eight,'' in* School Library Journal, *Vol. 29, No. 9, May, 1983, p. 56.*

For the very young an effective bedtime book provides a happy transition between late afternoon revelry and the sometimes less than inviting prospect of going to bed—unlike sentimental ditties or didactic fantasies that offer little incentive to the obdurate night owl. Far more successful are books, which, like Margaret Wise Brown's *Goodnight Moon* (Harper), create a quiet, playful mood within the small child's frame of reference. In this loving tradition the author-artist has devised an appealing countdown book in . . . direct, lilting rhymes accompanied by handsome full-page paintings executed in rich, intense colors. The style is representational, the composition uncluttered; the total effect is one of elegance and warmth. From the opening chant . . . to the final lines . . . the book has the enduring charm of a favorite lullaby. (pp. 428-29)

*Mary M. Burns, in a review of ''Ten, Nine, Eight,'' in* The Horn Book Magazine, *Vol. LIX, No. 4, August, 1983, pp. 428-29.*

There's nothing so special about [the theme of *Ten, Nine, Eight*] . . . but it is distinguished by its tenderness. There is real love in the gentle portrayal of the little girl and her father: unselfconscious, innocent, non-cloying. A rare, rare achievement.

> *Jenny Woolf, in a review of "Ten, Nine, Eight," in* Punch, *Vol. 285, No. 7447, August 17, 1983, p. 51.*

The pictures in warm, glowing colours evoke a mood of loving security, and as well as providing things to count, offer opportunities for further storying: '7 empty shoes / in a short / straight row'. Where is the missing one? And this is revealed four pages further on. The few well-chosen words are a pleasure to read aloud, the soft sound of *s*'s weaving a strangely soporific spell. A perfect bedtime book.

> *Jill Bennett, in a review of "Ten, Nine, Eight," in* The School Librarian, *Vol. 31, No. 4, December, 1983, p. 341.*

---

### *DAWN* (1983)

One of those rarefied concoctions of portentous folk motifs that never quite coalesces into anything. The first-person text is calligraphic; the facing, full-page illustrations are most often in color, and in the jewel-like mode of miniatures—but some are soft black-and-white pencil drawings. There is no significance, either way. In the text, a father, once a boat-builder, tells his daughter how he nursed an injured Canada goose back to health; a woman appeared, asking if he needed a sailmaker, and proved to be a remarkable one; the two were married, their daughter Dawn was born, and the father built the three of them a sailboat . . . ; a customer wanted similar sails, the mother objected, then gave in; finishing the sails, she turned back into a goose. . . . On the last page, the text shifts into the third-person—and we're told that Dawn set off, "in the boat made for the three of us," to find her. Mawkish folderol—which probably would strike some girls (and lots of grownups) as appealingly romantic.

> *A review of "Dawn," in* Kirkus Reviews, *Juvenile Issue, Vol. LI, Nos. 13-17, September 1, 1983, p. 145.*

Bang illustrates her new book with such beautiful pictures—arresting drawings and paintings in incomparably rich hues—that the creation surpasses even her most honored works like *The Grey Lady and the Strawberry Snatcher*. . . . No less entrancing is the graceful text. . . .

The emotional impact of Bang's story is strong, particularly at the end when Dawn tells her father what she intends doing

From Ten, Nine, Eight, *written and illustrated by Molly Bang. Greenwillow Books, 1983. Copyright © 1983 by Molly Garrett Bang. All rights reserved. By permission of Greenwillow Books (A Division of William Morrow & Company, Inc.).*

about their loss and we are left wondering over the daughter's future.

*A review of "Dawn," in* Publishers Weekly, *Vol. 224, No. 10, September 2, 1983, p. 81.*

Though Molly Bang has taken the Japanese tale of "The Crane Wife," moved the setting to a nineteenth-century America, and added a daughter as a focus for the story, she has retained the powerful feeling of love betrayed and so lost. . . . Bang uses both vividly colored artwork and soft penciled illustrations to bring the story to life in this milieu. Of special interest are the unusual borders that frame the color pictures, which are both evocative and decorative. . . . The story's dreamy, subtle nuances may be lost on the youngest, but other readers, even those in the middle grades, will be taken with it.

*Ilene Cooper, in a review of "Dawn," in* Booklist, *Vol. 80, No. 2, September 15, 1983, p. 162.*

Bang's rich full-color illustrations are magnificent, portraying the goose's human life; they are bordered with nature scenes

*From* Dawn, *written and illustrated by Molly Bang. William Morrow & Company, 1983. Copyright © 1983 by Molly Bang. All rights reserved. By permission of William Morrow & Company, Inc.*

and are effective in conveying the opposing forces in folk stories. The alternating black-and-white drawings are not as effective in sustaining the mood and one particular scene in which the husband grasps his goose wife, trying to prevent her departure after he has learned her secret, resembles a poorly choreographed scene from *Swan Lake.* The facial characteristics of the goose wife and Dawn are an amalgamation of many minority groups, but reflect the identity of none. . . . The telling lacks the magic and beauty of language and strength of emotions found in Sumiko Yagawa's *The Crane Wife* (Morrow, 1981), translated by Katherine Paterson. The power of the husband's greed and the goose wife's love is missing here, as is the urgency with which the goose woman begs her husband not to make her weave again. . . . [This version has] an unlikely ending for the folk tale genre, which does not usually offer second chances. However, the major question ought to be whether or not this perpetuation of female subservience is necessary in a library collection for children.

*Trev Jones, in a review of "Dawn," in* School Library Journal, *Vol. 30, No. 2, October, 1983, p. 155.*

Attention to detail marks this beautifully illustrated fairy tale. (p. 10)

As in many good folktales, the boatmaker's ambition leads to disaster for all concerned (though there is a bit of hope at the very end). What makes this version so powerful are, of course, Bang's illustrations. Watercolors alternate with pencil and charcoal drawings . . . , and the whole book [is] pleasingly designed. The paintings especially stand out—in themselves, of course, but also for their frames (backgrounds of sail cloth, of feathers, of the sea) and for their adultness. The stranger at the doorstep is just a girl; at the loom she is a pretty young woman; as she cradles her new baby her face shines with maternal fulfillment. And when the rich man pretends to look at the plans for his new boat, his eyes glance sideways with wanton interest in the boatbuilder's attractive wife. Dawn herself charms throughout, as she lifts a mallet while her father works, plays with bits of paper, cringes before the transmutation of her mother into a Canada goose. This is a haunting picture book, as affecting to adults as it is entrancing for children. (p. 11)

*Michael Dirda, in a review of "Dawn," in* Book World—The Washington Post, *October 9, 1983, pp. 10-11.*

Bang's story is a variant of a traditional folk theme, the animal-mate who resumes his or her original shape; the author has made a touching and effective tale of this, and has illustrated it handsomely. . . . The addition of a child to the story, and the open ending, add little dignity to the tale, but it is possible that having a child character may be appealing to young readers. (pp. 82-3)

*Zena Sutherland, in a review of "Dawn," in* Bulletin of the Center for Children's Books, *Vol. 37, No. 5, January, 1984, pp. 82-3.*

# Remy Charlip

## 1929-

American author, author/illustrator, and illustrator of picture books, dramatist, reteller, critic, and journalist.

Charlip is recognized as a versatile creator of picture books whose works are known especially for their inventiveness and the engaging childlike quality of their art. Puns and riddles, jump rope chants and jokes, a play, a legend, an alphabet—he transforms them all into something joyously different. Charlip's books range from the simplicity of the reading preparatory exercise *Where is Everybody?*, to the sensitivity of the retold legend *Harlequin and the Gift of Many Colors*, to the informativeness of *Handtalk: An ABC of Finger Spelling and Sign Language*, which enables communication with the deaf. He occasionally translates his plays from the stage into other writings, as with *The Tree Angel* (play and story) and *Mother, Mother, I Feel Sick, Send for the Doctor Quick, Quick, Quick* (shadow play and picture book). Charlip's willingness to experiment is expressed in his illustrations as well as his texts. Working variously with line drawings, tempera, watercolors, silhouettes, paper collages, and cartoons, he produces art that is noted for its use of color and movement. Charlip often employs naive art in his books, a style which demonstrates action and drama without superfluous detail and which appeals directly to children. *Harlequin*, the tender tale of a poor lad who becomes the star of a pre-Lenten festival through the generosity of his friends, marks a departure from the starkness of some of Charlip's earlier works. After making two trips to Bergamo, Italy, where the character of Harlequin originated, he found himself fascinated with such artistic details as shading and perspective. The illustrations he produced for *Harlequin* highlight a new concern with particulars like cobblestones, tree leaves, and eyelashes. Charlip's expression of naive art is still evident, however, in his unembellished, interpretative style; for example, he represents the people in the story as universal members of humanity rather than as individuals.

Charlip's diverse contributions reflect his lifelong involvement with dance, the theater, and children. A former member of the Merce Cunningham Dance Company, he has been an actor and choreographer with The Living Theater, a dancer and director with several other companies including his own, and has made costumes, handbills, posters, and stage sets. While attending Reed College, Charlip taught painting and arts and crafts to children. He helped to found the Paper Bag Theater in 1958; later, he and Shirley Kaplan directed the Children's Theater at Sarah Lawrence College. Charlip has also staged "happenings" (popular multi-media events), conducted drama workshops, written dance articles and criticism, designed textiles and wallpaper, and directed the opening presentation of the National Theater of the Deaf, which toured the United States in 1971-72.

Whether simple or complex, Charlip's works are considered creative, well-executed, and fun. Although reviewers complain that some of his books lack story lines, that not all of his transitions between mediums succeed, and that his humor is occasionally strained, they agree that he is a gifted entertainer. For the most part, critics welcome Charlip's rendition of *Har-*

© *Thomas Victor 1984*

*lequin*, but they are divided as to the effect of his delicate pastel watercolors. Although *Thirteen* is faulted for being too sophisticated, it is usually hailed as an ingenious innovation for simultaneously unfolding its thirteen visual mini-stories. Charlip is commended for appealing to the adult in the child and the child in the adult. *Fortunately* may help kindergartners expand their working vocabulary, third and fourth graders may master *Handtalk* for their own secret code, and adults may find delight in the octopuses who go "arm in arm in arm . . ." down the wedding aisle. Charlip's propensity to break barriers, crossing from one art form to another—from dance to play to story, from dramatization to design—makes him a unique figure in children's literature. *Harlequin* won the Irma Simonton Black Award in 1974 and *Thirteen* received the *Boston Globe* Horn Book Award for illustration in 1976.

(See also *Something about the Author*, Vol. 4 and *Contemporary Authors*, Vols. 33-36, rev. ed.)

---

## GENERAL COMMENTARY

### SHELLEY G. McNAMARA

One style increasingly found in children's picture books is called naive art. It is a style based totally on individual styles and operates from a premise which says that the world is not what is revealed to our glance, but what the artist intuitively senses. The naive book artist creates so as to make a personal statement about an inner reality. She or he uses a sense of harmony and composition to reveal a childishly naive, retiring world. . . .

In a picture book, the visual and verbal must supplement one another; neither can hold the story line alone. Yet artwork can extend and enhance prose. In Remy Charlip and Burton Supree's *Harlequin and the Gift of Many Colors,* the harmonious blending of both elements is obvious. With beautiful pastel shades, Charlip meshes this French tale of the Carnival events which take place just prior to Lent with his naive illustrations and shows, so effectively, the importance of love, sharing, and sacrificing for another. His drawings capture the authenticity of detail, yet they appear simple, direct and fanciful in the naive tradition. (p. 473)

Charlip uses the naive style because he believes it communicates a personal message that children readily understand. Having spent a great portion of his life in working in direct relationships with children through theater, schools, and dancing, Charlip tries to be both child and artist when he creates a story book. He feels the naive art frees children's imaginations while its repetitiveness helps them learn. In actual fact, the structure of many of his ideas has come directly from children themselves. (p. 474)

Remy Charlip has selected his naive style for his artwork in *Fortunately.* Here he achieves a sense of wonder and spontaneity as the reader, teetering the whole time between fortunate and unfortunate adventures, is compelled to turn the pages. His use of color in contrast with black and white emphasizes the power of the illustrations in a child's picture book. He elicits humor, fun, and gaiety from readers through magnificent manipulation of naive art. He reaches all viewers with his common life experiences. (pp. 475-76)

> *Shelley G. McNamara, "Naive Mural Art As a Vehicle for Teaching Elementary Social Studies," in* Social Education, *Vol. 43, No. 6, October, 1979, pp. 473-76.\**

---

### WHERE IS EVERYBODY?   (1957)

Combining a game and practice reading for the six-year-old, [Charlip] offers a really imaginative text-picture book. The first blank page is labelled, "Here is an empty sky." If some one reads that to a child he can continue, for on the next page where a formalized outline of a bird appears, it is plainly labelled "bird." Each page adds something to the picture and as each new object is added to complete the landscape, its name or a brief phrase about it is printed on the picture. Only the new word or phrase is written on any one picture so the effect of each page is kept beautifully simple. We especially like the later pages which are gray and finally black, as "a rain cloud floats by in the sky." This gives an opportunity to ask "where is everybody?" as they lurk behind the raindrops. . . . We think this bright book, with its gay yellow sun on most pages and the cleverly simplified diagram-like pictures will please the children, give them amusing easy-reading, and perhaps inspire them to make similar booklets for themselves. With Dr. Seuss' "Cat in the Hat" it is certainly a happy season for the first readers.

> *"Fun, Beauty, Fancy for First Readers," in* New York Herald Tribune, *May 12, 1957, p. 24.\**

A beginner's book that strikes the adult at once as ingenious in content and design, and, more important, proves its purpose with the first-grade child eager to read to himself. . . . [Pages] change color from white to light gray, darker gray, and almost black with the density of the shower. During this development, the reader is asked to locate each creature hiding from the storm. Compelling fun.

> *Virginia Haviland, in a review of "Where Is Everybody?" in* The Horn Book Magazine, *Vol. XXXIII, No. 3, June, 1957, p.212.*

Not quite like any other easy-to-read book, this one is an original invitation to learning and to look. . . . Simple as the story is, it has a forward movement and the teasing quality of a puzzle. The top trick for the beginning reader, however, is the way in which the words are introduced. The name of each object . . . is enclosed in its picture, thus making for easy recognition. Of the sixty different words, seven are of two syllables, the rest are monosyllables, which as anyone knows, makes reading a pleasure.

> *Ellen Lewis Buell, "Looking and Learning," in* The New York Times Book Review, *June 23, 1957, p. 22.*

---

### IT LOOKS LIKE SNOW: A PICTURE BOOK   (1957)

["It Looks Like Snow"] is the type of stunt that gives children's books a bad name: Twenty-two palm-sized pages, stark white except for a single line of text at the bottom of each. The book begins with "If you look closely you will see that it is snowing . . ." Get it? It's a joke—of sorts. The book comes in a red envelope and is suitable for mailing to your friends, who will undoubtedly think you're an easy mark.

> *George A. Woods, in a review of "It Looks Like Snow," in* The New York Times Book Review, *February 13, 1983, p. 30.*

---

### THE TREE ANGEL: A STORY AND PLAY   (with Judith Martin, 1962)

Originally a dance, later adapted as a play, the book is rather halting as a story; as the subtitle suggests, the simple dialogue can be used in a dramatic version. The cartoon-like treatment of the text seems pointless if the book is read aloud (printed upside down, the words "I wish" in very small type) and equally pointless if the book is to be used as a script. The adult who reads the book aloud can see that a dramatic version might be successful, but a small child could hardly visualize this. Three little whispering pines are in danger of being chopped down, and the tree angel gives them feet. They escape the would-be destroyer by making horrible faces and running away to a very nice new hill. On the page, the white face-circles on a conventionally-outlined Christmas tree look quite wrong, yet the photograph (taken in performance) at the back of the book shows an acceptable theatrical convention: holes cut in cardboard, with actors' faces showing. The story does not translate successfully from the original medium.

> *Zena Sutherland, in a review of "The Tree Angel: A Story and Play," in* Bulletin of the Center for Children's Books, *Vol. 16, No. 4, December, 1962, p. 62.*

---

And where is the sailboat?

From Where Is Everybody?, *written and illustrated by Remy Charlip. William R. Scott, 1957. Copyright 1957 by Remy Charlip. Reprinted by permission of the author.*

## FORTUNATELY  (1964)

This is fun. It's more of a word game for group use than a story. The text and pictures follow the adventures of a New York boy who received an invitation to a birthday party in Florida. "Fortunately a friend loaned him an airplane. Unfortunately the motor exploded. Fortunately there was a parachute in the airplane. Unfortunately there was a hole in the parachute . . .'' and so it goes until quite fortunately, he made it to the party. Solid, uncluttered illustrations in the bold color pages are excellent. These alternate with dull, grayish black and white spreads which are not so successful. Nevertheless, the book should spark imaginative, endless juvenile imitation.

> *A review of "Fortunately," in* Virginia Kirkus' Service, *Vol. XXXII, No. 15, August 15, 1964, p. 808.*

An engagingly zany nonsense story, attractively illustrated; the humor is the sort enjoyed by almost all small children. Each line of text is used with a double-page spread, so that there is a page to be turned in anticipation of the next cliff-hanger situation. (pp. 83-4)

> *Zena Sutherland, in a review of "Fortunately," in* Bulletin of the Center for Children's Books, *Vol. XVII, No. 6, February, 1965, pp. 83-4.*

---

## MOTHER, MOTHER, I FEEL SICK, SEND FOR THE DOCTOR QUICK, QUICK, QUICK: A PICTURE BOOK AND SHADOW PLAY (with Burton Supree, 1966)

The title line is an old jump rope chant and to it, Mr. Charlip has appended a series of rhymes revealing why the boy was sick. He'd eaten everything in sight including furniture and machinery and the doctor removes all this one by one. The illustrations are cleverly conceived silhouettes in white and black on backgrounds of bold colors. It turns out to be the great shadow play favorite of nursing schools—*The Operation.* . . . [Kids] always think that it's a lot of fun. It is. (pp. 299-300)

> *A review of "Mother Mother I Feel Sick Send for the Doctor Quick Quick Quick," in* Virginia Kirkus' Service, *Vol. XXXIV, No. 6, March 15, 1966, pp. 299-300.*

[Remy Charlip] has a lot of fun with this tale. . . . It can be made into a shadow play to the accompaniment, I'm sure, of much laughter from the young audience. The book is useful because really good slapstick comes seldom.

> *Alice Dalgliesh, in a review of "Mother Mother I Feel Sick Send for the Doctor Quick Quick Quick," in* Saturday Review, *Vol. XLIX, No. 16, April 16, 1966, p. 49.*

There are suggestions and instructions for dramatizing the story in shadow play, and it may come off in that form. The illustrations are colorful and unusually sophisticated; the idea is absurd. See it before you consider purchase.

> *Beatrice M. Adam, in a review of "Mother Mother, I Feel Sick. Send for the Doctor, Quick, Quick, Quick," in* School Library Journal, *an appendix to* Library Journal, *Vol. 12, No. 9, May, 1966, p. 138.*

[This] book succeeds in one of its intentions: to offer a humorous idea and suggested script for a shadow play. . . . [The] wildly absurd plot, told in somewhat effortful rhyme, is the result of the authors' appreciation of nonsense. . . .

As reading entertainment, the book comes off less well. There is a lack of harmony in the design and illustrations, partly the result of an over-indulgence in vibrant hues.

> *Rachael R. Finne, in a review of "Mother Mother I Feel Sick Send for the Doctor Quick Quick Quick," in* The New York Times Book Review, *August 21, 1966, p. 20.*

A read-aloud story, the illustrations establishing a pattern some pages after the story starts. The text, more or less in rhyme, is pleasant nonsense. . . . Very gay to see, and quite amusing. The book has tall-tale appeal, and it may stimulate a home performance, but it is weakened by being slow to start and by a rather flat ending. (pp. 5-6)

> *Zena Sutherland, in a review of "Mother Mother I Feel Sick Send for the Doctor Quick Quick Quick," in* Bulletin of the Center for Children's Books, *Vol. 20, No. 1, September, 1966, pp. 5-6.*

*From* Mother, Mother, I Feel Sick, Send for the Doctor Quick, Quick, Quick, *written by Remy Charlip and Burton Supree. Illustrated by Remy Charlip. Four Winds Press, 1966. Text copyright © 1966 by Remy Charlip and Burton Supree. Illustrations copyright © 1966 by Remy Charlip. All rights reserved. Reprinted with permission of Macmillan Publishing Company.*

### ARM IN ARM: A COLLECTION OF CONNECTIONS, ENDLESS TALES, REITERATIONS, AND OTHER ECHOLALIA  (1969)

This is a book without a message. This is a book without a story. This is a book that is unadulterated fun. Fun with words, fun with pictures. (Maybe *that* is the message? Fun is *great* when it's the bright, rollicking, walking-in-space fun of Remy Charlip.)

> *A review of "Arm in Arm: A Collection of Connections, Endless Tales, Reiterations and Other Echolalia," in* Publishers Weekly, *Vol. 195, No. 15, April 14, 1969, p. 97.*

Confetti from the antic world of Remy Charlip where anything goes . . . on and on . . . or around and around . . . or backward ("The moon sees me . . . I see the moon") or nowhere . . . replete with visual and verbal puns, strategic lettering, equivocal cartoons, elliptical riddles and rhymes . . . recalling sometimes Klee, sometimes Steinberg, sometimes the extravagant nonsense of children . . . whom Mr. Charlip invites to extend his ideas on and on. . . .

> *A review of "Arm in Arm," in* Kirkus Reviews, *Vol. XXXVII, No. 10, May 15, 1969, p. 555.*

When octopuses marry, it stands to reason that they walk "down the aisle arm in arm in arm in arm in arm . . ."—but who ever thought of it that way? Remy Charlip, and it is this particular perspective of his wherein lies the delight of one of the most kinetic picture books to appear in a long time.

The book provides an experience in word play complete with puns, riddles, mirror images, dramatic playlets and free-verse poems that bear the typographical shape of their ideas, all of which contribute toward creating a concentrated, imaginative awareness of language. The verbal gymnastics are accompanied by a melange of black and white and rainbow-colored illustrations which often speak independently of the text and lines of type which frequently twist and coil about themselves.

There is amusement here, endless diversion and a bit of well-placed philosophy—such as from the egg who tells the inquisitive chicken, concerned about the order of their origin, "Don't question it. Be grateful we have one another."

> *Ingeborg Boudreau, in a review of "Arm in Arm," in* The New York Times Book Review, *July 20, 1969, p. 22.*

["**Arm in Arm**" is] a picture book "happening" . . . where puns are outrageous, where the illustrations are delicately embroidered doodles and where you will be entertained for hours by the ingenious improvisation.

> *A review of "Arm in Arm," in* The New York Times Book Review, *November 9, 1969, p. 62.*

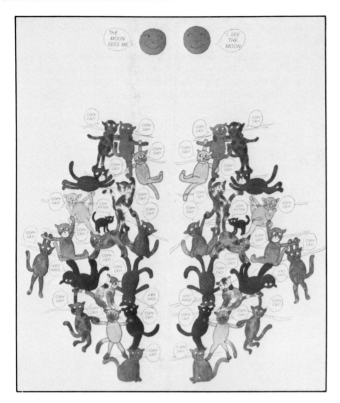

*From* Arm in Arm, *written and illustrated by Remy Charlip. Parents' Magazine Press, 1969. Text copyright © 1969 by Remy Charlip. Illustrations copyright © 1969 by Remy Charlip. All rights reserved. Reprinted by permission of Scholastic, Inc.*

**HARLEQUIN AND THE GIFT OF MANY COLORS** (with Burton Supree, 1973; British edition as *Harlequin and the Gift of Many Colours*)

### AUTHOR'S COMMENTARY

[*Charlip details his experiences in writing and illustrating* Harlequin *in the following interview by Paul Doebler.*]

For graphic artists, the children's book is potentially one of the most rewarding commercial ventures they can become involved with, offering a creative freedom unavailable in other print media.

For Remy Charlip, . . . the children's book has become the outlet for a writing and illustration talent as varied as his abilities in theatrical fields. . . .

Mr. Charlip first heard of the Harlequin legend of a boy who had no costume for the town festival from a fellow dancer in 1959. He suggested the idea of a book.

"I identified immediately with Harlequin, in that I felt I had nothing of my own, was not whole but rather a patchwork of all the bits and pieces learned from the people I admired or given me by those I loved," Mr. Charlip says.

["Harlequin"] tells the story of the origin of the familiar Harlequin costume, which is based on an outline found for Mr. Charlip by a friend in the "Larousse Dictionnaire Universel du XIX Siecle, 1865." The earliest drawings of 400 years ago show Harlequin wearing a suit of irregular patches roughly sewn on, Mr. Charlip recalls. Only later was it formalized into

the familiar diamond shapes. The costume is also traced back to St. Francis and others who wore tattered robes.

After doing the initial research, "I couldn't stop thinking about the story," Mr. Charlip remembers. "I tried to do it as a theater piece. I did it as a cover story for *This Week* magazine, updating it for UNICEF's Halloween collection drive. I tried it as a dance. I tried writing it as a picture book. But since I have difficulty writing, I asked many friends to help me.

"Finally, Burton Supree and I sat down and tried again. It was still difficult. We sat and wrote separately. We wrote together. Burt took it upstairs to work on it. I tried alone. We spoke into tapes. In enlarging from the bare outline in 'Larousse,' the difficulty was in keeping the story from being sentimental." During the research, the authors made two trips to the historic town of Bergamo, Italy, where the famous Commedia dell'Arte had originated the character Harlequin.

In Bergamo, the authors stayed near the town square, studied the people and surroundings, took photographs, bought postcards and books, collected tourist booklets and maps. "But we didn't find much on Harlequin," Mr. Charlip says. . . . The rest of the research was done in the New York Public Library's picture and book collections, and the Lincoln Center theater and dance collections.

The illustrations, which followed the completed manuscript also took Mr. Charlip much longer than anticipated—in all, two years. . . .

"I had no idea when I started that the book would take so long. I had never before made drawings or paintings like this. And I can't say now how it happened, but I started to become interested in reflections in people's eyes, eyelashes, hair, color and shading on skin and cloth, cobblestones, leaves on trees, perspective, shadows. It was most unexpected. I thought after [my last book] I would do something weirder, with more fantasy, certainly nothing so realistic.

"I could have gone on longer with '**Harlequin**' and worked to make it better, but, after two years, I just had to stop." . . .

"I learned something about drawing and painting while working on '**Harlequin**,' " he says. "But I know from experience it is of no use once I start on a new project. The next book has a completely new concept and I know I will have to struggle through again to find its own form."

*A conversation with Remy Charlip, in* Publishers Weekly, *Vol. 203, No. 17, April 23, 1973, p. 62.*

Opening this picture book, we see a child sleeping in bed while a huge and symbolic Harlequin—his costume spangled with stars—looms in the window. On the next page, the Harlequin has disappeared and his costume has become the sky. Then the child rises, walks to the window to gaze at the sparkling heavens, and we learn that *he* is Harlequin—the traditional acrobatic figure of French and Italian comedy. It is a stunning opening to a stunning book, and if there are faults to be found with it, they are definitely minor.

The encyclopedia tells us that Harlequin was found in folk literature as early as 1100—the proverbial ragamuffin—and that only later did he turn up as the Ariecchino of the commedia dell'arte. In his original French version, he was a spirit of the air, capable of invisibility, and all of these characteristics are conveyed by Remy Charlip's exquisite paintings. The text, which is somewhat less successful, tells of the child Harlequin who is unable to go to Carnival because he is poor and lacks a costume. Loving him, his friends each donate a scrap of their own costumes for his mother to sew together, and the traditional patchwork ensemble of Harlequin is born. He goes to Carnival and stuns the crowd with his beauty.

One must return to the illustrations, however, to taste the full flavor of the story. Limpid, finely drawn, and painted in the palest of pastel colors, Mr. Charlip's designs are distant echoes of 14th-century art. The groupings of his characters remind one of Giotto's angels, and the rural Italian setting he has chosen seems sun-washed and baked, like stucco and old clay. An enormous amount of thought and feeling has gone into these paintings. . . .

> *Barbara Wersba, "He Rose to Find His Costume Had Become the Sky," in* The New York Times Book Review, *March 11, 1973, p. 8.*

Here's an exquisite adaptation of the legend of the famed theatrical symbol. . . . There's even a hint of commedia dell'arte in Charlip's concluding illustrations amid a pre-Lenten carnival setting. . . . The soft water-color illustrations and the appealing text should provide a meaningful reading-listening experience for any adult-child duo.

> *Michael J. Bandler, "Harlequins, Dinosaurs, Ducks in the Bathtub," in* Book World—The Washington Post, *July 8, 1973, p. 13.**

[*Harlequin*] is illustrated in soft, soft colors, the first scenes of a small boy alone in his room a dramatic contrast to later pages, swirling with the action of a festival. . . . The writing style is subdued, but the story has enough conflict-resolution and the perennial appeal of a granted wish to compensate.

> *Zena Sutherland, in a review of "Harlequin: And the Gift of Many Colors," in* Bulletin of the Center for Children's Books, *Vol. 26, No. 11, July-August, 1973, p. 167.*

Two picture books [*Harlequin and the Gift of Many Colours* and *A Peck of Pepper,* illustrated by Faith Jacques] illuminate one of the hazards into which this form is liable to fall. They are both elegant, most carefully designed, and true to the artist's vision. They seem however to turn in upon themselves rather than to look out upon the world and their readers. *Harlequin* is so washed in moonlit colours that the effect is consistently insipid. *A Peck of Pepper* [is] far better drawn. . . .

> *Marcus Crouch, in a review of "Harlequin and the Gift of Many Colours," in* The Junior Bookshelf, *Vol. 38, No. 6, December, 1974, p. 334.*

"How splendid you look," his mother said proudly. He spun around and around, as bright as a butterfly. "Oh, thank you, I love it," Harlequin said as he put on his mask and his big hat. "It's wonderful!" And in a moment he ran off down to the square.

*From* Harlequin and the Gift of Many Colors, *written by Remy Charlip and Burton Supree. Illustrated by Remy Charlip. Parents' Magazine Press, 1973. Text © copyright 1973 by Remy Charlip and Burton Supree. Illustrations © copyright 1973 by Remy Charlip. All rights reserved. Reprinted by permission of Scholastic, Inc.*

A sentimental tale need not be unenjoyable, but when the text is as colourless as in this book, and is written without wit or insight, one is impelled to pick up another book as soon as one gets to the end, in order to reassure oneself that one's taste-buds have not suddenly ceased to function. In the case of *Harlequin* one has first to cough up the moral, which sticks in one's throat at the end of the book, before one can thus proceed.

The illustrations demonstrate a feeling for a certain range of pastel colours; unfortunately their effect is to make everything look washed out, not only the carnival itself, but also Harlequin's costume, the colours of which hardly 'gleamed and flashed . . . like jewels'. The drawing is somewhat naïve, and one understands why the townspeople wear masks to the carnival: without them their lack of individuality is such that they all look the same.

> *Clive Phillpot, in a review of "Harlequin and the Gift of Many Colours," in* Children's Book Review, *Vol. V, No. 1, Spring, 1975, p. 11.*

---

### HANDTALK: AN ABC OF FINGER SPELLING AND SIGN LANGUAGE   (with Mary Beth and George Ancona, 1974)

The exuberance and dedication of the team responsible for a unique book is felt on every page. People in the pictures act out strikingly the concepts of Finger Spelling (each word spelled letter by letter) and Signing (a word or idea conveyed by making a picture with one or both hands). Children should love this way of expressing themselves to friends, not only to the deaf, and it is also an effective prod to the imagination of teachers involved in language arts.

> *A review of "Handtalk: An ABC of Finger Spelling & Sign Language," in* Publishers Weekly, *Vol. 205, No. 6, March 11, 1974, p. 49.*

This is far from just another photo-illustrated handbook of finger spelling, nor is its appeal limited to those with a need to communicate with the deaf. Instead . . . [Charlip, George Ancona, and Mary Beth] have put together an expansive, energizing performance which would be its own excuse for being even if children were not intrigued, as so many are, with sign language and secret communication—and even if the finger alphabet of the deaf were not spelled out one letter at a time in photo insets through the pages and all together on the end papers and the accompanying chart. Full color and kinetic, a mixed media hit.

> *A review of "Handtalk: An ABC of Finger Spelling & Sign Language," in* Kirkus Reviews, *Vol. XLI, No. 6, March 15, 1974, p. 304.*

["**Handtalk: An ABC of Finger Spelling & Sign Language**"] is a marvelous initiation into what has largely been inaccessible and mysterious to adult and child alike. . . . Now, we who hear but cannot "speak," can easily learn finger spelling . . . and get the "feel" of Signing. . . .

Remy Charlip has designed "**Handtalk**" with the same clarity, humor and refreshing good sense found in his other books. . . . No one comes near Mary Beth in projecting an image of stunning immediacy; I would have preferred her singular use to the variety of subjects pictured. Also, the action shots are misleading. Though signing involves movement, catching a sign in flight distorts it. Without careful reading of the introductory material, the reader might assume from such photographs that signs are totally interpretive. They are not. Signing

should have been made clear as is the finger spelling chart so intelligently placed inside the book's dust jacket and on the end papers. But these are minor points. "**Handtalk**" is both novel and useful.

> *Cynthia Feldman, "Speaking of Other Ways," in* The New York Times Book Review, *May 5, 1974, p. 41.*\*

*Handtalk* provides a delightful introduction to the two modes of manual communication used primarily by the deaf. . . . Using imaginative photography and the highly expressive poses of several actors and actresses, the authors have created a work of considerable charm and appeal for all ages. The format includes full-page scenes of persons making various signs, with insets at the bottom of each page which illustrate the finger-spelling of the word represented by the sign. Thus, the learner may test his memory of the manual alphabet to discover the word being shown. While the book could be used as a basic text in learning the manual alphabet, it would be only of supplemental value in the learning of signs because of the more animated nature of signing. Its most basic function would be that of educating children and adults about the language and communication methods of a little-known minority group. For these purposes, *Handtalk* is highly recommended. It comes as close as any inanimate medium can to capturing the liveliness and sparkle of a beautiful, expressive and often humorous method of communication.

> *A review of "Handtalk: An ABC of Finger Spelling and Sign Language," in* Science Books, *Vol. X, No. 2, September, 1974, p. 160.*

[*Handtalk: An ABC of Finger Spelling and Sign Language*] shows how much more meaning can be conveyed when a signer's face and body are included. The exuberant photos of a variety of people—different races, ages and types—make this a most appealing book. Large photos illustrate signs (but why include the stereotypic word "crazy"?). . . . It would be nice to see a book like this totally devoted to ASL.

> *Albert V. Schwartz, in a review of "Handtalk: An ABC of Finger Spelling and Sign Language," in* Interracial Books for Children Bulletin, *Vol. 11, Nos. 1 & 2, 1980, p. 24.*

*Handtalk* is a book which builds children's curiosity about ways of communicating without speech. If you introduce the book by describing the world of a deaf person who must rely on eyes alone for communication, you can create sensitivity to the handicap of deafness. Experience with the book should help children to develop empathy with deaf people and admiration for the way they are able to communicate. (p. 560)

> *Zena Sutherland, Dianne L. Monson, and May Hill Arbuthnot, "Introducing Literature to Children: 'Handtalk'," in their* Children and Books, *sixth edition, Scott, Foresman and Company, 1981, pp. 560-61.*

---

### HOORAY FOR ME!   (with Lilian Moore, 1975)

["**Hooray for Me!**" tells] about a great variety of people all giving answers to the question: "Who are you?" "I'm me," all answer in a book which is an original and lighthearted way to help girls and boys identify themselves. [The pictures by Vera B. Williams and the text] also point out relationships within the family and within society. And we see roles filled:

From Thirteen, *written and illustrated by Remy Charlip and Jerry Joyner. Parents' Magazine Press, 1975. Words and pictures copyright © 1975 by Remy Charlip and Jerry Joyner. All rights reserved. Reprinted by permission of Scholastic, Inc.*

"That's not all I am: I'm my cat's pillow. I'm my dog's walker. I'm my shadow's body, I am my best friend's best friend. . . ." The creators of **"Hooray for Me!"** will make many best friends.

> *A review of "Hooray for Me!" in* Publishers Weekly, *Vol. 207, No. 12, March 24, 1975, p. 48.*

This book could be a bright spot in anyone's day. . . . There is no real story, just a happy celebration of the "me" in each of us. . . . The text might . . . be slightly confusing in spots for the young so an adult nearby to clarify might be helpful. Recommended for setting a happy "hooray" tone at the beginning or end of a story hour.

> *Marilyn Darch, in a review of "Hooray for Me!" in* Children's Book Review Service, *Vol. 3, No. 9, April, 1975, p. 65.*

Much rereading of **"Hooray for Me"** could drive an adult bonkers. But it is nonetheless a winsome book for the very youngest. A child would soon make the words his own and "read" the book himself. . . . The unusual bright watercolors and word play mesh to give a feeling of flatout celebration, making it no wonder adults like to read children's books—at least once.

> *June Goodwin, in a review of "Hooray for Me," in* The Christian Science Monitor, *May 7, 1975, p. B3.*

---

**THIRTEEN** (with Jerry Joyner, 1975)

A happy collaboration of the two gifted author-illustrators has resulted in an unusual, imaginative book. Luminous paintings in pastel shades tell even more than the brief text of 13 stories going on simultaneously on each page. One of the astonishing features is the subtle change in pictures which show a snail becoming swans, then swans becoming water, water becoming stars and so on, in eye-filling sequences. There is a poignant tale of a ship in a bottle; there is an innovative ABC; there is a wealth of surprises in a welcome contribution to children's books. Readers will also be intrigued by the notes which tell how the book came to be.

> *A review of "Thirteen," in* Publishers Weekly, *Vol. 208, No. 6, August 11, 1975, p. 117.*

Most picture books are arranged like the Guggenheim museum—you start at one end and work through to the other, with no distracting options. **Thirteen** is more like MOMA, with no certain route through the labyrinthine arrangement. . . . Chances are you'll cover the ground more than once, *Hopscotch*-style. In any case the whole non-linear enterprise is clearly more a creative kick for the author/artists than a made-to-order entertainment for the picture book age, but, being cleverly conceived and beautifully executed, this is one you float with the expectation that it will find an audience . . . somewhere. (pp. 1060-61)

*A review of "Thirteen," in* Kirkus Reviews, *Vol. XLIII, No. 18, September 15, 1975, pp. 1060-61.*

Few books can be called unique, but **Thirteen** deserves the tribute. More than just a picture book, this includes 13 separate stories simultaneously unfolded over 13 double-page spreads. Each can be read page-by-page to its ending, or along with the others, or backwards, or flipped through for motion sequences. The unusual format will inspire all ages to compare objects, watch the changing reflections, and find new visual experiences. The graphic variety allows unlimited possibilities for the simple stories to be expanded, pondered over, and discussed for meaning. Using pale watercolors that blend but vary, Charlip . . . [and] Joyner have brought new perspective to the physical properties of the book.

*Barbara Elleman, in a review of "Thirteen," in* Booklist, *Vol. 72, No. 3, October 1, 1975, p. 231.*

In creating **"Thirteen,"** Remy Charlip and Jerry Joyner have succeeded in a collaboration that extends and enriches each man's *oeuvre*. It is a complex work, at its heart concerned with the issues of time and change, heavy stuff for a children's book, but executed with such decorative grace that it can be understood and experienced without discomfort. . . .

Of the 13 stories I am particularly susceptible to **"The Mystery of the Pyramid"** in which a pyramid is first seen contained in a desert landscape by a 16-sided geometric figure. An Arab approaches in a series of steps and is revealed to be carrying a rug and hourglass. He spreads his rug, sits down and places the hourglass before him. We close in on the hourglass and observe the flow of falling sand. We pull back to discover that the falling sand has recreated a pyramid in a desert landscape. Absolute visual magic. Among the other stories, I especially liked **"Card Trick,"** where a leopard redraws himself into a more favorable environment, and the pleasantly mournful **"Unwanted Alphabet."** . . .

Charlip and Joyner have a winner here.

*Milton Glaser, in a review of "Thirteen," in* The New York Times Book Review, *October 5, 1975, p. 8.*

The book shows great cleverness on the part of its authors; however, young children who must go from one page to the next 13 times to get any continuity are apt to be confused. Certainly, without the guidance of an adult who has figured out how the book works, few youngsters will follow it on their own, though older children might find it amusing. All and all, a disappointment. . . .

*Catherine A. Coté, in a review of "Thirteen," in* School Library Journal, *Vol. 22, No. 4, December, 1975, p. 41.*

**Thirteen** is not only original in its use of imagery, but it also suggests an entirely different approach to picture books from the one recognized in the United States and in Europe. The pictures do not illustrate a story, nor are they simply drawn as works of art; the images respond to each other—not to any verbal concept. . . . Some of [the graphic sequences] are narrative, but most of them are concerned with changing and evolving visual forms. So a tree becomes a lobster; a lobster, an angel. . . . All of these images, beautifully executed in pastels, have been carefully arranged on the pages. The book may have to be introduced to children because it is not immediately obvious. But books that break new ground seldom are.

*Anita Silvey, in a review of "Thirteen," in* The Horn Book Magazine, *Vol. LII, No. 2, April, 1976, p. 148.*

# Beverly (Atlee Bunn) Cleary

## 1916-

**American author of fiction and picture books.**

Cleary is preeminent among writers of humorous realistic fiction for middle graders. Besides her universally popular *Henry Huggins* and *Ramona* books, she has done romantic fiction for junior high girls, picture books for a younger audience, and animal fantasies about Ralph, the motorcycling mouse. Using a blend of infectious humor and compassion, Cleary transforms everyday occurrences into hilarious incidents, yet the values of responsibility, perseverance, and unconditional acceptance prevail. She stresses them in an unsentimental, nondidactic manner, adopting a style that is easy to read both alone and aloud. The majority of her books are geared to the beginning independent reader and provide a happy transition from easy readers to more sophisticated reading matter. After her initial success with *Henry Huggins*, a story about the adventures of an irrepressible third grader, Cleary composed related books about the children on and around Klickitat Street. These works feature Henry, his dog, Ribsy, and such friends as spunky Ellen Tebbits and mischievous Otis Spofford. Perhaps the most winning personality, however, belongs to Ramona Quimby, an unlikely heroine who first appears in *Henry and Beezus* and later spawned several sequels of her own. Ramona is introduced as a tag-along terror who asserts her independence on every occasion, to the chagrin of her parents and big sister, Beezus. Readers identify with her attempts to grow up gracefully while still retaining her spirited personality. In all of Cleary's books for this age group, her protagonists gradually learn to cope with life and each other. Despite changing fads and family lifestyles, her novels about first dates and first loves published in the 1950s and 1960s continue to be read. Cleary's audience for these books has extended to pre-teen girls, who now vie with teenagers in taking the stories off library shelves. Above all, it is Cleary's extraordinary talent for inventing tales about ordinary third and fourth graders with not-so-ordinary problems that has won her prestigious national and regional literary awards as well as more than twenty-five child-selected awards.

A pioneer in writing about average American children and their world, Cleary often bases her stories on the life she knew as a youngster growing up in the Portland, Oregon area. Like Mr. Quimby, her father lost his job; like Mrs. Quimby, her mother went to work outside the home. *Emily's Runaway Imagination*, about a girl in the Oregon countryside who helps her mother start a library during the 1920s, appears to be autobiographical. As a child, Cleary longed for funny books about children like herself and the kinds of people she knew; as a librarian, she found boys and girls asking for the same kinds of stories. Recognizing the need for works of this type, Cleary began writing for young readers. Remembering her frustrations as a primary student in the low reading circle, she structures her works so that strugglers can experience the joyful power of reading by themselves and not be confined by a controlled vocabulary. Cleary's twins were the inspiration for her two picture books, *The Real Hole* and *Two Dog Biscuits*, and the story of nine-year-old Mitch and Amy. Over her long career, Cleary has spoken at many schools and has consci-

*Photograph by Marianne Cleary. Courtesy of Beverly Cleary*

entiously corresponded with thousands of young readers. She first ventured into the field of young adult literature at the request of some junior high girls who heard one of her talks. Her recent success, *Dear Mr. Henshaw*, was written in response to several letters she received asking for a book about a boy whose parents are divorced.

Critics often comment on Cleary's positive reputation with adults and children. Reviewers marvel at her recollection of the feelings and thoughts of a child—at four, at ten, at fifteen—regardless of sex. Parents, teachers, and librarians admire her obvious respect for her audience. Children trust Cleary's endings, knowing there will be no preaching or magic solutions. She assures all her readers that her protagonists will master their situations with courage and common sense. Cleary's attributes have made her one of the most widely read authors of children's literature. Critics credit her remarkable attention to detail with much of her success. Whether she is composing believable fantasy or imaginative realism, Cleary is commended for the accuracy of such settings as camps, classrooms, and hotels, and for her knowledge of motorcycles and tractor-trailer rigs. Critics acclaim her versatile, vivid use of language and note its appropriateness to its audience, whatever the age. They also applaud her ability to write on several levels at once—for the small child who identifies with kindergartner Ramona, for the older child who sympathizes with Beezus's predicament, and for the adult who enjoys the word play and nostalgic association. Adult characters in Cleary's earlier books conform to traditional roles and always provide background support; observers point out that more recent works show adult flaws as well as needs. In *Henshaw*, for example, Cleary does not attempt to hide the hurts in a divorced family. Reviewers note that her junior novels, such as *Fifteen* and *Sister of the Bride*, were among the first examples of quality literature written for adolescents. Impressed with Cleary's convincing characters and accurate depictions of love, dating, and the generation gap, critics praise the refreshing humor that enables her to take a subject like early marriage and communicate traditional values without moralizing. Although some reviewers accuse Cleary of sexual stereotyping or complain that her books lack strong plots, most laud her as a natural storyteller who makes reading a pleasure. Cleary's books are distinguished by the detailed realism of their small-town settings, their lively dialogue, characters whom readers can come to know as well as members of their own families, and themes on the innate needs to love and be loved, to belong and to achieve. Her unique gift for understanding the fears and joys, the conquests and calamities of childhood and adolescence keeps Cleary's books relevant after more than thirty years. *Ramona and Her Father* was a Newbery Honor Book in 1978 and was added to the International Board on Books for Young People (IBBY) Honour List in 1980; *Ramona and Her Mother* won the American Book Award for children's fiction in paperback in 1981; *Ramona Quimby, Age 8* was a Newbery Honor Book in 1982. Cleary was awarded the Newbery Medal for *Dear Mr. Henshaw* in 1984. She received the Laura Ingalls Wilder Award in 1975, the Regina Medal in 1980, and the University of Southern Mississippi Silver Medallion in 1982.

(See also *Children's Literature Review*, Vol. 2; *Something about the Author*, Vol. 2; *Contemporary Authors New Revision Series*, Vol. 2; and *Contemporary Authors*, Vols. 1-4, rev. ed.)

---

## AUTHOR'S COMMENTARY

About the time I began to feel I might survive my career as a [new children's librarian in Yakima, Washington, a] Sister of St. Joseph told me she had in her class a group of boys who were not interested in reading. She thought perhaps the fault lay in their school books. She asked if she might send the boys to the library once a week for help in selecting books that they might find interesting and which would stimulate them to read.

I was pleased to undertake this little program; as a child who had trouble learning to read and who had suffered the humiliation of the low reading circle with a group of unhappy boys, I had always sympathized with the problem of boys in school. (p. 22)

However, they soon presented a problem I had not met in work with children who came voluntarily to the library—there was very little in the library those boys wanted to read. They all demanded funny stories just as I had demanded funny stories from the children's librarian when I was their age. Like the librarian of my childhood, I was forced to turn to folk tales for easy humor, only to have the boys reject the books I offered.

"Don't you have any books about kids like us?" they asked. No, I did not. The boys compromised by accepting animal stories, and most of those were too difficult for these readers. I consulted lists and catalogs and concluded there were very few right books for these children.

For the first time I began to question the books published for children. . . . Where were the funny stories for children past picture books? Why were there almost no stories, lively and easy to read, about ordinary middle-class children and ordinary middle-class pets? Why did book dogs always live in the country? Why were all the stories about the Pacific Northwest pioneer stories? Didn't authors know the West had been won and that Oregon and Washington had been settled long enough to have cities? Where were the books about children who attended parochial schools? (I still wonder about this.) And why did children in books have to reform at the end of the story? These were questions the non-readers forced me to consider, questions that took me back to my own childhood reading.

By the time I was in the third, fourth and fifth grades, the most important years of childhood reading, I had overcome my reading handicaps and become an opinionated young lady who wanted to read about children, preferably children in my own neighborhood, as they were, not as they should be in the opinion of adults. An avid reader of all sorts of books, particularly fairy tales, I wanted most of all to read about problems children could solve themselves. I found disappointing, even objectionable, any book in which a child accepted the wisdom of an adult and reformed, any book in which a child reformed at all, any book in which problems were solved by a long-lost rich relative turning up in the last chapter, any book in which a family was grateful for the gift of a basket of groceries, usually on Christmas Eve, or any book in which a child turned out to be lord of the manor or heir to a fortune. These things did not happen in my neighborhood. Neither did I want to read about a noble dog who died in the last chapter after a long journey home on bleeding paws nor any book in which a pioneer girl ran through the forest to warn settlers of Indians. . . .

Ten years after leaving Yakima, I finally sat down to write the children's book I had planned to write since childhood, a book that was to be a girls' story about the maturing of a sensitive female who wanted to write. Instead, I found myself remembering the boys of St. Joseph's and the children who had once come to Saturday afternoon story hour and my own childhood reading, and to my surprise I found myself writing a book about a boy named Henry Huggins who lived in the neighborhood in which I had grown up in Portland, Oregon. I wrote the book as if I were telling each chapter as a story in a story hour at the library. Writing came with surprising ease. I simply told stories I would like to have read as a child. . . .

In my early books about Henry Huggins, Ellen Tebbits and Otis Spofford, I deliberately kept adults in the background. They were there to be supportive when needed—the proper role, I had felt as a child, for adults. Children wanted to read about children; adults should mind their own business and stay out of the story as much as possible. My characters worked out their own problems. They did not reform, although they sometimes got their comeuppance. I cannot help smiling when I recall that *Otis Spofford* was considered controversial when it was published in 1953, and some school libraries did not buy it because Otis threw spitballs and did not repent.

In the thirty years since *Henry Huggins* was published, the world has changed; so have children's books, and so have I. (p. 23)

Today, when children's books about problems children are powerless to solve are the trend, I feel that children who must endure such problems want to read about children who do *not* have the same problems. I am impatient with didactic books that are supposed to help a child understand problems, and I feel it is presumptuous of adults to feel they can offer solutions in fiction to troubled children. Writers, I feel, should write of childhood as they know it and leave children free to discover what they need.

Children turn to books for comfort. They tell me so, and letters of children who long for fathers influenced me, not to try to solve the problems of a fatherless child, but to write a book, partially drawn from my own childhood, in which a loving father was a central character. When *Ramona and Her Father* was published, I was astonished to have several librarians remark that I had finally written about contemporary problems. I had? I feel I have been writing about small problems contemporary to children all along. And fifty years ago my father, like Ramona's father, lost his job through a merger, tried to give up smoking and became irritable, which made me fear he might not love me. A man's loss of livelihood, grimmer in those days before unemployment insurance, comes under the heading, not of contemporary problems, but of universal human experience which is the proper subject of a novel, adult or juvenile.

Because parents deserve equal time, *Ramona and Her Mother* followed. In my childhood, when inflation threatened us as it threatens many families today, my mother sometimes worked outside the home. Her life was not easy, and neither was mine, for I sometimes felt that in her hurry and fatigue she did not have time left over for love. All children, I feel, long to have their mothers say they love them, so this became the theme of *Ramona and Her Mother*. Mrs. Quimby's work as a doctor's receptionist brings about changes in the life of the family and some feelings of insecurity in Ramona. Women have told me they are glad Mrs. Quimby is working outside the home, and so am I, for she enjoys her work even though it was begun out of necessity, and I feel that every woman should have an interest outside her family. Whether Mrs. Quimby is liberated or enslaved remains to be seen and will probably depend upon whatever attitude is current, for these days children's books are pushed about by trends.

Take the case of Mrs. Huggins. When *Henry Huggins* was published in 1950, reviewers commented with approval that Henry's parents were supportive. Times and trends changed, and in 1978 there appeared in a reference book on children's writers a short critical essay which stated that "... Henry's mother is something of a stereotype, always cooking and keeping the house neat—though she did help Henry pick up nightcrawlers." This critic overlooked the fact that Mrs. Huggins also delivered Henry's papers when Henry forgot and pitched in and helped when he was involved in a paper drive. Since Mrs. Huggins appears in the story only when she becomes involved in Henry's problems, there is no telling what she may be up to the rest of the time. Her activities, unless they concern Henry, have nothing to do with the story.

Now let us consider the dilemma of the author who receives the first chapter of *Henry Huggins* with changes proposed for its inclusion in a textbook. When Henry telephones his mother to ask if he can keep the dog he has found, Mrs. Huggins must not say in one editor's reader, "I don't know dear. You will have to ask your father," a line I felt was funny because we have all heard a version of it so many times from both male and female parents. The editor informs the author that this line does not show Mrs. Huggins as a strong person. The author mulls this over. Must every female in fiction be a strong person? Fiction should mirror life. How dull fiction would be if all female characters were portrayed alike. And is poor Mrs. Huggins really weak because she suggests her husband should be consulted, is she stalling a bit to give herself time to consider the situation, or is she considerate? Should not a father be consulted before a dog is added to the family? But wait. Farther down the page Mrs. Huggins relents and tells Henry he may keep the dog if he can bring it home on the bus. Here another thought occurs to the author but apparently not to the editor. Just possibly Mrs. Huggins is a weak person because she gives in to her son. Should the author point this out to the editor? No. Mrs. Huggins is a human being. She has both strengths and weaknesses.

Another textbook editor will allow Mrs. Huggins to say to Henry, "I don't know dear," but crosses out, "You will have to ask your father." He apparently feels that consulting Henry's father would make Mrs. Huggins a weak role model for girls. But might not girls, observing that Mrs. Huggins does not consult Mr. Huggins about a dog, grow up to become wives who add dogs to their families without consulting their husbands? Will this make them strong or overbearing? The author wonders about a generation of unwelcome dogs and their affect on the divorce rate.

Still another textbook editor will not allow poor Mrs. Huggins to wipe her hands on her apron. It seems this simple act turns her into a stereotype. The author is chagrined, for she often wipes her own hands on her apron. Has she unknowingly become a stereotype, perhaps even a weak person? But what about her husband? At times he has not only worn an apron but wiped his hands on it. Does this mean she is a stereotype while he is an individual? The author tries to think of a male character in fiction who has been labelled a stereotype but cannot. She suspects that if Mrs. Huggins had wiped her hands on the seat of her jeans the editor would have been pleased. This somehow would make her a non-stereotyped strong person. Messy, perhaps, but strong in his eyes.

But what about children? What do they think of Mrs. Huggins? As with real mothers, they seem to take her for granted, although once in a while a child remarks that Henry has a nice family. . . . [To] most children, a mother is the center of the family.

The two books about Ramona and her parents were written in rebellion against the portrayal of family life in many contemporary children's books. To this author the mother who wipes her hands on her apron is no more a stereotype than the familiar insensitive parents who do not understand their unhappy children, or the cheerful jean-clad single mother who copes with a child and a job, usually in the arts. Today's individual, I have noticed, is tomorrow's stereotype.

Religion is a part of Ramona's life. . . . I always felt that I had religion, sometimes as a worry (did God have to be everywhere when I was doing something I shouldn't?) but more often as a protection. So it is with Ramona. She is not a pious child, but she is very much aware of God. She has a quick word with Him now and then, and when she is doing something wrong she hopes He won't look until she gets things straightened out. She says her prayers, sometimes twice, in case He is too busy to listen the first time. Children often feel small and insignificant when frightened, and Ramona is often frightened.

In travels around the country I meet many parents, some who wear jeans and others who, I am sure, wipe their hands on their aprons, but all are concerned with their children and are doing the best they can in whatever circumstances an increasingly complex society has handed them. These are the parents—rich, poor, married or single—who care enough about books and reading to bring their children . . . to a bookstore or library to meet an author. . . . These are the parents whose children write happy letters that tell of reading aloud, sometimes the parent to the child or sometimes the child to the parent. . . . These to me are the non-stereotyped parents who need support in fiction for children. (pp. 24-6)

I receive in these times when many adults feel that anything is permissible in fiction for children, letters complimenting me on not feeling that I have to be "with it." I feel that I have always been with it, for the only way a children's writer can be with it with young readers, in my opinion, is to write honestly in realism or fantasy about childhood as he or she has experienced or observed it. Writers who do this may illuminate problems; they do not offer easy solutions. They may start trends; they do not try to get in on them. . . .

My intention is to continue wiping my hands on my apron and writing stories that I enjoy telling, for I always have several ideas in mind and faith that they will work themselves out as I write. (p. 26)

> *Beverly Cleary, in a "Regina Medal" award acceptance speech given at the Regina Medal Luncheon on April 8, 1981, in* Catholic Library World, *Vol. 52, No. 1, July-August, 1981, pp. 22-6.*

---

## GENERAL COMMENTARY

### EVELYN GELLER

Play, said the famous Viennese doctor, is the child's way of shaping reality to please his fancy. And it is an essential source of his charm; for in it he parodies—through his exposed needs, transparent motives, unabashed egoism, and grandiose schemes—the preposterous wishes that most of us would blush to divulge yet sneakingly entertain.

It is for this reason, perhaps, that Beverly Cleary delights in capturing children at their most characteristic occupation. With a rare talent for making them seem "pathetic and funny at the same time," the prolific and capable writer . . . creates a little world whose problems children can understand and adults, from their Brobdingnagian heights, enjoy. . . .

To her teen-age novels Beverly Cleary has brought the same blend of humor and sympathy. Although reviewers and librarians recommend these books primarily for slower readers, they praise the simplicity and tenderness with which Mrs. Cleary describes the inevitable ordeals of that chrysalis stage—mother-daughter conflicts, father's teasing, dating and popularity, first love. "Mrs. Cleary understands teen-agers inside and out, their language, their behavior, their dreams," wrote Charlotte Jackson about the "featherlight" comedy *Fifteen*. . . . [*The Luckiest Girl* and *Jean and Johnny*] show less sparkle and keen humor than the earlier novel, but are perceptive and consoling enough in their portrayal of "almost embarrassingly true to life" situations to mitigate some of the terrible bewilderment of adolescence.

In 1960 Mrs. Cleary turned her efforts to some funny and effortless little books [*Hullabaloo ABC, The Real Hole*, and *Two Dog Biscuits*] that reveal the "devastating logic" of the child's world.

> *Evelyn Geller, "W.L.B. Biography: Beverly Cleary," in* Wilson Library Bulletin, *Vol. 36, No. 2, October, 1961, p. 179.*

### PAUL C. BURNS AND RUTH HINES

[Children are] delighted when they first meet Henry, Ellen, Otis, and all the many lovable characters in Beverly Cleary's stories. Even reluctant readers are likely to become devoted "**Henry**" fans. (p. 743)

Particularly loved by children is *Otis Spofford*. . . .

When *Otis Spofford* was published, many librarians seemed to feel that it should not be placed on their shelves. Mrs. Cleary says: "This attitude astonished me because this type of boy is not malicious—he just likes to stir up a little excitement. There seems to be a real-life Otis in every classroom and I cannot see why anyone would object to him in a book." Otis appeals to children perhaps because he dares to try many of the things they have been tempted to do. They enjoy the fun and mischief, but they also sense the attitudes of fair play and consideration for others that pervade the story. (p. 745)

[In her] books for teenagers, Mrs. Cleary shows the same skill in creating true-to-life characters and situations that is found in her stories for the middle grades. She understands the real and imagined problems of adolescents and interprets them in a manner that tends to place them in proper perspective.

Beverly Cleary also writes well for the kindergarten and primary grade group. (p. 746)

Each of Mrs. Cleary's books is written in a simple style well suited to the subject matter. The characters have the virtues and faults of normal, everyday people. Their conversation is natural and realistic. They face problems familiar to most children and solve them in a childlike manner. Parents are warm and loving, interested and concerned, but not overly indulgent, so a good picture of family life is presented. Though not of the controlled vocabulary type, the books are easy to read and attract the interest of a wide range of ages. (pp. 746-47)

In schools and libraries everywhere, children often ask, "When are we going to get another Beverly Cleary book?" They know that when it comes, they will find that it was well worth awaiting. (p. 747)

> *Paul C. Burns and Ruth Hines, "Beverly Cleary: Wonderful World of Humor," in* Elementary English, *Vol. XLIV, No. 7, November, 1967, pp. 743-47, 752.*

### MARGARET NOVINGER

Someone has said that every good writer creates his world, peopled by his characters in the time and place in which he sets them. The world has not existed before the writer's creation and yet once created we cannot imagine a time when the author's world did not exist, though undiscovered.

In her "**Henry Huggins**" stories Beverly Cleary has created a world within the field of children's literature. It is not, to be sure, a large and majestic world; neither is it a slight nor insignificant one. The world is bounded by childhood and humor and welcomes all children, usually in what we term the middle-years group, to enter and enjoy.

When the stories began in 1950 Henry was an eight-year-old boy, a third grader who lived with his most understanding parents in a house on Klickitat Street in an average small city in Oregon. (It must quickly be added that in the very first episode of *Henry Huggins* a most unusual dog, Ribsy, is added to the family household.) The time on the clock was probably set at "now." Through the years Henry and his friends—Beezus (who is both an understanding friend to Henry and an older sister), Ramona (the four-year-old younger sister to Beezus (most exasperating, but a sister!), Scooter McCarthy (older boy in the neighborhood with a bicycle and a paper route of his own), and Byron Murphy (who was often busy building his robot)—have grown but at a slower chronological pace so that they are still within the 8 to 12 year-old-age group, of course, with the exception of Ribsy who seems always about the same. In this town, too, lives Ellen Tebbits, another eight-year-old, on Tillamook Street. But she and her friends—Austine Allen (her very best friend) and Otis Spofford (who really isn't a friend but a tease)—have not gotten around yet to meeting Henry and his friends, but maybe they will one day. Henry might be described as the typical American boy next door, but, of course, he is not average. Beverly Cleary has portrayed Henry as living, growing and experiencing the problems and pleasures of contemporary childhood. Adults, too, as parents, relatives, neighbors, teachers and bystanders, live in this world. Mrs. Cleary has presented a very human picture of the relationships between adults and children, often sympathetic and understanding, yet at times troubling and confusing. But on the whole, the children seem to be understanding and on occasions make use of one-upmanship. But above all this is a world of childhood—its language, its humor, its happenings, and its normal ups and downs.

As a librarian I learned at first hand the enthusiasm of children when they make the acquaintance of Henry and his friends. Henry is almost a catalyst. Give one book to a youngster and he will be back to finish the series. There are so many funny episodes to enjoy in the stories that one could start a list and keep right on going. My favorites have been: Henry's attempt to bring Ribsy home on a bus at the rush hour from *Henry Huggins;* Ribsy's bubble bath when he got lost—and found—in *Ribsy;* Ellen Tebbits' secret that she shared with Austine Allen, that they both wore woolen underwear, in *Ellen Tebbits;* Otis Spofford's nutritional help with the class's experimental rat in *Otis Spofford;* and Henry's comeuppance with Ramona when he got her favorite television fellow, Sheriff Bud, to announce on his TV program that he hoped a little girl called Ramona would stop pestering a boy called Henry Huggins in *Henry and the Clubhouse.*

All the episodes are funny, normal and believable. Almost any child in the age group of the stories could identify with the children in the situations.

While the stories together form a series, each book can stand upon its own merit. The characters and the setting tie them together. Beverly Cleary maintains their individuality as books because of her ability as a writer. To each book she brings humor and an unusual ability to understand children. Her stories are told in everyday dialogue about everyday life as most children in the United States know it. (p. 196)

Jane Purdy of *Fifteen,* Barbara MacLane of *Sister of the Bride,* Jean Jarrett of *Jean and Johnny,* and Shelley Latham of *The Luckiest Girl,* have much in common. They are all between the ages of 15 and 16, in junior high school, confronted with both the normal problems of growing up into womanhood, and meeting and adjusting to the special problems of contemporary society.... Mrs. Cleary has brought to bear her craft of writing, her unusually sensitive ear for language, and her understanding and humor.

The heroines of the stories have problems—boy-girl relationships, family relationships, search for values, school problems, relationships with friends, and simply the problem of growing up. The problems seem of the kind that must be widely shared by many average American girls, yet this does not mean that because the problems are common to the group they are not perplexing and individualized for each teenager who shares them. The value of the books would seem related to the opportunity they provide for identification and the comforting knowledge that problems are shared and that others have been able to adjust and grow as a result of the similar experiences.

The backgrounds of the stories again follow the pattern of the familiar and known as in the stories Mrs. Cleary has written for children in the middle years. Oregon and California are the regional settings and yet there is no feeling of provincialism in any of Mrs. Cleary's stories, because they could just as well have happened to children in Florida or North Dakota.

Thinking back to my own time as a teenager, in the 1940s, I remembered how few books there were for this age group, or, of the ones available, how few were written with the honesty and style of these teenage books by Mrs. Cleary. The one book I can remember is Maureen Daly's *Seventeenth Summer.* I felt such a sense of identification with the book that I read and re-read it. Mrs. Cleary has brought to her stories this quality of interest in and about junior girls.... *The Luckiest Girl,* I felt, was the best developed of Beverly Cleary's stories for this age group. The period of one school year for Shelley Latham, an only child, when she leaves her home in Oregon, her parents, her friends and her school to spend her junior year in southern California with a classmate of her mother's college days who has a large family, presents a realistic picture of the problems of adjustment to the large family of the Michies, especially of her relationship with Kate, the 13 year old, at a difficult time of life. The problems of boy-girl relationships are presented in a normal way. And yet the ability of Shelley to recognize the difference between infatuation and love and to distinguish between love that is lasting and love that will pass, is movingly portrayed as a sense of growth for the heroine. The relationship between Shelley and her mother is very honestly presented. The story ends with the implication that it may be Shelley who will end the period of separation by coming to understand the reasons for her mother wanting her daughter to be happier, more popular and attractive than she was as a girl.

Beverly Cleary has dealt often with the only child—Henry Huggins, Ellen Tebbits, Shelley Latham, Otis Spofford—in a more consistent number of stories than I can, at the moment, remember being attempted by any other author. Speaking from my own background as an only child, I think she has treated the only child in a very natural way. She has pointed out, as in *The Luckiest Girl,* the problems of adjusting to other children and learning the give and take of relationships in the family. And yet being the only child, as with twin-ness in her preschool stories, is a natural condition for many children and often their childhoods are normal and filled with many of the same frustrations, and happiness of children with brothers and sisters. The bond of childhood seems for Mrs. Cleary to unify children together in a way that children are not always unified with their parents who happen also to be adults.

*Sister of the Bride* has many of the qualities of Mrs. Cleary's books in the teenage group, yet it deals with a most temporary happening, early marriage. However, Mrs. Cleary treats the problem in such a normal and common-sense way that it seems to be just another aspect of contemporary society that young people have adjusted to and accepted and that the problem is now one for adults and parents to accept and live with. In particular the difference in outlook of Rosemary, the nineteen-year-old college freshman and bride-to-be, as she planned her marriage was delightfully handled in the specific question of stainless steel vs. silver flatware for the table. In my own experience this seems to be a point of separation between generations—the rather simple, everyday things and how our point of view toward them reflects a fundamental attitude toward life and how it is to be lived. The compromise on the flatware reflected the coming together of modern Rosemary, her rather starry-eyed sister, Barbara, and her mother's generation. While the story is about Barbara MacLane and her problem of always being two years behind her sister Rosemary, the wedding itself seems to bring together adults, teenagers and young adults into much more of a relationship than any of the other stories in the group.

While the stories in this age group are well written, humorous and contemporary, they do not seem to have the distinction of the **"Henry"** and **"Ellen"** stories. Other books written by other authors in this field might be compared with Mrs. Cleary's books and the former found to be more significant. But the degree of significance may be more a judgment of the adult than the teenager for whom the stories were written. (pp. 197-98)

Beverly Cleary seems to have an ability to understand the teenage girl in junior high and to write in such a way about this period of life that her books are marked with honesty as well as style and readability. If the adolescent can identify with the characters in the stories then possibly this is the meaningful measure of "significance" as applied by the readers of the books. (pp. 198-99)

Mary Stevens' lively and humorous illustrations match the sincerity and simplicity of Beverly Cleary's two stories in [the] picture book group, *The Real Hole* and *Two Dog Biscuits*. . . . Twins are rather an interesting combination in the stories because they are simply used as characters without the stories being tied to the quality of twin-ness. . . .

While Beverly Cleary has written only two books for this age group and in both the plots are rather slight, yet the humor in the stories, the ability of the author to catch the conversation of the children, and Mary Stevens' illustrations result in two delightful picture books. (p. 199)

Again, Mrs. Cleary has set [*Hullabaloo ABC*] in the background of the familiar. This book might be useful for a Head Start group since it gives a realistic picture of one aspect of American life—the farm, and provides an opportunity for the children to participate in making the appropriate "noises."

Two books written since 1960 seem to stand apart from the mainstream of Beverly Cleary's earlier books. Both books would be enjoyed by children in the 8 to 12 age group, but possibly one would be more enjoyed by girls than boys.

*Emily's Runaway Imagination* must surely be autobiographical fiction since the story is laid in a small town in rural Oregon during the 1920s, which corresponds to Beverly Cleary's time and place of childhood. Yet the period of the book lends color without distracting from the plot or the characters. Emily Bartlett is a character in her own right and not simply a reflection of Beverly Cleary. As in all the earlier books, Beverly Cleary tells about the adventures of Emily in a humorous and honest way. (pp. 199-200)

This is one of the most delightful of Beverly Cleary's stories both because of the charm of the story and the author's ability to convey the importance of books and reading as felt by Emily herself. . . .

[*The Mouse and the Motorcycle*] has been described as modern fantasy. The story is quite straightforward and might have happened to any average American boy. . . . The adventures of Keith and Ralph with the mice and human boarders at the Mountain View Inn are told in the usual artful, humorous and understanding style of Beverly Cleary. (p. 200)

I must say that I have given considerable thought on the one hand, to the lack of interest in the craft of Beverly Cleary as reflected in printed evaluations, summaries or criticisms, and on the other, to the lack of recognition of her works by significant awards in the field of children's books.

From personal experience in working with children in a public library, I know that the **"Henry Huggins"** and **"Ellen Tebbits"** stories are contemporary favorites of children in the middle-year group. The physical quality and constant need for replacement told an eloquent story of usage without reference to circulation records. Thinking back on it, the children that most often requested the Cleary books resembled Henry, Ellen, Otis and Beezus of the stories themselves. The children came wanting the books because friends or classmates had told them about the "funny" stories.

In my judgment the **"Henry Huggins"** books represent Beverly Cleary's unique contribution to the world of children's literature. Beverly Cleary is a versatile and creative writer at all age levels she has attempted: stories for boys and girls in the age group 8-12; stories for teenage girls; picture books for preschool children; and probably many adults at the age level from parent to grandparent. She has also been successful in various forms of writing: contemporary humor, picture books, autobiographical fiction, and modern fantasy.

As librarians we use standards of quality to judge books of value for the collection. While it is not possible for any one writer to constantly reach all standards with each book yet there is a consistent effort evident in Beverly Cleary's work. The following evidence can be cited: 1) she is an author who always writes with integrity and respect for her readers, 2) her characters and plots are believable and lively—though sometimes the plots seem slight in holding together a series of episodes or happenings, 3) she has accuracy and authenticity of background or setting, 4) she has a special style of writing—and it might be added she has an ear for the natural vocabulary of her reader, and 5) she attempts to give the reader something to wonder and think about—as well as a good story to enjoy and laugh about.

Simplicity of style and manner is almost deceptive in Beverly Cleary's stories. She seems to be a natural storyteller with an ear for the language of the contemporary child and an intuitive understanding of the unique personality of the child and his world. While Mrs. Cleary must have called upon many places, people and incidents from her own experience, her stories are not remembrances of things past. Beverly Cleary's stories are about the contemporary, average American child or teenager and most often the time of the story is today. The adults—parents, neighbors, teachers—seem average too. The joys and sadness, the successes and failures, the frustrations, the problems in relationships seem to be the ones that are expected in childhood and adolescence. But there is a need in children's literature for all sides of childhood to be presented. Mrs. Cleary may be called the Boswell of the average child. (pp. 201-02)

*Margaret Novinger, "Beverly Cleary: A Favorite Author of Children," in* Southeastern Librarian, *Vol. 18, No. 3, Fall, 1968, pp. 194-202.*

## CHARLOTTE S. HUCK AND DORIS YOUNG KUHN

[A] genuinely funny series of books about a very natural and normal boy are the *Henry Huggins* stories. . . . Mrs. Cleary's intimate knowledge of boys in the middle grades is very evident as she describes their problems, adventures, and hilarious activities. (p. 374)

Beverly Cleary has followed the adventures of Beezus in the book, *Beezus and Ramona,* to make one of the funniest stories ever written for girls. In this book, four-year-old Ramona becomes a real trial to both Beezus and her mother. Probably, the funniest episode is the day Ramona casually invites her entire kindergarten class to a party at her home without mentioning it to her mother. Girls with younger brothers and sisters will find this story hilarious. They certainly will sympathize with Beezus and may be helped to understand their own feelings toward the youngest members of their families. (p. 375)

*Charlotte S. Huck and Doris Young Kuhn, "Modern Fantasy and Humor," in their* Children's Literature in the Elementary School, *second edition, Holt, Rinehart and Winston, Inc., 1968, pp. 331-84.**

## JOHN ROWE TOWNSEND

American teachers and parents have long had cause to be grateful for the unpretentious books about Henry Huggins and his friends. . . . The formula for most of the [stories in *Henry Huggins*] is the same: a probable incident developed into hilarious improbability. . . . [*Ramona the Pest*] is a misnomer; Ramona is not really much of a pest, she's only a little girl beginning kindergarten. It seems just the thing for children who can remember that stage in their past, and condescend a little, but who are still near enough to understand and sympathize. (p. 280)

*John Rowe Townsend, "Realism, American-Style," in his* Written for Children: An Outline of English-Language Children's Literature, *revised edition, 1974. Reprint by The Horn Book Incorporated, 1981, pp. 272-82.**

## JUDITH ALDRIDGE

[In *The Mouse and the Motorcycle,*] Ralph is a mouse who craves excitement. Life behind the skirting of a seedy hotel bedroom lacks incident and adequate nourishment. So when a visiting boy leaves his model motorcycle accessible, Ralph immediately tries to ride it. Having mastered the technique ('These cars don't go unless you make a noise.') Ralph can explore the hotel and satisfy his desire for speed and incident, to almost disastrous limits at times.

Such a situation could become 'twee' but the writer totally avoids this danger. She has so clearly imagined and succinctly conveyed the setting, the human and mouse personalities involved, and relates the whole with such a delightfully astringent humour that the reader easily succumbs to the book's logic and atmosphere. The vocabulary is likely to be taxing for some readers and a few Americanisms may momentarily baffle, but the style and plot are direct enough for the book to hold the attention.

The sequel, *Runaway Ralph,* is a little more ambitious and perhaps less successful as a result. Tired of giving all his young relatives rides up and down the hotel corridors, Ralph decides to make for a nearby children's holiday camp. He is nearly killed by a cat, rescued, only to be put in a cage, and eventually redeems the reputation of one of the boys suspected of theft. Here the plotting and underlying ideas are a little too elaborate for their context. Nonetheless, there is much lively description, shrewd comment and a particularly amusing account of cat-and-mouse play as seen by the mouse.

*Judith Aldridge, in a review of "The Mouse and the Motorcycle" and "Runaway Ralph," in* Children's Book Review, *Vol. V, No. 1, Spring, 1975, p. 18.*

## CAROLINE FELLER BAUER

Who is Beverly Cleary? The author who has given us *Henry Huggins, Ramona the Pest, The Mouse and the Motorcycle, Ribsy,* and so many more. She is the woman who knows the importance of losing a first tooth and of having brand new boots. She knows how annoying it can be to have a little girl tagging after you on your paper route and how gratifying it is to make your Dad proud of you. She understands how frightening it can be to sleep alone in your own room at night, even if you had wanted the room more than anything in the world. . . . She writes about girls and boys with equal ease. She writes naturally and charmingly of the problems and pleasures of growing up, of going to school, and of getting along with friends and family in small-town America. She writes memorably of animals: dogs, cats, guppies, and a mouse named Ralph. . . .

Who is Beverly Cleary? A former librarian . . . who has written over twenty warm, funny, true-to-life books during a period of twenty-five years. Her books make us laugh out loud over such simple episodes as washing a dog or becoming a kindergarten dropout. Who is Beverly Cleary? She is the author who has made books exciting to children—hundreds and thousands and generations of children. How can you repay Beverly Cleary for such an outstanding contribution? (p. 359)

*Caroline Feller Bauer, in a "Laura Ingalls Wilder" award presentation speech given at the American Library Association in San Francisco on July 1, 1975, in* The Horn Book Magazine, *Vol. LI, No. 4, August, 1975, pp. 359-60.*

## SAM LEATON SEBESTA AND WILLIAM J. IVERSON

Today the dominant figure in happy-intermediate-childhood fiction is Beverly Cleary, whose . . . books have made readers the next-door neighbors of Beezus, Ellen Tebbits, Otis Spofford, Ramona, and especially Henry Huggins. . . .

Beverly Cleary's characters don't remain forever in a happy age of childhood. They grow older from book to book. They learn how to deal with each other, and successive episodes build on these changes and developments in character. Ramona in *Beezus and Ramona* . . . is something of a preschool-age tyrant. But in *Ramona the Pest* . . . we have hopes for this youngest member of the Quimby family. She may still be a nuisance to Henry, who is now on school patrol, and she does become a kindergarten dropout, but sympathy is on her side. She has moved from tyranny to trying to cope. At this writing, Beverly Cleary is reported working on the further adventures of Ramona. We await these eagerly. (p. 252)

*Sam Leaton Sebesta and William J. Iverson, "Realistic Fiction," in their* Literature for Thursday's

Child, *Science Research Associates, Inc., 1975, pp. 243-306.*\*

**MYRA POLLACK SADKER AND DAVID MILLER SADKER**

Beverly Cleary's stories, tremendously popular with children in the intermediate grades, are permeated with the sense of small-town security and comfort in the 1950s. Her convincingly realistic children emerge from essentially happy homes where parents remain on the periphery but are always ready with help and understanding when the children's problems become more than they can handle alone. (p. 26)

> *Myra Pollack Sadker and David Miller Sadker, "Life's Cycle," in their* Now Upon a Time: A Contemporary View of Children's Literature, *Harper & Row, Publishers, 1977, pp. 11-126.*\*

**MARY JUNE ROGGENBUCK**

Ask children "What author writes good stories?" Ask teachers "What author captures the interest of children in the middle grades?" Ask librarians "Whose books are children reading?" Beverly Cleary is a name you hear from each group. . . .

Cleary's philosophy of reading is the key to her kind of writing. What does she most want children to take from her books? "The feeling that reading is pleasure that can be enjoyed alone, that the written word has something to say that is worth discovering, and most of all, the feeling that *now* the reader is free to go on as far as he wants to go." . . . Without a doubt, this is the heritage that Cleary gives her young readers. (p. 55)

Her conviction that young children need to enjoy reading does not mean that Cleary has avoided children's problems in her books. In her stories, children must cope, for instance, with the teacher who doesn't understand, fear of the dark, anxiety about parents, fear of a dog, guilt feelings. To children these are serious problems.

All along, perceptive children have demonstrated greater insight into Cleary's writings than the typical adult reviewer. She has observed, "Since the publication of **Henry Huggins** I have noticed a difference between comments of children and the comments of adults. Reviewers said the **"Henry"** books were written purely for amusement. For almost thirty years children have been telling me the **"Henry"** books are 'funny and sad.' Funny and sad express my view of life, and I am pleased that children understand." . . . Cleary's view of life is genuine, and children intuitively recognize this. (p. 59)

> *Mary June Roggenbuck, "Profile: Beverly Cleary— The Children's Force at Work," in* Language Arts, *Vol. 56, No. 1, January, 1979, pp. 55-60.*

**CONNIE C. EPSTEIN**

[Beverly Cleary is an] author whose ability to see a situation from almost any point of view borders on the uncanny. (p. 274)

What has made Beverly Cleary such an important writer of her time? The immediate answer that comes to mind is her humor. But it is a very special kind of humor—the kind that can contrast two points of view, make us laugh at the difference, and show us with laughter, not a message, how the other person feels. (p. 275)

> *Connie C. Epstein, "Beverly Cleary: An Outstanding Children's Books Author for Our Time," in* Catholic Library World, *Vol. 51, No. 7, February, 1980, pp. 274-75.*

**MARGERY FISHER**

Beverly Cleary is deservedly popular for her shrewd humour and brisk prose, and [**Henry and Beezus** and **Henry and Ribsy**] are among her best. **Henry and Ribsy,** now a quarter of a century old, is as fresh as the new collection of tales, **Henry and Beezus,** and Thelma Lambert's drawings underline the energy and impetuosity of the characters. . . .

> *Margery Fisher, in a review of "Henry and Beezus" and "Henry and Ribsy," in her* Growing Point, *Vol. 19, No. 2, July, 1980, p. 3736.*

**LIZA GRAYBILL BLISS**

Back in the days of loafers and red convertibles, when a girl's world revolved around bobby pins and white piqué dresses, and the cutest boy looked "clean and tan in his letter sweater," Beverly Cleary wrote [**Fifteen** and **The Luckiest Girl**]. They both have '50-ish storylines involving high school-aged heroines who want to get ". . . the kind of boy every girl dreamed of. . . . And wouldn't it be wonderful if . . . she got to wear his letterman's sweater?"

Seems dated? Only at first glance. Beneath the surface is a germ of truth that keeps the writing far from superficiality, and keeps appreciation of the books from being trapped in the 1950s. Cleary's writing in both books features her characteristic sensitivity to personal feelings (with emphasis on the adolescent needs to be understood and to belong), and her perception into how relationships work. These elements are handled so effectively that they burn through the stories' oldish trappings and speak directly to any reader today—or tomorrow.

The result is a great combination: a meaning so on-target that it's not confined by a very specific and permeating time setting, plus a delightful dose of '50s nostalgia (the real McCoy; with an integrity that couldn't have been approached retrospectively). It is a terrific compliment to the author that these books written for contemporary consumption in the 1950s succeed out of the context responsible for their original appeal.

> *Liza Graybill Bliss, in a review of "Fifteen" and "The Luckiest Girl," in* Kliatt Young Adult Paperback Book Guide, *Vol. XIV, No. 6, September, 1980, p. 5.*

**DAVID REES**

[It is only in recent years] that critics have realized what has always been obvious: that Beverly Cleary is a marvelous writer. A superficial reading of the **"Ramona"** stories might suggest formula books and second-hand material: the adventures of a standard naughty little child who is far too boisterous and imaginative for her placid middle-class family and school, each chapter of each book concerning one self-contained incident that follows the same pattern—Ramona upsetting the Hallowe'en plans or the nativity play preparations, or ruining her mother's cooking or her sister's property or her teacher's lessons—an American version of Dorothy Edwards's *My Naughty Little Sister* or Richmal Crompton's *Just William* stories. But a judgment of this sort ignores the number of different ways in which the **"Ramona"** books work, the subtle shape of the narrative, and the distinction of the author's wit.

Beverly Cleary writes for varying levels of response, and this reflects an immense skill. Obviously the novels are of interest to the young child of Ramona's age, but they also give the appearance of looking back to that age from an older child's (sister Beezus) point of view, and, on a third level, one is constantly aware of an adult writing about children—for adults as well as children. These three quite different viewpoints are combined—concealed might be a better word—not only in every chapter, but in nearly every paragraph, sometimes in a single sentence. An excellent example of this occurs in *Ramona the Pest,* when Ramona, thrilled that she is wearing a fearsomely ugly witch's costume for the Hallowe'en parade, suddenly becomes frightened because nobody recognizes her. It's worth quoting the passage in full:

> "Ooh, what a scary witch!" said Miss Binney, rather absentmindedly, Ramona thought. Plainly Miss Binney was not really frightened . . . Ramona was. Miss Binney did not know who this witch was. Nobody knew who Ramona was, and if nobody knew who she was, she wasn't anybody.

> "Get out of the way, old witch!" Eric R. yelled at Ramona. He did not say, "Get out of the way, Ramona."

> Ramona could not remember a time when there was not someone near who knew who she was. Even last Hallowe'en, when she dressed up as a ghost and went trick-or-treating with Beezus and the older boys and girls, everyone seemed to know who she was. "I can guess who this little ghost is," the neighbors said, as they dropped a miniature candy bar or a handful of peanuts into her paper bag. And now, with so many witches running around and still more witches on the big playground, no one knew who she was.

> "Davy, guess who I am!" yelled Ramona. . . .

> "You're just another old witch," answered Davy.

> The feeling was the scariest Ramona had ever experienced. She felt lost inside her costume. She wondered if her mother would know which witch was which and the thought that her own mother might not know her frightened Ramona even more. What if her mother forgot her? What if everyone in the whole world forgot her? With that terrifying thought Ramona snatched off her mask, and although its ugliness was no longer the most frightening thing about it, she rolled it up so she would not have to look at it.

The simplicity of the sentence structure and the frequent repetition of ideas show that this kind of writing can be grasped by the young child, but the vocabulary—"miniature," "absentmindedly," "which witch was which," and the reference to trick-or-treating with Beezus—hold the interest of older children (they can regard with amusement the time when they did these things), while the main point being made—that wearing a mask causes a sense of loss of identity—is an ageless concept, experienced by adults as well as children.

The humor also works on the same three levels. Ramona's ingenuity—making stilts out of coffee tins and clanking around the block, singing at the top of her voice, or her literal interpretation of her sister's suggestion that she play Hansel and Gretel (she puts her doll in the oven and inadvertently ruins Beezus's birthday cake)—will doubtless entertain younger children, while her mistakes—thinking "the dawn's early light," for instance, is a dawnzer lee-light, a kind of lamp—will amuse

older readers. And there is an adult humor too; when Mrs. Quimby and Mrs. Kemp give their children endless advice about being careful in the traffic, "Ramona and Howie, weighed down by the responsibility of walking themselves to school, trudged off down the street." And sometimes all three come together; the episode in *Ramona and Her Father* when Ramona is bewildered by the sight of three girls dressing up for the nativity play is a good example:

> "Are you Jesus's aunts?" she asked.

> The girls found the question funny. "No," answered one. "We're the Three Wise Persons."

> Ramona was puzzled. "I thought they were supposed to be wise *men,*" she said.

> "The boys backed out at the last minute," explained the girl with the blackest eyebrows. "Mrs. Russo said women can be wise too, so tonight we are the Three Wise Persons."

The use of the word "Persons" and "Mrs. Russo said women can be wise too" are neat bits of satire, well above the heads of eight-year-olds, but, no matter—they will still be laughing at the remark about Jesus's aunts.

Nancy Chambers's comment in *Signal* on Judy Blume, that "she can encapsulate an emotion or a perception in a single sentence that makes the reader know it for himself as well as knowing it for the character in the book," and Lance Salway's agreement that Judy Blume "really does know how children feel and think and react," seem much more applicable to Beverly Cleary than to Judy Blume. Again and again the adult reader finds himself agreeing with the accuracy Beverly Cleary shows in her portrayal of her characters' feelings and thought processes, particularly in children's mistaken assumptions about what they only half-understand: Ramona thinking that a truant officer is something like a dog catcher and that he will take naughty children away just as the dog catcher took "an elderly overweight Basset hound" from the school playground; "he shut the dog in the back of his truck and drove away with it." There is the same insight when adults underestimate what children feel—Mr. Quimby trying to soothe Ramona when the cat has eaten the Hallowe'en pumpkin, not realizing that she is upset because he is smoking too much, that she's worried "his lungs will turn black." And in the absurd fears children experience, often so absurd that adults just don't understand the strength of the emotions involved: in *Ramona the Brave* Ramona has her own room at last; she no longer has to suffer the irritations of sharing with Beezus; it's something she has looked forward to for months. But she had not realized how frightened she would be, lying in bed, alone in the dark. She dare not tell her parents in case she loses the privileges and status of having a room of her own, and they never discover how terrified she is. She diverts their suspicions by making them think she is afraid of a picture of a gorilla.

Most children love a series of books about the same characters, but they rarely appeal to adults, the reason probably being that the first of a series is usually the best and its success has prompted the author into writing sequels that don't always match up to the inspiration of the original story. But the opposite, fortunately, is true of Beverly Cleary. The first of the "Ramona" books, *Beezus and Ramona,* is the weakest, the least amusing, with a final chapter that is a bit too cozy and cloying, but after that she never puts a foot wrong; the invention in its successors never flags and the wit and the narrative skill are always first-rate. This is a rare ability; Rodie Sudbery, for instance, despite the excellence of much of the writing in the Polly Devenish stories, does not . . . achieve the same consistency.

The appeal of Rodie Sudbery's and Beverly Cleary's work will be chiefly to those children who are readers, but who want something less intellectually demanding than the literature that usually claims most of the experts' attention. Books like theirs not only have an obviously useful function for the young, but they should also be read by adults. (pp. 98-102)

> *David Rees, "Middle of the Way: Rodie Sudbery and Beverly Cleary," in his* The Marble in the Water: Essays on Contemporary Writers of Fiction for Children and Young Adults, *The Horn Book, Inc., 1980, pp. 90-103.\**

## BERNICE E. CULLINAN WITH MARY K. KARRER AND ARLENE M. PILLAR

Beverly Cleary's work has wide appeal and lasting value. (p. 91)

Cleary's characters remind you of children who live down the street in many neighborhoods across America; therein lies part of the secret of their universal appeal. (p. 92)

> *Bernice E. Cullinan with Mary K. Karrer and Arlene M. Pillar, "Expanding Language through Literature," in their* Literature and the Child, *Harcourt Brace Jovanovich, Inc., 1981, pp. 71-114.\**

### EARLY YEARS

It is Beverly Cleary who brings imagination and the real world of contemporary children into schools and homes in this country and throughout the world. Little wonder the books are so widely read; hardly a parent or child could fail to appreciate the humor, or fail to recognize real-life situations that probably remind readers of what happened yesterday, or last week. (p. 24)

Although spinning a tale comes easily to Beverly Cleary, she approaches it as serious work, but work she enjoys. Each book is written first in longhand, then edited and typed. This version is then edited and typed again, before the final version is typed and sent to the publisher. Indeed, a Beverly Cleary book doesn't leave home until it's "right."

She has no pattern to how she writes her books, other than to start them on January 2nd. Why that date? "I started my first book, *Henry Huggins,* on that date." A book usually takes about six months to write, but before she starts she's been thinking of the book for three years or more. . . .

How does she write a book? It depends. With one book she'll start at the beginning and march straight through to the end. With another, she'll have a conclusion in mind, and the book will grow as Mrs. Cleary works out the ways in which the characters got to where they are.

She usually begins a book with whatever incident comes to mind and sometimes has absolutely no idea how the book will end. . . . It is obvious she approaches writing as a craft, and it is equally obvious she enjoys it immensely. (p. 25)

Beverly Cleary has a deep sense of humor, one that finds a chuckle in the familiar. . . . Her humor is not the slipped-on-the-banana-peel variety, but subtle, human and real. (p. 36)

> *"Beverly Cleary: A Practicing Perfectionist," in* Early Years, *Vol. 13, No. 1, August-September, 1982, pp. 24-5, 36.*

## SUSAN KENNEY

Ramona Quimby made her first appearance back in 1950 in ["Henry Huggins"]. . . . Clothed in increasingly tattered overalls, clutching a water pistol or a pet slug (yes, a slug), even in her brief appearances she managed to take over the action and usually, if inadvertently, save the day. In the seven books about Ramona that have followed—and in some 20 other books spanning more than 30 years—Beverly Cleary has portrayed with humor, and with the reality of detail that brings instant recognition, most of the ordinary predicaments and problems of childhood, the difficulties (and rewards) of growing up. In case you've forgotten what it felt like to have bubble gum in your hair, loose front teeth flapping every time you said a word, or a gorilla hiding under your bed, these books will refresh your memory.

From the beginning, Ramona has been one of the most popular, if not always the most appealing, of Beverly Cleary's characters. (She is, in fact, that most difficult of creatures, a perfect terror with whom we have complete sympathy. Well, almost.) She combines a rich fantasy life with canny if often misdirected ingenuity, exhausting energy and the spunky insouciance that leads her to answer the inevitable infuriating grown-up who asks "What's the matter, little girl, has the cat got your tongue?" by demonstrating clearly that the cat has not. At the end of the first book devoted entirely to the Quimbys, "Beezus and Ramona" . . . , Mrs. Quimby sighs, "All we can do is wait for her to grow up."

And that is what delighted generations of readers have done in the six "Ramona" books written since. Chronological and continuous, . . . they take Ramona from kindergarten—from which she is briefly expelled—through third grade.

So we find the Quimbys are a nice family, but not a perfect one. Mrs. Quimby, a working mother, is often harassed and sometimes irritable; Mr. Quimby loses his job and sits around the house smoking too much ("Ramona and Her Father," . . .); the family becomes financially overextended in the midst of the 1970's recession, the parents quarrel ("Ramona and Her Mother," . . .). The girls find themselves in predicament after predicament in school, at home, around the neighborhood, they experience fears of the dark, of teachers and parents not loving them or each other, of not doing well. They have to wear hand-me-down (worse yet, boys') snow boots, suffer home haircuts and unjust treatment at the hands of the baby-sitter. All these problems are humorously described but never made light of—they are real, and they are ours too.

But what is ultimately so reassuring is that the relationships between parent and child are based on mutual respect and understanding. The Quimby parents take the time to listen to their children, and somehow they always find the right things to say, the things that children long to hear and most parents wish they had said after it's too late.

"Nobody is nice all the time," says Mr. Quimby, "or if they are, they are boring" ("Ramona Quimby, Age 8," . . .). The Quimbys are not boring. Nor does everything always turn out perfectly. In this newest book, "Ramona Forever," Ramona is going on 9. Mr. Quimby has completed a degree in art education, begun after he lost his job two years ago, but now he can't find a job teaching. Ramona is allowed to leave her detested baby sitter and stay home with Beezus after school, but the Quimby cat, Picky-Picky, dies while the two girls are home alone. Aunt Beatrice announces she is getting married and moving to Alaska and last but not least, Ramona's mother is expecting a baby.

It's enough to make any 9-year-old's head spin, and Ramona's does; she feels as though her whole world is falling apart. Still, everything works out, or almost everything. Ramona finds the dropped ring at the wedding and is proclaimed a heroine; her mother's first words to her after the baby is born—"Oh, Ramona, how I've missed you!"—are the most beautiful she has ever heard. But Mr. Quimby doesn't get a job teaching, and has to return to the supermarket, though to a better job. "We can't always do what we want in life," he says, "so we have to do the best we can."

"Growing up is hard work" Mr. Quimby says. At the end, Ramona, who has seen herself in her bridesmaid's dress in a three-way mirror, going on forever, sums up her life, and in a way, all the books. "She thought about loose teeth, real sore throats, quarrels, misunderstandings with her teachers, longing for a bicycle her family could not afford, worrying when her parents bickered, how terrible she had felt when she hurt Beezus's feelings without meaning to, and all the long afternoons when Mrs. Kemp looked after her until her mother came home from work. She had survived it all . . . She was winning at growing up." And so she is. Luckily for her readers, she still has a long way to go.

> *Susan Kenney, "Growing Up a Winner," in* The New York Times Book Review, *November 11, 1984, p. 47.*

---

### HENRY HUGGINS (1950)

Enchanting small-boy adventures—a grammar school Odyssey. Henry Huggins, third grade man, is a neighborhood immutable—the boy with the limp mongrel, the boy whose parents feel compelled to root out night crawlers by flashlight so their son's business obligations might be fulfilled, the boy who winces and slides down in his seat when parts for the school's dramatic productions are assigned. Mrs. Cleary must have had her ear to the door many times to catch the flavor of third grade manners and mores. Young readers will sympathize with Henry's horror at the loss of prestige involved in being required to play the part of Little Boy and be kissed by a dumb eighth-grade girl on the stage; Henry's determination in sheltering the rapidly spawning progeny of two busy guppies; and the gloomy tragedy when the original owner of Henry's dog, Ribsy, appears triumphantly on the scene. A collection of light, gay episodes, sure to please.

> *A review of "Henry Huggins," in* Virginia Kirkus' Bookshop Service, *Vol. XVIII, No. 14, July 15, 1950, p. 386.*

Henry is a very normal boy with all the problems and fun of a third grader anywhere. . . . There is plenty of humor in each episode with none of the coy, tongue-in-cheek style that usually characterizes this type of story.

> *A review of "Henry Huggins," in* Bulletin of the Children's Book Center, *Vol. 3, No. 9, September, 1950, p. 54.*

Nine- and ten-year-old boys will appreciate Henry's dilemma in adopting a stray dog, trying not to raise too many guppies, etc. However, author made a mistake in referring to Henry in the first sentence as being in third grade; he acts and talks like a fourth- or fifth-grader. Definitely not in a class with *Homer*

*Readers of Cleary's books know Klickitat Street as Henry Huggins's address. Cleary told* Children's Literature Review *that children ask her constantly if such a street exists; indeed it does, as this photo proves. While living in Portland, Oregon, Cleary resided on 37th Avenue, one of Klickitat's cross-streets (as pictured above). She liked the sound of Klickitat so much that she used it throughout the* Henry Huggins *series. Courtesy of Beverly Cleary.*

*Price* but still very funny. . . . Good characterization of small boys; natural dialogue. . . . Recommended.

> *Margaret E. Martignoni, in a review of "Henry Huggins," in* Library Journal, *Vol. 75, No. 16, September 15, 1950, p. 1513.*

[This story] is written for younger boys and girls but we defy anyone under seventy not to chuckle over it. The humor is so much a part of the story that it is difficult to define. It is on every page, almost in every word. . . . If Henry complained that nothing ever happened to him before he acquired Ribsy, he certainly could not say that life was dull afterward. It is hard to decide which of these incidents is the funniest.

> *Mary Gould Davis, in a review of "Henry Huggins," in* The Saturday Review, *Vol. XXXIII, No. 45, November 11, 1950, p. 48.*

[Both **Henry Huggins** and *Homer Price*] appear at first glance to have a great deal in common. Both are about small town boys who become involved in ridiculous incidents; both are humorous, both in text and illustrations; both are episodic in form; both are very popular and have become minor classics. But actually, these are about the only things they have in common. Basically, they are completely different, although their appeal is universal.

Despite the realistic-seeming situations, *Homer Price* is a fantasy, and **Henry Huggins** is, in the best sense of the term, a nonsense book. . . .

The characters in *Homer* are not realistic, either. They are caricatures or farcical creations. . . . The book is, strangely, primarily about adults. Only in the Super-Duper Man incident are children important. And most of the time, Homer does not initiate the action. He is a rather passive character to whom things happen—he doesn't go out looking for adventure. . . .

*Henry Huggins* is very different. In each case, the situation starts out as a realistic one, but it slowly evolves to become logically absurd. There is nothing more normal than that an eight-year-old boy would like some guppies. Only Henry would wind up with thousands, and only Henry would trade them for one catfish. The other situations are equally as possible—the collection of night crawlers, the soaking in green paint, the hilarious dog show, and the acquisition of Ribsy. But as the author adds one detail after another, the whole incident gets further away from plausibility, although the reader cannot actually say any detail is impossible. This "it's always possible" approach is one of the factors that makes Henry's adventures so appealing to children. Also, the characters are typical, rather than farcical, as in *Homer Price*. There is not a single eccentric or unrecognizable person anywhere in the book. Nor are the situations at all unusual. They are things most children will be familiar with. The Christmas play, for example, is typical of every school play ever given, and Henry's reaction to his assigned part is just what the reader expects. But his way of getting out of the part is what makes the incident so funny, and the fact that his new role is perfectly wonderful for him completes the incident to everyone's satisfaction.

Henry is a much more active boy than Homer is, with many of the stories being started by a definite act of his own. The book is all about children—adults figure in it as minor characters. The approach is much more emotional in *Henry* than in *Homer*. Though the book is episodic, there is a thread of plot, and the last chapter, wherein Henry gets to keep his dog, is frankly emotional in nature. Since Henry is so much younger than Homer, naturally his audience is younger.

Miss Cleary writes only of things in an eight-year-old's world. She may have some wry comments on P.T.A.s or teachers or other children, but not on unionism or police efficiency or social progress with which her readers are unfamiliar. Mr. McCloskey, on the other hand, writes for older children who can appreciate his barbed comments and caricatures. Henry's small town is hardly described. Homer's becomes very familiar. Henry's enthusiasms lead him into difficulties. Homer's problems seek him out.

Despite the differences in the basic approach, both books depend for much of their humor, on exaggeration. And exaggeration is something children always love!

> *Phyllis Cohen, in a review of "Henry Huggins," in* Young Readers Review, *Vol. II, No. 6, February, 1966, p. 12.*

Frequently a child makes the transition from picture books to "real" books via the light, even slapstick *Henry Huggins* . . . , and Carolyn Haywood's the "Betsy" books. . . . These books are not "classics" in the old sense. Their characters are jauntily rather than finely drawn; but while they contain little depth in their portrayal of child life, they do offer fun and the secure family situation that makes such simple fun possible. (p. 25)

> *Sheila A. Egoff, "Survival of the Fittest: Selection from the Golden Ages of Children's Literature," in her* Thursday's Child: Trends and Patterns in Contemporary Children's Literature, *American Library Association, 1981, pp. 18-30.\**

---

## *ELLEN TEBBITS* (1951)

It seems obvious from this entrancing successor to *Henry Huggins* that the author is as well acquainted with the whisperings, weeps and whoops of third grade distaff side as she is with the ways of young men like Henry. Third grader, Ellen Tebbits, has her happiest dreams realized when she acquires a Best Friend, in the person of Austine Allen, who not only lives near enough to share after schools and Saturdays, but also is undoubtedly the only girl in the school besides Ellen who is forced to wear winter underwear. Together the friends weather crises— Ellen's campaign to win the honor of clapping erasers at school; a misadventure with a horse; and the shattering witticisms of the class's "uncooperative boy", Otis. Therefore when a quarrel divides the friends, the tragedy is overwhelming—not even Ellen's appointment as Substitute Rat in the "Pied Piper of Hamelin" can lift the gloom. An eraser clapping session, however, patches the quarrel.

> *A review of "Ellen Tebbits," in* Virginia Kirkus' Bookshop Service, *Vol. XIX, No. 13, July 1, 1951, p. 319.*

The trials of an 8-year-old in school and out will be a favorite with many young readers. I was especially fond of the chapter in which Ellen . . . is given the part of a Substitute Rat in case one of the regular Rats was ill. How she stole the show and got mixed up with the Maypole dancers because her rat mask slipped and she couldn't see what she was doing, is one of the funniest incidents I have read in a long time. (pp. 484-85)

> *A review of "Ellen Tebbits," in* Publishers Weekly, *Vol. 160, No. 5, August 4, 1951, pp. 484-85.*

[The serious preoccupations of third-graders] are delightfully presented in the person of **"Ellen Tebbits"**. . . . Ellen takes her place beside Henry as an original and endearing character— a welcome addition to children's bookshelves.

> *Ethel C. Ince, in a review of "Ellen Tebbits," in* The Christian Science Monitor, *September 6, 1951, p. 13.*

The creator of that riotously funny boy, **"Henry Huggins,"** now brightens the lives of third grade girls. . . . Ellen and her troubles are both funny to the young and touching to older readers. . . . [Children] will laugh hard at Ellen riding a horse she cannot control. Austine proves an original, understanding friend, who makes Ellen's complicated days happier. All is told with a downright realism that is almost believable, and the school scenes are choice. Girls of eight to ten will be immensely cheered to find that Ellen had worse troubles than theirs, and that they all came out happily in the end.

> *Louise S. Bechtel, in a review of "Ellen Tebbits," in* New York Herald Tribune Book Review, *October 14, 1951, p. 20.*

Beverly Cleary has a special gift for making the children in her stories funny and pathetic at the same time. . . . Through all Ellen's joys and sorrows there runs a thread of humor that makes the reader chuckle even when he is sympathizing with her.

> *Mary Gould Davis, in a review of "Ellen Tebbits," in* The Saturday Review of Literature, *Vol. XXXIV, No. 45, November 10, 1951, p. 60.*

*Henry Huggins* has had such a success with boys and girls everywhere (it is wonderful for reading aloud to groups of children) that I am sure *Ellen* will have a warm reception. To me the book seems a bit contrived and not quite so good as *Henry,* but nevertheless Ellen is a real girl and her adventures full of zest and interest.

> *Jennie D. Lindquist and Siri M. Andrews, in a review of "Ellen Tebbits," in* The Horn Book Magazine, *Vol. XXVII, No. 6, December, 1951, p. 408.*

---

### HENRY AND BEEZUS (1952)

More doings of Henry Huggins and his friends—especially Beezus. This time Henry is on the trail of a bicycle—a trail that leads him through a sale of bubble gum, to an auction of lost bicycles at the police station, and finally to a supermarket opening where his dream is realized. Mrs. Cleary has again succeeded in capturing the feelings, actions, and dialog of real third-graders and her account of their minor triumphs and tragedies is spiced with humor that they will enjoy.

> *A review of "Henry and Beezus," in* Bulletin of the Children's Book Center, *Vol. 6, No. 1, September, 1952, p. 3.*

Since Henry Huggins made his appearance two years ago that small boy has charmed young and old alike with his deadly persistence, his spontaneity and his capacity for trouble. It is wonderful to have Henry back again, and of course Ribsy his dog—both of them as natural as ever.

Henry now has his heart set on a bicycle and will go to any honorable lengths to get one. His friend Beatrice, commonly known as Beezus, is anxious to help, although considerably hampered by her bratty little sister. The well-intentioned Ribsy frequently complicates Henry's efforts too. . . . It is all very funny and as true to life as Henry's "genuine Daniel Boone coonskin cap with the snap-on tail."

> *Ellen Lewis Buell, "Bicycle Quest," in* The New York Times Book Review, *September 14, 1952, p. 30.*

The mere mention of [the incidents in **"Henry and Beezus"**] does not invest them with the well-established Huggins humor. It is now increased by Beezus' share in the plot, and the doings of her little sister Ramona.

It is small-town stuff put down with a loving pen and a keen ear for small boys' ways. Overflowing good humor pervades all three of the **"Henry"** books and you can read them in any order.

> *Louise S. Bechtel, in a review of "Henry and Beezus," in* New York Herald Tribune Book Review, *October 12, 1952, p. 16.*

Episodes are funny, and boy readers won't object to the two minor girl characters. Excellent to lure non-readers. Henry should enjoy the same popularity as Homer Price. Reading aloud will bring out all the humor. . . . Recommended for home, school, and public libraries.

> *Mary Jo Meade, in a review of "Henry and Beezus," in* Library Journal, *Vol. 77, No. 18, October 15, 1952, p. 1821.*

Although a book for younger primary children, even older ones—and adults—cannot help chuckling at Mr. Grumbie bar-

becuing his roast or Henry getting a ticket for parking Ribsy. Well-developed characters and humorous incidents make this book a laugh from one chapter to the next.

> *S. McD., in a review of "Henry and Beezus," in* Book Window, *Vol. 8, No. 2, Spring, 1981, p. 15.*

Both adults and children will find much to enjoy here—including further encounters with the infamous Ramona. Her elder sister's comment when Ramona sits on a box playing 'waiting for a bus' will strike a universal chord: 'She thinks it's fun and I don't want her to find out that it isn't. It keeps her quiet.' . . . Individual chapters have plenty of incidental fun, much of it provided by the exploits of Ribsy. . . . Beverly Cleary knows how children's minds work and she writes convincing dialogue: 'And if you don't behave I'll . . . I'll tell mother about the time you waited until she went to the shops and then tried to give the cat a bath in the Bendix. Then you'll be sorry!' . . . [This book] is likely to be popular with juniors and their teachers. (pp. 128, 131)

> *Peter Kennerley, in a review of "Henry and Beezus," in* The School Librarian, *Vol. 29, No. 2, June, 1981, pp. 128, 131.*

---

### OTIS SPOFFORD (1953)

Perhaps not as spontaneous as her **"Henry Huggins"** and **"Ellen Tebbits"** stories, this still has some mighty funny moments and follows the infectious misdemeanours of Ellen's contemporary, Otis. Dressed for the part of a bull in a bull fight at a school festival, Otis gets rambunctious and is due for a "come-uppance" but he goes unpunished on that day and heads on toward bigger and better escapades. . . . [He] and Ellen—whom he bullies continually—finally have it out on the ice pond.

> *A review of "Otis Spofford," in* Virginia Kirkus' Service, *Vol. XXI, No. 13, July 1, 1953, p. 387.*

A really hilarious story of a mischievous, impudent boy who is a classroom comedian, a show-off and a pest, but still very lovable. Young readers will understand Otis and recognize his type. They will be delighted when he is given his come-uppance by the gentle, timid, feminine Ellen Tebbits. . . . There is a brief but devastating parody of books designed to teach American history to children. It is called "With Luke and Letty on the Oregon Trail," and Otis doesn't think much of it.

> *A review of "Otis Spofford," in* Publishers Weekly, *Vol. 164, No. 7, August 15, 1953, p. 647.*

Children who find most book heroes too good to be true will be immensely taken by Otis Spofford, a boy who likes nothing better than to stir up a little excitement—and is a master at it. . . . As always the author's writing is marked by a freshness and naturalness stemming from an understanding of children and the brand of humor that appeals to them.

> *A review of "Otis Spofford," in* The Booklist, *Vol. 50, No. 1, September 1, 1953, p. 18.*

[Mrs. Cleary] has her elementary school down pat, and manages to report her growing boys, teachers, and P.T.A. meetings so that parents chuckle and boys laugh out loud. The incidents follow through the school year. An adult feels increasing pity for Otis' teacher and wonders at what ideas such a character will put into other boys' heads. We cannot say that we find Otis a really memorable bad boy, funny as he is, partly because there is no continuous plot and no change in Otis. But a lot of small boys are getting much-needed laughter from all the Cleary books.

> Louise S. Bechtel, in a review of "Otis Spofford," in New York Herald Tribune Book Review, September 27, 1953, p. 10.

[Otis is], unconsciously, just a little bit pathetic for he is the son of a hurried and harried dancing school teacher. He is the kid who hasn't much to come home to. Mrs. Cleary doesn't stress this point—she is no sentimentalist—but this reader couldn't help wishing that Otis' mother had more time for him. This in itself is proof of the strength of his personality—the brasher he is, the better you like him.

> Ellen Lewis Buell, "The Cut-Up," in The New York Times Book Review, October 4, 1953, p. 28.

Remember [Beverly Cleary's] *Henry and Beezus*? Well, *Otis Spofford* . . . has just as much small-boy deviltry and nonsense as the first. Probably won't be endorsed by P.T.A. groups, but it certainly has enough of a *Peck's Bad Boy* quality to make children between eight and twelve chuckle in secret, sympathetic glee.

> Margaret Ford Kieran, in a review of "Otis Spofford," in The Atlantic Monthly, Vol. 192, No. 6, December, 1953, p. 98.

---

### HENRY AND RIBSY  (1954)

One of Mrs. Cleary's most hilarious books. . . . Henry is promised a fishing trip if he can keep Ribsy out of trouble, not at all an easy task. There is a very funny scene involving Henry's friend, Beezus, and her little sister, Ramona, who makes off with Ribsy's bone and soon has the neighborhood in an uproar. We hope that Mrs. Cleary will write a whole book about Ramona very soon.

> A review of "Henry and Ribsy," in Publishers Weekly, Vol. 166, No. 2, July 10, 1954, p. 131.

[This third book about Henry Huggins is] better if possible than its predecessors. . . . Only a person who knows the minds and ways of children could continue to create such natural characters and such unhackneyed, genuinely funny situations.

> A review of "Henry and Ribsy," in The Booklist, Vol. 51, No. 1, September 1, 1954, p. 21.

Few writers for children can handle everyday comedy so briskly and so realistically as Beverly Cleary. Ribsy's entanglement with the garbage man (under the impression that he was protecting his master's property); Ribsy's misunderstanding with the embattled ladies of the P.T.A.; Henry's agonizing encounter with his friends after a home haircut—all these and other ordeals are built up with a fine sense of timing, an accurate ear for a small boy's speech and a genuine compassion for a small boy's tribulations. It's no wonder that real-life contemporaries of Henry—and of Ellen Tebbits and Otis Spofford—recommend Mrs. Cleary's books enthusiastically.

> Ellen Lewis Buell, "A Boy's Best Friend," in The New York Times Book Review, September 26, 1954, p. 34.

The adventures of Henry Huggins and his lovable shaggy dog, Ribsy, could happen to a boy and dog combination any-where. . . . This is a very readable story for the 7 to 10 year old boy. The style is flowing, although the action is a little "padded" at times. . . . The loyalty and love between boy and dog comes over very well, and is an essential ingredient of the story.

The only distasteful parts were the "clubbing" of the salmon, and, for British children, the frequent mention of "horsemeat" as a dog food. They can probably accept the rest of the Americanisms.

> A review of "Henry and Ribsy," in The Junior Bookshelf, Vol. 43, No. 3, June, 1979, p. 156.

---

### BEEZUS AND RAMONA  (1955)

A new and, of course, hilarious book by Beverly Cleary which concentrates on the antics of Beatrice Quimby's 4-year-old sister, Ramona, a character familiar to readers of **"Henry Huggins," "Henry and Beezus"** and Mrs. Cleary's other entertaining stories about the trials and embarrassments of the young of Portland, Oregon. Adults will be able to follow the infant logic that leads Ramona into her various escapades, but to the 9- and 10-year-olds who will read and love this book she will doubtless remain a nasty little villain in homemade paper rabbit ears, determined to spoil everyone's fun.

> A review of "Beezus and Ramona," in Publishers Weekly, Vol. 168, No. 7, August 13, 1955, p. 670.

The unpredictable, funny things done by this imaginative baby sister make humorous reading for girls in the third and fourth grades and for slower readers in even the fifth and sixth grades who baby-sit. As usable as the Haywood books.

> Miriam Snow Mathes, in a review of "Beezus and Ramona," in Junior Libraries, an appendix to Library Journal, Vol. 2, No. 1, September, 1955, p. 39.

All of us who know Henry Huggins know Beezus, and we've had glimpses of her little demon sister Ramona. Now they have their own book, just as funny and real as those about Henry. It will bring wonderful comfort to nine-year-old girls who suffer from characterful, bright, naughty little sisters. In every chapter, this little imp . . . dreams up some new mischief. Discipline from her parents, varied tactics of child-care applied by Beezus—nothing affects her.

Poor Beezus is most truly horrified when she suddenly discovers she doesn't LIKE Ramona! Mrs. Cleary resolves this unhappiness cleverly, in a book full of laughter and extraordinary family situations, all drawn with skillful realism. The talk is ever so true to children of these ages.

> Louise S. Bechtel, in a review of "Beezus and Ramona," in New York Herald Tribune Book Review, November 6, 1955, p. 8.

The adults in this sometimes humorous book are sympathetic to Beezus's problems, but they appear to assume that Ramona will outgrow her tantrums and willfulness with little discipline. Although she suffers abuse from her sister, Beezus feels guilty when she realizes she does not always love Ramona. Through the understanding of her elders, she learns that such feelings are natural and acceptable.

> Sharon Spredemann Dreyer, in a review of "Beezus and Ramona," in her The Bookfinder: A Guide to Children's Literature about the Needs and Problems

of Youth Aged 2-15, *American Guidance Service, Inc., 1977, No. 190.*

Beezus is nine and Ramona is four. . . . The ideal reader is perhaps in the in-between-age. She must be old enough to read and young enough to enjoy the discomfiture of Beezus. Sisters are inveterate rivals and reading lightheartedly about the quarrels and reconciliations of others might be a soothing process.

> *A review of "Beezus and Ramona," in* The Junior Bookshelf, *Vol. 43, No. 1, February, 1979, p. 28.*

---

### FIFTEEN (1956)

The author of the **"Henry Huggins"** books which depict younger children so surely, demonstrates an equal understanding of adolescence in the story of an average fifteen-year-old girl, Jane Purdy, and the ups and downs of her friendship with Stan, her first real boy friend. The boy-girl and family relationships, the worries, the joys, and the anguish common to adolescent girls are portrayed with perceptiveness, warmth and kindly humor in the thoroughly enjoyable story, perfect for junior high readers.

> *A review of "Fifteen," in* The Booklist and Subscription Books Bulletin, *Vol. 53, No. 1, September 1, 1956, p. 28.*

In her stories of Henry Huggins, Ellen Tebbits, their friends and foes, Beverly Cleary has given us intimate glimpses of the fourth- and fifth-grade worlds, thereby bringing a great deal of pleasure to the inhabitants of that world. Now she applies her perception and her remarkable gift for comedy to the problems of the younger teen-ager. . . .

[If Jane's] ordeals seem less complicated than those of other fictional, teen-aged heroines, she herself would not agree. . . . Featherlight in style, this is good comedy, underlaid with common sense and insight.

> *Ellen Lewis Buell, "Teen-Age Troubles," in* The New York Times Book Review, *September 16, 1956, p. 38.*

The author of the inimitable **"Henry Huggins"** proves her versatility and her understanding of adolescence in this story of Jane Purdy. The same humor that has endeared Mrs. Cleary to younger boys and girls marks this story. . . . Fifteen-year-old girls, girls not yet fifteen, and anyone who has ever been fifteen will love this story of [Jane] . . . , as lovable a fifteen-year-old as ever agonized over a phone call that failed to materialize.

> *Ruth Gagliardo, in a review of "Fifteen," in* The Saturday Review, New York, *Vol. XXXIX, No. 46, November 17, 1956, p. 60.*

"Teen-age story" has come to connote a thin dish of high school chatter flavored with a tantalizing dash of romance, enough to keep eleven and twelve year olds reading on in the hope of learning how to be popular when their time comes, but so weak in characterization that they fail to be satisfying. . . . [Jane met Stan] under odd circumstances and has to do a bit of explaining to her parents when she plans to go out with him. You feel for her as she desperately asks, "Do you have to refer to him as 'This Stanley Crandall'? . . . Oh, Mom, do you have to act like the F.B.I. or something?" But you also sympathize with her mother who finally says sharply:

"Will you please get that look of exaggerated patience off your face." High school chatter? Yes. Dash of romance? Yes. Well, what's the difference? Beverly Cleary. She has the light touch, humor, the seeing eye and her characterizations ring as true at fifteen and sixteen as they did at nine and ten. In short, she knows how to write.

> *Robin Gottlieb, "Satisfying Romances for Girls 12 to 16," in* New York Herald Tribune Book Review, *Part II, November 18, 1956, p. 28.\**

In their early teens, girls find a foretaste of growing up in all kinds of reading, absorbing women's magazines, adult novels (from light romantic to ultra-sophisticated) and those junior novels in which young love and young ambition are carefully watered down. To them I would offer *Fifteen* as a better key to life. This story lays bare with unglossy candour the follies, the false values and the dangerous whole-heartedness of Jane Purdy. . . . The author is sure as a rock on the emotional background of her story. Jane does not want any physical manifestations of emotion yet. Her worries are whether Stan will give her his identification-bracelet, whether he will fetch her for a date in his father's car or in the Doggie Diner truck which he drives as a spare-time job. Excellent in its detail, this is a subtle, sympathetic picture of youth.

> *Margery Fisher, in a review of "Fifteen," in her* Growing Point, *Vol. 1, No. 8, March, 1963, p. 123.*

[*Fifteen*] represents one of the earliest images of adolescence written for the adolescent. Jane Purdy exemplifies the viewpoint of a more modern fictional teenager that 'the really terrible thing about being young is the triviality'. *Fifteen* reads like a teenage version of *The Diary of a Nobody*: it is far less engaging, but the main protagonists in each book have the same obsessional tendency to endow small matters with great significance. Unlike *The Diary of a Noboby*, Cleary's novel is intended as an honest portrayal, not as a parody. Jane's chief preoccupation is securing an eligible male. There are undeniable touches of reality in her experience—all the agonizing about what to wear for a date, the feeling of embarrassment about parents, the joy and relief in finding that one is attractive to the opposite sex—but this does not compensate for the general impression of superficiality and triviality. The detail of Jane's progress is painstakingly recorded, from meeting Stan . . . , to the moment when he presents her with his identity bracelet and deposits a first chaste kiss on her lips. Along with the trivia, the insistent adulation of the male is one of *Fifteen*'s most irritating qualities: 'She was Stan's girl. That was all that really mattered'. (pp. 43-4)

> *Susan Thompson, "Images of Adolescence: Part I," in* Signal, *No. 34, January, 1981, pp. 37-59.\**

---

### HENRY AND THE PAPER ROUTE (1957)

Irrepressible Henry Huggins is carried away with his own ambitions in another situation comedy. Henry goes on being exasperatingly and familiarly funny with a resemblance to everybody's younger brother. With his heart set on a paper route, Henry never expected assistance from his inescapable little [friend] Ramona. But to his surprise, her sabotage of "genius" Murphy's paper route brought him the chance he longed for. Easy reading and a chuckle a page.

*A review of "Henry and the Paper Route," in Virginia Kirkus' Service, Vol. XXV, No. 13, July 1, 1957, p. 439.*

More humorous episodes with Henry Huggins are told with as much zest as the previous stories of Henry and his friends Ramona and Beezus. A good family story where father and mother rally round when necessary, it will please children who enjoyed the other Cleary books or "Homer Price." . . . Recommended.

*Juanita Walker, in a review of "Henry and the Paper Route," in Library Journal, Vol. 82, No. 16, September 15, 1957, p. 2190.*

When a young boy or girl wants a book to read just for fun, we can confidently give them any of the rollicking stories by Beverly Cleary about Henry Huggins. Henry is growing up now—he is 11—and he feels it is high time he did something important. . . . The fun is an unpredictable and zestful as ever, and we are happy to see a new addition to the Huggins household: Nosy, who may be either a small cat or a large kitten, but who is indubitably a premium, to use Henry's own term. In fact, one of the delights of Mrs. Cleary's books is that they are always filled with premiums, of one sort or another.

*Marion West Stoer, "Widening Horizons: 'Henry and the Paper Route'," in The Christian Science Monitor, November 27, 1957, p. 15.*

Warm humor and skillful storytelling shine through in this story. Henry's acceptance of responsibility and use of creativity in solving problems are woven into the text in a nonmoralizing way.

*Sharon Spredemann Dreyer, in a review of "Henry and the Paper Route," in her The Bookfinder: A Guide to Children's Literature about the Needs and Problems of Youth Aged 2-15, American Guidance Service, Inc., 1977, No. 192.*

---

**JEAN AND JOHNNY**   (1959)

[Jean Jarrett] was overwhelmed when handsome Johnny Chessler deigned to notice her. However, she eventually faced squarely the fact that Johnny accepted her attention only because he was flattered, not because he cared for her. Johnny's friend Homer, who had also recognized Johnny's selfishness and conceit, helped her to profit by the experience. A not-unusual plot, handled with freshness and restraint. Excellent characterizations and natural touches of everyday incidents enhance the warmth and humor of the style.

*Zena Sutherland, in a review of "Jean and Johnny," in Bulletin of the Center for Children's Books, Vol. 13, No. 1, September, 1959, p. 5.*

Another delightful girls' story with those typical Cleary touches (e.g. re Daddy: "his voice had already registered Impatience, well above Medium but not yet to Explosive"). . . . Story is light, yet a little sad and very typical of teen-age crushes. . . . Recommended especially for slow readers, but everyone will enjoy it.

*Beatrice Bailin, in a review of "Jean and Johnny," in Junior Libraries, an appendix to Library Journal, Vol. 6, No. 2, October, 1959, p. 164.*

Again as no surprise, the liveliest of [this fall's nearly fifty new] stories for girls in the early years of high school is "**Jean and Johnny**" . . . , which tells lightly, sympathetically, with some humor but not as much as in the earlier story "**Fifteen**," of Jean's experience [with Johnny]. . . .

*Margaret Sherwood Libby, "Even in Fall a Young Girl's Fancy Lightly Turns to Thoughts of Love," in New York Herald Tribune Book Review, November 1, 1959, p. 28.\**

Mrs. Cleary has drawn another fifteen-year-old heroine with as sure a touch as that which pictured Jane in **Fifteen,** and younger teen-age readers will discover just as complete an empathy for the new Jean. Blithe humor freshens the ordinary enough incidents while a perceptive inclusion of details important to Jean's contemporaries makes everything as real as next door.

*Virginia Haviland, in a review of "Jean and Johnny," in The Horn Book Magazine, Vol. XXXV, No. 6, December, 1959, p. 485.*

---

**THE REAL HOLE**   (1960)

Four-year-old Jimmy, unlike his girl twin, likes real not imagined things. And so when his father gives him a real trench shovel, he is in transports and determines to dig himself a perfectly enormous hole. This he does. But what to do with it? His family hits upon a delightful solution, and the denouement of this charming story takes into consideration the nature of the reader at whom it is directed.

*A review of "The Real Hole," in Virginia Kirkus' Service, Vol. XXVIII, No. 13, July 1, 1960, p. 494.*

[Beverly Cleary] has now written her first story for little children. The plot is slight, but the whole is as natural as life . . . , and I think a great many young realists will get a vicarious satisfaction out of purposeful, single-minded Jimmy's feeling of accomplishment.

*Ellen Lewis Buell, "Biggest in the World," in The New York Times Book Review, October 9, 1960, p. 52.*

---

**TWO DOG BISCUITS**   (1961)

[What fun for Jimmy and Janet] when they discover something as new to Mother as it is to them. Look as they may, the children cannot find a dog whom they like well enough to offer their dog biscuits to. Thus when they spy a cat who seems worthy of their offering, they are delighted to find the feline's appetite relishes dog biscuits, contrary to Mother's prediction. The joke is on Mother as the twins make an independent discovery. A sound idea which really needs a more credible situation.

*A review of "Two Dog Biscuits," in Virginia Kirkus' Service, Vol. XXIX, No. 3, Feburary 1, 1961, p. 100.*

A very pleasant book to read aloud, with illustrations [by Mary Stevens] that have the same ingenuous appeal as does the text; both have simplicity and humor. Beverly Cleary's four-year-old twins, Janet and Jimmy, are completely real.

*Zena Sutherland, in a review of "Two Dog Biscuits," in Bulletin of the Center for Children's Books, Vol. XV, No. 1, September, 1961, p. 5.*

### EMILY'S RUNAWAY IMAGINATION (1961)

Miss Cleary, who has been writing books for teen-agers and pre-schoolers, has returned to the middle-age group, the field in which she does her best (and funniest) work. Emily is a delightful child who lives on an Oregon farm in the 1920's. Her imagination, which is really wonderful, leads her into all kinds of hilarious difficulties as, for example, when she tries to transform a farm horse into a snow-white steed by washing it with Clorox. It is one of the most delightful of the season's storybooks, and Emily is one of Miss Cleary's most charming characters.

> *A review of "Emily's Runaway Imagination," in* Publishers Weekly, *Vol. 180, No. 11, September 11, 1961, p. 62.*

A slight plot holds amusing adventures together. . . . A chapter for this or any time of year is **"The Scary Night,"** in which Emily's cousin June comes to stay with her. . . . A good picture of the period, but fortunately Emily is too lively to seem a "period child." (pp. 35-6)

> *Alice Dalgliesh, "Things That Go Bump in the Night," in* Saturday Review, *Vol. XLIV, No. 43, October 28, 1961, pp. 35-6.\**

Acquisition of a library for the small town is the thread holding the story together. Uneven as to humor; not as funny as **"Ellen Tebbits"** or the **"Beezus"** books, but Cleary fans will probably enjoy it. Third-graders would enjoy hearing it read aloud.

> *Palmer Price Clark, in a review of "Emily's Runaway Imagination," in* School Library Journal, *an appendix to* Library Journal, *Vol. 8, No. 3, November, 1961, p. 50.*

### HENRY AND THE CLUBHOUSE (1962)

Beverly Cleary does it again. Henry, with his paper route and his clubhouse project interfering with each other and Beezus' pest of a little sister interfering with him, is as much all boy as ever. Ribsy is in the story, too, getting into a fight with an economy-size Dalmation. At the end, there are faint indications that Henry may be beginning to start to begin to grow up. Recommended, of course.

> *Siddie Joe Johnson, in a review of "Henry and the Clubhouse," in* Library Journal, *Vol. 87, No. 16, September 15, 1962, p. 3200.*

The hazards run by sequels—repetitiveness, a contrived effect, a watering down and spreading thin of incident and character—are once again triumphantly avoided in the case of Henry Huggins, whose latest adventures are as lifelike and funny as ever. . . . **"Trick or Treat,"** the Halloween chapter, creates just the right atmosphere of crisp autumn night and peculiar happenings.

> *Margaret Warren Brown, in a review of "Henry and the Clubhouse," in* The Horn Book Magazine, *Vol. XXXVIII, No. 5, October, 1962, p. 484.*

Henry Huggins, that modern day Penrod, is back with us. . . . Henry's adventures are amusing and as normal as your own neighborhood. His efforts to build a clubhouse strictly "No Girls Allowed" will make it easy for 8-12's to identify with him.

> *Marian Sorenson, in a review of "Henry and the Clubhouse," in* The Christian Science Monitor, *November 15, 1962, p. 5B.*

[This book] reinforces Beverly Cleary's claim to be one of the most honest observers of the American scene. . . . Poor Henry! His troubles are so real and child-sized, his adventures never straining credulity.

Beverly Cleary first came to attention in this country with a picture of adolescence. She is as much at ease at the other end of the age-scale. Gentle humour, attitudes devoid of condescension or sentimentality, she has just the right touch, and a clear and unfussy style to go with it.

> *Marcus Crouch, in a review of "Henry and the Clubhouse," in* The Junior Bookshelf, *Vol. 45, No. 5, October, 1981, p. 193.*

Small-town America comes to life in linked episodes, good-humoured and racy, reflecting the author's shrewd appraisal of the vicissitudes of everyday. This enlivening domestic comedy has lost none of its sparkle since it was first published . . . : it should certainly be added to earlier tales of Henry and his dog Ribsy.

> *Margery Fisher, in a review of "Henry and the Clubhouse," in her* Growing Point, *Vol. 22, No. 1, May, 1983, p. 4088.*

### SISTER OF THE BRIDE (1963)

Pleasantly realistic, lightly humorous, a sister's-eye view of a wedding; Barbara, sixteen, is not so excited about her sister Rosemary's wedding that she isn't concerned about her own affairs but, since she is fancy-free, all her romantic energy is directed toward Rosemary's marriage. Barbara, seeing her sister change, begins to appreciate a more mature viewpoint toward love and marriage. Good writing style, good values; a family story that has warmth, honest sentiment, and affectionate humor.

> *Zena Sutherland, in a review of "Sister of the Bride," in* Bulletin of the Center for Children's Books, *Vol. XVII, No. 2, October, 1963, p. 24.*

A lighthearted novel on a serious theme. . . . The author's understanding of today's young people and her remarkable ability to express it in their terms, with warmth and humor, are put to good use in a fast-moving story rooted in the serious contemporary problem of early marriages.

> *Margaret Warren Brown, in a review of "Sister of the Bride," in* The Horn Book Magazine, *Vol. XXXIX, No. 5, October, 1963, p. 507.*

This author's deft briskness brings to life even the second-string players in her story. . . . She writes dialogue with spontaneity that characterizes the two sisters, the two generations, two patterns of homemaking without wordy exposition.

> *Ann M. Seeley, "Giving a Gal a Hand," in* Book Week—The Sunday Herald Tribune, *November 10, 1963, p. 40.\**

"'I'm falling in love,' she whispered experimentally to herself, and found the words comfortable on her tongue." Sounds a little out-of-date? The quote is from *Sister of the Bride,* written almost twenty years ago. At the time of its first publication

..., a reviewer from *The Horn Book* praised Beverly Cleary's "understanding of . . . young people and her remarkable ability to express it in their terms" [see excerpt above]. Those terms have evolved almost beyond recognition between then and now. Cleary's understanding of young people, though, was so clear at the time this book was written, that it still applies today. This leaves us with an unusual dichotomy: a novel graced by on-target insights which are expressed in such strange terms that they almost defy readers to identify (a considerable obstacle for an audience as fussy about idiom as are young adults). . . .

Some of the book's characteristic reflections on marriage, stemming from this situation, may help you decide whether the writing style would seem prohibitively outmoded to your young adults: Marriage was "love and moonlight and orange blossoms," "new dishes, new clothes, everything brand-new all at once." But it was scarey, too, because "it sounded so permanent," and "it was such a short step from a ring to a lifetime of dishwashing" and, besides, "their father was sure to feel that there was a big difference between asking a boy home to dinner and marrying him."

Yesterday's context; today's concerns.

> *Liza G. Bliss, in a review of "Siser of the Bride,"* in Kliatt Young Adult Paperback Book Guide, *Vol. XV, No. 6, September, 1981, p. 6.*

---

### RIBSY (1964)

Ribsy, who belonged to Henry Huggins, was the kind of dog that no one could resist patting or familiarly calling Mutt or Pooch. So when this friendly dog jumped out of the station wagon at the supermarket simply to hunt for Henry, his friendliness led him into hilarious situations one after another, until a whole month flew by before he found Henry again. This latest story by the author of several humorous books for the under-twelve group tops them all and is guaranteed to produce chuckles in girls and boys alike.

> *Charlotte Jackson, in a review of "Ribsy," in* The Atlantic Monthly, *Vol. 214, No. 6, December, 1964, p. 162.*

Henry Huggins' dog makes a prime hero in an exceedingly fast-moving, varied, and original sequence of adventures in being lost. His dealing in a series of temporary homes with such strange matters as a bubble-bath, Henry's voice on the telephone, and an apartment-house fire escape, has high comedy and pathos, sure to make his story immediately recommended, reader to reader. Mrs. Cleary has a deft touch in characterizing adults as well as children and the various kinds of domestic life they create.

> *Virginia Haviland, in a review of "Ribsy," in* The Horn Book Magazine, *Vol. XL, No. 6, December, 1964, p. 615.*

---

### THE MOUSE AND THE MOTORCYCLE (1965)

[Mrs. Cleary's book] recounts the wonderful adventure of a mouse who finds that he is a motorcyclist. . . . Ralph is a young and reckless mouse, who lives with his family in an old hotel. Keith, the boy who owns the motorcycle, is a guest at the hotel. And a very nice boy he is, as Ralph discovers. When Ralph is trapped in the wastebasket, it is Keith who saves him

from being thrown out with the trash; it is Keith who allows him to ride the precious motorcycle; it is Keith who brings the mouse family food; it is Keith who makes Ralph a crash helmet from an old ping-pong ball.

But the friendship isn't all one-sided. Ralph does his best for Keith, and manages to find an aspirin for the sick boy when there are no aspirins to be had. The dark and dangerous journey through the hotel in search of a pill is the high point of the book. Ralph's adventures are hair-raising, and in the course of his trip he proves himself to be a responsible young mouse. . . . He has become so responsible that Keith actually gives him the motorcycle for his very own.

This fantasy is so realistic that it is almost plausible. The mouse-eye view of life in an old resort hotel is certainly different, and the love of a mouse for a mechanical contrivance is made believable. The rapport between boy and mouse is nonchalantly handled: "Neither the mouse nor the boy was the least bit surprised that each could understand the other. Two creatures who shared a love for motorcycles naturally spoke the same language." With equal nonchalance the author ignores or explains away any points that her usual down-to-earth, realistic fans might boggle at. She never strains for an effect, so that the entire story seems natural, unforced, and serious. This does not mean that it is a solemn book—can Mrs. Cleary possibly write a book devoid of humor? There are a few *very* funny touches. The mouse mother, worried about "doing the right thing" and trying to leave a tip for Keith for his "room service" is hilarious. The conflict between the generations (among the mice) is a funny echo of that among humans. . . . Even boys who do not care for fantasy may find this fantasy much to their liking. (pp. 7-8)

> *Phyllis Cohen, in a review of "The Mouse and the Motorcycle," in* Young Readers Review, *Vol. II, No. 3, November, 1965, pp. 7-8.*

[Beverly Cleary] has ventured into the demanding realm of fantasy. Her foray . . . is a success. ***The Mouse and the Motorcycle*** has unavoidable overtones of *Stuart Little*, but both Ralph, the mouse with mechanical aptitudes, and the small boy, Keith, are believable characters.

> *Margaret Sherwood Libby, "Young Man's Fantasy," in* Book Week—New York Herald Tribune, *December 5, 1965, p. 50.\**

The logical put inside a frame of the illogical is a prerequisite of fantasy. Unfortunately, Beverly Cleary, whose **"Henry Huggins"** books were a success, fails to establish the difference in her new book. . . . [Keith's and Ralph's] ventures are swiftly paced and amusing, although the crises, at times, seem a bit contrived and numerous. The mouse is clever about elevators, vacuum cleaners, maids, peanut butter and aspirins and room service—and that is just too clever for credibility or fancy either. At one point, while Ralph is in the grandfather's clock, we are reminded that his ancestors ran up and down it. Come now!

> *Polly Burroughs, in a review of "The Mouse and the Motorcycle," in* The New York Times Book Review, *December 26, 1965, p. 18.*

On second thought, why be surprised that Beverly Cleary has done a delightful fanciful story? What other kind of fantasy would she write? The illustrations [by Louis Darling] are, like the story, a combination of prim detail and an incongruous or wildly imaginative situation.... The human-to-human dialogue is good, too.

> *A review of "The Mouse and the Motorcycle," in* Good Books for Children: A Selection of Outstanding Childrens' Books Published, 1950-65, *edited by Mary K. Eakin, third edition, The University of Chicago Press, 1966, p. 76.*

Surprisingly, this talking mouse seems more realistic than the same author's kindergarten pupil, Ramona. In a lighthearted story, the ability of the mouse to talk to sympathetic humans is handled particularly well.

> *A review of "The Mouse and the Motorcycle," in* The Junior Bookshelf, *Vol. 39, No. 1, February, 1975, p. 33.*

---

## MITCH AND AMY  (1967)

It's twins this time at Mrs. Cleary's—nine years old and doing fine, thank you, after a slow start. When Mitch and Amy hit their stride, the air crackles. Mitch is a whiz at math and Amy is intimidated by the multiplication tables; Amy is in the top reading group and Mitch is still on Dr. Seuss. Mitch is good at games and Amy is good with her hands.... A nicely restrained understanding of childhood dilemmas permeates the wildest episodes.

> *A review of "Mitch and Amy," in* Kirkus Service, *Vol. XXXV, No. 3, February 1, 1967, p. 130.*

It is a rare author who can describe a sibling relationship with all the authority of a case study and have it emerge as a smoothly written and entertaining story. Mrs. Cleary ... has written such a book.... The scene in which Mother patiently hears Mitch stumble through his required daily dose [of reading], while Amy hovers nearby, unable to resist the opportunity to flaunt her superiority, will probably be long remembered....

> *Zena Sutherland, in a review of "Mitch and Amy," in* Saturday Review, *Vol. L, No. 11, March 18, 1967, p. 36.*

And if Mrs. Cleary could have listened in on the children's comments on that TV program, "Children Explore Books," she would echo Oscar Wilde's aphorism. "There is only one thing in the world worse than being talked about and that is not being talked about." The children talked and talked about her books. She would also risk bursting with pride, for they not only talked about her books, they raved about them. They (and booksellers) will be delighted to know she has written another book for them, a typical Cleary which introduces two new, but typically Cleary characters: twins, who fight like blazes with each other but present a united front against a common enemy. (To Cleary partisans, a typical Cleary is code for a book they can't contemplate missing, and booksellers can't miss selling.)

> *A review of "Mitch and Amy," in* Publishers Weekly, *Vol. 191, No. 14, April 3, 1967, p. 56.*

The writing style and dialogue, the familial and peer group relationships, the motivations and characterizations all have the ring of truth. Written with ease and vitality, lightened with humor, the story is perhaps most appealing because it is clear that the author respects children.

> *Zena Sutherland, in a review of "Mitch and Amy," in* Bulletin of the Center for Children's Books, *Vol. 20, No. 9, May, 1967, p. 136.*

This vivid, realistic presentation of the problems and the joys of being fraternal twins is lightened with humor. The mother in this story is present when her children need her. However, the father's involvement is limited to repetitions of his two standard lectures to the children.

> *Sharon Spredemann Dreyer, in a review of "Mitch and Amy," in her* The Bookfinder: A Guide to Children's Literature about the Needs and Problems of Youth Aged 2-15, *American Guidance Service, Inc., 1977, No. 193.*

---

## RAMONA THE PEST  (1968)

### AUTHOR'S COMMENTARY

I thought consciously about *Ramona The Pest* for fifteen years before I set a word of the story on paper. The book began in a taxicab on Fifth Avenue in New York when my editor, who was discussing the three books I had written at that time, said she would like me to write a book about Ramona who was a minor character in the *Henry Huggins* books. At the moment I dismissed the suggestion rather lightly for a number of reasons. Ramona went to kindergarten, and never having gone to kindergarten, I knew nothing about the behavior of children in that school situation. Also, I was not sure that Ramona would be funny when her story was told from her point of view. Ramona was funny to readers because she was such a pest to other children, but Ramona did not see herself as a pest. And hadn't teachers and librarians been saying for years that children do not like to read about children who are younger than themselves? Besides, I was full of ideas for other books which I wanted to write. However, an idea was planted that June afternoon in 1953 and once an idea is planted in the mind of a writer, that idea usually grows even though it may never flower or bear fruit.

By 1953 Ramona herself had done considerable growing as a character. Her first appearance in *Henry Huggins* was somewhat accidental and she speaks only two lines. When I had finished the first draft of the book, the thought crossed my mind that all the characters appeared to be only children, although to explain her unusual nickname, I had mentioned that Beezus, whose real name was Beatrice, had a little sister who called her Beezus. Rather casually I gave the little sister a small part of the story and named her Ramona because at that moment in the writing of the story, a neighbor called out, "Ramona!" to another neighbor of that name.

There was nothing casual about the fictional Ramona. She was a stubborn young lady who began to appear in stories whether I expected her or not. Sometimes she took over whole chapters. Letters from children asking for more about Ramona began to arrive. Ramona, it seemed, was exactly like the pesty little sisters of many of my readers. I enjoyed Ramona and had great sympathy with her, for some of the things she did I had done but with a difference. Where I had been reserved, Ramona was the opposite. Ramona did not hesitate to express herself, to kick and scream and demand her own way. She was not a child to suffer in silence. Where I had only thought of scenes I could have made, Ramona took action and made the scenes. I admired her courage. I also began to see that Ramona represented a facet of my own personality which I enjoyed enlarging upon in fiction. Her popularity, I suspect, lies in the fact that she is a facet of every child's personality. All children are eager, impatient and frequently baffled by the world around them. All children want to kick and scream and demand their own way though they may not actually do so.

For fifteen years I thought about Ramona, sometimes writing about her and sometimes not. During those years I had children of my own, twins, who . . . [went to] nursery school and then kindergarten. School was a much happier experience for them at the age of five than it had been for me at the age of six. I watched my children and so did the person with whom I collaborate, the child within myself. (pp. 17, 29)

Several years later, in 1967, I wrote three chapters of a fantasy which I was enjoying when suddenly I found I could not go on. No matter how long I sat at my desk, I could not write another word of that book at that time, although a year later I was to finish it. I picked up a fresh sheet of paper and began *Ramona The Pest*. That the book was about a child younger than the future readers was no longer the obstacle it had seemed . . . , for I had learned much from the letters that children write me and from observing my own children. I had learned that the rules one learns about the books children will or will not read do not apply if the story is funny. Boys will read about girls, girls will read about boys, junior high school students will read about fourth graders if the stories will make them laugh. Today's children, I sometimes think, are starved for laughter, true-to-life laughter that springs from character and not the synthetic laughter that comes from the pow-pow-pow of cartoons on Saturday morning television. Today's children want to recognize themselves in books and to be able to laugh at themselves, for then they know they have grown.

My own children, I had observed, found their own younger behavior hilarious. They often asked me to tell them what they had done when they were in nursery school or kindergarten, and invariably they found these reminiscences funny because they had grown past that stage of their behavior. If they had not grown, they would not have been able to laugh at themselves.

The age of my protagonist no longer worried me. If my story was true to life, children would read about a girl who was younger than they. The words appeared on the paper with unusual speed; indeed, the story of Ramona's clash with the school system, her eagerness for attention, her stubbornness, her misunderstandings, her fears, her longing to love and be loved, almost seemed to write itself.

The several months spent setting *Ramona The Pest* to paper passed quickly, but two generations went into that little book. To observe children in kindergarten would not have been enough, for then I would have written a story about children for adults. Neither would remembering childhood be sufficient, for then I would have written a reminiscence for adults. The writer for children must fuse memory and observation and go back into childhood as he writes. He must be the child he is writing about.

To be Ramona in kindergarten was easy, for in a sense I had already lived part of the story as the child within myself had accompanied my twins to kindergarten. The book brings back to me the truth of the statement made by the late Elizabeth Enright, a writer whom I have long admired. She said that all true fiction is fantasy compounded of imagination; of wish and of memory. This is true of *Ramona The Pest* which is the story

of the child within the author attending the kindergarten she wishes she might have attended.

I count the hours spent writing *Ramona The Pest* among the pleasantest hours of my life. (p. 29)

*Beverly Cleary, "How Long Does It Take to Write a Book?" in* Oklahoma Librarian, *Vol. 21, No. 3, July, 1971, pp. 14-17, 29.*

Your reviewer wishes she had read **"Ramona the Pest"** before she went to lunch, because she was challenged at lunch by an important man in the book world—challenged and defeated. He . . . challenged my wariness about series books—my conviction that each title in a series must stand (or fall) as a unique book, that it can't get by because it belongs to a "good family" (a good series). And if I'd read **"Ramona the Pest"** I could have crowed "I *have* the perfect example! Mrs. Cleary's new book is her best! Children love all her stories. And booksellers sell all her titles. But this one, of Ramona who is a pest, a pest *nobody* will want to miss, is the tops. And children will love it and booksellers will sell it, as a book not to be missed, not as the latest book of a series." Too bad, but if he (the I.M.) ever asks me to lunch again, *I'll* be triumphant, thanks to Mrs. Cleary—and Ramona.

*A review of "Ramona the Pest," in* Publishers Weekly, *Vol. 193, No. 16, April 15, 1968, p. 97.*

This book is all Ramona's—Henry, Beezus, and the others figure in it only occasionally—and at last we learn about Ramona's side of things. She's not a pest. "No matter what others said, she never thought she was a pest. The people who called her a pest were always bigger and so they could be unfair. . . . She was not a slowpoke grownup. She was a girl who could not wait. Life was so interesting she had to find out what happened next." What happened next, was that Ramona Geraldine Quimby started kindergarten. And who but Ramona would be a kindergarten dropout?

As in all her other books about the boys and girls of Klickitat Street, Mrs. Cleary invests this one with charm, humor, and complete honesty. There are some adults who can remember many incidents from their early childhood; there are few who can remember how they felt about things and why; there are fewer who can communicate these feelings. And fewer still who can retain the humorous aspects. Mrs. Cleary is one of those rare ones. . . . Even boys and girls who dislike stories about children younger than themselves enjoy the incidents in which Ramona makes a pest of herself in the *Henry* and *Beezus* books. They should adore this book. And with good reason. Ramona has never been funnier and has never been so sympathetic a character.

On the first day Ramona misunderstands her teacher and thinks that she's going to get a present ("Sit here for the present"), asks her teacher the first unanswerable question of the term ("Miss Binney, I want to know—how did Mike Mulligan go to the bathroom when he was digging the basement of the town hall?"), is the first child to have to sit on the isolation bench, and snores (delicately) to prove that she's a good rester (and breaks up the class). The pace doesn't let up. (pp. 1-2)

Needless to say, Mrs. Cleary has great sympathy for rascally Ramona, and children will at last see beyond Ramona's naughtiness to her very sweet, if direct self. As usual, this is a giggle-all-the-way-through book. . . . As usual, this is standard Cleary first rate entertainment. (p. 2)

> *Phyllis Cohen, in a review of "Ramona the Pest,"*
> *in* Young Readers Review, *Vol. IV, No. 9, May,*
> *1968, pp. 1-2.*

Admittedly Ramona is very American, and the song about 'the dawnzer lee light' which puzzles Ramona will puzzle English children much more, but for sheer exuberance she is unbeatable and almost every child will respond to the hilarious results of her efforts to shine in school. . . . [Less] able readers may find American terms daunting even though the spelling is English. For teacher to read aloud; this book is guaranteed to grip a class of seven- to nine-year-olds.

> *Joyce Taylor, in a review of "Ramona the Pest," in*
> The School Librarian, *Vol. 22, No. 2, June, 1974,*
> *p. 195.*

Though quite certainly a two-level book (grown-ups will relish some of the situations and word play that may pass over the heads of small children, whilst the young will identify with the heroine and share her tribulations and joys), *Ramona the Pest* is a welcome addition to the select number of books that read well aloud and are entertaining and supportive to the school beginner.

> *Elaine Moss, "Fiction I, Stories for 5-8 Year Olds:*
> *'Ramona the Pest'," in* Children's Books of the Year:
> 1974, *edited by Elaine Moss, Hamish Hamilton, 1975,*
> *p. 30.*

Ramona is one of the best little girl characters in children's literature. . . . Her exploits will be relished in retrospect by children who have left those first experiences of school comfortably behind so they can enjoy reading about Ramona's comic mistakes.

> *A review of "Ramona the Pest," in* Books for Your
> Children, *Vol. 11, No. 3, Summer, 1976, p. 14.*

It is easy for readers to sympathize with Ramona, having probably once had similar feelings themselves. The relationships in the story are quite credible, although the adults never seem to lose their tempers nor to have much insight into the world of children.

> *Sharon Spredemann Dreyer, in a review of "Ramona*
> *the Pest," in her* The Bookfinder: A Guide to Children's Literature about the Needs and Problems of
> Youth Aged 2-15, *American Guidance Service, Inc.,*
> *1977, No. 195.*

---

### RUNAWAY RALPH (1970)

Ralph, resident mouse at the Mountain View Inn, has found that he could communicate with any human being sensible enough to understand that to make a toy motorcycle real you have only to say, "Pb-pb-b-b-b!" Tired of giving rides to his little cousins, Ralph decides to run away, and goes zooming off. He is caught by a homesick camper who is supected of having stolen a watch. Ralph, who knows that the thief was a cat, makes a deal with the camper—a boy intelligent enough to go "Pb-pb-b-b-b!"—and thus achieves freedom. The combination of reality and fantasy is deft, the depiction of camp life delightfully wry, and the saga of Ralph's adventures a musine triumph.

> *Zena Sutherland, in a review of "Runaway Ralph,"*
> *in* Saturday Review, *Vol. LIII, No. 19, May 9, 1970,*
> *p. 44.*

Recipe for a best seller—bring back a character who made a best seller of the first book he was in, put him in a topical crisis, in a timely setting, and blend well. Ralph was the mouse-hero of **"The Mouse and the Motorcycle."** The crisis for him in this story is the generation gap, the setting is a summer camp. And Beverly Cleary is better than a Waring Blender anytime. She, Ralph, *and* booksellers, can't miss with this one.

> *A review of "Runaway Ralph," in* Publishers Weekly,
> *Vol. 197, No. 18, May 14, 1970. p. 64.*

It is inevitable that the sequel to *The Mouse and the Motorcycle* should lack some of the impact of the first book; but the new story is constructed with much the same combination of simplicity, realistic detail, ingenuity, and humor that made the earlier book a resounding success.

> *Ethel L. Heins, in a review of "Runaway Ralph,"*
> *in* The Horn Book Magazine, *Vol. XLVI, No. 4, August, 1970, p. 386.*

The tale is a rather trivial one, made so not by the actual story which shows some originality but in the somewhat dull, pedestrian and offhand way in which it is written. There is some attempt at characterisation and interplay of feeling amongst the inhabitants of the holiday camp, but one feels constantly that the author never really becomes sufficiently interested in the people involved, or in the action of the story. Imagination on the part of the author seems to stop short when feelings and reactions could have been explored in greater depth. Younger children will enjoy the story but it will leave no lasting impression, while older children who may read the book will sense the absence of the exploration of undertones which are only implied or touched upon very superficially. (p. 104)

> *A review of "Runaway Ralph," in* The Junior Bookshelf, *Vol. 39, No. 2, April, 1975, pp. 103-04.*

---

### SOCKS (1973)

Socks has white paws, hence his name. The kitten is bought from a little girl who has set up a stand with the message, "Kittens 25¢ or Best Offer." Pregnant Ms. Bricker can't resist the bargain so Socks gets a fine home. All too soon, however, it's threatened by the arrival of Charles William Bricker, new human, who gets much of the attention the cat has come to take for granted. All's well when Socks and Charles William become friends, as expected. . . . [The] story, for all its triteness and predictability, will no doubt be popular, for the prolific author has legions of fans.

> *A review of "Socks," in* Publishers Weekly, *Vol. 204, No. 9, August 27, 1973, p. 282.*

This wonderful author has once again turned out a warm story about an animal that every child will long to have. . . . The story is told by Socks and has some humorous touching moments that will be enjoyable to anyone who reads it. . . . [The] story is clearly Cleary and great!

> *Judy N. Staley, in a review of "Socks," in* Children's
> Book Review Service, *Vol. 2, No. 1, September, 1973,*
> *p. 3.*

[Socks is] resentfully jealous until the baby gets big enough to turn into a playmate. Socks always behaves and thinks like a cat, never a person, yet Cleary invests him with a definite personality in this delightful tale. (p. 346)

> *Zena Sutherland, Dianne L. Monson, and May Hill Arbuthnot, "Modern Fiction: Animal Stories," in their* Children and Books, *sixth edition, Scott, Foresman and Company, 1981, pp. 344-46.\**

---

### RAMONA THE BRAVE  (1975)

Beverly Cleary is at her best, which is very good indeed, in this book about the troubles and triumphs of Ramona Quimby. Readers who have met the Quimby family in earlier books will be delighted to find how Ramona keeps earning her father's admiration for spunkiness. Brave she has to be as she enters first grade and has to cope with a well-meaning but dull teacher, a cheating classmate, a fierce dog who attacks her on her way to school and other challenges. The author's story is vivid, laced with her gentle humor.

> *A review of "Ramona the Brave," in* Publishers Weekly, *Vol. 207, No. 13, March 31, 1975, p. 50.*

A sequel to **Ramona the Pest** is equally diverting, written with the ebullient humor and sympathy that distinguish Cleary's stories. Ramona is as convincing a first-grader as a fictional character can be, trying to be compliant but too independent a child to be conforming. . . . This is a perfect book for installment reading to younger children as well as a pleasure trip for independent readers.

> *Zena Sutherland, in a review of "Ramona the Brave," in* Bulletin of the Center for Children's Books, *Vol. 28, No. 11, July-August, 1975, p. 175.*

Through a few simple scenes, in the classroom or at home, Beverly Cleary makes shrewd points about one of her most wittily and sympathetically drawn characters. This is straight domestic writing at its liveliest and most skilful. (p. 2798)

> *Margery Fisher, in a review of "Ramona the Brave," in her* Growing Point, *Vol. 14, No. 7, January, 1976, pp. 2797-98.*

Beverly Cleary's picture of the transition from being an important top Infant to a small, insignificant member of a Junior school is delightfully recognisable for children anywhere, despite the American terminology. . . . There is excellent understanding of the child's viewpoint, particularly over relative sizes—the hugeness of the older children, and the new-found detachment from "the messy sort of a child known as a toddler"—and the difficulty of reconciling the contrast between Ramona's own daydreams of herself as "the brave", and other people's view of the matter. (pp. 20-1)

> *A review of "Ramona the Brave," in* The Junior Bookshelf, *Vol. 40, No. 1, February, 1976, pp. 20-1.*

**Ramona The Brave** describes the trials and tribulations of a six-year-old girl who wants desperately to grow up, and who seeks her identity through adult approval. Ramona is a very sensitive little girl who lacks a sense of self-worth, and all of her actions are geared to finding that self-worth—her competition with her sister for their parents' love, and her efforts to elicit her teacher's approval. Given the nature of her prob-

lem, Ramona's drives are understandably individualistic and materialistic.

The author writes with humor and wit but usually at the expense of Ramona's painful feelings. Her portrayal of Ramona perpetuates the image of little girls as being frightened, unhappy, competitive, bitchy, manipulative and emotional. Furthermore, Ms. Cleary depicts boys/men as strong, responsible figures and suggests that girls/women must rely on them to resolve problems or to achieve an identity. Thus, a boy, Howie, is a "great one for thinking things over" and Ramona "gets excited but Howie remains calm."

If **Ramona The Brave** is typical of Ms. Cleary's many books for young readers, this reviewer would recommend avoiding them. Human feelings and needs are mocked in this book, and the sexist, competitive and individualistic values it promotes are not the least bit cute. (pp. 159-60)

> *"The Analyses: 'Ramona the Brave'," in* Human— and Anti-Human—Values in Children's Books: A Content Rating Instrument for Educators and Concerned Parents, *edited by the Council on Interracial Books for Children, Inc., Racism and Sexism Resource Center for Educators, 1976, pp. 159-60.*

Many of the sexist attitudes and stereotypes found in the earlier book, **Ramona The Pest,** have been dropped from this one. Ramona is a distinct individual, who will attract the interest of children. A genuinely funny book, written cleverly. Good for older, reluctant readers.

> *Enid Davis, "Fiction, Grades 3-10: 'Ramona the Brave'," in her* The Liberty Cap: A Catalogue of Non-Sexist Materials for Children, *Academy Press Limited, 1977, p. 111.*

---

### RAMONA AND HER FATHER  (1977)

Ramona is justifiably one of the most famous and loved characters in children's fiction. . . . Cleary infuses ["**Ramona and Her Father**"] with believability, pathos and comedy. Hard times fall upon the Quimby family because father loses his job and can't find another. Mrs. Quimby goes to work outside the home fulltime and relations become understandably strained. Ramona alternately exacerbates and relieves the situation with her ideas. A boffo chapter reveals how the child copies kid actors in television commercials in the hope of making a million dollars so "her father would be fun again." There is no forced happy ending but a total picture of a happy family, even with its troubles.

> *A review of "Ramona and Her Father," in* Publishers Weekly, *Vol. 212, No. 9, August 29, 1977, p. 367.*

With her uncanny gift for pinpointing the thoughts and feelings of children right down to their own phraseology—while honoring the boundaries of clean, simple writing—the author catches a family situation that puts strain on each of its members, despite their intrinsic strength and invincible humor. . . . True, warm-hearted, and funny. (pp. 285-86)

> *Betsy Hearne, in a review of "Ramona and Her Father," in* Booklist, *Vol. 74, No. 3, October 1, 1977, pp. 285-86.*

Her many friends will rejoice to know that on the precarious journey toward growing up, Ramona Q has somehow slipped through the double binds of Mrs. Griggs's first grade into grade two, her gutsy soul intact. . . .

Ramona Quimby, once known as Ramona the Pest, is the kind of child that drives her elders to the brink. If they could only understand that the hair full of burs which must be cut out one by one started out as a magnificent crown. . . . Ramona, like many of her tribe, never, or hardly ever, sets out to be malicious, and she's certainly not thoughtless. Her schemes are painstakingly crafted and bravely launched, only to be dashed again and again on the uncharted rocks of the grown-up world. . . .

[Beverly Cleary] is, and I do not exaggerate, wildly popular with children. So I came to her books, not only as a reviewer but as a writer, to ask why.

Is it because she is easy to read? She is, but so is "Run, Spot, run." Is it because her settings are contemporary and her characters familiar? They are, but there are thousands of books fitting both descriptions which never capture a fraction of Cleary's devoted readership.

Last week I carried home a stack of Cleary books from the local library to see if I could discover her secret. My two teenagers spotted the books on the dining room table and smiles spread across their faces. "Oh, yeah," one said, as though hearing the name of an old friend after many years. "I remember reading those." "Yeah," said the other. "They're funny."

When I was young there were two kinds of funny—funny ha-ha and funny peculiar. A lot of funny ha-ha things happen in Cleary's books, but her real specialty is another kind of funny, which is a cross betwen funny ha-ha and funny ahhh. Cleary has the rare gift of being able to reveal us to ourselves while still keeping an arm around our shoulder. We laugh (ha ha) to recognize that funny, peculiar little self we were and are and then laugh (ahhh) with relief that we've been understood at last.

The librarian from whom I borrowed the books said that Cleary is loved because she can describe simply the complex feelings of a child. But even more, Cleary is able to sketch clearly with a few perfect strokes the inexplicable adult world as seen through a child's eyes. *Ramona the Brave* should be required reading for all teachers just as *Ramona and her Father* should be read by all parents. . . .

Amidst the traps and hurdles strewn along the path toward growing up, (People are always telling Ramona to "Grow up!" and she's trying, really she is!) there are rare patches of undiluted joy. Cleary captures these as gently as my 11-year-old catches fireflies. Who will ever forget the day Ramona and her friend Howie make tin can stilts and *clank clank* through the twilight, singing "Ninety-nine bottles of beer on the wall" all the way down to the last bottle? Or the Christmas pageant for which Ramona's harassed mother has only had time to devise a sheep costume out of faded pajamas upon which prance, sometimes upside down, an army of pink bunnies? Howie's grandmother has made him and his bratty baby sister, who doesn't even need one, glorious sheep skins of woolly acrylic with zippers up the front. I won't tell you how this particular mortification is transformed into joy. Read it aloud with someone you love. I've asked my nine-year-old to read it to me. She loves Cleary, too, and is less likely than I to spill tears all over page 186.

*Katherine Paterson, "Ramona Redux," in* Book World—The Washington Post, *October 9, 1977, p. E6.*

Another warm, funny, pithy story about Ramona, now in second grade, has some problem situations, large and small, but it is the engaging candor of Ramona, expressed in Cleary's impeccably authentic dialogue and exposition, that gives validity to the book.

*Zena Sutherland, in a review of "Ramona and Her Father," in* Bulletin of the Center for Children's Books, *Vol. 31, No. 4, December, 1977, p. 58.*

As in her previous books, the author delineates the contemporary family with compassion and humor, unerringly suggests the nuances of suburban conversation, and develops as memorable a cast of characters as can be found in children's literature.

*Mary M. Burns, in a review of "Ramona and Her Father," in* The Horn Book Magazine, *Vol. LIII, No. 6, December, 1977, p. 660.*

A warm family story on the surface, this title deeply reinforces the early school age youngster's need for harmony and repeated exposure to the love and affection of an adult. The approval that is bestowed consistently upon Ramona, in spite of real problems, is something that all children seek. To find it given, in this story, by a father to a young daughter belies myths to the contrary. The nonsexist style is commendable. (p. 173)

*Diana L. Spirt, "Identifying Adult Roles: 'Ramona and Her Father'," in her* Introducing More Books: A Guide for the Middle Grades, *R. R. Bowker Company, 1978, pp. 171-74.*

---

### RAMONA AND HER MOTHER (1979)

[The sequel to *Ramona and Her Father*], but without quite the tense central situation that made it so cohesive, this develops and resolves Ramona's doubts about her mother's loving her. The first incident highlights the problem when Ramona feels left out of a party situation because she's too old for the kind of special attention naughty little Willa Jean gets and too young to be included with the adults the way sister Beezus is; various other family or school conflicts deepen her worry. Cleary is at her best when she simultaneously honors straight-laced traditional lifestyle (not to mention writing style) and pokes fun at it, too. . . . Children enjoy both the comfort and the everyday humor to be found in the scenes generated by this perpetually normal family. (pp. 1360-61)

*Betsy Hearne, in a review of "Ramona and Her Mother," in* Booklist, *Vol. 75, No. 17, May 1, 1979, pp. 1360-61.*

What's left to say about Ramona? Cleary has created a wholly delightful personality, she writes in a deceptively casual and conversational style, she has a fine ear for dialogue, and her family scenes are vividly real and funny. . . . There's no real story line, but each incident focuses on Ramona's feelings, her relationship with her mother, and her place in the family, and each is a small gem.

*Zena Sutherland, in a review of "Ramona and Her Mother," in* Bulletin of the Center for Children's Books, *Vol. 32, No. 10, June, 1979, p. 172.*

[The lofty announcement that Ramona's leaving home] creates a gloriously happy ending to Cleary's latest story. [Alan] Tiegreen's drawings again match the spirit of the funny, warm, artless style of the author who has made Ramona irresistible to readers of all ages.

*A review of "Ramona and Her Mother," in* Publishers Weekly, *Vol. 216, No. 5, July 30, 1979, p. 63.*

Cleary's sociology lags behind her child psychology when she has Ramona's average-American family celebrating, after several months of her father's unemployment, his finding a job as supermarket cashier—in our experience, a near-minimum-wage spot usually filled by 18-year-olds and part-time house-wives.... Meanwhile, with Cleary's pipeline to childhood as faithful as ever, second-grader Ramona struggles for recognition, fuming when a guest remarks that a pesty four-year-old neighbor is "Ramona all over again."... Ramona's friends will be gratified to see her coming along, and even her lapses remain endearing.

*A review of "Ramona and Her Mother," in* Kirkus Reviews, *Vol. XLVII, No. 15, August 1, 1979, p. 852.*

A sense of belonging is just about the most secure feeling anyone can have, and Beverly Cleary's family of books—books of a family—provide that reassurance and comforting continuity. Her characters grow and change, but the more they change, the more they stay the same.

For instance, when Ramona first appeared, in 1952, she was the same age as my friends and I. Since then, we've entered school and finished it, gotten married, had jobs and are now the same age as Ramona's parents. But Ramona's current concerns are still the most basic concerns of our lives—"Does my mother love me as much as my sister? Is anyone guessing my guilty secret? If I say I'm going away, will somebody stop me?"

Ramona may not be much older, but she's as alive and true as ever—to the 4-year-old, the 5-year-old, the 6-, 7- and 7½-year-old alive in all of us, whether we're older, younger or exactly the same age.

*Kathleen Leverich, in a review of "Ramona and Her Mother," in* The New York Times Book Review, *October 14, 1979, p. 41.*

[Even] when she's up to such antics as adorning the bathroom with toothpaste rosettes, Ramona is hard to dislike. So skillfully has Cleary presented the viewpoint of a child coping with strained family relationships in difficult times that it is easy to sympathize with Ramona's attempts to be grown-up even when they fail....

In this, as in her 23 previous books, the author's gift for nuances and realistic detail gives a genuine picture of suburban family life right down to the meals cooked in a Crock-Pot, trips to the shopping mall, and the ever-pervasive influence of TV commercials. As always, Cleary chronicles the experience of being young with compassion, humor, and insight.

*Maria Lenhart, "Ramona Reformed," in* The Christian Science Monitor, *October 15, 1979, p. B11.*

---

## RAMONA QUIMBY, AGE 8 (1981)

Although the age level suggested on the new adventure of Ramona is 8-12, the best way to convey her influence is to point out that grownups and even *small boys* count Ramona among their top favorites. In Cleary's fifth, utterly beguiling story, our heroine wrestles with a teacher's putdown [and]

straitened Quimby finances.... Ramona has many challenges for her doughty character but handles them all with the aplomb of a brand-new third-grader. Again, Cleary writes with the light touches of humor and seriousness about a loving family that has its problems but its share of joys as well. More than most highly touted authors, she earns her devoted public. (pp. 91-2)

*A review of "Ramona Quimby, Age 8," in* Publishers Weekly, *Vol. 220, No. 2, July 10, 1981, pp. 91-2.*

Many children will greet Ramona Quimby's return happily, as they would greet an old friend. All of her stories ... are notable for their humor and for the precision with which Beverly Cleary gets inside children, presenting their intense excitements, longings and traumas....

Cleary fills her books with sensations that are redolent of real life. Who does not recall with Ramona the smell of a new soft Pink Pearl eraser? Who would not be shattered, as she is, to discover that radio cat food commercials may distort the truth? The mirror held up to her life reflects sharply her disillusionments as well as the pleasures and vicissitudes of family life. Nowhere are more amusingly seen the efforts of daughters cooking Sunday dinner; nowhere are more sympathetically portrayed the languors of being sick with the flu.

*Virginia Haviland, "Cybil Rivalry and the Romps of Ramona," in* Book World—The Washington Post, *July 12, 1981, p. 6.**

Cleary has brought her "nice sticking-together family" into the 1980s. She's taken the best from the 60s and 70s—she's freer now (viz., neighbor Willa Jean Kemp's playmate Bruce "doesn't wee-wee in the sandbox") and more feelings-centered. And, she's done it without sacrificing any of the decency or laughter that makes the Quimbys a favorite happy family. As if answering critics of her "perfect" family, Cleary puts the Quimby's under real pressure and lets the strains show. The elder Quimbys are trying to make do on one-and-a-half paychecks (when they were struggling on two) so that Mr. Q. can go to college. Straight-arrow Beezus is turning into a temperamental teen. Ramona and bratty Willa Jean are taken care of after school by doting Grandmother Kemp, and Ramona has to put up with other things that are unfair, embarrassing or both.... But Ramona hangs in there and earns the highest honor, being "big enough for her family to depend on." No doubt about it, *Ramona Quimby, Age 8* gets better with every year.

*Pamela D. Pollack, in a review of "Ramona Quimby, Age 8," in* School Library Journal, *Vol. 27, No. 10, August, 1981, p. 54.*

With her unrivaled knack for juggling ordinary happenstances and catching the unexpected effect, Cleary again shows the Quimbys pulling through hard times, with full focus on Ramona.... The insights into child and adult behavior are sharp as well as funny, with the episodes adding up to a convincing, comfortable family portrait. (pp. 42-3)

*Betsy Hearne, in a review of "Ramona Quimby, Age 8," in* Booklist, *Vol. 78, No. 1, September 1, 1981, pp. 42-3.*

It is no small thing to have one's 25th book published, and that's what Beverly Cleary's new story about Ramona Quimby represents. Even better, Mrs. Cleary has won a whole closet full of awards since her first book was published in 1950. And even better than *that*, 25 of those awards came to her in state-wide contests where the voters were young readers. This last seems especially significant. It is a rare thing to be hailed by audience and critics alike. In our field, children do occasionally take up a writer critics have spurned; this was the case, for instance, with L. Frank Baum's Oz stories. More often, children spurn writers that critics have taken up. But in Mrs. Cleary's case, everyone seems delighted.

The new "**Ramona**" is much like its predecessors. The language is relatively uncomplicated—though by no means simple—and the story blends comedy and tragedy as it builds to a happy ending that is not a sweep of the wand but rather a coming to terms with things as they are. Mrs. Cleary's popularity surely gives the lie to both of the common assumptions that children are, on the one hand, jaded and street-wise or, on the other hand, dear little bundles of innocence. For "**Ramona Quimby, Age 8**" lives in a real world of financial woes, arguing parents, sibling rivalries and school anxieties, including that deepest of all humiliations, throwing up in class.

But Ramona also lives in the equally real world of school success, closeness with a sibling and loving parents. In other words, it's an everyday world full of ups and downs that finally—if only temporarily—find their balance.

Part of the secret of Mrs. Cleary's success with her readers is surely that she very seldom slides into the role of Amused Observer; she manages instead to see things exclusively through Ramona's eyes—no mean feat. A lot of the time, in books for young children, the writer-as-adult seems not to be able to resist raising an eyebrow here and there, or hiding a smile. Children pick that up, and must laugh with the author at the hero rather than identifying. When that happens, the heart of the story is lost.

This "**Ramona**" story is mainly episodic. There is no unifying problem as there was in "**Ramona and Her Father**," where Mr. Quimby lost his job and had a hard time finding another. Instead, the episodes are held together by the simple business of Ramona's being in the third grade and being especially sensitive to difficulties both at school and at home. It's a relief to find that these difficulties are average rather than bizarre, that a story about a pleasant, normal young WASP is still O.K. It all says something reassuring—to me, at least—about the state of the Union's grade-schoolers. A great many writers seem to believe that only a cup of hemlock can catch their interest. How nice to find, instead, that a glass of milk is as popular as ever. . . .

Mrs. Cleary's many fans will be happy with this new book, and I hope she goes on to give them 25 more.

> *Natalie Babbitt, in a review of "Ramona Quimby, Age 8," in* The New York Times Book Review, *November 1, 1981, p. 38.*

I was not enthusiastic about this book. . . . But remembering how thoroughly I enjoyed Cleary's books when I was a child, I brought the book to my classroom of third and fourth graders—and they loved it! The author's gift is that she can plug into the minds of young children, identify with and accurately present their problems, issues and concerns. As an adult, I had missed that.

To the author's credit, this is a story of a working-class family. Issues of financial hardship, usually ignored in children's literature, are mentioned as a regular part of the Quimbys' daily life. (p. 33)

Ramona's concerns are typical for her age. She understands that the family will have to "cut back," but she is supportive of her father's return to college, even though she is sad that she will get less attention from him.

The Quimbys are presented realistically. The parents—who are both caring, yet firm—do not always get along, and they are concerned about making ends meet. Ramona and her sister are sometimes enemies, sometimes allies against their parents. Ramona both accepts and resents her responsibilities within the family. (pp. 33-4)

[When reading about Ramona's mishap with the raw egg,] I thought, "This is ridiculous. What a pain in the neck that child would be in my classroom." My students found that incident absolutely delightful. Again, this is the author's gift. (p. 34)

> *Jan M. Goodman, in a review of "Ramona Quimby, Age 8," in* Interracial Books for Children Bulletin, *Vol. 13, Nos. 2 & 3, 1982, pp. 33-4.*

---

### *RALPH S. MOUSE*   (1982)

Ralph S. (for Smart) Mouse is back again, still living at the Mountain View Inn in Cucaracha, California. His many little relatives are pestering Ralph for motorcycle rides in the Inn's lobby, and the resulting accumulation of droppings is getting his handyman friend Matt in trouble with the Inn's management. To save Matt's job and to avoid his pesky relatives, Ralph convinces his new friend Ryan Bramble, son of the Inn's housekeeper, to take him to live at the Irwin J. Sneed Elementary School. Ralph's adventures there, avoiding detection and then becoming the basis of a class project on mice, are the major focus of the novel. . . . All the elements that make Cleary popular with children are present here. Although the plot is not as interesting nor as fast moving as the previous "**Ralph**" titles . . . , children will eagerly read these further adventures of Ralph and will ask for more. A natural choice for reading aloud.

> *Ellen Fader, in a review of "Ralph S. Mouse," in* School Library Journal, *Vol. 28, No. 10, August, 1982, p. 94.*

[This is] a sequel worthy of *The Mouse and the Motorcycle* and *Runaway Ralph*. . . . The scenes in the fifth grade classroom are most diverting; Cleary captures the essence of classroom bickering and the warm relationship between a good teacher and her students. . . . The story is a deft blend of realism and fantasy, quietly and consistently funny, and occasionally touching without being the least saccharine. Again, bravo. (pp. 5-6)

> *Zena Sutherland, in a review of "Ralph S. Mouse," in* Bulletin of the Center for Children's Books, *Vol. 36, No. 1, September, 1982, pp. 5-6.*

The anthropomorphic mouse is among the most popular literary stock characters created for children. In fact, there is a whole genre which could perhaps be called "mouse picaresque." Its inventor was Beatrix Potter; among its most skillful practitioners are Margery Sharp, E. B. White, and now Beverly Cleary. . . .

[Ralph S. Mouse] is much like Stuart Little, although Ralph lacks Stuart's big city polish. . . .

[Ralph's exploits] are pretty standard for literary mice: foraging for food in unusual places, nesting in mittens and boots, buzzing about on a toy motorcycle. What makes this story so successful is Cleary's perfect ear for children's conversation, and that certain wryness most of her characters, whether they be mice or children, possess.

For the fans of Ramona and Ribsy, and Henry and Beezus, and now Ralph, Beverly Cleary has served up another treat.

> *Alice Digilio, in a review of "Ralph S. Mouse," in* Book World—The Washington Post, *September 12, 1982, p. 7.*

Fans of Ralph and of his motorcycle adventures will be glad to know that the author's ability to perceive the thoughts of children—and of mice—has not deserted her. . . . Full of amusing vignettes and sudden insights, the classroom is vividly set forth, with each child thoroughly individualized. The book reflects two levels of experience—an unsophisticated child's (or mouse's) and, at the same time and in some magical way, that of the adult with its hopeful, but worldly, point of view.

> *Ann A. Flowers, in a review of "Ralph S. Mouse," in* The Horn Book Magazine, *Vol. LVIII, No. 6, December, 1982, p. 648.*

Is fantasy changing direction? The adventures of Ralph the mouse and his magically propelled motor-cycle started seventeen years ago as a kind of Dinky-Toy dream in which Ralph's education as a rider was described with the charm of incongruity. Over the past decade at least, and perhaps for longer, an increased didacticism has been creeping into fantasy-adventures: for instance, animals now apply the principles of conservation as automatically as humans do. In the third adventure of Beverly Cleary's miniature hero, **Ralph S. Mouse,** she has complied with the trend. When Ralph persuades Ryan Bramble . . . to take him along to school in his pocket, he falls victim to the zeal of Miss Kuckenbacker, who seizes the chance to demonstrate animal behaviour by testing the mouse in a cardboard maze. Ralph takes a practical view of the exercise:

> He knew he was really a smart mouse. Why should he have to run around banging his nose in front of all these tacos and sandwich gobblers? Nimbly he leaped to the top of the partitions, caught a whiff of pure peanut butter, and took off across the top edges of the maze. He would show them who was smart.

If Ralph profits from the education system, it is by proving to his satisfaction that humans may be larger and more powerful than mice but they are surely not as sensible. Perhaps this book is not so different from its predecessors after all. In all three of Ralph's encounters with people he is a vehicle for a Gulliver-scrutiny of Brobdingnag as well as a splendidly entertaining character in his own squeakily confident right. (pp. 4007-08)

> *Margery Fisher, in a review of "Ralph S. Mouse," in her* Growing Point, *Vol. 21, No. 5, January, 1983, pp. 4007-08.*

Readers who have not come across Ralph S. in the earlier books may miss the immediate rapport that is established, for instance, with the Quimby household in Beverly Cleary's **"Ramona"** books. . . . The story of **Ralph S. Mouse** contains humour and the fascination of building up detail about a particular world (the Irwin J. Sneed Elementary School from a very particular angle), but there is also a reflective quality and a touch of sadness in Ralphs' equivocal position: a solitary mouse in a man's world. . . .

[Both **Ralph S. Mouse** and *The Cricket in Times Square*] invite children into the pleasures and demands of really absorbing reading. The authors understand children and coax them to grow. Ramona's mother would approve.

> *Mary Steele, "Fiction: 'Ralph S. Mouse'," in* The Signal Review 1: A Selective Guide to Children's Literature, *1982, edited by Nancy Chambers, The Thimble Press, 1983, p. 40.*

---

***DEAR MR. HENSHAW*** **(1983; British edition as *Dear Mr Henshaw*)**

### AUTHOR'S COMMENTARY

Readers often suggest books for me to write about Henry or Ramona or books featuring themselves as central characters. The suggestion that stayed with me came in 1982 from several boys unknown to one another: "Please write a book about a boy whose parents are divorced."

For some time I had been thinking about writing a different sort of book because I find change refreshing and because I had noticed that, although I have written a variety of books, I was being stereotyped as always writing a certain kind of book. The new one would be about a boy. Girls, it appeared to me, had taken over children's literature. A story began to fall into place. Leigh Botts, child of divorce, living with his mother, longing for his father. Those thoughts that are jumbled in an author's mind began to separate themselves and cling to this nucleus. An overheard sentence spoken in grief by a strange woman: "It's so terrible when his father promises to call and doesn't." A remark by a teacher: "This kid in my class rigged up a burglar alarm for his lunch box. It made a terrible racket." These were joined by boys' pride in fathers who drive tractor-trailer rigs, grief at the loss of a pet, loneliness in a new school. My own idle thoughts about sending children lists of questions were no longer idle. Letters to an author who sends questions and demands answers followed by a diary seemed right; let the boy reveal his own feelings, for I believe children who want to write should look within themselves, not within the books of others.

One problem was the author Leigh was to write to. He must be a young foot-loose male whose books did not resemble mine. Creating Mr. Henshaw, from a name plucked from an obituary column (I read names anyplace I can find them!) was great fun, for he writes the books I have wanted to write but could not. His *Ways to Amuse a Dog* goes back to the 1940s, when I first heard that booksellers' legend of the woman who misunderstood the title of a book called *Forty Days of Musa Dagh* and asked for *Forty Ways to Amuse a Dog*. This struck me as a splendid idea for a book because most of the dogs I knew were bored. *Moose on Toast* came out of a visit to Alaska, where a librarian asked, with a touch of desperation in her voice, whether I would like to take home some moose sausage. Her husband had shot a moose, and the family of three was faced with eating a thousand pounds of moose meat from their freezer. When I mentioned this to other librarians as having humorous possibilities for a story, no one was amused. All had a moose or part of a moose in their freezers. This discouraged me but would not discourage Mr. Henshaw, who would spend his time in Alaska climbing mountains instead of speaking at banquets and would be hungry enough to eat moose, even though I was told it is dry and stringy. Mr. Henshaw's third and more serious book *Beggar Bears*, about bear cubs in Yellowstone National Park, who are taught to beg instead of forage and whose mothers die from eating plastic bags, is another book I could not write because I lack a naturalist's knowledge. Foot-loose Mr. Henshaw was free to travel and research bears.

When *Dear Mr. Henshaw* was published, almost every note on the Christmas cards we received asked, "How come *you* know so much about trucks?" Fortunately, our son had been able to answer my questions. When he was in college, he worked summers in produce warehouses and packing sheds, where he came to know the ways of truckers. I also visited a truck repair yard in Salinas—not an easy experience, for the dusty truckers found my asking questions amusing and I had to be wary of having my leg pulled. Our son also rigged for me a lunch box with an alarm that does indeed go off with a racket. (pp. 435-37)

*Dear Mr. Henshaw* was a most satisfying book to write. It seemed almost to write itself. Because I find life humorous, sorrowful, and filled with problems that have no solutions, my intent was to write about the feelings of a lonely boy and to avoid the genre of the problem novel. . . . As soon as the book was published, more letters—the first, from adults—arrived. Some said it was the best book I had ever written; others expressed disappointment, even indignation, that I had not written a book as funny as the *Ramona* books. This surprised me. Writers of humor for children often hear that they "just write funny stories" and are made aware, even though they know it is wrong, that serious books are considered superior. A couple of people said they liked the book themselves but expressed doubts about giving it to children because it wasn't funny and because Leigh's parents were not reconciled at the end—a conclusion that I felt would be sentimental, dishonest, and a source of false hope to many children. Teachers wrote that the book would be valuable for classroom discussion because so many pupils came from single-parent homes. Mothers struggling to rear sons without help from fathers wrote moving letters of appreciation.

Then letters from children began to arrive. The first came from a boy with two parents, whose father owns a gas station in Leigh's town. He said he read *Dear Mr. Henshaw* straight through the day he bought it and five times the next week. Others said it was my best book. Children found more of the humor in the story than adults and expressed interest in Leigh's lunchbox alarm, although one girl wrote a wistful letter saying she never had anything good in *her* lunch. Another girl said she was *so* glad Leigh's parents didn't get together at the end. Many told me how hard life is in a new school, that their lives were very much like Leigh's, or that there were "lots of kids like Leigh" in their school. Several letters ended "Please don't send *me* a list of questions." (pp. 437-38)

Other children wrote that they liked Leigh, but they liked Ramona better. And why shouldn't they? The rallying cry of my library training was "the right book for the right child." In a world in which children's lives vary so widely, there is no reason why every child should like every book, even Newbery books. . . .

No, when I wrote *Dear Mr. Henshaw,* I did not expect every reader to like Leigh as much as Ramona. Although I am deeply touched that my books have reached two generations of children, popularity has never been my goal. If it had been, I would have written *Ramona Solves the Mystery of the Haunted House and Finds a Baby Brother* or followed trends and written

something like *Henry and Beezus Play Doctor,* instead of a book about the feelings of a lonely child of divorce.

"Who is Leigh Botts?" adults now ask. "Is there really a Leigh Botts?" children want to know. "Is he a friend of yours?" There is not one Leigh Botts; there are many. Leigh Botts is all the brave and lonely children I have ever known who have found books and libraries to be their best friends. (p. 438)

> *Beverly Cleary, in a "Newbery Medal" award acceptance speech given at the meeting of the American Library Association in Dallas on June 24, 1984 in* The Horn Book Magazine, *Vol. LX, No. 4, August, 1984, pp. 429-38.*

---

"Dear Mr. Henshaw . . ." It all begins when Leigh Botts is in second grade and writes a letter to an author. "My teacher read your book about the dog to our class. It was funny. We licked it." In third, fourth, and fifth grades the letters are perfunctory as well as predictable ("If you answer I get to put your letter on the bulletin board . . ." "Our teacher is making us write to authors for Book Week . . ."). In sixth grade there is another teacher and another assignment. It is here that what has been a smattering of letters turns into a correspondence in earnest. . . .

It is in the answers to [questions asked by Mr. Henshaw] and in the letters and diaries that follow that we learn about Leigh and about his family.

Since his parents' recent divorce he and his mother (clearly a sensible type) have lived in Pacific Grove, on California's Central Coast, where Leigh is still considered a new boy in school and his only friend is Mr. Fridley the custodian. His father, meanwhile, is a long distance trucker, happy-go-lucky and not much given to settling down. In fact, Leigh spends a lot of time waiting for him to call, to come for a visit, to notice him in some way. From his description of a life that is at times both dreary and lonely, it is easy to see why Leigh (who calls himself "the mediumest boy in the class") puts so much importance on his letters to Mr. Henshaw. And it is through this correspondence that Leigh learns to confront the facts of his life and to handle his anger at his parents' divorce. . . .

Epistolary novels, by their very nature, are apt to limit a writer, but Beverly Cleary, pitfalls not withstanding, has peopled her story with a group of fully realized characters. Even Mr. Henshaw comes alive as a likable yet slightly irreverent person who claims that the reason he writes books is that he has "read every book in the library and because writing beats mowing the lawn or shoveling snow."

The letters themselves are so real they make your teeth ache—a fact that should come as no surprise given the mail Cleary reads and answers every year.

And if Leigh isn't Henry Huggins or Beezus or Ramona or Ellen Tebbits—well, here I feel like one of those teachers who ask a child why he isn't as bright/clever/winsome as his older sister/brother/cousin. By this time we all know that, like a child, a character is who he is. So let me just say, "Welcome, Leigh Botts."

> *Colby Rodowsky, "Life through the Letter Box," in* Book World—The Washington Post, *August 14, 1983, p. 7.*

Cleary succeeds again. . . . [Leigh's] resolution to continue loving his difficult-to-love father and to try to get along and make friends in a new home and school will certainly move young readers, regardless of their own situations. And, as usual, Cleary's sense of humor leavens and lightens what might otherwise be a heavy work of social realism.

> *Ruth K. MacDonald, in a review of "Dear Mr. Henshaw," in* School Library Journal, *Vol. 30, No. 1, September, 1983, p. 120.*

Cleary deftly characterizes the feelings Leigh has for his absent father, and the book stacks up well against any in the middle-grade problem genre; it nevertheless lacks the wit and ingenuity for which Cleary's stories are known. An applicable quote appears in one of Leigh's letters to Mr. Henshaw about his latest book: "I was surprised because it wasn't funny like your other books, but I got to thinking . . . and decided a book doesn't have to be funny to be good, although it often helps." Indeed it does.

> *Ilene Cooper, in a review of "Dear Mr. Henshaw," in* Booklist, *Vol. 80, No. 1, September 1, 1983, p. 80.*

Beverly Cleary has adapted an old novelistic device, the epistolary form, in a poignant story with an unmistakable ring of truth. . . . [The] story is by no means one of unrelieved gloom, for there are deft touches of humor in the sentient, subtly wrought account of the small triumphs and tragedies in the life of an ordinary boy.

> *Ethel L. Heins, in a review of "Dear Mr. Henshaw," in* The Horn Book Magazine, *Vol. LIX, No. 5, October, 1983, p. 570.*

Beverly Cleary has written many very good books over the years. This one is the best. It is a first-rate, poignant story in the form of letters and a diary—a new construction for a Cleary book—and there is so much in it, all presented so simply, that it's hard to find a way to do it justice.

Mrs. Cleary knows the voices of children. Dialogue has always been one of the strongest parts of her work. And here, where all is dialogue, that strength can shine alone and be doubly impressive. . . .

What makes **"Dear Mr. Henshaw"** so special is Leigh's candid acceptance of all that happens to him. He hasn't the least idea how brave he is. One letter to Henshaw ends this way: "I don't think Dad is that much interested in me. He didn't phone when he said he would. I hope your [new] book wins a million awards." Leigh is a normal boy with a life full of things to occupy his attention. If his parents' divorce is giving him pain, it has not made a monomaniac of him—he can still care about Henshaw's books. A P.S. to a later letter says, "I bought a copy of [your book] 'Ways to Amuse a Dog' at a garage sale. I hope you don't mind." That's wonderful. It clangs with reality.

The story closes as it should. There will be no reunion between Leigh's parents; he has come to understand that and accept it. Wisely, Mrs. Cleary does not fix things so that the lunch box thief is caught; she does not arrange a meeting between Leigh and Henshaw; and she never allows Leigh's writing to slide a millimeter away from the natural humor and unconscious pathos that make it work so honestly.

What a lovely, well-crafted, three-dimensional work this is. And how reassuring to Mrs. Cleary's fellow writers to see that

a 27th book can be so fresh and strong. Lots of adjectives here; she deserves them all.

> *Natalie Babbitt, in a review of "Dear Mr. Henshaw," in* The New York Times Book Review, *October 23, 1983, p. 34.*

The fly-leaf proclaims that the correspondence changes his life. In fact nothing much changes but our understanding grows with the growth of Leigh's understanding and his ability to express himself. It isn't much maybe, but what there is is sound, good, lively and alive.

> *Dorothy Nimmo, in a review of "Dear Mr Henshaw," in* The School Librarian, *Vol. 32, No. 2, June, 1984, p. 151.*

---

## *LUCKY CHUCK* (1984)

The cautionary tale of a teenage cyclist who flouts the Motor Vehicle Code—in picture-book format and spoofy Dick-and-Jane form. Exactly who is meant to make what use of this odd item is a puzzlement. The publishers age it, like the run of picture-books, 4-8. But it's full of technical information and technical lingo, and, with its close-up drawings [by J. Winslow Higginbottom] of the motorcycle's parts, it does obviously intend to be a guide to motorcycle operation. At the same time, the mock-primerese—"This is Chuck's motorcycle-driver's license. He earned it by studying the Motor Vehicle Code and passing a driver's test. . . . This is Chuck's mother worrying about Chuck and his motorcycle"—has a satirical tone out-of-sync with both the technical detail and Chuck's reckless driving. . . . There may be some kids around nine or ten, who'll recognize the Cleary name, think fondly of mouse Ralph, see the authentic motorcycle poop, and lap it all up. But the book resembles nothing so much as a public-service offering from the motorcycle folk, jollied up for popular appeal.

> *A review of "Lucky Chuck," in* Kirkus Reviews, *Juvenile Issue, Vol. LII, Nos. 1-5, March 1, 1984, p. 2.*

The Newbery Medalist's new story has all her hallmarks. The odds are against anyone but Cleary weaving facts about a motorcycle, rules of the Motor Vehicle Department and a lesson in safety into a slyly humorous picture book.

> *A review of "Lucky Chuck," in* Publishers Weekly, *Vol. 225, No. 9, March 2, 1984, p. 94.*

The indomitable Beverly Cleary has come up with something new: a picture book about an adolescent motorcycle rider. It's the style that lends humor here, for the text follows a pattern: This is Chuck—this is Chuck's motorcycle—this is Chuck's mother (worrying about Chuck) and so on. . . . [It] depicts a ride in which Chuck is careless, has a spill, is lucky to be unhurt, and even as he's saying, "See, Mom, nothing to worry about," is worrying about how he's going to pay his traffic fine. This is informative and funny, a deft blend of fictional framework and informative text.

> *Zena Sutherland, in a review of "Lucky Chuck," in* Bulletin of the Center for Children's Books, *Vol. 37, No. 9, May, 1984, p. 162.*

Cleary's writing is humorous, yet serious in content and easy to read; however there is a monotony to her device of starting most pages with the phrase, "This is. . . ." . . . Nevertheless,

*Lucky Chuck* does introduce important content within the confines of its weak story.

*Peggy Forehand, in a review of ''Lucky Chuck,'' in* School Library Journal, *Vol. 31, No. 1, September, 1984, p. 100.*

---

### RAMONA FOREVER (1984)

A gentle comedy, a warm and realistic family story, and a perceptive study of a child: *Ramona Forever* is all three, a sequel as beguiling as its predecessors. The title refers to Ramona's glimpse of eternity as she sees herself in the endlessly reflecting mirrors of a bridal shop. She and Beezus are to be attendants at an aunt's wedding, and the ceremony is the final episode of a story that focuses on family relationships with a keen eye and a light touch.

*Zena Sutherland, in a review of ''Ramona Forever,'' in* Bulletin of the Center for Children's Books, *Vol. 38, No. 1, September, 1984, p. 2.*

Ramona is back! Everyone's favorite heroine has returned to find herself facing more changes and problems than she ever knew existed: her father's search for a teaching job, which could uproot the family; the marriage of her Aunt Bea; the death of a pet; her relationship with big sister Beezus. Perhaps the biggest change is her mother's pregnancy. This causes all sorts of problems (Ramona's case of ''acute siblingitis'' when she can't visit the new baby is priceless.) Cleary's can't-fail style is evident in this sure-fire winner. She can deal with sensitive subjects without becoming gushy, and injects every situation with her unbeatable humor. Don't miss it!

*Sharon A. McKinley, in a review of ''Ramona Forever,'' in* Children's Book Review Service, *Vol. 13, No. 1, September, 1984, p. 7.*

Fans who worried when *Dear Mr. Henshaw* and *Lucky Chuck* appeared can relax—Ramona is back, and Beverly Cleary has lost none of her ability to produce a book of sure-fire popularity. . . . With her customary deftness, Cleary guides Ramona through the ambivalent feelings that accompany [the new events in her life], all the while retaining her ability to convey Ramona's difficulties with humor and understanding. The Quimby family emerges as strong as ever, and readers can close the book with the assurance that Ramona will remain Ramona—forever.

*Annie L. Okie, in a review of ''Ramona Forever,'' in* School Library Journal, *Vol. 31, No. 1, September, 1984, p. 115.*

Happy days, Ramona is back! . . . Sandwiched between all the laughs and hustle-bustle are some realities that give the story depth. . . . As in her other work, Cleary provides laugh-out-loud scenes, memorable characters, and keen perceptions. When it comes to writing books kids love, nobody does it better. (pp. 62-3)

*Ilene Cooper, in a review of ''Ramona Forever,'' in* Booklist, *Vol. 81, No. 1, September 1, 1984, pp. 62-3.*

Cleary forever! And then we can have Ramona and Beezus and Henry Huggins and Ribsy and Ralph S. Mouse and Ellen Tebbits forever too. This reviewer devoured his first Beverly Cleary book—it was the unforgettable *Henry and Ribsy*—at least 25 years ago, this latest only last week. Which was better? It's like asking which is your favorite Trollope. Cleary's work is so much of a piece, of so consistently high and even a standard, that any child who likes her work will eventually want to read it all. . . .

Again like Trollope's, Cleary's books may not be masterpieces, but they remain sprightly, spring-like, and exceptionally readable. Try one and see.

*Michael Dirda, in a review of ''Ramona Forever,'' in* Book World—The Washington Post, *September 9, 1984, p. 11.*

The seventh book about the spirited girl reveals a more mature, reflective Ramona who can now laugh at herself. Reassuring to young readers, the story detailing this change—if less hilarious—is still very funny and is as astutely observed and alive with palpable characters as are its predecessors. . . . The old, ingenuous Ramona still peeks through; for example, she responds to Beezus's suggestion that their mother is pregnant, '''Why would Mother do a thing like that when she already has us?''' And she still exhibits the contradictory behavior and the conflicting emotions that have made her so human and endearing; but these attributes are now tempered by self-restraint. Howie's younger sister carries on Ramona's uninhibited ways while Ramona knows that ''she had grown past Willa Jean's kind of behavior, which had been fun while it lasted.'' Appreciative readers may experience similar conflicts—cheering Ramona's coming of age but also suffering a twinge of regret.

*Nancy C. Hammond, in a review of ''Ramona Forever,'' in* The Horn Book Magazine, *Vol. LX, No. 5, September-October, 1984, p. 590.*

# Penelope (Jane) Farmer

## 1939-

English author of fiction and short stories, reteller, script-writer, critic, editor, and translator.

Farmer's ease in juxtaposing reality and fantasy as well as her talent for capturing mood and character have brought her to the fore of contemporary British literature for children. Best known for sophisticated "introvert" fantasies which explore psychological concepts and feelings, she has also produced realistic and historical fiction and mythological tales for younger readers. Farmer uses the structure of myth, magic, and dream to provide unique and occasionally disconcerting variations on the themes of identity, maturity, and the nature of reality. She uses the time-shift technique to describe children who are caught between the worlds of fantasy and actuality. Farmer's protagonists are often faced with life-altering choices, such as whether or not to remain in their fantasy dimension. Depending on themselves to solve their own problems, they ultimately reject immortality and return to familiar surroundings. Farmer illuminates the lives of her characters by investing them with important insights from their experiences which they can apply to their everyday lives. Claiming to have few original ideas, she adopts the symbols and images of mythology to express literary concerns that are personal but universal.

Born the second of fraternal twins, Farmer has had a lifelong preoccupation with establishing a separate identity. After obtaining a degree in history and a diploma in social studies, she began writing, sometimes unknowingly giving voice to her inner needs. A story originally intended for Farmer's first book, a collection of short stories called *The China People*, provided the framework for her fantasy, *The Summer Birds*. Likened to *Peter Pan* because a strange boy teaches some village children to fly, the book has a different theme: the children must choose to remain human or become birds. It is acclaimed for its haunting aura, realistic social interaction, and successful evocation of human flight. *The Summer Birds* introduces Charlotte Mary Makepeace and her sister, Emma, who are later featured separately in *Charlotte Sometimes* and *Emma in Winter*. Farmer draws on her experiences as a teacher in the London slums for *The Magic Stone*. Regarded as an accurate presentation of class differences, the book also receives negative comment for its sluggish pacing and obvious Arthurian imagery. Farmer employs vivid dream sequences in *Emma in Winter*, a sequel to *The Summer Birds* which has a similar theme but deeper psychological overtones. Emma and Bobby Fumpkins fly backwards in time to the creation of the earth, where they must consciously decide to return to everyday life or lose humanity by entering the unknown. Critics commend the controlled tension which pervades the book while pointing out that some children may find the narrative too introspective. Perhaps Farmer's most popular work is *Charlotte Sometimes*. Charlotte grapples with doubts about who she really is and what constitutes reality after she exchanges places with Clare, who had attended the same boarding school in 1918. Reviewers praise *Charlotte Sometimes* as one of Farmer's finest novels. They especially admire her deft handling of relationships, her skill in maintaining suspense, and

Courtesy of The Bodley Head

her attention to detail in forming the moods of her dual time periods.

With *A Castle of Bone*, Farmer established herself as a major fantasist. Basing her framework on Celtic tree alphabets and calendars, she uses the unpredictability of an enchanted cupboard, the amusing and sometimes troubled relationship of four youngsters, and Hugh's strange nightly dream-journeys to examine the mortality and insularity of the adolescent. *Castle* is deemed Farmer's most ambitious and original work for children, one demanding a knowledge of Celtic mythology to fully appreciate the allusions. Farmer approaches a less complex but no less serious topic in *William and Mary*. Two school friends enter various sea-related paintings to search for the other half of a magical shell which, when found, would signify to William that his parents are reunited; reviewers praise the book's picturesque language and solid characterization. Farmer has written three books of realistic fiction, *Saturday Shillings*, *The Seagull*, and *Dragonfly Summer*, and three books of historical fiction, *August the Fourth*, *The Coal Train*, and *The Runaway Train*. These works show her ability to compose simple, believable narratives for the primary grades. *Daedalus and Icarus*, *The Serpent's Teeth*, *The Story of Persephone*, and *Heracles* point to Farmer's intense interest in myths and legends. While some critics find her language occasionally strained, these retellings are noted for their drama and clarity. Farmer has also edited a book of mythology called *Beginnings: Creation Myths of the World.*

**Most critics recognize Farmer as an imaginative and inventive writer who works well in several genres. They appreciate her well-defined characters, convincing atmospheres, and often lyric prose. Farmer is occasionally called an unconventional writer for the intensity of her imagery and her experimentation with word usage. Although some observers consider her overly symbolic and pretentious, many believe that she has reduced the distinction between literature for children and adults. Farmer is usually acclaimed as an author who transforms her personal concerns into challenging and relevant books. *The Summer Birds* was a runner-up for the Carnegie Medal in 1963.**

**(See also *Contemporary Authors New Revision Series*, Vol. 9 and *Contemporary Authors*, Vols. 13-16, rev. ed.)**

---

## AUTHOR'S COMMENTARY

I used to be surprised that adult readers should sometimes try to distinguish fantasy from fairy tale, myth and legend, because all seemed to me to have roughly the same function: to interpret human and imaginative experience in terms of symbol or image. Fantasy and fairy tale in any case are usually hopelessly confused, so that any short story tends to be called fairy tale while the longer ones are called fantasy. Yet the more I think about it, the more I begin to find one clear distinction. Myth, fairy tales and legend all relate to general experience and come from the mass subconscious—myths, obviously, dealing with much grander matters than fairy tales, concerns of a more universal kind—yet the difference being of degree not kind, since both relate to the minds of a people rather than of an individual. Fantasy, on the other hand, though it may use universal symbols, springs from purely private experiences— it is psychological image coloured and transformed by the workings of a single mind. This does not mean that a modern fairy story from some particular modern writer cannot, *per se*, be a fairy story, or that it cannot be told in an individual idiom or style; only that the writer has to maintain some distance from the material, to let the feeling of the story come from his interpretation and reworking of themes within the fairy tale convention, even if in a fairly original way, rather than from unknown recesses of his own mind. (p. 23)

In an article in a short-lived newspaper called *Play*, Helen Cresswell made a distinction between phantasy in the psychological sense spelt with a 'ph' and fantasy in the literary sense spelt with an 'f'. I regard this more often than not as an entirely false distinction. Many kinds of literary fantasy are just psychological phantasy given form, narrative and coherence; the staple themes are, after all, the stuff of dreams—witches, ogres, time shifts, flying, changes of shape or size. The same thing, of course, is true of myth and fairy tale, though there the phantasy (with a 'ph') is of a more general kind. In one sense, though, myth here is the reverse of fantasy. The more sophisticated a culture, the more coherent are its myths. In the primitive myths of the Australian aborigines, for instance, it is hard to find or to follow any story line; they have a totally dreamlike incoherence, compared with the strong narrative lines of, say, the Greek myths. Conversely, the more sophisticated an audience, the less does the creator have to disguise the subconscious of his fantasy; it can, even should, retain that kind of incoherence, or at least appear to do so, as in Kurt Vonnegut whose brilliant fantasies, particularly *Slaughterhouse Five*, have this surface incoherence—or rather perhaps illogicality, like

the process of consciousness or of dream—but an enormously strong and conscious structure underlying them. This says more about war in a hundred pages than Norman Mailer does in a thousand, and should disabuse anyone of the idea that fantasy has only something to say to children. Probably only in film, though, has the thing been taken to its logical extent, as in Fellini's *Satyricon*, which abandons narrative entirely in favour of the incoherence of the subconscious and the dream.

Jonathan Miller's television version of *Alice* brought home to me the fluid, illogical, totally dreamlike shiftings of Lewis Carroll's narrative—so that almost for the first time I saw what *Alice* was really about: not only a dream but having the structure of dream itself.

As a child, though, I read *Alice* straight. For children are not a sophisticated audience, and therefore—and this is my second point—if you write fantasy for children, whatever its origins, you must provide or, as Lewis Carroll did, appear to provide, a strong narrative line. You must create a beginning, a middle and an end; a process which can, I think, make it much clearer to yourself from where your ideas spring, even if disguising it from the audience. It is not that you cannot or must not play with form. Event does not have to be extrovert, it can go on in people's heads, or within the most simple domestic situation. But the form must be there and be seen to be there, otherwise children will not read you.

Here I must make a distinction. Up till now I have been considering fantasy as an introvert form, but it does not necessarily have to be.

Roughly, extrovert fantasies rely more on surface mechanics, or machinery. They may use the themes and devices of introvert fantasy, yet the source and consequence of event is basically exterior to both the author and his or her characters. And though the failings of the characters, such as stupidity, cowardice, idleness or overenthusiasm, may land them in danger or embarrassment, there is not so much a sense of terror below terror, joy below joy as you will find in fantasy of the other sort. (pp. 23-5)

Once you make categories of course it is hard to find anything that fits them exactly. Tentatively, though, I would call Joan Aiken's fantasies extrovert rather than introvert (especially her short stories). Perhaps it is no coincidence that she is probably also one of the most inventive and fertile of present children's writers. Do the writers of introvert fantasies have to go deeper into smaller areas precisely because they are less inventive, even if no less imaginative?

Lewis Carroll, Alan Garner, Lucy Boston, Russell Hoban I would call introvert fantasists. Mary Norton is harder to categorize but I think I would put her among the introverts, especially in her first two borrower books. The sense of human littleness in an enormous universe is a basic human fear or feeling—even more literally true for children—and the Borrowers' shifts and artifices to turn objects from the giant human world to their own use, go beyond invention; they have a quirkiness, an oddity, which makes them precisely right, which moves an imagination on, as well as satisfying it.

I need not make any too high claims for my books when I say that they tend to fall into the same category, because I find myself dealing with the same interior kinds of subjects—often, unknowingly—and quite often again touch on problems of my own, even if I do not always recognize this and certainly do not know how or why. For instance, halfway through ***Charlotte***

*Sometimes* I realized that I was writing a book about identity. I am a twin, a nonidentical one, and apparently one of the chief problems of nonidentical twins is always the establishment of a genuine and separate sense of identity. Looking back I can see this has in fact been an obsession with me, since the age of twelve or so at least. Margery Fisher has said that *Emma in Winter* is also about a search for identity, [see excerpt below for *Charlotte Sometimes* (1969)], which is interesting because it is quite certainly something that I did not recognize at any stage while writing it. And it is true, if you write this kind of book, that though some of its concerns may become apparent to you as you write, some never do, unless they are brought to your attention when other people comment on what you have written. One reviewer for instance, talking about *Charlotte Sometimes,* said it was full of images suggesting the gap between appearance and reality—an acorn which didn't quite fit its cup, a huge bell which was cracked and so only made a small sound, marbles which looked huge in water and smaller outside. I still do not know myself if, subconsciously, this was for me an underlying concern.

I wonder if other writers too have experienced, in the middle of some emotional or nervous crisis, a totally blinding and startling sense of *déja-vu*. Or again, have had some curious emotion, say an enormous feeling of elation, or again, of terror, when reading or describing some passage from an earlier book which is much more powerful than the feeling that at the time appeared to generate the passage? It almost seems as if what you write previews some future state of crisis, or alternatively previews its resolution. (pp. 26-7)

In fact these decidedly personal origins of my kind of fantasy make it very hard to discuss. To say much more about what appears to be the genesis of one or other of my books would involve revelations which I have no intention of making. Equally, to investigate the origins of books written by other writers could well lead one into exceedingly impertinent assumptions—unless they are safely dead, that is. (p. 27)

I should now like to turn to the effect of fantasy on its audience. But perhaps I had better start briefly, and I fear gradiosely, by talking more generally about the function of art, and of images in art. For me, chiefly, their function is to communicate, and particularly to communicate the almost incommunicable: that is feelings and experience of every kind—emotional, spiritual, intellectual, aesthetic; all of which helps to lessen the huge distances between ourselves and other people, so making us feel less isolated, less alone. This can be done more effectively often by symbol or image—even by abstract image—than by direct statement, precisely because images are so much more powerful. They can be almost limitless in their reverberations. . . . Art, through images, analyzed and began to comprehend the states of the human mind long before there was any science available to do it. . . . I think of *Hamlet,* a complete portrait of a manic depressive, long before there were psychologists, let alone a clinical recognition of manic depression; and of Blake whose prophetic books set out almost precisely the same fourfold analysis of the mind of man as Freud did a century later.

Poetry, via images, compresses the deepest and most complex ideas into the space of a few lines. (pp. 30-1)

[Fantasy] does precisely what poetry does, but in a way which children can take. Poetic images, except of the simplest kind, are too compressed and elliptical—while fantasy images are extended through narrative and character and are, therefore,

more approachable. Children need such images quite as much as adults do, because so much of what goes on around them, and even more what goes on in their minds and the minds of other people, is totally inexplicable intellectually; because explanation would involve terms and concepts way beyond their grasp. Only through images, therefore, can they begin to recognize and understand many of their own feelings and much of their emotional experience, or at least to recognize that they are not alone in it. You might say . . . [that images of fear] are not ones you ought to give to children at all, that you frighten them unnecessarily. This is, I think, why [Catherine Storr's] *Marianne Dreams* has never been read on *Jackanory* [a BBC children's television program]—it is considered too frightening; and again, this was the reason why some people were very dubious about Maurice Sendak's picture book *Where the Wild Things Are* when it first came out. But the point is that what goes on in children's heads—hate, fear, aggression—is just as frightening, if not more so, and needs to be externalized in some intuitively recognizable form. The importance of both *Marianne* and *The Wild Things* is that the fears are both examined and resolved—or overcome for the time being—in a satisfying and logical convincing way. . . .

Even where children might be able to accept a more direct intellectual explanation, through imagery they can be given a great deal more; the idea can be taken a great deal further. In *Charlotte Sometimes* I did not immediately realize I was writing a book about a search for identity; but by taking a literal situation—an extended image if you like—making Charlotte take the place of Clare who had lived fifty years earlier—I could take the matter, both consciously and unconsciously, a good deal further than if I had just made the schoolgirl sit down and debate to herself 'Who am I?' Apart from anything else, if she had debated it for a hundred and fifty pages or so, what child would have read it? (p. 32)

[All] good writing for children has to be highly selective and precise, but with a sense of underlying richness, of immensity left out, as in some lyric poetry. You do not forget adult consciousness or adult experience as a writer for children, you rather push it underground, so that it is like a stream making the ground above more fertile, though remaining unseen. But in fantasy particularly you can use fully your own feelings as an adult because you are not using them directly, but working around them; in a way you can, in the fullest sense, write for yourself, indeed I think you must. William Mayne has said that he writes for himself as a boy, but I do not find it possible myself to differentiate so sharply between adult and childhood. Most of the time in memory one state melts into the other; they are inextricable.

But now I return to the question of the audience. For though the origins and functions of fantasy may in some sense be constant, its effect on the audience varies greatly, particularly when that audience is made up of children, whose reading is much more related to psychological need than that of most adults. A child does not read a book making cool assessments of its aesthetic qualities (though he may of course without knowing it, gain aesthetic pleasure). He takes from the book what he most needs, from wish fulfilment at the lowest level, upwards to the pointing and even partial resolving of the most complex of subconscious dilemmas. Sometimes a child recognizes the need quite consciously. I can remember myself that as a child, if I needed comfort or security, if I was depressed, I went straight off and read either the cooking chapter of *Little Men*—when Daisy is given a stove and has a gloriously cosy, domestic day; or else Rat and Mole's long stay in Badger's den in *Wind in the Willows*. But unconsciously, in other ways, books can trigger off sets of the most powerful psychological responses, fear, uncertainty or joy, without anyone quite knowing why.

Fairy tale, as I suggested earlier, arouses these responses in a fairly ritualistic way and is therefore often easier for a child to take, because he sees precisely what frightens him and what makes him sad. And there is no doubt that a child, like an adult, likes both to be frightened and made sad sometimes. How do we otherwise explain the continuing popularity of books like *Black Beauty* or the stories of Edgar Allan Poe? As an adult I read Grimm horrified by the sadism, the gougings and stickings, the tearing out of eyes, the cutting off of heads and limbs—all of which must have gone straight over my head as a child because I don't particularly remember them, though I knew Grimm almost by heart.

Fairy tales resolve themselves so neatly, too. Goodies are happy and cruelties perpetrated on them avenged; the baddies die miserably. Perhaps if anything they are almost too predictable, as my six year old daughter suggested when she said in a bored voice, 'I don't want to hear *any more* of those stories when the woodcutter's son has to do three tasks before he's allowed to marry the princess.' Probably fairy tales are only really disturbing to a child if they touch on some very particular but hidden fear. . . . (pp. 33-4)

I don't think overt sadism worries children so much—just as it did not worry me in Grimm. They tend not to notice it, any more than they notice or are sickened by the sentimentality. What might disturb them is being shown, if only subconsciously, that all is not straightforward in the adult world; that growing up solves nothing, but merely introduces more intractable problems, more moral subtleties and endless emotional shades of grey. (p. 36)

I do not have any conclusions. Introvert fantasy may well be a dangerous affair but no one can legislate for everyone, so heaven forfend that we should try to keep the more uncomfortable writers from the children they write for. If you did get rid of Hans Andersen you would still be left with children frightened by Beatrix Potter (as well they might be—*The Tale of Samuel Whiskers* gives me a goodly chill to this day). You certainly cannot submit writers to psychological tests before letting them loose to write children's books, though you might well think that many of us need them.

Children need this kind of writing. They need fantasy of all kinds. It is up to the adults round them to mediate, if necessary to explain and reassure. They should know something about children's literature, if for no other reason, in order to judge its effects on children in their care, and to mediate between child and book where this seems necessary. (p. 37)

> Penelope Farmer, "'Jorinda and Jorindel' and Other Stories," in Children's literature in education, *No. 7 (March), 1972, pp. 23-37.*

---

## GENERAL COMMENTARY

### *THE JUNIOR BOOKSHELF*

[*The Summer Birds*] is Penelope Farmer's first full-length story for children; her first book of fairy-tales, **The China People,** showed great promise. Here, many readers felt, was an artist in words, a writer with a keen and witty imagination whose stories could be read aloud with pleasure and success to most children of about 6-8 or older. This new book shows the same light, poetic touch, and for all who appreciate fantasy could well be "a winner." A mysterious boy, with the powers of invisibility, appears in a country lane one summer morning and for two weeks teaches all the schoolchildren to fly. . . . This boy is no Peter Pan, teaching children to fly by "thinking wonderful thoughts which lift you up in the air;" flying, here, is a matter of leg and arm exercises, and some of the children never become good at it. (pp. 318-19)

The children are drawn realistically, but it seems unnecessary to have given them such ugly names; there seems no need to call village children "Scragg," "Scobb" or "Fumpkins"; there are usually a few "Smith's" or "Jones's" or something similar, in every walk of life. . . .

Apart from one or two tricks of style which could become irritating, Miss Farmer's book is well done; she is an author to watch. (p. 319)

> A review of "The Summer Birds," in The Junior Bookshelf, *Vol. 26, No. 6, December, 1962, pp. 318-19.*

### MARION R. HEWITT

I came upon Penelope Farmer's first book when searching for something new to read at a story hour. I had already been told that it was good, but thought that my informant might be prejudiced having known the author from childhood. Also, knowing it to be fairy stories, I shied away from the possibility of happy pixies and jolly elves. . . .

Penelope Farmer's fairy stories are in a very different class and I realise now how very wrong I was to delay acquaintance. She has had two books published: [**The China People** and **The Summer Birds**]. (p. 20)

Her books reflect a close knowledge of traditional fairy stories, but her own style is far from traditional.

Her first book, **The China People,** takes its title from the first of the short fairy stories that it includes. None of them is of the "little people" variety and all are unclouded by sentimentality. Her portrayal of witches, wizards and princesses shows a very shrewd appraisal of more mortal beings.

There is no trace of the cruelty so common to many traditional fairy stories, no sharp line between good and evil, the good are often rather silly and the evil only mildly so. Her charm lies in the combination of magic and commonsense, the slight touch of malice and disconcerting humour that underlies each story. Not all end happily, there is never the feeling that she is "writing down" for children, the immortals are far from infallible. Fairy Godmothers forget, spells go awry and beautiful princesses even when they have reformed their fiendish tempers, do not always get the handsome princes. (pp. 20-1)

Of all this collection I like best the **Park Witch,** a very short story about a Victorian household whose nanny is a retired witch. Discipline is maintained kindly with the aid of a little magic, naughtiness being punished by transformation into a caterpillar, while a flick of the wand replaces all the tedium of baths and buttons for the good. It is a very practical arrangement until a moment's carelessness results in disaster, but it is a very appealing disaster, and all children know that accidents will happen!

At first reading I thought these stories might hold more appeal for adults than for young children, but not so. I gave them first to my elder daughter, a reliable ten year-old guinea pig who read them through into the night by the light of a torch under the bedclothes, and voted them "Super," an accolade never lightly awarded. Next I read them to a story hour audience of three to eleven year-olds, not always an easy group to satisfy at the same reading. They were enchanted, no wriggles and whispers, they sat quite still and silent, their faces reflecting their pleasure. At the end they sat and waited for more, and surely there could be no higher praise from a young child who has kept still for a whole hour!

The second book, *The Summer Birds,* more than fulfils the promise of the first. (p. 21)

All the children in this book are real and vital, the adults form part of a shadowy background. Charlotte, in particular, is beautifully drawn. A solid, sensible child but so sensitive that she feels everyone's hurts. One knows, with deep pity, that she will always carry the weight of the world on her shoulders. She is all children's conscience as the boy is their fantasy.

This is a beautiful book. The description of the Downs at night has an ethereal poetry and the sadness of the farewell [when the nameless boy returns to his island home] is delicately and truthfully shown. It is part of growing up, and the author never cheats by glossing over unhappiness. But just as truthfully the joy of living, happiness and excitement of childhood is shown as the children fight and clown their way through the summer.

This book should appeal to all children from nine upwards, for its vitality and adventure, but for the more perceptive child it will have a very special charm. The twelve and thirteen year-old will be better able to appreciate the finer qualities.

Penelope Farmer's work shows an acute sense of observation and the skill to transcribe what she sees. Her description captures the feeling as well as the sight of the countryside, and her people are made up of odd details that give them real life. Her sense of timing is excellent, no point is laboured and the story slips faultlessly from humour to sadness, from magic to realism. She never falls into the trap of whimsy but always keeps a balance between logic and fantasy.

The world of childhood is made of the inextricable mixture of magic and reality, and it is because she has captured this so completely and easily, that I feel she will take her place among the finest children's authors writing to-day. (p. 22)

> *Marion R. Hewitt, "Emergent Authors: Penelope Farmer," in* The Junior Bookshelf, *Vol. 27, No. 1, January, 1963, pp. 20-2.*

### THE GUARDIAN WEEKLY

["**The Serpent's Teeth**" and "**Daedalus and Icarus**" are] old tales retold with great freshness and simplicity. Miss Farmer's elegant narrative style dissolves the worn familiarity and false solemnity which so easily encrusts the Greek myths, and tells them with unaffected directness for their own sake. The more interesting of the two stories is "**The Serpent's Teeth,**" which in contrast to the obvious universality of the Daedalus story, tells the strange tale of the founding of Thebes—a local myth with an oddity and inconsequence about it that reminds one of its alien origins.

> *J.P.W., "Myths Retold," in* The Guardian Weekly, *Vol. 104, No. 23, June 5, 1971, p. 19.*

### THE JUNIOR BOOKSHELF

[*The Serpent's Teeth: The Story of Cadmus* and *Daedalus and Icarus*] are brilliantly and briefly told with such poetic consistency that [Penelope Farmer's] use of words is truly striking.... Both books can be highly recommended.... (pp. 215-16)

> *A review of "The Serpent's Teeth: The Story of Cadmus" and "Daedalus and Icarus," in* The Junior Bookshelf, *Vol. 35, No. 4, August, 1971, pp. 215-16.*

### MAY HILL ARBUTHNOT AND ZENA SUTHERLAND

*Charlotte Sometimes* is a fantasy adventure that borders on science fiction. Its time-shift theme is a familiar one in that genre, but it has seldom been used more dramatically, perhaps because Charlotte alternates between two worlds.... The mystery and suspense are maintained to the end.

In *Emma in Winter* . . . , Charlotte's sister finds that she shares the same dreams as a boy she dislikes, a boy she and Charlotte met in *The Summer Birds,* the most moving of these books.... In these three books and in *The Magic Stone* as well, the style is smooth, the mood subdued, and the characterization perceptive, but *The Summer Birds* has an almost palpable aura of magic and an ending that has the inevitability of Greek drama.

> *May Hill Arbuthnot and Zena Sutherland, "Modern Fantasy: 'Charlotte Sometimes', 'Emma in Winter', and 'The Summer Birds'," in their* Children and Books, *fourth edition, Scott, Foresman and Company, 1972, p. 256.*

### MARGARET K. McELDERRY

[*The Summer Birds*] is a haunting story.... Rare characterization, fine writing, and great originality make this a book of distinction. (p. 799)

*The Summer Birds* actually grew out of a collection of short stories, *The China People*.... Through Penelope's agent, page proofs of this book had been submitted to the adult division of the trade department at Harcourt, Brace & World . . . where I was then the Editor of Books for Children. The head of the department felt the collection of stories was not quite right for the U.S. adult trade market, but sent it along to me in case it might have young adult potential. While I did not feel that was so, I did feel the author, if interested, might write something very good indeed for children. I queried her agent, who replied that Penelope was "interested" and had an idea for such a book.

The idea for *The Summer Birds* came from a short story that had originally been included in the manuscript of *The China People,* but was later taken out because, as Penelope said, "It was too big an idea, too bony as a short story." In it was a sequence in which a child learns to fly. Penelope then wrote a synopsis for a children's book that changed totally as she began the actual writing. As she explained in a letter,

> I find synopses very hard to write, like trying to describe a baby before it's been born: . . . in the course of writing the book, ideas and situations start slipping into place, and suddenly it becomes clear from the context what should happen in a particular place, which is impossible to know with the bare bones of a synopsis (with the possible exception of the beginning which is already fairly fully imagined and perhaps partly written).

After the manuscript of *The Summer Birds* was delivered, a lively correspondence ensued between Penelope and me. We had not yet met each other, we had not previously worked together, and so this was a feeling-out process, an immensely important moment in the development of the author-editor relationship, the establishment of a basis for future trust and mutual understanding. Unless each finds the other sympathetically intelligent, with ideas and tastes and commitments to writing that are broadly similar, basic misunderstandings will occur and the results can be disastrous. The editor must show infinite respect for the fact that the manuscript, in the final analysis, does belong to the author and that suggestions for revision and change can be pressed only so far.

As Penelope and I thrashed out at long distance our areas of agreement and difference regarding the *The Summer Birds* manuscript, not only were the usual editorial problems solved, but also the more special problems, some minor, some of greater importance, that cannot help but arise in an Anglo-American project. There were no vast or threateningly insurmountable difficulties.

I had sent back to Penelope a copy of the manuscript marked with all my queries, large and small, and with my suggested cuts and word changes. Two of the areas in which we then had most stimulating exchanges were *style* and *word usage*. About the question of style, Penelope wrote:

> This is obviously a very idiosyncratic thing. I know my style is not always conventional, but I do feel that grammar is something that can legitimately be played with. All the people I most admire have done so—Virginia Woolf, Henry Green, Dylan Thomas—and what about Shakespeare? I'm not exactly equating myself with any of these! But they do demonstrate how fluid grammar can be. I agree that with a children's book you have to be more careful, but the only crucial thing is that language is not so complex as to be indecipherable to them. If that is so, I see no reason why there shouldn't be liberty to experiment as in any other kind of writing.

My reply was: "Only where a trick of style seems to strain for effect and therefore get in the reader's way do I question it." We struggled over such sentences as, "Charlotte tight to his hand thought she had never gone so fast . . ." which eventually became, "Charlotte, holding tight to his hand, thought she had never gone so fast. . . ." Penelope liked to leave out small words like "of" and "for" as "it sounds neater in most places without making the sense any less comprehensible." I felt often that the small words were necessary for clarity and a child's comprehension.

On word usage, Penelope had this to say:

> I tend to use them in odd contexts, but isn't this part of the art of writing? To find the unexpected word which is exact? Further, made-up words, e.g. *skimmering:* I think it's better than just *skimming* because it's a more delicate word and describes more how swallows fly, I think. Jabberwock word-making is surely a legitimate thing for a writer? This one is a combination of *glimmering* and *skimming.* Similarly, *squirly,* you say, isn't a word. Isn't it

quite clear what it means? Anyway, *squirly* is a perfectly good word.

To which I replied:

> *Skimmering* and most others that you want I have left. I will still raise a point about *squirly* which is not in Webster's unabridged. I assume you mean to indicate a whirly feeling or design by its use, but the image is not clear in my mind, I confess, and is more likely to a child to suggest the animal.

Penelope continued:

> What I do think is important is that no word in a children's book should contain sophisticated ideas because these cannot be explained to a child. But this is not true of my words here. Even *affinity* is not too hard, I think, though it is very hard to find a substitute. Certainly it does not mean *likeness. Sense of kinship* is more my idea. Perhaps this is too hard for a child? What do you think?

(Much later, Penelope told me that she now agrees with "lots of the things you said then, particularly on questions of style, but which I fought you mightily on at the time! So often you were right. I *hate* 'squirly' now.")

A third area of consideration between us was what Penelope called "the translation of some English into American." Expanding on it, she stated:

> I believe very strongly that we here want to retain our own language! I remember when I read American children's books published over here. It used to intrigue me to have them talk about *sidewalks* and *elevators* and *candy.* Isn't the reverse true? Can't American children realize that everywhere is not America? Don't they like differences?

My answer was:

> I agree that English usage in a book written by an English person about the English scene is all to the good, but I think a few word changes help the reader here to have a clearer understanding and are therefore legitimate and to be desired. There are actually very few places where this comes up. . . . We do here, I think, tend to give an author a harder time than in England. At any rate, I suspect we make more suggestions than some of our counterparts, but I suspect you and I are not really so far apart as you may have thought in your first horror upon looking at my hentracks [penciled suggestions on the manuscript].

Penelope and I did do battle on one small detail where each was sure she was dead right. Penelope referred to lobsters as "navy blue." I suggested that dark green with orange claws was correct. She said she'd picked out many a live lobster from the sea and they were always navy blue. I replied that I'd had the same experience and they were dark green with orange claws and orange undersides. At last we discovered that European and American lobsters are different and that we were *both* right! We laughed about it then and have used it as a touchstone many times since then!

In all our exchanges, the form and shape of the story itself never were questioned. As Penelope said much later, "When I sat down to write a book for the first time, for some extraordinary reason, it worked—just like that."

This was not so of the second book, *The Magic Stone*. . . . When Penelope began to write this, she expected it to go just as easily as had *The Summer Birds,* but she discovered very quickly that "I hadn't a clue to what I was doing." The manuscript required an enormous amount of reworking. In referring to it recently, Penelope said: "That was a very painful experience, that book. It just went on and on and on." . . . She refers to this book now as "my sociological book." In it, she drew on her experiences while doing odd jobs and later teaching in the slum areas of London's East End. The girl going off to boarding school was based partly on her own knowledge of going off to school and what happened to certain friendships that ultimately vanished as a result. A certain indignation at her parents, who were rather cavalier in their treatment of her younger sister because of her friendship with a girl who lived in a housing development, also crept in here. (pp. 799-802)

One of the elements in the book that needed to be re-thought was the development of the magic theme, the piece of metal embedded in stone that, singly, the girls could not remove but together could pull out effortlessly. In writing to me about this, Penelope explained that she was

> afraid of overplaying the magic. If you use magic it must be subtle; it must be used to increase perception of reality and must also spring logically from reality. Four-square fantasies about ogres and witches, etc., I think may be delightful but little else. What I'm saying in effect is that I do up to a point believe in magic; at least in so far as strange behaviour of time and the reality of extrasensory perception is concerned. I mean there are things that cannot scientifically be explained and that, because they exist, extend imagination and understanding, which improbable, four-square kinds of magic do not do; in fact they belittle magic, bring it down to a tangible nursery level which is no longer mysterious or illuminating. Thus I think if I use magic it mustn't ever be fully explained or developed. It can't be cut and dried at all, and I'm always terrified of doing this. With the result, in this case, that I didn't develop it enough. When you write one thing, there're always about ten things in the back of your mind you haven't written, and you tend to read in some of those when you re-read what you've written and forget that this won't be so with anyone else! So I will develop this if I can and maybe in this way also bring some narrative and action into the girls' friendship as you suggest.

With *The Magic Stone,* Penelope as a writer was beginning to use all the things that were happening around her, as well as her extraordinary sense of fantasy and imagination, but she wasn't yet skilled at integrating them, which is why *The Magic Stone* proved so difficult to put into shape. However, it was then that Penelope began to learn to write and to feel now and again that she was in control of what she was doing.

*Charlotte Sometimes* . . . was the first of her books in which Penelope consciously and very skillfully used a series of tricks, or illusions, to give her book form and structure, and her control of her material was markedly stronger and surer. . . . [*Charlotte Sometimes*] is a fascinating exploration of the fragile barriers between layers of time, handled with great skill in the writing and delicacy of perception. The chief complication with this book was in the middle sequence, where Charlotte is caught for weeks out of her own time. Very little in the way of incidents actually happened, yet it was essential to keep the tension high as to how and whether Charlotte would get back into her own time. This had to be achieved against a background of ordinary, unexciting, day-to-day events and of what was actually happening then in World War I. [Penelope said]:

> To keep the thing moving was really a series of tricks—illusions you create where the plot doesn't help you too much, using climaxes and apparent climaxes even when there aren't any. . . . When the girls were changing around in time there was always the actual device of the notebook they shared [they could leave messages in it for each other], but when Charlotte got into the past totally it was very difficult because there wasn't that much happening, yet you had to make it appear that there was. What I had to do was to try and advance the attitudes of the two girls and their worrying about whether they'd get back to their own time. As a kind of counterpoint, this gave tension and tautness to what was going on every day.

The illusion of events, given through her characterization, carried the story along and gave it more depth.

> In *Charlotte* I used a lot of incidents which I already knew about, based on family experiences. It was a kind of mosaic technique, a cutting up and putting together. The book has a more mechanistic plot. Not mechanistic in a bad way, but just that things had to happen in a certain sequence. This in itself gave it plot and structure, though I'm usually not very good at plot.

Here Penelope knew where she was going from beginning to end. It was inherent in her story from the start.

By contrast, *Emma in Winter,* her third book, . . . had suffered because it had less structure than *Charlotte Sometimes,* and Penelope, less sure then of her techniques as a writer, was desperately trying to think of incident and event at which she was not then very skilled. . . . The manuscript was predominantly descriptive when it first came in. Penelope re-wrote it a bit, putting in a few more specific incidents at my suggestion. Looking back at them now, she says she could have developed them more fully and that would have improved them.

By now, of course, Penelope is much more skillful at analyzing her own writing, realizing something must happen to carry the story line forward and planning a series of such happenings. "Some people have too much sense of plot and some people just don't have enough of it. You have to learn to space things out or pull things up more." (pp. 802-03)

[*A Castle of Bone*] marks an enormous development in Penelope's power as a writer, both imaginatively and technically. Both elements fuse into an overwhelmingly powerful and extraordinarily original narrative. . . .

Whereas the previous book, *Charlotte Sometimes,* was very consciously structured, as the material and story dictated, *A Castle of Bone* structured itself more internally, less consciously, without having to be revised and rearranged too much once it had been set down.

> Various things I had put down very tentatively, such as the form the dream sequences took, worked as they stood and didn't need anything done to them. In *Charlotte* I arranged a lot of incidents which I knew about ahead of time based on family experiences, but *Castle* didn't have any kind of plot like that. It had a beginning and an end, which more or less defined it in advance, but I don't think I had any idea of how I would get to that end. It was a book which was internally defined and ordered in ways that were uncomfortable.
>
> (p. 804)

[Penelope observed recently]:

> Perhaps some books are kinds of peaks. . . . You head towards one and it's a peak that uses all the experiences you've had and techniques you've learned over a period of time. Therefore it appears to be a book of enormous ease technically. Suddenly, the knowledge—all you've previously been through—is inside you and you use it without having to be aware of it all the time. But then, for the next book, you may have to go back and start learning other techniques and absorbing other experiences, so your technical devices are perhaps more apparent. It will be a while till you build to another peak.

Now Penelope is hard at work on what she terms "a less serious book." "It's more upbeat; some of it's funny." It is about a girl whose father is headmaster of a boys' school so that she normally lives in a very male atmosphere. But the story takes place out of term time, with only one boy there whose family is abroad. The children have free access to all the rooms in the school, each an evocative setting in itself, suggesting ideas for what incident will occur next. This is the device that will structure the book. "But," says Penelope,

> writing comedy is no pleasure. There's nothing more unfunny than something you've read through or written three or four times. But some funny ideas are coming into my head as opposed to gloomy ones. On the technical side, I'm fascinated by the structural device this setting offers.

For a creative writer like Penelope Farmer, there is no end to seeking, experimenting with, absorbing new ideas, new sensations, new perceptions, new ways of expression. There is no such thing as self-satisfaction. Rules are made only to be broken. What was true for one book may have not the slightest meaning for the next one. This is a tremendously demanding gift that sometimes pushes its possessor to extreme limits of endurance. It results in books that cannot be predicted, that become part of the living literature of a period, that offer readers new realms of experience and understanding, that reflect life from unexpected angles, illumine fascinating perspectives, and leave the reader with a heightened sense of wonder and expectation.

This thrust for the new, the fresh, the different, this striving to discover the unknown out of the known is as inevitable as it is eternal. It was a Greek philosopher, long before the Christian era, who suggested that you cannot step into the same river twice, for you will have changed and so will the river. Change is with us. It is the hallmark of the fine creative writer that he or she inherently tries to make that change for the better and ideally, in the Aristotelian sense, reaches for the very best. (p. 805)

> *Margaret K. McElderry, "Penelope Farmer: The Development of an Author," in* Elementary English, *Vol. 51, No. 6, September, 1974, pp. 798-805.*

## HUGH CRAGO

*The Summer Birds* bears few signs of being its author's first published novel. Except for the extreme formality and slight stiffness of the opening chapter, which reads as though it was worked over again and again, there are almost no traces of the clumsiness we expect in debut performances. The book moves smoothly from beginning to end, its author fully in control throughout. So much is she in control that she cannot resist constantly anticipating what is to come. From the very first page, with its mention of swallows "skimming like cream off the green lawn", the imagery of birds and flying is an insistent presence; it is inevitable that the children should learn to fly, inevitable that the Boy should turn out to be a Bird in disguise, inevitable that the power of flight cannot continue beyond the golden, unreal summer with which the writer constantly associates it.

Ultimately the symbolic imagery becomes almost irritating— but it has served its purpose. Because we have been soaked in verbal suggestion beforehand, nothing that happens seems incredible—it merely *had* to happen that way. Only once, really, is our confidence shaken, and this is in a place where there has been no preparation of the kind just mentioned. Up till now, the Boy has been a lone figure, self-sufficient and demanding no explanation. Now, in the moment of revelation, he is seen to be part of something larger, a Bird hierarchy which fails to ring true because of its ramifications which are too shadowy, too unrooted in the minutiae of day-to-day experience that hold the rest of the book solid:

> He was a bird he said, of a bird kind dying out, extinct almost in memory but for a museum skeleton. He alone existed, the last bird of his race. The summer had been given to him by the mighty birdlord, the fiery Phoenix, as a last chance to restore his kind. "Renew yourself," the lord had said. "Renew yourself as I renew myself, by fire. Fly to the furnace of the human world, find fellows for yourself, take them to your island, and your race will go on. Of any kind or form they may be. Your form and kind they will become. Go, the summer is yours. Use it well."
>
> So the boy had taken human shape and loitered uncertain in the lane that May morning where Charlotte and Emma had come on their way to school.
>
> "So you were taking us to your island to become birds," said Charlotte slowly.
>
> "Yes," said the boy, downcast.

"And we would never have come back?" went
on Charlotte more slowly.

"You could never have come back," said the
boy.

Perhaps the main cause of the trouble here is the "fiery Phoenix". Left as "the mighty birdlord", he would still have been
open to the objection of being shadowy, but at least we would
not have the sense of a traditional mythology intruding into
the new mythology created within the novel. This sort of clash
is a pitfall into which many modern fantasies have fallen,
conscious as they are of being heirs to the myths of the past,
yet sensing the need to create them anew. The myth that *The
Summer Birds* is remaking hasn't anything to do with the Phoenix—it is, of course, *Peter Pan* (as the author recognizes,
though she says she was quite unconscious of it at the time of
writing). *The Summer Birds* is *Peter Pan* pared down, the
whimsy, the sentimentality and the extravagant pantomime
mythmaking cut away, leaving the essential core of genuine
wonder—some children learn to fly under the guidance of an
alien being—and the essential dilemma: should the children
stay children (for "children", read "birds" in Penelope Farmer)
and fly, or should they grow up and cease to fly? The choice
for Penelope Farmer's children seems a more serious and a
more frightening one than it is for Barrie's, just as her children's learning to fly is difficult and exhausting, no mere matter
of being touched with instant-acting magic dust. Yet ultimately, the choice is still not a real one. The children cannot
become birds. As Charlotte says: "I don't know why I stopped
us coming. I didn't want to. I'm sorry; but I had to, you see.
I don't know why."

There might be a number of reasons why, theoretically, this
should be so, but the practical reason is that Penelope Farmer's
book will not *let* the change be acceptable. As we saw earlier,
the end of the flying has been anticipated many times before
it happens. The whole book is about the onceness of experience—whether flying or making love (with which Charlotte's
teaching by the Boy has something in common), it doesn't
matter. Innocence, the openness to new experience, can only
happen once, and it cannot be prolonged. And the pity of it is
that in the very moment when the experience is new, discomfort
or anxiety distracts us from being fully immersed in it. And
then it is too late. There would be no *point* in the children
becoming birds, for the moment of new awareness has already
passed. All that remains is jealousy—a wish to hug the experience to oneself (to one's friends) because this is a reflex
action, a desperate association of the experience with the only
reality one knows: oneself.

Though jealousy, a recurrent theme in Penelope Farmer's work,
also plays a part in *The Magic Stone*, it is a smaller part. There
is little question here of hugging experience to oneself for long;
the magic that Caroline and Alice find in the Arthur stone is
intended precisely to bring them together: the problem of the
book is whether shared experience will win over the class and
age barriers that otherwise separate the two girls. It does (though
it is part of the author's refusal to compromise that she leaves
open at the end the question of whether the friendship will
continue after the magic has gone and the social gulf becomes
greater), and somewhat as in the earlier book, we are constantly
*told* that it does:

> In contrast to the growing enmity between the
> boys, the friendship of Alice and Caroline took
> the normal course of such things; they forgot,

for the most part (where it was not forced on
their attention by the grown ups), that Caroline
was a boarding-school girl and Alice a girl from
the estate; and in the fields and woods where
they went the differences were unimportant.
They remembered only that one was Caroline,
the other Alice, and that they were friends.

Where the earlier book conveys its message by repeated images, this one, far more clumsily, simply states it. Much of
its greater length is made up of long, flat analytic passages
like that quoted above—embarrassingly unnecessary in view
of the skill with which Penelope Farmer can handle more direct
insight into relationships through characters' words and actions. The stone itself is a clumsy image, too obviously symbolic (only if both girls pull together will the blade slide from
the stone), and its associations with King Arthur are reminiscent of the "mighty Birdlord" in being basically irrelevant
intrusions of a traditional mythology.

The magic the stone creates—a much-developed form of the
heightened sense-perception that was fleetingly associated with
flight in *The Summer Birds*—is impressively realized in itself,
yet spoilt by being so obviously and explicitly merely an exaggeration and a speeding-up of what is happening naturally,
as the girls' senses become more aware of all that is going on
around them. We are told several times that even without the
magic, Caroline and Alice are noticing more, that it is hard to
tell where the magic ends and ordinary life begins. If magic
is only a heightening of real life, and the novel is really about
the relationship of the two girls, why introduce the magic
element at all?

What has happened here is that the author's sophistication of
concept has outrun her technical skill. The magic of *The Summer Birds* can be symbolic, and a vehicle for statements about
relationships and growing up, but it is simply, recognizably,
paranormal experience as well. The magic of the stone, less
clearly "magic", has more trouble being allegory, which is
probably why the author labours so hard to make sure we know
just what the allegory is. In its didacticism, its overstatement
and its occasional false notes (Alice's speech, for all its *cors*,
doesn't always ring true to the social class it is intended to
belong to), *The Magic Stone* reads much more like a first novel
than its predecessor, except that it is pleasingly free from the
tendency to "fine writing" and carefully polished rhetoric that
occasionally spoils *The Summer Birds*. Significantly, *Emma in
Winter* returns to the setting and characters of the first novel.

*Emma* is about a growing relationship, too, but this time there
is far less obvious "pushing" of the theme. More important,
the magic bears a different relationship to events on the human
plane. True, there are certain parallels between what happens
in the dream-flying sequences and what happens in Emma and
Bobby's friendship, but the parallels only account for a small
part of the magic, which is too "huge" (to use one of the
author's favourite words) to be contained by mere allegory.
Why does there seem to be some connexion between the dream
flying and the unnatural winter that grips the village? Why does
the flying lead Bobby and Emma backwards in time? Why
those two, of all the children? Why does the evil presence of
the dreams resolve itself into the image of Miss Hallibutt, the
not-unkind schoolmistress whom neither child has any cause
to hate? Only the last of these questions can be easily answered:
by the end it is clear that Miss Hallibutt—in the dream—is a
psychic projection of parts of Emma herself. Indeed, at this
stage Penelope Farmer almost steps too far into explicit allegory

again, replacing the figure of Miss Hallibutt with twin projections, one of Bobby, one of Emma, the falseness of which they must perceive if they are to escape the dream:

> Bobby never knew what checked him. Perhaps it was seeing the real blinded, gasping Emma beside him, perhaps the feel of her hand brushing past his ear, he could not have said. Yet somehow he heaved back from the image and it was like dragging himself out of a powerful marsh, his skin sucked and pulled most painfully. But the real Emma by him grew clearer to his eyes and the false Emma more remote. And he looked at the images and shouted with all his strength.
>
> "You're not real either; any more than she was real. I'm Bobby and there's Emma, you're not real at all, not real at *all*." And with each word it was easier, his body was light suddenly, his skin free.

A well-known fantasy ploy this—to convince oneself of the reality by shouting at, or *unthinking,* the illusion—and one which never fully convinces me, though when you think of the immense power of language, which has created the entire fictional world in which human beings live out their lives, it may well be a genuine psychic weapon. At all events, the sudden way in which the protagonists' personal psychological images flood into the hitherto objectively determined flying dreams upsets our expectations and unbalances us. But that is what all dreams tend to do anyway. To this extent, the unpredictability of the action, the series of unanswered questions posed earlier, are marks of the author's success. This magic, for the first time in Penelope Farmer's work, is in itself a wholly satisfying symbol for the unconscious mind—and the more satisfying for *not* being explained as such. *Emma in Winter* is charged with a sense of the enormous stature of emotions, which dwarf the humans who "have" them in a most frightening way. As in the earlier books, the fundamental "objectivity" of jealousies, envies and even affections shines out: this, it seems to me, is what distinguishes these books from other novels ("realistic" or "fantasy") which tackle the same problems of the interactions of characters in depth; this takes Penelope Farmer beyond the "will-he-smile-at-me-yes-he-will" school, beyond the danger she herself courts when she, confidently sharp-tongued, introduces a character as "a long vague selfish man, thin as a pen" (*The Magic Stone*). This tendency towards being the witty amoral prober of suburban character-types, pleasing though some of its effects are, is ultimately a dead-end. She can move past it, and she does.

Both *The Magic Stone* and *Emma in Winter* had a tendency to move uneasily in and out of what I privately call a "children's book style", writing recognizably (for one reason or another) directed at a child audience. Nowhere in *Charlotte Sometimes* is this the case, until the very last page: "Yet, as the bus crept on through the neon-lighted town, Charlotte too began to sing, to chant out with the rest. After all she was Charlotte now, safe in the present, going home to Aviary Hall, to her grandfather, Elijah, and her sister Emma."

It is only in its anxiety to cross *t*s and dot *i*s, to emphasize cosily that "fantasy time is over now, folks" that this strikes a note different from that of the rest of the novel; specifically, the redundant information ("to her grandfather, Elijah, and her sister Emma") is oddly out of phase with the economy of the

earlier pages. It's easy enough to see why the ending should have called forth this manner; there the urge to "tie it all up" is especially strong. Yet the whole triumph of *Charlotte* is that it *cannot* be all tied up. For the first time since *The Summer Birds* the magic is more important than the relationships it expresses, not only because it is larger and more irrational than the characters, as in *Emma,* but because the experience of the magic *is* the experience of the book. And it is a perfect magic for this purpose, since there is no visible sign of it whatever. The magic "is" in the sleep that separates Charlotte now, from Charlotte in 1918, and since both worlds are fully realized in convincing detail, there can be no faltering in the actual experience. Only the *explanations* offered for the occurrence of the magic might be a source of trouble, as they are in so many fantasies, yet here again the potential weakness is avoided. The bed in which Charlotte sleeps is the magic instrument, yet no one ever speculates on *why* it operates. Our attention, with Charlotte's, is wholly focused on how to cope with the time-shift in terms of day-to-day living. And, at the end, when the neat pattern of relationships and coincidences that explains the whole thing falls into place, it seems, not over-contrived, but eminently right.

Why exactly the neatness of *Charlotte* should seem acceptable where the neatness of *The Magic Stone* did not, I'm unsure; but it may well have to do with the fact that *Charlotte,* though it expresses a lot about relationships, is not consciously about them, that it is about one person's experience of a magic which is only referred to as such once or twice in the whole novel. And though the magic is controlled within the neat limits we have been talking about, the terror of the irrational depths, as in *Emma,* is still present; most obviously in the gripping and entirely convincing seance sequence, more evanescently in the way the imagery of the latter half of the novel comes increasingly to reflect Charlotte's desperation in the manner in which it evolves towards the paranoid, climaxing in the frightening ending to the Victory celebrations: "Faces seemed to leer like masks, the light part dim, part bright, catching half-faces, noses, eyes or teeth, never all at once." But the parallels between descriptions of externals and the inner experience of Charlotte are never predictable: even after the return to the present there is the peculiar scene in the park:

> The sun came. It made garish, deep, deceptive colours; made the tumbled bracken bright as red earth . . . Near the ponds there was a group of trees with sick green trunks, but their twigs and branches were glowing red, as if they shed their own light instead of taking it from the sun . . . The wind had come so suddenly and now was gone.

Behind this lie hundreds of literary wastelands, yet the emphasis on colour introduces a new and altogether disquieting note. Something is awry in nature, as in the human world, and a book in which everything is so deeply imbued with the puzzling and out-of-phase cannot be closed with the old comforting formulas ("back to her sister Emma . . ."). This measured book keeps its power so much in check that one puts it down still agitated by what Penelope Farmer does not say in the novel, but which she has said elsewhere: that in the real world, the smallest piece of "magic" could have the effect of almost unhinging the mind. And come unhinged it surely does in *A Castle of Bone.*

To write about the fifth of Miss Farmer's novels is no easier than to read it with full comprehension. To say, as I did after a first reading, that the rampant paranoic imagery dominates the characters proves on lengthier consideration to be a misleading statement. As you reread the novel, its clipped, compacted sequences of phrases yield up their secrets in such a way as to build an overwhelming impression of conscious planning, conscious control—*The Summer Birds,* but on a vastly more sophisticated level. Everything that happens on the magic/unconscious level has a reason, or seems to have, but because the web of relationships on the human level is so intricate and so subtly delineated, one is not aware of many of the connexions.

Only slowly did I become aware of the jealousy that causes Anna to wish so fiercely to dominate her big genial brother, and of the detachment that prevents Hugh doing anything about her manipulation of him—that same "artist's" detachment that characterized the author herself when she produced those coldly dismissive character-sketches we noted earlier. Perhaps because the situation where two brother-and-sister teams undertake adventures together is so common, it is doubly hard at first to see the retiring, baffling younger sister as the centre of a *triangle,* to see Penn and Hugh as in a sense rivals for the regard of a goddess who is more ancient than either, to see that this goddess is not only Anna but her mother also, the White Goddess of Robert Graves' wrongheaded yet immensely powerful study. Anyone who doubts the influence of Celtic myths on the novel is recommended to try pp. 51-3 and 170-1, especially if he wondered why Penn was called Penn, and what on earth that black crow was doing on the snow! In no sense am I claiming that Penelope Farmer's book can only be understood if glossed from Graves; I'm merely offering proof that what at first seemed so full of the arbitrary and irrational can be seen ultimately to be almost as neat and ordered as *Charlotte.* It proceeds by statement and antithesis (Hugh led becomes Hugh the leader; Jean the organizer becomes Jean the disorganized) via the medium of the cupboard, the agency by which the status quo can be reversed.

As in *The Summer Birds,* almost every image prefigures future action, or comments obliquely on present action: "The sun gave no brightness. It was as if its brilliant edges dwindled to a black centre." Penn dominated by Anna? Given this degree of verbal suggestion, it seems superfluous that the writer should need to "explain" so often; some of the magical experiences in the novel's latter half are conveyed in terms so painstakingly descriptive that we almost lose the experience in the effort to comprehend it:

> There was a sound in the cupboard now, a single note, yet containing all notes. At first it emerged from a single point, but then it hissed and swelled, spread further as if beyond the walls, as if thrown out into an enormous void. But at the same time it seemed to have joined itself into a narrower line of sound, like a telegraph wire above Hugh's head. . . .

Being concrete is normally what good descriptive style is about—but here the degree of concreteness is an embarrassment.

The same tendency to be over-explicit is responsible for the way in which authorial explanation leaps ahead of the characters themselves. Thus, early in the novel, Hugh is made to speculate that "Thomas [the Rhymer] and Sir Orfeo had left time as well as space when they went to fairyland, and now he and Penn and Jean and Anna were outside time too because

what had happened could not belong to time, which was reality, or the reality they understood."

I find it hard to credit that Hugh could have thought the thing out quite so fully, and abstractly, at this stage. Indeed, the author has given him unfair access to her own stock of insights into time-conventions in fantasy. And this brings us to the point that, even more than some of its predecessors, *A Castle of Bone* embodies many of the conventions of the traditional two-world fantasy—a magic cupboard purchased in a junk shop; Otherworld time unrelated to real-world time; even a moment of choice precipitated by physical pain (remember Puddleglum and the Queen of Underland?):

> She undid her brooch . . . and jabbed the pin into his arm with all her strength. She was yelling at him at the same time. Then Hugh yelled too, with pain and fright, and for a moment, briefly, it cleared his mind. He gathered all his effort, snapped the succession, stilled the thought he seemed to need. "Stop Anna," he said slowly, thickly. It was hardly a decision, more a pressure to which he had at last acceded; whether it was what he truly wanted he did not know.

The setting-up of a "choice" scene prompts expectations on our part of a choice: yet, as the author herself tells us in the line just quoted, there *is* no choice, any more than there was in *The Summer Birds.* "Choice" belongs to the two-world fantasy of the Lewis type, because here there *is* a clear distinction between good and evil. What Penelope Farmer seems to be aiming at in *A Castle of Bone* is to remake this, and other conventions of what she calls "extrovert" fantasy into the stuff of "introvert" fantasy, but to my mind she does not totally succeed in doing so. Like the "note" Hugh hears in the cupboard, the book is trying to be two things simultaneously, and the burden is too great for it to carry.

It seems to me that in her attempt to evolve increasingly towards a sophistication both of form and content the author has reached a point where sophistication becomes counter-productive. Conscious control is a fine thing, but when its threads criss-cross the supposedly "irrational" parts of the novel's experience, it may be time to cry halt and ask how true a feeling of the irrational the book can then convey. In that sense, the unpretentious *Emma in Winter* seems the culmination of Penelope Farmer's work. It maintains a subtle tension between control and chaos that she has never repeated. *Charlotte,* though a more ambitious and artistically substantial book, is good not because it is a fantasy, but because of its brilliant juxtaposition of two realities. It may be an oversimplification to say that the author is a realist trying to work within fantasy, yet the shoring-up of her own structures with King Arthur, with Ulysses, with the Phoenix, seem marks of an uneasiness at working half in one convention and half in another. But should she abandon the Otherworld totally, she would perhaps lose that accuracy and power which the mirror of dream logic alone can give.

It is not her problem alone, but the dilemma of the whole movement to which she belongs, created in part by what Elaine Moss would call the "adult-eration" of children's books, in part by a literary climate in which the old labels "fantasy" and "realism" are becoming increasingly irrelevant. Whatever way the dilemma resolves itself, Penelope Farmer's work is intelligent enough to demand our close attention and, I think, flexible enough to benefit from it. (pp. 81-90)

Hugh Crago, "Penelope Farmer's Novels," in Signal, No. 17, May, 1975, pp. 81-90.

**MARGERY FISHER**

With all the implications and intricacies of these three delicately pointed fantasies [*The Summer Birds, Emma in Winter,* and *Charlotte Sometimes*], Penelope Farmer never forgets the duty of a novelist to create believable character. In a sense both Charlotte and Emma stand for any girl who is at the stage of questioning and defining her own personality, yet they are never less than individuals.

Margery Fisher, "Who's Who in Children's Books: 'The Summer Birds,' 'Emma in Winter' and 'Charlotte Sometimes'," in her Who's Who in Children's Books: A Treasury of the Familiar Characters of Childhood, Holt, Rinehart and Winston, 1975, Weidenfeld and Nicolson, 1975, p. 69.

**DAVID REES**

[Penelope Farmer's] achievement seems to be a number of successful books for children arising from preoccupations which are strongly personal, themes and ideas that might easily have found voice in novels written for an adult audience. These preoccupations recur, sometimes obsessively: The wish every one has had at least once in his life to be able to fly, for example, is the main theme of both *The Summer Birds* and *Emma in Winter* and also of her picture book *Daedalus and Icarus;* it reappears, disguised as a desire to swim underwater like a fish, in *William and Mary*. Obviously it would be possible to use such a theme in a totally adult way, to use it as a means of expressing some kind of liberation from the body, perhaps sexual; but in Penelope Farmer's books the theme is simply the child's wish to fly like a bird come true.

Penelope Farmer's books come under the convenient label of *fantasy,* and this is a label that may unfortunately suggest that a writer is unable to, or chooses not to, write realistic fiction. . . . [Penelope Farmer] is just as much at home in writing about the interior of chemists' shops, the smell of school kitchens, or the relationships between children and adults as she is about cupboards that turn matchboxes into fir trees or the inside of a whale that seems to be a plush hotel. Three of her books—*The Dragonfly Summer, Saturday Shillings,* and *The Seagull*—dispense with fantasy altogether, and they are good examples of how well she can write in a medium with which we do not normally associate her. In fact, it could be argued that *Charlotte Sometimes,* probably her most widely read novel, is not a fantasy at all, for the only nonrealistic device in this book is the bed that turns Charlotte into Clare . . . ; the world of the last few months of the 1914-1918 war is just as realistic as Charlotte's boarding school in the present. It is the only book of hers in which dream sequences or events that are completely fantastic are not employed in the parts of the book which are supposedly fantasy.

In four of the seven novels—five, if we include the 1918 passages of *Charlotte Sometimes*—two different worlds are sharply contrasted, the everyday and the extraordinary. The extraordinary involves only the child protagonists, and their problems usually occur because the dream world has its good and its evil just as the real has; but the children can never turn for help to the real world—the safe security of home and parents—because they will either not be believed or the trouble will be worse if they do. Hugh, Anna, and Jean, for example, in *A Castle of Bone,* have to manage on their own. The magic cupboard has turned adolescent Penn into a baby. To ask his

parents or Hugh's parents for assistance would obviously be impossible; the recriminations and the anguish would be extreme and would not help to turn Penn back into his normal self. In any case it is the children's own fault; Penn was shut in the cupboard as a result of a violent quarrel between him and his sister, which Hugh and Jean did nothing to stop—a scene which is a microcosm of what is fundamentally at fault in the relationships among the four. It is only right that the children extricate themselves unassisted from the difficulties they have made; only by doing so can they achieve a more mature relationship with each other.

The dream sequences in *Emma in Winter* have a similar function. They become, on the whole, increasingly unpleasant and are mirrored in the everyday world by the mounting tensions in the village caused by the unusually lengthy period of frost and snow. At first the dreams are delightful, the sense of liberation and happiness caused by the ability to fly being predominant, just as Emma and her friends take delight in the snow, which turns the ordinary landscape into a fairy-tale paradise and pleasantly disrupts the tedium of the day-to-day rhythm of their lives. . . . But something is wrong: Emma's selfishness and unmerited sense of superiority cause a great deal of unhappiness, particularly to the clumsy fat boy, Bobby Fumpkins, who adores her, and also to her teacher, Miss Hallibutt, who overlooks her faults too easily because Emma has brains. It is only by learning to compromise, by growing up in these two relationships in the dreams that Emma is able to mature in her actual relationships with these people, and the dreams—now nightmares—can stop.

Poor Charlotte is a different case. It cannot be argued that she is responsible for what happens to her, that she in any way deserves it; nor can it be said that the book, like *Emma in Winter* and *A Castle of Bone,* is about growing up, growing awareness, maturing relationships. In fact, with the exception of *Year King,* it seems to be much more of an adult book than any other novel by Penelope Farmer. This may seem to be an odd judgment, when it is remembered that it has sold extremely well in the Puffin edition, has been serialized on children's television, and that *A Castle of Bone* is often unfavorably commented on—by adults—as being either too adult, sinister, or even evil, whereas no one has said this of *Charlotte Sometimes*. What disturbs many people about *A Castle of Bone*—adults again, not children—is that Penn is shut in the cupboard, more or less deliberately, by his sister. However, it seems a common enough action to children, a sister shutting her brother in a cupboard, an everyday family event, even. The prevailing mood of *Charlotte Sometimes* is, perhaps, not part of the child's world. Whatever may happen in *Emma in Winter* and *A Castle of Bone,* they remain in essence happy books, even joyous at times. Hugh's pleasure in his own adolescence, the shifts of his moods, the achieving of new experiences are, for instance, very positive, as is the sequence where Bobby Fumpkins helps his father dig in the snow. Both books are often comic; the passage where Molly Scobb thinks she has given Emma her come-uppance is a very amusing and realistic piece of observation, and Hugh's attempts to buy baby food and nipples have a zany, almost clown-like quality. . . . Such moments are absent from *Charlotte Sometimes,* the atmosphere of which is low key, one of depression. Its most memorable passages are poignant or resigned or concerned with absence, loss, or death in action during the war. . . . Its theme is not so much maturing relationships, but identity. This is a perfectly proper theme for children's fiction, of course, for why am I I, and not John Smith or Julie Bloggs, is a normal preoccupation of the thoughtful child. But the book goes further than this. Charlotte begins to wonder, with increasing dismay, if she really is Charlotte; perhaps she has turned into Clare, rather than just substituted for her. This may be an adult fear—the fear of not being everything you and other people have always said you are, the realization that you may be someone totally different, that maybe there isn't such a thing as yourself at all, only a series of different images other people have of you that don't add up to anything coherent.

A key passage in *Charlotte Sometimes* occurs in chapter sixteen:

> But when she put her fingers into the water and pulled a marble out, it was small by comparison with those still in the glass, and unimportant, too. It was like the difference between what you long for and what you find—the difference, for instance, between Arthur's image of war and his experience of it. It was like other times, her own and Miss Agnes's proper childhood times that seemed so near to her memory and yet so far away. It was like everything that made you ache because in one sense it was so close and in another unobtainable.

One might find similar paragraphs in other children's books that deal with the idea of illusion and reality. . . . But the context of this passage in *Charlotte Sometimes* makes it particularly heartfelt, coming just after the pathetic Agnes—doomed for the rest of her unfulfilled life to a sad spinsterhood—reveals to Charlotte that the image of her brother dying heroically in battle, an image her parents believe in and which she tries hard to subscribe to, is very far from the truth. It seems to have a wholly adult feeling about it, which is added to by Charlotte's inability to cope with the adult reactions and emotions of Agnes.

Inability to cope with adult situations: This might be said of Charlotte's response to her predicament as a whole. In the other books the children grapple with problems, often with zest, and either overcome them or come to terms with them. Charlotte does not; she struggles only feebly with the situation, just keeping her head above water. It is significant, perhaps, that it is not she who organizes her return to her own world, but Emily.

None of this is a criticism of *Charlotte Sometimes;* the book is none the worse for breaking the conventional bounds of the children's novel. It is probably Penelope Farmer's finest novel—complex, taut, not a word wrong—and it thoroughly deserves the popularity it has attained. *A Castle of Bone* ought to be her best book; its central idea is more strikingly original, the characters more vivid and varied, its potential, both serious and comic, greater. But it remains a flawed achievement. In her lecture **"Patterns on a Wall"** [see excerpt below in Author's Commentary for *A Castle of Bone* (1972)], Penelope Farmer says that the castle of bone image, taken from a Welsh triad, was

> . . . not relevant to the book I was proposing to write; nor could I see any way of making it so. But the image took over, took me and the book over, wormed its way into the plot till it was central.

It is central enough at the end; indeed, the denouement could not work without it, but in most of the book it isn't central. Hugh's dreams do not seem to fit into the rest of the story; there is a strong temptation to skip over them and return to

what is happening to the children and to the cupboard. For most of the time the castle image does not seem apposite or even very interesting, and one might say that it is a pity that "the image took over, took . . . the book over," as the author reveals, rather than the other way round.

It is difficult to find anything wrong with either *Emma in Winter* or *William and Mary,* but neither of these books compete with *Charlotte Sometimes,* because they do not aim at anything quite so rich or profound. It is perhaps appropriate here to say something about *William and Mary* and Penelope Farmer's first two novels, *The Summer Birds* and *The Magic Stone,* and why they do not measure up to *Charlotte Sometimes. William and Mary* comes after *Charlotte Sometimes* and *A Castle of Bone,* but it seems in many ways a return to an earlier manner, the simpler world of *Emma in Winter.* It has the same kind of central relationship, a boy and a girl whose friendship helps at least one of the two to mature, and the fantasy, juxtaposed in self-contained sections with the everyday world, has the same episodic nature as Emma's dreams. The real world as in *Charlotte Sometimes* is a boarding school; only now it is the holidays; Mary is the headmaster's daughter, alone in a vast empty building, alone even during term time in being the only girl among hundreds of boys. She has some of Charlotte's sense of being apart from everyone else. . . . But William has the shell, the talisman—that most popular of devices in fantasies . . .—which transports the children to another world, in this case under the sea to Atlantis or Dunwich or the depths of the Pacific Ocean. William's search for the other half of the shell is mirrored in real life by his wish to bring his separated parents together. The book is perfectly done; the relationship between William and Mary is full of insights, the fantasy comic or bewildering or sinister (one is constantly aware in this book of fishes' teeth and claws and the murky depths of the sea). . . . Nevertheless, after the previous two books it seems slight, the kind of novel which the author knows she can do well because by now she is well practiced in this kind of thing, but it does not seem to be one that has engaged the whole of her attention nor the whole of the imaginative power that the preceding two have revealed.

*The Summer Birds* and *The Magic Stone* are essentially apprentice books in which the author is trying to make up her mind what kind of book she can write. This is especially true of *The Magic Stone,* most of which is a realistic analysis (if somewhat labored) of the relationship between two adolescent girls. . . . It has some striking passages, particularly its opening description of Caroline watching Alice who is bringing in the washing; trying to cope with her younger brother, she is full of annoyance that Caroline can see her. But the fantasy is very obscure. What powers does the stone have? Is it King Arthur's? Neither the characters, nor the author, it seems, are at all sure.

*The Summer Birds* is the better book. Flying is the central theme, and the pleasures and sensations of this impossible human activity are effectively explored. For a first novel it is fine; nothing much wrong with it anywhere except for some awkward stylistic lapses, but it remains a small thing, for the relationships, though perfectly convincing, are not shown in any depth. It is the book of Penelope Farmer's which is the least adult, the one that is contained most entirely in a child's world.

One might well ask why a children's book shouldn't be contained entirely in a child's world. Many people, C. S. Lewis included, have said that a really good children's book ought to appeal to adults as much as to children, for then it is not limited by saying something to only a certain group of readers; it is simply a good book. And this appeal is what *Charlotte Sometimes* has that *The Summer Birds* has not; it enhances the perceptions of all of us, helps our imaginations, whether child or adult, to grow in the most pleasurable of ways. And that is what reading and writing should be about. (pp. 1-10)

What is the sum of her achievement so far? Her use of fantasy is probably more personal in origin than that employed by most children's writers yet it has been successfully manipulated to produce seven books that deal with not personal, but universal, problems and ideas in a way that they could not be dealt with in more realistic books, at least for children. [Penelope Farmer writes in **"Jorinda and Jorindel and Other Stories"**:]

> I doubt if you could find any piece of realistic fiction for adolescents that says a quarter as much about adolescence as Alan Garner's *The Owl Service*.

The same claim is true about certain aspects of childhood and adolescence in her own novels that she should be more widely known and read than she is. She deserves much greater recognition; she's one of the finest of English authors and the most underrated of them all. (p. 12)

> *David Rees, "The Marble in the Water: Penelope Farmer," in his* The Marble in the Water: Essays on Contemporary Writers of Fiction for Children and Young Adults, *The Horn Book, Inc., 1980, pp. 1-13.*

---

### THE CHINA PEOPLE (1960)

I tend to look askance at fairy stories which are sharp with adult reality. Or, perhaps, what I find in [*The China People*] to make me uneasy is the overt awareness of the disappointment that lies in store. This awareness leads Penelope Farmer into being literary, polysyllabic and poetic. Her characters are incompetent witches, a princess who cannot keep her temper and is turned into a bee for her crimes, a boy suddenly cursed with ambition, a lovely slug, an ugly princess, and a silver flower which extinguishes all its admirers. This last story, in spite of its coy ending, has the ambivalence and fragility of fairy stories and china. And the story called **'The Farmer's Year'** has a definable wisdom.

> *Ralph Lavender, in a review of "The China People," in* The School Librarian, *Vol. 17, No. 3, September, 1969, p. 320.*

The title story, like the others in this volume, has something of the sub-ironic manner of Edith Nesbit's comic fairy-tales. The elegant posturings and manoeuvres of the china figures belong to an artificial fancy which has its own place in literary tradition.

> *Margery Fisher, in a review of "The China People," in her* Growing Point, *Vol. 15, No. 1, May, 1976, p. 2901.*

---

### THE SUMMER BIRDS (1962)

A fantasy unusual in sustained mood and quiet style. Two sisters meet a strange boy who teaches them to fly; one by one, all the children in school are taught and they spend the summer secretly enjoying the joy of flight. Until the end of the summer, the children do not learn who the strange boy is, and when they find out, he must leave them and they lose their ability to fly. The sedate writing and the lack of humor will limit the audience for this book, which will appeal—even amongst the lovers of the fanciful—to the more sophisticated reader who can enjoy the subtleties of style and mood.

> *Zena Sutherland, in a review of "The Summer Birds," in* Bulletin of the Center for Children's Books, *Vol. XV, No. 8, April, 1962, p. 124.*

The pictures that this story brings to mind, of all the school children in air, each one's manner of flying in accord with his personality, are enchanting ...; and the story has overtones and meanings below the surface. [One] feels that for Charlotte, at least, the summer could never quite be lost—nor for the reader. (pp. 176-77)

> *Ruth Hill Viguers, in a review of "The Summer Birds," in* The Horn Book Magazine, *Vol. XXXVIII, No. 2, April, 1962, pp. 176-77.*

It is atmosphere, mood and human reactions that make the story so extraordinarily moving. With Charlotte, the reader sees and smells the growing things of an English countryside; with her he shares the ecstasy of conquering a new element. She is 12 years old and in most ways childish still, but she is mature in her nostalgia for the golden summer which is slipping past, in her realization of the tragedy of growing up, in her awareness of the impermanence of human happiness. She loves and understands the nameless boy as no one else can, yet it is she who must make the decision to sever the relationship.

Penelope Farmer is a young author worth watching for her freshness of outlook, her felicity of expression, and her economy of plotting, though her touch is still a little uncertain at times, and one might wish that she would employ more euphonious names for her characters.

> *Ethna Sheehan, in a review of "The Summer Birds," in* The New York Times Book Review, *April 1, 1962, p. 38.*

["**The Summer Birds**"] is written with distinction about children easy to believe in. Penelope Farmer uses words that send 9-12-year-old readers soaring and swooping with the children.... With so many adventures set in such admirably created atmosphere, it would be ungrateful to wish that the children's flying had led to some more thrilling deeds.

> *Pamela Marsh, "Widening Horizons," in* The Christian Science Monitor, *April 5, 1962, p. 19.*

A strange fantasy.... There is conflict when [the mysterious boy's] authority is challenged and surprise when his origin is explained, but readers will be intrigued most by the feeling of flight which the author deftly conveys.... A refreshing book which will provoke differing opinions and have most appeal for the reader of delicate fantasy.

> *Janice H. Dohm, in a review of "The Summer Birds," in* School Library Journal, *an appendix to* Library Journal, *Vol. 8, No. 9, May, 1962, p. 100.*

Characters are sharply defined, the ecstasy of flight and the spell cast by the boy are vividly conveyed, and a haunting atmosphere of strangeness permeates this original, gracefully written fantasy.

> *A review of "The Summer Birds," in* The Booklist and Subscription Books Bulletin, *Vol. 58, No. 20, June 15, 1962, p. 728.*

## THE MAGIC STONE (1964)

The story is partly a fantasy and partly a realistic account of the problems girls face in different family situations and in adjusting to friends with different outlooks.

When Caroline and Alice first meet each other, they find a stone with a steel inset which they believe to be magical because the steel will not move unless both hold the stone together. At first they resent this, but after strange and sometimes dangerous experiences with the stone, they become excited and curious. Absorbed in their own tensions and satisfactions, they ignore the ominous gang warfare starting up between their small brothers and their respective followers until a shocking occurrence jolts them.

The author has no easy answers. She depicts life as she sees it. Young girls of 11 to 14 years will find she has real insight into their questionings and difficulties. And she suggests here that magic is as much in the individual as in a talisman. Remarkably interesting, good reading and provocative.

> Margaret Sherwood Libby, "Battling Blokes and Blighters," in Book Week—The Washington Post, November 22, 1964, p. 20.*

The psychological implication of [Caroline and Alice's] relationship is deftly handled: before they go their ways . . . both girls have changed, each broadening her understanding. Characterization is sharply etched, the familial patterns being wonderfully candid and perceptive. Beautifully written, a story in which the fanciful element gives depth to an honest picture of class differences.

> Zena Sutherland, in a review of "The Magic Stone," in Bulletin of the Center for Children's Books, Vol. XVIII, No. 4, December, 1964, p. 53.

The author of **The Summer Birds** has again penetrated, and captured in words, the mysterious emotions of children, their uneasy relationships, and the sometimes terrifying awareness of their encompassing worlds. Too introspective for some children, the story has overtones and insights that will make it exciting and satisfying for others.

> Ruth Hill Viguers, in a review of "The Magic Stone," in The Horn Book Magazine, Vol. XLI, No. 1, February, 1965, p. 52.

After the excitements of **The Summer Birds**, Penelope Farmer's readers may be a little disappointed in the more subdued charms of her new book. . . . This is an ambitious book, but unfortunately it does not quite come off. The two major characters are all-important, and Caroline is very shrewdly drawn, but Alice, who is intended to be the more dynamic, is shadowy and less convincing. Indeed, the author seems altogether less sure of herself when dealing with the housing estate side of the community. The slow pace and uneventfulness of the book make it unlikely that it will attract a wide readership, which is a pity, for, dealing as it does with concepts and ideas, it provides valuable material for the thoughtful child. (pp. 217-18)

> A review of "The Magic Stone," in The Junior Bookshelf, Vol. 29, No. 4, August, 1965, pp. 217-18.

The child who has Arthurian echoes in his mind has a poetic truth that may stand him in good stead all his life. Something like this might be said to be the point (or one point) of **The Magic Stone**—that children of all classes and all temperaments need imagination for their proper development. More concretely, the theme is the class-feeling which is modified when children talk and act like themselves and not as other people expect them to. Thus, the power of the stone can be called truth or love or magic or anything else you like, or you can simply read the story letting its effect (and it is a powerful one) do your thinking for you. In the sense that there is an intellectual point, this might be taken as a story for the above-average, even the middle-class reader: but in so far as it is a well-told, exciting story, illuminated by honesty, it is one I would try on children of all kinds and all backgrounds. . . . [This] is no airy-fairy tale; it is firmly based on personality, on the freedom of youth to experiment, a freedom threatened at the end of the book, when Alice leaves school to go to work and Caroline (who is younger) goes off to boarding-school. Too wise to tell the reader that everything will be all right, the author is only prepared to suggest that because the girls have learned to trust themselves and each other, they are all the better equipped for the future. . . . Let me be clear—the book is not priggish nor over-weighted with theory. It is exciting, delicately balanced between realism and fantasy, with a properly drawn domestic and natural background to keep it from whimsy. The moods of sea and fields impose themselves on the girls through events which are partly real and partly imagined, running alongside the world we live in, with the adults afraid of the awkward friendship and the little boys expressing their social differences with their fists. In this outstanding book, Penelope Farmer has handled a tricky subject with success. (pp. 554-55)

> Margery Fisher, in a review of "The Magic Stone," in her Growing Point, Vol. 4, No. 3, September, 1965, pp. 554-55.

---

## THE SEAGULL (1965; U.S. edition as Sea Gull)

[Stephen] was hoping to cage the sea gull after it recovered the use of its broken wing and return with it to his London apartment. His grandmother inserts gentle admonishments about the cruelty of confining wild life and Stephen responds with a petulant obstinacy that may be realistic but certainly isn't engaging. The best part of the book is the author's depiction of the gull, which roosts around the seaside home with unsentimental ingratitude for first aid rendered, regarding his would-be owner with a viciously bright stare. Stephen, of course, sees the error of his ways and releases the bird on his own initiative. It is an over-focused incident sharing the theme and the faults of Edith Brecht's Ada and the Wild Duck (1964) with an emphasized, completely telegraphed moral and a central character who seems babyish by American standards.

> A review of "Sea Gull," in Virginia Kirkus' Service, Vol. XXXIV, No. 1, January 1, 1966, p. 4.

Where "Storm Boy" [by Colin Thiele] suffers from too much plot, **"Sea Gull"** suffers from too little. The pattern—Boy Wants Pet, Finds Pet, Must Set Wild Pet Free—is obvious and the story predictable from beginning to end. However, this weakness is well-compensated for by interesting characters and an attractive writing style. More than a pet story, this is the tale of a selfish, impatient, petulant boy's adjustment to the inevitable, told in a text full of choice images and rhythmic prose.

> Donald J. Bissett, in a review of "Sea Gull," in The New York Times Book Review, May 1, 1966, p. 30.

An interesting variant on the child meets animal, loves animal, loses animal theme. Here the child is relieved at losing the creature he had at first hoped would become an unusual pet.... The mood, atmosphere, and dialogue are excellent; the relationship between Stephen and his grandmother sympathetic but utterly realistic. All of these assets are embedded in a sedate, but competent, writing style.

> *Zena Sutherland, in a review of "Sea Gull," in* Bulletin of the Center for Children's Books, *Vol. 20, No. 1, September, 1966, p. 8.*

---

### EMMA IN WINTER  (1966)

[*The Summer Birds*] ceased their flight with satisfying finality so that it is a surprise to come upon a sequel which centers on two minor characters from the first book.... Emma, alone and lonely finds herself drawn toward Bobby, still friendless. A tentative sort of friendship develops between them, all unspoken. It is sealed by their discovery that they have been dreaming the same dreams each night, in which they fly progressively backward in time. Gradually the dreams seem the most vivid part of their lives, finally they reach the beginning of the world, and find, not the Garden of Eden, but only endless sea and rocky shore. A kaleidoscope of images bursts before their eyes, climaxing with another Bobby and another Emma, who threaten to swallow them up. With great effort, Bobby rejects the phantoms, shouts at them, and drags Emma away. They are able to return to reality only by consciously choosing it—all the familiar loved and despised aspects of their daily life. The theme, then, is the same as that of *The Summer Birds*, a "special" book which succeeded by involving the reader with a variety of people and events steadily building toward a resolution. In *Emma in Winter* the focus is narrow, the development internal. The author displays her usual wizardry at evoking sensations, but youngsters are likely to become impatient with the psychological and psychic unravelling of Emma and Bobby long before the end.

> *A review of "Emma in Winter," in* Virginia Kirkus' Service, *Vol. XXXIV, No. 16, August 15, 1966, p. 835.*

This is not an improving story but one which uncovers the subconscious a little and gives tangible form to the emotions of children in a dream-sequence brilliantly sustained in the author's elegant, rhythmic style. It is not everyone's book but for some it may become a key to more than just a story.

> *Margery Fisher, in a review of "Emma in Winter," in her* Growing Point, *Vol. 5, No. 5, November, 1966, p. 791.*

This lovely, imaginative fantasy is a sequel to Miss Farmer's first book, *Summer Birds*, and will appeal to the same readers.... Miss Farmer has a gift for creating character and mood, with the natural setting of a small English village or the larger world of the dreams. The book won't appeal immediately to the child looking for a fast-moving plot, but all children should have a chance at it. (pp. 5747-48)

> *Amy Kellman, in a review of "Emma in Winter," in* Library Journal, *Vol. 91, No. 20, November 15, 1966, pp. 5747-48.*

Admirers of *The Summer Birds* will almost certainly be disappointed in its sequel.... [The author's use of dreams] is a clever idea, but not very carefully worked out. Why does the dream always start at the point at which it last left off? Dreams do not usually behave like that. And if they are not in fact dreaming but actually caught up in the time spiral, why do they always return to their own time by day? Much of the book is repetitive and boring. It is an anticlimax when the menacing presence of the early dreams resolves into a stupid caricature of the children's teacher, just at a time when their dream experience should have been at its most terrifying. Nor is the author's touch in social relationships so sure as it was in her earlier novels.

> *A review of "Emma in Winter," in* The Junior Bookshelf, *Vol. 31, No. 2, April, 1967, p. 120.*

---

### CHARLOTTE SOMETIMES  (1969)

*Charlotte sometimes* has the same depth [as André Norton's *Fur Magic*] in its delineation of character through fantasy. This is a remarkable story, emotionally rich and very ingenious—indeed, it needs an intelligent reader of twelve or so to appreciate just what happens to Charlotte in terms of plot, as well as a reader who is responsive to her feelings. Charlotte belongs to today, Clare to the world of 1918, and by a series of chances the two find themselves interchanging in their daily lives—first alternating and then, alarmingly, apparently fixed for ever in each other's world. Like *Emma in winter* this is really a study in disintegration, the study of a girl finding an identity by losing it. The book is well-found in every respect. The prose is grave, flexible and rich in texture, the social and domestic detail sharp and fascinating; the moments of terror and affection are given their full value. Above all, here is a dream-allegory which teaches not through statement but through feeling. We sense the meaning of Charlotte's changes of identity in the way that she senses them herself.

> *Margery Fisher, in a review of "Charlotte Sometimes," in her* Growing Point, *Vol. 8, No. 5, November, 1969, p. 1408.*

Penelope Farmer knows that magic works only when it is as integral a part of the story as is any character. And that's what she makes of it in *Charlotte Sometimes*....

Charlotte and Emily are real girls with real problems, extraordinary as some of them may seem. Their fears and their hopes, their dreams and their nightmares are totally in character and totally believable.

> *Marion Simon, "Magic Goes Awry in 'The Apple Stone,' but 'Charlotte' Is a Spellbinding Tale," in* The National Observer, *November 3, 1969, p. 20.\**

[*Charlotte Sometimes*] is a book of quite exceptional distinction....

The action takes place in an English boarding school for girls and in a stiff, sad English household during World War I. Out of this simple and dangerous material (the opportunities for banality are enormous) the author has built a haunting, convincing story which comes close to being a masterpiece of its kind.

There is little physical adventure. The real drama takes place in the hearts and minds of the three girls where the suspense and the mystery, the echo of tragedy and the honorable anguish of compassion are all held in tension.

The publishers suggest 10-14 as the age group for their book. This reviewer would remove the upper limit altogether.

It is not just about young female humans; the children are not primarily girls, or even children; they are primarily people. The book is essentially about humanity caught in the still trickery of time.

If the first few pages seem a little unpromising—well, so do many other doorways which open on strange, moving, homely landscapes.

Not easily forgotten.

> *Neil Millar, "Tales from School," in* The Christian Science Monitor, *November 6, 1969, p. B5.**

The situation is fascinating and the author controls it well. . . . The atmosphere of boarding-school life both in 1918 and the present is evoked, and the varied and subtle relationships of the other girls in the school add interest to an intriguing fantasy which deftly navigates some fairly deep psychological waters without really coming to terms with the questions it raises.

> *Sidney D. Long, in a review of "Charlotte Sometimes," in* The Horn Book Magazine, *Vol. XLV, No. 6, December, 1969, p. 675.*

It was brave, but perhaps foolhardy, to attempt a wrinkle in time so near the present that the heroine Charlotte . . . can encounter two characters grown up from her other life in 1918. Her exchange with . . . [Clare] does not quite come off. It is altogether too complicated, particularly when Emily, sister to the other girl Clare, has to be party to the changes. Unlike the best examples of this genre, the time-jump here seems quite inexplicable. However, personal relationships, particularly within the earlier period, are very well-drawn and show a deeply sympathetic understanding of people, most moving when Charlotte seems imprisoned for ever in the past and is in danger of forgetting that she is not Clare. Emily's reactions to this are sensitively imagined, and there is a disturbingly frightening moment when Charlotte is nearly caught up in a different, far more tragic relationship.

> *A review of "Charlotte Sometimes," in* The Junior Bookshelf, *Vol. 33, No. 6, December, 1969, p. 385.*

[Farmer] has written another unusual, sometimes disturbing, fantasy. . . . [Shuttling back and forth from one time and one personality to the other] is unsettling both for Charlotte and readers; there is neither lightness nor pleasure, only anxiety, and the gripping uncertainty and suspense will prompt some compulsive reading to discover if Charlotte does escape from the past. It's learned at the end (a shattering denouement) that Charlotte's alter ego had died of influenza shortly after Charlotte manages to get back to her own time. Throughout, Charlotte remains her strangely timid, literal-minded self, and it may well be these qualities that make her adventures so much more startling.

> *Frances M. Postell, in a review of "Charlotte Sometimes," in* School Library Journal, *an appendix to* Library Journal, *Vol. 16, No. 4, December, 1969, p. 50.*

### DAEDALUS AND ICARUS  (1971)

[This is the] story of Daedalus from his arrival in Crete to his son's fall into the Icarian Sea. . . . Ian Serraillier's *A Fall from the Sky,* which covers more of the Daedalus myths, is a far more engrossing story which is also more faithful to its sources (here, for example, the Minotaur is the son of King Minos). Reluctant readers assigned the story at school might be attracted to this version for its brevity . . . but would be more likely to finish Serraillier's account. (pp. 437-38)

> *A review of "Daedalus and Icarus," in* Kirkus Reviews, *Vol. XXXIX, No. 8, April 15, 1971, pp. 437-38.*

The tragic ending of the tale is neatly told, but the author's improvisations on this myth are strange. She adds details of no importance while removing others of interest, and commits what I believe to be a serious error: it was not Daedalus who escaped the labyrinth but Theseus, slayer of the Minotaur. Only a few versions of the story have placed Daedalus in the labyrinth, and that was to help Minos's wife couple with a white bull. Perhaps it was thought that this latter bit of information would be disturbing, but the book is more disturbing without it.

> *Barbara Wersba, "Tales of Mortals and Immortals," in* The New York Times Book Review, *Part II, May 2, 1971, p. 46.**

Penelope Farmer's version [of the tale of Daedalus] invites comparison with Ian Serraillier's. . . . His version was cunningly shaped into a satisfying whole: the master craftsman's life in Athens was described, and his jealousy for his clever nephew Talos carefully demonstrated; so that the flight to Crete with Icarus made proper dramatic sense. But this new version is set wholly in Crete: this has the curious effect of diminishing the justness and the sadness of the final accident, in which Daedalus is punished for his earlier crime through his son. A small point of detail is that Ian Serraillier had Talos inventing the saw, and this is confirmed by the *Oxford Companion to Classical Literature;* whereas Penelope Farmer credits Daedalus with this particular invention. An eleven-year-old boy asserts that '*Fall from the Sky* describes things better . . . It also uses more adjectives . . . it is longer as well.'

Nor is the new version dramatically convincing at the point where Daedalus and his son are shut in the labyrinth by Minos. There are occasional perverse oddities in the writing. For example, the story begins: 'To Crete across the sea there fled a man called Daedalus. He was an engineer, the most brilliant inventor of his time and no one more aware of that than he.' There is an uncomfortably conscious striving for effect here, as if the words are not good enough to speak for themselves in their natural order. (pp. 181-82)

> *Ralph Lavender, in a review of "The Serpent's Teeth" and "Daedalus and Icarus," in* The School Librarian, *Vol. 20, No. 2, June, 1972, pp. 181-82.*

### DRAGONFLY SUMMER  (1971)

People are fascinating and difficult. . . . Stephen reached [this conclusion] when he paid a second visit to his grandmother at Mill House (the first was described in *The seagull*) and found his cousin Peter was also invited. *Dragonfly summer* with subtle simplicity shows how Stephen learns by stages that because his cousin is not aggressive or competitive there is little satisfaction in scoring points against him. . . . Penelope Farmer makes her points within a pleasant picture of summer work and play, using words with discrimination and showing the personalities of her actors clearly despite the brevity of her tale.

Margery Fisher, in a review of "Dragonfly Summer," in her Growing Point, Vol. 10, No. 6, December, 1971, p. 1847.

---

### THE SERPENT'S TEETH: THE STORY OF CADMUS (1971)

Cadmus, whose sister Europa has been borne off to sea by a white bull, is exiled by his father because he did not stop his sister when she climbed on the bull's back. He goes off with a band of warriors who are slain by a snake with several heads, kills the reptile, and is told by Athene that an army of men will rise where he sows the serpent's teeth. Cadmus does this, and from the most stalwart of these men come the beginnings of a new city, Thebes, which he rules. . . . [The] retelling loses none of the action of the myth, but the style is compressed, so that occasionally there is a shift from dialogue to a new subject; for example, Athene tells Cadmus to seek a white heifer and, where she bends her head to graze, "there found your city. There lies your fate." On the next page, "The heifer might have been sired by Europa's bull," the text goes on, with no description of finding her. (pp. 105-06)

Zena Sutherland, in a review of "The Serpent's Teeth: The Story of Cadmus," in Bulletin of the Center for Children's Books, Vol. 25, No. 7, March, 1972, pp. 105-06.

This myth contains some of the most fantastic antiwar propaganda in literature, plus a plug for conserving cities. . . .

The somber, theatrical text has the same relentless drive as Cadmus moving toward his fate.

Flo Morse, "When Gods Were Human, All Too Human," in The New York Times Book Review, August 27, 1972, p. 24.*

A dramatic treatment of the Cadmus myth. . . . The cadenced prose and a vivid, forceful word choice perfectly suit the tale for reading aloud. . . . A standard retelling of the Cadmus story is included in D'Aulaires' Book of Greek Myths (Doubleday, 1962), but both text and pictures are flat in comparison with Farmer's version [illustrated by Chris Connor].

Elva Harmon, in a review of "The Serpent's Teeth: The Story of Cadmus," in School Library Journal, Vol. 19, No. 1, September, 1972, p. 78.

---

### A CASTLE OF BONE (1972)

#### AUTHOR'S COMMENTARY

It seems that I need symbols and images, symbols being formalized, ritualized, often universal images—the sun, for instance, or the dark, or the power of flight. Since I have very few ideas (I envy the prolific, more extrovert fantasists like Joan Aiken), I have to nurture each idea carefully, squeeze it to the uttermost, digging very deeply into myself in the process, though often unaware of what is happening, and letting each idea develop as it always must, via images. Without these images I cannot frame my idea and expand it into narrative.

For while poetry uses images straight, more or less, and usually very compressed ones, fantasy marches head-on into them. People actually fly, move about in time, swap identities; inanimate objects become animate. For me, the extraordinary is

a means of looking at people sideways and finding out more about them—and me. But looking straight at them, at real instead of at imagined life, I feel eyeless and earless; I can see, hear, describe precisely nothing. Without symbols, and the images they give me, I can find no form or structure anywhere. It was not till I came across the Celtic tree alphabets and calendars and took the tree for one central symbol that I found a framework for A Castle of Bone . . . and was able to set about writing it.

Once I have such a structure, I can begin to work out a narrative, or so it was with A Castle of Bone. Obviously, no two books are absolutely alike, and in Castle the mythological framework was a good deal more logical and complete than in anything else I've done. For instance, the Celtic tree calendar not only assigns a tree to each day of the week but gives each tree—and hence each day—a particular mood or character. Thus, Monday, is the day of the willow; and the willow is the tree associated with death, the color black, and witchcraft. It is also the tree from which cricket bats and aspirin are made. For Monday, then, I had not only an atmosphere but also props which, in their turn, suggested activities and preoccupations; and this was very helpful to me since I find it hard to know what to do with my characters most of the time. I suppose you could say that learning to be a writer is discovering various tricks to get over, round, and under the things you aren't good at, just as much as developing the things you are good at. So I need a framework.

In Castle, the structure works on two levels: the practical, as with the cricket bat; and the symbolic, as with the meaning of the tree (in the case of the willow—paralysis, witchcraft, and death). But while the practical aspect is fairly conscious and obvious to me as I write, the symbolic aspect is quite otherwise. Up to a point, I can tell where I am going with symbolism. I knew that in Castle I wanted a sense of depression and helplessness, but beyond that I did not know what to do. For symbols can jump uncannily, in ways you do not expect. You can find you've made symbolic associations without realizing you've done so, because they touch echoes in yourself, even if you do not know what they stand for. This has been true for me particularly, probably because I have—or used to have—a very literal mind. I know now that in Castle two of the symbols pursued me rather than the other way about. The image of the castle I took initially from the Welsh triad which I quote at the beginning of the book: "The achievement of Manwyddan the wise / After lamentation and fiery wrath / Was a construction of the bone fortress of Oeth and Anoeth." Fortress, you see, not castle. But I translated it unconsciously. For when I went back to look for the passage, I was looking for castle, not fortress. Anyway, it made a good title I thought—A Castle of Bone. Only, sadly, it was not relevant to the book I was proposing to write; nor could I see any way of making it so. But the image took over, took me and the book over, wormed its way into the plot till it was central. Yet, I did not myself realize what had happened till I wrote the last sentence in the next-to-the-last chapter, "But this castle of bone was himself." Then, for the first time, I saw that the image I had been using stood for man himself. And don't tell me the Anglo-Saxons did that before; I know they did—now. But I did not know then, and that's the point.

Even uncannier was the old man who sold Hugh the cupboard and to whom Hugh returned for help. I saw him, I suppose, mainly as a deus ex machina; certainly not, as someone suggested to me later, as Tiresias, the archetypal blind seer who explains the world in riddles for our own deciphering. And yet, every time he appeared, I referred carefully to the blind bust in the shop; even, eventually, giving it the old man's face. I find all this alarming. It certainly makes me believe wholeheartedly in Jung's theory of the universal subconscious. A child wrote to me recently, "I don't really like your books, but I can't help reading them. . . . **'Castle of Bone'** gave me a funny feeling." Well, it gave and still gives me some pretty funny feelings, too. (pp. 172-74)

> *Penelope Farmer, "Patterns on a Wall," in* The Horn Book Magazine, *Vol. L, No. 5, October, 1974, pp. 169-76.*

---

"Eyes take time to adjust from light to dark" and Hugh takes time to adjust to the dream-landscape in which a rugged castle each night seems to get nearer. At first he doesn't try to find any connection between his recurrent dream and the cupboard, bought from an old man in a junk shop, which has the power to reduce objects to their original elements. . . . Fantasy does not take kindly to bald summary and no short quotation could really do more than hint at the way Penelope Farmer integrates the actual and the extra-ordinary; nor would an account of the things ab-evolved by the cupboard be much help.

Readers already alerted to echoes of C. S. Lewis and Alan Garner will add E. Nesbit to the list when they learn that athletic, matter-of-fact Penn becomes first a lusty infant and then a newborn baby, to the dismay of the others. The situation does recall the Psammead's double-edged magic and there is something of the same lurking humour. But this is more than a comic-fantastic adventure resolved with common-sense. Penelope Farmer takes the search for identity that runs through all her books to an unexpected conclusion. Not so much 'Who am I?' but 'How many I's are there?' With amusement and nervous curiosity the four friends, slowly accepting the nature of the cupboard, try it out with raisins, a button, a brush, but already Anna has reached a more serious conclusion—'Anyone old could get into the cupboard and be made young again. They could grow old again and be made young again. They needn't ever die.' The alarming thought haunts them all. It is only partly by accident that Penn is eventually shut in the cupboard and it is only by an extraordinary effort of will and imagination, when dream and reality merge inside the castle, that Hugh performs the action that stops the magic and restores normality.

Hugh learns most from the adventure; he learns that the castle of bone that is his body contains his past, present and future, and is locked in unity with his thoughts and feelings. Anna plays a crucial part in the resolution but her remark to Hugh about changing—'I feel years older than Jean. Sometimes I feel years older than you'—is a clue to her character. She is one of those girls with an early intuitive knowledge of life. For Jean, the adventure is personal. Strongly attracted to Penn, and piqued because he rarely notices her, she sees the danger to him and little more. And Penn himself, snatched back so suddenly in time, emerges unchanged and unaware; he is a doer, not a thinker. Subtle points of personality and a steady domestic documentation balance the fantasy and make a complete whole. I have suggested that quotation is useless but without quotation I can't praise properly the intense power of Penelope Farmer's writing. The gaiety and aptness of talk between the characters, the ease of the narrative—it would be possible to analyse these, I suppose; but the deepening magic

is another matter. Here the reader must let words carry meanings that need no gloss:

> The studs in the huge oak door were like eyes too, as they had been before. Yet they were more brilliant today when threatening, multiple brilliancies, each stud reflecting another little bright sun like the pupil in an eye, and together he saw now, forming the same five-pointed star shapes as the apple trees had. The bird handle of the door stared out from among them fiercely as ever. But its eyes went beyond Hugh and Jean as if the enemy lay elsewhere. The whole effect was of enormous energy and splendour, the more so in their setting, that quiet grey court. Hugh turned the bird head, wrenching it with both his hands; and this time it moved and the door fell open. He felt as if he was being sucked inside by some invisible, inaudible force and pulled Jean with him, after him. The door closed itself behind them.

With this book (reality lit with fantasy which is itself lit by myth) Penelope Farmer emphatically claims her place in the front rank of writers for the young. (pp. 1983-84)

> *Margery Fisher, in a review of "A Castle of Bone," in her* Growing Point, *Vol. 11, No. 3, September, 1972, pp. 1983-84.*

In fantasy, magic cupboards come in the category of antique furniture, yet Penelope Farmer is not only fully aware of the pedigree of the device she is using, but also most subtly gets her characters to sort out the magic in modern, sceptical, adolescent terms. This is not the only way in which the strange credibly invades normality: the other is the insidiously inevitable way the sinister world of the cupboard takes over the world they know around them, at the zoo, on stamps, on buttons. Contrast is made between 'nice' and 'horrible', words fluid enough to allow the author to exploit the unreliability of each and to point out the coexistence of both in everything nice and horrible, which is perhaps what growing up is all about.

Mere fun for all too short a while, the cupboard turns one of them into himself-as-a-baby, and the 'nice' family world is turned upside down; but not farcically, for—unwritten law—parents cannot be told. The anxiety is internalised, as Garner describes the magic of his later books. It is in this spirit that they challenge the magic by going *deliberately* into its power, where, in a kaleidoscope of firelights and reflections, ambiguities surround them and where each succumbs to change except Hugh, whose mind is under siege like a castle. His decision sums him up as a being in *both* worlds, acknowledges the reality and the fantasy, the circumstantial and the illusionary.

In a most original way the story explores the 'shut-offness' of adolescents, their spasmodic panic at being isolatedly 'themselves', their reaction to an unforeseeable world. Fantasy rarely probes reality as deeply as this.

> *C. S. Hannabuss, in a review of "A Castle of Bone," in* Children's Book Review, *Vol. II, No. 5, October, 1972, p. 150.*

Equally powerful [as Mollie Hunter's *The Haunted Mountain*], though ultimately less successful, is Penelope Farmer's *A Castle of Bone*. . . . Here the author has tried something even harder: a novel with admirably convincing contemporary children co-existing with a dark, frightening world of fantasy that must eventually be resolved. . . . Miss Farmer's technique, though, involving a succession of jumps between the here and the not-here, is difficult to settle down to, and the force of her imagination tends to become squandered in too much explaining and scene-changing. A pity—perhaps she can choose a framework next time that will release more of her obvious potential. (p. 692)

*Nicholas Tucker, "Catching Fire," in* New Statesman, *Vol. 84, No. 2173, November 10, 1972, pp. 690-92.**

[This is] an exhilarating, troubling book, unlike any other, and unforgettable. Certainly, it is for children, and about children: Ones who say "Jesus!", scratch their groins, have far more complicated feelings than children in books are usually given credit for, and whom—though we aren't told their ages, last names, parents' jobs, or what town they live in—we end up knowing better than we do many people in real life.

The book invites extraordinary thoughts: How would it be to have to grow eternally older, or remain eternally the same? Or, to relive a certain stage of life an endless number of times? And what are the limits of I and Other? And how much does fulfilling one's innermost self necessitate giving others their due? . . .

[Hugh] has a passion for observing things, and his need for privacy is so great that part of him stays aloof from everyone. In a way the cupboard shatters this aloneness. Once Hugh and Penn and their sisters know about the cupboard's power, they have to unite to test it and try to cope with it. For the cupboard changes not only things—wallet into sow, matches into fir tree, sweater into hank of wool—but *people.* How one of them gets shut inside—not so accidentally—and is reduced to smiling, bawling helpless baby, and how the others react is terrifying, yet wildly funny and, in the end, a triumph.

The cupboard's second, equally awesome, power makes Hugh's aloneness more complete by drawing him nightly into a dimension outside time, through woods to a castle at once forbidding and beckoning, into which he cannot penetrate. These wanderings reflect the day's events, as dreams do. But when Hugh finds himself back in his bed, snow clings to his pajamas, or holly leaves to his feet. He knows—and so do we—that the castle is real. It is his own self. And in a stunning ending, he enters it, not by passively being drawn there but by being willing to go, in conjunction with, not rejection of, his sister and his friends.

Behind other fantasies and dream novels, one usually senses the storyteller's presence, inventing and pacing in order to entertain, scare a bit, then reassure and enlighten. Not here. The story bursts forth like a torrent, sweeping one along. In fact, a rarer category than fantasy or dream novel comes to mind: Necessary writing. What a writer "must write—or burst," as C. S. Lewis said; what readers' lives are changed by.

*Doris Orgel, "A Magic Cabinet, Kissing Wolves and a Running Nose: 'A Castle of Bone'," in* The New York Times Book Review, *January 21, 1973, p. 8.*

Farmer's fantasy is perhaps less a novel and more a tapestry of words with the rich elaboration that metaphor conveys. Complex ideas permeate the adventure as concepts of time and substance collapse, reappear, and dissolve. Vocabulary generally unexpected in a child's story—for example, *affectation, suffused, plinth, reanimate*—are found throughout the narra-

tive. Both real and imaginary characters enter whose speech or behavior is not fully explained, and assumptions must be made as to their motives and other actions. A clue to the novel's tone may be inferred from the references to Welsh mythology and to Blake, whose poetry and thought serve as an inspiration for the title. Readers must bring background—Odysseus, for example—to the story and be able to shift easily between the many transitions, time perspectives, and ideas that may be bluntly, partially, or only inferentially expressed. (p. 130)

*Barbara H. Baskin and Karen H. Harris, "A Selected Guide to Intellectually Demanding Books: 'A Castle of Bone'," in their* Books for the Gifted Child, *R. R. Bowker Company, 1980, pp. 129-30.*

In her specialized definition of fantasy—"psychological image coloured and transformed by the workings of a single mind"—Penelope Farmer sets up two categories [see excerpt above in the Author's Commentary which precedes General Commentary]. She labels as "extrovert" fantasy those stories which rely on surface mechanics with the source and consequence of the event basically exterior both to the author and to his characters. "Introvert" fantasy, on the other hand, probes "interior kinds of subjects"—psychological problems which concern the individual author and his protagonist. Her own novel, *A Castle of Bone,* is a prime example of such fantasy.

On the surface, introvert fantasy such as *A Castle of Bone* incorporates many of the conventions of the standard time fantasy for children: a magical cupboard of mysterious origin transports four young people, two boys and their sisters, into a fantasy world dominated by a turreted castle where, we are led to believe, an important choice is to be made. Hugh, the protagonist, is a dreamer, an artist, an awkward adolescent with "legs of late grown inconveniently long." As owner of the strange cupboard, he is drawn each night into the mysterious realm of the castle. His sister, Jean, a down-to-earth, sensible, well-organized girl, is attracted to Penn, her brother's friend. Penn is athletic, graceful, ebullient, logical, and assertive, the perfect complement to the introverted Hugh. Penn's sister, Anna, provides sharp contrast to her large, positive brother. She is small, black-haired, seemingly timid, quiet, and always dressed in black, which accents the paleness of her skin; she exudes a sense of mystery. (p. 171)

When Penn is shut in the cupboard by his sister, he is returned as a toddler. The plot begins to take shape. The young people must learn how to restore Penn to his proper age.

In addition to this surface dilemma, Miss Farmer develops her theme through the symbolism of Hugh's nightly journeys into the fantasy world of the castle. Drawn into this world in what seems to be a dream, Hugh sees a girl with black hair, a red dress, and white feet, feeding a fire in an alder grove. Across the river on a hill stands a square and turreted castle. Hugh breaks through the circle of hostile alder trees but cannot reach the castle. The dream ends (or so he thinks) but the next morning, when he awakens, he finds green alder bark under his fingernails. (In the *Odyssey,* the alder is the first named of the three trees of the resurrection that formed a grove around the cave of Calypso, daughter of Atlas, on her Elysian island of Ogygia. These alder thickets confined the hero on the oracular island by growing around its shores. Odysseus was detained by Calypso on Ogygia, but, declining her offer of immortality, escaped.)

The second visit finds Hugh in a terrain empty of all things but the castle. He is again in a woods where he sees a dead crow, its black feathers scattered on the white snow which glistens with drops of red blood. He awakens in his bedroom wearing slippers soggy from the snow, though the month in his own time is August.

A third trip finds him seeking the castle through a grove of willow trees. He touches one and is frozen to the tree, immobilized while a horse and rider pass by. In a subsequent encounter the horse and rider again appear as Hugh struggles through a holly grove. Yet another sequence finds him struggling up an avenue of oak trees. The sun gives no light, its brilliant edges dwindling to a black center. Hugh feels a force trying to suck him into the back center which is both the pupil of an eye and a tunnel, yet, at the same time, he is still walking along the road, screaming with fear yet not screaming. Between each pair of trees, the pressure grows stronger until finally he enters the castle courtyard and stands in front of a door whose handle is shaped like a crow. (p. 172)

Inside the castle, in a nightmare sequence, Hugh and Jean watch Anna hold the infant Penn over a basin of fire. Spurred by Jean, who jabs him with a pin, Hugh chooses to stop Anna, and Jean rescues the baby from the fire. Tension drains from the scene and they return through the cupboard to the present, Penn being restored to his normal age in the process. So much for the surface plot.

Though one might expect a neat pairing of Hugh and Anna, Penn and Jean, it becomes obvious as the book progresses that the central tension arises out of the triangular relationship between the two boys and Anna. Anna is the center of the triangle and jealousy is the recurring theme. Anna is jealous of her brother yet attracted to him. The strength of her emotion is revealed in her violent attack on Penn before she shoves him into the cupboard. Hugh is attracted to Anna though he feels her presence as strangely irritating. He is glad when she chooses him in preference to her brother when the four go rowing on the lake. Watching Penn and Anna from his bedroom window, Hugh feels jealous because they have so much to say to each other when he is absent. On another occasion, Anna's mother accuses her of being obsessed with Penn.

This strange relationship becomes clearer when the reader is aware of the sources of the author's symbolism. (p. 173)

[Miss Farmer] confirms the fact that Celtic mythology exerts significant influence over her symbolism [see excerpt above in the Author's Commentary for *A Castle of Bone*]. Penn is described in terms which suggest that he is a Celtic sun-god, Bran or Lugh or Llew Llaw Gyffes, or perhaps Gwern, Bran's sister's son, who was burned in a bonfire. In his study, *The White Goddess: A Historical Grammar of Poetic Myth*, Robert Graves writes:

> For each year that the reign of this agricultural Hercules [a year king] is prolonged he offers a child-victim in his stead; which explains the Greek legends of Hercules killing children by accident or in a fit of madness, and the destruction by fire, after a temporary investiture as king, of various unfortunate young princes, among them Gwern, nephew of Bran. . . .

Graves explains that this primitive ritual of the Year King permitted a single king to rule for a term of years. The custom of burning a child to death as an annual surrogate for the king conferred immortality on the child by the burning process. In *Mythology: the Voyage of the Hero*, David Adams Leeming

provides another example of the Year King motif in the myth of Isis and Osiris. Acting as a nursemaid to the infant son of the Queen of Byblus, Isis began to burn "all that was mortal of him away." The queen spied what Isis was doing and rescued the child, thereby preventing him from becoming immortal. That this motif of the Year King intrigues Miss Farmer is indicated by the fact that five years later she published a novel entitled *Year King*, dealing with the psychological conflicts of identical twin brothers, Lan and Lew, characters very similar to Hugh and Penn. In *A Castle of Bone*, the infant Penn is held over the fire at Lammas according to the sacrificial pattern. Is Penn then a surrogate for Hugh, who, in stopping Anna at the book's climax, rejects both the goddess and immortality as did Odysseus?

Anna is Graves' White Goddess, the triple deity of birth, life and death, as her name and color symbolism, white, red, and black, indicate. In his analysis of the goddess, Graves offers the opinion that "Anna" means "queen" or "Goddess-mother." She appears in Irish mythology as the Danaan goddess Ana or Anan, who had two aspects, one of which was the beneficent mother whose name came to symbolize "plenty." In Celtic myth, she is connected with the mid-summer fire festival. In her maleficent aspect, Ana is the leading person of the Fate Trinity, Ana, Badb, and Macha, together known as the Morrigan or Great Queen, a death goddess. Other forms of the name appear in various mythologies and can be traced back to the Sumerian goddess, Inanna, c. 2000 B. C. Graves concludes: ". . . if one needs a single, simple, inclusive name for the Great Goddess, Anna is the best choice" (p. 372). Earlier in his book Graves notes: "I write of her as the White Goddess because white is her principal colour, the colour of the first member of her moon-trinity, . . . the New Moon is the white goddess of birth and growth; the Full Moon, the red goddess of love and battle; the Old Moon, the black goddess of death and divinations" (p. 70).

In addition to suggesting that Anna is an aspect of the White Goddess, Miss Farmer draws on the Fourth Branch of the *Mabinogion*, the story of "Math, Son of Mathonwy," in which the goddess appears under two aspects, Arianrhod and Bloudeuwedd. The second part of that tale relates how Gwydion, son of Don, tricked Arianrhod into naming and arming a son she did not wish to acknowledge. In attempting to circumvent her vow that the boy, Llew Llaw Gyffes, "shall never have a wife of the race that is now on this earth," Gwydion and Math, the High King, by magic and enchantment, conjure a wife for Llew Llaw Gyffes out of flowers and call her Bloudeuwedd. She ultimately betrays him to her lover, Gronw Pebyr, but at the end of the tale, Llew Llaw Gyffes is restored to human form and healed by Gwydion. In revenge, he turns the faithless Bloudeuwedd into an owl and slays Gronw Pebyr to regain his kingdom. Hugh would seem to be either Gwydion, son of Don, or perhaps Gronw Pebyr. Graves states that Gwydion and Gronw share a kind of twinship with Llew Llaw Gyffes and that together they are year king and tanist [successor].

Trees provide major symbols throughout the book, the most significant being the apple tree. Hugh is told that his cupboard is made of the wood of *the* apple tree and is asked if he knows what *that* signifies. Later Hugh connects the apple with King Arthur, Avalon, and immortality. In the final trip to the castle, when the four young people enter the applewood cupboard, they find the castle surrounded by an orchard of apple trees laid out in a triangular pattern representing a five-pointed star, the emblem of immortality. In *The White Goddess*, Graves devotes two chapters (pp. 165-204) to a discussion of the Celtic tree alphabets and calendars, including extensive discussion of the trees Miss Farmer employs in her fantasy sequences—alder, willow, birch, holly, ash, oak, and finally, apple. Of all the trees, the apple was considered the noblest, being the tree of immortality (p. 253).

Though at times Miss Farmer's fantasy seems the product of Hugh's rampant paranoia, her book is in fact carefully structured to develop her theme, the adolescent's first intimations of mortality. Immortality is balanced against mortality; the irrational is contrasted with the rational. Hugh is a boy in the throes of adolescence. His legs are inconveniently long; Anna's presence irritates him, but it makes him aware of "a beautiful sense of growing out of himself." His relationship with his mother is compared to two loose ends of a charged wire, an effective simile in describing the tensions which exist between parent and teenage child.

Miss Farmer details Hugh's rite of passage through her second major symbol, the castle of bone, an image borrowed from a Welsh triad. The castle is a potent mythological symbol. Speaking of various heroes, in *The White Goddess,* Graves says: "The castle that they entered—revolving, remote, royal, gloomy, lofty, cold, the abode of the Perfect Ones, with four corners, entered by a dark door on the shelving side of a hill—was the castle of death or the Tomb, the Dark Tower to which Childe Roland came in the ballad" (p. 107). She claims that she herself was not aware of its full significance until the final chapters. In the story, the castle appears on such mundane objects as bone buttons, postage stamps, and at an army display, as well as in Hugh's fantasy world. As Hugh reaches the castle in his fantasy world, he realizes: "Walls had closed around . . . confining him, imprisoning him in the narrowest of castles; a castle of bone . . . But this castle of bone was himself." Spirit is imprisoned in flesh and bone and subject now to death.

It would seem that Hugh is given a choice between immortality and mortality when he enters the castle of bone, but which is the right choice, or whether he ever had any choice at all, seems to me ambiguous. Is immortality in this context a refusal to grow up, or does it stand for artistic immortality? Anna and Hugh discuss the possibilities of achieving immortality: "Anyone old could get into the cupboard and be made young again. They could grow old again and be made young again. They needn't ever die". . . . Anna observes that she wouldn't like immortality if it meant no change. Hugh adds that some people don't want to be immortal at all, alluding to Odysseus.

Early in the novel, in an evaluation which seems out of character for a young adolescent, Hugh says:

> It [the park] looked as unreal as elfland, a place to which men were enticed in fairy tales and from which they never returned—like Sir Orfeo, or Thomas the Rhymer—except that both those had returned at last . . . Not even time seemed real any more . . . Thomas and Sir Orfeo had left time as well as space when they went to fairyland, and now he and Penn and Jean and Anna were outside time too because what had happened could not belong to time, which was reality, or the reality they understood. . . .

In consulting the old man about restoring Penn to his rightful age, Hugh looks from the baby to the old man and realizes: "Almost for the first time he could see a progression between birth and youth and age; not as unlinked stages . . . but as one steady progression from each stage to the next. That would be his own progression. He had never related it to himself before, or only vaguely, not with this total, piercing comprehension". . . .

In the fantasy castle of bone, Hugh stops Anna from making Penn immortal, but whether or not it was what Hugh truly wanted, he did not know. He realizes, however, that his choice has imprisoned him in a castle of bone, his mortal self. One last dialogue between Hugh and Anna again expresses Hugh's uncertainty that he has chosen properly. Hugh recalls for the second time the myth of Calypso and states again that Odysseus refused the gift of immortality she offered him, preferring a natural life. Anna points out that Penn didn't object and asks, "Do you wish you hadn't then?" Hugh only answers: "What else could I have done?". . . .

In the closing pages of the book, Hugh removes the traces of the things the cupboard, no longer magic, has changed. Each item gives him pain, a sense of loss, but it is a fading progression, a lessening of pain. He does not like this and tries to reanimate the feeling, but to no avail. He cannot feel the loss of magic because, almost, he does not believe in it any more. An estrangement grows between Penn and Anna and Hugh. The old man's warning—"You must destroy something"—comes to mind. But the reader is left to decide just what has been destroyed.

*A Castle of Bone* is a striking example of a growing trend in children's time fantasy toward introspection and personal symbolism based on psychological compulsion. Garner's *The Owl Service* and *Red Shift,* William Mayne's *A Game of Dark,* and Miss Farmer's work all suggest an "otherworld" which is an interior landscape of the mind rather than some other time or place in our world or "elfland." With their protagonists often teetering on the brink of psychosis, the novels produce neither the joy of the happy ending nor a tragic catharsis for the reader.

Great emphasis has been put recently on the psychological value of the folk fairy tale, but Miss Farmer herself points out the difference between these fairy tales and the type of fantasy she writes [see excerpt above in the Author's Commentary which precedes General Commentary]. Fairy tales arouse fear, uncertainty, or joy in a fairly ritualistic way; they resolve themselves neatly. Virtue triumphs. Even overt sadism found in many folk fairy tales doesn't worry children too much. Miss Farmer states: "What might disturb them is being shown, if only subconsciously, that all is not straightforward in the adult world; that growing up solves nothing, but merely introduces more intractable problems, more moral subtleties, and endless emotional shades of grey. This unresolved, unfocused fear and anxiety . . . is too complex for a child to face."

This seems to me exactly why *A Castle of Bone* is unsuitable for children, though it is intellectually stimulating for an adult reader who brings to it the necessary experience or who enjoys hunting out its mythological sources. For the child reader, the novel starts off with a promising burst of action—turning a purse back into a sow's ear (and all the rest of the animal as well). The child does not need to know that the white sow represents Cerridwen, a form of the triple goddess, but he does require a strong narrative. He is denied this as the story bounces back and forth between Hugh's fantasy journeys, which make no sense, and the minimally interesting interaction among the four adolescents. The cryptic conversation with the old man, the baffling climax in the castle, and the equally obscure conclusion further weaken the story. The resolution of the plot, which Miss Farmer describes as "a kind of dissociation," has exactly the effect she admits may be really disturbing to the child. There is no resolution. One is left wondering about Hugh's choice, not even sure he really had one.

In his essay, "Penelope Farmer's Novels" [see excerpt above in General Commentary, 1975], Hugh Crago gets to the heart of the problem when he remarks: "It seems to me that in her attempt to evolve increasingly towards a sophistication both of form and content the author has reached a point where sophistication becomes counter-productive." In exchanging the world-creating fantasy of external action with its victory of good over evil for the internalized psychological journey which has no clear resolution, are she and others leading fantasy into a cul-de-sac?

Miss Farmer herself seems fully aware of the dangers implicit in the type of fantasy she is attempting. In **"Discovering the Pattern"** . . . , she admits: "Perception of all kinds tends to become, perhaps dangerously, less a process of appreciation than a kind of personal decoding of symbols and ideas. And what effect does that have on writing, on discovery and creation of form? Is it ultimately destructive? Or does it lead on toward new tunnels, areas of darkness with new hidden patternings to sense and to explore?"

That indeed is a key question for all who are interested in fantasy literature. (pp. 174-78)

> *Margaret P. Esmonde, "Narrative Methods in Penelope Farmer's 'A Castle of Bone'," in* Children's literature in education, *Vol. 14, No. 3 (Autumn), 1983, pp. 171-79.*

---

### THE STORY OF PERSEPHONE  (1972)

[Here is a book which] stresses the awesome side of myth without forgetting its relevance to human behaviour. Penelope Farmer writes in a spare, precise prose that makes scenes and situations compelling. . . . This book could only deepen a child's understanding of that quality in myth that has kept it alive over the centuries.

> *Margery Fisher, in a review of "The Story of Persephone," in her* Growing Point, *Vol. 11, No. 7, January, 1973, p. 2093.*

Penelope Farmer tells the story of Persephone's capture by Haded, Demeter's search for her daughter, almost explaining the Ice Age, and finally the compromise by Zeus which led to the seasons, with simplicity, clarity and purity. This last may sound an odd word but it is the key to the book. I think it would be an excellent introduction for the six to eight-year-old, or perhaps even the older but less able reader, to the subject of Greek mythology. Some explanation of the background may be necessary for the very young. (pp. 23-4)

> *A review of "The Story of Persephone," in* The Junior Bookshelf, *Vol. 37, No. 1, February, 1973, pp. 23-4.*

Farmer asks us to take Persephone's story very seriously but what she takes seriously is her own ponderous prose, which sometimes imposes annoying delays on the action and often lapses into heavy cliche ("Then the torn earth heaved itself," and later, when Persephone is visited in Hades by her mother, "The hand she gave Demeter felt as cold, as unyielding, as

ice"). (Another casualty of her making too much of things is the mother-daughter relationship, which she magnifies into something overtly unhealthy, with no acknowledgment of the problem; the two are "more like lovers" than like mother and daughter. . . .)

Far better the genuine stateliness of Proddow's prose . . . [in the] 1972 *Demeter and Persephone.*

> *A review of "The Story of Persephone," in* Kirkus Reviews, *Vol. XLI, No. 19, October 1, 1973, p. 1099.*

Farmer's retelling takes the myth seriously, and though her prose is not so smooth as Proddow's lyrical translation in *Demeter and Persephone* . . . , it is several cuts above Tomaino's *Persephone; bringer of spring.* . . . Here the myth takes on a dark, foreboding quality. . . . An unusual, unsweetened interpretation and an interesting contrast to the Proddow version.

> *A review of "The Story of Persephone," in* The Booklist, *Vol. 70, No. 13, March 1, 1974, p. 740.*

[The] sophistication of the writing [gives] this retelling . . . more impact than Margaret Hodges' *Persephone and the Springtime;* while it is for slightly more mature readers than the audience for Sarah Tomaino's *Persephone: Bringer of Spring,* Farmer's style may pose difficulties for some readers. Compare her description of Hades: ". . . he, too, fell passionately in love. Obsessed by Persephone, determined to have her, he watched continually, invisible. A black rock, a hawthorn tree, a cloud on the hillside," with Tomaino's simpler presentation, in which Hades simply appears and sweeps Persephone into his chariot, or with Penelope Proddow's poetic brevity in *Demeter and Persephone.* . . . Farmer devotes more attention to the involvement of the Olympian dwellers than do the others, and the often-lyric prose contributes also to achieving more of a sense of majesty than is found in the other versions.

> *Zena Sutherland, in a review of "The Story of Persephone," in* Bulletin of the Center for Children's Books, *Vol. 27, No. 11, July-August, 1974, p. 175.*

---

### WILLIAM AND MARY: A STORY  (1974)

Readers who remember **"A Castle of Bone"** will look forward to this new fantasy from the English writer. Mary's father is headmaster at a boys' school, and she is usually the only girl in a boys' world. During the holidays, William, a boy as cool and poised as Mary is gruff and uncertain, befriends her and shares with her the secret of his magic shell, which can whisk them into any picture—a painting, photo or one of their own drawings. During their adventures the two children draw together and also learn something of themselves. This is an awfully uneven book. At times it's inspired—the children's first trip into a daft Atlantis is equal to the very best of P. L. Travers, and other episodes are fine, too. But there's something unfinished about it: Mary, in particular, is a character who seems far too complex for her role. One leaves the novel feeling that the author grew suddenly bored and thus left a fine character and a delicate situation dangling.

> *A review of "William and Mary," in* Publishers Weekly, *Vol. 206, No. 9, August 26, 1974, p. 306.*

[*William and Mary: A Story*] skillfully mingles and integrates elements of fantasy and realism, of characterization and smooth-flowing narrative. . . . [Finding] the other half-shell becomes a simple but powerful symbol of William's reunion with his parents and of Mary's growing sensitivity to the people in her circumscribed world. Even the minor characters in the story are superbly drawn: Miss Pitt, the dyspeptic school secretary, who constantly refers to her niece in Australia; Mr. Penny, the school cook, who was an ex-naval chef; and Mrs. Trent, "a rather down-at-heel and faintly grubby old woman with sagging clothes and straight grey hair." The shift between realism and fantasy is smoothly accomplished; for William and Mary are always immediately able to adjust themselves to unbelievable circumstances. The language is rich with the feeling of the concreteness of things: The shells "were more exotic than William's shell, yet somehow less interesting. There were huge, pale spiky ones, smoother, shinier, freckled ones, the open sides rather like mouths without faces Mary thought, because their curling upper lips were lined with indentations like little teeth." (pp. 690-91)

> *Paul Heins, in a review of "William and Mary: A Story," in* The Horn Book Magazine, *Vol. L, No. 6, December, 1974, pp. 690-91.*

Miss Farmer's writing is, as always, highly original and imaginative, and the worlds which she creates in this her latest story are sparkling and imminently close, bringing with them the iridescence and fluidity of water, which becomes a reflection and revelation of the tone and movement of life itself. Her characterisation is deft and sure and one factor which helps to link the everyday with the fantasy world until they both become as one, intermingling and overlapping "as if reality was intermittent or even not more real than unreal", as Lucy M. Boston said in one of her books. Indeed the two authors have much in common—an awareness of deeper truths that lie below the surface of life and which can only be expressed by probing sharply into thought and feeling until something of the complexity of life in its fullness is seared apart. This is not always a happy process but fantasy is a combination of wonder and fear, and so is life. Mary and William have to face both, and in doing so grow in self knowledge and wisdom. The writing has all the rippling variety and nuance of language which bring the seen and unseen into enveloping proximity until the reader too becomes aware of a wider, more exciting, and turbulent world. A simple story of a search transformed into a universal theme that impinges on, and stirs the heart and mind of each one of us.

> *A review of "William and Mary," in* The Junior Bookshelf, *Vol. 38, No. 6, December, 1974, p. 361.*

Less complex and terrifying than some of Penelope Farmer's novels (notably *Castle of Bone*, . . .) *William and Mary* is nevertheless attractive reading. . . . The imagery is powerful, the prose poetic, the dialogue between William and Mary themselves and the strange characters they meet, perfectly pitched.

> *Elaine Moss, "Fiction 2, Stories for 8-11 Year Olds: 'William and Mary'," in* Children's Books of the Year: 1974, *edited by Elaine Moss, Hamish Hamilton, 1975, p. 50.*

Like that remarkable early work, *The Summer Birds*, *William and Mary* seems in some ways like the extended image in a poem. The immediate subject—the effect on William of his parents' separation—seems curiously separate from the main theme, the sensuous and precise exploration of a certain element. Everything seems to happen under water; even the first vision of Atlantis hardly seems to be on land, for the movements of the terrified people are almost aquatic, and once

during the story dancing (the undulating kind of dance suitable for pop tunes) suggests an under-water scene. So, most strongly of all, does the dreamlike pace of the various explorations the children are empowered to make through the influence of the half-shell whose other part William is seeking. In the end the most deeply placed theme of all is seen to be (as in all Penelope Farmer's books, perhaps) the move out of childhood into a next stage which for want of a better word one must call adolescence; though "a move into new possibilities" is perhaps nearer to what the author intended to show in this very tender and searching story. Whatever setting she chooses for her books, she seems always to be looking for new artistic ways to explore the comical-tragical days and ways of childhood.

> *Margery Fisher, in a review of "William and Mary," in her* Growing Point, *Vol. 13, No. 7, January, 1975, p. 2556.*

[This is] an adroit blending of fantasy and realism. . . . Farmer excels in the dramatic composition of a book such as this: strongly defined characters, a sustaining theme, a convincing antiphonal structure of real-unreal, and, as background, a strong evocation of place.

> *Zena Sutherland, in a review of "William and Mary: A Story," in* Bulletin of the Center for Children's Books, *Vol. 28, No. 6, February, 1975, p. 93.*

---

### AUGUST THE FOURTH   (1975)

A tightly wrought story, told in retrospect, of the events in a single day—August 4, 1914. The story opens as a telegram arrives announcing that Meg's brother Robert has been killed in battle. With numb feelings, Meg recalls the day two years earlier when England declared war on Germany. The air seemed charged with electricity as older brothers rushed off with great bravado to enlist, as cheerful soldiers on troop trains passed by, and as her sister burst into tears over her tennis party being left in ruins. Meg's plans that day had been for a carefree bicycle and picnic outing with three friends. Flaunting instructions to be home early, the four enjoy the day fully expecting to be punished later. Upon arrival home they find, instead, parents preoccupied with the reality of war and unaware of the children's lengthy absence. Being shunted aside and ignored for the moment makes Meg realize that many changes will come into all their lives. Although the children's misdemeanor might seem insignificant in light of the freedom allowed today, Farmer's counterbalancing a simple incident of childhood against a crucial day in history is extraordinarily successful. (pp. 1404-05)

> *Barbara Elleman, in a review of "August the Fourth," in* The Booklist, *Vol. 72, No. 19, June 1, 1976, pp. 1404-05.*

The author's sense of realism encompasses the bickering friendliness of the children, the social stratification of the village, and the pleasantness of the countryside; but the undercurrent of momentous events is suggested by casual details: The village children accuse Mr. Rosen, the chemist, of being a spy; a trainload of soldiers goes by the level crossing. Meg's experiences are distilled in the irony of her seemingly naïve observations: "I'd still like to have one brother left, I think one medal's plenty for any family." (pp. 395-96)

> *Paul Heins, in a review of "August the Fourth," in* The Horn Book Magazine, *Vol. LII, No. 4, August, 1976, pp. 395-96.*

A wistful reminiscence. . . . [Farmer] paints a realistic picture of the period. . . . The story depends more on mood than action, and Farmer successfully communicates Meg's increasing realization of what war is really about. . . . Briticisms will be a problem so this will best be appreciated by skillful readers.

*Susan Lister, in a review of "August the Fourth," in* School Library Journal, *Vol. 23, No. 1, September, 1976, p. 132.*

---

## THE RUNAWAY TRAIN   (1980)

Penelope Farmer's story of *The Runaway Train* set in the not-so-long-ago of 1947 is a companion to [her 1977 book] *The Coal Train*. [*Fanny and the Battle of Potter's Piece* by Penelope Lively and *The Runaway Train*] are both competent books written to a successful formula [*Long Ago Children's Books*]. . . .

Characterisation is stronger in *The Runaway Train*. Rosie Dudd, daughter of the unstoppable driver of the excursion train, tells the story. She, however, is repeating what her friend Beryl told her about the outing when the train ran away. Thus Rosie's comments on her friend are cleverly superimposed on Beryl's interpretation of events.

Beryl is an attractive character, a forthright, plump girl who thinks one must be sharp to compensate—"if you are fat like me". The actual episode of the runaway train is less satisfactorily drawn and is anticlimactic.

*Sophie Last, "A Sharp Slap from Her Grandmother," in* The Times Educational Supplement, *No. 3349, August 22, 1980, p. 20.**

The atmosphere of the immediate post-war world and the excitement of train excursions are re-created in vivid detail, as is also the holiday pleasures of a day at the sea. . . .

[This is an] enjoyable little book.

*A review of "The Runaway Train," in* The Junior Bookshelf, *Vol. 44, No. 6, December, 1980, p. 290.*

# Gail (Gretchen) Gibbons

## 1944-

American author/illustrator and illustrator of nonfiction and fiction.

Gibbons is noted for creating clear, concise information books for children from preschool to fifth grade. Focusing on such familiar subjects as clocks, the postal service, and holidays, she carefully constructs works which are simple, yet full of interesting facts. Initially, Gibbons presented concepts within the framework of a fictional story. Her later works center on straight nonfiction, and are recognized for successfully explaining complicated ideas in an uncondescending manner.

While in college, Gibbons became interested in children's literature through the enthusiasm of her illustration instructor. Before pursuing a career as a children's book illustrator, she worked in television production as a graphic artist and as an illustrator and animator for the NBC-TV children's program "Take a Giant Step." Her first book, *Willy and His Wheel Wagon*, was prompted by a meeting with an editorial representative who suggested that she be author as well as artist for a story detailing the basic set theory of new math.

Critics applaud Gibbons's ability to combine her illustrations and texts into a digestible whole. Many of her works, however, receive mixed reviews. Critics often disapprove of Gibbons's unusual formats—such as the inclusion of jokes, puzzles, and other asides in books like *Things to Make and Do for Columbus Day*, *The Too-Great Bread Bake Book*, and *Paper, Paper Everywhere*—and suggest that she limit her presentations to the facts. Several critics complain that her prose is bland, stuffy, and overly cute, especially in her fiction. Reviewers defend Gibbons's writing by blaming the complexity of her subjects; many praise her explanations as precise and well-organized. Illustrations and diagrams are often considered strong points in her works. Gibbons uses brightly colored, attractive pictures to provide additional, often more technical information, thus complementing her texts and making it easier for children to comprehend the concepts being discussed. She is most successful in her works on mechanical functions (clocks, locks, tools) and public services (fire fighting, department store, post office), where she discusses specifics such as type, operation, and terminology while adding historical perspectives and unusual facts. Gibbons is appreciated for composing understandable introductions to often difficult subjects in works that entertain while they inform.

(See also *Something about the Author*, Vol. 23; *Contemporary Authors New Revision Series*, Vol. 12; and *Contemporary Authors*, Vols. 69-72.)

---

### WILLY AND HIS WHEEL WAGON (1975)

Willy, whose sole characteristic is that he loves wheels, builds a wheel wagon to house his collection. But then when all his friends ride up and request that he fix their broken . . . wheels or give them new ones, Willy cracks. He jumps into his wagon to hide, it rolls downhill, and he is only rescued from who-knows-what danger by the intervention of his friends on their assorted wheels. Gibbons has evidently decided near the end

*Photograph by Howard R. Search*

to make this a lesson in the value of friendship, but the three items which are enclosed in hearts on the last squiggly-lined page—wheels, wheel wagon and friends—never do mesh, let alone go anywhere.

> *A review of "Willy and His Wheel Wagon," in* Kirkus Reviews, *Vol. XLIII, No. 6, March 15, 1975, p. 300.*

Lavish illustrations are a recompense for thin stories, but some books fail on both counts. In **"Willy and His Wheel Wagon"** . . . Gail Gibbons introduces basic set theory, using as a vehicle Willy, whose passion is wheels. He collects them—in sets—and his friends trade with him for their nonfunctioning wheels. Finally everybody rolls along except Willy . . . and the reader, who has had a short, bumpy ride.

> *Alice Bach, in a review of "Willy and His Wheel Wagon," in* The New York Times Book Review, *May 4, 1975, p. 1818.*

---

### SALVADOR AND MISTER SAM: A GUIDE TO PARAKEET CARE (1975)

[Gibbons] dresses up the three-color cartoons with some oppy floor patterns and collage-like representations of old tablecloths, mantles, etc. By us, she might as well have done a straight manual—or left parakeet owners to look up the appropriate section in a bird book.

*A review of "Salvador and Mister Sam: A Guide to Parakeet Care," in* Kirkus Reviews, *Vol. XLIII, No. 22, November 15, 1975, p. 1291.*

This slim primer on parakeet care incorporates generalized information into a mild story that features young Sonia describing her friend Salvador's two parakeets Sidney and Sue. Sonia's running narrative tells about the birds' sex, behavior, mating habits, and feeding and housing needs. Salvador's pair mate, and when their offspring are old enough, Sonia chooses one for herself and teaches it to talk, surprising Salvador at the conclusion. Gibbons' glib, blunt prose flows surprisingly well after a coy beginning, and though the story device seems ultimately unnecessary, it does present the essentials.

*Denise M. Wilms, in a review of "Salvador and Mr. Sam: A Guide to Parakeet Care," in* The Booklist, *Vol. 72, No. 8, December 15, 1975, p. 578.*

[This] worse than useless offering is intended to get children interested in caring for, training, and following the development of their own pet parakeet. Unfortunately, the unbearably stodgy prose frustrates this objective. Even the bright blue, yellow, and green cartoon-like illustrations are too ordinary to provide a sufficient lure.

*Daisy Kouzel, in a review of "Salvador and Mister Sam: A Guide to Parakeet Care," in* School Library Journal, *Vol. 22, No. 5, January, 1976, p. 37.*

---

### THINGS TO MAKE AND DO FOR HALLOWEEN   (1976)

Still another holiday scrapbook, beginning with still another set of directions for making a paper bag mask, a witch's hat and a folded paper bat. . . . Done up in flashy, forgettable cartoons, it will go about as far as those prepacked loot bags supermarkets stock for the occasion. (pp. 129-30)

*A review of "Things to Make and Do for Halloween," in* Kirkus Reviews, *Vol. XLIV, No. 3, February 1, 1976, pp. 129-30.*

The first half of this book offers five simple if unoriginal Halloween craft projects. . . . A smattering of jokes, a one-paragraph story, visual puzzles, and the basics of planning a Halloween party complete the slim volume. The book's most commendable feature is its potential for giving readers a sense of accomplishment. Brightly colored illustrations lend a festive air; unfortunately, the juxtaposition of instructions and side comments occasionally breaks visual continuity, a bad feature for an easy reading book. Not a comprehensive craft project source; nevertheless, it could be rewarding for readers on their own.

*Judith Goldberger, in a review of "Things to Make and Do for Halloween," in* The Booklist, *Vol. 72, No. 14, March 15, 1976, p. 1052.*

This potpourri of Halloween ideas offers easy-to-follow instructions. . . . Youngsters will enjoy the colorful cartoon-like drawings which are visual reinforcements of the minimal text. Hardly unique but pleasant.

*Eileen Blumberg, in a review of "Things to Make and Do for Halloween," in* School Library Journal, *Vol. 22, No. 9, May, 1976, p. 50.*

A hodgepodge of Halloween activities plus a few moldy jokes. . . . The projects are all ordinary and can be found in many other sources, . . . and the cartoons of costumed kids, though humorous, are too busy for the intended audience.

*Lisa Landes, in a review of "Things to Make and Do for Halloween," in* School Library Journal, *Vol. 23, No. 5, January, 1977, p. 82.*

---

### THINGS TO MAKE AND DO FOR COLUMBUS DAY   (1977)

A compilation of craft ideas and diluted history that would find an appropriate home in the Sunday funnies. Readers are instructed on how to carve the *Niña, Pinta* and *Santa Maria* from soap, how to make a sea monster from a sock, and how to make a Columbus Day lunch from tuna fish. The comic book style illustrations are at the same low ebb as the text which includes some ancient riddles and incredibly dumb games. First through third graders deserve a better Columbus Day than this.

*Phyllis Ingram, in a review of "Things to Make and Do for Columbus Day," in* School Library Journal, *Vol. 24, No. 1, September, 1977, p. 107.*

Gail Gibbons has written and illustrated a "must" book . . . ! Here is the way she has organized history and activities: A few appropriate facts are given (such as, "Columbus took 90 men with him on the trip. They sailed in three boats. Pinta, Santa Maria, Nina.") followed by an activity (such as, "You can make your own Columbus Day boats." EXPLICIT directions ensue!) The book goes on with imaginative activities to couple with those fabulous Columbus adventures!

*Barbara Ann Kyle, in a review of "Things to Make and Do for Columbus Day!" in* The Babbling Bookworm *Vol. 5, No. 9, October, 1977, p. 2.*

Instructions are clear and easy to follow but the crafts and recipes will require some adult supervision. Some of the games are part of the book (double-page spread for a board game) which could lead to exhausted binding and worn-out pages. This should provide a lot of fun for an often neglected holiday.

*Elizabeth Monette, in a review of "Things to Make and Do for Columbus Day," in* Children's Book Review Service, *Vol. 6, No. 2, October, 1977, p. 15.*

---

### THINGS TO MAKE AND DO FOR YOUR BIRTHDAY   (1978)

Every primary-grade teacher knows how excited children become on their birthdays. To add a note of specialness to school-day birthdays, without disrupting regular lessons calls for skillful planning. Here is a book that offers many ways to celebrate that very special day.

By letting each birthday child borrow the book just before his day, he could pick the way he would most like to be honored and it might become a part of the class's planned learning activities.

Choices offered range from simple crafts to cooking activities especially aimed at junior chefs. Riddles, games, and jokes might be expanded to introduce a variety of reading or language arts projects. Just the act of borrowing the birthday book would give most youngsters a feeling of important recognition! Bright and lively illustrations are bound to inspire even the shiest celebrator.

> *Diane Crane, in a review of "Things to Make and Do for Your Birthday," in* Instructor, *Vol. LXXXVII, No. 9, April, 1978, p. 169.*

This book is a jumble of ideas in picture book format. The games suggested are too juvenile, while the piñata and finger puppet projects are too hard. If there's a demand for this type of thing, buy it; otherwise, let your craft and cookbook collections fill the need.

> *Nancy Bilbie, in a review of "Things to Make and Do for Your Birthday," in* Children's Book Review Service, *Vol. 6, No. 13, July, 1978, p. 124.*

This offers a meager selection of activities suggested for birthdays. The ideas . . . all appear elsewhere. Moreover, the cookie recipe calls for boiling molasses—far too dangerous for this age group. . . . [All] in all, a very slender return for the price of the book. Other better birthday and party books abound. . . .

> *Phyllis Ingram, in a review of "Things to Make and Do for Your Birthday," in* School Library Journal, *Vol. 25, No. 3, November, 1978, p. 62.*

---

### CLOCKS AND HOW THEY GO (1979)

Inside movements of the weight and spring clock seemingly tick into action with Gibbons' concisely worded text and clean line work over bold, contrasting colors. Use of orange, green, blue, and red against a pale blue background with arrows noting movement, for example, individualizes segments such as wheels, pendulums, pallet forks, and mainsprings and allows easy understanding of a clock's workings. The clear style will facilitate classroom use as an adjunct to lessons in telling time. A summary of clock parts appears in chart form at the book's conclusion.

> *Barbara Elleman, in a review of "Clocks and How They Go," in* Booklist, *Vol. 76, No. 5, November 1, 1979, p. 448.*

**"Clocks and How They Go"** has bright, bold pictures and a text intended for the very young reader. A 5-year-old may be able to digest it. First, it's perplexing to be told that "the old ways"—candles, sundials—"were a lot of trouble" and "not good enough." Then come descriptions on this order: "Below the pallet fork is a wheel called an escape wheel, with specially shaped teeth. The pallet fork, the escape wheel, and the pendulum together are called the escapement. The escape wheel turns with all the other wheels of the clock. As it turns, its teeth are stopped by the pallets on the pallet fork, first one pallet and then the other. The pallet fork tips one way and then the other way, and the pendulum swings back and forth."

No doubt. But the accompanying diagrams are unmarked, reference to the table on the last page is awkward, and to determine what the author means can be a frustrating experience. On the other hand, she often writes too simply. Her explanation of the digital clock is hardly adequate. (p. 31)

> *Nora Magid, in a review of "Clocks and How They Go," in* The New York Times Book Review, *November 18, 1979, pp. 31-2.*

Bold, straightforward illustrations in clear bright colors accompany simple explanations. . . . In the illustrations each part is color-coded so that their functions in different types of clocks are seen to be related. An admirable example of the kind of book that explains for the young reader how mechanical things work; it even tells why some clocks go "tick-tock" and others go "tick-tick-tick-tick-tick."

> *Ann A. Flowers, in a review of "Clocks and How They Go," in* The Horn Book Magazine, *Vol. LV, No. 6, December, 1979, p. 676.*

The explanation is difficult to follow, for on the one hand the workings are complicated, yet on the other, the explanation has been oversimplified, so the result is a straightforward account of the drum turning the main wheel turning the center wheel and so on—but the why and how questions remain unanswered. For instance, the balance wheel prevents the other wheels from unwinding too fast—but how? Gibbons has possibly done as good a job as can be done for this age group; the problem seems to be the complexity of the subject matter. (p. 32)

> *Christine E. Rowan, in a review of "Clocks and How They Go," in* Appraisal: Children's Science Books, *Vol. 13, No. 2, Spring, 1980, pp. 31-2.*

More than half of each page is a picture, either of one or more clocks or watches, or of the works that make them go. The written descriptions are brief but satisfying. Many parents will learn more about clocks than they ever dreamed. It is a very good book to arouse interest in the insides of clocks and watches; and to introduce children to simple mechanics. Parents! Beware! There well may be a bit of encouragement here for dissection. The results will be good for the child but not for the clock.

> *R. Gregory Belcher, in a review of "Clocks and How They Go," in* Appraisal: Children's Science Books, *Vol. 13, No. 2, Spring, 1980, p. 32.*

---

### THE MISSING MAPLE SYRUP SAP MYSTERY; OR, HOW MAPLE SYRUP IS MADE (1979)

Story and information combine painlessly in a lightweight, four-chapter picturebook "mystery." Its protagonists are Mr. and Mrs. Mapleworth, who enjoy tapping their maple grove in early spring but are shocked when their buckets turn up empty. They decide to camp nearby and catch the thief, who turns out to be their horse, Max. The rest of the story briefly shows how the collected sap is poured into an evaporator and boiled until it is syrup. A warm finale sees the Mapleworths happily indulging in syrup-laden pancakes and "sugar on snow." The pictures are lively, detailed pen-and-wash drawings that sit framed on the page. Some of the colors and shading techniques recall Mercer Mayer's work. Lines are loud but not harsh; the elderly, apple-cheeked Mapleworths project a cheery efficiency that's appealing.

> *Denise M. Wilms, in a review of "The Missing Maple Syrup Sap Mystery; or, How Maple Syrup Is Made," in* Booklist, *Vol. 76, No. 8, December 15, 1979, p. 611.*

Gibbons's decorative paintings convey the special feel of early spring in Vermont and also, unfortunately, her story's unregenerate archness. Cutesy Mr. and Mrs. Mapleworth take much too long to catch the thief. . . . As straight nonfiction, this book could have been an interesting, informative account of how New Englanders make syrup. As a quasi mystery and fact combination, the result is sappy in more ways than Gibbons had in mind.

> *A review of "The Missing Maple Syrup Sap Mystery; or, How Maple Syrup Is Made," in* Publishers Weekly, *Vol. 216, No. 25, December 24, 1979, p. 58.*

Gibbons has contrived a dull story to explain how maple syrup is made.... Alert readers will spot the couple's horse, Max, lurking behind the trees, and will pin down the culprit long before the Mapleworths do. The handy solution allows the author to return to the sugaring operation.... The washed ink illustrations are homey and cheerful. Unfortunately, they cannot carry the pedestrian—sometimes syrupy—text.

> *Janet Smith, in a review of "The Missing Maple Syrup Sap Mystery; or, How Maple Syrup Is Made," in* School Library Journal, *Vol. 26, No. 6, February, 1980, p. 45.*

Gibbons gets right to work with old Mr. and Mrs. Mapleworth tapping maple trees, and she keeps this going for a while with a little trumped-up mystery concerning empty sap buckets.... Gibbons reports that the book grew from her fascination with her Vermont neighbors' annual sugaring, and the procedure will probably interest readers too, though the story is thin and the folksy pictures of the cute old couple (amidst Anglund-like gnarled trees) are a bit too corny to charm.

> *A review of "The Missing Maple Syrup Sap Mystery," in* Kirkus Reviews, *Vol. XLVIII, No. 3, February 1, 1980, p. 121.*

Young children love a mystery and this book should appeal.... The lay-out on the page and the colours used do much to enhance the appeal of this story and older children could find the book instructive. In fact, they would probably wish that they lived in Vermont! A very attractive book.

> *Margaret Walker, in a review of "The Missing Maple Syrup Sap Mystery," in* Book Window, *Vol. 7, No. 2, Spring, 1980, p. 11.*

---

### THE TOO-GREAT BREAD BAKE BOOK  (1980)

Innovative additions to Gibbons's illustrations result in eye-arresting views of a country landscape and the interiors of Mr. Simon's store and Missy Tilly's homey cottage. The pictures, in soft tones of pink, brown and sepia, show Missy Tilly baking her great bread and explaining the functions of "yeastie beasties" as well as kneading the dough before she takes a nap. She dreams that the dough keeps growing and becomes a monster that threatens the village before she awakens, a part of the book that could be dispensed with, as could the reference to cutesy "yeastie beasties" and to Missy Tilly's "whining," out of character for the heroine. On the plus side, the text explains clearly how to make the mouth-watering loaf according to the recipe appended.

> *A review of "The Too-Great Bread Bake Book," in* Publishers Weekly, *Vol. 218, No. 5, August 1, 1980, p. 50.*

The cuteness throughout is overwhelming: ingredients are referred to as "goodies," and yeast is called "yeastie-beasties," over and over again. There is a possibility of humor when the dough rises out of control, but this idea is accomplished more

effectively in de Paola's *Strega Nona*.... The line drawings with two-tone brown wash are cluttered and cloying: for example, in Missy Tilly's house there lives a duck which has its own chair and four-poster bed. The bread recipe calls exclusively for whole wheat flour: this makes a very heavy loaf which does not rise much and is not considered delicious by everyone. Also, there is no warning about the danger of killing the yeast by adding liquid which is too hot. A more satisfying book for beginning bread bakers is *Let's Bake Bread* by Hannah Johnson (Lothrop, 1973). (pp. 61-2)

> *Carolyn K. Jenks, in a review of "The Too-Great Bread Bake Book," in* School Library Journal, *Vol. 27, No. 3, November, 1980, pp. 61-2.*

---

### LOCKS AND KEYS  (1980)

Gibbons, who so precisely demonstrated the inner workings of timepieces in **Clocks and How They Go** ..., turns her careful attention to another specialized subject for young readers. Using more text and a different artistic style here, she traces the history of locks and keys from early times (cavemen's boulders, Egyptians' first mechanical lock) to the present, describing the development of increasingly complex locks and how they operate. The workings of tumbler locks, Yale locks, padlocks, combination locks, and time locks are simply explained and clearly visualized in the gray-shaded line drawings accentuated with reds and blues. The mechanically minded youngster will soon be puttering on his own.

> *Barbara Elleman, in a review of "Locks & Keys," in* Booklist, *Vol. 77, No. 2, September 15, 1980, p. 114.*

[Beside **Clocks and How They Go**], with its brightly colored, boldly geometrical illustrations, the blurry, confusing quality of the three-color illustrations alternating with black-and-white pencil drawings of **Locks and Keys** are pale and ineffective. The text ... is brief yet lucid, thorough yet not too technical in its explanation. Based on the lack of information on this interesting subject for young readers ... and the clarity of the text, **Locks and Keys** is a reasonable purchase.

> *Connie Tyrrell, in a review of "Locks & Keys," in* School Library Journal, *Vol. 27, No. 2, October, 1980, p. 146.*

[This] is a generally colorless explanation, which could interest mechanically-minded kids simply by virtue of the subject matter.... The pictures help to demonstrate how each one works, but like the text they are plodding and uninspired.

> *A review of "Lock and Keys," in* Kirkus Reviews, *Vol. XLVIII, No. 19, October 1, 1980, p. 1301.*

[The author-artist of **Clocks and How They Go**] has once again skillfully combined a concise, clean text with explicit, attractive illustrations to acquaint young readers with a mechanical subject.... A two-page display of latches and bolts, locks and keys ends the book.

> *Karen Jameyson, in a review of "Locks & Keys," in* The Horn Book Magazine, *Vol. LVI, No. 6, December, 1980, p. 653.*

Using clear and somewhat whimsical line drawings, the author skillfully explains in simple language the historical development of locks and their mechanisms. Because these mechanisms are sometimes intricate, the young reader must make some effort to follow the straight-forward, step-by-step explanation and understand how a key can enter and selectively allow the bolt to be thrown. However, the student should be well rewarded in personal satisfaction in completing this short book.

> *David G. Hoag, in a review of "Locks and Keys," in Appraisal: Science Books for Young People, Vol. 14, No. 2, Spring, 1981, p. 18.*

It may be a bit hard for a child to visualize exactly how some of the locks described in this twenty-eight page book work, but I hope they will persevere, because the subject is a most interesting one. Perhaps a teacher or parent could help. The amusing, only fairly explicit drawings show the workings of various types of locks. . . . The book is deceptive—it looks like a picture book but it really is too hard for anyone under seven.

> *Heddie Kent, in a review of "Locks and Keys," in Appraisal: Science Books for Young People, Vol. 14, No. 2, Spring, 1981, p. 18.*

---

### THE MAGNIFICENT MORRIS MOUSE CLUBHOUSE (1981)

The animals are building a clubhouse, but Morris Mouse is excluded from helping because his long tail keeps knocking over ladders, paint buckets, and everything else. So Morris builds his own clubhouse and finds he can *use* his tail to measure, mark lines, raise ceiling beams, and so on. When a storm hits both houses, Morris' holds up better, and so he's enlisted to help the others rebuild theirs. The story holds up less well: Morris' switch from klutz to master builder is too sudden, the storm too convenient, and the whole too hastily erected.

> *A review of "The Magnificent Morris Mouse Clubhouse," in Kirkus Reviews, Vol. XLIX, No. 20, October 15, 1981, p. 1295.*

Some original ideas here, but nothing that animates the whole. . . . Gail Gibbons' ink-and-wash drawings are only mildly entertaining; even the slapstick bits don't come off very comically.

> *Nancy Palmer, in a review of "The Magnificent Morris Mouse Clubhouse," in School Library Journal, Vol. 28, No. 4, December, 1981, p. 76.*

Many children have habits or handicaps they think are in their way. They and others will empathize with Morris. This book offers a challenge beyond the very easy books. The illustrations show all the action and should help those who don't know all the words.

> *Annette C. Blank, in a review of "The Magnificent Morris Mouse Clubhouse," in Children's Book Review Service, Vol. 10, No. 6, Winter, 1982, p. 54.*

---

### TRUCKS (1981)

Pure, crisp color and tidy pen lines give this largely visual introduction to trucks a neat appearance that keeps the sometimes complex arrangement of shapes easy to decipher. There are few words. "Trucks go everywhere—" says the first page; "Delivering things," says the second, with "Moving heavy loads" on the subsequent double spread. Each named function comes with a picture sequence, sometimes a double spread, sometimes a boxed series of miniscenes, that shows the truck

accomplishing its work. It's a slick production, instructive, easy to follow, but with sufficient detail to keep the lesson effortlessly intact.

> *Denise M. Wilms, in a review of "Trucks," in Booklist, Vol. 78, No. 4, October 15, 1981, p. 304.*

Alongside Donald Crews' *Truck* (1980), totally flat as an evocation; alongside any number of other books (reaching back to *The Great Big Car and Truck Book*), extremely limited as a vehicle of information. We see assorted delivery trucks, for instance, each labeled; and then, opposite, small uncaptioned pictures (not always easy to make out) of things in them or being delivered from them. . . . The text is as banal as any very few words can be . . . ; the pictures clearly delineate each truck (they are also distinctly colored), so that a child could learn to recognize some of the more esoteric kinds (a power grapple, say, or a backhoe). But this has no more imagination or extension, really, than an aircraft-spotter's manual.

> *A review of "Trucks," in Kirkus Reviews, Vol. XLIX, No. 20, October 15, 1981, p. 1291.*

Clean-lined, precise drawings of brightly-colored trucks show the variety of functions they perform. . . . This serves its primary purpose very well, with drawings and captions combining to make it easy for children to identify types of trucks. Its minor weakness is that the drawings are crowded on some pages, creating awkward perspectives; its major strength is that some of the double spreads are paired: after the two pages that show five types of trucks that lift things, for example, there's a double-page spread in which the same trucks are shown (each in three small boxes of a cartoon-style ministrip) functioning, not labelled, but identifiable by function as well as by color.

> *Zena Sutherland, in a review of "Trucks," in Bulletin of the Center for Children's Books, Vol. 35, No. 3, November, 1981, p. 46.*

The bright, primary colors and crisp, precise, geometric lines of the illustrations make *Trucks* very appealing to the eye. The colored trucks are sharply defined and stand in contrast to the black-and-white illustrations of the background. . . . Often the trucks presented on one page are shown in smaller detail on the next to explain visually how they operate. The repetition helps clarify and is fun for the picture book group.

> *Connie Tyrrell, in a review of "Trucks," in School Library Journal, Vol. 28, No. 3, November, 1981, p. 75.*

---

### TOOL BOOK (1982)

An array of common tools—from a hammer to a coping saw—is displayed in a colorful picture book. A minimal text describes their use in general terms: "Some tools grip . . . and others make holes. Screwdrivers turn screws." Various tools—labeled in boldface type—are pictured to demonstrate each function; for instance, a shovel, a hand drill, and a brace and a bit are examples of tools that make holes. Set against areas of flat bright colors, the clean line drawings show clearly the shape and design of the hardware. As in *Clocks* and *Locks and Keys* . . . , the author-illustrator shows, in a simplified, visually appealing manner, how things work. Although the new book is comparable in attractiveness and format to Anne and Harlow Rockwell's *The Toolbox* (Macmillan), the tools shown are more numerous and complex, and the concepts more advanced. (pp. 154-55)

> *Kate M. Flanagan, in a review of "Tool Book," in* The Horn Book Magazine, *Vol. LVIII, No. 2, April, 1982, pp. 154-55.*

**Tool Book** is nothing more than a pictorial toolbox. Through the use of bright colors, impeccably neat layouts and a narrative of never more than a few words per page, we become acquainted with all kinds of tools, their functions and related uses. Cross sections of wood show how screws, nuts and nails do their jobs. Close-ups of hammers and drills have arrows to show how they work. . . . Gibbons' use of color is always as bright and as crisp as her line. Objects still have the same two-dimensional quality as seen in some of her previous books, but are not always confined to their colored backgrounds. Only the plaster trowel is difficult to recognize until it is shown in use.

> *Patricia Homer, in a review of "Tool Book," in* School Library Journal, *Vol. 28, No. 9, May, 1982, p. 52.*

A non-mechanical adult, wishing to share the **Tool Book** with a two to six year old, may be frightened by the first three pages! Because nothing is labelled or explained, just precisely and invitingly drawn like the book's jacket. But take heart, turn to page four and all will be revealed! . . . Although the pictures are completely simplistic, they are expressive and show clearly how each tool is used. The only slight confusion comes from a lack of shading in some cases (the chisel, for instance, and the sledge hammer) which makes the shape of the tool a bit hard to visualize. (p. 27)

> *Heddie Kent, in a review of "Tool Book," in* Appraisal: Science Books for Young People, *Vol. 16, No. 1, Winter, 1983, pp. 26-7.*

**Tools help us build.**

*From* Tool Book, *written and illustrated by Gail Gibbons. Holiday House, 1982. Copyright © 1982 by Gail Gibbons. All rights reserved. Reprinted by permission of Holiday House, Inc.*

Gibbons presents clear, attractive, and colorful drawings of common hand tools. . . . The illustrations show no people using the tools, so no sex bias is presented. Also, only U.S. common linear measurement units, not metric units, are included in the drawings of rulers and tapes. Young readers, however, should enjoy this book.

> *Richard J. Merrill, in a review of "Tool Book," in* Science Books, *Vol. 18, No. 3, January-February, 1983, p. 149.*

Precise drawings and bright colors distinguish this introduction. . . . Categorizing the items into their use for cutting, shaping, measuring and making holes imposes a fairly sophisticated concept of unity. . . . Should appeal to children two or three years older than the audience for Rockwell's *Toolbox.* A pleasure.

> *Kathleen R. Roedder, in a review of "Tool Book," in* Childhood Education, *Vol. 59, No. 4 (March, 1983), p. 281.*

---

### THE POST OFFICE BOOK: MAIL AND HOW IT MOVES   (1982)

Chiefly a mechanical recap, efficiently if uninvolvingly pictured, of how the post office department handles mail. . . . The step-by-step depiction of the original sorting has the interest of any closely described process, and the whole has utility as the only rundown of postal operations at this age level, but it's all generalized and impersonal to the point of resembling an official handout.

> *A review of "The Post Office Book: Mail and How It Moves," in* Kirkus Reviews, *Vol. L, No. 13, July 1, 1982, p. 730.*

Primary-grade units on the post office will surely benefit from this orderly, brisk description of the way the post office moves the mail. . . . Gibbons touches briefly on the history of mail delivery and traces the route of a letter from posting to delivery. Though young readers may need some adult explanation about the inset drawings, which tend to be confusingly placed, and are given no explanation as to why six of the zip codes on the U.S. map are in red (others are all shown in black), the text is generally informative and interestingly presented.

> *Barbara Elleman, in a review of "The Post Office Book: Mail and How It Moves," in* Booklist, *Vol. 79, No. 1, September 1, 1982, p. 42.*

The book is bright and cheerful, with its patriotic post office colors of red, white and blue and drawings of happy patrons and bustling, efficient workers. Text and pictures greatly simplify a complex operation and reveal the postal system to be most expeditious. Uh-huh. For this age group, however, stamp the book first class.

> *George A. Woods, in a review of "The Post Office Book: Mail and How It Moves," in* The New York Times Book Review, *September 26, 1982, p. 31.*

Because the illustrations are carefully designed to explain concepts, much information is conveyed with a minimum of text. Emphasis is placed on the kinds of detail which young children find particularly useful and fascinating—such as the scales for weighing items, various styles of mailboxes and, of course, trucks. The narrative's forthright tone complements the style of the pictures; the concluding page, labeled **"More Mail Facts"**

*From* The Post Office Book: Mail and How It Moves, *written and illustrated by Gail Gibbons. Thomas Y. Crowell Co., Inc., 1982. Copyright © 1982 by Gail Gibbons. All rights reserved. Reprinted by permission of Harper & Row, Publishers, Inc.*

and designed like an oversized postage stamp, adds an appropriate fillip to the appealing book.

> *Mary M. Burns, in a review of "The Post Office Book: Mail and How It Moves," in* The Horn Book Magazine, *Vol. LVIII, No. 5, October, 1982, p. 510.*

Another winner by Gail Gibbons, who has a wonderful ability to choose a daily occurrence or a familiar object, something adults take for granted but children are curious about, and succinctly make sense of it. . . . The crisp, precise illustrations . . . are appropriate and eye-catching. . . . A useful and attractive book for any child who has puzzled over mail delivery.

> *Connie Tyrrell, in a review of "The Post Office Book: Mail and How It Moves," in* School Library Journal, *Vol. 29, No. 3, November, 1982, p. 67.*

Red, white, blue, and grey are used in small-scale pictures with a minimum of clutter; some of the pictures are in cartoon-strip style. . . . Useful information, succinctly conveyed, this is a book that can also be used for reading aloud to younger children. The use of parallel lines to indicate dark skin is a bit disturbing; since the features are much the same for all the people depicted, there is no indication of an effort to show true racial diversity. (pp. 106-07)

> *Zena Sutherland, in a review of "The Post Office Book: Mail and How It Moves," in* Bulletin of the Center for Children's Books, *Vol. 36, No. 6, February, 1983, pp. 106-07.*

---

## CHRISTMAS TIME  (1982)

***Christmas Time*** covers secular and nonsecular aspects of Christmas—Jesus's birth, Santa Claus, and Christmas trees. Though the message of love, joy, and peace is unquestionably sound, and Gibbons's bright, bold illustrations appealing, the book's prose is choppy and the story does not flow.

> *Margo Showstack, in a review of "Christmas Time," in* Children's Book Review Service, *Vol. 11, No. 1, September, 1982, p. 6.*

It takes a great deal of talent to present the oftentimes conflicting values and traditions of Christmas to very young children. Gail Gibbons in ***Christmas Time*** offers a simple yet not condescending look at why and how we celebrate Christmas. . . . Even the secular tale of Saint Nicholas presents goodness and love, and Gibbons manages to maintain the theme of joy and peace at Christmas time. The bold, vibrant full-color drawings offer the perfect combination with the basic text to attract very young readers and listeners. If you are looking beyond a standard purchase, select this attractive picture book to reflect the real reason for the season. (p. 165)

*Peggy Forehand, "Top of the Tree," in* School Library Journal, *Vol. 29, No. 2, October, 1982, pp. 165-66.\**

Though some may find that the integration of Nativity and secular or family celebrations fragments the book, others will use it as a very young introduction to the many aspects of Christmas. Gibbons' strong colors and flat surfaces lend a folk-art nuance that matches the holiday tone.

*Barbara Elleman, in a review of "Christmas Time," in* Booklist, *Vol. 79, No. 3, October 1, 1982, p. 244.*

Holiday-bright hues spice the illustrations in Gibbons's simplified narrative, ideal for explaining the Nativity and the origins of Christmas observances to tiny boys and girls. Endearing lambs star in the introduction, describing the first Christmas, as recorded in the New Testament. . . . Grownups may find that some legends—honoring generous St. Nicholas—are news to them as well as to their children.

*A review of "Christmas Time," in* Publishers Weekly, *Vol. 222, No. 17, October 22, 1982, p. 56.*

---

## PAPER, PAPER EVERYWHERE (1983)

Gibbons's works have been honored as innovations that entertain and teach children about things encountered in daily life. This is on a par with her **"Tool Book," "Clocks and How They Go"** and other winners, with pictures in sunny colors showing boys and girls making multiple uses of paper. . . . Gibbons follows [examples of how paper is used] with explanations and more pictures detailing steps in manufacturing pa-

*From* Christmas Time, *written and illustrated by Gail Gibbons. Holiday House, 1982. Copyright © 1982 by Gail Gibbons. All rights reserved. Reprinted by permission of Holiday House, Inc.*

per. The author also gives children puzzles to solve in the pages, a zesty game represented by clues in flags on each page.

*A review of "Paper, Paper Everywhere," in* Publishers Weekly, *Vol. 223, No. 7, February 18, 1983, p. 129.*

Paper is an integral part of our lives. All the more reason for Gibbons' simple and interesting approach. The first section of this book for very young children is actually a gimmick—"a paper puzzler." Readers are expected to find all the paper products in a picture of a picnic, a birthday party, etc. Wordless answers can be found at the book's end. . . . The treatment is light and simple as are the illustrations featuring a collection of children accompanied by assorted animals. Illustrations and carefully delineated simplified diagrams are less vibrant than the author's other works. The inclusion of animals and children playing with paper is intended to supply visual humor and provide a light approach. Though this device seems unnecessary, the book as a whole works as a unique introduction for young children.

*Brenda Durrin Maloney, in a review of "Paper, Paper Everywhere," in* School Library Journal, *Vol. 29, No. 9, May, 1983, p. 61.*

Given as how paper is one of the most common, unmistakable substances around, it's not really much of a "puzzler" to identify paper objects. . . . The process [of making paper] is extraordinary, even when seen in real life—and it's a fair bet that no child of picture-book age, looking at these diagrammatic drawings, is going to comprehend what's happening. Does it make any particular sense to try to teach papermaking to small children this way, when it can be demonstrated, with a hand-held screen, so satisfactorily? Is there ever any reason to mix ersatz games with real learning?

*A review of "Paper, Paper Everywhere," in* Kirkus Reviews, *Vol. LI, No. 9, May 1, 1983, p. 526.*

---

## BOAT BOOK (1983)

[Gibbons] scores again with this volume, a collection of all sorts of seafaring craft. Minimal text and simple, clear drawings depict the busy doings on rivers, on seas and in harbors. Tots will be entertained as well as informed as they turn each color-splashed page, spying speedboats, sailboats, canoes, cruise ships, police and fire boats, and commercial and military vessels. Various means of propulsion (wind, oars and paddles, engine power) are explained, as are the uses of each type of boat. "Boats are fun to watch," concludes Gibbons, and so are those she's drawn in this **"Boat Book."**

*A review of "Boat Book," in* Publishers Weekly, *Vol. 223, No. 10, March 11, 1983, p. 86.*

[Like *Trucks,*] this is an illustrated catalogue; unlike *Trucks*, it isn't clearly bested by a Donald Crews' entry (Crews' *Harbor* has its own problems) and it does have a little shape, a little tempo, a little variety: some organized information, in short, and some signs of life. . . . We see various kinds of sailboats and motor boats, "boats that help us when there is trouble" (fireboats, police boats, Coast Guard boats), as well as the inevitable "boats that carry heavy loads." Moreover, there are sailboats racing, and speedboats racing—and they really do look it. (The Coast Guard boat is coming to rescue a woman with an overturned canoe.) So altogether this serves its purpose with a certain dash—even the colors have more character than Gibbons sometimes manages.

*A review of "Boat Book," in* Kirkus Reviews, *Vol. LI, No. 6, March 15, 1983, p. 304.*

Simple, one-line captions and labels are the extent of the information given, but that will be enough for littlest readers who can point out their favorites after paging through this several times. Once again, Gibbons uses simple shapes and flat Day-Glo colors to illustrate her subject, a tack that should appeal to her audience.

*Ilene Cooper, in a review of "Boat Book," in* Booklist, *Vol. 79, No. 19, June 1, 1983, p. 1276.*

It may be considered a regrettable coincidence that an excellent new book should appear barely seven months after one so similar in aim and in design—Anne Rockwell's *Boats* (Dutton). But in these days of visual mediocrity one should not decry some accidental repetition. . . . [The new book] does contain slightly more technical information and terminology . . . ; moreover, human figures are shown in functional roles in the carefully drafted, brilliantly colored drawings. Each of the books is inviting and handsomely done; surely there is room for both.

*Ethel L. Heins, in a review of "Boat Book," in* The Horn Book Magazine, *Vol. LIX, No. 4, August, 1983, p. 431.*

*Boat Book* is a fine example of a nonfiction book that will provide an engrossing and entertaining learning experience for preschoolers. The text, though stilted, is logically presented in a non-condescending manner. . . . Most of the illustrations are full page, and all of them are playfully bordered with a scalloped edge that resembles an ocean wave. Gibbons gives plenty of detail to pore over, yet retains a remarkably uncluttered look. Clarity and simplicity characterize this attractive book. (pp. 105-06)

*Lauralyn Levesque, in a review of "Boat Book," in* School Library Journal, *Vol. 30, No. 1, September, 1983, pp. 105-06.*

---

### *NEW ROAD!* (1983)

There's a chipper, Tinkertoy aspect to Gibbons' depiction of the road-building process that weighs strongly in its favor—and so do some interesting bits of information. It's even possible to think you know something about how a new road is planned (without really understanding any of the considerations); how the route is cleared and leveled (by removing dirt and rock from high places ''to fill in lower places''); and, close to actuality, how a roadbed is paved—because it is indeed a straightforward, mechanical process. Here, too, the pictures are good fun—as, from the same, mid-road vantage point, we see a final layer of asphalt spread, the paint truck marks the lanes, signs and lights are set in place, and grass and trees are planted. Environmentalists might not call the finished road ''beautiful''—but it is unmistakable, and children from the block-building age up can pretend they know how it was built. (pp. 168-69)

*A review of "New Road!" in* Kirkus Reviews, *Juvenile Issue, Vol. LI, Nos. 13-17, September 1, 1983, pp. 168-69.*

The crisp lines and bright poster colors of this road-building exposition are inviting. . . . The picture is comprehensive, with attention to details. . . . Because this is a picture book rather than a photo essay, as was Kehoe's *Road Closed* . . . , it will have built-in appeal for younger audiences. They'll find the information simply stated and never overwhelming—with the pictures providing as much information as the text. This author/artist is proving a master of picture-book nonfiction.

*Denise M. Wilms, in a review of "New Road!" in* Booklist, *Vol. 80, No. 4, October 15, 1983, p. 358.*

Fireboats . . .                                    police boats . . .

*From* Boat Book, *written and illustrated by Gail Gibbons. Holiday House, 1983. Copyright © 1983 by Gail Gibbons. All rights reserved. Reprinted by permission of Holiday House, Inc.*

This book is a stylized study of the process of making a high-way. . . . A fascinating addition is a briefly illustrated history of roads from the Roman stone slabs to the present-day concrete.

The book is simple in concept, yet accurately depicts the construction process. The clear writing style is enhanced by excellent explanations, a brief narrative, and the addition of specific terminology imposed on each page.

Intensely bold, the bright colors increase the sharpness of line and detail in this simplistic visual interpretation. Although broadly generalized by design and geometric shapes, the illustrations surprisingly contain much detail to intrigue the readers.

> *Ronald A. Jobe, in a review of "New Road!" in* Language Arts, *Vol. 60, No. 8, November-December, 1983, p. 1019.*

Two pages of text and illustration integrate bibliographic data into the overall book design by depicting a plethora of traffic problems as prelude to the idea that "it's time to build a . . . NEW ROAD!" The various stages of highway construction . . . are then carefully explained through a series of bright, posterlike drawings accompanied by a concise, uncondescending narrative. Technical terms, such as names for equipment, materials, or processes, are inserted unobtrusively within the illustrations—a technique that permits instant identification and avoids cumbersome description. The colorful, stylized landscapes are aesthetically appealing; the human figures, while varied, are prototypes rather than individuals so that they do not distract from the book's primary focus. Changes in page design, size, and placement of drawings and an occasional use of diagrams or maps provide interest as well as information. . . . [The historical description of highway building techniques] is an added bonus and an imaginative conclusion for a book as vigorous as its subject. (pp. 724-25)

> *Mary M. Burns, in a review of "New Road!" in* The Horn Book Magazine, *Vol. LIX, No. 6, December, 1983, pp. 724-25.*

---

## THANKSGIVING DAY (1983)

Bright paintings, simply composed and with large blocks of unrelieved color, illustrate a text that is equally simple, if a bit flat, in writing style. It describes the advent of the first settlers in New England (although it omits some of the story) and how they celebrated, with the Indian friends who had helped them, their first harvest. The remainder of the book describes how we celebrate the holiday today. Not unusual in coverage or outstanding for its visual impact, this is an adequate first book on Thanksgiving.

> *Zena Sutherland, in a review of "Thanksgiving Day," in* Bulletin of the Center for Children's Books, *Vol. 37, No. 2, October, 1983, p. 27.*

The colorful illustrations are captivating; the minimal text lacks sparkle though it does accurately detail holiday customs and history. However, the pictures more than make up for the unexciting text, making this a good purchase for those needing easy non-fiction holiday books. (pp. 12-13)

> *Maxine Kamin, in a review of "Thanksgiving Day," in* Children's Book Review Service, *Vol. 12, No. 2, October, 1983, pp. 12-13.*

Parents looking for a simple way to introduce Thanksgiving to young children will find this eminently suitable. As in her other books, Gibbons uses an easily worded text to explain a rather complex topic. . . . The neatly laid-out artwork is done in flat shapes and bright, festive colors (oranges, browns, yellows, and greens predominate), which children will enjoy paging through on their own when there is no reader about. Because of its good-sized artwork and easy-to-understand information, this will do well in holiday programs or story hours. An adroit piece of work that should be given extra credit for making the difficult look easy.

> *Ilene Cooper, in a review of "Thanksgiving Day," in* Booklist, *Vol. 80, No. 4, October 15, 1983, p. 358.*

A good book about Thanksgiving for young readers would certainly be something for which to give thanks, but Gibbons doesn't come close with **Thanksgiving Day.** Opening with the erroneous statement, "Thanksgiving is celebrated on the last Thursday of November" (the holiday actually falls on the fourth Thursday of the month), Gibbons describes the first Thanksgiving and how the holiday is celebrated today. While the text is simple—no more than three lines of text per page—the writing is static and uninspired. Her description of the Pilgrims' journey and first winter, though bland, is clear enough for young children to understand, but at other times her simplification leads to confusion: her concluding statement, "On Thanksgiving Day there is much to be thankful for," follows references to decorations, food, games and parades. No mention is made of the sort of things for which children today might be thankful, and they will probably miss the point of the holiday from this description. The illustrations—flat areas of intense color within black borders—show nearly identical cherubic faces on all the people. In spite of the difficulty of presenting this holiday to young people, and the paucity of available material for this age group, this is disappointing. (pp. 55-6)

> *David Gale, in a review of "Thanksgiving Day," in* School Library Journal, *Vol. 30, No. 4, December, 1983, pp. 55-6.*

---

## SUN UP, SUN DOWN (1983)

This is a strikingly colorful look at the sun's effect on the daily life of a little girl, told in first person. From the sun's first beam through her window in the morning to the dark night, the little girl focuses on the sun. She sees patterns (from the sun's beams through the window) on her floor; shades her eyes from looking at the sun and eats cereal made of wheat ("My dad tells me the sun made the wheat grow"). Most of the information provided is explained by the child, who has an understanding of seasons, the concept of east and west and a firm grasp of distance and other concepts related to facts about the sun. The significance of some statements may elude younger children but the basic ideas, i.e., the sun's warmth and its power to help plants grow, will come through. The illustrations clarify the text with bold, clear drawings in full color. Gibbons has created a picture book that is less fact oriented than Branley's The Sun: Our Nearest Star (Crowell, 1961) but **Sun Up, Sun Down** is a colorful introduction to the subject.

> *Sharron McElmeel, in a review of "Sun Up, Sun Down," in* School Library Journal, *Vol. 30, No. 5, January, 1984, p. 64.*

Gibbons, who has been so successful at explaining topics such as Thanksgiving and road building to primary-graders, takes on a more scientific subject here—the sun and its effect on the earth. She packs a surprising amount of information into the spare text, but there are a few instances where what's given is not enough. For example, the statement that the sun's "brightness colors the sky and clouds" is one that could well elicit the response, "How?" from young listeners. . . . [This] does cover a good bit of territory: what the sun does, what makes shadows, how the sun helps form rain clouds, and how it keeps the planet warm are included with explanations varying in detail. Gibbons's trademark flat shapes and poster colors are used to fine effect here in the larger-than-usual format. Add this one to primary-grade science shelves.

*Ilene Cooper, in a review of "Sun Up, Sun Down,"
in* Booklist, *Vol. 80, No. 9, January 1, 1984, p. 680.*

### DEPARTMENT STORE  (1984)

Gibbons has done a remarkable job of bringing order and organization to a complex topic: the people, departments, and "goings on" in a department store. Cartoon blurbs are juxtaposed with text and the colorful illustrations are detailed yet easy to follow. Only the hidden cameras and the shoplifter problem are omitted from this excellent presentation.

*Barbara S. Worth, in a review of "Department Store,"
in* Children's Book Review Service, *Vol. 12, No. 12,
Spring, 1984, p. 122.*

Although simply told, this is a rather thorough presentation of solid information especially suited to youngsters who shop with their parents but also serving to remind the adult reader of the complexity of running such an organization. The book can be of use both in and out of the classroom, especially for youngsters learning about community helpers and services. It is an excellent blend of text and illustration.

*Susan Roman, in a review of "Department Store,"
in* Booklist, *Vol. 80, No. 21, July, 1984, p. 1548.*

[This is an] attractive, informative book. . . . The last page gives a brief historical perspective of the department store. Throughout, bright illustrations in Gibbons' modern realistic style offer information visually; dialogue balloons reinforce the brief text that appears below the large pictures. Perfect for preparing primary classes for a trip to a department store, it will also be popular for story hours. Similar to, but more attractive than, *This Is a Department Store* (Follett, 1962; o.p.).

*Harriet Otto, in a review of "Department Store,"
in* School Library Journal, *Vol. 30, No. 10, August,
1984, p. 59.*

Illustrations with clean lines, almost garish colors, and tidy composition show the many departments, the store layout, and some of the special services of a department store. The text is direct and simple; some of the pictures use balloon captions to give additional information. For most children, the variety and bustle of a large store is interesting; this will give them some background to help them understand the complexity and diversity of a department store.

*Zena Sutherland, in a review of "Department Store,"
in* Bulletin of the Center for Children's Books, *Vol. 34,
No. 1, September, 1984, p. 5.*

### TUNNELS  (1984)

Gibbons looks at different kinds of tunnels, from the simplest varieties made by animals to complex, man-made structures. Using her familiar, neat layouts and bright, primary colors, Gibbons succinctly explains the four major types of tunnels constructed by humans: the rock tunnel, drilled and blasted through solid rock; the soft ground tunnel; the underwater tunnel; and the cut-and-cover tunnel, in which a trench is dug and covered with dirt. Brief captions describe how tunnels are dug, along with their many uses. While the details on the shapes of tunnels and several of the diagrams may be a little difficult for some children to understand, readers who are not ready for this information will simply turn the page. A well-conceived and -illustrated explanation.

*Ilene Cooper, in a review of "Tunnels," in* Booklist,
*Vol. 80, No. 16, April 15, 1984, p. 1189.*

With bright colors, simple layouts, and no more than one sentence per page, Gibbons gives a clear description of types of tunnels and their functions. . . . An excellent and attractive concept book, great for young children who have ever wondered about man or animal-made tunnels.

*Anne F. Saidman, in a review of "Tunnels," in* Children's Book Review Service, *Vol. 12, No. 10, May,
1984, p. 101.*

The bold colors in Gibbons's admirably precise drawings and her clean, quickly grasped text combine to make an absorbing primer on tunnels for tiny children. . . . This fine presentation ranks with ***Tool Book, Boat Book*** and the author's other lauded works. (pp. 152-53)

*A review of "Tunnels," in* Publishers Weekly,
*Vol. 225, No. 20, May 18, 1984, pp. 152-53.*

Vibrantly colored illustrations indicate setting and size yet keep attention firmly on the concepts; the hard-hatted workers and the populace are similarly representative with just enough detail to suggest racial and sexual diversity. A final page of facts adds historical perspective.

*Nancy C. Hammond, in a review of "Tunnels," in*
The Horn Book Magazine, *Vol. LX, No. 3, June,
1984, p. 348.*

### FIRE! FIRE!  (1984)

Hurray for Gail Gibbons! She consistently comes up with colorful, factual and well presented books on topics of great interest to young children. . . . The pictures are too small for group viewing, but many items are clearly identified for solo enjoyment. Feminists will be pleased to see some women firefighters.

*Beverly Woods, in a review of "Fire! Fire!" in* Children's Book Review Service, *Vol. 13, No. 1, September, 1984, p. 2.*

In a refreshing change from the usual fireman books, Gibbons explores different types of fires (in the city, in the country, in the forest and on the waterfront) and the firefighters' approach to them. She uses bright colors and simplified diagrams to convey the excitement and teamwork necessary in fire-fighting. There are details for children to pore over and the equipment in the illustrations is clearly labeled. Charts at the end of the book show other fire-fighting equipment, ways to prevent fires and how to deal with a fire. Although the illustrations are not big enough to share with large groups, smaller groups of young children will enjoy listening to this book while examining the illustrations, and older children will find that the text is not condescending. Unforgiveably, though, one of the illustrations shows a man calling the fire department from his burning apartment, while the fire safety tips state that one should leave the building and call from outside. Still, this is colorful and informative and will be a welcome addition in most collections.

> *Diane Pozar, in a review of "Fire! Fire!" in* School Library Journal, *Vol. 31, No. 1, September, 1984, p. 102.*

The big, big plus of Gibbons' report on firefighting is its coverage not only of familiar city procedures, but also of how volunteers respond and operate in the country—and, for special interests, how fires are fought in the forest and on the waterfront. In each instance, there's a *lot* of up-to-date detail for the picture-book format: the city fire first sets off an apartment smoke-alarm; communications, organization, equipment all get attention; women-firefighters are visible; and the labeled pictures provide still further particulars. In the country the payoff is even greater—because most of us don't think about volunteers keeping their gear in their cars, or know where the water comes from. Like Gibbons' books generally, this one substitutes a semblance of movement and action for drama—but there is indeed vitality in the total, word-and-picture presentation of the information.

> *A review of "Fire! Fire!" in* Kirkus Reviews, *Juvenile Issue, Vol. LII, Nos. 10-17, September 1, 1984, p. 75.*

A concise text and clear, colorful pictures explain the different ways fires are fought. . . . [Information] comes through efficiently. . . . The only flaw is the occasional confusion between trucks and engines: it is the engines, rather than the trucks, which control the water pressure and push the water through the hoses.

> *Denise M. Wilms, in a review of "Fire! Fire!" in* Booklist, *Vol. 81, No. 3, October 1, 1984, p. 247.*

---

## HALLOWEEN (1984)

Though not as successful as some of her other books on holidays, Gibbons' Halloween book will still provide festive moments. Concise captions underscore the bold, splashy artwork, but at times the text is so brief it obfuscates meaning, especially in the short historical introduction. Each picture portrays a different aspect of Halloween tradition; there are drawings of jack-o'-lanterns (along with the legend that brought them into being), trick-or-treating, and Halloween parties and parades, all done in Gibbons' signature solid-shaped, bright-hued style. Although it is problematical whether this is the proper forum for Halloween safety tips, there is no mention of them. Despite its shortcomings, children will enjoy looking at this ebullient depiction of a favorite holiday, and librarians will find it handy to have on the shelves or to use in Halloween story hours.

> *Ilene Cooper, in a review of "Halloween," in* Booklist, *Vol. 81, No. 1, September 1, 1984, p. 64.*

The text is terse, the subject one in which most chidren will be interested, although there is little here that is not general knowledge, and there is no adequate explanation of the name of the holiday. The illustrations are bright and bold, with filled pages but no fussy details.

> *Zena Sutherland, in a review of "Halloween," in* Bulletin of the Center for Children's Books, *Vol. 38, No. 2, October, 1984, p. 25.*

Gibbons tells the history and customs of Halloween in one or two sentences below each full-page illustration in vibrant colors. Current practices such as trick-or-treating, parties and visiting "haunted" houses are shown in spirited scenes that convey the excitement children feel for this holiday. All of the familiar creatures children will expect to see are here—witches, ghosts, pumpkins and skeletons—and there's just enough information for them to understand the origins of this holiday and how the various traditions came about. For younger readers than Cass Sandak's *Halloween* (Watts, 1980) and with larger, more colorful illustrations than Joyce Kessel's *Halloween* (Carolrhoda, 1980), this will be welcome in any collection serving primary grade children. (pp. 107-08)

> *Candy Colborn, in a review of "Halloween," in* School Library Journal, *Vol. 31, No. 3, November, 1984, pp. 107-08.*

# Norman (Alfred William) Lindsay

## 1879-1969

Australian author/illustrator and illustrator of fiction and non-fiction, essayist, autobiographer, and editor.

One of Australia's best-known writers, Lindsay is certainly its most controversial. His adult novels focus on Australian subjects with humor and often biting satire, elements which also characterize Lindsay's most prominent work for children, *The Magic Pudding*. Considered Australia's finest contribution to juvenile literature as well as its first outstanding fantasy, *The Magic Pudding* is a rollicking, boisterous nonsense tale interspersed with witty verses, songs, and illustrations. Organized into chapters called "slices," it revolves around the adventures of Bunyip Bluegum, a koala bear who sets out to see the world. He meets Sam Sawnoff, the penguin, and Bill Barnacle, a sailor, who own Albert, the pudding. Albert is ill-tempered and sharp-tongued, but he is also capable of providing his owners with a magically constant supply of delicious meals. This quality makes him especially appealing to a sly pair of puddin' thieves, a possum and a wombat. The capturing and recapturing of the talking pudding prompts fast-paced action—daring hints of murder, kidnappings, slapstick fights, and a trial before a judge—while the dialogue's Australian colloquialisms supply local color. Lindsay pokes fun at hypocrisy, curiosity, and greed, romanticizes world wanderers, and flaunts authority and the law, all with musical-comedy verve. The book remains irresistible to this day, especially when read aloud. *The Flyaway Highway*, Lindsay's only other work for children, was never published in the United States and is largely unsuccessful with children and adults. Despite Lindsay's illustrations and use of Australian idiom, it is thought to lack the simplicity and universality of *The Magic Pudding*.

Lindsay was born and raised in the small mining town of Creswick, Victoria, in New South Wales. This community served as the model for Redheap, the setting for his adult semi-autobiographical trilogy about boyhood and post-adolescence: *Redheap, Saturdee,* and *Halfway to Anywhere*. The iconoclastic Lindsay appears to delight in shocking Victorian readers in these and all his works. He aligns himself with youngsters by expressing their views, their quarrels with the establishment, and their frank hedonism with vigorous wit and lively dialogue which is amply laced with Australian slang. Although *Redheap* was banned in Australia for its nineteen-year-old hero's dalliance with sex and drink, the book was warmly received in America as a hearty expression of youthful curiosity and rebellion under the title *Every Woman's Son*. *Saturdee*, about a Tom Sawyer-esque eleven-year-old, is praised with *Halfway to Anywhere* for Lindsay's understanding of childhood and youth. During his lifetime, Lindsay wrote over a dozen novels, produced a number of books on art, and also published essays, a collection of letters, his autobiography, and *Siren and Satyr: The Personal Philosophy of Norman Lindsay*. Better known for his gifts as an artist than as a writer, he began his career at sixteen, serving as free-lance illustrator and later as editor on various Melbourne papers until he joined the Sydney *Bulletin*, where he became chief cartoonist. A versatile craftsman, Lindsay worked with oil, watercolor, etching, lithography, wood-engraving, cement-molding, and model-ship building, but is

*Taken from the 1975 edition of* The Magic Pudding. *Reproduced by permission of Angus & Robertson (UK) Ltd. Publishers.*

most acclaimed for his pen drawings. He illustrated close to forty books by other authors, particularly such uninhibited writers as Casanova, Boccaccio, and Petronius. All of his creations, which range from the comical to the blasphemous, reflect his unconventional attitudes towards sex, religion, and art. Reacting against the sham and pretense he saw around him, Lindsay defied tradition and society by affirming life and freeing the human spirit. He suffered public denunciation from church and press as well as personal abuse, but survived both to become recognized for his genius. Lindsay remains best known today, however, for *The Magic Pudding* and a separate resulting volume, *Puddin' Poems, Being the Best of the Verse from "The Magic Pudding."*

Lindsay began writing his first children's book in response to a bet. When noted editor Bertram Stevens challenged that children would rather read about fairies than food, Lindsay created *The Magic Pudding* to prove otherwise. Critics immediately hailed the work an enormous success, referring to it consistently as Australia's *Alice in Wonderland*. They applaud Lindsay's prolific imagination and unique characters—the peripatetic poet, Bunyip, his pugnacious friends, and especially the irascible pudding, with his naughty tongue and insatiable lust to be devoured again and again. Critics also praise Lindsay's knack with verse, which they ascribe to the influence of Gilbert and Sullivan and the English ballad-opera, and delight in his outrageous freedom with language. They laud Lindsay's skills as an artist and book designer, noting the professional cartoonist's touch in his comic characters and the attractive arrangement of his pictures and text. Above all, reviewers commend Lindsay's understanding of what children like to read. *The Magic Pudding* is criticized for the similarity and inferiority of its trial scene when compared to the one in *Alice;* a few critics also complain about the unnecessarily big words. However, Lindsay's reputation as the creator of a purely Australian fantasy remains undisputable. He is recognized for contributing Australia's only true classic to the world of juvenile literature as well as his country's first modern children's book. The fact that Lindsay continues to be read and enjoyed today attests to the success of his combination of magic, adventure, and animal comedy; the timelessness of his wise-cracking text, precise caricatures, and tongue-in-cheek laughter at human folly; and his remarkable affinity with children.

(See also *Contemporary Authors*, Vol. 102.)

---

GENERAL COMMENTARY

**COLIN RODERICK**

[With *The Magic Pudding*] Lindsay entered a field which it is to be regretted he has not more fully explored. It records the hilarious adventures of Bunyip Bluegum, [Bill Barnacle, and Sam Sawnoff]. . . . Their wit and ingenuity are capably employed in retaining possession of the magic pudding, which, in addition to qualities like those of Elijah's celebrated cruse of oil, possesses the power of speech. Children of all ages chuckle over this fantasy. One cannot but feel that the fertility of Lindsay's imagination, his insight into child psychology and his ability as an artist form a trinity capable of creating distinctively Australian work that would be equally as attractive to children as that of Walt Disney. (pp. 177-78)

[*The Flyaway Highway*] captures the child mind. Its recital of the adventures of the two children under the guidance of Silvander Dan—who significantly wears a beard and horns—disregards logic to the delight of the child. Runaway lovers, modern detectives and medieval monks are jumbled into a glorious pie that provides fare eminently suited to the palate of the eager youngster. (p. 179)

> Colin Roderick, "Norman Lindsay: 'Saturdee'," in his 20 Australian Novelists, Angus and Robertson, 1947, pp. 177-89.

**H. M. GREEN**

[The spirit of movement and adventure in *The Magic Pudding* and *The Flyaway Highway*] is accentuated by the fact that both of these tell of a road, along which the characters travel. *The Magic Pudding* is as much a classic in this kind as *Saturdee* is in another; the acquirement of the pudding . . . and the repeated contests between the pudding owners and the pudding thieves is shown with Lindsay's characteristically humorous extravaganzas of fancy and language. In Lindsay's second book it is the road itself that is magic, running through houses and everything and providing its own scenery . . . ; [a small boy and girl] travel along the magic road through various areas of legendary romance, independently of space and time. These two books are for both boys and girls. . . . (p. 1144)

> H. M. Green, "The Novel," in his A History of Australian Literature, Pure and Applied: 1923-1950, Vol. II, Angus and Robertson, 1961, pp. 1122-52.*

**JOHN HETHERINGTON**

It could be argued that "children's fiction" is a misapplied term of identification [for *The Magic Pudding* and *The Flyaway Highway*]. Each of them, and *The Magic Pudding* in particular, is read with no less pleasure by adults than by children; if a survey were practicable, it might well disclose that at any given time more adults than children are reading *The Magic Pudding*. (p. 46)

Both tales were illustrated by the author, and these illustrations are, in each instance, an integral and indispensable part of the work. It is valueless to attempt to explain why one book had, and continues to have, high success, while the other has made no impact worth mentioning. Perhaps the explanation lies in the simplicity of *The Magic Pudding,* alongside the relative complexity of *The Flyaway Highway*. Of *The Magic Pudding,* Norman Lindsay says: "Roughly stated the theme is eating and fighting, which is child psychology at its simplest." Those words probably hold the complete answer to the mystery of *The Magic Pudding*'s great, and enduring, popularity.

Any attempt to make a subtle analysis of *The Magic Pudding*'s theme would be doomed; one might as profitably try to define in words the charm of *Alice in Wonderland*. All that need be— or, for that matter, all that can be—said of *The Magic Pudding* is that it is a masterly example of story-telling, whether for the eyes and ears of adults or children. The narrative flows as naturally, as smoothly, as unaffectedly as a tale told by the fireside; its triumph is that nowhere is the reader aware of the craftsman who is telling the tale, but only of the tale itself. (pp. 46-7)

It is beyond doubt . . . that *The Magic Pudding* will outlive Norman Lindsay, and will outlive also the youngest child reading it today; for no circumstances are conceivable which could destroy or diminish its freshness, its originality, and its power to enchant. It is not only a wholly original tale, told with consummate skill, but, like *Alice in Wonderland*, an emanation of genius. (p. 47)

> *John Hetherington, in his* Norman Lindsay, *second edition, Lansdowne Press, 1962, 48 p.*

---

**THE MAGIC PUDDING: BEING THE ADVENTURES OF BUNYIP BLUEGUM AND HIS FRIENDS BILL BARNACLE AND SAM SAWNOFF** (1918)

AUTHOR'S COMMENTARY

> [*Lindsay was interviewed in 1961 by John Hetherington of the* Age *newspaper. The following is Lindsay's account of why he wrote* The Magic Pudding.]

For me there was only one flaw in the "Alice" books and that was that Alice got nothing to eat in them. On the event of that great dinner party, when Alice was introduced to the leg of mutton and on that proposed to carve it, she was not permitted to do so, on the understanding that it was bad manners to cut a friend one had been introduced to. In order to get in this feeble little grown-up joke, Carroll put a blight on the spiritual gastric juices of his little readers, all primed up to enjoy a gustacious dinner party with Alice.

If I may intrude here about my own modest contribution to literature for the young, that frustrated dinner party of Alice's had a good deal to do with it. Away back about the year 1915, I became involved in an argument about the best literary pabulum for young readers with a friend of that era, Bertram

Stevens. In his opinion, fairies constituted its major theme for subject matter. I contested that, on the infallible evidence of the infant belly, what sublimates a concept of bliss is nice things to eat, and I was ready to bet that if a kid was given a choice between fairies and food in typematter it would plump for food.

Shortly after that talk, I was sitting in my studio one evening, striving to combat a fit of depression over the infernal 1914 war, . . . and as a feeble device to escape thinking about it, that argument about Food versus Fairies recurred to me, and I started writing some nonsense verses about an inexhaustible pudding as literary nutriment for the young and that begot that little book, *The Magic Pudding*! (pp. 54-5)

> *Norman Lindsay, in an extract from "Children's Authors: Norman Lindsay," in* The Singing Roads: A Guide to Australian Children's Authors and Illustrators, Part I, *edited by Hugh Anderson, fourth edition, Wentworth Books, 1972, pp. 53-5.*

———————

Keep an eye on this book with its many uproarious drawings. Maybe its publication will turn out to be an Event. It is a nonsense story, genuine luscious nonsense, which every one used to books for children knows is the first thing a writer for them attempts and the last he is likely to bring off. This one turns the trick. It succeeds in being original in spite of a central situation impossible without "Alice in Wonderland" and a technique no one could have brought off who had not been brought up on Gilbert and Sullivan—indeed on English ballad-opera in general, as it has developed from Gay's masterpiece to this year's "The Two Bouquets" of the Farjeons. The story further runs true to form in being the work of a man whose reputation has been made in other fields . . .—who writes in this field for the sheer fun of it, letting his pen trot under power long stored up. . . .

A technique arising from a natural feeling for ballad-opera, especially of the Savoyard type, makes it the easiest and most natural thing in the world for characters to burst into song at any moment and on any page. This would ordinarily kill it for small boys, who shy from any page on which poetry interrupts the action, but these verses do not interrupt at all; they carry the story along as the lyrics of Buttercup or Bunthorne do. Strictly speaking, the story is carried along a trifle too far; a judicious pruning toward the close would have improved it. I doubt if a child will think so; he usually goes on the good principle that the more he gets of what he likes, the better.

The third feature that may keep the book alive past the probationary year for such productions is a trained and natural writer's feeling for words, and for finding zest in their humorous possibilities. Bunyip, being a solemn sort of koala bear, uses them as if addressing a meeting; the Kookaburra, being a low sort of larrikin, has a rich Australian vocabulary of invective; all the others—and Mr. Lindsay as an Australian can draw on some fancy fauna—speak each after his own kind, all funny. You can tell them apart whenever they speak, just as you can distinguish all the characters in the ancient saga of Amos and Andy.

In short, . . . this is a nonsense book that I think a child will like if he likes nonsense, and this means one that an intelligent adult may be grateful to get for his hours of ease.

> *May Lamberton Becker, in a review of "The Magic Pudding," in* New York Herald Tribune Books, *September 13, 1936, p. 9.*

[This] tale of the great war between the puddin' owners and the puddin' thieves is as rollicking a bit of nonsense as has been turned out since Gilbert and Sullivan parted company.

To Australian children the koala bear, the bandicoot and the wombat may be as familiar as Br'er Rabbit is to us, but on this side of the map the story takes on an added flavor of fantasy because of its animal characters with the incredible names. The saga starts with the departure from home of Bunyip Bluegum, a staid little koala, with the manner of a Junior Warden and a speech as sonorous as the Book of Common Prayer. Aimlessly wandering down the road he ran into Sam Sawnoff, the penguin, and Bill Barnacle the Sailor, owners of a pudding, and was promptly invited to lunch. It was a magic pudding, with a variety of flavors, ranging from steak and kidney to plum duff; a cut-and-come-again pudding, which never gave out no matter how many slices were cut. A thin-legged, crochety pudding, Albert's chief delight was in being eaten, and invariably after being retrieved from the puddin' thieves, he had insulting comparisons to make between the lean appetites of the owners and the gustatory powers of the thieves. . . .

This is the epic tale of the taking and retaking of the puddin', a contest of wits and fists and speech-making in which rules were laid down before the other side could think, and which had to be inexorably obeyed, a dodge which any child recognizes as part of the game.

It is a gusty, absurd saga, told in rolling, high-flown phrases, as quotable as "Pinafore." Its characters indulge in impassioned oratory at the drop of a pudding, and the next instant swing into ballads which combine the most rhythmical qualities of Kipling and Robert W. Service. Fortunately their most emotional moments have been faithfully preserved in pen and ink by their creator in drawings as daft and delightful as the text.

> *Ellen Lewis Buell, in a review of "The Magic Pudding," in* The New York Times Book Review, *September 13, 1936, p. 10.*

[*The Magic Pudding*] is definitely a funny book. To boys of eight, I believe it will be wildly amusing. That is not to say that its appeal is narrow, but rather that it exactly meets one particular demand.

The magic pudding is a real inspiration. . . .

The story is interspersed with some very slick and amusing rhymes which add to the really excellent entertainment which the whole book affords.

> *Eleanor Graham, in a review of "The Magic Pudding," in* The Junior Bookshelf, *Vol. 1, No. 1, November, 1936, p. 32.*

[Having unlimited pudding of every kind is] a state of affairs peculiarly satisfying to children. One wonders why the idea was not thought of before in this fashion. It seems obvious—but so, I suppose, a wheel does now.

For good measure there are the theft of the pudding and the devices to recover it. There are songs and poems and some of the best illustrations for children that have ever been printed. Each aspect has its appeal. Some children know slabs of the verse by heart. . . . The colloquial vulgarity of Sam and Bill's conversation is another infallible source of laughter. Such expressions as "Clout him on the snout" make children laugh out aloud.

It is too much to expect, of course, that all should be so good. The big words have no meaning for children and no particular humour for adults; and the court scene, so like that in *Alice*, suffers greatly by the comparison. But all in all the book is the best thing of its kind in Australia.

With so much of such different appeal, it is perhaps profitless to pick favourites. But even if the pictures as a whole are not the best thing, one picture is. It is the last in the book. There the three friends are seen at their ease in a house built on a tree-top, while Ben works in the garden below and the Pudding is kept safe in a small enclosure. It is a picture that fascinates children, who can pore over it endlessly, picking out fresh objects of noisy contemplation. And like good pictures it can be approached at different levels. The adult cannot but appreciate the considerable insight that went to its composition, to the selection of details calculated to appeal to the interest and curiosity of children. If the book were better known overseas, it would be acknowledged to rank among the tiny group of really successful children's books.

The book reveals a most unusual Lindsay, one that those who know him by his paintings and etchings would find it hard to credit. It may be, for all we know, the real Lindsay, and the paintings may be the cocking of a snook by the young at the old, the rigid, the spoilsport, the wowser. (pp. 67-8)

When [Lindsay] writes a book not about children but for children, he shows an imaginative and uncanny insight not into what children are but what children like. And if *The Magic Pudding* is not a novel, and if we can hardly call it literature, it turns out to be at any rate a little classic. (p. 68)

> C. H. Hadgraft, "Four Ages—Youth and Norman Lindsay," in Southerly, Vol. 12, No. 2, 1951, pp. 62-8.

[*The Magic Pudding*] is a splendid, racy, jovial Australian story which is, in fact, one simple expanded joke.... [The to-ing and fro-ing of the Puddin'] is magnificently varied, in a story that moves quick and sharp as the crack of a stockwhip, never overdoing a detail, never missing a chance for one more absurd variation on the theme. It is the simplicity that does the trick. (p. 154)

One word too many, and the joke might become tedious; but it never does.

This wonderful little story has in it both the types of humour that particularly appeal to children—the humour of situation (horseplay and accident) and verbal wit. The various stratagems of pudding-thieves and pudding-owners, illustrated in rollicking style, are introduced by absurd touches. When the friends come upon the thieves disguised by curious headgear, the Possum stumps them by remarking 'No removing people's hats. Removing hats is larceny, and you'll get six months for it.' Bunyip Bluegum's solution is to stand to attention and strike up God Save the King, whereupon the crooks are revealed. In the other vein, there are conversations in the height of lunatic vigour, like the one between Bill Barnacle and Henderson Hedgehog the deaf Horticulturist [about the singed possum].... Or, in a different idiom, the Kookaburra's rude comeback to the staring sailor, 'all I can say is that if yer don't take yer dial outer the road I'll bloomin' well take an' bounce a gibber off yer crust'.

*From* The Magic Pudding: Being the Adventures of Bunyip Bluegum and His Friends Bill Barnacle and Sam Sawnoff, *written and illustrated by Norman Lindsay. Angus and Robertson Publishers, 1918. Copyright Janet Glad, 1918. Reprinted with the permission of Angus & Robertson (UK) Ltd. Publishers.*

There are echoes of *Alice in Wonderland* all through this book, but its raw, violent, bustlingly energetic humour is unique. (pp. 155-56)

I would put *The Magic Pudding* on a level with *Alice* in its lively inventiveness.... (p. 167)

> Margery Fisher, "Climates of Humour," in her Intent Upon Reading: A Critical Appraisal of Modern Fiction for Children, 1961. Reprint by Franklin Watts, Inc., 1962, pp. 153-69.*

[*The Magic Pudding*] should, I feel, be widely appreciated on three different levels: first it is an hilarious book for children, fast-moving with many funny situations; second it is a fascinating and unusual animal story, comically drawn, featuring Australian animals which have been given human attributes not at all at variance with their personalities as animals; third and largely through the characters of these "animals" it is a brilliant satire on the Australian man and portrays various traits and qualities of the "typical Australian." (p. 28)

Albert—the pudding—appears generous in urging others to feed gluttonously upon him.... But he is not really a generous fellow. He simply has a mania to be eaten. Rather he is ill tempered, complaining, aggressive and envious. He does nothing out of kindness to, consideration of, or politeness for his owners.... (pp. 28-9)

Albert is the main character in the story and it is impossible to describe him adequately without the help of Norman Lindsay's illustrations.

Norman Lindsay was working as a cartoonist on a famous Australian newspaper, *The Bulletin,* when **The Magic Pudding** was first published in 1918. And his pudding does reflect many of the tricks and techniques that he and other "Bulletin" artists, journalists and poets used.

*The Bulletin,* according to Vance Palmer, was the "bushman's bible", "a sharpshooter dancing about on the fringes of society and firing squibs with gay malice", "its weapons were the pointed paragraph and the satirical drawing. . . ."

These, too, were Norman Lindsay's weapons and this is the tradition in which **The Magic Pudding** was created. (p. 29)

[Speaking of the book, Norman Lindsay said:]

> I had used the small bear as a journalistic asset for years, and it had become so popular that there was an incessant demand for it, so much so that I frequently cursed myself for ever having perpetrated it. All the same, I naturally slid into using it as the central character of that kid story. Within limits, it amused me to write it, especially experimenting with the nonsense verses which are not so easy to write as their simplicity would appear to suggest. . . .

**The Magic Pudding** is a "kid's book"—an hilarious, fast-moving story with all the ingredients to appeal to children. Lindsay's characters trot about the world with wonderful freedom, sometimes in retrospect, sometimes in imagination, and it is only in the **Last Slice** that they meet up with the forces (and restrictions) of the law.

The way in which they pull each other's noses, end up with their heads in bags, engage in a kind of "cops and robbers" game, are pursuers and pursued—whatever they do, their actions are comprehensible, amusing and always interesting.

The only really adult character in the story is Uncle Wattleberry, who is the cause of Bunyip Bluegum leaving home. He is the adult, the bewhiskered symbol of authority against which all young people would want to rebel.

He expresses his indignation in **Slice Three**, where that "sacrilegious whiskerplucker", Bill Barnacle, acts on the assumption that they are stuck with glue and hide the identity of a pudding stealer, in a dignified manner. . . . But his dignity soon collapses and the Uncle proceeds to bound and plunge in rage, shouting all the while in a thoroughly childish manner. . . . This bounding has probably been imitated by many children and not only is it extremely funny when an Uncle does it, but understandable too. (pp. 29-30)

[Australian poet and playwright Douglas Stewart has said:] "I am suspicious of Norman Lindsay's uncles. He seems to regard the very word as instantly and automatically funny. . . . Norman Lindsay's are small, mean, decrepit uncles. They have red noses. . . ." And his animal characters—they are comically drawn but never sentimentalized. Certainly they behave like humans and somehow each animal's behavior seems altogether appropriate and just what one would expect of him if he did magically become human. Each is a thoroughly acceptable character with actions comically and aptly justified in verse and illustration. . . .

[There's] Finglebury, the Flying Fox, the well-known and respected "fruit stealer"; Henderson the Hedgehog, the "horticulturist"; the "hooknosed, peevish" Parrot; the Rooster "the fine upstanding, bumptious skite, who loved to talk all day in

the heartiest manner, to total strangers, while their wives did the washing."

All these animals—the minor characters—are drawn as children see them, but their speeches and actions are essentially comic.

Then, at another level, there is the satire which gives the Australian parent reading **The Magic Pudding** to his children something more than the comic delights he is providing for them. Lindsay takes in the passing scene, analyses the social habits, customs and conventions, and pokes fun at us all. (p. 31)

[In] the **Second Slice** he introduces us, painlessly and hilariously (through the animals), to many human failings.

The pudding owners win the wonderful everlasting, ever-growing pudding back from the pudding stealers by the device of a potion that will make the pudding even larger—it is *greed* that loses the stealers the pudding just as it was *curiosity* which made the foolish owners surrender their much publicized caution and end up with their heads in a bag.

Then there is the much discussed "sense of humour" [scene at the breakfast table] and that very human failing of not being able to laugh at oneself. . . . (pp. 31-2)

All these are human failings in general but naturally enough Norman Lindsay was even more interested in firing his "squibs with gay malice" at Australians in particular.

When in the **First Slice** Bunyip Bluegum decides to take to the road we are asked to laugh at the Australian romanticizing of the "swaggie," the man who "humps his bluey" and wanders the world. And who but someone brought up on *The Bulletin* would go to a poet for advice? . . .

And Bill Barnacle: he is the typical Australian digger—energetic, courageous but with a chip on his shoulder. Full of mistrust, but never apologizing and ready to punch anyone on the snout, who argues with him.

In the last, the **Fourth Slice,** we laugh at authority, legality, all epitomized in the police and the judges. Although this last episode is rather reminiscent of Gilbert and Sullivan, (or, as some have claimed, of *Alice in Wonderland*) and may seem less original and funny than the other slices, it must be remembered that Australians tend to be anti-authority and particularly anti-police! There is something peculiarly Australian in the beating over the head with beer bottles. (p. 32)

To sum up. All these ingredients—children's fun, animal comedy, universal and Australian satire—have combined to put the magic into this pudding. They have been mixed together and beaten well with the cartoonist's skill in black and white, and the illustrator's clever use of colours. Add to all this the vitality and gusto of Norman Lindsay himself, his wonderful use of techniques in the telling—verse, narration and dialogue—and you have something exceptional in children's literature.

But like *Alice in Wonderland,* and *The Hobbit,* for example, **The Magic Pudding** is not an easy book for a child to read for himself. It is the sort of book that is best read aloud the first time, and then savoured quietly on one's own. (p. 33)

> *Marjorie Roe, "A Magic Pudding from Australia,"*
> in Bookbird, *Vol. VI, No. 3 (September 15, 1968), pp. 28-33.*

It was not until the last year of the first world war that a timeless Australian book for children was to appear. This is a book which has retained its appeal over the passing years, and is as fresh and as popular today as it was when it was first published in 1918—a book of magic and adventure, belonging to both children and adults—a ''rip-roaring'' expression of the author's own exuberant personality—Norman Lindsay's *The Magic Pudding*. (p. 106)

*The Magic Pudding* is a book to surprise the imagination, but its essence is difficult to distil. The title page gives a hint of its magic. . . . Lindsay's own sketch of the three friends appears underneath the title. In it he catches something of the book's gaiety, vigour, drollness and magic. Indeed, the author's illustrations for the whole book, mainly in black and white, but with a coloured wash here and there, are as much part of the story as his verses that punctuate the text. . . .

At its most obvious, . . . the story has the appeal of conflict and adventure. . . .

The constant clashes between the Puddin'-owners and the Puddin'-thieves assume epic proportions, the many battles being reported in mock-heroic style. . . . (p. 107)

On the surface the story moves realistically but within a framework of fantasy. . . .

[When Norman Lindsay] turned to children's books, he created the best fantasy in Australian writing for children.

In *Alice in Wonderland*, with which Lindsay's book is often compared, the fantasy is more in evidence than the realism. Here, as in another children's classic, *Mary Poppins* by P. L. Travers, the fantastic impinges upon the world of the possible.

Given the existence of ''the puddin''' itself and the unlikely friendship of the trio, the events of the book have their own internal logic. And that brings up the question of the puddin', and the lasting appeal of magic. Here is a puddin' that speaks and grumbles; is never diminished; and supplies meals of unlimited variety. It is exactly the blend of humour and magic that surrounds Mary Poppins' medicine bottle; the bottle from which she pours successive doses of strawberry ice, lime-juice cordial, milk and rum punch. In *Alice* there is similar humour and magic in the situations where the heroine finds cakes inscribed ''Eat me'', or bottles commanding, ''Drink me''. But, of all three, the puddin' makes the greatest appeal to the imagination, for it has a personality of its own. . . . What the three friends object to and yet what delights the reader are the puddin's ''treacherous 'abits''. (p. 108)

The characters themselves are slightly ludicrous, yet are real enough to make them appeal to the reader's sympathy. . . .

Their actions are at times reminiscent of an animated cartoon—as when Bunyip Bluegum visits Watkin Wombat's Summer Residence in the guise of a Pudding Enlarger, yet like the best cartoon characters the Puddin'-owners reveal the follies and inconsistencies of real people. The rich satire would probably be lost on most children. Nothing is sacred to Lindsay, and at times he lampoons society in the manner of Gilbert and Sullivan. English, as well as Australian traits, are ridiculed as when the Puddin'-thieves appear disguised in bell-toppers. . . . (p. 109)

Lindsay's satiric portrait, too, of the Rooster—''one of those fine upstanding, bumptious skites who love to talk all day, in

*From* The Magic Pudding: Being the Adventures of Bunyip Bluegum and His Friends Bill Barnacle and Sam Sawnoff, *written and illustrated by Norman Lindsay. Angus and Robertson Publishers, 1918. Copyright Janet Glad, 1918. Reprinted with the permission of Angus & Robertson (UK) Ltd. Publishers.*

the heartiest manner, to total strangers while their wives do the washing'' the reader would like to think of as more English than Australian! But when the Puddin'-thieves appear before the court at Tooraloo, the satire is at its most biting and is much more than an imitation of Gilbert and Sullivan or of Lewis Carroll's court scene from *Alice*. It is an expression of Lindsay's own iconoclastic humour.

Perhaps it is Norman Lindsay's style that makes the story so funny and at the same time gives it spice. The language is always vigorous, at times almost vulgar, but often with an alliterative quality and a richness of imagery which has immediacy of appeal. There is no mistaking the characteristics of the Puddin'-thieves after Lindsay's description of them:

> One was a Possum, with one of those sharp,
> snooting, snouting sort of faces, and the other
> was a bulbous, boozy-looking Wombat in an
> old long-tailed coat, and a hat that marked him
> down as a man you couldn't trust in a fowlyard.

Round Australian abuse is hurled by Bill at the insolent Parrot: ''Of all the swivel-eyed, up-jumped, cross-grained, sons of a cock-eyed tinker!'' he calls him.

Lindsay can move quickly from vigorous punning—''bungfoodling tricks'' and ''foodbungling tricks'' are all the same—to a mock-serious style. . . . (p. 110)

Throughout the text, nonsense verse is freely interpolated and the three friends break into a lusty rollicking song on occasions of both joy and of sorrow. The verses themselves, like Carroll's, frequently couple incongruous ideas to create bizarre imagery:

> It's worse than weevils, worse than warts,
> It's worse than corns to bear,
> It's worse than havin' several quarts
> Of treacle in your hair.

At other times Lindsay allows himself warm touches of homely humour as when the friends sit down with tea and sugar and ''half a pound of mixed biscuits'' to celebrate their victory over the Puddin'-thieves.

All this is blended into a wonderfully inconsequential whole, with shrewd insight into the motives and actions of human beings. For the weaknesses of the animals are the weaknesses of mankind everywhere.

The metaphor holds the book together, and slice by slice, rather than chapter by chapter, the plot progresses to the inevitable end of the road. . . . (p. 111)

*The Magic Pudding* cannot be said to mark the development of general maturity in books for children in Australia. Unfortunately, it may be questioned whether any other children's writer, since 1918, has attained the stature of Norman Lindsay. . . . Lindsay did not have to apologize for not having a didactic purpose. He could write a book appealing directly to children's needs and interests without excuse or explanation, and it was immediately accepted on its face value.

In this sense the book is a bridge, from a period when books were expected to instruct or preach, to the time when they were free to provide delight. . . .

*The Magic Pudding* is a bridge in another sense, too. It is readily recognizable as Australian—the flavour is undeniably so—but it is also universal and timeless. The characters are Australian, so at the same time British, yet they belong to any country, and any age. So, too, do the illustrations. Although the Australian idiom is evident—the ''Parrot who was a Swagman'' is a good example—they are expressed in a language that can be understood anywhere. (p. 112)

Because Norman Lindsay was an artist as well as a writer, he designed a book especially for children, and one which was aesthetically pleasing as an example of book production. In an age dominated by the drab Ward, Lock series, issued in uniform size and binding, it must have been a tremendous step forward to have an Australian book for children not looking like an adult novel. The format was larger than that of the conventional story book; the type was well spaced on the page; and the illustrations were the antithesis of the tasteless, conventional half-tone, tipped-in plates that were the usual concession to the juvenile market.

*The Magic Pudding* was a modern book in every sense of the word. (pp. 112-13)

With *The Magic Pudding* began a new era of Australian books for children. . . .

Norman Lindsay, more than any other writer before or since, helped satisfy children's love of humour, and at the same time met their interest in magic and adventure. (p. 113)

> *H. M. Saxby, ''Old Themes Recurring 1900-1918,''
> in his* A History of Australian Children's Literature,
> 1841-1941, *Wentworth Books, 1969, pp. 99-113.*

In Australia fantasy has often been attempted but has never been the most successful type of writing for children. The first notable Australian fantasy was published in 1918, and up to the time of writing it remains the best. This was *The Magic Pudding* . . . ; and it is a solid, strongly-flavoured fantasy whose recipe is (it seems to me) uniquely Australian. (p. 169)

It is firmly related to the stomach (for which most children have a proper regard) and it is thickly stuffed with corny verses and nonstop knockabout humour. (p. 170)

> *John Rowe Townsend, ''Fantasy between the Wars,''
> in his* Written for Children: An Outline of English-
> Language Children's Literature, *revised edition, 1974.
> Reprint by The Horn Book Incorporated, 1981, pp.
> 163-77.*

---

**PUDDIN' POEMS: BEING THE BEST OF THE VERSE FROM "THE MAGIC PUDDING"** (1977)

The somewhat grotesque drawings of bad-tempered puddings, puddin' thieves, puddin' owners, sailors and penguins are fitting accompaniments to the virile verses that they illustrate. As it is entirely unsuitable for young children, being all about greedy, guzzling pudding eaters, some of whom come to a bad end, not to mention captains who have their hats thrown overboard, they are likely to enjoy the book very much. The verses ask to be read aloud, in all their ungrammatical beauty. Recommended as good fun for upper infants and juniors.

> *David Churchill, in a review of ''Puddin' Poems,
> Being the Best of the Verse from the Magic Pudding,'' in* The School Librarian, *Vol. 26, No. 3, September, 1978, p. 252.*

# L(ucy) M(aud) Montgomery

## 1874-1942

Canadian author of novels, short stories, and nonfiction, poet, and journalist.

Montgomery is the most enduring Canadian author of fiction for girls. Although she wrote many works for adults—romantic novels, short stories, poetry, her autobiography, and *Courageous Women*, a collection of biographical sketches—her books for young readers are her most important achievement. They emphasize the imaginative, emotional, and nostalgic aspects of childhood and adolescence while underscoring the importance of their Prince Edward Island (P.E.I.) settings. Characterized by both realism and sentimentality, they document the conflicts and successes of heroines who are motherless or orphaned. Montgomery's protagonists are natural children, frequently blessed with imagination and talent. Through their vibrant personalities and self-directed actions, characters such as Sara Stanley (*The Story Girl*), Pat Gardiner (*Pat of Silver Bush*), and Jane Stuart (*Jane of Lantern Hill*) influence their rigid guardians to become more compassionate and receptive towards their charges. The girls in turn are nurtured by their communities and comforted by nature. Montgomery's first novel, *Anne of Green Gables*, introduces her most famous creation, Anne Shirley. An orphan, Anne is sent by mistake to Matthew and Marilla Cuthbert, who had asked to adopt a boy. Anne possesses a well-rounded character, complete with unrefined thoughts and manners. Utilizing her innate honesty and perceptiveness, she shows her elders and peers the fallacies of their narrow beliefs and becomes loved and accepted for herself. *Anne of Green Gables* was followed by a series of five novels which document Anne's maturation. Works such as *Anne of Avonlea* and *Anne's House of Dreams* depict her life as a school teacher, doctor's wife, and mother of six. In many of Montgomery's other stories, Anne's children (*Rilla of Ingleside*) and the people in her town (*Rainbow Valley*) take the lead, while Anne is often given a subsidiary role. Montgomery also produced a trilogy about Emily Byrd Starr, an aspiring young author. *Emily of New Moon*, *Emily Climbs*, and *Emily's Quest* are considered autobiographical, and reflect Montgomery's struggles as a female Canadian writer.

Critics repeatedly parallel Montgomery's life with the people and incidents in her narratives. There are many similarities, especially in Anne's imaginative personality and enchantment with P.E.I., but Montgomery insisted that her characters would be flawed if they imitated living people. Until Emily, Montgomery did not admit personal identification with any of them. Her life and works do, however, reveal the influence of her background. Montgomery's relatives helped to settle Prince Edward Island, and she revelled in the romance of her historical ties. When her mother died, Montgomery was sent to live with her strict maternal grandparents. Until she was eleven, she resided in an old-fashioned Cavendish farmhouse surrounded by apple orchards, where she based a personal fantasy world on the beauty around her. She began writing about her environment at the age of nine, and was first published at sixteen. Early in her career, she worked strenuously on poetry, essays, and short stories which were printed in various Canadian and American periodicals. For financial reasons,

*Public Archives Canada/C11299*

Montgomery learned to cater to the styles and subjects of these magazines as well as to public taste. She wanted to be a poet or sophisticated adult novelist, but believed—with some merit—that she was better at composing the unpretentious romances which provided the bulk of her income. Montgomery originally intended *Anne of Green Gables* to be simply a Sunday school serial, but found Anne's personality so captivating that it prompted an entire book. *Anne*'s success caused Montgomery's publishers to demand a sequel. After *Anne of Avonlea*, Montgomery said, "If I'm to be dragged at Anne's chariot wheels the rest of my life, I'll bitterly repent having 'created' her." Nevertheless, Montgomery continued writing about Anne and other youthful heroines. In 1920, she complained that Anne "weighed on me like an incubus when she ceased to be an inspiration." Montgomery died without realizing that the serious work she longed to produce was within her juvenile books.

Montgomery's critical reception has been mixed. Many reviewers label her works non-literary, pointing to her use of excessive sentiment, flowery prose, and inconsistent characterization. They regret the fact that her popularity has deflected attention from greater Canadian writers. Montgomery's plots and characters are regarded as derivative, and she is censured for not representing real growth except in Emily and Anne. Some critics hold that Anne's appeal diminishes as she gets older and more conservative. Others say that none of Montgomery's works equalled her first book. Most reviewers, however, commend her as a true storyteller whose charm and honesty transcend her faults. They praise her evocative picture of the geography and culture of P.E.I. and her use of landscape to give pleasure and solace. They appreciate her incisive analyses of the Island's inhabitants and their values, and are especially impressed with Montgomery's attacks on prejudice, lack of imagination, and tyranny over the young. They also note the mocking sweetness that adds humor and substance to Montgomery's reflections of nineteenth-century morality.

Montgomery's greatest gift, most critics say, is her understanding of children. Reviewers admire her sensitivity towards her heroines as they fight to maintain their identity against the opposition of home and community. During a period when he was highly critical of mawkishness in literature about children, Mark Twain wrote to Montgomery, "In *Anne of Green Gables* you will find the dearest and most moving and delightful child since the immortal Alice." Many critics agree with Twain, and *Anne* is now acclaimed a classic. The scholarly value of the *Emily* series is currently being acknowledged for its link with Montgomery's life and artistic philosophy; readers have also taken a renewed interest in the trilogy. Montgomery is recognized as an author whose works are still debated as genuine literature, but whose popularity is undeniable. She was awarded the Order of the British Empire in 1935. Several museums dedicated to her on Prince Edward Island receive visitors from around the world. *Anne of Green Gables* has been adapted into three movies, several plays, and a television series.

(See also *Yesterday's Authors of Books for Children*, Vol. 1 and *Contemporary Authors*, Vol. 108.)

---

## AUTHOR'S COMMENTARY

[*Montgomery was asked by the editor of* Everywoman's World, *a Toronto-based magazine, to relate the story of her career. From June-November, 1917, six installments appeared under the title* "The Alpine Path." *The articles were later published in book form.*]

Many years ago, when I was still a child, I clipped from a current magazine a bit of verse, entitled "To the Fringed Gentian," and pasted it on the corner of the little portfolio on which I wrote my letters and school essays. Every time I opened the portfolio I read one of those verses over; it was the keynote of my every aim and ambition:

> Then whisper, blossom, in thy sleep
> How I may upward climb
> The Alpine path, so hard, so steep,
> That leads to heights sublime;
> How I may reach that far-off goal
> Of true and honoured fame,
> And write upon its shining scroll
> A woman's humble name.

It is indeed a "hard and steep" path; and if any word I can write will assist or encourage another pilgrim along that path, that word I gladly and willingly write. (p. 10)

[The] incidents and environment of my childhood . . . had a marked influence on the development of my literary gift. A different environment would have given it a different bias. Were it not for those Cavendish years, I do not think *Anne of Green Gables* would ever have been written.

When I am asked "When did you begin to write?" I say, "I wish I could remember." I cannot remember the time when I was not writing, or when I did not mean to be an author. To write has always been my central purpose around which every effort and hope and ambition of my life has grouped itself. I was an indefatigable little scribbler, and stacks of manuscripts, long ago reduced to ashes, alas, bore testimony to the same. I wrote about all the little incidents of my existence. I wrote descriptions of my favourite haunts, biographies of my many cats, histories of visits, and school affairs, and even critical reviews of the books I had read.

One wonderful day, when I was nine years old, I discovered that I could write poetry. (pp. 52-3)

Poems, however, were not all I wrote. Very soon after I began to write verses I also began to write stories. The "Story Club" in *Anne of Green Gables* was suggested by a little incident of schooldays when Janie S—, Amanda M— and I all wrote a story with the same plot. I remember only that it was a very tragic plot, and the heroines were all drowned while bathing on Cavendish sandshore! Oh, it was very sad! It was the first, and probably the last, time that Janie and Amanda attempted fiction, but I had already quite a library of stories in which almost everyone died. (p. 57)

Nowadays, my reviewers say that my forte is humour. Well, there was not much humour in those early tales, at least, it was not intended there should be. Perhaps I worked all the tragedy out of my system in them, and left an unimpeded current of humour. I think it was my love of the dramatic that urged me to so much infanticide. In real life I couldn't have hurt a fly, and the thought that superfluous kittens had to be drowned was torture to me. But in my stories battle, murder and sudden death were the order of the day. (p. 58)

A story I had written in a prize competition was published in the Montreal *Witness*, and a descriptive article on Saskatchewan was printed in the Prince Albert *Times*, and copied and commented on favourably by several Winnipeg papers. After several effusions on "June" and kindred subjects appeared in that long-suffering *Patriot*, I was beginning to plume myself on being quite a literary person.

But the demon of filthy lucre was creeping into my heart. I wrote a story and sent it to the New York *Sun*, because I had been told that it paid for articles; and the New York *Sun* sent it back to me. I flinched, as from a slap in the face, but went on writing. You see I had learned the first, last, and middle lesson—"Never give up!" (p. 59)

After leaving Prince of Wales College I taught school for a year in Bideford, Prince Edward Island. I wrote a good deal and learned a good deal, but still my stuff came back, except from two periodicals the editors of which evidently thought that literature was its own reward, and quite independent of monetary considerations. I often wonder that I did not give up in utter discouragement. At first I used to feel dreadfully hurt when a story or poem over which I had laboured and agonized came back, with one of those icy little rejection slips. Tears of disappointment *would* come in spite of myself, as I crept away to hide the poor, crimpled manuscript in the depths of my trunk. But after a while I got hardened to it and did not mind. I only set my teeth and said "I will succeed." I believed in myself and I struggled on alone, in secrecy and silence. I never told my ambitions and efforts and failures to any one. Down, deep down, under all discouragement and rebuff, I knew I would "arrive" some day.

In the autumn of 1895 I went to Halifax and spent the winter taking a selected course in English literature at Dalhousie College. Through the winter came a "Big Week" for me. On Monday I received a letter from *Golden Days,* a Philadelphia juvenile, accepting a short story I had sent there and enclosing a cheque for five dollars. It was the first money my pen had ever earned; I did not squander it in riotous living, neither did I invest it in necessary boots and gloves. I went up town and bought five volumes of poetry with it—Tennyson, Byron, Milton, Longfellow, Whittier. I wanted something I could keep for ever in memory of having "arrived."

On Wednesday of the same week I won the prize of five dollars offered by the Halifax *Evening Mail* for the best letter on the subject, "Which has the greater patience—man or woman?"

My letter was in the form of some verses, which I had composed during a sleepless night and got up at three o'clock in the wee sma' hours to write down. On Saturday the *Youth's Companion* sent me a cheque for twelve dollars for a poem. I really felt quite bloated with so much wealth. Never in my life, before or since have I been so rich!

After my Dalhousie winter I taught school for two more years. In those two years I wrote scores of stories, generally for Sunday School publications and juvenile periodicals. The following entry from my journal refers to this period:

> I have grubbed away industriously all this summer and ground out stories and verses on days so hot that I feared my very marrow would melt and my gray matter be hopelessly sizzled up. But oh, I love my work! I love spinning stories, and I love to sit by the window of my room and shape some 'airy fairy' fancy into verse. I have got on well this summer and added several new journals to my list. They are a varied assortment, and their separate tastes all have to be catered to. I write a great many juvenile stories. I like doing these, but I should like it better if I didn't have to drag a 'moral' into most of them. They won't sell without it, as a rule. So in the moral must go, broad or subtle, as suits the fibre of the particular editor I have in view. The kind of juvenile story I like best to write—and read, too, for the matter of that— is a good, jolly one, "art for art's sake," or rather "fun for fun's sake," with no insidious moral hidden away in it like a pill in a spoonful of jam!

It was not always hot weather when I was writing. During one of those winters of school teaching I boarded in a very cold farmhouse. In the evenings, after a day of strenuous school work, I would be too tired to write. So I religiously arose an hour earlier in the mornings for that purpose. For five months I got up at six o'clock and dressed by lamplight. The fires would not yet be on, of course, and the house would be very cold. But I would put on a heavy coat, sit on my feet to keep them from freezing and with fingers so cramped that I could scarcely hold the pen, I would write my "stunt" for the day. Sometimes it would be a poem in which I would carol blithely of blue skies and rippling brooks and flowery meads! Then I would thaw out my hands, eat breakfast and go to school.

When people say to me, as they occasionally do, "Oh, how I envy you your gift, how I wish I could write as you do," I am inclined to wonder, with some inward amusement, how

much they would have envied me on those dark, cold, winter mornings of my apprenticeship. (pp. 60-2)

In June, 1902, I returned to Cavendish, where I remained unbrokenly for the next nine years. For the first two years after my return I wrote only short stories and serials as before. But I was beginning to think of writing a book. It had always been my hope and ambition to write one. But I never seemed able to make a beginning.

I have always hated beginning a story. When I get the first paragraph written I feel as though it were half done. The rest comes easily. To begin a book, therefore, seemed quite a stupendous task. Besides, I did not see just how I could get time for it. I could not afford to take the time from my regular writing hours. And, in the end, I never deliberately sat down and said "Go to! Here are pens, paper, ink and plot. Let me write a book." It really all just "happened."

I had always kept a notebook in which I jotted down, as they occurred to me, ideas for plots, incidents, characters, and descriptions. In the spring of 1904 I was looking over this notebook in search of some idea for a short serial I wanted to write for a certain Sunday School paper. I found a faded entry, written many years before: "Elderly couple apply to orphan asylum for a boy. By mistake a girl is sent them." I thought this would do. I began to block out the chapters, devise, and select incidents and "brood up" my heroine. Anne—she was not so named of malice aforethought, but flashed into my fancy already christened, even to the all important "e"—began to expand in such a fashion that she soon seemed very real to me and took possession of me to an unusual extent. She appealed to me, and I thought it rather a shame to waste her on an ephemeral little serial. Then the thought came, "Write a book. You have the central idea. All you need do is to spread it out over enough chapters to amount to a book."

The result was **Anne of Green Gables.** I wrote it in the evenings after my regular day's work was done, wrote most of it at the window of the little gable room which had been mine for many years. I began it, as I have said, in the spring of 1904. I finished it in the October of 1905.

Ever since my first book was published I have been persecuted by the question "Was so-and-so the original of such-and-such in your book?" And behind my back they don't put it in the interrogative form, but in the affirmative. I know many people who have asserted that they are well acquainted with the "originals" of my characters. Now, for my own part, I have never, during all the years I have studied human nature, met one human being who could, as a whole, be put into a book without injuring it. Any artist knows that to paint *exactly* from life is to give a false impression of the subject. *Study* from life he must, copying suitable heads or arms, appropriating bits of character, personal or mental idiosyncracies, "making use of the real to perfect the ideal."

But the ideal, his ideal, must be behind and beyond it all. The writer must *create* his characters, or they will not be life-like.

With but one exception I have never drawn any of my book people from life. That exception was "Peg Bowen" in *The Story Girl.* And even then I painted the lily very freely. I have used real places in my books and many real incidents. But hitherto I have depended wholly on the creative power of my own imagination for my characters.

Cavendish was "Avonlea" to a certain extent. "Lover's Lane" was a very beautiful lane through the woods on a neighbour's

*The "Green Gables" house, located in Prince Edward Island National Park. Designed to represent the Cuthbert home from* Anne of Green Gables, *it actually belonged to Montgomery's uncle. Now a popular museum, the house is close to her childhood residence and gravesite. Reproduced by permission of Ian Gillen.*

farm. It was a beloved haunt of mine from my earliest days. The "Shore Road" has a real existence, between Cavendish and Rustico. But the "White Way of Delight," "Wiltonmere," and "Violet Vale" were transplanted from the estates of my castles in Spain. "The Lake of Shining Waters" is generally supposed to be Cavendish Pond. This is not so. The pond I had in mind is the one at Park Corner, below Uncle John Campbell's house. But I suppose that a good many of the effects of light and shadow I had seen on the Cavendish pond figured unconsciously in my descriptions. Anne's habit of naming places was an old one of my own. I named all the pretty nooks and corners about the old farm. I had, I remember, a "Fairyland," a "Dreamland," a "Pussy-Willow Palace," a "No-Man's-Land," a "Queen's Bower," and many others. The "Dryads Bubble" was purely imaginary, but the "Old Log Bridge" was a real thing. It was formed by a single large tree that had blown down and lay across the brook. It had served as a bridge to the generation before my time, and was hollowed out like a shell by the tread of hundreds of passing feet. Earth had blown into the crevices, and ferns and grasses had found root and fringed it luxuriantly. Velvet moss covered its sides and below was a deep, clear, sunflecked stream.

Anne's Katie Maurice was mine. In our sitting-room there had always stood a big book-case used as a china cabinet. In each door was a large oval glass, dimly reflecting the room. When I was very small each of my reflections in these glass doors were "real folk" to my imagination. The one in the left-hand door was Katie Maurice, the one in the right, Lucy Gray. Why I named them thus I cannot say. Wordsworth's ballad had no connection with the latter, for I had never read it at that time.

Indeed, I have no recollection of deliberately naming them at all. As far back as consciousness runs, Katie Maurice and Lucy Gray lived in the fairy room behind the bookcase. Katie Maurice was a little girl like myself, and I loved her dearly. I would stand before that door and prattle to Katie for hours, giving and receiving confidences. In especial, I liked to do this at twilight, when the fire had been lit and the room and its reflections were a glamour of light and shadow.

Lucy Gray was grown-up and a widow! I did not like her as well as Katie. She was always sad, and always had dismal stories of her troubles to relate to me; nevertheless, I visited her scrupulously in turn, lest her feelings should be hurt, because she was jealous of Katie, who also disliked her. All this sounds like the veriest nonsense, but I cannot describe how real it was to me. I never passed through the room without a wave of my hand to Katie in the glass door at the other end.

The notable incident of the liniment cake happened when I was teaching school in Bideford and boarding at the Methodist parsonage there. Its charming mistress flavoured a layer cake with anodyne liniment one day. Never shall I forget the taste of that cake and the fun we had over it, for the mistake was not discovered until tea-time. A strange minister was there to tea that night. He ate every crumb of his piece of cake. What he thought of it we never discovered. Possibly he imagined it was simply some new-fangled flavouring.

Many people have told me that they regretted Matthew's death in *Green Gables*. I regret it myself. If I had the book to write over again I would spare Matthew for several years. But when I wrote it I thought he must die, that there might be a necessity for self-sacrifice on Anne's part, so poor Matthew joined the long procession of ghosts that haunt my literary past.

Well, my book was finally written. The next thing was to find a publisher. I typewrote it myself, on my old second-hand typewriter that never made the capitals plain and wouldn't print "w" at all, and I sent it to a new American firm that had recently come to the front with several "best sellers." I thought I might stand a better chance with a new firm than with an old established one that had already a preferred list of writers. But the new firm very promptly sent it back. Next I sent it to one of the "old, established firms," and the old established firm sent it back. Then I sent it, in turn, to three "Betwixt-and-between firms", and they all sent it back. Four of them returned it with a cold, printed note of rejection; one of them "damned with faint praise." They wrote that "Our readers report that they find some merit in your story, but not enough to warrant its acceptance."

That finished me. I put **Anne** away in an old hat-box in the clothes room, resolving that some day when I had time I would take her and reduce her to the original seven chapters of her first incarnation. In that case I was tolerably sure of getting thirty-five dollars for her at least, and perhaps even forty.

The manuscript lay in the hatbox until I came across it one winter day while rummaging. I began turning over the leaves, reading a bit here and there. It didn't seem so very bad. "I'll try once more," I thought. The result was that a couple of months later an entry appeared in my journal to the effect that my book had been accepted. After some natural jubilation I wrote: "The book may or may not succeed. I wrote it for love, not money, but very often such books are the most successful, just as everything in the world that is born of true love has life in it, as nothing constructed for mercenary ends can ever have.

"Well, I've written my book! The dream dreamed years ago at that old brown desk in school has come true at last after years of toil and struggle. And the realization is sweet, almost as sweet as the dream."

When I wrote of the book succeeding or not succeeding, I had in mind only a very moderate success indeed, compared to that which it did attain. I never dreamed that it would appeal to young and old. I thought girls in their teens might like to read it, that was the only audience I hoped to reach. But men and women who are grandparents have written to tell me how they loved **Anne,** and boys at college have done the same. The very day on which these words are written has come a letter to me from an English lad of nineteen, totally unknown to me, who writes that he is leaving for "the front" and wants to tell me "before he goes" how much my books and especially **Anne** have meant to him. It is in such letters that a writer finds meet reward for all sacrifice and labor.

Well, **Anne** was accepted; but I had to wait yet another year before the book was published. Then on June 20th, 1908, I wrote in my journal:

"To-day has been, as Anne herself would say, 'an epoch in my life.' My book came to-day, 'spleet-new' from the publishers. I candidly confess that it was to me a proud and wonderful and thrilling moment. There, in my hand, lay the material realization of all the dreams and hopes and ambitions and struggles of my whole conscious existence—my first book. Not a great book, but mine, mine, mine, something which I had created." (pp. 71-7)

*Montgomery in 1908, the year* Anne of Green Gables *was published. Courtesy of Archival Collection, University of Guelph and E. Stuart Macdonald estate.*

With the publication of **Green Gables** my struggle was over. I have published six novels since then. . . .

**The Story Girl** was written in 1910 and published in 1911. It was the last book I wrote in my old home by the gable window where I had spent so many happy hours of creation. It is my own favourite among my books, the one that gave me the greatest pleasure to write, the one whose characters and landscape seem to me most real. All the children in the book are purely imaginary. The old "King Orchard" was a compound of our old orchard in Cavendish and the orchard at Park Corner. "Peg Bowen" was suggested by a half-witted, gypsy-like personage who roamed at large for many years over the Island and was the terror of my childhood. (p. 78)

[The] story of Nancy and Betty Sherman was founded on fact. The story of the captain of the *Fanny* is also literally true. The heroine is still living, or was a few years ago, and still retains much of the beauty which won the Captain's heart. **"The Blue Chest of Rachel Ward"** was another "ower-true tale." Rachel Ward was Eliza Montgomery, a cousin of my father's, who died in Toronto a few years ago. The blue chest was in the kitchen of Uncle John Campbell's house at Park Corner from 1849 until her death. We children heard its story many a time and speculated and dreamed over its contents, as we sat on it to study our lessons or eat our bed-time snacks. (p. 79)

The "Alpine Path" has been climbed, after many years of toil and endeavor. It was not an easy ascent, but even in the struggle at its hardest there was a delight and a zest known only to those who aspire to the heights. (p. 95)

L. M. Montgomery, in her The Alpine Path: The Story of My Career, Fitzhenry & Whiteside Limited, 1974, 96 p.

---

## GENERAL COMMENTARY

### EPHRAIM WEBER

[Weber was a Canadian author who wrote to Montgomery because he admired her poetry. They only met three times, but established a friendship through steady correspondence that lasted for forty years.]

To write with third-rate interest about the common people and their daily doings is easy; to write about them with second-rate interest is not extra hard; but to do it with first-rate interest is surprisingly difficult. L. M. Montgomery has depicted the common people of Prince Edward Island with first-rate interest; for, having grown up among them, she knows their ways, their traditions, their souls, as Dickens knows his islanders. And yet some of her critics are not won over; one of them, reviewing the later Canadian literature some years ago, called the Montgomery novels "the nadir of Canadian fiction". Of course the thrilling romantic plot is missing. To a reader of the old school, addicted to those far-spun yarns of romance vibrating with heroic excitement, the humbler affairs of the community novel may well be piddling neighborhood fusses. But many of the best late novels, highly rated and widely read, are quite without large-scale plot interest. What, no terrific tenseness between mighty antagonistic forces! No Himalayas scaled in pursuit of the villain! No war over the duchess! Well then, has the community novel any compensating substitute? The compensating substitute in the first-rate community novel is the interest of reality.

The interest of reality in the new Canadian novel is mainly character interest, heightened by concentrated regional setting; and not far behind is the interest of incident. To make up in this way for lack of plot structure is obviously no easy assignment. Before you know it, you have the dry rot of dullness—unless you scrape into unsavory realism. Then, too, this kind of fiction, far more than the heroic romance, attracts the spoiling imitator. Even so, if your author knows his kind and knows his art, the interest of reality fills the bill excellently.

Every day we meet people who have read a few of the "Anne" books, and there are those who have made a clean sweep of the Montgomery shelf, or have re-read parts of it. (pp. 64-5)

A German Mennonite girl of eleven comes to my study these times twice a week for a next "Anne" story, because "At the public library "Anne" books are always out, and the last one I had was all worn out and dirty". I quiz her a bit on these stories; her knowledge is surprising. What is there in them that fascinates this child, who is being brought up in a different social world and on a different language? It is surely her heart's response to the author's friendly human note and the living vividness of it all. "Montgomery girls", reported a bright tenth grade lass I was quizzing, "act just like we girls act; they're just so many of us. They just step out of the book and are with us." Her gusto in saying it showed how this middle-'teener enjoyed the illusion of reality. Herein is our author's opportunity: her upward trend and idealization of life is so naturally

veiled as entertainment that our girls are off guard against being made better, and so are made better. (pp. 65-6)

So, are these Montgomery tales not nearer the zenith than the nadir? Can so many people of so many kinds in so many lands be charmed by cheap fiction with its anaemic reality? The adverse critics can still keep their souls in clover on ripping adventure, dashing romance, bigwig intrigue and unlimited realism.

Though it is still the Creator's secret how a talent produces its precise effects, let us visit the Montgomery study and see at least what distinguishing elements, what salt and savor, this creator puts into her characters. No, this is not an interview. Delicately sensitive to personality, she gets sharp impressions of people's inner selves, and is downright happy in exercising her resourceful inventiveness on all kinds of circumstances in which to show their behavior in action and to let us feel their atmosphere. To get us perfectly acquainted with her Island folks, she treats us to a liberal range of incidents, all the more engaging for their local color: Scotch Presbyterian and such. The reason her machinery does not creak is that she never proceeds by a technique she is learning, but just by an original instinct for her characters. Warm with emotion and animated by zest, she enters into them like a dramatist.

How she understands Matthew Cuthbert of Green Gables! When this lonely, taciturn soul speaks, he has something to say; his few words, so coolly spoken, make impressions. About such self-suppressing persons there emanates an aura of pathos, which we feel in this rude Scotchman, long-haired old farmer bachelor with a refined soul, a fair type of our pioneering bushwhackers. He has no one to love but a freckled, carrot-haired little thing of an orphan—and is afraid it may be discovered! (p. 68)

Quite as convincing a reality is Marilla, his old-maid sister. Are there, or have there ever been, such stern, dour, uncommunicative Scotch Presbyterians? Well, isn't this their very race-brand back a generation or two? Not on their sleeves but in their deep dense interiors they wear, or wore, their hearts. Added to years of the orphan's softening presence, it took Matthew's funeral to make Marilla confess she loved the child, loved her like her own flesh and blood; and in spite of her crabbed discipline she managed to tell her, "You've been my joy and comfort ever since you came to Green Gables". Her Scotch stubbornness—or shall we graciously call it her dogged consistency with her original grudge against the child for being a girl?—was sturdy stuff, backed up by the traditional asceticism, which supported her hard attitude; backed further by Matthew's secret love of the girl. The complexity is left nicely veiled, and makes good reading for those who know the old Scotch temperament. Though Marilla's earlier scoldings and denials give us heartache, we do not find it hard to forgive her in the end: "It's never been easy for me to say things out of my heart." Even some of us not exactly Scotch might give the old spinster a brotherly handshake on that if we could get ourselves to do it. But what a clean job she made of it once she got round to it! What a mother heart now has room to expand in her bosom! A reader told the author she regretted Matthew's early death; the author replied she had come to feel the same way, explaining her object had been to bring Anne a needed sacrifice [see excerpt above in Author's Commentary]. Right or wrong, one fine thing accomplished by it is the highly-due humanization of Marilla. (pp. 68-9)

After a closer look at [Anne], all this about Marilla and Matthew needs to be re-read. Let us see what kind of energy, what sweetness and light, we can find in this World-Anne, whose major early troubles, next to her homelessness, were her carrot hair, her freckled nose, and the abomination of seeing her name without an *e*. (p. 69)

[At] the very start of the **"Anne"** fiction we have first class interest between humble character and humble circumstance: the anguish this sensitive child endures because she is a mistake and is to be driven out of her Eden to make room for a boy. An insipid character in this fine suspense would be boring. . . . Next comes the process of mistress bringing up ward—and ward "bringing up" mistress. "Father" had been brought up while listening to Anne's charming chat during the long buggy ride home. The old ascetic restraint and the new rebellion against it carry on the action, until by degrees the mistress is nine-tenths conquered and doesn't know it, at least hates to own it, even to herself. Not that the ward plotted it; her unconscious influence brought it about. Not Anne's outbreaks, but her quiet innate force liberalized the old-school Calvinist into healthy discipline. Still, the early strictness, though marred by harshness, had the effect of giving the child a compensating appreciation of life's blessings. Interesting reciprocity!

Anne is charming when she gets stormy. The abuses she suffers win her our tender feelings, which make her outbursts all the more startling. When the too neighborly Mrs. Rachel Lynde discharged her blunderbuss at her over her freckles, skinniness and carrot hair, she was "properly horrified" at the response she got; and nobody who was at Avonlea School the day Gilbert Blythe made fun of Anne's hair before the whole room when school was on will ever forget the scene she put up in dealing with him. Small events, these, but character and incident cooperate to make appealing young people's literature of them in their contexts; and appealing young people's literature makes no dull reading for older generations.

The **"Anne"** series of the Montgomery novels has as its main interest the development of this scrawny, sensitive orphan into a toughened and enlightened mother. To those who have not read **Green Gables,** the initial volume, this may sound blank and bleak, but only to those. Across the territory of these volumes her personality runs like a power line, distributing energy and light and love, right and left, wherever there is human material that can take the current. Naturally and satisfyingly her presence dominates the whole sequence. In letting such a mite evolve to such a power, the author has nowhere strained the laws and ways of reality to contrive an artificial perfection. Evolution has no grudge against the unlucky. To see Anne through her girlhood, 'teens and mature life is a great way for a girl to learn what unfading satisfaction can be got out of life without either sinking into drudging ambitionlessness or chafing to soar into flighty careering in public life and high society. Here we have that basic middle course which circles enduringly and fulfillingly about a woman's centre of gravity: a childhood home with nature's health and refinement playing about; enough choring to learn housekeeping; preparatory school, then college with its enlarging culture; a spicy nip of public life (school principal); a lovely courtship—such letters!—a fine married life &c. with its creative mystery; and in time that pleasant easing-off into lighter duties. (pp. 69-71)

Anne's unique originality, live imagination, precocious wisdom, optimistic energy, versatile hearty serviceableness—all these in peculiar combination may well make her stand out. . . . (p. 71)

Reporting to the author on my complimentary copy of **Anne of Ingleside,** I noted how my wife and I were further impressed

by her understanding of children, and how at spots our mellow smiles became 'teenish laughs; for the story was a delightfully undulating streak of entertainment. She replied I needn't have been so nice with my compliments: the yarn, spun to order as a fill-gap in Anne's life, was mainly padding. "But yarn and eiderdown, not hay," I retorted, bound to have the last word, "make nice padding." If this story lacks strict organic unity, it has at any rate the continuity of family raising, and such a family! Anne's, of course. One must know them, see them in action, overhear their remarks, be asked their questions, and feel the atmosphere, to get all there is.

As to gap-fillers: the Montgomery novels fall mainly into the **Anne,** the **Emily,** and the **Pat** groups. The first in each is written out of fascination for the dominating heroine, succeeding ones came at the insistence of readers and publishers of the first. L.M.M. did not experience heavenly joy in writing them all. . . . It is hard to think the author got no enjoyment out of the writing once she got warmed up to it; there is a live glow in it all. (pp. 71-2)

Are not these **"Anne"** stories as interesting as the coarse thrillers—to all but the sophisticated Smart Set and their following? The characters, Dog Monday and all, are normal and walk the plane we tread. After re-reading the books, can you imagine Anne as *fiction*? This Anne whose unconscious influence liberated, liberalized Marilla, Mrs. Lynde, Miss Barry; who stood her ground against the Pyes, the Sloanes, the Pringles; who meant so much to groping little Elizabeth and Paul, to gray-haired lonely Matthew, rugged Captain Jim, love-sick Charlotta the Fourth, gruff old Rebecca Dew; this Anne who, while making herself pluck roosters, roamed the Milky Way—can you doubt that if your daughters got to know her well, they would feel a stimulating lift from her toward becoming the girls they would like to be? (p. 73)

> *Ephraim Weber, "L. M. Montgomery's 'Anne'," in* The Dalhousie Review, *Vol. 24, No. 1, April, 1944, pp. 64-73.*

### ARTHUR L. PHELPS

An interesting Canadian literary fact admits of varying interpretations. The fact is: romantic and sentimental writers, handling Canadian material, have a pretty wide circulation outside of Canada. . . . By the standards of discriminating literary criticism none of these writers [Robert W. Service, Mazode la Roche, Ralph Connor, and L. M. Montgomery] is important. No critic would think of any one of them as having made a serious contribution to literature. Yet these writers have carried the name of Canada here and there throughout the English-speaking world, and, in some cases, through translation, much beyond the English-speaking world. (p. 85)

Now I come to a confession which is partly a proclamation. I have been going through a lot of this popular Canadian writing. It is rapid and easy reading for the accustomed reader. By contemporary standards it lacks realism and penetration. It makes no parade of being philosophic. There are few rich passages of really good writing. It raises no great issues and seems unaware of problems that habitually vex the contemporary mind. It is soft reading. It is simple, ordinary and straightforward and makes no pretensions whatever to being "literary" in quotation marks. Yet it has its public and it performs a function for that public. My confession is that, coming at it freshly and with an attempt at open mindedness, to my surprise, I enjoyed some of it as a relief from the tension and self-conscious craftsmanship and experimental techniques of many contemporary works presumably much more important and widely publicized. The proclamation is, I suppose, that one need not be ashamed of this sort of writing. If to say it has its place seems like condescension and dismissal, there still remain for the critic the questions: what is that place, and how important in relation to literature is that place?

Such questions can bring us at once to L. M. Montgomery. L. M. Montgomery's work stands as representative of the kind of writing I have been discussing. It is unpretentious to the point of being naive. Its innocence seems always on the edge of suggesting close cousinship with ignorance—ignorance of life. Yet, as one reads, the sophisticated reader is uneasily aware that the argument might turn and go in another direction. The unpretentiousness and innocence may be the kind of honest simplicity that does have life and even art in it. One critic at least has been able to say of *Anne of Green Gables* that it is "deservedly a classic of its kind not because of its excellence of style or plot, but because of the altogether charming character of Anne." To that one is tempted to add that if a novel can create a character with capacity to enter alive into the imaginations of hundreds of thousands of readers, may one not say also of that novel that it must possess some of the vital qualities of style and plot that suggest a respectable artistic achievement? It may be that L. M. Montgomery, one of our popular so-called mediocre story tellers, should not be dismissed too casually just because she has been popular. Widespread popularity in any form of expression usually suggests the presence of positive and fundamental qualities. (pp. 87-9)

Of course the Montgomery popularity has been, in the main, popularity with young girls and their amiable ordinary parents. L. M. Montgomery is a category story teller. She writes girls' stories. Anne of Green Gables is a girl in whom every girl can see a good deal of herself. But what if as well, those of us, male and female, who are not girls, can see in Anne something of that precious commodity, universal girlhood, made into such engaging flesh-and-blood reality that we laugh or weep and are tender with solicitude over the bright vulnerability of happy youth? What if L. M. Montgomery has given to all of us an enduring symbol in Anne? That might put L. M. Montgomery at least among the respectable story tellers.

Now I know there is one further thing to say. For many it is the damning thing. **Anne of Green Gables** is old fashioned. L. M. Montgomery is old fashioned. She belongs indeed to the age of innocence. Modern young girls brought up on the funnies, the movies, the slick magazine stories, cannot tolerate the soft well-meaning goodness of Miss Montgomery's portrayal. That portrayal belongs to an earlier time and is gone with the winds of change. Old fashioned stories are revived and enjoyed, it is said, only by the nostalgic and the sentimental or read today as current fare only by the uncultured and unsophisticated. For the modern there is stronger meat. Even for the modern little girl there is stronger meat. But the alternative reading is most often the current spate of wholly superficial magazine stories and the lurid empty sorts of pocket books. Contrasted with that type of writing, L. M. Montgomery's stories have qualities of range and subtlety and fine comprehension which make them relatively worthy even today. That they are still popular can be a kind of reassurance. The local librarian from whom I got the four *Anne* volumes said to me, "Don't keep them too long. They are out all the time." There may still be a place for the stories of L. M. Montgomery. (pp. 89-90)

*Arthur L. Phelps, "L. M. Montgomery," in his* Canadian Writers, *McClelland and Stewart Limited, 1951, pp. 85-93.*

**ELIZABETH WATERSTON**

Many women *have* lived "fabulous" lives. But in L. M. Montgomery's case the real miracle is that she could exploit her experience in an enduring art-form. She universalized her story; she recreated it against vivid regional settings; she structured it into mythical patterns. She retold the legends she had lived, in haunting and memorable style. (p. 198)

We find in her life, her letters, her journals, the story of an important craftsman, a professional writer fighting to clarify and improve the conditions of an artist's work. And in her novels we find a subtle and illuminating use of archetypal patterns, particularly of the recurring myths of girlhood. (p. 199)

Her established audience—girls between ten and fourteen—continues to read and love the L. M. Montgomery books. But she may also lay increasing claim to our attention as adult critics. The books have an intensity because they *were* written as "children's books." The same kind of sesame that unlocked Lewis Carroll's inhibitions and let him write the classic of fantasy and repression that we now see in *Alice*—that same magic releasing power seems to have operated with the Canadian, late-Victorian, provincial spinster. Writing "for children," she could re-enact the rituals of childhood. Recreating her own remembered yearnings and anxieties, she could create a myth of the hesitant desires and worries of the virginal years.

*Montgomery at eleven, the same age at which Anne was introduced to young readers. Courtesy of Archival Collection, University of Guelph and E. Stuart Macdonald estate.*

Modern psychology explains some of the hidden power of L. M. Montgomery's books, especially for adolescent girls. Most teen-aged girls find it hard to get along with their mothers, the psychologists say, yet not daring consciously to dislike the mother, they are torn by mixed emotions of admiration, rivalry, dependence, hostility, all operating at a subconscious level. The heroines of L. M. Montgomery have no mothers. They do have aunts and grandmothers (who can safely be hated). Indeed, they usually have a range of aunts, some restrictive, some permissive. The adolescent reader can discriminate ambivalent feelings by loving one aunt (mother-substitute), while hating another. Also, in adolescence there is a normal intensity of feeling for the father, a feeling that must be outgrown or re-directed, but that is very powerful in the transitional stage between family relations and extra-familial ones, and correlates with the transition from homosexual to heterosexual devotion. In most of L. M. Montgomery's books, the father, safely distanced by death, stirs deep feelings of attachment (usually disapproved of by the aunts or grandmothers).

Other tenets of the psychologists who study adolescence can similarly be illustrated from the Montgomery books. "Girls may feel unconscious jealousy of boys": in the novels girls replace boys, as Anne replaced the asked-for boy orphan, as Valancy replaced her mother's desired son. Many times, also, names are used to suggest crossing of boundaries: "Peter" in **The Quarantine** is a girl; "Bev," the boy-narrator in the **"Story Girl"** series has an ambivalent name, as have "Phil", "Jo", Jamesina, Pat, and a long list of others. The theory would be that reading such tales gives young girls an outlet for their fantasies of changing sex. Another tenet: "The adolescent longs for yet dreads the coming of physical passion." No doubt this accounts for the pleasure girls find in reading the long, long sequence of tales in which consummation of a romance is suspended, usually by some illogical tabu. Item: "The ending of virginity may be symbolically accepted in dreams, as a prelude to reality." Re-reading the L. M. Montgomery books with even a reserved acceptance of Freudian symbolism would surprise most of us! Once again, the theory is that such gentle, sublimated acceptance into the young reader's consciousness can be a healthy form of gradual adjustment. Such a Freudian re-reading, besides increasing our interest in the **"Anne"** and **"Emily"** books, may lead to a revaluation of *The Blue Castle,* where many of the suppressed themes are directly stated.

The basic assumption in this revaluation is that L. M. Montgomery was probably not conscious of the forces she was releasing. She was, however, honest enough to use the patterns her memory suggested. Furthermore, she was a good enough craftsman to lift the stories from the level of clinical confession to that of archetypal statement.

We may guess, also, that this author was increasingly conscious of the basic equation she had established, almost by chance, in her first successful novel. "The Island" is adolescence. And Adolescence, that time of intense dreaming, of romantic yearning and disturbing hostility, remains as a part of every consciousness. Encircled by the mature sands of logic, pragmatism, utilitarianism and conformity, the island of youth exists for us and in us still. Perhaps art can be the channel by which we rediscover the island. L. M. Montgomery's world of poetry, virginity, and pantheism still opens for the adult reader the way back to his own world of young realization: he "wakes, to dream again."

This brings us to the final claim of L. M. Montgomery on our attention and respect. She is the novelist for the bookish child,

the word-conscious child to whom she gives reassurance about a sense of the magic of 'naming.' She knows that words are her tool, and have been so ever since as a child, by naming, she made her own Island in time. (pp. 218-19)

> *Elizabeth Waterston, "Lucy Maud Montgomery," in* The Clear Spirit: Twenty Canadian Women and Their Times, *edited by Mary Quayle Innis, University of Toronto Press, 1966, pp. 198-220.*

### FRANCIS W. P. BOLGER

Lucy Maud Montgomery, throughout her literary career, derived her principal inspiration from the beauty of nature and from her family associations. Her novels, poems and short stories reflect the cultural, intellectual and emotional climate of her childhood and adolescence. Her descriptions always mirror the familiar background of pastoral Prince Edward Island. The beauty of her environment, the warmth of human relationships, the sheer happiness of life are the *stuff* of Lucy Maud Montgomery's stories. Her creative writings have a wholesome purity which was nurtured by her intimate association with forebears of strong character and high ideals. (pp. 18-19)

> *Francis W. P. Bolger, in his* The Years Before "Anne," *The Prince Edward Island Heritage Foundation, 1974, 229 p.*

### SHEILA EGOFF

To denigrate the literary qualities of *Anne of Green Gables* is as useless an exercise as carping about the architecture of the National War Memorial. Anne arrived and she has stayed. There is no doubt that the first book in the twenty-two titles by L. M. Montgomery . . . was an improvement on what little was being written for children at the time. The spirited redhead from Prince Edward Island added a note of girlishness and mischief to Canadian children's books that was hitherto lacking. But when we have mentioned the Prince Edward Island setting, which is lushly described, there is little else to comment on. Montgomery belongs to that breed of writers who give themselves away in their second and succeeding books. Of Anne, we are inclined to say, 'Her I can accept,' but the increasingly sentimental dishonesty of the succeeding books tends to destroy the first. Only the most avid **"Anne"** fans will refuse to admit that the appealing qualities of the first book are soon dissipated. It is sad but true that the **"Anne"** books continue to evoke great nostalgia from many adults to whom much vastly superior modern Canadian writing is unknown. (p. 304)

> *Sheila Egoff, "Early Canadian Children's Books," in her* The Republic of Childhood: A Critical Guide to Canadian Children's Literature in English, *second edition, Oxford University Press, Canadian Branch, 1975, pp. 292-309.\**

### MOLLIE GILLEN

[Maud's] young heroines find their fulfilment in soul-satisfying relationships: not necessarily in success through money or fame, but through perfect communion of the spirit with the right people, in the right environment and the right niche in life, though they often have to suffer before gaining their Promised Land. Jane Stuart (*Jane of Lantern Hill*) had to endure an unendurable old grandmother before finding a father after her own heart and reunited parents. Maud herself made the best of what she had, but in her private letters she sometimes writes like a woman short-changed by life, despite her public success.

Nevertheless, her rich endowments of spirit and imagination were, she must have realized, compensation enough—or almost. Who, with that intense love of beauty, could not be grateful for such a refuge from the slings and arrows? (p. 148)

And who, with Maud's sense of humour, could not find relief in comedy from darker moods? No wonder Leaskdale folk caught her laughing to herself as she wrote: describing, perhaps, the frigid politeness with which an aspiring Emily and the successful editor she is interviewing suffer the madly destructive living-room romp of an uninhibited dog each believed to be owned by the other; or picturing Aunt Frances, refusing an aspirin to relieve a headache and "still enduring God's will in her bedroom"; or embedding a whole world of shocked folk-morality in one amber sentence: "How would you like to die in your sleep and go before your Maker in *pyjamas*, Patricia?"

She had another refuge—her lifelong personification of inanimate objects, a trait shared by her youthful heroines: the child in her flower-girl finery who runs upstairs to comfort a weekday dress for temporary neglect; the little girl who ached for the lonely, tumble-down house that needed to be loved and lived in; Emily saying goodbye to her trees—"to the Rooster Pine and Adam-and-Eve . . . to the spider crack in the kitchen window—to the old wing chair—to the bed of striped grass—to the silver birch-ladies."

And of course, for Maud, there was also the intoxication of words and phrases. (p. 149)

Like her Emily, Maud had felt near to the secret heart of the mystery, only a fragile veil's-width away from all the answers she would never find in church. Her gods were beauty and truth; and reality, for her, lay in her writing where, through the thoughts and actions of her characters, she could safely express unorthodoxy, hit out at remembered injustices, and relive the joyous world of her youth. Yet in that world, her sharp eye saw the human flaws, her keen ear heard the note of protest. Few writers have better portrayed the plight of sensitive children under the authority of uncompromising adults. All her heroines are hag-ridden to greater or lesser extent by these guardians, well-meaning but obtuse: they are adolescent girls alone in a world more or less hostile, unprotected by the parents with whom they had once lived or (they passionately believed) would have lived in close and sympathetic companionship. Only Jane Stuart, of all Maud's heroines, once she had discovered her charming father—and perhaps Pat, with her happy home life at Silver Bush and full complement of parents—really escaped the tyranny of nagging adults. Anne and Emily and Marigold constantly ran head-on into the prejudices of the period in those small, infinitely important crises erupting in the daily round of life in school and home. All too well Maud understood and was able to depict the soul-destroying power of the trivial, and the incurable scars small stabs can leave. "I think the little things in life often make more trouble than the big things," said Anne with Maud's own insight.

Her books, by their very nature, are more powerful than her short stories . . . : especially those with romantic plots frequently based on the emotional reconciliation of people who had let some stupid tiff keep them apart into middle age, a theme that appealed to her romantic nature. Stories featuring children are much more successful. Maud's child characters are natural little creatures with human flaws, neither all bad nor all good, and she uses them skilfully for sly digs at absurd adult behaviour or the prim conventions of the day. The chil-

dren scold each other with the virtuous morality they have imbibed from their elders. (pp. 173-74)

In her almost plotless books—a series of anecdotes and incidents strung on the thread of a child's journey to adulthood—Maud's strength in capsule characterization is particularly marked. She has made telling and effective use of the kind of detail every reader will recognize. Every story she was ever told, every person she met, every human situation she encountered, every phrase she read or heard, all were noted down, stored away, to be used unchanged or brought to sparkling new life by the touch of her darting imagination. Everything was the stuff of stories for Maud. Even [her] terrible premonitory dreams during the war were used, grafted onto the schoolteacher Gertrude Oliver in *Rilla of Ingleside.*

The inescapable power of natural beauty to haunt and compel her, the tormenting need to purge her soul of its ecstasy in verbal expression, led her often into the excesses she was able to mock through the characters she created, but could not correct in her own writing. Her purple patches, and the clichés of her romantic and frankly commercial short stories have led many critics to overlook the real flashes of insight and often wit in her characterizations, especially those of adolescent girls and crusty eccentrics.

"You're too fond of purple, Emily," the young Emily is told by a candid teacher. "Cut out all those flowery passages," was Anne's teacher's advice. "And I'd let the sun rise and set in the usual quiet way without much fuss over the fact."

But when it came to sunsets and sunrises, Maud was lost. Morning and evening were new miracles that had to be captured and recaptured on her pages. In one book alone (*Anne of the Island*), sunset after sunset trailed glory through successive pages. (p. 175)

It was impossible for Maud to leave natural beauty well alone. . . . But then, this is part of her continuing appeal. She speaks for so many inarticulate people in the grip of emotions they cannot release, particularly the young for whom she writes who are making their own first discoveries about the joy of living. (p. 176)

> *Mollie Gillen, in her* The Wheel of Things: A Biography of L. M. Montgomery, Author of "Anne of Green Gables," *Fitzhenry & Whiteside Limited, 1975, 200 p.*

**MARGERY FISHER**

The long popularity of the eight stories of Anne and Avonlea owes much to the Pollyanna stories and *Rebecca of Sunnybrook Farm*, books which set a fashion for the orphan who becomes a ray of sunshine in dark lives. But there is nothing dark about Green Gables, nor has Anne the ineffable joyousness of Pollyanna. Her irruption into other people's lives is less dramatic and she is herself a more natural character than either of the earlier heroines. The atmosphere of the **"Avonlea"** books (at least of the first two, *Anne of Green Gables* and *Anne of Avonlea*) is good-humoured and light, with an outdoor feel about it, depending on episodes at home or in school in which Anne shows her bursting high spirits, her imagination (poetic and engagingly absurd in the manner of the early 'teens), her gift for friendship, her quick temper and equally quick affection.

A remark made about Anne by old Miss Barry may provide another key to the long life of this fictional character. 'That Anne girl improves all the time . . . [She] has as many shades as a rainbow and every shade is the prettiest while it lasts.' A heroine who is observant and genuinely interested in people is an asset to a novelist. Anne's creator was able to use her in later books as an excuse for anecdotes about local worthies, keeping Anne herself in the background to avoid repetition. The books concerning Anne's high school and college years, her marriage and growing family, are less entertaining than the first two in the series—to adolescents at least, for whom Anne's decorous romance with Gilbert Blythe must seem dull after the sprightly quarrels they indulged in as school-fellows. It is best to forget that the freckled, red-haired orphan ever grew up, for there is still much to enjoy in following her through the lively years between eleven and sixteen.

Margery Fisher, "Who's Who in Children's Books: Anne Shirley," in her Who's Who in Children's Books: A Treasury of the Familiar Characters of Childhood, Holt, Rinehart and Winston, 1975, p. 23.

**GILLIAN THOMAS**

It is a cliché of popular literature that sequels tend to be disappointing, and students of children's literature are all too sadly familiar with the decline of writers who turn themselves into human factories on the basis of a successful first book. After the phenomenal success of **Anne of Green Gables** in 1908, L. M. Montgomery wrote well over a dozen more books with a similar setting, five of which concentrate on Anne herself as the central character. Although these five other "**Anne**" novels are by no means without interest, they lack many of the qualities which make the first book so appealing. (p. 37)

The progressively unsatisfactory nature of the five "**Anne**" sequels reveals a good deal about why their forerunner was so successful. Several important factors are missing from the grown-up Anne. When we meet the young Anne, she is an orphan sitting alone in a railway station. As most children's librarians know, "books about orphans", evoking, as they do, a mixture of pity and envy, enjoy an immense popularity among child readers. However, far from being alienated and unwanted, Anne in the later books is totally absorbed in a dense social network of family and rural community. Similarly, much of the young Anne's appeal to female readers stems from the substance of the book's initial episode, in which Anne is almost sent away because Marilla and Matthew had wanted a boy but the orphanage has sent Anne by mistake. In a world in which most female children rapidly become aware that they would have enjoyed a higher status both within the family and in the outside world had they been born male, this episode is bound to have a powerful effect on its readers. By contrast, the grown-up Anne enjoys (at second-hand) the social status of her doctor husband [Gilbert Blythe] and willingly accepts the social restrictions which result from that role.

If the Anne of the first book is often considered a spirited individualist, then the Anne of the final book seems a rather dreary conformist. A somewhat priggish tone is established at the very beginning of **Anne of Ingleside** where, when Anne remarks to her old friend Diana that Marilla still makes redcurrant wine "in spite of the minister and Mrs. Lynde . . . just to make us feel real devilish", Diana giggles at the piece of wickedness and thinks that she "did not mind 'devilish' as she would if anybody but Anne used it. Everybody knew Anne didn't really mean things like that. It was just her way."

One of the episodes in **Anne of Ingleside** which is most revealing of the adult Anne is the one in which her eight year old daughter, Di, becomes friendly with Jenny Penny, a new

pupil at her school. Jenny's "background" is told to Anne by Susan, the Blythe family servant:

> They are a new family that have moved to the old Conway farm on the Base Line, Mrs. Dr. dear. Mr. Penny is said to be a carpenter who couldn't make a living carpentering . . . being too busy, as I understand, trying to prove there is no God . . . and has decided to try farming. From all I can make out they are a queer lot. The young ones do just as they like. He says he was bossed to death when he was a kid and his children are not going to be.

Jenny, although a distinctly tougher character, has much of the storytelling ability of the young Anne and constantly fantasizes a more alluring family history for herself. Di is forbidden to go and stay overnight with Jenny because the Penny family are obviously "unsuitable" friends for the Doctor's children. When Di, at Jenny's instigation, sneaks away to the Pennys' house, she is appalled by its run-down appearance because she is "accustomed to the beauty and dignity of Ingleside". As the episode progresses, the Penny family fit more and more into the stereotype of the feckless working class and the sequence culminates with the terrified Di playing dead and being dumped outside Ingleside by the equally terrified Penny children. Interestingly, however, there is no hint throughout this episode that Jenny's storytelling has a source similar to the fantasies of the young Anne in a lonely childhood, or that her behaviour merits any response short of condemnation.

The first few chapters of **Anne of Ingleside** are taken up with the deadening and interminable visit of Gilbert's Aunt Mary Maria. The old woman is an intolerable prude and bully, but Anne, out of loyalty to Gilbert, is unable to exert pressure to persuade her to leave despite the fact that it is very clear that the situation is something of a nightmare for her:

> "I feel as you do in dreams when you're trying to run and can only drag your feet," said Anne drearily. "If it were only now and then . . . but it's every day. Meal times are perfect horrors now . . ."

This Anne, who seems the willing victim of social convention, is bound to disappoint the readers who so admired the spirited Anne of the first book. The child who stamped her foot at Mrs. Lynde and who walked the ridge-pole for a dare has vanished and left in her place a woman intent on observing the social proprieties and for whom "imagination" has come to mean something which very closely resembles sentimentality.

Curiously enough, in the midst of its flights of sentimentality, the final "pot-boiler", **Anne of Ingleside,** and its predecessor, **Anne's House of Dreams,** touch on much darker themes than the previous "**Anne**" novels. Anne's first baby dies. Her friend, Leslie Moore, lives out a death-in-life existence with her brain-damaged husband. Neither of these situations is permitted to become a permanent blight on the House of Dreams, however, for the stork (sic) brings Anne another child, and a highly contrived series of events, culminating in successful brain surgery, leads to the discovery that Leslie Moore's husband has been dead for many years and that "Dick Moore" is in fact her dead husband's amnesiac cousin. In **Anne of Ingleside** there is also the recurring theme of Anne's own death. Early in the novel, Anne's little son Walter, who is sent away in a state of mystification to stay with neighbours while his mother is due to give birth to another child, develops the obsession that she is dreadfully ill and likely to die. Naturally the episode ends cosily with hot milk, cookies and comfort being dispensed, but the same theme recurs soon after when Anne almost dies of pneumonia.

Amid these reminders of death, the final "Anne" novel contains two other very odd episodes. In the first of these, Anne "remembers" what happened at Peter Kirk's funeral. Kirk had evidently treated both his wives quite brutally and was generally disliked in the community. His first wife's sister, Clara Wilson, attends the funeral and delivers a tirade against the dead man. . . . This episode, the strangest and most powerful one in the novel, is immediately undercut by the "explanation" provided by Stephen Macdonald that Clara Wilson had been jilted in her youth by Peter Kirk. Thus the source of her hatred which was originally shown as outrage at her sister's suffering becomes instead the trivial vindictiveness of the jilted woman.

The novel, as a whole, ends on a muted note after an odd episode in which Anne believes that she is "losing" Gilbert to an old college acquaintance of theirs. They go to dinner with Christine Stuart, in whose company Gilbert is animated while having been quite remote and abstracted when with Anne. In the familiar Montgomery pattern, the darkness is quickly dispelled with the explanation that Gilbert's abstraction has been caused by his concern over a seriously ill patient who has now made a dramatic recovery. The book ends with a determined celebration of marriage and family which remains curiously unconvincing.

Marian Engel has remarked that Margaret Laurence's novels, "unlike the sentimental novels of . . . [L. M. Montgomery] pull no punches about their community." This remark, taken in relation to some of the elements in the later "Anne" novels discussed here, leads to some interesting conclusions about the nature of L. M. Montgomery's writing. If "serious" literature tends to explore individual consciousness and awareness, then popular literature tends more frequently to celebrate social bonding. The re-union with the long-lost relative and the cunningly engineered marriage of true minds make up the familiar fabric of 19th century melodrama and "romantic" novels as well as of contemporary television soap opera.

If the young Anne's role is to transform Green Gables and its surroundings by the exercise of her "imagination", then the role of the grown-up Anne is more and more that of social engineer, bringing about the unions and re-unions on which popular literature is so dependent. Once she is married, Anne becomes an indefatigable matchmaker. . . . Despite the incident at Peter Kirk's funeral which raises the spectre of sadism, and despite Anne's temporary apprehension that her own marriage may be failing, all of Anne's matches are presented as bringing about nothing short of perfect and permanent bliss for the objects of her schemes. The only one of her matches which goes awry does so because the couple she has marked out for one another have already secretly planned to marry, and thus her scheming is merely superfluous. The idea that some marriages can be unfulfilling or destructive is scarcely allowed to intrude on Anne's world. Similarly, while *Anne of Green Gables* and *Anne of Avonlea* incorporate and come to terms with some of the narrowness and petty meanness which is a familiar component of life in a small community, this element is more and more firmly thrust aside in the later "Anne" novels.

In part the shortcomings of the sequels to *Anne of Green Gables* develop naturally from the genre of the sentimental novels to which they belong. Their failings also spring from the social

limitations on Anne Blythe who must behave appropriately for her role as "Mrs. Dr." It is a sad thought that, if the young Anne Shirley with her sharp eye for social hypocrisy were to meet her own grown-up self, she would probably not find that she was a "kindred spirit". (pp. 37-41)

*Gillian Thomas, "The Decline of Anne: Matron vs. Child," in* L. M. Montgomery: An Assessment, *edited by John Robert Sorfleet, Canadian Children's Press, 1976, pp. 37-41.*

**ANN S. COWAN**

Writers are not always their own best critics nor is the market always the best judge of a writer's work. In Montgomery's case, her own favourite books, *The Story Girl* and *The Golden Road*, and the most popular, *Anne of Green Gables*, *Anne of Avonlea*, and *Anne of the Island*, are inferior, in my opinion, to the "Emily" books, and it is on the strength of these that Montgomery's reputation as a children's novelist must rest.

In *Emily of New Moon*, *Emily Climbs*, and *Emily's Quest*, L. M. Montgomery tempers the romantic fantasies of a book for girls with autobiographical notes from the life of a struggling young writer. The resultant trilogy fascinates the young reader and holds the interest of the adult. As Emily matures as a woman and as a writer, she must resolve the large questions of the human condition, and, in this, the books move into the realm of literature.

Because of their autobiographical nature, the "Emily" books hold a special interest for Montgomery's readers. She thoroughly disapproved of biographies and forbade her friend Weber to "write her life":

> So "if I die before you do, you'll write my life?" No, you won't! Nobody shall. . . . Biography is a *screaming farce*. No man or woman was *ever* truly depicted. Biographies, even the best, are one—or at most two-sided—and every human being has half a dozen different sides. It must always be that way until some medium of communication is found for "soul moods".

The creation of Emily Byrd Starr afforded L. M. Montgomery an opportunity for a wide range of soul worlds. Since many of the facts of Emily's life correspond with Montgomery's own, perhaps we can assume that they shared as well a few of the "soul moods". . . .

Emily Byrd Starr's writer-father was much resented by the Murrays of Blair Water whose youngest daughter, Juliet, had disgraced herself by marrying. According to the Presbyterian ethic of Montgomery's milieu, writers are irresponsible dreamers (see *Jane of Lantern Hill* and *The Story Girl*) and earn only grudging respect when they achieve financial success. They are always adored by Montgomery's heroines for their sensitivity to suffering and joy and for their appreciation of nature (*Blue Castle*). Even their understanding of religion is different from the accepted social view. Emily contrasts "Father's God" with "Aunt Elizabeth's God". But the heroine always finds a society of "kindred souls" to compensate for the insensitivity of the larger society. (p. 44)

The acknowledgement that society is not receptive to the poet marks a development in Montgomery's attitude to her young audience. Her earlier heroine, Anne, had a flair for writing too, and although Marilla scolded her occasionally, she never faced the hostility Emily encounters. Both Anne and Emily write wildly romantic tales and choose exotic names for their heroines. (A fault shared by L. M. Montgomery; see *The Story Girl* and *Chronicles of Avonlea*.) They both learn, however, to exercise artistic restraint. Anne is told to write only of what she knows and to criticize her own work sharply. Emily's Mr. Carpenter, on reviewing all of her work, finds ten good lines. He becomes a stern critic of Emily's work, far beyond the role of teacher. Montgomery suggests in *Emily of New Moon* that the child writer is father unto the man-writer and as such must not be sheltered from the trials and hardships of life and literature—a marked change from the "Anne" books. (p. 45)

Aside from their literary gifts, Emily of New Moon and Lucy Maud Montgomery share many similarities. Both were aware of death in early childhood. Emily's description of the death of her mother corresponds almost word-for-word with the description in Montgomery's biography of her childhood memory of her mother's death. Mr. Carpenter remarks on reading Emily's poetry that she "knows something of death", while Anne, though an orphan, is seemingly unaware of death except in her abstract imaginings. Emily and Lucy were both solitary children who imagined playmates. . . . All children understand loneliness—even if their only experience is the occasional exclusion from playground games. L. M. Montgomery offers her personal solution, a retreat into the imagination.

In her later books, Montgomery allows her heroines more suffering and consequently greater strength to overcome it. Anne is immediately loved and accepted by her schoolmates; Emily, like young Lucy, is teased about her high button boots and baby apron and persecuted because "you ain't a bit like us". Childhood prejudice is painful and it is a mark of Montgomery's literary progress that she skilfully copes with it in her later novels. The devotion of Anne and Diana is far less realistic than the stormy friendship of Emily and Ilse. Emily had "loved" Rhoda Stuart with the same sentimentality that colours Anne and Diana's friendship—only to discover Rhoda unworthy. Emily's friendship with Ilse allows for Ilse's quick temper and Emily's stubborn pride.

Emily's discoveries about writing parallel her discoveries about life. In a sense her literary progress provides a framework for the three novels while her growing maturity supplies the supporting interest and detail. One of the most dramatic examples of the close relationship of personal and literary growth occurs in *Emily's Quest*. When Emily becomes engaged to marry Dean Priest, her cousin, friend, confidant, and critic from early childhood, she senses that her marriage will end her literary career. Dean has always praised her writing but has laughed at her for taking "these trifles" seriously. Since Dean saved Emily's life as a child he has always half-jokingly half-seriously claimed that her life belongs to him. Montgomery does not admit the right of one person to possess or dominate another, and characters who try to do so in her novels are always foiled. Teddy Kent's mother, in her attempt to possess her son, jealously discourages the friendship between Emily and Teddy. This conflict mirrors the Emily-Dean relationship.

Dean's greatest crime is to lie to Emily about her writing. In his jealousy of her work, he discourages Emily who, in faith, burns her first book. Emily agrees to give up her writing and marry Dean even though she loves someone else. Of course, Montgomery cannot let this happen. To change the course of events, she gives Emily the gift of "second sight". Emily is able, with this gift, to prevent Teddy from sailing on a boat that sinks. The incident makes Emily realize how close she is "spiritually" to Teddy and how wrong of her it would be to marry anyone else. Unfortunately, Emily's pride and Mrs. Kent's

jealousy delay the mutual discovery of their love until many years later, but Emily learns two significant things. She cannot give up her writing nor can she deny her heart, both important aspects of L. M. Montgomery's own experience.

Anne does give up her writing. When Gilbert suggests that she has sacrificed, Anne replies that her family is more important than the "few children's stories" she wrote, an attitude Montgomery certainly never shared. Despite her busy life as a minister's wife and a mother, Montgomery always found time for her writing. She always acknowledged the right of both men and women to fulfill their destinies. (pp. 45-6)

One of the most striking qualities Emily shows is her compassion. Even though Mrs. Kent has greatly wronged her, and even though Dean has lied to her, Emily is able to forgive them readily because she can see that pain and weakness have motivated them. Compassion was Mr. Carpenter's most valuable lesson. Carpenter saw himself in Emily's satire of old Peter DeGeer and chastized her sadly. . . . Mr. Carpenter's last lesson is delivered on his death bed in *Emily's Quest*. He makes her promise that she will write to please only herself:

> Keep that—and you'll be—all right. No use trying to please everybody. No use trying to please—critics. Live under your own hat. Don't be—led away—by those howls about realism. Remember—pine woods are just as real as—pigsties—and a darn sight pleasanter to be in. You'll get there—sometime—you have the root—of the matter—in you. And don't—tell the world—everything. That's what's the—matter—with our—literature. Lost the charm of mystery—and reserve.

Neither Emily nor Montgomery write of pigsties, but Montgomery does write of pain with compassion and truth, romance tempered with the realism of experience. While Emily's lapse from the writer's faith is only temporary, it is an important element in her growth. Emily must justify her decision to write in her own fashion. While she has the moral courage to believe she is right, she must have some form of tangible success and finally the approval of her family. Predictably, this comes for Emily because of her maturity and compassion. (pp. 46-7)

Both Emily and L. M. Montgomery received contradictory reviews. One of the most significant for Emily is the one from Janet Royal in New York. Miss Royal had been angry when Emily refused her offer of a position in New York. . . . Emily replied that she would create her own atmosphere,

> And as for material—people *live* here just the same as anywhere else—suffer and enjoy and sin and aspire just as they do in New York. . . . Some fountain of living water would dry up in my soul if I left the land I love.

Miss Royal's letter affirms Emily's understanding of the nature of her literary gift:

> You were right not to come to New York. . . . You could never have written the *Moral of the Rose* here. Wild roses don't grow on city streets. And your story is like a wild rose, dear, all sweetness and unexpectedness, with sly little thorns of wit and satire. It has power, delicacy, understanding. It's not just story-telling, there's some magicry in it. Emily Byrd Starr, where

do you get your uncanny understanding of human nature—you infant.

Aunt Elizabeth pronounces the final dictum: "Well I never
believed that such a pack of lies could sound as much like the
real truth as that book does."

The novel is justified, the *Canadian* novel is justified, and
Emily has found success. L. M. Montgomery, in the **"Emily"**
trilogy, has successfully expanded the themes of her novels
for girls to create a work of literature that sensitively explores
the problems and conflicts facing the young Canadian female
novelist in a society which places a literary career second to
the role of wife and mother. The work, though fiction, is
successful in its truth-telling because Montgomery wrote from
her own understanding of life and literature. (pp. 47-8)

> Ann S. Cowan, "Canadian Writers: Lucy Maud &
> Emily Byrd," in L. M. Montgomery: An Assess-
> ment, edited by John Robert Sorfleet, Canadian Chil-
> dren's Press, 1976, pp. 42-9.

### MURIEL A. WHITAKER

It was with some hesitation that I recently returned to [**Anne
of Green Gables, Emily of New Moon, The Blue Castle,** and
**Pat of Silver Bush**] . . . ; a hesitation stemming partly from
reluctance to burst the bubble of nostalgia, partly from an
awareness of critical disapproval. . . . On rereading, *Anne* seemed
not at all bad and *Emily* interested me so much I wanted to
read the rest of the series to see how things turned out. Admittedly, the charm was partly that of a period piece. Canadiana
is "in" at the moment: though we no longer use gin jars for
hot water bottles or keep up a parlour for serious occasions,
hooked rugs, patchwork quilts, and butter churns are highly
prized and highly priced. Is the appeal of L. M. Montgomery's
novels simply a matter of nostalgia or do they contain something of lasting, if minor, literary value? In what context do
her child heroines operate? What makes Anne and Emily particularly interesting, and Valancy and Pat less so? (p. 50)

[We] can neither sympathise with Valancy [in *The Blue Castle*]
nor admire her. The Castle in Spain fantasy, realised as an
island retreat in the wilds of Ontario, is pure corn, but not less
so is the heroine's marriage to frog prince Snaith who turns
out to be not only the famous nature writer, John Foster, but
also the son of a multi-millionaire Purple Pill producer (a fact
that brings Valancy's disapproving relatives round in a hurry).
Nor are we surprised to learn, after a Perils-of-Paulinish episode involving a shoe heel caught in a railway track before an
onrushing train, that Valancy's fatal heart condition really belonged to another Sterling and that violet-eyed Barney has
married Valancy out of love not pity. It is tempting to exculpate
L. M. Montgomery by regarding *The Blue Castle* as a parody
of romance rather than as a serious attempt at the genre, but
I cannot quite convince myself that such is the case. . . .

Pat Gardiner is the fourth of five children. Because her mother
is sickly and occupied with a new baby, Pat's upbringing, like
that of Anne and Emily, is left to a surrogate parent. Judy
Plum is a shanty Irish family retainer whose influence on the
"quare child—touched wid a liddle green rose-thorn" by a
leprechaun on the day she was born—is, from the modern point
of view, deplorable. Judy can speak "English" when the Gar-
diners' fine relatives are present, but in the bosom of the family
she affects an Irish brogue in which dialect she fills the child's
head with fairy nonsense, assures her that babies are found in
parsley beds, passes on malicious gossip, and instills in her a
conviction that she is socially superior. . . . (p. 54)

*Pat of Silver Bush* contains many of the ingredients found in
*Anne* and *Emily*—the P.E.I. setting, the clan feeling, the visits
to eccentric relatives, the bosom friend, the admiring boys, the
education at Queen's—yet when I read *Pat* as a child I found
it a disappointment. Pat seems a bore and a snob. Rereading
has not changed my mind. Part of Pat's failure to interest us
results from the lack of development in her character. Petted
by the family and Judy, she is never placed in a position of
real crisis where strength of character is required. Moreover,
the love of nature which she shares with the other heroines is
expressed in such tritely sentimental rhetoric that the character
cannot help being diminished. Whether running about in the
garden to kiss the flowers or dancing naked under the impression that she is a bewitched princess, she comes across as a
girl who is queer to the point of being dim-witted.

Why are Anne and Emily such memorable characters while
Valancy and Pat are best forgotten? It is not a question of time
bringing to slow fruition a writer's skill, for Anne, the first of
Montgomery's creations, is also the best. The answer must be
found in the fictional character's relationship to reality. Much
of the interest in *Anne* and *Emily* results from the tension
between the adults, with their rigid view of how a child should
act, and the children, with their strong sense of justice and
clear-eyed awareness of adult shortcomings. Though the heroines' characters may have been influenced by such fictional
rebels against the establishment as Lewis Carroll's Alice and
Mark Twain's Huckleberry Finn, they must also represent the
way in which real children reacted to the authoritarian adults
who controlled their destinies. (p. 55)

When Anne shouts furiously at Mrs. Lynde,

> "How dare you call me skinny and ugly? How
> dare you say I'm freckled and red-headed? You
> are a rude, impolite, unfeeling woman!"

she is expressing a justifiable sense of outrage at the insensitivity of adults. And when Emily confronts Aunt Elizabeth
with "How dare you touch *my private papers?*" she is asserting
her right to be treated as an individual.

Moreover, in *Anne* and *Emily* there is such genuine interaction
between children and adults that the adults themselves are
changed. Matthew and Cousin Jimmy, the weak but kindly
father figures, are given an interest that lifts them out of the
humdrum routine of their daily lives and enables them to stand
up to formidable females. Aunt Elizabeth learns that she cannot
treat children according to standards that differ from those
applied to adults. And Marilla so far overcomes her distrust
of emotion that after Matthew's death she confesses her true
feelings about Anne. (pp. 55-6)

By the same token, what makes Valancy and Pat inadequate
is their lack of influence. Valancy's pert put-down of the rid-
dling uncle and boring aunts strikes us as rudeness rather than
as a courageous expression of ego, while the self-dramatisation
which brings Anne so vividly to life seems, in Valancy, to be
maudlin play-acting. There is no better testimony to the adults'
immobility in *The Blue Castle* than the fact that, regardless of
how queerly Valancy behaves, her mother and Cousin Stickles
continue to sit "drearily, grimly knitting. Baffling and inhuman
as ever."

In *Pat of Silver Bush* there is no lack of incident—births, wed-
dings, the departure of a brother, the death of a friend—but
all is surface fussiness. Because the characters fail to interact
with one another we remain uninterested. The lachrymose seems

the dominant mood but there is no sense of proportion. Tears gush forth as profusely when Father shaves his beard as when the bosom friend dies. At the same time, there is no development of Pat's character. The woman who becomes ''the Chatelaine of Silver Bush'' is really no different from the seven-year-old listening to Judy's stories.

In the end, what contributes most of all to the sense of reality projected by Anne and Emily is the fact that the fabric of their lives is that of L. M. Montgomery's own experience. Lucy Maud, too, was a motherless child brought up by relatives in a farmhouse at Cavendish, Prince Edward Island. She, too, struck callers as ''queer'' because she talked to objects, individually named apple trees, and imaginatively created child companions who were ''kindred spirits''. She suffered from the tension between Puritan expectations and the working of original sin. (p. 56)

> Muriel A. Whitaker, '''Queer Children': L. M. Montgomery's Heroines,'' in L. M. Montgomery: An Assessment, *edited by John Robert Sorfleet, Canadian Children's Press, 1976, pp. 50-9.*

## JANE COWAN FREDEMAN

For all their differences, Valancy and Marigold illustrate the primary theme of Montgomery's work, the encroachment of the real world on the child and the need to leave childhood behind. Only two, the Story Girl and Emily Starr, will not become exiles from fairyland, though for all a contented future is envisioned. Her heroines share further common traits which serve to accentuate their solitude.

Perhaps to mark the individuality of growth and perhaps because it echoed her own experience, with the exception of Pat Gardiner all Montgomery's heroines are isolated from the normal pattern of family life. Marigold and Valancy have only one living parent, and neither mother is able or willing to help her child. Jane Stuart believes her situation to be the same until she learns that her parents are separated. Anne, Emily, and Kilmeny are orphans living with elderly people who cannot, even when they try, comprehend their private worlds. The Story Girl whose mother is dead and whose father is abroad, is a further variation; her home is with an aunt and uncle, near, but not with, her numerous cousins. (p. 64)

The heroines also tend to be isolated or differentiated from the other girls in the books by their plainness and by the oddity of their clothes, aspects almost as frequently commented upon as the gratitude expected from them by their surrogate and real parents. The truism that beauty is only skin deep is documented dramatically in Montgomery's novels where internal rather than external beauty is a prerequisite for the final emergence of the character; frequently too, it separates those other characters who recognize the depth and uniqueness of the heroines' visions and dreams from those who are incapable of doing so. Though all recognize that they are ''nae beauties,'' Anne seems more keenly self-conscious about her carrot hair and freckles, and in none of the other novels are the episodes involving the recognition of plainness so hilarious as the hair-dying scene in *Anne of Green Gables.* The burden falls lightest on Marigold and Pat; neither are jealous children, and the former's most earnest hope is to have her hair bobbed, while Pat learns at eleven that her eyes, her smile, and her capacity for love will carry her further than any amount of golden curls. Emily's good points are like Pat's, though she inwardly rages, like Anne, at her old-fashioned clothes and earnestly wants the ''band'' she feels will make her prettier. The Story Girl's too

long and too white face is more than compensated for by the rainbow voice which in the future, the reader is told, will make kings delight to honour her. (p. 65)

The naming of places, trees, and objects is another personal trait which Montgomery transfers to her heroines. Whether or not these secret names are shared with others, it is the meaning the heroine invests them with that makes them live. Thus, for example, Diana Barry, though she wants to share Anne's games, lacks the depth of Anne's feelings to actualize for herself the ''Lake of Shining Waters,'' ''White Way of Delight,'' and ''Dryad's Bubble,'' among others. So, too, all of the children and adults in *The Story Girl* know the names of the trees in the old orchard, but only she can revivify the long gone people for whom they were named and create the sensation Beverley says the children could feel but were unable to analyze.

The betrayal or outgrowing of these childhood names often separates the heroine from her peers. Just as Budge thought Sylvia ''silly,'' so there comes a day when Pat's beloved brother Sid turns his back on their ''Secret Field'' by showing it to May Binnie to whom it is only ''a hole in the woods.'' For Pat, May is the equivalent of Anne's Josie Pye, and through her and the many other stodgy, unimaginative, or cruel children, L. M. Montgomery introduces a view of childhood which contradicts the assumption that all children are inhabitants of fairyland. . . . Sid was one of the few, but ''down he forgot'' by the time he married May. Pat's story illustrates another use of emblematic names. Throughout [*Pat of Silver Bush* and *Mistress Pat*] her home, "Silver Bush," represents everything to Pat. She thinks she is free and happy to have it alone when she finally decides not to marry David Kirk, but after Rae's departure and Judy's death, there are signs that for Pat, too, things must change. Alone, she decides to light up the house:

> It did not like to be dark and silent. Yet she paused for a moment on the door-step, the prey of a sudden fancy. That shut door was a door of dreams through which she might slip into the Silver Bush of long ago. . . . A world utterly passed away might be her universe. . . .

Pat knows the fancy is ''nonsense,'' but it cannot be dissipated until the emblem is gone. Her dreams go through fire as Silver Bush burns. . . . Silver Bush and her devotion to it were not her life but her protection against it, as she finally recognizes when Hilary Gordon, who has not forgotten to remember, comes to her among the ashes to tell her that he has built her a new home by another sea. (p. 66)

One character above all others illustrates and summarizes the workings of fantasy in Montgomery's novels—Emily Starr, whose story is told in a trilogy in many ways superior to the far longer **"Anne"** series. Though L. M. Montgomery was and still is identified with Anne, any reader of *The Alpine Path* will recognize at once that Emily's biography, appearance, and career more nearly parallel her own. Despite superficial similarities, however, it is dangerous to press character analogues in the novels too closely. Montgomery would have endorsed wholeheartedly Thomas Wolfe's disclaimer in the proem to *Look Homeward Angel* that whereas ''all serious work in fiction is autobiographical . . . fiction is not fact,'' and ''a novelist may turn over half the people in a town to make a single figure in his novel.'' Like Wolfe, Montgomery meditated no man's or girl's—especially not her own—portrait in her books, as she makes plain in *The Alpine Path* [see excerpt above in Author's Commentary]. . . . She is to be included in this stricture, and those incidents in Emily's life which do or do not accord with her own are therefore not noted.

The eight-year-old Emily to whom the reader is introduced in *Emily of New Moon* has all the accoutrements of a full-blown child of fantasy. For companions she has the Wind Woman, Emily-in-the-glass, and various trees. But above all she has her writing, through which she can record her joys and dissipate her sorrows, and "the flash." (p. 67)

At her father's death, Emily is turned over to her mother's reluctant family, who eventually draw lots to decide who must take her. The first impressions Emily makes on them are even more unpropitious than Anne's on Marilla. But from the moment when "the flash" returns and with it "courage and hope" for "her cold little soul," Emily never falters in her sense of justice or in her forthrightness. When her Aunt Elizabeth demands to see the account book in which she keeps her writings, she burns it; when her father is called a failure, she retaliates. So, too, as she settles into New Moon, she learns she can master both the children—who reject her "because you ain't a bit like us"—and even her Aunt Elizabeth, when "some formidable power in [her] soul" brings Archibald Murray's expression to her face.

After various minor disappointments, she is soon friends with Ilse, Teddy, and Perry, and the characteristics of the fantasy worlds of Montgomery's other heroines begin to become part of the way in which she enlarges her solitary imaginings. Names are provided in abundance for their haunts, the most important among them for the future being "The Disappointed House" and the Roads of Today, Yesterday, and Tomorrow. Playacting, though frowned upon, flourishes, and she has repeated clashes with her first teacher and her aunt over her writing, particularly of "untrue" things, as time passes. But these reactions are compensated for by her relationships with such adults as Aunt Laura, who sympathizes without understanding, "queer" Cousin Jimmy, who soon becomes the provider of the Jimmy books in which her fancies take form, and Mr. Carpenter, who recognizes her talent and savagely corrects her writing.

Above all there is Dean "Jarback" Priest, a college friend of her father's, who, perceiving an inner beauty which he describes as "prismatic—palpitating—elusive," calls her, poetically, Star. Their special relationship builds through the years. To Emily "Dean Priest was sealed of her tribe and she divined it instantly. He had a right to the inner sanctuary and she yielded it unquestioningly." . . . For Dean, a different fantasy takes form: he "became a boy again with a boy's untainted vision," and he dreams of possessing his Star.

Dean Priest is probably the most difficult of L. M. Montgomery's characters to comprehend. The reader is not normally shown so much of the character of any of the heroines' lovers and is, consequently, not so torn when a choice between them comes. Perhaps Montgomery intended him as a figure to replace the equally sensitive Douglas Starr in Emily's life, for in certain ways he can be compared to the fathers her other heroines regain—the bohemian Blair Stanley, dissipating his talents and energies as he tells fascinating stories of his wanderings around the world; and the stronger Andrew Stuart who encourages his child to grow as she will. However, despite his external deformity, the inner "strength and tenderness and humour"—with which Montgomery imbues Dean from the outset and which he constantly demonstrates—makes him equally suitable as lover.

In *Emily of New Moon,* Dean defines fairyland as "everything the heart desires." In *Emily's Quest* he has to lose his fantasy, though he comes close to having it in his grasp. Perhaps Dean is voicing Montgomery's feeling when he says at the time their engagement is broken, "I should have known that only youth can call to youth—and I was never young. If I ever had been, even though I am old now, I might have held you." . . . But this explanation is not satisfactory; it could have been said to Pat by David Kirk. Dean's jealousy of Emily's work and his criticism of it, which led her to burn her first novel, provocatively entitled *A Seller of Dreams,* is perhaps intended to show more truly why he could never capture and hold her as Teddy Kent can.

Though the relationship between Emily and Teddy is not as fully developed as that with Dean, the reader is not unprepared for Emily's realization that she loves Teddy. Throughout their years apart, sufficient reminders of the days when they dreamed of sharing "The Disappointed House," when Emily always responded to Teddy's whistle, and when they vowed always to think of one another at the sight of Vega of the Lyre, are given to keep Teddy in mind, as do the intermittent references to the way in which Emily's eyes and smile continue to inform his paintings from his earliest days until he is recognized as an artist.

Emily's awareness of the totality of their bond comes as a result of one trait, occasionally implied in other heroines, but defined only in Emily. Closely connected with "the flash," but coming to her in dream or illness instead of waking hours, are moments of prescience. Through some kind of vision the child Emily had discovered the mystery of Ilse's mother's disappearance; in adolescence, she divines the location of a lost child; and, finally, calling to him through space, drawing "aside the veil of sense and time and see[ing] beyond," Emily saves Teddy from sailing on the *Flavian.* These moments are frightening and enervating for Emily, but through them

> She *knew,* beyond any doubt or cavil or mockery, that she had seen Teddy—had saved, or tried to save him, from some unknown peril. And she knew, just as simply and just as surely that she loved him—had always loved him, with a love that lay at the very foundation of her being.
>
> (pp. 68-9)

Anne may be, in Bliss Carman's words, "one of the immortal children of fiction," and so she certainly has been for several generations of L. M. Montgomery's readers. But it is Emily who fully encompasses the complex fantasy worlds which Montgomery shaped in her novels. (p. 69)

*Jane Cowan Fredeman, "The Land of Lost Content: The Use of Fantasy in L. M. Montgomery's Novels," in* L. M. Montgomery: An Assessment, *edited by John Robert Sorfleet, Canadian Children's Press, 1976, pp. 60-70.*

## JEAN LITTLE

[Montgomery] remembered exactly how it was to be a child. More than that, she was able to record the experience of being a child so faithfully and vividly that reading children, years later, find themselves in her stories. These two linked gifts, first the almost total recall and second the craft which enabled her to use this rich material, are what keep L. M. Montgomery alive. Her writing is flawed. She is overly sentimental and whimsical, although these qualities were welcome in children's fiction at the time when she wrote her books. She has an irritating preoccupation with matchmaking. She revels in describing whole clans of eccentric relations who have little or nothing to do with the plot. As a matter of fact, she seems to find it extremely difficult to leave any place, person or thing without giving it a full description. She frequently loses control of her ''minor'' characters. In *Pat of Silver Bush,* for example, the heroine is thoroughly upstaged by the family servant who gets to say at least fifty words to Pat's one. Montgomery's sense of humour saves her time and time again but also deserts her sometimes when she is badly in need of it. All of these weaknesses and more are to be found in Montgomery's many, many pages. Yet they are cancelled out to a great extent by the fact that Lucy Maud Montgomery knows about children.

She understands exactly what humiliates a child and how that child responds to it. She knows the way a child's conscience will magnify a small misdeed into a Sin of major proportions, a torment to be wrestled with in the darkness. The terrors children suffer in her books are gargantuan and usually the child perceives them as something that will pursue him forever. Montgomery is always aware that, for her heroes and heroines, the present is all that has actuality. She knows, too, the fatal ease and rapidity with which an adventure can become a disaster and how powerless and angry a child feels as adults manipulate his life without thought of consulting him. That sounds like enough but there is so much more this author understands. How confusing it is for children to be well-behaved in a world where the rules keep changing! How bitterly a child can resent casual well-meant teasing! And how sweet, how passing sweet, are the moments of victory, revenge, and eventual understanding! In *Emily of New Moon,* the child Emily Starr writes:

> A good many things I don't understand but I will remember them and find out about them someday.

This vow each of us made and, later, kept. But how many of us would remember without writers with Montgomery's perceptive memory to remind us? . . .

[Much] of L. M. Montgomery's awareness reaches us through mediocre writing. I could devote the rest of this article to outlining the limitations of her talent as a creative writer and as an objective editor and rewriter of her own work, giving chapter and verse as proof. I would find this a pointless exercise. Given these limitations, plus the handicap of writing in a time when sentimentality was not only accepted but immensely popular, Montgomery still did achieve something memorable. What was it?

> Or would the question be better put Who were they?

Anne Shirley is, of course, Montgomery's famous heroine. Whether or not you personally like, love or loathe Anne, I think it is safe to say that she will outlive anybody now reading this article. . . . Yet, in spite of Anne's popularity or perhaps because of it, I plan to ignore her, as much as possible, for the remainder of this article. I was devoted to her once and I have not lost my fondness for her during her harumscarum childhood, though I find her less engaging as she matures. But she was never my favourite among Montgomery's heroines. Jane was, in *Jane of Lantern Hill.* And, after rereading masses of Montgomery, I find I remain partial to Jane.

I want, therefore, to look more closely at Jane and at some of the other children Montgomery created, for I believe it was the children who kept us reading all those books, except for the one small space in time when we were twelve or so and became captivated by *The Blue Castle.*

This one lapse is easily understood by those of us who remember ourselves as reading twelve-year-olds. The book is purely and simply a dream, more literate and enchanting than those found in Love Comics. When dreaming is the biggest part of life, *The Blue Castle* is more than satisfactory. The current booming sales of Harlequin Romances and their ilk show that many people do not grow beyond the need for the fantasy world in *The Blue Castle.* Montgomery's effort is much better than some, which is not to heap praises upon her head but merely to give her her due. She at least spices it with humour.

Often, throughout all her books, Lucy Maud Montgomery's sense of the ridiculous or her abrupt return to the mundane saves her from banality. Also her wit is delightful when she does not exploit it. This bit, from *Magic for Marigold,* is one illustration chosen from among hundreds.

> Gwennie stuck out her tongue at Grandmother. It gave Marigold a shock to realize that anybody could do that and live.

To return to the children! Not every child coming from Montgomery's busy pen does her credit. She seems, to me, to have written about four types of children: Stock Children, Non-Children, Exaggerated Children and Real Children. These classifications are not as neat and airtight as I make them sound because Montgomery occasionally loses track of what kind of child she has in hand and lets him or her slip momentarily into being somebody else. This does not trouble child readers unduly since they too step out of character every so often. Critical adults accept such lapses with less equanimity.

The best illustrations of Stock Children are to be found in *The Story Girl* and its sequel *The Golden Road.* Since these two books are in no way separate stories, I shall discuss them as one. Eight children are involved and every one is what I call a Stock Child. Each is early given certain identifying characteristics which never vary. Felix is fat and sensitive about it. Felicity, more complex, is pretty, vain, a good cook, and a snob. She is also always jealous of her cousin Sara and at odds with her brother Dan. Dan is sarcastic. . . . Cecily, sister to Dan and Felicity, is almost a carbon copy of Beth in *Little Women* (although Beth will be remembered long after Cecily is forgotten). Cecily is good, gentle, timidly brave, and patient throughout. We are given to understand, after making our way through seven-hundred-and-nineteen pages, that dear Cecily will not live to grow up and we feel not the slightest twinge of shock at the news. Peter, the hired boy, is lively, irreverent, and smitten with Felicity. (When Montgomery writes about hired boys, she makes it crystal clear that they are not made of the same stuff as The Family, but she gives them gumption and intelligence and hints, if she does not spell it out, that they will rise in the world and make their mark. An interesting essay could be written on her whole treatment of class distinctions. Anne, for instance, although definitely an orphan, is discovered to have sprung from genteel stock. By their relatives shall ye know them.) Sara Ray, a neighbour child, cries. Always! Sara Stanley, the fabled Story Girl herself, is a heroine who is not a heroine because Montgomery never gives her a plot within which she can develop into a real person. She remains another

Stock Child, although the most complicated. She is always vivid, mysterious, charming, slightly humanized by her inability to learn to cook, and so ever ready with a story that I, for one, sometimes longed to tape her mouth shut. Beverley, the narrator of the whole thing, is pompous and ordinary. He also, for a very good reason, sounds middle-aged.

In *The Alpine Path* [see excerpt above in Author's Commentary] Lucy Maud Montgomery declares:

> *The Story Girl*. . . . is my own favourite among my books, the one that gave me the greatest pleasure to write, the one whose characters and landscape seem to me most real.

When she wrote this, she had not reached the end of her career as a writer, but she had had seven novels published. Why, one wonders, was she so partial to this early effort? I suspect the reason lies, in part at least, in the fact that the book took so little effort to write. She did not have to struggle with plot or search for ways to reveal change and growth in her characters. There is no sustained plot and nobody changes. At the same time, through the handy vehicle of the babbling Story Girl, Montgomery was able to relish retelling all the family and local legends to which she had listened with fascination during her own childhood. And she provided herself, alias the Story Girl, with a highly satisfactory audience, always ready to drop everything and listen spellbound. She failed to realize that a story told has an immediacy which is missing in that same story written down, unless the writer is someone with a storytelling gift far exceeding Montgomery's. It is only fair to say that few and far between are the writers who can successfully interject the telling of a tale which is not vitally linked to the plot of the characters. It has been tried, time and again, by the ablest of authors, and it has been my observation that children invariably simply skip to where "the real story" picks up again.

*The Story Girl-Golden Road* succeeds seldom, but that is not due simply to the fact that the children are Stock Children. Such boys and girls are the heroes and heroines of many excellent books. Arthur Ransome's characters, to a much lesser extent than Montgomery's, are Stock Children much of the time. . . . But so much happens in his books and his writing draws you on with its magic so skilfully that you do not notice, mind, or even believe that the children remain static in character. Montgomery, also, can make her Stock Children come alive. Before I reread the books, I found I remembered only one incident clearly, but I did remember one and at least thirty years had passed since I had read the story. It was the time when the children learned that the coming of the end of the world had been prophesied and the date had been printed in the newspaper! The group grew more and more terrified as the fateful hour approached. I shared their terror. What child has not spent uneasy minutes pondering over this eventuality? The children in the book plagued adults with questions which sought reassurance but brought upon them nothing save amusement and teasing. I found I still recalled their solemn vows to reform their entire lives if only the world be permitted to remain as always. I felt with them intense relief, joy, and freedom when the hour passed and the Last Trumpet had not sounded. Why did I recollect this when every single story Sara Stanley told had vanished from my memory leaving no trace? It was not because the eight acted unpredictably; it was because they acted. Something dramatic was actually happening instead of being recounted. We read other L. M. Montgomery books till they were in tatters; we left these two looking almost as untouched as the day they were purchased.

The author made two other major mistakes with this book. The worst was that the entire story is told in retrospect by an adult forty years or so after the action, what there was of it, took place. Yesterday is not the world children inhabit, not unless an artist can, like Hester Burton or Geoffrey Trease, turn "the olden days" into now. Sentences like the following, which comes fairly early in *The Story Girl,* destroy the reader's feeling of being himself right in the thick of things.

> Never had I heard a voice like hers. Never, in all my life since, have I heard such a voice.

Compulsive readers or devoted Montgomery fans will keep going. The others, and there are far more of them, will drop the book and look for something offering more involvement.

Montgomery also gave in to the temptation to help fill up her manuscript by including examples of writing ostensibly done by her child characters. This is fun for an author to do. Do you really know your characters so well and do you have the skill necessary to do their writing for them, allowing each his or her individual style? Style or idiosyncrasy? Many authors, often unconsciously I would guess, end up with one eye on their adult audience who will enjoy grammatical absurdities, flowery or wildly inappropriate descriptions, and hilarious spelling errors. I remember shrinking inside as my grandmother laughed heartily over these parodies. "Do they laugh like that at the things I show them, when I'm not there?" a sensitive child asks. The answer is clearly "Yes".

I must make clear, before leaving this point, that there are times when a child's writing forms an integral part of the book itself. Emily Starr, in *Emily of New Moon* is a child in the first apprenticeship stages of becoming a writer. She has to fight her formidable Aunt Elizabeth for her right to keep what amounts to a journal and to keep what she writes in it private. From her schoolmates, she wins both praise and mockery for her efforts. She suffers cruel ridicule from one teacher and, later, accepts severe yet encouraging criticism from another about her writing. The reader needs evidence of Emily's ability or lack of it to make all this plausible. Also Montgomery uses Emily's writing to reveal something of her inner longings, aloneness, resolution, despairs, and so on. Still, Emily's outpourings, while often delightful, should have been cut in half, I think, for here again Montgomery falls back on Emily's telling about things happening instead of letting the reader be there at the very instant. A different sort of example of a child's writing being important to a book is Faith Meredith's open letter to her father's congregation in *Rainbow Valley*. Instead of slowing the plot, this frank epistle sends it forward with alacrity.

The Non-Children, among whom neither Faith nor Emily belong, are hardly worth commenting upon since no child believes in them for an instant. Little Elizabeth, in *Anne of Windy Poplars,* is one. Paul Irving is another. There are others sprinkled here and there. Montgomery fails to give them life. They have not one redeeming flaw. They are always small for their age and they have huge wistful eyes with long lashes and they make impossible speeches. . . . I doubt that Montgomery herself was excessively fond of these creatures. They seem to be the type of child appearing least often in her books, and almost never in her best. The Stock Children have fun; the Non-Children may have heard of it but certainly never take part in any.

The Exaggerated Children, on the other hand, usually know far more about fun than is needful. *Magic for Marigold* has two such in rapid succession, Princess Varvara and Marigold's cousin Gwendolen. They are wild, almost amoral children. They are diabolical and outrageous. They are occasionally repentant for the moment or two, but this is never convincing and does not last. Children read about them with awe-struck delight. They are so impossibly wicked and yet they often escape unscathed. But these Exaggerated Children are so busy being bad that they have no time left in which to think or feel, respond or question. The shocks come at one with the staccato quality of the Sesame Street commercials. To have number facts presented in rapid fire succession is one thing; to be so introduced to a person is another. It may leave the reader gasping with a combination of horror and pleasure, but it also leaves him definitely on the outside, looking on. On the other hand, all children have exaggerated days or wish they dared, so these "holy terrors" of Montgomery's have their place.

"But what about Jane?" a voice demands with pardonable impatience.

Jane is one of the Real Children. Yet among the Real Children there are further divisions. There are the inferior Real Children, those lacking in Imagination but strong on faithfulness like Diana Barry in *Anne of Green Gables* or those who begin as irritating prigs but become people like Cousin Phyllis in *Jane of Lantern Hill*. And there are the superior Real Children who experience "The Flash" like Emily Starr or have Imagination like Anne Shirley. These superior beings, the ones who really matter, usually talk a blue streak, often astonish and/or shock their elders with their precocity, suffer agonies—but believable ones which the reader suffers with them—are humiliated, misunderstood and misjudged, but come out victorious over all in the end. They are totally alive, exceedingly human, and yet possess an added something. Could it be that this plus factor, whatever it may be, removes them just slightly from the rest of us? Are they, maybe, every so often, too wonderful?

Saying so is heresy because we love them, Anne and Emily at least. Marigold might have fared better if she had been allowed into the story before page forty. Pat, in *Pat of Silver Bush*, was, as far as I was concerned, close to being a Non-Child. I could not understand her stifling fear of change. It seemed not only excessive but silly. So what if her father shaved off his moustache! As a niece of mine, an ardent Montgomery fan, succinctly put it, "Pat's really quite dumb." That this feeling of dread stemmed from real emotion Montgomery herself vividly remembered feeling is a matter of record, but most children's only memory of their mother is not the sight of her lying in her coffin. There can be little doubt that the child Lucy Maud was had more reason to be apprehensive about life than most.

Emily and Anne, however, remain strong heroines, not allowing themselves to be overshadowed or pushed aside by other characters. Ilse Burnley, Emily's friend, is a girl who is both Exaggerated and Real, fiery, unpredictable and interesting, but she never usurps Emily's position as central figure. These Real Children change. They get into trouble and learn how to get out again. They suffer consequences and experience both deep joy and sorrow. They are all heroines should be, if only they were not quite so . . . super-sensitive?

And now, Jane! Jane is the heroine of L. M. Montgomery's last novel and Jane was not met with quite the acclaim her predecessors had won. Why not? Nobody seems to have wondered. Could it be simply that people were startled to encounter a child who was just a child?

I do not for one moment claim that *Jane of Lantern Hill* is a book without flaws. Jane's parents are two of the most far-fetched creatures Montgomery ever concocted. Mother is so fluttery and ineffectual that one longs to swat her. Jane's loyalty to her surprises the reader and even Jane has her moments of doubt. Dad is easier to take because he is cast as the hero with Jane as his heroine. His problem is that he is far too good to be true. He is always ready to spend time with his beloved daughter (even though his love is a trifle late in manifesting itself; for years, Jane does not know she has a father), so handsome that Jane, still unaware of his identity, cuts his picture out of a magazine and fantasizes over it, and so willing to go along with Jane's least whim that it is a good thing for all concerned that Jane is a child with sense. Dad is given only one character defect, and one feels that Montgomery hated to mar him even this much and only did so because it was necessary to the plot. He has a blind faith in and fondness for his sister who, with Jane's maternal grandmother's help, managed to wreck Mother and Dad's marriage before Jane was old enough to set things straight. As I reread the book, I found Mother and Dad as foolish as ever and concluded that Jane was going to have uphill work holding the marriage, mended at the book's happy ending, together.

As I earlier indicated, however, I believe the children, not the adults in Montgomery's books, were what held us. The story of Jane, pitted against adult forces she does not understand, being undermined and nearly destroyed as an independent person by a grandmother who is all the wicked witches and selfish stepmothers rolled into one, and yet somehow managing to keep fighting for her selfhood, still found me involved. I was delighted all over again when, with some help but largely through her own tenacity and maturation, Jane wins through to becoming a person with whom others must reckon.

Jane is described in a few sentences early in the book:

> . . . Jane was not very good at games. She always felt awkward in them. At eleven she was as tall as most girls of thirteen. She towered among the girls of her class. They did not like it and it made Jane feel that she fitted in nowhere.

Does this sound like the same writer who, years before, wrote of Anne Shirley:

> Her face was small and white and thin, also much freckled; her mouth was large and so were her eyes, that looked green in some lights and gray in others.

> . . . an extraordinary observer might have seen that the chin was very pointed and pronounced; that the big eyes were full of spirit and vivacity; that the mouth was sweet-lipped and expressive; that the forehead was broad and full; in short . . . that no commonplace soul inhabited the body of this stray woman-child. . . .

Or who wrote concerning Emily Starr:

> She put the faded blue hood on over her long, heavy braid of glossy, jet-black hair, and smiled. . . . The smile began at the corners of her lips and spread over her face in a slow, subtle, very wonderful way. . . . In all else . . . she was like the Starrs—in her large purplish-grey eyes with their very long lashes and black

brows, in her high, white forehead . . . in the delicate moulding of her pale oval face and sensitive mouth, in the little ears that were pointed just a wee bit to show that she was kin to tribes of elfland.

Whom do most eleven-year-old girls see when they look in their mirrors? Anne? Emily? I saw Jane.

The theme of *Jane of Lantern Hill* is similar to that of the other two, *Anne of Green Gables* and *Emily of New Moon.* At the beginning, the child is found unacceptable as she stands and the adults, or most of them, try to kill, figuratively, the unacceptable person and create another made to their liking. All three girls resist. All have allies: Anne in Matthew, Emily in Cousin Jimmy and Aunt Laura, Jane in her father. But the outcomes or solutions differ. Anne and Emily eventually win love for their true selves from those who earlier sought to reshape them, and the two girls, without conscious effort, succeed in softening the harshness and implacability of Marilla and Aunt Elizabeth. As the children gain in power, the adults lose. Jane wins no love from her antagonists nor does she want to, since they are essentially evil rather than merely old-fashioned and strong-willed. Instead Jane becomes strong enough to be herself in spite of them. As she gains self-confidence, her grandmother and her Aunt Irene lose much of their power to hurt her but they are, in no way, redeemed, nor are they reconciled to her as Jane. She is still unacceptable at the end of the book, but their acceptance has become of no importance to her. She has outgrown them.

Jane's position at the outset of the book is shown clearly in the names by which she is called. Jane was christened Jane Victoria, the names of her two grandmothers. Grandmother, who longs to be rid of Jane, calls her Victoria which is her own name. She gives a great deal of herself in an effort to obliterate anything in Jane which suggests that Jane was fathered as well as mothered. Her mother, who loves her child but cannot stand up to her own mother's corroding possessiveness, calls her Jane Victoria. Her father and Jane herself, both of whom want her to be the person she really is, call her Jane. Montgomery's feeling for the importance of names to children is interesting. Anne's insistence that her name be spelled with an 'e' is now famous. Also every book with a strong heroine in it has her name in the title.

Ways of attacking and diminishing a child's sense of her own worth have not changed. The following scene demonstrates this and also shows Montgomery at her best:

> "Tut, tut," said Uncle William, "Victoria could get her grade easily enough if she wanted to. The thing is to study hard. She's getting to be a big girl now and should realize that. What is the capital of Canada, Victoria?"
>
> Jane knew perfectly well what the capital of Canada was but Uncle William fired the question at her so unexpectedly and all the guests stopped eating to listen . . . and for the moment she couldn't remember for her life what the name was. She blushed . . . stammered . . . squirmed. If she had looked at mother she would have seen that mother was forming the word silently on her lips, but she could not look at any one. She was ready to die of shame and mortification.

> "Phyllis," said Uncle William, "tell Victoria what the capital of Canada is."
>
> Phyllis promptly responded.
>
> "Ottawa."
>
> "O-t-t-a-w-a," said Uncle William to Jane.
>
> . . . Jane dropped her fork and writhed in anguish when she caught grandmother's eye. Grandmother touched her little silver bell.
>
> "Will you bring Miss Victoria *another* fork, Davis," she said in a tone implying that Jane had had several forks already.

Every child has sat at that dinner table and not known the right answer. Every child has dropped her fork when all she had left was her dignity. Every child has not been Emily or Anne for they were children with something special about them. We all hope we possess that magic extra ingredient that sees Emily and Anne through, but underneath that hope lies the hard knowledge that we are fork-droppers. (pp. 71-80)

Did Montgomery, in writing this last book, deliberately turn away from writing about the special children who had made her famous? Was she looking for more reality?

I doubt that she was consciously doing so for the reality is always there even when it is less easy to find than in *Jane of Lantern Hill.* The burning embarrassment of having to wear the wrong clothes to school, the shock of betrayal when your "best friend" turns out to be a snake in the grass, the desolation of homesickness, the impossibility of communicating the urgency of childhood to adults who never doubt that tomorrow will be soon enough, the naming of special places with private names, the fear of Judgement Day and of cows, all of these and so much more Lucy Maud Montgomery records faithfully and with complete identification. So children will continue to find themselves in her pages. They will have to skip because there is a lot of waste space there too, but rage, wonder, laughter, misery, resentment, panic, ecstasy, failure, love, and insight wait therein between the inconsequential parts. And the dreams are there! Because if Anne, who was taken in by mistake, if Emily, who was given a home by the drawing of lots, and if Jane, who did not know the capital of Canada, can all make it through to victory, maybe we can too. (pp. 80-1)

> *Jean Little, "But What about Jane?" in L. M. Montgomery: An Assessment, edited by John Robert Sorfleet, Canadian Children's Press, 1976, pp. 71-81.*

**THOMAS E. TAUSKY**

[*Emily of New Moon, Emily climbs,* and *Emily's quest*] can be read as the fictionalized confession of a troubled personality alternating between confidence in creativity and despairing self-doubt. Before the first of these novels was completed, Montgomery confided to a friend that Emily was an autobiographical character. . . . Critics have subsequently remarked upon the abundant parallels between Montgomery's literary career and the "Alpine Path" climbed by Emily. The comparison extends to deeper matters of the spirit, as is indicated by the juxta-position of Montgomery's January 8, 1908 letter to [G. B.] MacMillan with a passage from Emily's diary in *Emily's quest:*

> Do you take the "blues" too . . . I cannot fully describe these experiences . . . They *are dreadful,* far worse than physical pain. In so far as I can express my condition in words, I feel a

great and awful *weariness*—not of body or mind but of *feeling,* coupled with a strange dread of the future—*any* future, even a happy one—nay, a happy one most of all for in this strange mood it seems to me that to be happy would require more *emotional energy* than I will possess.

Gloom settles on my soul. I can't describe the feeling. It is dreadful—worse than any actual pain. In so far as I can express it in words I feel a great and awful weariness—not of body or brain but of *feeling,* coupled with a haunting dread of the future—*any* future—even a happy one—nay, a happy one most of all, for in this strange mood it seems to me that to be happy would require more effort—more buoyancy than I shall possess.

The duplication of phrasing in passages written more than a decade apart is astounding. Montgomery was in the habit of making one set of reflections serve more than one correspondent, and in this instance one must suspect that she attributed her innermost feelings to Emily by referring either to the original letter or to her personal diaries. In any event, the passages certainly demonstrate Montgomery's sense of identification with her protagonist.

Emily's story does not always take such a melancholy turn. Indeed, it follows the pattern of Montgomery's life in being on the surface a story of triumph. Emily finds a place in her family and community despite the opposition of disagreeable relatives and narrow-minded fellow citizens; she succeeds as an author, first with money-making potboilers and then with more artistic works, despite negative reactions from both family and publishers; she achieves happiness in love despite malicious attempts to separate her from her partner. Yet throughout all three books, as much emphasis is placed on the obstacles to success (both external and within Emily herself) as upon the ultimate victories.

*Emily of New Moon* concentrates on Emily's integration within the Murray family, and on her initial attempts to make herself into an artist. As the story of an isolated individual finding a new self-definition within a family, *Emily of New Moon* superficially resembles *Anne of Green Gables:* in both cases an orphan learns how to gain the affection she desperately craves, and in return transforms the character of her guardians. Yet, in several respects, the process of mutual adjustment is more complex and troubled in *Emily* than in the earlier novel. Anne quickly wins Matthew Cuthbert's heart, and although her conquest of Marilla is more gradual, it is evident from an early stage that Marilla has the warmth of heart to respond to Anne's charm. Emily has an ally corresponding to Matthew in Cousin Jimmy Murray, but in Elizabeth and Laura Murray, she has to contend with the two sides of Marilla's personality split into separate characters: Laura is all sympathy but ineffectual, and Elizabeth, the dominant spirit in the New Moon household, is cold, moralistic and self-righteous. Marilla's increasing acceptance of Anne is clearly indicated before the middle of *Anne,* whereas the turning-point of Emily's relationship with Elizabeth does not occur until *Emily* is nearly at its conclusion. When Elizabeth chooses to read unflattering descriptions of herself contained in Emily's confessional "letters" to her dead father, the resulting confrontation is presented at a level of seriousness altogether lacking in *Anne.* . . . (pp. 5-7)

For much of *Emily of New Moon,* our heroine is not even certain she wants to be accepted as a Murray. Here again, she differs from Anne, who has nothing but bitter memories to serve as an alternative to life with the Cuthberts. Emily can think of herself as a Starr, her father's child, and it is not until the aftermath of her quarrel with Elizabeth that she gives up the allegiance to her father implicit in her habit of writing letters to him.

Douglas Starr leaves a lasting imprint on his daughter in another respect: he constitutes her first image of the life of a writer. . . . Speaking to Emily on his deathbed, he has to admit that "from a worldly point of view I've certainly been a failure," . . . but takes consolation in the idea that "You have my gift . . . you will succeed where I have failed." . . . The prophecy proves to be correct, partly because Emily is determined to play out the role her father has cast for her. The image of the artist as an alienated outcast, financially insecure and scornfully regarded as a failure, is established through the character of Douglas Starr in the trilogy's opening pages, and is never completely abandoned in the nine hundred pages that follow. (p. 7)

If the oppressive events of real life can threaten to snuff out Emily's artistic flame, writing itself can sometimes counteract the pains of reality. Over and over again, Emily assuages the humiliation of a public defeat by retreating to the private world of her imagination. Her capacity to weave the distorted elements of reality into a healing fantasy often gives a necessary boost to morale in her vulnerable early years. Moreover, it is an indication of the talent Montgomery ascribes to her heroine that in the process of working out her tales, Emily moves from simple wish-fulfillment to a genuine absorption in the imagined world. . . . So far, fiction has simply cured Emily of her distress. But the entry into a creative world is suggested immediately afterwards, in the paradox of artistry that "she forgot the Murrays although she was writing about them."

The seriousness of Emily's self-image as a writer is particularly evident in *Emily of New Moon*'s final pages. Emily is determined not to give up her art, even when ordered to do so by her aunt. . . . Emily's consciousness of the similar dedication of her artist friends strengthens her resolve. . . . Montgomery also chooses to make Emily's compulsion to write the subject of the novel's concluding scene, in a chapter revealingly entitled **"Emily's great moment."** She nervously submits her work to Mr. Carpenter, a stern judge. He acidly denounces the failings of her poetry; however, like both Father Cassidy and Dean Priest before him, he is less concerned with the modest achievement of the present than with the character of the artist: "I think there's *something* trying to speak through you—but you'll have to make yourself a fit instrument for it." . . . He cross-examines her on her basic motivation, and only when she assures him that apart from loving to write she feels she *has* to write does he utter his benediction, urging her to "go on—climb!" . . .

Father Cassidy had already advised Emily to "keep on" . . . , but the metaphor of ascent is given a more prominent place in the novel, as it seems to have had a more prominent place in Montgomery's own imagination. Montgomery had already chosen *The alpine path* as the title of her autobiographical sketch . . . , and the phrase is mentioned innumerable times throughout the *Emily* trilogy. . . . [The] poem does provide an external sanction for Emily's own guiding principles: the reliance upon Nature, the need for determination, confidence that literary success constitutes a worthy goal. (pp. 9-10)

*Emily climbs,* the second volume of the trilogy, shows Emily making considerable progress along the literary slopes. . . .

This success is achieved, however, in the face of obstacles every bit as discouraging as those encountered in *Emily of New Moon.* (p. 10)

In *Emily of New Moon,* becoming a artist was not, on the whole, incompatible with becoming a Murray; in *Emily climbs,* however, the necessity for Emily to make painful choices becomes evident.

The inner drive to escape the suffocating confinement of a conventional milieu is a common subject in novels of the *bildungsroman* type. In *Emily climbs,* Shrewsbury and Aunt Ruth are certainly all one could wish as a justification for shaking the red dust of the Island from one's feet. Yet Emily does not go; indeed, in the major scene of the novel, she consciously rejects an opportunity to go. In taking this decision, she makes a gesture similar to Anne's loyalty to Green Gables, but Emily does not face the tangible crisis that overwhelms the Cuthberts; hers is a totally voluntary act of renunciation. This episode gives *Emily climbs* its greatest interest. Though this novel, more than its companions, often seems shapeless, it ultimately turns into a meditation upon inner freedom, particularly the freedom of the artist.

The choice is created for Emily when a Shrewsbury native who has become a successful New York editor offers to introduce her to the literary life of the big city. Until the moment of choice, Emily develops a sense of identification with and loyalty towards the Murray tradition, all the while preserving, with equal passion, the sense of detachment, the aloneness, of the artist. The intrinsic contradictions in Emily's values are revealed in a passage a few chapters before the appropriately-named Miss Royal arrives with her autocratic summons to literary glory. Emily reproaches herself on one page for confiding too much in Ilse because "it is not a Murray tradition to turn your soul inside out," . . . in the same diary entry, however, she complains bitterly about the obstacles to freedom:

> Nobody is free—never, except just for a few brief moments now and then, when the flash comes . . . All the rest of our years we are slaves to something—traditions—conventions—ambitions—*relations.*

(pp. 11-12)

Emily's rejection of the temptation offered by Miss Royal appears at first sight to be a vote in favour of the Philistine Murray tradition, and even against literary aspiration. Miss Royal argues, plausibly enough, that "you mustn't waste your life here. . . . You must have . . . the training that only a great city can give.". . . The basis for Emily's response seems clear enough: "I belong to New Moon—I stay among my own people." . . . Yet on close examination, Emily's decision is not as unequivocal as it seems. Miss Royal offers herself, not just as a friendly adviser, but as a surrogate guardian. . . . Indeed, the repeated suggestion that Miss Royal has a penchant for attractive girls implies the interest of a sublimated Lesbian as well as substitute mother and frustrated author. In short, Emily has reason to suspect that Miss Royal would pose a greater threat than any Murray to her creative and personal independence. Just before Emily makes her final decision, her meditations show that she has come to feel that freedom and stimulus to the imagination are to be associated with New Moon, not New York:

> Would the Wind Woman come to her in the crowded city streets? Could she be like Kip-

ling's cat there? "And I wonder if I'll ever have the flash in New York," she thought wistfully.

(p. 12)

It is appropriate that Emily should think of Kipling's cat at this crucial moment, for she has already used this literary animal as a symbol of her need for independence. The allusion is to "The cat that walked by himself," from *Just so stories;* it is necessary to recall the fable briefly in order to evaluate its significance for Emily. The Cat desires the comforts of cave life, and yet will not give up his separateness. After a series of tough negotiations with the Woman, he agrees to provide needed services, and gains the privileges he desires. But he continues to insist on his lack of attachment to humanity, and at the end the narrator affirms his victory:

> But when he has done that, and between times, and when the moon gets up and night comes, he is the Cat that walks by himself, and all places are alike to him. Then he goes out to the Wet Wild Woods or up the Wet Wild Trees or on the Wet Wild Roofs, waving his wild tail and walking by his wild lone.

Much of Emily's character and behaviour can be understood in the light of the Kipling passage. Like the Cat, Emily has a need to make an alliance with human society; like the Cat, she brings benefits with her coming. But she is resentful of attacks upon her freedom, and remains faithful (like the Cat in the quoted passage) to a kinship with Nature in its untamed aspect.

Emily is given to associating herself with the Cat as a means of bolstering her identity when it is under attack from the Murrays. In the aftermath of the scene in which Aunt Elizabeth outlaws fiction, Emily defines her consciousness of being different from a Murray:

> I'm like Kipling's cat—I walk by my wild lone and wave my wild tail where so it pleases me. That's why the Murrays look askance at me. They think I should only run with the pack. . . .

The same allusion is used later on when Emily finds herself in disgrace with the Murrays yet again:

> I hate to go mincing through life, afraid to take a single long step for fear somebody is watching. I want to "wave my wild tail and walk by my wild lone." . . .

In an introspective passage of a letter to [Ephraim] Weber, Montgomery reveals that Emily's emotional identification with Kipling's cat springs from her own feeling:

> I have generally been considered a "good mixer" myself—but I am *not.* I am only an excellent imitation of one—compelled to play the part by the circumstances of my existence. In reality I detest "good mixers" and despise myself for aping them . . . The only people I ever knew who were really worth while were cats who walked by themselves, rejoicing in their own peculiar brand of cathood and never pretending to be Maltese if they were tortoise shell.

The vehement tone of this passage and the image it develops, as much as its content, are indications that Emily's creator had very much at heart her protagonist's struggle to assert independence in the face of the circumstances of her existence.

*Emily's quest,* the third volume of the trilogy, explores the consequences of Emily's decision to wave her wild tail in New Moon. Emily is not, however, allowed in the end to walk by her wild lone; the novel concludes with the marriage, not exactly a surprise to the reader, between Emily and Teddy Kent. Though *Emily's quest* is more tightly knit than *Emily climbs,* and contains much psychological interest, it subordinates Emily as artist to Emily as lover, and thereby disappoints some of the expectations aroused by the earlier books.

Yet there are some episodes and introspective passages in which Emily's dedication to her craft returns with the former seriousness. For example, the effects of a diseased love upon creativity are dramatized when Dean Priest deliberately condemns Emily's newly written first novel in order to claim her undivided heart. Montgomery underlines the magnitude of the evil inherent in this design by having Emily burn her manuscript . . . and then blunder into a fall that nearly costs her life: physical danger symbolizes the danger to the soul. When Emily recovers and forces herself to contemplate marriage with Dean, he wins an apparent victory in that she temporarily turns against writing; it is only after she frees herself from the incubus of Dean that the "miracle" . . . of a return to creativity occurs.

After this crisis has been resolved, Emily is finally able to reap the benefits of her long apprenticeship to art. A second novel is accepted by a very prominent publisher. Within her family, Emily is finally forgiven for being a writer: "It was better to have won her standing with the New Moon folks than with the world." . . . The opinion of the literary judges Emily values most is also favourable: Dean is won over, and Miss Royal is forced to admit that "You could never have written *The moral of the rose* here [i.e. in New York]." . . . With this concession, Emily can feel that the decision to remain at New Moon, which she herself questions through much of *Emily's quest,* has been justified in literary as well as personal terms.

So, after many stumbles, Emily has climbed her Alpine Path. Nevertheless, for the young woman Montgomery portrays in *Emily's quest* (quite a different person from the girl of the two earlier novels), literary success alone is no guarantee of happiness. Montgomery has Emily avow throughout the final novel that Teddy means more to her than the Alpine Path. Just before Teddy returns to provide the necessary happy ending, Emily feels utterly abandoned. . . . The character who had once resolved never to marry and to be *"wedded to my art"* . . . (emphasis Montgomery's) has certainly changed her outlook.

Montgomery's own changes of heart about the trilogy, as revealed in her correspondence, help to explain the shift in direction one may detect in *Emily's quest.* Her mood while at work on *Emily of New Moon* is strongly enthusiastic. . . . But when she turns to *Emily climbs,* she comments

> I am working on a second Emily book now and later there will be a third. These two will be only hack-work. But I enjoyed writing *Emily of New Moon* and I do think it is good *of its kind.* The charm went out when I finished it and cannot be recaptured for a whole series.

This passage was written well before *Emily climbs* was published; in retrospect, when she got stuck attempting to finish *Emily's quest,* Montgomery came to feel that the task of writing *Emily climbs* was not so bad after all:

> I wrote *Emily of New Moon* with intense pleasure. I wrote *Emily climbs* not unenjoyably. But

> I have written Emily III so far with reluctance and distaste. So it will not amount to anything.

One reason for Montgomery's gloom is that as an author no less than as a minister's wife, she feels compelled to meet public expectations she is not inclined to satisfy. . . . In another complaint, Montgomery blames her own incapacity, rather than external pressures, for her difficulties with *Emily's quest:*

> You ask about my literary activities. Well, just now I am trying to marry Emily off and am finding her a bit of a handful. Not because of any special perversity on her part—but simply because—alack!—I can't write a young-girl-romantic-love story. My impish sense of humour always spoils everything.

We do not have to accept without qualification Montgomery's somewhat contradictory expressions of despondency about the last two volumes of the trilogy. Writers have often disparaged some of their best work. In this instance, I think Montgomery was right to feel that *Emily of New Moon* was the best novel in the trilogy, and *Emily's quest* the least satisfactory, but the falling off does not seem to be quite as dramatic as she believed it to be. It does appear evident, however, that Montgomery's view of the restrictive conventions she faced and the limited success she was achieving greatly affected the tone of the final volume. Emily's despair is her despair, just as Emily's earlier delight in "the flash" was Montgomery's own tribute to the joy of life and literary creation. The emotional depths of *Emily's quest* are sounded, not in the exhilaration Emily still sometimes feels as a creator or even in her happiness when finally united with Teddy, but rather in the passages nakedly revealing moods of profound depression.

Yet another factor in Montgomery's complex attitude towards her work in this period appears to have been a feeling of guilt about her failure to develop a more ambitious project. She blamed herself, in essence, for not attempting to climb a higher Alpine Path. Even in her initial enthusiasm for *Emily of New Moon* she writes that the novel is "along the old lines" because she does not have the "unbroken leisure I want for a more serious attempt." . . . Four years later, Weber attempts to compliment Montgomery by suggesting that *The Blue Castle* is her adult book, but she will not be flattered. She finally reveals the exact nature of her cherished *magnum opus:*

> I take this to be a reference to a long-ago confession of mine that I wanted some day to write a book for adults. Oh, no, this is not the book of my ambition . . . "The" book is still unwritten. Though I hope to write it still: a book portraying the life among the big "clan" families of the Maritimes. I come of three of them . . . and I know the life from A to Z if I can only get it on paper *alive.*

Montgomery's view of herself as an unwilling slave of public taste whose best work remains unwritten cannot have worked to the advantage of the trilogy. There is a sad irony in all of this: the *Emily* books are far more a personal expression, far less the product of external pressures, than their author seems to have realized. Whatever the potential merit of her projected saga, it could not possibly have contained much more of Montgomery's inner spirit, or even of her particular insight into Island society, than may be found in the *Emily* trilogy.

The mixture of reverence for literary creation and persistent melancholy that we find in the *Emily* novels is, I have tried to show, related to Montgomery's character and conception of herself. No writer is an island, however; in Montgomery's case, the effect of the literary backgrounds one can associate with her—the inheritance of Romanticism, the situation of the woman writer, the influence of the Canadian milieu—may well have been to reinforce the tendency toward soul-searching and sorrow in her work.

The *Emily* novels are intensely Romantic works. Especially in *Emily of New Moon,* the protagonist's delight in Nature (which extends to symbolic identification: she is called a star, a skylark, a young eagle and a wild cherry tree) and joy in the "flash" define her being. In one extended and passionate scene, the narrator uses the Romantic vocabulary of Nature-worship as religion and poet as priest to describe Emily's emotions upon gazing at the Northern lights. . . . (pp. 12-17)

When Romantic visions fade, however, there are also specifically Romantic forms of depression. In a passage which in its entirety alludes to both the "Intimations Ode" and "Tintern Abbey," Emily wonders whether she might lose "the flash." . . . In sympathy with Shelley's lament that "the mind in creation is as a fading coal," Emily regrets that "*Nothing* ever seems . . . as beautiful and grand . . . when it is written out, as it does when you are thinking or feeling about it." . . . In the account of Emily's "great and awful weariness" of the soul, already quoted, one can find a parallel with the "grief without a pang" of Coleridge's "Dejection: An Ode," particularly since Emily, like Coleridge, attributes tragic utterances to the wind. . . .

If Romantic poets fear the loss of visionary power, women novelists (or fictional women novelists) may have cause to fear the harmful consequences of divided interests. . . . At the conscious level, Emily experiences little of this conflict, since Teddy is himself an artist, and interests himself in her work. Yet, as we have seen, love for Teddy gets in the way of Emily's devotion to her art; even more fundamentally, Emily's feeling for Teddy is directly contrary to the state of mind which best suits her Romantic art. As an artist, Emily needs to walk by her wild lone; as a lover, Emily literally comes to Teddy's whistle, feeling "in the mad ecstasy of the moment" . . . that she is "helpless—dominated" . . . and reveling in her abasement.

Yet, if in this episode Emily's conduct seems to recall the behaviour of the Victorian heroine, she also may be linked with the women novelists who were contemporary with her creator. In her influential book, *A literature of their own,* Elaine Showalter suggests that women novelists of the 1920s "found themselves pulled apart by the conflicting claims of love and art." Consequently, novels of Montgomery's own time portray heroines subject to the kind of distress from which Emily suffers in much of *Emily's quest.* . . . Like her creator, Emily seems half-Victorian, half-modern; half-submissive, half self-sufficient; half the socially acceptable public mask, half the intensely private creative personality. The conventional ending of *Emily's quest* does not really unify these divided selves.

To add to Emily's plight, she has to bear the burden of being a Canadian artist. This aspect of her misfortune is not strongly emphasized on the surface, but it emerges if one compares her trials with the difficulties other artist figures in Canadian fiction have to face. Like David Canaan or Philip Bentley, Emily has to live among rural people whose imaginations are shown to be limited, and whose sympathies are narrow. Like David Newman of Patricia Blondal's *A candle to light the sun* and the artist heroines of Margaret Laurence's fiction, Emily has to struggle to define her own individuality while groping with ambivalent feelings about the stern representatives of the Celtic tradition in Canada. Like Rose, the protagonist of *Who do you think you are?,* Emily learns to adopt disguises as the best defence against public scorn of the unconventional sensibility.

Emily shares with most of the characters already mentioned the representative dilemma of the Canadian artist figure: on the whole, she is not in harmony with the local society of her upbringing, yet she cannot bring herself to shake off its influence. . . . To satisfy herself or public expectations (or both) Montgomery allows Emily to have both artistic success and loyalty to her culture. The happy ending enabled Montgomery to experience vicariously the delights of the road not taken: Montgomery herself, after all, had forsaken P.E.I. for Ontario manses, and had come to feel that "a certain part of my soul" had been "long starved" in "years of exile." Emily's choice to remain at New Moon can be viewed more generally as representing the Romantic's preference of the rural to the urban world, the traditional heroine's preference of the familiar to the unknown, and the Canadian artist's inability to break free.

For Kipling's untamed cat, "all places are the same." For Emily and her fellow Canadian artists, attachment to place can mean both spiritual discipline and spiritual confinement. Emily's triumphant self-mastery and conquest of the outer world reflect the lessons learned by her creator, who could write of herself:

> Yes, I agree with you that all the trials of an uncongenial environment should be regarded as *discipline* . . . I used to be a most impulsive, passionate creature . . . It was a very serious defect and injurious to me in many ways, mentally, morally, physically. I see now that it needed to be corrected and the life I have had to live has been of all others the one best calculated to correct it.

The darker passages of the *Emily* trilogy tell another story. The penalty of bondage to more limited minds is inevitable alienation, an unbridgeable gap between the real and the ideal. In another letter, Montgomery writes:

> So, as a rule, I am very careful to be shallow and conventional where depth and originality are wasted. When I get very desperate I retreat into my realms of cloudland. . . .

The ecstasy and despair of a life dedicated to art and hindered by social pressures is the real subject of the *Emily* trilogy. This is an ambitious theme; moreover, it is also the underlying theme of Montgomery's own life. In the *Emily* novels, Montgomery wrote her own spiritual autobiography, and these works would have been even finer achievements if their author had realized that in writing them she had climbed the Alpine Path to heights as lofty as any she might have attained by composing an "adult novel." (pp. 17-19)

*Thomas E. Tausky, "L. M. Montgomery and 'The Alpine Path, So Hard, So Steep',"* in Canadian Children's Literature: A Journal of Criticism and Review, *No. 30, 1983, pp. 5-20.*

## ANNE OF GREEN GABLES (1908)

A farmer in Prince Edward's Island ordered a boy from a Nova Scotia asylum, but the order got twisted and the result was that a girl was sent the farmer instead of a boy. That girl is the heroine of L. M. Montgomery's story, **"Anne of Green Gables,"** . . . and it is no exaggeration to say that she is one of the most extraordinary girls that ever came out of an ink pot.

The author undoubtedly meant her to be queer, but she is altogether too queer. She was only 11 years old when she reached the house in Prince Edward's Island that was to be her home, but, in spite of her tender years, and in spite of the fact that, excepting for four months spent in the asylum, she had passed all her life with illiterate folks, and had had almost no schooling, she talked to the farmer and his sister as though she had borrowed Bernard Shaw's vocabulary, Alfred Austin's sentimentality, and the reasoning powers of a Justice of the Supreme Court. She knew so much that she spoiled the author's plan at the very outset and greatly marred a story that had in it quaint and charming possibilities.

The author's probable intention was to exhibit a unique development in this little asylum waif, but there is no real difference between the girl at the end of the story and the one at the beginning of it. All the other characters in the book are human enough.

*"A Heroine from an Asylum," in* The New York Times Book Review, *July 18, 1908, p. 404.*

**"Anne of Green Gables"** is one of the best books for girls we have seen for a long time. It is cheerful, amusing, and happy.

*The first manuscript page of* Anne of Green Gables. *Courtesy of Confederation Centre Art Gallery and Museum.*

Anne is a sort of Canadian "Rebecca of Sunnybrook Farm" in her imaginativeness, love of high-flown language, and propensity to get into scrapes. But the book is by no means an imitation; it has plenty of originality and character. Moreover, it will please grown-up people quite or nearly as well as the school-girls for whom it is primarily designed. It ought to have a wide reading. (pp. 956-57)

*A review of "Anne of Green Gables," in* The Outlook, *Vol. 89, No. 17, August 22, 1908, pp. 956-57.*

[*Carman, considered the leading Canadian poet of his lifetime, was named poet laureate in 1928. The following is excerpted from a letter he wrote to Montgomery in the fall of 1908.*]

I see that Anne has become one of the popular young ladies of the season, but I can assure you that if she had no one else to love her, I should still be her most devoted admirer. . . . And I take it as a great test of the worth of the book that while the young people are rummaging all over the house looking for Anne, the head of the family has carried her off to read on his way to work.

*Bliss Carman, in an extract from a letter to L. M. Montgomery in 1908, in* Canadian Author & Bookman, *Vol. 44, No. 3, Spring, 1969, p. 7.*

[*MacMechan was Montgomery's English literature professor at Dalhousie College. He wrote the following in 1924.*]

[**Anne of Green Gables**] just misses the kind of success which convinces the critic while it captivates the unreflecting general reader. The story is pervaded with a sense of reality; the pitfalls of the sentimental are deftly avoided; Anne and her friends are healthy human beings; their pranks are engaging; but the 'little more' in truth of representation, or deftness of touch, is lacking; and that makes the difference between a clever book and a masterpiece. . . . Miss Montgomery has created her public and she supplies it with what it wants. The conclusion to be drawn from Miss Montgomery's achievement is that the great reading public on this continent and in the British Isles has a great tenderness for children, for decent, and amusing stories, and a great indifference towards the rulings of the critics.

*Archibald MacMechan, in an extract from "Fans and Critics," in* The Wheel of Things: A Biography of L. M. Montgomery, Author of "Anne of Green Gables," *by Mollie Gillen, Fitzhenry & Whiteside Limited, 1975, p. 162.*

**Anne of Green Gables** is unquestionably one of the best-known examples of Canadian children's fiction. But much of the book's appeal consists in its catering to a desire for wish-fulfilment and, on the part of the older reader, nostalgia for a sentimentally-envisioned past; and these desires are catered to largely through the use, or misuse, of myth and fairy tale, which are so distorted that only their pleasant associations remain.

The rags-to-riches theme which appears in so many tales is a feature of **Anne of Green Gables,** but we see precious little of Anne in rags. We are asked to believe in a Cinderella-like pathos for which there is small evidence. The stepmother figures, Mrs. Thomas and Mrs. Hammond, do not come into the story directly, and Marilla Cuthbert, well-meaning but severe, is not so much a mother figure of any kind as a representation of what Anne might be were it not for the saving grace of her imagination. This is clearly reflected in the east gable room, which, untenanted and under Marilla's management, is "of a rigidity not to be described in words". But when Anne has been there for some time, "the whole character of the room is altered''; the ''icy white muslin frill'' which Marilla put across the window is transformed into the ''splendid filmy tissues of rainbow and moonshine'' with which Anne's dreams have, apparently, tapestried the whole room.

The more obvious references to fairy tales (and many of them are obvious indeed) tend to be on the ''splendid filmy tissues of rainbow and moonshine'' level. Particularly distressing, especially in a girl of almost fourteen, is Anne's comment on the Haunted Wood in autumn, its plants covered by leaves: ''I think it was a little gray fairy with a rainbow scarf that came tiptoeing along the last moonlight night and did it.'' ... Mercifully, Miss Stacey and the progress of adolescence eventually convince Anne that ''it's nicer to think dear, pretty thoughts and keep them in one's heart, like treasures.'' ...

The habit of attributing human qualities to inanimate nature—often very appealing both to the sentimental adult and to the pre-adolescent child—is central to L. M. Montgomery's concept of the imagination and colours Anne's observations of nature. This can be extremely tiresome. At eleven, it is pardonable enough to go around naming geraniums and so forth (the fairy tale element becomes pronounced when Anne calls the cherry tree outside her window the Snow Queen). But Anne's sentimentalities about flowers are hard to take even at that age—''do you think amethysts can be the souls of good violets?'' ...—and still more at twelve—''Do you know what I think Mayflowers are, Marilla? I think they must be the souls of all the flowers that died last summer and this is their heaven.'' ... Not even the sobering reality of Matthew's death, when she is seventeen, can erase this extravagant conceit; ''I hope he has roses ... in heaven. Perhaps the souls of all those little white roses that he has loved so many summers were all there to meet him.'' ... Once L. M. Montgomery has got hold of a good thing, she does not relinquish it easily.

At every point in her development Anne is to be found clutching or even kissing bunches of flowers. This is sometimes more revealing than the author herself is aware.... More deliberately, flowers are used to indicate Anne's innocence. ''I'm to have a wreath of white roses on my hair'', she tells Marilla when she is discussing her costume for the part of, of all things, a fairy.... The heroine's innocence is frequently emphasised; on several occasions she is referred to as a maiden, or, worse still, a small maiden, in a manner somewhat reminiscent of the poem which prefaces Lewis Carroll's *Alice Through the Looking Glass,* and which has, contrary to its author's intention, attracted comments of a ribald and derisive kind.

The sentimental evocation of innocence pinch-hits reasonably well for pathos, an effect which is heightened by oblique comparisons of the heroine to Ophelia. Anne makes her debut at the Avonlea Sunday School with a bunch of wild flowers in her hat; she is late for school one momentous afternoon because she is at the far end of the grove, ''singing softly to herself, with a wreath of rice lilies on her hair;'' ... and she actually floats down the stream, escaping drowning by only a hair's breadth, although, in a glorious potpourri of myths, Anne is supposed to be Elaine (the ''lily maid'') at this point. The only genuine element of pathos in the situation, Anne's orphan status, is of course exploited for all it is worth, and this works well when Matthew is wretched at the thought of her impending disappointment ... or when Josie Pye is making some patronising remark about orphans. But when Anne herself takes up the strain, one feels that the author has gone too far. ''*You* would cry ... if you were an orphan and had come to a place that was going to be home and found that they didn't want you

because you weren't a boy,'' she sobs to Marilla. ... In her apologies to Mrs. Lynde and Miss Barry she successfully plays on being a ''little orphan girl,'' ... and after her disappointment over puffed sleeves she mutters, ''I didn't suppose God would have time to bother about a little orphan girl's dress.'' ... Only in the context of the sentimentality of the whole book is it possible to sympathise with a heroine who has so little pride.

In case all these associations with myth and fairy tale should not suffice to lift Anne above the level of the ordinary girl, we are constantly reminded of her powers of enchantment (beneficent, of course). ''Matthew Cuthbert, I believe that child has bewitched you!'' says Marilla on Anne's first night at Green Gables ..., and, not long afterwards, thinks ''She'll be casting a spell over me, too.'' ... Allusions to magic are also useful in obviating Anne's defects of appearance, for, while she is represented as painfully conscious of them for much of the book, L. M. Montgomery manages, somewhat disingenuously, to argue them away as soon as they are mentioned; it is not so bad to be covered with freckles if one can be described as a ''freckled witch of a girl.'' ...

Throughout **Anne of Green Gables,** in fact, the author writes of her heroine with an indulgence to which F. R. Leavis' criticism of George Eliot's portrait of Maggie, in *The Mill on the Floss,* might well be applied; ''in George Eliot's presentment of Maggie there is an element of self-idealization. The criticism sharpens itself when we say that with the self-idealization there goes an element of self-pity. George Eliot's attitude to her own immaturity as represented by Maggie is the reverse of a mature one.'' (There is, of course, a substratum of autobiography in **Anne of Green Gables**). Matthew is conscious that ''Anne had a brighter face, and bigger, starrier eyes, and more delicate features than the others;'' ... her inferiority boils down to the purely external question of clothes. And at the other end of her career—at least in this novel—the same kind of judgment is made, for, at Queen's, ''Stella Maynard carried off the palm for beauty, *with a small but critical minority in favour of Anne Shirley.*'' ... But the technique of praising with faint damns is employed most ingeniously in Mrs. Lynde's appraisal of the fourteen-year-old Anne's appearance, for, while apparently giving the preference to other girls, Mrs. Lynde is really setting her above them.... (pp. 247-50)

Hans Andersen's duckling is ugly to start with—indeed until the very end of the tale—but L. M. Montgomery reminds the reader constantly that Anne has lain in a swan's egg. And, whereas the duckling is mistreated and lonely until the last page, Anne suffers no real hardships, after her initial pain and suspense, until Matthew's death in the closing chapters of the novel. The imaginary friends of the past are swiftly replaced by flesh-and-blood friends who, since they can so far violate realism as to forgive childhood's cardinal sin of oddity, may well be expected to acknowledge, without resentment, their admiration of and dependence on Anne's superior gifts. There is always the exception of Josie Pye, of course—but she is universally despised. The heroine's original insecurity is allayed early in the book by her attainment of a new identity as Anne of Green Gables (she celebrates the moment of realisation by kissing her reflection affectionately in the mirror). Every catastrophe is calculated to engage the reader's sympathy and amusement and is followed by some incident that more than compensates for the preceding disaster (her hair grows darker, for example, after she has dyed it green and perforce had it cut). There is barely time for an interval of suspense; every wish is gratified, not, as in the approved fairy tale tradition, at the end of the story, but during the course of the book, so that there is a continual "onwards and upwards" drift; "Hills peeped o'er hill and Alps on Alp arose," as L. M. Montgomery cannot help (incorrectly) quoting.... At the end, where a reversal of fairy tale procedure seems intended, Anne is deprived of her reward; but even her surrender of the Avery scholarship (a matter of circumstance rather than choice, since so many obstacles are placed in the way of her leaving Avonlea) is compensated for by a convenient teaching position, Gilbert's friendship, and the ever-present prospect of "the bend in the road." ...

The use of myth and fairy tale in *Anne of Green Gables* is typified by the Snow Queen, as the cherry tree outside Anne's bedroom window is called; the tree is white and beautiful, but the association with Andersen's queen is reduced to banality, since her cruelty is entirely overlooked and lip-service only is paid to her coldness. Such distortions of myth and fairy tale sentimentalise not only Anne but her world, for this is life as it might be pleasant to suppose it; a life where the agreeable always outweighs the disagreeable, the good the bad, and where one can progress from good to better against a background of "frogs . . . singing silverly sweet" . . . and "Mayflowers . . . peeping pinkly out." ... What L. M. Montgomery really wants is to engage for Anne the same kind of sympathy which might be given to a fairy-tale heroine, but without making her undergo the same trials; and, thanks largely to affective transference on the part of many readers, she succeeds to a quite remarkable degree. (pp. 250-51)

*Lesley Willis, "The Bogus Ugly Duckling: Anne Shirley Unmasked," in* The Dalhousie Review, *Vol. 56, No. 2, Summer, 1976, pp. 247-51.*

[*Earlier in this essay, Rubio writes of the similarities in background between Montgomery and Mark Twain as well as the similarities between* Anne of Green Gables *and Twain's* Tom Sawyer *and* The Adventures of Huckleberry Finn. *The critic contends that both "Montgomery and Twain, writing from mature perspectives, treat their respective communities and characters with humor and affection. Each had an eye for the incongruous, the comic dimension in human behavior which results when adults and children alike take themselves too seriously . . .".*]

Aside from *Anne's* comic and satiric elements, what has been responsible for its initial and continuing success? In spite of parallels between *Anne* and Twain's two novels of boyhood, Montgomery's work owes its success to elements distinctively its own: Anne is not a female Twain character. There are, in Anne, other areas which deserve comment: Montgomery's combination of realism and romanticism, her treatment of the imagination, and her perceptive dealing with the psychological needs of humans, both children and adults.

*Anne of Green Gables* is best considered as an example of literary realism, despite the fact that it contains such elements as haunted woods which are typical of romance. One of the realities which children can build up is a world of imaginative romance and dreams, and we must keep in mind that most of the highflown romance in *Anne* exists because Anne creates it in her mind. Her imagination takes over early in the book, and it is primarily from her point-of-view that we see much of Avonlea. She may be a pretentious little girl who has read too much without digesting it, but as such she represents a type of precocious adolescent who is familiar and realistic. Montgomery places her in a specific and realistic setting, and we

finish the book with a good sense of what it was like to be a child living in a small Prince Edward Island town around 1900.

Anne Shirley uses the worst sentimental clichés when she talks. These serve a greater function than to create humour or to characterize her, however: through Anne's overly dramatic and flowery speech, Montgomery is able to satirize romance. Montgomery, writing of her own childhood, tells us that she was brought up with such "Literary pablum" as *Godey's Lady's Book....* Montgomery, who also spent a considerable amount of her own time doing hack writing for money, was obviously quite aware of the distinction between fresh and hackneyed expression. Anne's overripe diction is clearly intended to be comic, not only because it is inappropriate speech for a girl her age, but also because it is very trite and hackneyed in itself. Montgomery is clearly satirizing the popular literary taste for sentimental clichés just as Twain does in *Huck Finn* when he exposes us to the poetry of sweet little dead Emmeline Grangerford, poetry which outdoes the worst of the sentimental female versifiers who were then popular.

L. M. Montgomery was a highly disciplined and efficient writer who was, in some of her other novels, too aware of her reading public, and too willing to conform to their taste so as to sell. She turned out a great amount of material which she herself seems to consider "hack" work in her letters to [Ephraim] Weber. The general tone of her letters to him indicates that she was quite gratified by the money which her pen brought, but she had no illusions that she was creating great literature in the stories and poetry which she ground out before and after *Anne* for the Sunday school magazines. She wrote him that she hoped her novels would sell so that she could quit the "Sunday School stuff": she had learned to cater to the public taste to satisfy publishers and as a financial necessity. When Weber complained that he did not like two things about *Anne of Green Gables,* namely Anne's superlative success in school and Matthew's death, Montgomery replied that she didn't either, but that she felt they would be demanded by the reading public, the first as a reward because Anne had been a good girl, and the second to enforce a choice upon Anne. When the publishers asked her for an immediate sequel to the immensely successful *Anne,* Montgomery immediately churned one out, but observed that it lacked the spontaneity and freshness of the first *Anne* book.

Perhaps another of the factors which has made *Anne of Green Gables* so successful both with adults and children is Montgomery's treatment of the imagination. (pp. 32-3)

The term "imagination" is one of the key words and concepts in *Anne of Green Gables.* What, however, does Montgomery mean when she speaks of it?

Anne possesses imagination in both the worst and the best of senses. When we first meet her she retreats to imaginary worlds from an unhappy real world. But she also possesses an unique ability to take ordinary sensory data from the external landscape of Avonlea and arrange it within her own imagination into a fascinating world. Whereas Anne looks through a window and sees a world that is "wonderful" outside, Marilla looks through the same window at the same time and sees only a big tree that "blooms great, but the fruit . . . [is] small and wormy." Most people are very much influenced by the constructions which other people place on reality; a political orator, a popular singer, an evangelist—each can completely catch us up in his own perception of reality. We can enter his imagination and see the world defined by his mood and by his particular arrangement of symbols. Some people perceive the world as a place of great struggle and probable defeat for them; external objects in their environment become threats. Other people regard the world as a challenge and a pleasure; the same factors which threatened the first group are a stimulus to the second. Anne Shirley possesses a perception of the world close to the second: readers love her for it.

The "imagination" has been much maligned by religion. Certainly we can see Marilla's distrust of it: "I don't believe in imagining things different from what they really are," she says; "When the Lord puts us in certain circumstances He doesn't mean for us to imagine them away." . . . What Marilla's literal mind fails to discern is the difficulty of determining how things *really* are in reality. The external world does not exist for us until our senses gather data and our minds interpret it. Marilla might well reflect that a literal reading of the Bible tells us that one of the first requirements which God made of man after creation was that man use his imaginative faculty to name the animals which He had created.

Like Adam, Anne Shirley's first important act after coming to Avonlea is to rename the external world which she finds. "The Avenue," a stretch of blooming apple trees, is rechristened "the White Way of Delight," and "Barry's Pond" becomes "The Lake of Shining Waters." The names she chooses show us the particular quality of her perception of reality. She takes the commonplace and makes it beautiful. Marilla and Matthew do not have enough literary sophistication to realize that the particular phrases which Anne chooses to externalize her vision are somewhat hackneyed—they are merely enchanted with the positive nature of the vision itself.

Anne's stay in Avonlea is a fascinating study of how one's imaginative perception of the world can in effect metamorphosize the actual structure of the world. One of the most exciting and satisfying aspects of the novel is Anne's transformation of an ordinary farm into a fairyland and of an inarticulate old bachelor and a cheerless old maid into people who can articulate their love.

Dour old Aunt Josephine Barry, in her selfish way, speaks for many readers when she summarizes her responses to Anne: "She makes me like her because she is interesting." Most humans are a little short on imagination and, like Aunt Josephine, enjoy being lifted out of commonplace lives by a free spirit like Anne.

I think that ultimately what readers respond to in *Anne* is not the momentary, amusing diversion of Anne's imaginative flights of fancy, but rather something far more powerful—the recognition that our perception of reality often becomes the blueprint for our lives. Our expectations can create our future. . . . Anne herself is aware of the importance of one's own perception of reality. She says "I read in a book once that a rose by any other name would smell as sweet, but I've never been able to believe it. I don't believe a rose *would* be as nice if it was called a thistle or a skunk cabbage." (pp. 33-5)

That the vision of the individual imagination gave existence and shape to the external world was a tenet of literary romanticism; it is also, in the 1970's, an idea being explored by modern psychologists who have demonstrated, for instance, that a child who perceives himself as a failure is quite likely to become one, no matter how great his native abilities may be. But in 1908 when *Anne of Green Gables* appeared, such a doctrine ran counter to the sociological and biological determinism of the age. Other contemporary literary heroines of

serious adult fiction had little or no ability to control the direction of their lives. . . . In an intellectual climate where people were presented as helpless either because of their own biological make-up or because of the social atmosphere in which they lived, novels such as *Anne of Green Gables* suggested that one's imagination could influence the external world.

Today, children of the Anne Shirley age (11-15 in the novel) are beginning to test their wings outside the family. They can watch Anne manipulate her environment. When she first meets Marilla and Matthew they are most unpromising parents; all humanity in them seems to be repressed, and what is more, they don't want her because she is a girl. Yet, they are better than the alternative, and Anne determines to find warmth and human kindness in them. At first, her manipulations are obvious—she tells Matthew and Marilla that she is an orphan that nobody ever loved and that she expects to be treated as badly by them as by everyone else. But her ability to control her environment is achieved by far more than such obvious manipulation: she presents herself as an interesting and impulsive child, one the Cuthberts need because she can furnish them with the psychological, emotional, and imaginative dimensions which are lacking in their own lives. And she does the same for us, the readers. (p. 35)

> Mary Rubio, "Satire, Realism & Imagination in 'Anne of Green Gables'," in L. M. Montgomery: An Assessment, *edited by John Robert Sorfleet, Canadian Children's Press, 1976, pp. 27-36.*

---

### ANNE OF AVONLEA (1909)

Readers of **"Anne of Green Gables"** do not need to be told that the story of the next few years of Anne's life is a story of crystal clearness, of tenderness, humor, and fancy. If the fancy is sometimes exaggerated, it is not in the least morbid, but walks always in lock-step between fun and common sense. To an Anne who has reached the age of discretion and become a teacher in her old school at Avonlea, it is naturally not permitted to be so consistently impossible and so hilariously freakish as in her tender years; nor may she dream quite so recklessly. Accordingly the author, with happy respect to her own forte, provides an orphan boy who is all pranks and a half-orphan boy who is all aerial dreams, and the two supply what was earlier found in Anne.

Anne herself, meanwhile, has by no means wholly graduated from either her imaginings or her talent for predicament. When she is found telling the irrepressible Davy that it is "wrong for little boys to use slang," it seems that Anne must have been changed at rebirth. But again, there are reassuring scenes of catastrophe in respect to mistaken potions which link her joyously with the past. Interest in sentimental adventure naturally waxes, but it does not even yet carry the drama beyond the bounds of youth. As before, the atmosphere of Prince Edward Island prettily surrounds the story.

> A review of "Anne of Avonlea," in The Nation, *Vol. LXXXIX, No. 2305, September 2, 1909, p. 212.*

To do a thing twice and to be as successful with the latter as with the former effort is apparently almost impossible to humanity. Either the second attempt is really not so good as the first, or else the rest of the world, mixing up its memories with subsequent fancies and glamours, is disappointed, however unjustly, with number two. . . .

*Anne of Avonlea* contains much the same gentle charm that made *Anne of Green Gables* so delectable a book.... [The characters] continue their hushed, secluded, leisurely lives in a way calculated to yield the reader weary of the steam riveter and the automobile, the career and the fad, a refreshing sense of peace. None of the problems of modern life enter the quiet pages. But there is plenty of sunshine and green shadow, of the timid and yet serene faith of untried youth, and not a little blue and silver love making. Childhood still pervades the pages, for Anne has her schoolful of youngsters, and Marilla adopts twins—twins as opposed as the poles and filling every waking hour with mischief perpetrated or endured.

There is a Miss Lavendar, sweet as her name, pretty, faded, full of quaint fancies, pretending people out of fairyland to fill her lonely life, and ending in a bloom of romance. And that is all. The book is as simple as a daisy, and if not quite as bewitching as the first we were given, the fault is doubtless with ourselves rather than the little flower.

> *Margaret Merwin, "L. M. Montgomery's 'Anne of Avonlea'," in* The Bookman, *New York, Vol. XXX, No. 2, October, 1909, p. 152.*

An unknown Canadian writer published a girls' story a year ago or so which had that peculiar quality which makes the person who reads it tell some one else to do the same; and just this thing probably has more to do with the success of play or story than any amount of booming. **"Anne of Green Gables"** was funny without being silly, quite naïve, but honest as it was simple. Naturally Miss Montgomery has written a sequel, and evidently meditates another. **"Anne of Avonlea"** is a little more sentimental than the earlier **"Anne"**, but it is jolly and friendly ... The story will surely be read.

> *A review of "Anne of Avonlea," in* The Outlook, *Vol. 93, No. 5, October 2, 1909, p. 276.*

[*Anne of Avonlea*] is by no means a great work but is rather a somewhat commonplace story of a school teacher of some imagination, a type of thousands of other teachers all over the land who are doing conscientious work in and out of school and who draw old and young to them by means of pleasing personality. The character drawing is sketchy and in no instance does it rise into the realm of a masterpiece.

> *A review of "Anne of Avonlea," in* The Independent, *Vol. LXVII, No. 3185, December 16, 1909, p. 1355.*

---

## KILMENY OF THE ORCHARD (1910)

The author omits Anne of Green Gables from this, her third venture into fiction, although we have the familiar setting of Anne's Prince Edward Island. Its salt shore and spring blossoming have their wonted charm, and one reflects that an island is a portion of land bounded by perpetual fitness for romance. Never, surely, did romance glide onward so gently, so balmily, so florally as this. Never did the roughnesses inherent in the course of true love disappear so gracefully. Hard-hearted guardians are melted by a kind word. Prohibiting parents yield at a touch. Critical friendship melts under beauty's first glance. How mildly the eerie mystery of Kilmeny's dumbness unfolds and later clears itself! How amiably the lions in the path of young affection take themselves off! How lightly falls the foot of crime that only treads on flowers!

> *A review of "Kilmeny of the Orchard," in* The Nation, *Vol. XC, No. 2345, June 9, 1910, p. 587.*

["**Kilmeny of the Orchard**"] is a simple tale, with never a hint of problem or analysis of character, but abundant sentiment, and a pervading flavour of the Scots Nova-Scotian atmosphere of "the Island." This is a clean, unsophisticated atmosphere, admirably suited to the heroine of the tale, who is beautiful, dumb, and a musical genius all untaught. The scene of the tale will be new to many readers, and we can recommend it for holiday reading.

> *A review of "Kilmeny of the Orchard," in* The Atheneum, *No. 3418, July 30, 1910, p. 122.*

[*Kilmeny of the Orchard*] is a title connoting a blossom romance—a romance as wholesome as the bread and milk that the hero eats at dusk. This hero is a young school teacher; his Kilmeny a gentle figure out of that sentimental fiction we seem about to lose. To the young man who discovers her, and loves her in the fragrant coolness of the orchard, she is a lady in distress—not any problematic distress of morals or mind, such as civilization imposes, but that kinder distress imposed by Nature.... This story is as refreshing—and perhaps rather more stimulating—as a drink from a cool spring set back from the novel reader's dusty road.

The story of *Kilmeny,* however, in spite of its rural garb, could be set in the sophisticated garden of some fashionable country house and lose none of its atmosphere thereby. (pp. 362-63)

> *A review of "Kilmeny of the Orchard," in* The Independent, *Vol. LXIX, No. 3220, August 18, 1910, pp. 362-63.*

It is partly a lessening of [the] quality of close study which makes Miss Montgomery's *Kilmeny* less appealing than *Anne of Green Gables*. There was a distinctness about the former, an artistic truth in the portrait of the quaint child with individual fancies. This story is pretty and fanciful, in the green and gray setting of a Prince Edward Island orchard, but vagueness replaces the close rendering of real things, and, in spite of the poetic touch, the tale does not hold the reader. Only the genuine poet, one to whom the invisible is more real than the visible, dare write the story 'all made up of the poet's brain.' (p. 808)

> *Margaret Sherwood, "Lying Like Truth," in* The Atlantic Monthly, *Vol. CVI, No. 6, December, 1910, pp. 806-17.** 

---

## THE STORY GIRL (1911)

The many admirers of this author will welcome her new book. And those who, in the cases of the later Anne and of **"Kilmeny,"** found cause to temper praise with comparison will give double welcome to a story which returns to the plane of the author's best work. The scene is still in Prince Edward Island, the actors are a group of merry children spending their lives or their vacations on ancestral acres. The acres bloom in the old picturesque and fragrant way. The children are of all sorts, except very bad. Inevitably one of them must be dowered with a fantastic soul, and this one is the Story Girl who has the gift of remembering, inventing, and, above all, of telling. Fairy tales, Norse legends, the family ghost stories, the domestic ancestral joke are alike fuel for her fire. She becomes, in a way, the mouthpiece for much anecdotage, but through it all preserves a marked personality, compounded, in the author's agreeable manner, of fancy, fun, loftiness, and perversity. She is the leading spirit, but there is no lack of individuality among the boys and girls with whom we spend the summer, and pass long hours in the old grand-paternal orchard, where every member of the clan is represented by a tree. We go to school, do chores, gather apples, burn potato stalks, and after the manner of youth attack the problems of the universe. To sit in the grassy aisles of the orchard with the cousins and listen to the Story Girl's witching voice, to assist at counsels of mischief, at the drolleries, scrapes, and inter-squabbles of the young folk, and to have clear if brief glimpses of the elders is to be left with a lively sense of lively and actual acquaintance.

> *A review of "The Story Girl," in* The Nation, *Vol. XCIII, No. 2406, August 10, 1911, p. 122.*

It is a genuine pleasure to be able to say of a new story that it is equal to the very best thing the author has previously done. . . . Her other stories have also been liked, but none, we suppose, has pleased readers quite as much as the first **"Anne"** book. Now Miss Montgomery's **"The Story Girl"** is being read everywhere, and everywhere it is liked and praised. . . . [Instead] of one interesting child, as in **"Anne of Green Gables,"** we have a group of several girls and boys, quite unlike one another, each with characteristics which are strongly marked. Their play and adventures, and, above all, the stories told them by the girl who has gained the name of "The Story Girl," make capital reading. Like its predecessors, this story is clean, wholesome, and unsensational, but alive with character and rich in amusement. (pp. 46-7)

> *A review of "The Story Girl," in* The Outlook, *Vol. 99, No. 1, September 2, 1911, pp. 46-7.*

The children's chatter is often funny and perceptive, and their characters are neatly differentiated, but the thread on which the story is strung is a frail one, and there is little to move the action forward or to invite continued interest except a gentle pleasure in the mood and setting. Anne and Emily both carry the reader on to new discoveries about developing personalities and life stories, and arouse a desire to learn what happens next. One becomes involved with Anne and Emily as one does not with Sara Stanley and her circle. These children have no passionate problems, no hearts bursting with love and hate and frustration. (p. 84)

> *Mollie Gillen, in her* The Wheel of Things: A Biography of L. M. Montgomery, Author of "Anne of Green Gables," *Fitzhenry & Whiteside Limited, 1975, 200 p.*

---

### CHRONICLES OF AVONLEA, IN WHICH ANNE SHIRLEY OF GREEN GABLES AND AVONLEA PLAYS SOME PART (1912)

[This] is less distinctively an **"Anne"** book than its predecessors, as that charming and energetic girl appears only incidentally in one or two of the stories. The several tales which make up this volume are in turn gently sentimental and enjoyably humorous. Miss Montgomery seems to have great store of excellent material for this kind of writing.

> *A review of "Chronicles of Avonlea," in* The Outlook, *Vol. 101, No. 9, June 29, 1912, p. 500.*

[Anne] is not the leading figure in any of the tales, which might have been called "Romances of Middle Age," so strongly does a single motive dominate them. Ten out of the dozen stories deal with belated love-affairs, or with the pathetic devotion of age for youth. Perhaps this is why the group as a whole reminds one of Mrs. Deland's "Old Chester Tales"—

this and certain resemblances of style which are probably not due altogether to accident. The resemblance does not go very deep. The essential difference between the two chroniclers is the difference between sentiment and sentimentality, restraint and exuberance. . . . [Miss Montgomery's Avonlea] is a place which furnishes types about which pretty stories may be invented. This writer has that fatal gift of neatness which is ready to sacrifice everything else to finish of plot. So she does not balk at the absurdity of a twelve-year-old boy who has never been taught to fiddle improvising masterpieces on the slightest provocation. This is a pity, because Miss Montgomery has certainly the story-teller's instinct, genuine humor, and a sentiment altogether clear of sentimentality—when she chooses to keep it so.

> *A review of "Chronicles of Avonlea," in* The Nation, *Vol. XCV, No. 2460, August 22, 1912, p. 171.*

Miss Montgomery has written a series of short stories full of pathos and humor. *Old Lady Lloyd* and *Old Man Shaw's Girl* are quaint and original stories of foolish pride and perfect human love. . . .

For quaint, clean sparkling humor, *The Winning of Lucinda, Aunt Olivia's Beau, The Courting of Prissy Strong,* and *The Quarantine* are remarkable. The author is very fond of one particular theme, namely, the marrying of old spinsters to their lovers of twenty or thirty years ago. She succeeds in disposing of at least five such hopeless cases.

Frequently in these stories we are reminded of J. M. Barrie; the author has not his finished style, but she does share his sympathetic and kindly understanding of human nature.

> *A review of "Chronicles of Avonlea," in* Catholic World, *Vol. XCVI, No. 571, October, 1912, p. 103.*

---

### THE GOLDEN ROAD (1913)

Again this always readable writer about boys and girls (but not solely for boys and girls) tells of the doings and sayings of a group of young people in Prince Edward's Island with whom her readers are already acquainted. We will not say that the story is the equal of **"Anne of Green Gables,"** but it has the same wholesome and natural fun, and again there are interspersed little stories and incidents which have quaintness and sometimes imagination.

> *A review of "The Golden Road," in* The Outlook, *Vol. 105, No. 5, October 4, 1913, p. 280.*

[Miss Montgomery] pilots a happy, fun-loving crowd along "The Golden Road" to the parting of the ways. . . . Sara Stanley, the "story-girl," the weaver of dream stories, is the guide and leading spirit in all the daily adventures, but the group of boys and girls, brothers, sisters, cousins, and friends, pursue the natural methods of children. They love and squabble, they play and plan, and their adventures and doings charm by their very spontaneity. Fun and pathos alternate in these interesting pages, and a glimpse of romance is not lacking. The editing by the children of "our magazine" provides a clever and convincing incident.

> *A review of "The Golden Road," in* Literary Digest, *Vol. XLVII, No. 6, October 18, 1913, p. 692.*

---

## *ANNE OF THE ISLAND* (1915)

Like its two predecessors in the **"Anne of Green Gables"** stories, this book is wholesome, friendly, and spontaneous in its fun and bits of odd character. Anne is as lovable as ever, although a little staid and altogether womanly now; but there are other children here who are quaint and amusing.

> *A review of "Anne of the Island," in* The Outlook, *Vol. 110, No. 17, August 25, 1915, p. 1009.*

[Anne] threatens to become another Elsie for sequels. She is here brought to the verge of matrimony; so the worst may be over, since this is the kind of fiction which naturally ends with wedding bells. It is an altogether foolish and adequate account of Anne as a "co-ed." An adoring Gilbert appears on page three, who is clearly Anne's chosen, but, of course, the author puts him off by a series of transparent expedients till it is convenient for him to do the trick. It all "comes out right" in the end, which is the main thing. All that is desirable in this kind of fable is a perfunctory fumbling with obstacles in the interest of sentimental contrast.

> *A review of "Anne of the Island," in* The Nation, *Vol. CI, No. 2617, August 26, 1915, p. 263.*

Anne is back, not the little prankish Anne, Canadian cousin of Rebecca of Sunnybrook Farm yet with an individuality and charm quite her own, but a grown up Anne ready for college and the more serious things of life. As one says of the delectable bit of fur and mischief, the romping kitten, one is tempted to say of Anne.—Why does she have to grow up? . . .

**"Anne of the Island"** is the chronicle of the doings of Anne and her friends during four years spent at Redmond, pleasant adventures of the sort which might happen to any likable young people in a small co-educational college. . . .

In the intervening vacations, the scene shifts from Kingsport, Nova Scotia, the seat of Redmond, back to the Island, Prince Edward Island where the author's pen and heart are so much at home. Here are the old school friends of former books, the gossipy but usually warmhearted old ladies, and a pair of twins whose liveliness suggests early Green Gable days.

One wonders why an unmistakable Halifax has been veiled behind the name Kingsport, but to Anne-lovers, it will not be of serious moment whether she is educated at Halifax or Honolulu, so long as Anne occupies the centre of the screen. And they as well as others will find in **"Anne of the Island"** a wholesome and pleasant story of young life in the Maritime Provinces.

> *A review of "Anne of the Island," in* Publishers Weekly, *Vol. LXXXVIII, No. 12, September 18, 1915, p. 790.*

---

## *RAINBOW VALLEY* (1919)

Here is another **"Anne"** story in which Miss Montgomery has succeeded in recapturing some of the elements which made her first book such a popular success. She is at her best in creating without exaggeration delightfully natural children—naughty or rather, lively ones, in particular—and in reflecting with an insight not always found in the native writer the rural life of her beloved Island. The present book keeps the adults well in the background and confines itself for scene to a little village near Anne's first Island home.

Anne Shirley, now in village parlance Mrs. Dr. Blythe, has six healthy youngsters who figure in the story and contribute the title, their own name for their favorite playground, but it is the manse family of four which holds the center of the stage. Now minister's children are always entertaining in fiction and the Merediths are no exception, not because they have to scrimp and save to keep up appearances, but because the word "appearances" is not in their vocabulary at all. (p. 484)

The Meredith children are a jolly engaging set of youngsters who are likely to have a large following among youthful and older readers. (p. 485)

> *A review of "Rainbow Valley," in* Publishers Weekly, *Vol. XCVI, No. 7, August 16, 1919, pp. 484-85.*

The author of **"Anne of Green Gables"** shows in this book, as in her other popular stories, an unusual knowledge of girls' character, a cheerful spirit, and a sense of humor. This is less distinctly a girls' book and more distinctly a novel, properly speaking, than some of its predecessors.

> *A review of "Rainbow Valley," in* The Outlook, *Vol. 123, No. 3, September 17, 1919, p. 95.*

It is a pretty story, enlivened with much talk and play, innocent roguery and eager interest in life of a dozen children, part of them Anne's, part of them the new minister's, and one a naughty waif who pops up in the community and develops great ingenuity and energy in the matter of keeping things in general well stirred up. The children are all strongly individualized and each one is portrayed carefully and made to keep his own place in the picture. Miss Montgomery's thousands of admiring readers will welcome many of their old acquaintances whom they have delighted to meet in her previous books. There are also some new people whom the neighborhood takes into its arms and at once begins, after its friendly fashion, to arrange their lives and futures. They are very amusing in their efforts to settle the future of the widowed new minister with his house-

*Cavendish Capes, located close to the home of Montgomery's grandparents, the Macneills. It is one of many scenes on Prince Edward Island that inspired Montgomery's descriptions of nature. Reproduced by permission of Ian Gillen.*

ful of children. And there is much humor in the conversation and incidents which the author narrates in detail. The reader feels that she loves all these people whom she has created and that she takes keen delight in writing about them. They are racy of their region, each one a sturdy bit of individualism and a true son or daughter of their island soil. The book has a homey charm and its descriptions of the region are likely to make all its readers wish to visit Prince Edward's Island.

*A review of "Rainbow Valley," in* The New York Times Book Review, *September 21, 1919, p. 484.*

## RILLA OF INGLESIDE  (1921)

Even those who never read **"Anne of Green Gables"** or **"Rainbow Valley"** will find agreeable entertainment in this new novel by the same author; while people already acquainted with Anne will doubtless experience exquisite pleasure in going through the volume with her impulsive, pretty, warm-hearted daughter. For Rilla is Anne Shirley's offspring, and she has been named Marilla, after her aunt at Green Gables, and she lives at Ingleside, on Prince Edward's Island, and is surrounded by the same kind of amiable, chatty folk as laughed and gossiped and sometimes suffered through the other books. Life at Ingleside is tranquil enough in itself, but the period of the story is during the great war, and the reaction of the European horror upon the even existence of Rilla and those about her makes it rumble subconsciously with the beat of drum and the roll and roar of machine gun and great cannon. . . .

For the rest, the novel is mainly a pleasing recital of the doings, thoughts and aspirations of a very human young girl. We go with her to her first party, and peep over her shoulder while she reads her first love letter in a shady nook in Rainbow Valley, and we know that she has confided her most intimate conclusions and ambitions to her diary. Rilla is a charming girl, of the type which the author depicts so naturally and sympathetically, and the reader of either sex will love her. There is a cat of unusual propensities, and a good-natured, blundering dog of the most lovable kind, both of whom have several paragraphs to themselves here and there. The friends and acquaintances of Rilla are as attractive in their several ways as she is herself, and if some of them are inclined to be snippy and ill-natured, why, that is to be expected even in so Elysian a region as Ingleside where there are human beings. The author seldom touches a deep heart note, but it does not appear that she desires to do so. She writes a captivating, sunny story, and when one lays the book down after reaching the end, it is with the feeling that one has been in thoroughly wholesome company.

*A review of "Rilla of Ingleside," in* The New York Times Book Review, *September 11, 1921, p. 23.*

## EMILY OF NEW MOON  (1923)

There seems to be still afloat in the literary world a popular fallacy that all unhappy, imaginative children possess a kind of sixth sense which serves as a medium of communication with a world of unreality. It seems also that this sixth sense, through enabling its possessor to consort with elves and fairies, quite successfully compensates for any minor financial or domestic misfortunes which may beset the imaginative child. Whether science will ever succeed in proving to a world of adults that only imaginative children can ever be utterly and

miserably unhappy is extremely doubtful. In the meantime L. M. Montgomery . . . has written another book.

Miss Montgomery has created a charmingly winsome character in little Emily Starr, who, after the death of her parents, goes to live with two iron-bound old maid aunts. (One begins to wonder if iron-bound old maid aunts are always to be set before the public in groups of two.) Emily brings the proper amount of sweetness and light into the household and gradually the aunts are won over and become mellowed as old maid aunts should.

The characters are largely stock characters, from the brusque schoolmaster with his crop of bushy hair to the cousin, more than twice Emily's age, who presents himself as a prospective suitor and who flaunts a sad but sweet smile on a mouth that "connotes strength and tenderness and humor." Of course, the love affair never matures. Emily is far too young for that; but the reader is given a general idea of the type of affair it is likely to be when Emily and her admirer make a pact that they are "never to say good-bye, but always to smile and go."

There is a splash of color in Emily's old Aunt Nancy, yet another relative who crosses the child's path, and who, having once been quite a successful flirt, gives Emily a few instructions, bidding her to remember that her ankles would always do more for her than her brains. On the whole, however, Miss Montgomery lacks the dash and the spontaneous humor that Kate Douglas Wiggin, for instance, puts into her stories of children; and even "the Wind Woman" and "the flash" and a suggestion of second sight fail to create that poetic illusion which is a natural and effortless attribute of Frances Hodgson Burnett's style.

**"Emily of New Moon"** shows Miss Montgomery to be simply a pleasing story-teller. There is little originality in either her plot or her characters. Her greatest charm lies in a real understanding and sympathy for children, a sympathy which, even though it may degenerate at times into the sentimental, nevertheless has a certain appealing quality and a depth of sincerity that is disarming. (pp. 24, 26)

*A review of "Emily of New Moon," in* The New York Times Book Review, *August 26, 1923, pp. 24, 26.*

Both as a study of the early life of a very precocious child and for its original setting in Prince Edward Island, this story makes a considerable appeal. The little pictures of the island's coasts, with the pastures sloping up the valleys, and the long-settled homesteads and the quiet inland waters, are admirably done. No less interesting is the account of the life and peoples of the province, like us because essentially British in habits and feeling, yet unlike because here we have English, Scots, Irish, and French all living an intermixed and closely associated life.

In the story little Emily Byrd Starr, aged eleven, has been left an orphan. We are in time to see the death of her father, Douglas Starr, an unsuccessful journalist, and to learn that though he had never been forgiven for having eloped with Juliet Murray, yet the Murray pride is such that the family will certainly provide for Juliet's daughter. It is decided by the drawing of lots that she shall go to New Moon with two of her aunts. New Moon, called after the ship in which the Murrays sailed from the old country, had been built more than a century ago; the family had spread and prospered, its tentacles were deep down in the island soil, so that we may watch the founding of a new squirearchy as well as obtain glimpses of many aspects of an ordered colonial life.

*A review of "Emily of New Moon," in* The Times Literary Supplement, *No. 1130, September 13, 1923, p. 105.*

Though her creator always denied that Emily was another Anne, there are in fact many similarities between the two girls, not least the fact that each is articulate and independent of mind and ready to hold her own against the elders who order her life for her. (p. 3244)

In spite of likenesses between the two heroines, Emily has the distinction of being closer to her creator. There is much of the young Lucy Maud in this first book of the **"New Moon"** trilogy—with the "flashes" of perception that drive Emily to write poetry and the sense of justice which is so easily hurt by her disciplinarian aunt. The **"Anne"** books are perhaps richer in pen portraits of village worthies and have a fuller social scope, but Emily's story offers a sharper picture of a child fighting for her identity in a world of adult values. Some of the scenes in *Emily of New Moon*—confrontations at school with insensitive Miss Brownell, Aunt Elizabeth's decree about the stray kitten, a punitive session in the dark spare room "where a stuffed, white Arctic owl" stared at her "with uncanny eyes"— have a marked intensity that lift them from the particular to the world of childhood as a whole; though sentiments are often expressed in a way that now seems mawkish and embarrassing, the real crises of the book ring true. Moreover, the author keeps that firm balance between young and adult characters, that breadth of domestic experience, which junior novels are only just recovering after generations of tales in which boys and girls existed in artificial isolation. The long, bitter mistake over the fate of Ilse Burnley's mother, the so-called weakness of mind in Cousin Jimmy, Cousin Nancy's untimely coarseness of outlook, are evidence enough of a freedom of reference which deepens the effect of this kind of domestic story.

The children (mainly girls) who read this book may or may not identify with Emily. They are likely, at least, to respond to the background of farm, woodland and meadow which is so naturally revealed in Emily's artless secret letters of her dead father, and to the circumstantial detail so congenial in this kind of book. Description, when it comes from Emily herself, is suitably naïve and long-winded: when it comes from the author, it often has the precision and vitality of a Victorian conversation-piece. . . . Many a young reader will wish to be translated into a world so unfamiliar and so full of unusual possibilities. As well as creating a heroine brimful of life, believable and entertaining, L. M. Montgomery has created a world for her to inhabit which for the reflective reader could become at once real and magical. (pp. 3244-45)

*Margery Fisher, in a review of "Emily of New Moon," in her* Growing Point, *Vol. 16, No. 7, January, 1978, pp. 3244-45.*

---

## MAGIC FOR MARIGOLD  (1929)

Despite a cloying title, *Magic for Marigold* has some of the charm and freshness of its well-loved predecessor, *Anne of Green Gables*. Once past the opening chapters, which are cluttered with a motley assortment of doting, dim-witted elders whose peculiarities are not as amusing as their creator plainly supposes them to be, the story of a lonely and imaginative child growing up in a setting of rare natural beauty has a good

deal to offer the young reader of today sated with more robust fare.

It is an episodic, rambling story. By far the most memorable passage . . . brings little Marigold and her great-grandmother together in a darkened garden on the last night of the old woman's life, to share her memories of the past. Seldom has the delicate, precious relationship between the very young and the very old been so sympathetically treated.

The 'magic' of the title is the evanescent magic of childhood: the story closes as Marigold half-unwillingly parts from the imaginary playmate who has been her only and beloved companion to make the more demanding friendships the world of rude reality requires.

*Marigold* demonstrates many of L. M. Montgomery's weaknesses; her fondness for the maudlin moment; for passages which strain the most indulgent reader's credulity; for such insipid creations of two-dimensional femininity as Marigold's mother, whose spineless malleability is so trying to the modern reader's patience: but for all that, her work was founded on a solid bedrock of belief in the power of love and goodness; of the importance of tradition and wholesome family pride. Half a century after first publication, *Marigold* still has a meaningful message for a less confidently 'sure and certain' generation. (pp. 42-3)

*John McGrath, in a review of "Magic for Marigold," in* In Review: Canadian Books for Children, *Vol. 11, No. 3, Summer, 1977, pp. 42-3.*

---

## ANNE OF INGLESIDE  (1939)

Anne's literary debut took place some time in 1908, and much iconoclastic literary history has been made between then and now. Would she stand the test of being read about, as prelude to this 1939 sequel, by a reader to whom, even as a child, sentimental books had never appealed?

She did. Because, after all, the sentimentalism was only a slight overdose of sugar . . . in an original and far from unstimulating concoction. Anne herself, with her precocious love of long words and of pseudo-romantic phraseology such as may be studied in repositories of mid-Victorian sentiment of the "Family Herald" sort, was the eternal prototype of the romantic-minded feminine literary artist in embryo. She was also—and this, no doubt, explains her success with the girlhood of her own day and later—any girl with a dash of original devil in her, with the added fascination of the propensity for getting into unusual scrapes afforded by her individual talent and personality.

Well, she grew up, and here, without necessity to sample intervening states, is the same Anne, still young but married and with five small children and a sixth to appear before we have gone very far in the story. . . . Make no mistake about it. Anybody who has ever sat in the one classroom of a little red or whitewashed village school, or whoever, as a child, loved pirating or Robin Hooding or hanging round a harbor wharf, or who can still smell the home-made breads and cakes and pies and jams of earlier—and more peaceful—days is going to like **"Anne of Ingleside."**

But it is not, though it is full of children, six of them different varieties, from impish to dreamy, of the original Anne, a children's book. Personally one would style it, in the main, an anti-quack, anti-nostrum, wholesomely corrective study-drama based on the theme of the carelessly natural way of bringing up nice children—badly enough needed in these days of excessive regimentation and heartless, unleisured efficiency. But let not the shocked modern be deterred. There is the purely literary side as a village gossip book and as an album of queer village personalities spicily reminiscent of Jane Austen's provincial England and of "Cranford," but with a tang to it unmistakably North American. Be it here noted that nobody—not Sheila Kaye-Smith herself—makes you smell and see a lovely countryside better than Lucy Maud Montgomery does in "**Anne of Ingleside.**" If you are stuck tight in a city and cannot get out of it don't go near this novel!

To one who has not watched Anne's development and the literary development of Anne's creator the jump-in quality is particularly noticeable. The humor here is more closely knit and, at the same time, more omnipresent than before. Among its ingredients there is a new and pleasant tartness, and the villainesses are sketched with a wholly enjoyable maliciousness

not found in the earlier book; like Aunt Mary Maria, whose fifty-fifth birthday party had such a wickedly satisfying outcome, and the resurrected former flame of Gilbert's, of whom Anne was so haughtily jealous.

Mark Twain, had he been alive, would have approved of the later Anne. She has worn well; or rather, there is no sign of wear about her. Natural wit, a fine constitution and a zest for living nothing could dampen, plus the inherent capacity for doing the decent thing in a crisis (as when she gave up ambition for the sake of the aging woman who had mothered her), have kept her sweet as a sound-cored apple with a good sharp bite to it. Victorian bustles and hair-do's brought up to date have a delicate charm of their own, heightened by sophistication. Anne of Ingleside has the same charm in an intensified degree, but with no sophistication at all.

*Jane Spence Southron, "After Green Gables," in* The New York Times Book Review, *July 30, 1939, p. 7.*

# Arthur (Michell) Ransome

## 1884-1967

English author/illustrator and author of fiction, author of non-fiction, reteller, poet, journalist, essayist, critic, translator, and editor.

Ransome ranks among the giants of English juvenile literature for his *Swallows and Amazons* series, which extols the joys of holiday adventure. By writing simply and sincerely about subjects that mattered to him, Ransome created a plausible, satisfying picture of believable children who enjoy the freedom of outdoor activity while exercising their independence and self-reliance. The series spearheaded a sub-genre of realistic fiction that made these topics accepted and popular among writers for the young. It also channeled the emphasis of British children's stories from school to the outdoors. Setting his books primarily in the Lake District of his childhood, Ransome wove his tightly-crafted novels around a group of resourceful boys and girls, the "Swallows" (John, Susan, Titty, and Roger Walker) and the "Amazons" (Nancy and Peggy Blackett). Admirably free of adult supervision, the youngsters sail, camp, and explore on and around Lake Windermere. Five of Ransome's books take place among these northwestern lakes and peaks, an area which his descriptions have made familiar to readers; other volumes feature the Norfolk Broads and the Hebrides. The plots range from rivalry between the crews of the two sailboats in *Swallows and Amazons* to boat stealing in *The Big Six*, coping with the terror of being cast adrift in *We Didn't Mean to Go to Sea*, and wildlife protection in *Great Northern?*. *Peter Duck* and *Missee Lee* are imaginary adventures, one taking place in the Caribbean and the other on the China Sea. Ransome's themes deal with such values as cooperation, responsibility, and competence. His characters grow with each book and, because of their ages and personalities, appeal to a large number of readers of both sexes. A salient feature is the author's attitude of taking the children's side against the "natives," as they call the adults. The exception is the Blacketts' Uncle Jim, whom the youngsters nickname Captain Flint after the pirate in *Treasure Island;* this rotund, eccentric author is Ransome's characterization of himself. Whether he writes fantasy or realistic tales, Ransome's works communicate his love of the lakes and lowlands of England and demonstrate his passion for storytelling.

The son of a history professor who was an avid fisherman, Ransome associated his happiest early memories with Coniston Lake, where his family spent Long Vacations. After an unhappy boyhood at school, where poor vision and lack of skill at games doomed him, Ransome worked as an errand boy in a London publishing house by day and wrote by night. Whenever possible, he escaped to Coniston Lake to stay with the family of W. G. Collingwood, biographer of John Ruskin. Ransome painted, wrote, camped, and sailed in the *Swallow* with Dora and Barbara Collingwood, who were close to his age, and young Robin Collingwood, who later became known as a philosopher and historian. Ransome admitted that he based his fictional Walkers on the children of Dora Collingwood and the poet Ernest Altounyan—Susan, Titty, Roger, and Taqui, the oldest girl, whose name was changed for marketing purposes to John. In 1913, Ransome went to Russia to

*Courtesy of Rupert Hart-Davis*

learn the language and study folklore; three years later, he published *Old Peter's Russian Tales*, a collection of twenty-one stories he had heard from local peasants. During the First World War and the Russian Revolution, Ransome acted as correspondent for several English newspapers and became immersed in Russian politics. Recognized by the Bolsheviks as a sympathetic journalist, he interviewed Lenin, Trotsky, and other figures who usually refused to talk to foreign reporters; Ransome later married Trotsky's secretary, Evgenia Shelepin. Ransome's controversial commentary on Russia prompted the *Manchester Guardian* to appoint him as their Russian correspondent. In his spare time, he sailed about the Baltic in his own ship, the *Racundra*, began to fish in emulation of his father, and dreamed of escaping the demands of his job to write stories for children. The *Guardian* reassigned Ransome to England, but also sent him to cover political affairs in China, Egypt, and the Sudan. Finally, at the age of forty-five, he rejected the stress—and security—of their job offer as a Berlin-based correspondent and began *Swallows and Amazons*, which he dedicated to the Altounyan family in return for the children's birthday gift of red carpet slippers. Ransome skillfully weaves various facts of his life into his books. *Winter Holiday* is based on the Great Frost of February 1895, when Lake Windermere was frozen over for a week; *Missee Lee* owes its authentic setting to Ransome's Far East travels and no less a personality than Madame Sun Yat-sen, whom he met in China and Moscow. The character of the sailor Peter Duck is patterned after Captain Sehmel of the *Racundra*, while the Blackett sisters were inspired by a glimpse of two little girls in red caps whom Ransome saw playing on the shore. Before writing *We Didn't Mean to Go to Sea*, he actually sailed to Holland to make sure he would have the details of the journey correct.

Ransome's initial works for children spotlight his interest in nature and folklore. At the age of twenty-two, he was asked to write *The Child's Book of the Seasons, The Things in Our Garden*, and *Pond and Stream*, which were later compiled in *The Imp and the Elf and the Ogre*. Critical attention at the time was minor; it was not until Ransome had established himself as a major children's writer that reviewers returned to these sentimental books and found occasional seeds of strength. *Old Peter's Russian Tales* was well-received by critics and gives credence to Ransome's growing ability as a storyteller. *Aladdin and His Wonderful Lamp* appeared in 1919 and is appreciated for its vivacity; this marked Ransome's only venture into poetry, and was his first children's book to be published in the United States. *The Fool of the World and the Flying Ship*, taken from the *Tales* and popularized by Uri Shulevitz's Caldecott-winning edition, is praised for the dignity and rhythm of its prose. Reviewers also acclaim Ransome's rendition of *The Soldier and Death* for the simple, conversational style which captures the grandeur of the Tsarist era as well as the lowliness of peasant life. More than twenty-five years of experience in journalistic and creative writing preceded the publication of *Swallows and Amazons*.

By the time he decided to write exclusively for children, Ransome was a master of the succinct phrase and the lively narrative. Although initial sales and critical response to the first two *Swallow* books were slow, available reviews were overwhelmingly positive. Critics hailed *Peter Duck* and then its predecessors for their exacting plots, fresh dialogue spiced with nautical terms, and convincing characterizations. Reviewers continue to admire the sharpness and accuracy of Ransome's descriptions, whether of cooking over a camp fire, tying a knot, or sailing a rough sea. While there has been little adverse criticism, a few observers object to the almost exclusively middle class protagonists, their nearly constant equanimity, and the lack of emotional entanglements common to adolescents. The majority of critics, however, say that since Ransome concentrated on young people he knew and liked, class distinctions are irrelevant. Ransome firmly believed that any illustrations for his books should completely reflect their texts. He was infuriated, therefore, by the inaccuracy of the original pictures in *Swallows and Amazons* and *Swallowdale*, which were done by professional artists. Ransome began illustrating his books with *Peter Duck*, and later redid the art work in the first two books. In an attempt to underscore the reality of his works, Ransome did his black-and-white line drawings as if he were one of the children; in fact, he tried to make his pictures appear as if all the characters had participated in them. Aware that his artistic talents were limited, Ransome usually attributed his simple scenes, diagrams, and maps to Nancy Blackett; critics agree that they appear to be done by a child and note the innovation of his technique. Stylistically, Ransome's efforts are considered amateurish. His technical flawlessness and integration of text and picture, however, are consistently lauded.

Ransome is credited with raising the standards of children's fiction by moving away from the sensationalism and senti-

mentality of his time towards a more modern realism. He is recognized as an author who wrote naturally and uncondescendingly for children, one whose works continue to be appreciated for their understanding of childhood and delight in open-air pleasures. Without being didactic, Ransome communicates his immense knowledge of the outdoors. His unique ability to describe a technical process in such lucid detail that a layman can fashion a pigeon loft or raise a sunken sailboat has made his novels prized handbooks for hardy adventurers. Though Ransome's success was imitated by many of his contemporaries, their stories never equalled those of their mentor. Ransome once said: "A good book is not merely a thing that keeps a child (or a grown-up person) amused while reading. It is an experience he shares, something that he himself lives." Ransome's books exemplify his own definition. In 1936, he received the first Carnegie Medal for *Pigeon Post*. Besides reissues of the popular series, Ransome's books have been broadcast, televised, and translated into at least a dozen languages.

(See also *Something about the Author*, Vol. 22 and *Contemporary Authors*, Vols. 73-76.)

---

## AUTHOR'S COMMENTARY

*[The following excerpt was written by Ransome in response to a request from H. J. B. Woodfield, founder and editor of* The Junior Bookshelf. *It contains Ransome's often-quoted philosophy of writing books for children. See also Woodfield's excerpt below from* The School Librarian and School Library Review, *March, 1949.]*

You asked for an article, but, sitting here in my little cabin, with the coke glowing red in the stove, a kettle simmering, and old Nancy, in from the sea, lying quietly on her moorings, I don't feel like writing anything so formal. You wouldn't yourself, if you had been up at five in the morning and spent the whole long day beating to windward. You must forgive me for writing a letter instead. I will try to keep to the subjects you suggest.

First: on writing books for children. I do not know how to write books for children and have the gravest doubts as to whether anybody should try to do any such thing. To write a book *for* children seems to me a sure way of writing what is called a "juvenile," a horrid, artificial thing, a patronising thing, a thing that betrays in every line that author and intended victims are millions of miles apart, and that the author is enjoying not the stuff of his book, but a looking-glass picture of himself or herself "being so good with children" . . . a most unpleasant spectacle for anyone who happens to look over his shoulder. It is true that some of the best children's books were written with a particular audience in view—*Alice in Wonderland* and *The Wind in the Willows*, for example. Many others were not, and it is impossible to read even those that were without realising that one member of that audience and the one whose taste had dictatorial rights was the author. Lewis Carroll was not "writing down" further than to Lewis Carroll, and though Kenneth Grahame could count on a delighted listener in his small son, the first person to enjoy the exquisite fun of Mr. Toad and his friends was Kenneth Grahame himself. Stevenson was stimulated to the writing of *Treasure Island* by the presence of a young stepson, greedy for the chapters as they came, but his first delighted public was Robert Louis Stevenson. "If this don't fetch the kids," he writes, "why, they have gone rotten since my day." And, "It's awful fun, boys' stories; you just indulge the pleasure of your heart. . . ." That, it seems to me, is the secret. You just indulge the pleasure of your heart. You write not *for* children, but for yourself, and if, by good fortune, children enjoy what you enjoy, why then you are a writer of children's books ... No special credit to you, but simply thumping good luck. Every writer wants to have readers, and than children there are no better readers in the world.

Second: the country of my own books. Stevenson talks somewhere of the importance of maps, and says you should know the country of your tales "like your hand." If you know a bit of country really well, it takes a very active part in the making of your book. You can count on it. It is always there and, somehow or other, life flows from it into your story. In the case of one of my books, the country is that of the Norfolk Broads, where I had an enormous lot of pleasure during the years when I was too groggy to go to sea. In the case of another, I worked out with a fair amount of accuracy the proper course for a small sailing vessel between Lowestoft and the Caribbees. The one I am now busy on is about the North Sea, and I let my own little ship blow across to Holland while making sure that I had the details right. I like getting the details right. It lets me sail and call it work ... (That kettle is boiling. Just half a minute while I fill the teapot ...) But I think you meant the country of the Swallows and Amazons ... In those four books, *Swallows and Amazons, Swallowdale, Winter Holiday* and *Pigeon Post,* the places are not given their proper names. But, in actual fact, I know that country better than any other. It is the country of my own childhood. In the case of the first book, I steered clear of using real names, for quite practical reasons. The place had to be disguised. So the Swallows and Amazons had a country of their own. Their lake is not altogether Windermere, though Rio is, of course, Bowness, because I had to take a good deal from Coniston. No island on Windermere has quite so good a harbour as that among the rocks at the south end of Peel Island on Coniston where I first landed from a little boat I hardly like to say how many years ago. And a good many people have spotted that Kanchenjunga must be the Old Man. But Cormorant Island is Silverholme on Windermere, and until a year or two ago the cormorants were there.... Then, too, there had to be a little pulling about of rivers and roads, but every single place in all those books exists somewhere, and by now, I know the geography of the country in the books so well that when I walk about in actual fact, it sometimes seems to me that some giant or earthquake has been doing a little scene-shifting overnight.

Finally: as to how I began to write. I will tell you the truth, and let others take warning. I was not meant to be a writer at all. I was a cheerful small boy of action, very bad at lessons (as I remained) and with no thought of taking to a pen when, at about the age of eight, we were all playing at ships under and on an old dining room table, a really old one, with a heavy iron screw pointing downwards in the middle of it. It was my watch below when, suddenly, somebody else, who was on the bridge, on the top of the table, raised a shout for "All hands on deck!" I started up. That heavy iron screw made a horrible dent in the top of my skull, altering its shape and my character for life. I crawled out much shaken, played no more that day, but took a small blue notebook and wrote in it my first story, about a desert island. I have been at it ever since. (pp. 3-5)

> *Arthur Ransome, in a letter to Mr. Woodfield, in* The Junior Bookshelf, *Vol. 1, No. 4, July, 1937, pp. 3-5.*

---

## GENERAL COMMENTARY

### RHODA POWER

The author really does know how to write for children: in other words, he writes of what he himself delights in and so pleases without any effort both young and old. [*Swallows and Amazons*] has a worthy sequel in *Swallowdale* which is redolent of open air, camping, sailing, sunshine, rain, and all the picnic of a good holiday.

> *Rhoda Power, in a review of "Swallows and Amazons," in* The New Statesman & Nation, *Vol. 11, No. 41, December 5, 1931, p. xxii.*

### ANNE CARROLL MOORE

Mr. Ransome is unquestionably a magnetic writer for children of the present day; he is identified heart and soul with their out-of-door interests and gifted with an inexhaustible capacity for fresh invention and natural conversation.

> *Anne Carroll Moore, in a review of "The Coot Club," in* The Atlantic Bookshelf, *a section of* The Atlantic Monthly, *October, 1935, p. 16.*

### W. C. BERWICK SAYERS

[In 1930, Mr. Ransome] began the series of children's books, by which he has become a household word, with the one entitled *Swallows and Amazons.* It is a transcription of the ordinary experiences of childhood, intensified and lifted on to a plane which is literature.... [The children's adventures] are told with such skill, charm and verisimilitude that the whole fantasy is accepted and followed with the keenest interest by children of almost every age. The style of these books is admirable; they are long without being in the least tedious; the characters are alive, are real children; and a part of the charm are the quite unconventional, child-like illustrations. (p. 219)

> *W. C. Berwick Sayers, "The Library Association Carnegie Medal and Mr. Arthur Ransome," in* The Library Association Record, *Vol. 39, May, 1937, pp. 218-19.*

### L. A. G. STRONG

[The] best way to write for children is to write with adult conviction on all but purely adult concerns.

This is the secret of that paladin of writers for children, Mr. Arthur Ransome.... [He] gives himself up entirely to what he is doing. He enters a child's world, by right, not as a visitor looking around with benevolently disguised patronage. And he is very serious about important things.

> *L. A. G. Strong, in a review of "We Didn't Mean to Go to Sea," in* The Spectator, *Vol. 159, No. 5710, December 3, 1937, p. 1023.*

### MAY LAMBERTON BECKER

Arthur Ransome may go down in history as the one author who wrote books for young people in a series that began from the first every time. It is an art. He practices it in various ways. Sometimes the scene changes, sometimes the time of year transforms the scene: often a few favorite figures go on holiday to let new characters come in without clogging the stage; sometimes a minor character, staying through other books in the wings, suddenly takes the leading part. However it happens, the result is the same; you can start anywhere.

> *May Lamberton Becker, "Adventures by Land and Sea," in* New York Herald Tribune Books, *May 1, 1938, p. 12.\**

*Pearl diving. From* Swallows and Amazons, *written and illustrated by Arthur Ransome. Jonathan Cape, 1976. Reprinted by permission of David R. Godine Publisher, Inc. In Canada by Jonathan Cape Ltd, on behalf of the Literary Estate of Arthur Ransome.*

## ELEANOR GRAHAM

Arthur Ransome created a new standard [in children's books]. He writes always with the full weight of his mind and experience, while his personal integrity gives substance and reality to all his work. He chose to demonstrate the dignity of youth, trained to independence and responsibility, and to show the value in that training of constructive play. Neither the reader nor the onlooker has to fear being fooled by him. (pp. 59-60)

> *Eleanor Graham, "The Carnegie Medal and Its Winners," in* The Junior Bookshelf, *Vol. 8, No. 2, July, 1944, pp. 59-65.**

## DOROTHY NEAL WHITE

Arthur Ransome is, I think, the uncrowned king of modern English writers for children. Other people have written books that by themselves are better, but no contemporary British writer has such a long sustained record of success. Look at a list of his books. . . . The very titles have their own unique flavour, and it is noteworthy that all appeal equally to boys and girls. . . . [The adventures are] exciting at the time but not over-spectacular, garnished with the children's imagination (for no small brother can be a nuisance once he is named the ship's boy, and grown-ups are tolerable once called the 'natives').

His characters are delineated completely by their conversation and actions, by description never, except for such scraps of information as age and, where necessary, costume. Mate Susan's colossal sense of order and tidiness is built up with a hundred touches, until the reader becomes conscious of a cushion out of place (more or less) as soon as Susan appears on the scene. This probably is one of the reasons for the book's complete air of reality. . . . Arthur Ransome excels at clear explanations, given without patronage. Whenever his staple characters, the Walkers or the Blacketts or the Callums, embark on something about which the reader is likely to be in ignorance, Arthur Ransome makes it plain exactly what they are doing. In this respect he has a gift. (pp. 88-9)

[Arthur Ransome] follows the Stevenson precept that an author should know the country of his tales like the back of his hand. . . . All Ransome's books have good maps, and he has set quite a fashion for other children's novelists in this respect. (p. 90)

> *Dorothy Neal White, "Realistic Stories—Standards 5 and 6," in her* About Books for Children, *New Zealand Library Association, 1946, pp. 86-108.**

## MAY HILL ARBUTHNOT

Some of the adventures [of Ransome's young people] are genuinely hair-raising, but they are possible for well-trained, competent children, and they are just such adventures as every normal child dreams of.

The outstanding characteristic of these Ransome children is their competence. They know how to cook, clean fish, sail a boat, do their own laundry, scour their pans with sand, take care of themselves in a storm, on land or lake. They meet every emergency with resourcefulness and intelligence. No one talks about courage. It is taken for granted like cleanliness and a decent sense of responsibility. Their other striking characteristic is their power to plan and sustain these tremendous games of make-believe that last for days or weeks. These games are the plots of the stories—the children lay down the rules of the game and then the action starts.

The outdoor atmosphere of these stories is invaluable for indoor children. Everything happens outdoors. It is indeed almost impossible to imagine the Walkers and Blacketts cribbed and confined in schoolrooms or houses. You wonder if they don't perhaps carry their mattresses to the roofs for the winter and become arctic explorers. You also hope their mothers ply them with sufficient greens and milk during the winter to compensate for their somewhat sketchy holiday diets and their amazing consumption of strong British tea.

The nautical phraseology of these stories, together with the Britishisms, makes them heavy going for many readers. Good readers skip a lot of the nautical stuff, but the poor reader is bogged down with it and gives up.

One of the things children ought to learn in reading is the art of skipping, and with a little help on the first book more children could and would enjoy the whole series. (pp. 372-73)

> *May Hill Arbuthnot, "Here and Now," in her* Children and Books, *Scott, Foresman and Company, 1947, pp. 360-469.**

## JANET ADAM SMITH

Arthur Ransome's own illustrations to his classic series arouse mixed feelings. It is good to feel absolute confidence in the technical accuracy of the drawings of boats, wigwams, camp-

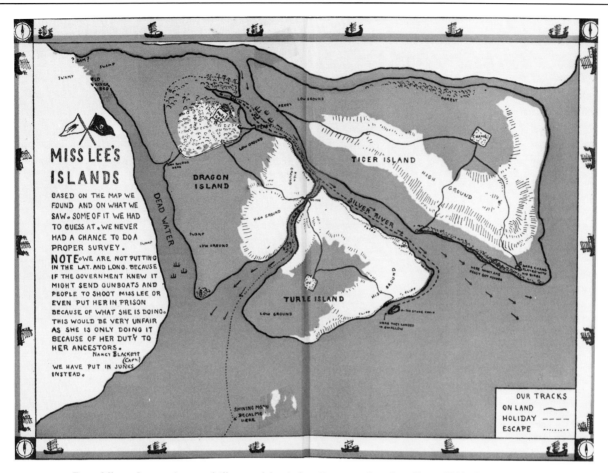

*From* Missee Lee, *written and illustrated by Arthur Ransome. Jonathan Cape, 1964. Reprinted by permission of Jonathan Cape Ltd, on behalf of the Literary Estate of Arthur Ransome.*

ovens, pigeon lofts and Great Northern Divers; but the charm of the gawky human figures soon wears thin. (pp. 48-9)

> Janet Adam Smith, ''Twentieth-Century Children's Books,'' *in her* Children's Illustrated Books, *Collins, 1948, pp. 39-50.\**

**GEOFFREY TREASE**

The outstanding literary landmark of [the mid-twentieth century] is Arthur Ransome. His name will go into the short list of writers like Talbot Baines Reed, who have deflected the stream of fiction into new channels. What Reed did for the school term, Mr. Ransome did for the holidays. As the holidays scarcely existed for Reed, so school plays no part in the Ransome world. (p. 161)

It is a fantasy world, disguised under a wealth of realistic practical detail. These children who run through the whole series, *Swallows and Amazons, The Coot Club* and the rest of them, whether the scene is the Norfolk Broads, the Lake District or the Hebrides, are practical beyond all else. They hammer, paint, cook, navigate, stow hammocks and swab decks. Their favourite reading is maps and charts, and they write mainly in logbooks. The dialogue is in keeping:

> ''Stern warp, John! Haul in and belay!''
> ''Aye, aye, Sir.''
> ''Port warp, Nancy.''

The child who has read and re-read **Great Northern,** not to mention its predecessors, should be just about qualified to sit for a master's ticket. Yet it is a fantasy world in that the child-group is almost independent of adult interference. (pp. 161-62)

Arthur Ransome's contribution must not be minimised. There is little enough danger of that, for his popularity is so high, not only with children but with those under-thirtyish librarians and others who had the advantage of meeting his work while they were themselves children, that adverse criticism of his work is practically unknown, if not unthinkable. His books are solid and genuine. He writes of the things he cares about, he does not ''cater''. Producing a new book at long intervals, he shames those prolific yarn-spinners who present their public with a litter of several books per season. He demonstrates, over and over again, that the interest of the child can be held without introducing improbable sensations. In his latest, **Great Northern,** the whole drama . . . is built round the nest of a rare bird, and the villain is nothing more sinister than a vulgar and unscrupulous egg-collector. He does not need to ''bring in the police'', because he can manage without that element of crime which so many authors (or rather, I am inclined to think, so many publishers) believe to be an essential ingredient of an enjoyable fictional holiday. Handiness, co-operation, decent behaviour and above all self-reliance . . .—these are the Ransome virtues, and very well worth preaching they are, especially when the writer never falls for a phrase or syllable into a recognisable preacher's tone.

All these things are excellent. It would be ungracious to expect more of any single writer. Unfortunately some of his less critical admirers—probably to his own vexation more than to anybody else's—have sometimes talked as though the Ransome books represented a kind of final, highest-attainable pinnacle in the range of juvenile fiction. Nothing could be less helpful to arriving at a fair estimate of their worth, and nothing more unjust to writers in other fields. There is a breezy healthiness about his stories which at times is suspiciously suggestive of antiseptic. These children are so busy hauling in and belaying that they seem untroubled by dreams or problems of personal relationship. They take plenty of soundings at sea, but they plumb no emotional depths. Arthur Ransome himself, who once turned aside to collect Russian fairy-tales, knows well enough that the world of his own stories is only one world. He who, as a young newspaper correspondent, witnessed the Bolshevik Revolution, is only too well aware of wider horizons than are scanned by his young voyagers. (pp. 162-63)

"Of course," a well-known publisher said to me recently, "Ransome merely discovered a new formula. Once the others found it, there was nothing to it. Everyone's using it now." That, I should say, was much less than the truth. There *have* been many imitators and a number of writers . . . who have been consciously or unconsciously influenced by him. . . . The fact remains that in his own field Arthur Ransome has no equal. He has created a new *genre* and, I am inclined to think, perfected it himself in a decade or two of his own writing life. (p. 164)

*Geoffrey Trease, "Home and Holiday," in his* Tales Out of School, *William Heinemann Ltd., 1948, pp. 160-79.\**

### H. J. B. WOODFIELD

Every year now we are given a flood of what can best be described as "holiday" stories, since they are all concerned with children on holiday. We need have no hesitation in saying that Arthur Ransome's books stand head and shoulders above all others in this type. Indeed there seems no doubt that he was the forerunner of the present glut of such stories. But the more recent publications show unpleasant signs of being written to a formula. All have much the same ingredients, of which the most important now seem to be escaped German prisoners, smugglers and black marketeers. Ransome never makes that mistake. His stories continue as true to life as the first he gave us, *Swallows and Amazons*. I imagine Ransome will be read for a long time.

*H. J. B. Woodfield, in a review of "Swallows and Amazons," in* The School Librarian and School Library Review, *Vol. 4, No. 5, March, 1949, p. 170.*

### FRANK EYRE

*Swallows and Amazons* led the way to a new conception of the children's adventure story. (p. 21)

So many imitations have since appeared that it is difficult for us today to remember how new and exciting that first book was. Ransome's contribution to the development of the modern children's story is not always sufficiently realized. It is a commonplace, nowadays, to say that "Ransome invented holidays," or "Ransome invented the sailing adventure story", or "Ransome invented the story about the country", or "Ransome first set children free from parents"; all these statements are true enough, but they miss the essential point of his contribution to children's writing.

I imagine that in fact he consciously invented very little. What he did do, almost for the first time since *Bevis*, was to write a book based on loving and detailed observation of the true characters and activities of a group of real children. Quite obviously the idea of inventing any new type of children's story never entered his head until afterwards. The important thing was that he had known and loved a group of children who enjoyed a way of life that happened to appeal to him. He had studied them with that delighted affectionate enjoyment Jane Austen derived from her own circle, and when the idea came to him to write a book for children the important thing was not to invent fantastic adventures but to get as close as he could to the truth. It would be, of course, imaginative rather than real truth. Like all true artists, he supplied here and there the interpretative touch that gives cohesion and significance to the story, but he permitted himself no extravagances and none of his children ever for a moment acts or speaks out of character.

Ransome carries his passion for accuracy and probability to unusual lengths—even going so far as to let himself drift across the North Sea in a small yacht to test the plot of one of his later books—and the practicalities that he introduces can be tried and tested at every point. Even the illustrations are unusual. . . . [His books] are not sequels in the accepted sense, nor do they constitute a series, but they are all about the same group of children, who grow older naturally throughout the series (no perpetual youth for Ransome). Most, though not all, of their adventures take place on or near water, and a boy or girl who has read the whole series must have a pretty thorough knowledge of small boat sailing; but there are a hundred and one other hints in his books of things to do and how to do them, for he contrives to get his excitement from probabilities and his suspense from the success or failure of child or adult in perfectly possible activities. One of his best stories, *Pigeon Post*, . . . is a perfect model of how to write a children's story, for in it he subjects his group of children to all the superficial ingredients of the conventional children's "thriller". There is a mysterious stranger, a search for treasure, midnight excursions, and so on; but how skilfully it is all handled and how differently the children themselves react. And yet how much more truly exciting it is than the usual nonsense.

Ransome's contribution to the twentieth-century children's story was incalculable. He led the way to a more natural approach; to a realistic and unsentimental characterization; to completely true to life dialogue, and to a new conception of the kind of excitement necessary to keep children reading for pleasure. He has had, of course, hosts of imitators. He launched a whole fleet of sailing adventure stories; . . . he started the immense flood of stories about the summer holidays (and in doing so more or less dealt the death-blow to the school story); he began the fashion for books with plenty of country lore in them. But above all the success of his books showed both authors and publishers that it was possible for a successful book to break away from the "reward" pattern. (pp. 56-8)

*Frank Eyre, "Historical" and "Fiction for Children," in his* 20th Century Children's Books, *Longmans, Green and Co., 1952, pp. 11-24, 50-64.\**

### RUTH HILL VIGUERS

[There is a] tendency in many English stories to present a group of children, often of varying ages, who share in activities and adventures, each child holding a special place in the group, with interest centering on no one child for any length of time.

The first writer to reach near-perfection in this type of story and to have a marked influence on realistic stories both in England and America was Arthur Ransome. . . . John and Susan, Titty and Roger, Nancy and Peggy and all the other children who people his books come as close to being living companions as book children ever can. Unhampered by grownups the children can lose themselves completely in their play, and demonstrate the self-reliance and common sense teamed with free imaginations which are natural to the average child but which are too seldom given a chance to thrive. Sometimes the children are up against a very real challenge, as they are in *We Didn't Mean to Go to Sea* . . . , when the yacht on which they are sailing around Harwich Harbor drifts out to sea, but their play life has amply prepared them for such an emergency. The only adults who are allowed to play any large part in their lives are those who make possible a more highly colored or romantic experience than they could have by themselves on the lakes, such as Captain Flint, who takes them with him on a trip around the world in *Missee Lee* . . . , or the old seaman *Peter Duck* . . . , who shares their adventures with buried treasure and pirates.

So reasonable are all the children's adventures, so spontaneous the fun, and so full of fascinating detail are the descriptions of their activities that readers are inspired to create for themselves similar adventures. Probably no other books have had so much influence on children's play as have Mr. Ransome's stories of the Swallows, the Amazons and the other tribes, and few writers of this century have had as many imitators here and abroad. (pp. 546-47)

> Ruth Hill Viguers, *"Experiences to Share," in* A Critical History of Children's Literature *by Cornelia Meigs, Anne Thaxter Eaton, Elizabeth Nesbitt, and Ruth Hill Viguers, edited by Cornelia Meigs, The Macmillan Company, 1953, pp. 539-60.*

**HUGH SHELLEY**

[Until Arthur Ransome wrote *Swallows and Amazons*,] that now famous book that changed the course of so much children's literature, no one had treated school holidays as more than the setting of a novel. . . . There had been on the serious side Mrs Molesworth's *The House that Grew* and, later, E. Nesbit's books. The latter were perhaps the true forerunners of Arthur Ransome's—certainly they were the first about children's life in the holidays to be written with some zest and humour—and it is interesting to learn that Arthur Ransome had singled their author out as the only writer of children's books he can remember reading as a boy . . . other than Robert Louis Stevenson. (pp. 7-8)

The reason why Arthur Ransome has become the Holidays' champion and chronicler is a very simple one; he has spent the greater part of his seventy-five years either looking forward to, enjoying or looking nostalgically back at them. That is mainly because he is a countryman whose profession alone has brought him to live at times in towns. (pp. 8-9)

[Not] just holidays but the right sort of holidays are the setting and in great part the substance of Arthur Ransome's books. (p. 12)

Arthur Ransome's twelve books 'for children' are really twelve volumes of one major work, as are the novels that compose the Forsyte Saga or the Dolittle Books. The holidays they chronicle are consecutive. . . .

The children grow naturally older volume by volume, and the (fictional) lapse of time between *Swallows and Amazons* and *Great Northern?* is between five and six years. For this reason, because the author is constantly referring to occasions and characters in previous books, and because both style and subject matter are simplest in the early books, would-be readers are strongly recommended by him and his publishers to begin with Volume I. (p. 13)

Who *are* the book's children? Did they really exist? (p. 15)

There does indeed exist a family of four sisters and a brother, who are intimately connected with the saga. . . .

It is not, however, true, as many people have imagined, that Arthur Ransome wrote his first book *about* this family. He had already written the greater part of *Swallows and Amazons* before getting to know the five children at all intimately. (p. 16)

[Soon] he was changing the names of his Swallows to those they now bear, and altering some of the circumstances of the story to make it seem possible for the real children to feel they were the originals of his heroes and heroines.

As the now grown-up John says, not one single adventure in any of the books sprang from anywhere but its author's imagination; only incidentals were taken from life. And there were no 'originals' of the Amazons, Nancy and Peggy Blackett, though Arthur Ransome does remember a sudden glimpse he once had when sailing on the Lake of two little girls in identical red woollen hats sitting on the bank.

It is satisfactory to be able to scotch so demonstrably the myth of 'originals', for it shows that both Swallows and Amazons, like all characters of stature, are entirely their author's creatures and yet become more real to the dedicated reader than his or her closest friend. And Arthur Ransome, in common with other authors, is far more pleased and flattered to learn that young readers have taken his characters to their hearts than that they are thrilled by the plot or entranced by the setting. (p. 17)

It is Arthur Ransome's triumph that both the scenes and characters of his books become so real to their readers, that people insist that there must have been models for both. . . .

His characters are even more lifelike, lively and memorable [than the scenes]. . . . Peggy is a normally healthy and sporting girl, but she shrinks to an insignificant, docile pawn, with neither mind nor will of her own beside her outrageous elder sister. Nancy is the tomboy of tomboys, the utterly uninhibited leader, whom all the others follow without question, the complete extrovert, who leaves her contemporaries and her elders breathless and speechless. (p. 18)

She could belong to no other sex, nation or background. (p. 19)

The second strongest character in the books . . . is, oddly enough, an adult. This is the Blacketts' idiosyncratic Uncle Jim. . . . His is to no small extent a self-portrait. He is large and rather bald and disguised only by the absence of his creator's very fine (and once piratical) moustache. He is a rover, a sailor, a writer, an angler and a would-be solitary. Being irascible by nature, and certainly no besotted child lover, he is extremely put out when he is led to believe that the young are deliberately annoying him. This is one of the principal themes of *Swallows and Amazons*. Uncle Jim grossly misjudges the Swallows and is despicably unfair to them. When he discovers his mistake, he is immediately and most honourably remorseful. . . . Amiable, omniscient bachelor uncles on the side of the children rather than of their parents, have long been commonplaces of children's fiction. But Uncle Jim is the doyen of them all, besides being by far the most convincing.

While Nancy is the moving spirit behind the Swallows' and Amazons' adventures, and Uncle Jim their benevolent and beneficent supporter, who can give the sanction and aid without which parental opposition would scotch their plans, it is the Walkers who are the real heroes of the saga, with whom the reader must identify him- (or her-) self. It is more than an incidental pleasure to discover that Arthur Ransome, unlike the majority of his contemporaries writing for children, does not pander to the ten-year-old's article of faith that all females, bar 'sporting' mothers and aunts, are inexcusable interlopers in a world created by Dr Arnold. (pp. 19-20)

[So] many reviewers and critics have praised the books primarily for their plots that people forget that the distinction of Arthur Ransome as a writer for children lies not in telling 'rattling good yarns' and becoming a twentieth-century Ballantyne, but in his ability to write about children who were not only credible, attractive individuals who grew up as they grew older, but also personalities with whom at least a million children have been able to identify themselves. (p. 22)

*Swallows and Amazons* is not the most professional of the twelve books, but in many ways it is the most endearing, the friendliest. Re-reading it as an adult, one senses the enjoyment and the enthusiastic application with which it was written. (p. 23)

[Whereas] a lesser writer would have plunged straightway into action and adventure, this leisurely tyro among children's writers is quite content to let his Swallows explore the island, set up camp, eat and drink, swim and fish for four whole chapters. (pp. 23-4)

The successor and sequel to *Swallows and Amazons* is *Swallowdale,* and what a worthy, satisfying sequel it is. It has the same endearing quality, the same characters and the same setting; it is better written and more exciting.

It is longer too, and by today's standards exceptionally so. Indeed, returning to Ransome after reading more recent children's books, one is struck by the length of his stories. Admittedly, *Swallowdale* is the longest, nearly 150,000 words, but they are all long. Whereas nowadays a children's novel of 60,000 words is quite usual, the shortest Ransome, *The Picts and the Martyrs,* is 64,000 and the average is nearly 90,000. (p. 25)

[We] get to know the Walkers far better [than the Blacketts]. By the end of the book they are as familiar as our closest friends, not only because Arthur Ransome identifies himself and makes us identify ourselves with them, but because he takes time over them. As in *Swallows and Amazons,* there is no rush to get on with the story. Pages are spent in describing the daily, even the hourly, life of the children. (pp. 26-7)

The other agreeably effective way in which Arthur Ransome brings one to know his characters is by frequent back reference. They are continually remembering, as children do, what happened the last time they were in such-and-such a place or predicament. The children are worth getting to know, because they always behave as children and not as cardboard heroes. The place or predicament is never taken in the children's stride as it usually is in the second-rate adventure story. They are ever new and strange; unfamiliar and little frequented country can be very unnerving to children, and Arthur Ransome knows this well. The Walkers and the Blacketts get tired and hungry and feel lonely as children do. And from time to time, their

tiredness, hunger and loneliness are such that only adults can assuage them. How different from those heroes and heroines of Cornish cove mysteries, who can retrieve the school cups, unmask the villain and uncover an international spy ring in twenty-four sleepless, foodless, waterless hours. Arthur Ransome is sufficiently familiar with physical discomfort and the disadvantages of solitude to appreciate two major facts of childhood: achievement in the face of ungauged difficulties and hardships is the most exciting thing; loneliness with neither physical nor moral support is the most daunting. In *Swallows and Amazons,* one of the best passages describes how Titty makes up her mind to stay alone on the Island and play her lone part in the night battle between the Amazon pirates and the crew of the *Swallow* rather than take her mother's offer of a row home to civilisation. In *Swallowdale* it is Titty again, who is left alone, this time with a frightened Roger, when the two of them lose their way on the moors in the fog. Roger sprains his ankle—and they have eaten the last of the chocolate. (pp. 27-8)

Roger is occasionally fanciful and often slightly—naturally—silly, while Titty is blessed and cursed with the most vivid of imaginations. Both are determined to overcome their several fears. Whenever they are successful, their heroism is in accordance with their age; their achievements are triumphs of their age. They are genuine heroes. (pp. 29-30)

[Ransome] also wrote some fairy stories that were, he says, 'as bad as they could be'. There are, however, two children's books outside the **"Swallow and Amazon"** saga that are worth consideration. In 1919 appeared his rhymed version of *Aladdin*. . . .

[The] story is told with despatch and humour in fine, spanking verse, with an occasional surprising subtlety of rhythm; and many parents must have read it to their children with zest. One must admit, however, that it is no landmark in chidren's literature and Arthur Ransome does not intend to reprint it.

The other book [*Old Peter's Russian Tales*] is a very different matter; it has been in print for nearly half a century. (p. 33)

The stories themselves are delightfully told and suit Arthur Ransome's taste in humour and for colour and magic. (p. 34)

The two books in the **"Swallow and Amazon"** saga that most closely resemble Arthur Ransome's earlier writings are *Peter Duck* and *Missee Lee.* These differ from the other ten books in that they are imaginary adventures supposedly invented by the Swallows and the Amazons to beguile winter evenings between their own summer holiday adventures. (p. 35)

Both *Peter Duck* and *Missee Lee* give Arthur Ransome full opportunity to indulge his taste for credibly outrageous fantasy. (p. 36)

The originality of *Peter Duck* and *Missee Lee* compared with the bulk of fantasies for the young lies, paradoxically, in their factual approach. Often they are more concerned with the mechanics of 'going foreign' than are the 'true' stories of the Swallows and the Amazons with the technicalities of sailing. *Peter Duck,* for example, contains detailed drawings of the ship in which they sail to the Caribbean, and Arthur Ransome tells how he carefully worked out the course from Lowestoft to 'Crab Island' so that the adventurous could actually sail there and back with the aid of the text and the end-paper map. As for *Missee Lee,* the author visited China and wrote a book about it, *Chinese Puzzle,* after being sent out there by the *Manchester Guardian* at the time of the Chinese Revolution.

Even more striking than the accuracy of the background is the consistency with which the children, in their own story, the one they made up, behave exactly as they would under the story's circumstances. With a sigh of relief one realises that it would be blowhard Nancy, by all the barbecued billygoats in the northern hemisphere, who was irremediably seasick as the *Wild Cat* lurched south down the North Sea. It is an agreeable surprise that the desperately keen John should be less confident than he was on the Lake. (pp. 36-7)

Arthur Ransome's ability to create fantastic reality is to me more exciting than his admittedly remarkable achievement in writing realistic fantasy. . . .

[*The Picts and the Martyrs* is], I think, the least successful [of the Lake books]. Ransomanes are so far united in refusing to criticise any of 'the twelve', but I must risk their giving me the black spot as Nancy memorably gave it to Captain Flint, by suggesting that we are brought back to the Lake—after sorties into strange parts of the British Isles—a little under false pretences. The plot mainly concerns the efforts of the Amazons and the 2 D's to outwit the abominable Great Aunt, whom we had not met since *Swallowdale*. But perhaps I am prejudiced by the absence of the Swallows. (p. 38)

[By the time *Winter Holiday* appears,] the position of the grown-ups in the stories has become clearly defined. Strangers who merely happen to cross the children's horizon are imagined to be something else that will not spoil the fantasy of their adventures. The skaters on the frozen Lake that has become the Arctic Ocean encasing the *Fram,* are counted as Eskimos or seals, just as in *Swallowdale,* when Titty and Roger went off exploring on their own, the hooting cars on the main road became trumpeting savages. Adults within the children's family circle become Natives for the purposes of fantasy, but they are acknowledged to have 'real' lives as well. All of them (with the exception of that Great Aunt) are remarkably good-natured and willing to give the children what assistance they can to make the games, adventures and expeditions a success. Uncle Jim is their mainstay, but the others help staunchly. At times, there is an almost feudal atmosphere, for not only parents and other relations join in, but the lower orders play their part. One is forcibly reminded that the first books were written in the early 'thirties, when the middle classes still had servants. However, one feels that the farmers' wives who lodge the children and the various locals they meet are friendly only because they are amused by and like the children. Other characters, such as the two Billies, the charcoal burners who appear in both *Swallows and Amazons* and *Swallowdale,* Mary Swainson in *Swallowdale,* and others, are all pleasant open folk. Their deference is the natural, often protective, politeness of country people. What is more, they are never mere ciphers; they have definite characters, unlike the background yokels of so many children's books. And their dialect, unlike the Mummerset of fictional coastguards, has the ring of authenticity. One of the nicest of Arthur Ransome's Westmorlanders (or northern Lancastrians) is Mr Dixon, the farmer who speaks to no one until the Callums appear on the scene, when he and Dick strike up a convincingly odd friendship that astonishes even Mrs Dixon.

On the whole, though, the children's relations with the adult world are a minor matter. It is their relationship with each other and their development that is most interesting. Some, like Susan and Roger, are simple characters, so simple that adult readers may weary of the constant repetition of their not very subtle characteristics. Susan's Native mind, her preoccupation with the domestic economy of each expedition and adventure,

its victualling, health and hygiene, is constantly reiterated, while Roger's ever-empty stomach and thoughts of chocolate recur in book after book. But these repetitions are not solely for the sake of opposing Susan's practical to Nancy's adventurous, Dorothea's romantic and Titty's imaginative approach, or, for that matter, of bringing in Roger's unworthy pangs as light relief. Children love repetition, both comic repetition (which, of course, is a basic ingredient of the most primitive comedy) and serious repetition that gives the sense of continuity and security their conservative natures require. (pp. 39-41)

*Pigeon Post,* sixth of the series, and one of the most complete, is an outstanding example of Arthur Ransome's ability not only to analyse character and show its development but to do so dramatically. And in terms any boy or girl of average sensitivity can appreciate. . . .

[The Carnegie Medal was awarded to Arthur Ransome] not so much, one is given to understand, for his achievement in *Pigeon Post* itself, but to honour the man who was unquestionably the foremost English children's writer at the time. *Swallows and Amazons, Swallowdale, Peter Duck, Winter Holiday* and *Coot Club* were the books it crowned. Because of this *Pigeon Post* and its successors are often underrated. (p. 42)

[*We Didn't Mean to Go to Sea*] is the one I suspect Arthur Ransome himself considers his best. Certainly, it is the most exciting. (p. 48)

The reality of the book lies . . . not in the plausibility of its plot, but in the naturalness of the children's behaviour, the effect [drifting at sea] has on each. As always, the main interest is not in the situation but in the way the boys and girls react to it. There are no phoney heroics. They are sick as cats, Titty, early on, goes below with a splitting headache, Roger—quite naturally—is scared stiff, and Susan, the stolid domesticated Susan, is at one moment in a flood of tears. So one is not surprised that they make it, that they win through—and even rescue a shipwrecked kitten on the way. (pp. 49-50)

One might have thought that the subsequent books would be anticlimaxes, particularly as the next one, *Secret Water,* is about nothing more exciting than surveying. (p. 51)

Although the make-believe adventures and one real one, when the three youngest are nearly cut off by the tide, make up the bulk of the book, the greatest interest is in a minor but to the young, most heart-searching question of loyalty to one's own gang in conflict with one's natural inclinations and desires. (p. 52)

[*The Big Six*], of all the twelve books, is the nearest to the conventional 'rattling good yarn'; it is a most competent thriller and the Big Six put in some excellent (and scientific) detective work. (pp. 52-3)

[*Great Northern?*] is as good as any of its predecessors, and some consider it better than any of them. If Arthur Ransome had to rest on his laurels, the publication of this book was surely the best of occasions. (p. 53)

The final chase is as excitingly told as any incident in any of the books. (p. 54)

All twelve of the books are very fully illustrated, with an average of twenty-six full-page plates (*Secret Water* has as many as forty-one), end-paper maps and numerous tailpieces to the chapters. Today, the illustrations must be regarded by many people as an integral part of the saga, yet the first edition of *Swallows and Amazons* contained no pictures at all. The second edition carried end-paper maps by Stephen Spurrier, and illustrations by Clifford Webb. Stephen Spurrier's maps have a nice swashbuckling quality, and Clifford Webb is a fine decorative artist. Why, then, are all the books now 'illustrated' by Arthur Ransome, who states that he cannot draw for toffee? What happened?

The answer is this: when Arthur Ransome wrote *Peter Duck* it struck him very forcibly that as the story was supposed to be written by the Swallows and Amazons themselves, it would add to the book's verisimilitude if they were also supposed to illustrate it. None of them (save, possibly, Titty?) could draw very well, so who better to make their pictures for them than the real author. A note at the beginning of *Peter Duck* states that all the children (even Roger) had a hand in the drawings, and is signed: 'Captain Nancy Blackett'.

Arthur Ransome decided that henceforth he would illustrate all his own books, and furthermore, that he would re-illustrate *Swallows and Amazons* and *Swallowdale*. . . . (p. 55)

Why did Arthur Ransome continue to illustrate all his books with the ham-fisted Nancy's assistance? Was it a gimmick suggested by the publishers, or is Arthur Ransome secretly rather proud of his pictures? Are they his Achilles' heel? Neither answer is the right one. Arthur Ransome points out very strongly that the pictures are not, in the true sense, illustrations; they are really part of the text. He sets out deliberately to give authenticity to the stories by drawing as he thought the children would draw. The pictures are intentionally amateurish and so aim to help the reader to trust in the reality of the story. They were, therefore, an extremely interesting innovation in the technique of illustrating—one must still use the word—children's books.

Whether or not Arthur Ransome's pictures do really make many children believe that the stories are true, they have one incontrovertible asset, they encourage the reader to identify himself or herself with a particular character. Not only are the figures in the drawings often shown at a distance, but they are frequently portrayed with, so to speak, their backs to the easel.

All this would make it sound as though none of Arthur Ransome's pictures had the merit of recognisable, critical portraiture. While I am prepared to accept Arthur Ransome's insistence on the value of bad drawing, I cannot agree that his drawings *are* so very bad. . . . Arthur Ransome has drawn a number of entertaining and occasionally most moving pictures; his portraits of Uncle Jim/Captain Flint are among the most endearing, particularly as the profile is that of his portrayer; his pictures of boats, quays and islands have the feel of place; and his explanatory diagrams, whether they be of ship's rigging or of pigeons-ringing-bells-in-lofts, are as clear as blueprints. His secret is hard to guess, but part of it may lie in an almost oriental emphasis on relevant shape and detail combined with a disregard of irrelevant setting. (pp. 56-7)

Ever since 1932, reviews [of the books] have been uniformly, almost boringly, favourable. (p. 60)

Have there been no adverse criticisms? The only ones I have been able to discover have taxed Arthur Ransome with making his characters too nice—too kind and game and loyal, never cheating or squabbling. Of course no children behave so well for so long in real life, but what purpose is served by picking holes in heroes and heroines unless you do not find them credible without faults? And the chief characteristic of the Amazons, the Swallows, the 2 D's, the Death and Glories and the

*The hidden boat. From* Swallowdale, *written and illustrated by Arthur Ransome. Jonathan Cape, 1955. Reprinted by permission of David R. Godine Publisher, Inc. In Canada by Jonathan Cape Ltd, on behalf of the Literary Estate of Arthur Ransome.*

Eels, is that they are supremely credible and memorable. The truth is not that they have no faults but that Arthur Ransome legitimately prefers to show them to us at their nicest, which is when they are happiest and at their most interesting.

The most valuable review of Arthur Ransome to have appeared so far is perhaps the long article that was published in the *Times Literary Supplement* of June 16, 1950, under the heading 'A Contemporary Classic' [not available for republication]. The writer concentrates on the characters rather than the plots. To my mind it is therefore all the more surprising that its author should wind up by acclaiming *Peter Duck* as 'perhaps the high-water mark'. To make amends for my admittedly rather summary and certainly prejudiced dismissal of the book, I should, I think, quote this: 'Here is something for every taste mixed together in an irresistible hotch-potch of humour and fantasy, realism and romance.' Another—and to the best of my knowledge the only other—detailed study of Arthur Ransome to date is by the Canadian Children's Librarian, Lillian H. Smith, in *The Unreluctant Years* (American Library Association, 1953) [see excerpt below for *Great Northern?* (1948)]. She makes an interesting analysis of *Great Northern?* and draws attention to the remarkable quality of what she finds to be Arthur Ransome's three quite distinct styles. . . . I would agree with her evaluation of Arthur Ransome's style, but cannot see that its character changes so noticeably according to his subject matter. Colloquial simplicity and a marked economy of words are its hallmarks. . . . He never wastes words in achieving his effect, whether it be humorous, dramatic or didactic, and it is due to this that he can slip from description to narrative to dialogue so easily and naturally. (pp. 60-2)

What sort of children are Ransome enthusiasts? Are they, as one would expect, predominantly middle-class? The immense sales would make one query this, even if Arthur Ransome himself did not violently contradict the notion, and produce letters from working-class schools in northern mining districts showing that whole classes of boys who could never afford the Walkers' type of holiday were fascinated by the books. I would say however that middle-class admirers are in the majority, and other readers on the decrease. This is the result, I should add, of only sketchy investigation among London librarians and booksellers and the librarian and some of the girls of a South London Comprehensive school. Middle-class children, however, seem to read him almost as avidly as ever, judging from enquiries of children at a London co-educational preparatory school.

As is the case with most authors, two or three decades after reaching the peak of their popularity, Arthur Ransome may well be read less and less for a while. But his popularity will return and return for good, because his basic stories are universal and even on the surface they do not date. One reason is that his dialogue though always colloquial is never spattered with contemporary slang.

In general the people who do not like Ransome's books are found to be those who do not share his hobbies and interests and who do not enjoy doing things for themselves. It is for this reason that many parents are mystified by the fascination the books exert over their children. The other most common cause for complaint is that the stories are too technical. (pp. 65-6)

[There] is nothing more delightful than [Arthur Ransome's] obsession with the workings of things and his passion for passing on odd lore. . . .

But these are incidental delights. What will remain will be the children, as secure of a place in literature as Jim Hawkins or the Bastables, Kay Harker or the Ruggles. (p. 67)

To my belief [Arthur Ransome's remark that he writes not for children but for himself] is not the amiable white lie of a nice man refusing to discuss the agony of writing what children read with careless ease. It is the honest statement of a very great craftsman who only cares about what he makes—and who makes only what he truly cares about. (p. 68)

*Hugh Shelley, in his* Arthur Ransome, *1960. Reprint by Henry Z. Walck, Incorporated, 1964, 71 p.*

**MARGERY FISHER**

Let children enjoy the ninety-nine readable but undistinguished holiday adventures which merge into one jumble of caravanning, toffee-making and stamp-collecting. The story with characters in it, the hundredth story, is the one I am concerned with; the book that children will read till its pages fall out. And that hundredth book may well be by the pioneer in the field of holiday stories, Arthur Ransome.

Now with Ransome the rule is 'Grown-ups not admitted unless accompanied by a child.' The Blackett and Walker parents know their place; they stay tactfully at home and act as ship's chandlers. Uncle Jim can approach a little nearer when he is needed as a pirate or a mining expert or a ship's captain, but even he is some distance away from the centre of action—like

Ransome himself, who watches, with evident delight, the important exploits of his creations, and lets them express themselves (even in the illustrations).

And they *are* important. Ransome's children always have something on hand—bird-watching, gold-mining, astronomy, tracking, innumerable outdoor projects, involving (usually) no serious expense of emotion but a great deal of energy and technical skill. As he never writes about anything unless he knows it from A to Z, his books have an accuracy and precision much appreciated by his readers. If they followed his clear indications they could probably become as accomplished as the Swallows and Amazons. And they will want to imitate Ransome's children all the more because he never cheats. He never makes things too easy. When in *Pigeon Post*, Dick has built his kiln to exact gold (as he hopes) from the pile of stone they have collected, he feels triumphant, but then comes the reaction:

> The miners looked at each other and at the stone furnace that was far too hot to touch. They were suddenly tired. It was as if the string of a necklace had snapped and the beads were rolling all ways on the floor. The work that had kept them all awake was at an end. With no bellows to work or furnace to feed they were no longer a team, and each one separately was wondering how it had been possible to keep awake so long. (pp. 274-75)

It is the writer who understands children who thus alters the pace of their schemes and their achievements. (p. 275)

Ransome does not give us a *round* study of family life, as Mayne does, for he is committed to the children's point of view; but they have among themselves very clear and changeable relationships, though their relations with grown-ups are static. If you want to read a shrewd account of child behaviour, look at **Winter Holiday,** where the Blacketts and Walkers cautiously approach Dorothea and Dick, newcomers to the district. See how the two strangers stand aloof, envying the solidarity of the little group, and see how each individual learns to get used to a change of friends. It is a wonderful piece of social management. And what child with imagination does not warm to Titty Walker, with her shrinking from noise and heartiness, her burning courage in a crisis? In **Pigeon Post** Titty finds she is a natural dowser. Terrified at first, she faces her responsibility (for their holiday plans depend on finding water in the hills). She goes away alone, screwing herself up to test her gift; and when she has found water, her first impulse is to boast about it. Every stage of her feelings is beautifully described, but within the action of the story, and at the same time we see how this incident affects the other children. To Nancy Blackett the new-found spring is a challenge: 'Barbecued billygoats!' she exclaims, 'If it's there, we'll get it out all right if we have to dig through to Australia', and you can hear the ring in her voice. But to Dorothea, a budding author, there is more to it than this:

> 'I'm going to put it in a story . . . Different, of course. I'm making you a boy, and you do that business with the stick all by yourself and you've got a spade with you and you start digging. It's at night, and the moon rises through the clouds, and all of a sudden you've dug deep enough and the water comes spouting up into the moonlight. . .'

'Go on,' said Titty. 'What happened next?'

'I'm not quite sure yet,' said Dorothea.

(pp. 281-82)

There are children who find Ransome's books tedious because they are not interested in sailing, camping or skating, but there are few who will not change their minds if they have the patience to look beyond the technical details to the characters. They will find, in the end, that Ransome's stories last them longer than the similar tales of Kitty Barne or Lois Lamplugh or Tyler Whittle. (p. 282)

> Margery Fisher, *"Little Birds in Their Nests Agree,"*
> *in her* Intent Upon Reading: A Critical Appraisal of
> Modern Fiction for Children, *1961. Reprint by Frank-
> lin Watts, Inc., 1962, pp. 270-96.*

## GEORGE BOTT

[Why] am I so completely and irrevocably a Ransomeite? . . . The explanation of my fanatical admiration is very simple: it is Ransome the story-teller, Ransome the writer, whose spell bewitches me and can still fix me firmly to a chair long enough to re-read any one of the *Swallows and Amazons* series at a sitting. (p. 16)

[A] dozen books crystallise the holiday dreams of a generation of children. . . . The mere bulk is impressive and may well deter some potential readers; but add to it the standard of the story telling and the achievement is little short of a miracle.

The tales have what Eleanor Graham has called "the thrill of probability" [see excerpt below for *We Didn't Mean to Go to Sea* (1937) from *The Junior Bookshelf* (January, 1938)]: the adventures are real and plausible, verging at times on the improbable but never tumbling into the impossible. (pp. 18-19)

One of the hallmarks of Ransome's plots is that he can maintain interest without resorting to the sensational or the spectacular. Things happen but excitement and suspense spring from situations which are handled with disciplined restraint and make no excessive demands on the characters involved. Once we start reading we are compelled to go on reading. E. M. Forster suggested that a story makes us ask, "And then . . .?"; a plot demands intelligence and memory. Ransome keeps us guessing and not only asking "And then . . .?" but also continually using our intelligence, recalling past incidents as the series unfolds, wondering anxiously what the next page will bring, struggling happily with the technical details of charcoal burning or photography. . . . (p. 19)

The idea of a group of children being swept out to sea may sound improbable but it certainly is not impossible. This episode epitomises so much that the children do; they are faced with challenges of varying difficulties but not challenges beyond their capacities, however far they may be stretched. The Walkers and the Blacketts are not called on to capture a criminal who has defied the whole of Scotland Yard and the police forces of ten counties. Even Dick's foolhardy rescue of a crag-fast sheep in *Winter Holiday,* a rock climb with an overhang facing a boy who had never climbed before, is made credible by having Dick securely roped.

The theme of responsibility is the pivot of many of the stories. The demands of sailing a boat across the North Sea, for example, in fog, rain and squalls call forth all the children's self reliance. Here, perhaps, they reach the acme of their adventures, adventures which are confronted with courage and resourcefulness. But this terrifying experience produces no false

heroics: the children realise their predicament, they are sick and scared and even Susan is in tears.

Arthur Ransome is right in realising that very often children can handle an emergency but I cannot help feeling that without the play adventures of *Swallows and Amazons* the realities of *We Didn't Mean to Go to Sea* might have been overwhelming. (pp. 19-20)

I have never been able to understand the objections to Ransome's children being middle class. If this was the type of boy and girl he observed closely and affectionately and recorded so faithfully, what grounds are there for protest? [Ruth Hill Viguers] has suggested that Arthur Ransome's children "come as close to being living companions as book children ever can" [see excerpt above, 1953]. She is right and the problem of class is irrelevant.

Perhaps at times they are idealised a little; perhaps they are uncomplicated and respectable, almost too friendly, too involved in their healthy pursuits ("better drowned than duffers"), too truthful, too inspired by a keen sense of fair play. But each in his or her own way is a lively individual, their growing personalities revealed in a battery of details in dialogue and plot, incident and predicament. (p. 20)

Ransome does not write down to his audience; children are far too important for condescension. His prose is direct, free from gimmicks, apparently effortless and artless—the art that conceals art. Hugh Walpole said of *Peter Duck:* "It is so well written that you don't realise it is written at all." This is the true craftsman at work, the story-teller holding his audience spell-bound, beguiling young and old readers into believing his fiction. There is no wasting of words; narrative dovetails smoothly and confidently into dialogue. The dialogue itself is natural and convincing, avoiding slang—except, of course, permitted nautical slang. His crisp prose eschews purple passages of description. . . .

What, then, is the key to Arthur Ransome's success? It can be summarised in one word: sincerity. He believes in the story he is telling; he believes in the children he writes about, he sympathises with them, he understands their point of view; he believes in the importance to the children of the incidents and adventures in the stories; he thinks as a child, he sees as a child, he feels as a child—a rare quality in an adult. (p. 21)

> George Bott, *"A Little Lower than the Angels: A
> Tribute to Arthur Ransome,"* in The Junior Book-
> shelf, *Vol. 28, No. 1, January, 1964, pp. 15-21.*

## RICHARD BAMBERGER

In his excellent treatise, *Children, Books and Men,* Paul Hazard writes: "No other country reflects its eternal image in its children's books as England does. A picture of England could be reconstructed from English children's stories." This goes for Arthur Ransome more than for any other writer of children's tales. In his books, we find the atmosphere of his country, the inter-relation of land and sea which we can smell and touch, and his characters, the young ones and the old ones, are drawn with a sound sense of reality, a subtle humour, a longing for adventure which, nevertheless, does not upset his heroes' deep-rooted conception of the necessity of order—all characteristics which the whole world admires in Englishmen.

To write about children as real human beings—which author, considering the entire international field of juvenile literature, has achieved this to the same extent as Arthur Ransome? Longing for great adventures, the children in his books have their feet on the firm ground of reality. The "conquest of the world" of which they dream takes place in the small happenings of every-day life, in thrilling events in the course of which the children grow up and extend their horizon—be it in the independence of camping, the excitement of climbing expeditions, in sailing, bird-watching, tracking, in any of the innumerable little or big adventures of outdoor life as thousands of children experience them in their holidays. Like Charles Dickens, Arthur Ransome has discovered a romantic world inside our real world.

A distinctive trait in Arthur Ransome's stories, very rare in children's books, is that his boys and girls develop as the tale progresses. Their knowledge of the world and of themselves increases owing to their natural curiosity, their eagerness to learn more and more about the mysterious and miraculous life that goes on around them. Ransome's young people thus become examples of youth as it really is, not only in England, but anywhere, examples of youth as the entire world needs it, in our time more than ever before. The children in Ransome's books have not yet fallen victim to the mass influences of our modern commercialised era; the forces that drive them on still come from their own souls and from sound traditions which youth should carry over from days past into days to come.

Arthur Ransome's books have been very well received in translations. . . . His style, however, is so personal that his translators have no easy task. In addition, his stories are long and therefore do not fit into the lists of publishers who follow the fashions of short children's books. These are the reasons why his books are less frequently translated than some stories by much less important writers. His books stand for themselves, as an entity, and deserve to be translated wherever it is feasible, not only because they would tell children of other lands much about English children and thus create a bridge between nations, but also because Arthur Ransome could exert a beneficial influence on writers in other countries. He takes his work and his readers very seriously, as the accuracy and precision of his style, his love of detail and his attitude towards his heroes all show. If other writers adopted his conception of writing for children, their work would doubtlessly improve. . . . (pp. 31-2)

> *Richard Bamberger, "Arthur Ransome and a Treasure Chest for the Whole World,"* in The Junior Bookshelf, *Vol. 28, No. 1, January, 1964, pp. 31-2.*

## ROGER LANCELYN GREEN

With most recent books we are too near to be able to judge properly [whether they will become 'classics']. . . . (p. 258)

There are a few exceptions to be made. The earlier part of the period since 1920 has already given us A. A. Milne and Hugh Lofting: as surely it will leave Authur Ransome to be one of the greatest of their company; probably John Masefield, C. S. Lewis, and J.R.R. Tolkien are assured of a place in the same hall of fame: some confidently aver that Walter de la Mare has already taken his place there.

All but one of these were writers of fantasy in one form or another. . . . But by far the greatest writer for children among living authors, and one whose works are undoubtedly among the great of all time in the hierarchy of children's books, stands head and shoulders above all those who write or have written of children in real life during at least the last half-century. . . . (pp. 258-59)

When Arthur Ransome sent the Walkers and the Blacketts sailing on Lake Windermere in *Swallows and Amazons* . . . ,

he achieved a success as great in its own way as that of Stevenson or E. Nesbit. His stories are about real children, individual, likeable, understandable children, doing the things we would all like to do—and not impossible or even unlikely things either. Here is the apotheosis of outdoor adventure, the realization towards which Mark Twain and Jefferies and Thompson Seton were all groping in their own ways—experiences in which children can share even more easily than in the doings of Bevis and Mark, or of Sam and Yan. But each of the dozen delectable volumes is an exciting story in itself, the kind of story that cannot be put down once it is started, and yet all so unexpectedly real and simple in appearance. Where a lesser author would need a hidden treasure, a foreign spy or a smuggler, Ransome gives us a rare bird which must be saved from a merciless egg-collector and photographed on its nest by Dick to show that he himself is the real discover. . . . (p. 262)

Perhaps the children are better tempered, more loyal and more reliable than those whom we usually meet, but they never for a moment cease to be real. Of course they are presented to us as always occupied, always eagerly busy doing those things which they want most to do—and hardly any children so fortunate would find the time or inclination for any form of mischief. And the things that they (or Ransome) most enjoy have such a perennial fascination for young and old alike that, as he presents them, they are utterly absorbing and memorable and as real as a remembered experience of childhood.

The two 'holiday romances', **Peter Duck** and **Missee Lee** . . . , improbable adventures even if not impossible, are only a shade less successful and less popular than the other ten volumes of the real saga. Some older readers, however, prefer these two to any of the rest. . . . **We Didn't Mean to Go to Sea** is held to be Ransome's own favourite; but it shows the greatness of his total achievement that any readers would argue over their own favourites, and no one has ever dared to name a categorical and indubitable best. . . . Of course we have our favourites: **Winter Holiday, Pigeon Post, The Picts and the Martyrs, Great Northern?** . . . but how can we omit **The Big Six** or **Swallows and Amazons** itself? . . . And so it is if we do try to make a list. (pp. 262-63)

> *Roger Lancelyn Green, "Arthur Ransome and Holiday Adventure,"* in his Tellers of Tales, *revised edition, Franklin Watts, Inc., 1965, pp. 258-68.**

## M. S. CROUCH

Whatever changes overtake children's literature, and however much reputations rise and fall, it is safe to predict that a history of children's books published in the 21st Century will include a chapter on the Ransome Revolution of the Nineteen-Thirties.

The nature of that revolution was expressed most briefly and effectively in Eric Linklater's splendid dictum: "He makes a tale of adventure a handbook to adventure". In all his writing he showed a passionate awareness of beauty and the interest of everyday things—or rather holiday things. What the Swallows and Amazons were like at school is beyond imagining—although the Ds no doubt did all right. Ransome replaced the undisciplined imagination and the crudely exotic settings of the Boys' Reward of the Twenties with finely written words, the action of which grew naturally out of the reactions of people to one another and to their environment. No man makes a revolution single-handed, but it is fair to say that every writer who draws children behaving naturally in a natural setting is paying unconscious tribute to Arthur Ransome. (pp. 219-20)

In the long muster-roll of children's books most of the great landmarks, the books which endure untouched by time or place, are fantasies, books which push back the frontiers of the real world. Ransome alone—if one excepts the isolated phenomenon of *Bevis*—brought a creative imagination to interpret the real world, shocking, delighting and enlightening children with a clear delineation of themselves.

Much of the social environment of these books has gone beyond recall, but the Ransome books date no more than do Nesbit's, and for the same reason. Both writers deal with unchanging values, and both write, unpriggishly and without self-conscious aim, about integrity, loyalty and pride in a job well done. So long as these values endure, so long will Ransome speak meaningfully to children and to their children's children. (p. 220)

> *M. S. Crouch, "Dr. Arthur Ransome, C.B.E.," in* The Junior Bookshelf, *Vol. 31, No. 4, August, 1967, pp. 219-20.*

## PAMELA WHITLOCK

[*At the age of sixteen, Whitlock wrote* The Far-Distant Oxus *with fifteen-year-old Katharine Hull. Inspired and influenced by Ransome, the book describes the holiday adventures of six children as they ride and camp on Exmoor. The authors wrote alternate chapters, each editing the other's work; Whitlock also added Ransomesque illustrations. Ransome encouraged this partnership, and took* Oxus *to his publisher, Jonathan Cape, with the words "I have here the best children's book of 1937." He also contributed a foreword to the first edition. The Far-Distant Oxus had two sequels,* Escape to Persia *and* Oxus in Summer.]

It was because he knew everything about boats that Arthur Ransome had to learn to do his own illustrations. No other artist was able to draw every rope and block in the right position in the many craft in his pages. He hated merely pretty pictures,

which funked details and did nothing to help the story. 'Pictures must be full of larkiness'. When none of the professionals proved competent with jibooms and bobstays he began to do his own pictures. They were not always elegant, but they did belong to the story, and were indeed often essential to explain how something was made or some passage sailed. . . .

The books are full of observations of river life and water birds. Titty watching the dipper in *Swallows and Amazons* is a classic passage. Bird-book detail and accuracy is suddenly brought to life and made exciting. Titty is seeing something real, and for the first time. Every reader shares her joy. (p. 222)

One reason why the 'Ransome books' stand out so far from those round them, is that they were written, not by 'a mere manufacturer of books,' but by a man of letters with all his lifetime's experience of storytellers and words.

The twelve books that started with *Swallows and Amazons* were never written particularly for children. They were written to please himself, mariner, angler, yarn-spinner, poet. That children liked them he felt was a lucky thing. Boys and girls loved the stories for the sailing, camping, exploring, birdwatching, and adventures, for the reality of the characters and the romance of the settings. Perhaps most of all they loved them because in the author they recognised someone who was on their side. He was one of them in the war with the unpredictable natives.

He was always on the side of the young. He is for the honesty of the young against the cheating of the old. He is for the thoughtfulness and patience of Coots or Picts against the brash Hullabaloos of the world. He is for the fun of the Jolly Roger, against Great Aunts and Sunday clothes.

It is too easy, and I believe quite wrong to think of him only as the Captain Flint of the stories. There was so much of himself in each of the children he invented. He was as much sailor

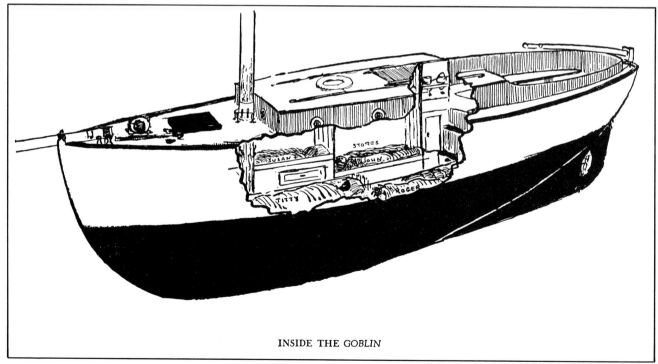

INSIDE THE GOBLIN

*Inside The* Goblin. *From* We Didn't Mean to Go to Sea, *written and illustrated by Arthur Ransome. J. Cape, 1937. Copyright, 1938, by Arthur Ransome. All rights reserved. Reprinted by permission of Jonathan Cape Ltd, on behalf of the Literary Estate of Arthur Ransome.*

John as practical Susan; he was the jokey schoolboy Roger, and—perhaps most of all—romantic, thoughtful Titty. Then again he was Dick with his inventive, inquiring, exact mind. He was Dorothea, forever taking notes for another story. He was Tom the born leader. He was the dashing, loyal Death and Glories.

The books have been criticised for being 'middle-class'; they have been praised for being moral; they have been imitated by those who only found in them children intent on practical occupations which were explained in detail. They have been read again, just because they are splendid unfolding yarns. What has been overlooked very often is the happiness and poetry in every one. In them the day to day business of boys and girls on holiday, is magnified and made marvellous. In the twelve stories written out of his own love and knowledge of happy things, Arthur Ransome captured what he once called 'that lovely rose-behind-your-ear feeling of youth, when everything in the world is possible'.

It has sometimes been, too quietly, recorded that the 'Ransome books' changed the course of children's literature; that they started a whole new era of books about the open air, and better written books for boys and girls. What has perhaps never been underlined enough, and what cannot be exaggerated, is the tremendous impact that they made on the first generation to enjoy them. They gave thousands of children a new way of looking and seeing; possibly the biggest eye-openers of their whole lives. They created an infinitely desirable country, so close to reality that it seemed to every reader only just over the hill. Probably many of those who read the books in the 1930's are looking for their Wild Cat Island still.

Arthur Ransome always despised his early work. He would have been surprised to find this sentence quoted from an essay he wrote in 1913. 'We ask from an artist opportunities of conscious living, which, taken as they come, multiply the possibilities of their recurrence, turn us into artists, and help us to contract the habit of being alive'.

When he found his way to what he wanted to write, 'with all sails set and a fair wind', he went on to become a considerable artist. Generations of children who read his books, have through this enchanting man become more alive. (pp. 223-24)

*Pamela Whitlock, "From Swallow to Sea Bear," in* The Junior Bookshelf, *Vol. 31, No. 4, August, 1967, pp. 221-24.*

**WALLACE HILDICK**

Note how often [Arthur Ransome] intermingles with relatively high adventure sprightly passages of the low, using the second to regulate the pace of the first. In the opening paragraphs of *Secret Water,* for example, the Swallows' high hopes of exploring a group of islands with their father are dashed when the Commander is ordered back to London by the Admiralty. By the end of that first chapter, however, they are somewhat cheered to learn that their parents have a secret plan:

> "Something to do with us," said Titty. "Didn't you hear what he was saying?"
>
> "What did he say?"
>
> "He said, 'Better keep mum about it till the morning.'"

End—very effectively—of chapter. The next opens at breakfast:

"All hands!" said Daddy, as they sat down to breakfast.

"Wait till they've had their porridge," said Mother.

Daddy laughed.

"Oh do tell us now," said Titty.

"You heard what your Mother said."

"Oh Mother!"

"You get your porridge down," said Mother. "But don't go and eat it too quickly."

"Or too slowly," said Roger, swallowing fast. "Slop it in, Bridget. Bridget doesn't know how to eat porridge. When you've got a mouthful in, don't just wave the spoon about. Get it filled while you're swallowing."

"Don't you hurry, Bridgie," said Daddy. "News'll keep."

"Anybody want any more porridge?" said Mother presently.

"Nobody does," said Titty.

"What about Roger?"

For a minute or two everybody had been watching Bridget, whose eyes wandered from face to face as she worked steadily on, spoonful by spoonful. Roger looked at the porridge still left in her plate. He could have a little more and yet be done as soon as she was.

"Yes, please," said Roger, and passed his plate.

Bridget eyed him balefully and put on speed. It was a very close thing. Roger was still swallowing his last mouthful while Susan was wiping a stray bit off Bridget's chin.

Daddy looked at Mummy. She nodded.

There was a breathless pause.

"Now look here," said Daddy. . .

And so the momentous secret is finally divulged.

The risk that Ransome has taken here is really quite considerable—that of making the delay as bothersome to the readers as it is to the characters—for it is a firm rule in any branch of fiction that the boring must never bore, always entertain. Here the author resolves the problem by interrupting, or braking, the larger drama with one of the miniature dramas of childhood, involving the technique of eating porridge, Roger's agonizing decision, and the brief race—the real prize for which is the justification of Roger's decision, the evident accuracy of his calculations. It is done so skillfully that one is able to bear the main delay without being moved to skip—an ever-present temptation where child readers are concerned, the succumbing to which can be ruinous to true appreciation.

Ransome's books are full of such passages, not all of them concerned with techniques as relatively unimportant as that of porridge-eating. Navigation, map-making, surveying, fishing, fire-making, cooking: readers can learn a lot about these and similar subjects from this author's pages of fiction, and do so almost unconsciously, (a) because they are presented as situations arising naturally out of the basic story, and (b) because the author handles them with great technical skill, taking care to unfold them in an atmosphere of possibility, good or bad. This is didacticism at its best. (pp. 48-50)

> *Wallace Hildick, "Making Them Wait: The Importance of Timing," in his* Children and Fiction: A Critical Study of the Artistic and Psychological Factors Involved in Writing Fiction for and about Children, *1970. Reprint by The World Publishing Company, 1971, pp. 39-61.\**

## MARCUS CROUCH

[Arthur Ransome] gave all his books the care and skill of an accomplished professional writer, . . . but he applied to them no aesthetic or sociological principles. He chose to write sincerely and modestly about things that mattered to him personally, and to associate them with children whom he knew and liked. The result was startlingly original. Here are stories about children passionately concerned with realities. We see them only at play, for they are always on holiday, but it is a serious play, applying hard-won skills to difficult and responsible tasks.

Ransome chose to look upon these books always as 'yarns' and never dignified them with a higher title. They have, nevertheless, some of the qualities of the novel. They offer detailed studies of society, a small-scale society but one in which the relationships between individual members and their responsibilities to the whole are examined closely. One might feel a theoretical regret that Ransome did not choose to show children and adults in partnership, and that, with the exception of Captain Flint and a few others, the adults are hostile and barbarous, like the Hullabaloos, or tyrannous like Great Aunt Maria. With Ransome, however, rather more than with most writers, one accepts gladly the writer's chosen limitations, recognizing that he knew precisely what he was about. He shows with beautiful clarity and conviction how children grow by contact with one another and with their environment, submitting to their own voluntary disciplines while retaining their personal integrity. Like a good novelist, too, he uses the setting of his stories as if it were an actor in them. He writes only about places for which he has a strong feeling, like the Lakes—their topography drastically reshaped but their spirit faithfully portrayed—and the Broads and the estuaries of Suffolk. To each of these settings his characters react according to their natures and according to the nature of the landscape.

For the first time in children's literature since *Bevis*—and this was an isolated phenomenon—Ransome showed not only *what* happened but *how* it happened. He and his characters are deeply concerned with the mechanics of living. (pp. 18-19)

> *Marcus Crouch, "Foundations," in his* The Nesbit Tradition: The Children's Novel in England 1945-1970, *Ernest Benn Limited, 1972, pp. 15-25.\**

## JOHN ROWE TOWNSEND

Ransome did not write the kind of story we now look on as 'realistic'; but, unlike the hack writers and some of the literary fantasists of the previous decade, he did write seriously and without condescension about the real lives of real children. His books gave a new direction and impetus to English children's writing. (pp. 183-84)

With the **"Lake District"** books especially, I suspect that the main appeal to children must be that of identification: of imagining oneself to be among this fortunate group who can actually sail dinghies on Windermere and spend nights camping on an

island in the middle of the lake. The author's attention to detail is a great help here. He explains so authoritatively how everything was done . . . that the reader is convinced it actually happened, and almost that he or she was there at the time.

The values of the **"Swallows and Amazons"** series are such as to meet with the approval of conscientious middle-class parents. There is a clear—and to most such people a welcome—preference for country over town, and for manpower or windpower over mechanization. It is entirely appropriate that these decent and sensible books should have been written by a stalwart of the old *Manchester Guardian*. Yet in some ways their scope is limited. Faced with a million words about the Walker children and their friends, we may wonder if they could really be so consistently right-minded; we may wish we could see them in a living relationship with their parents, instead of having the parents mainly as understanding figures in the background; we may even wish they were not always on holiday.

Ransome seems in fact to have deliberately avoided any serious approach to problems of personal relationship. 'Captain Flint' as a benevolent uncle is a very simple figure; the Blacketts' dreadful Great Aunt belongs strictly to fiction. The older children, though well into their teens before the series ends, maintain a sexless comradeship which does not quite accord with the facts of adolescence. And on the whole there are rather few insights; rather few of those moments when the reader is pulled up in sudden awareness that life is richer or stranger than he had realized. (pp. 185-86)

> *John Rowe Townsend, "Past into Present," in his* Written for Children: An Outline of English-Language Children's Literature, *revised edition, 1974. Reprint by The Horn Book Incorporated, 1981, pp. 178-93.\**

## BETTY LEVIN

Hailed by critics and children alike over nearly half a century, [Arthur Ransome's] books have inculcated in more than one generation the attitudes of a writer whose repeated pattern of storytelling reveals a deep seated need to get rid of parents.

Admirers may protest: they may argue that since all children fantasize about matricide and/or patricide, Ransome simply offers a healthy outlet for such fantasies. Young readers can identify with the Walkers and Blacketts, acting out those children's own delightful adventures, unhampered by guilt and reassured in the end by the timely emergence of one or more parents. But this parental resurrection may be more insidious than the complete annihilation of parents in more recent books (e g *Pippi Longstocking*, Donovan's *Wild in the World*, etc.). In not a few of Ransome's books there is a blurring of distinctions between authority figures and the children themselves. Moreover, there is a confusion of feeling which results, not only in the normal ambivalence of love-hate relationships, but in the substitution of other adults as surrogate parents who may also represent love objects, regardless of their sex. (pp. 99-100)

Analysis of a book like *Pigeon Post* would promptly prove the validity of my concern. This is the story in which Titty Walker discovers that she is a natural dowser. Her first reaction is one of horror. Remember, she is a small girl, already in awe of the aggressive tomboy Nancy Blackett. More than that, her gender is emblazoned by her name. The dowsing rod raises Titty to a new phallic awareness of her own power, which is underscored by the context Ransome provides. Here is Dorothea reacting to Titty's remarkable transformation:

I'm going to put it in a story. . . . Different of course. I'm making you a boy, and you do that business with the stick all by yourself and you've got a spade with you and you start digging. It's at night and the moon rises through the clouds, and all of a sudden you've dug deep enough and the water comes spouting up into the moonlight. . . .

Countless girls and boys have been subjected to this disturbing sexual symbolism, while parents and librarians, complacent and hearty, have approved such material for preadolescents.

Some titles alone should have raised suspicions among vigilant adults: *Swallows and Amazons,* for instance, with its castrating Amazonian heroines. But even those books whose innocent titles and apparent emphasis on self-reliance and fun might have passed a cursory examination reveal an underlying complex of anxiety-producing conditions. This is true of all the stories about boats (usually called vessels by Ransome's adult characters) in which this classic hermaphroditic symbol is the chief focus.

Viewed in its sexual context, *We Didn't Mean to Go to Sea* looms as perhaps the most pernicious of all, with the four Walker children shut in by the fog, lost and at sea, prisoners of the female cockpit and cabin and yet called on to manipulate the sail attached to the erect mast. For John, the oldest, each stage of the adventure threatens him: below the surface of suspense he is not merely a boy trying to cope and prove his manhood; he fumbles and falls, he slithers in the wet, fogbound female part of the boat, clutching and missing, while, like a reflection of his own impotence, the only object visible, the Beach End Buoy, riding upright on the surface of the water, slips past them as they slide helpless on the tide and out to sea.

It should not be necessary to enumerate the multiplicity of psychosexual symbols pervading this adventure story. They are as general as the sea, as specific as John's failure to keep the *Goblin* firm. For John, as for any sensitive reader, the chain that slips through his hands, the anchor that gets stuck in the muddy bottom, the failure of the kedge to hold its shape . . . and all the subsequent trauma that assails him build into a towering need to prove himself as whole, male, complete. In such a situation, the long arm of coincidence reaches out at the end of the nightmare with the appearance of father just when the Walker children, having crossed the North Sea, reach that absolute symbol of female sexuality, the harbor. At the moment when John may be said to have arrived, or come, it is his father who steps into the boat to resume his incontestable place as the dominant male of the family.

Little wonder that Ransome wrote book after book in which his child characters only flourished once their parents were set aside and forgotten. Considering the popularity of his books and their influence on so many other writers during the past forty years, surely it is time for someone to investigate the effect of Ransome's fixations on children in whom and for whom alienation and the generation gap have approached critical proportions. (pp. 100-01)

*Betty Levin, "Correspondence," in* Children's literature in education, *Vol. 17 (Summer), 1975, pp. 99-101.\**

### RUPERT HART-DAVIS

[Ransome] was remarkable in many ways, but chiefly because in himself he combined two very different characters. Half of him was a dedicated man of letters, with a passion for language and literature. He had read everything and was always deeply concerned with all branches of the literary life. His early writings were all literary, and though he later looked on most of them as false starts, they served one all-important purpose— they helped him to shape and perfect that lucid and seemingly effortless prose which he was to use in the work he always wanted to do above all, the writing of stories.

The other half of him was a perpetual schoolboy, with all the zest, fun, enjoyment and enthusiasm of youth—always ready to watch cricket or Rugby football, to sneak off to his beloved Garrick Club for a game of chess or billiards or simply to drink a little Burgundy with his cronies. The two greatest delights of his life—fishing and sailing—he enjoyed long after his doctors had told him to give them up, and to accompany him on any of these enterprises was like sharing them with a most articulate, knowledgeable and amusing boy.

It was the amalgamation of these two characters—the man of letters and the schoolboy—that produced his enduring memorial, his twelve books for boys and girls. He was as fond of children as the next man, but not excessively fond. The unique quality of these books is simply explained by the fact that their author was always partly a child. . . . Arthur Ransome's children's stories fully satisfied both his literary and his boyish ambitions.

As the books became more and more popular, he began to be deluged with letters from children—hundreds and thousands of them—varying from the enchanting and the droll, through the prosaic to the idiotic. (He answered them all courteously.) But of all the questions that his young readers asked him, one was predominant and recurring—the question 'Is it real?'

The stories seemed so lifelike that the children couldn't be sure if they were fact or fiction. And with this question they touched the heart of Ransome's secret. For everything in those books *is* real—every technical detail of sailing, camping, bird-watching, every aspect of the Lake District, the Norfolk Broads, the North Sea passage. They are all things that Ransome had seen and done and enjoyed, and continued to enjoy, so that he was able to turn them into fiction of such verisimilitude that his readers took it as fact.

No storyteller could hope for a richer reward, and Arthur Ransome seems assured of exactly the kind of immortality he would have chosen—not the writing of learned theses on his work, nor critical assessments of his talent, but the voices of generation after generation of children, delightedly asking their parents 'Is it real?' (pp. 10-11)

*Rupert Hart-Davis, in a prologue to* The Autobiography of Arthur Ransome *by Arthur Ransome, edited by Rupert Hart-Davis, Jonathan Cape, 1976, pp. 9-11.*

### MARY CADOGAN AND PATRICIA CRAIG

Arthur Ransome's stories come into the small category of those which appeal equally to children of both sexes; in them, moreover, sex roles are not insistently differentiated. Girls do the cooking, but are also "Amazons"; a boy is nauseated by the practical business of skinning a rabbit. (p. 334)

*Mary Cadogan and Patricia Craig, "Swallows and Ponies," in their* You're a Brick, Angela! A New Look at Girls' Fiction from 1839 to 1975, *Victor Gollancz Ltd., 1976, pp. 333-54.\**

**AIDAN CHAMBERS**

[Ransome's style] is essentially writing for children; no one, surely, can believe that, had Ransome been writing for adults— in the sense of an implied adult reader—he would have adopted the tone of voice so evident and so well created in *Swallows and Amazons*. . . . (p. 70)

Mention of Ransome calls to mind his famous much-quoted words about writing for children: "You write not FOR children but for yourself, and if, by good fortune, children enjoy what you enjoy, why you are a writer of children's books" [see excerpt above in Author's Commentary].

All very well and, obviously, what Ransome believed about himself. But it is difficult to believe on the evidence of Ransome's books that, had he really thought he was speaking to an adult audience primarily, he would have adopted the same tone of voice or would have treated his stories in the ways he does. Even a traditional critical examination of his books, eschewing all thought of the reader, implied or otherwise . . . , must surely reveal that Ransome's books are for children in quite specific ways, whatever Ransome himself said. Which is not to suggest that he, or any other writer who adopts this idea about himself as a writer, is dissembling. Rather, I want simply to reinforce [F. H.] Langman's observation: "An author may write for a single person or a large public, for himself or for nobody. But the work itself implies the kind of reader to whom it is addressed and this may not coincide with the author's private view of his audience." (pp. 70-1)

> Aidan Chambers, "The Reader in the Book: Notes from Work in Progress," in *Signal, No. 23, May, 1977, pp. 64-87.*

**W. A. WOODROW**

I staunchly maintain that the books [in the *Swallows and Amazons* series] have qualities that far outweigh their more obvious defects: which defects, incidentally, may be attributed to the changes in social structure and cultural opinions of their readers rather than to intrinsic faults in the books themselves.

Several charges have been levelled at the author and his work. It is claimed that the books perpetuate an elitist standpoint which is anathema to many contemporary critics (both literary and social). I cannot deny this. The whole fabric of the stories is woven from a filament in which school implies Public school or boarding school; where the concepts of property and ownership, along with its attendant ideas of domestic service and obligation, are just as strong as in Galsworthy. I agree that we are presented with a narrow canvas that barely touches upon the social problems of the age; the unemployment and poverty of a large percentage of the population; the sordidness of industrial towns and the bleakness of the struggle of rural people to adjust to changes that were beginning to pulsate beneath the surface of their landscape. In accepting these criticisms I ask the critics why such books ought to reflect these problems.

When Arthur Ransome began the series in 1929 he was already an established writer and correspondent. . . . He was much travelled and was himself the production of an "elite" social background. His approach to writing was that of a professional journalist. When he turned away from journalism to literature he wrote from experience and for an audience who were, themselves, under the same social umbrella. What is there to complain about in that? After all, this is exactly what a far greater contemporary, Ernest Hemingway, was doing.

If we are going to complain that the life of, say, John Walker is too circumscribed and restricted to be valid experience for readers to identify with—and I do not accept the premise— how many of us can claim to have lived the life of Nick Adams? One can argue that Hemingway became the spokesman of his generation: but Hemingway was a genius as well as being a great writer. As for being the spokesman for his generation, I'm not so sure. Perhaps it would be fairer to contrast and compare Arthur Ransome and his restricted canvas with Scott Fitzgerald, another contemporary whose range of experience, that is, meaningful and usable experience, was even more narrow than Ransome's. But comparisons of this sort are academic exercises and sterile, as so many academic exercises often are.

It is enough to say that within the self imposed limits of his work, Arthur Ransome gave us a plausible and satisfyingly complete picture of a section of life during the 1930/40 period. That the picture is circumscribed in the way we have described is not a valid criticism per se, as I have tried to show with the Hemingway analogy.

The other major criticism; that the books are lacking in emotional depth and that a true understanding of the emotional relationships of adolescents is missing, is one that I cannot deny. By contemporary standards certainly the characterisation is naive and shallow. I admit this as a serious intrinsic weakness, in retrospect at least. I cannot remember being troubled by it when I read the books [as a child].

Are we not once more in danger of using the wrong criteria? Do we criticise Malory in his treatment of Launcelot and Guinevere because he does not use the emotional intensity and vocabulary of Lawrence? No. We accept the convention of Malory within its context. Why then should we condemn Arthur Ransome for neglecting to use the emotional ideas and language of the 60's and 70's?

We have dwelt upon the defects. What about the virtues? These again must be qualified within the period context of their authorship. The books were written at a time when the majority of children's books were trivial and often downright bad, both in style and content. Arthur Ransome gave us plausibility spiced with imagination; realism tempered with fantasy; believable characters, with whom readers could identify their own internal world, whose dialogue was really the way children talk to each other—heightened by art to prevent it from becoming tedious.

The books are longer than most other children's books by many thousands of words. They were written for a more spacious and less hurried age than the present. But they are so artfully constructed, and move so smoothly towards their climax that the objective length does not obtrude itself.

Equally unobtrusive is the wealth of information that the books contain. . . . [One] can learn so much about doing all those things that have now become the province of Outdoor Pursuits and are hedged about with rules and regulations and clubs and certificates. In the Arthur Ransome books we see them in the pristine simplicity of simple enjoyment.

After all, that is what the books are about; simple enjoyment. And in defiance of all the extra-literary, social criticism that has been levelled at them they go on doing simply that. They have quality and charm, they are well written and they entertain. But the point that probably infuriates their detractors most is that they have, from their inception, always been bestsellers. (pp. 150-51)

*W. A. Woodrow, "Ransome in Retrospect," in* The Junior Bookshelf, *Vol. 43, No. 3, June, 1979, pp. 149-51.*

## GERALD HAIGH

As the Ransome centenary approaches, in 1984, the books will surely ride another surge of popularity. There were those in the sixties and seventies who saw them as quaint and "middle class" an attitude which now looks as grubby and dated as do some of the books which were written to placate it.

What Ransome's books do now is remind us of a world in which there was time and space for childhood adventure. In **Coot Club,** a motor cruiser crewed by "Hullabaloos" was a resented intruder. Now the Hullabaloos have taken over, and the veil beyond which the children live is even more impenetrable than it was for me.

This will surely, though, make young readers all the more eager to enter the world which Ransome created, and makes it a matter of faith for publishers, teachers and parents to ensure that it stays available for them.

*Gerald Haigh, "Inside the Coot Club," in* The Times Educational Supplement, *No. 3360, November 14, 1980, p. 20.*

## PETER HUNT

The obvious questions which we ask when reading a children's book—"is it good?"; "is it good for the child?"—are hardly as obvious as they seem. What do these judgements mean? The first question is really two—a distinction between "quality" and "value"; the second really a distinction between "suitability" and "accessibility." Certainly, when we come to look again at an author such as Arthur Ransome, who has been a major figure in children's books for fifty years, it is as well to get our terms clear. Is he a good writer for children but not for anyone else—with the horrific implications of that idea? Is he a "classic" writer, sustained by adult nostalgia and commercial inertia? Is he an historical figure who led the way to "a new conception of the children's adventure story" [see excerpt above, 1952] and showed "how to get along without parents just the same as if they were there"? . . . I would argue that critics and reviewers have been right about Ransome for the wrong reasons; he *does* deserve his status and his longevity, and he *is* a classic example of a "good" children's writer. Why this is so might give us some insight into the judgements which we tend to take for granted.

Briefly, then, what do we mean by "is a book 'good'"? We are making, first, a syntagmatic or stylistic judgement about an author's *qualities*—of style, or of coherence of character, or of arrangement of incident. It is, essentially, a comparative judgement, and has little to do with subject matter. A great or profound story can be ill-written, and vice-versa. Thus, with Ransome, it is fairly simple to note his "workmanlike prose"— which means that he is not much given to adjectives, or purple passages, or, significantly, clichés.

The second judgement is paradigmatic—a judgement of *value*. What lies beneath the style, the characters, the scenes? Do they express, or *transform*, a theme which is less than transitory? (*Transform* is used here in much the same sense as it is used in "transformational-generative" grammar. That is, deep levels of structure or meaning are transformed, or changed, by a series of "transform rules" into the "surface" expressions which we actually read.) Does that theme resonate up from less expressible depths of basic motivations? It is clear, I think,

that our common agreement on the "great" in literature—or, indeed, on what "literature" itself is—is based on a recognition of the levels of a book.

Of course, the two elements are very closely linked: at each level, the transform (character expresses theme, style expresses character) is detectable to the skilled reader, and by combining the judgements of *quality* and *value*, we end up with some consensus about *good.*

In theory, then, what a book is *really* about is far more important than the surface story; but, standing *in loco parentis* it is obviously not so simple. Most of the arguments about children's books are about suitability of surface content, rather than suitability of thematic levels. Equally, the implication that a "child" reader cannot take advantage of deeper levels tends to deny children's books the right of having accessible depths. What is more reasonable is to suggest that there may be themes more *appropriate* to the child audience—and these may or may not subsist above profounder levels, or be expressed in surface levels (stories) within the child's experience or competence. . . . *The Lord Of The Rings* contains a purely circular and secure tale of development in Sam Gamgee, a *bildungsroman* in Frodo, and an "adult" tale in the Elves. Hence, its critical reception, at least in terms of classification, has been mixed. More interestingly, these structures are reflected very accurately in the various styles which Tolkien (perhaps inevitably) employs to express them—hence the "uneven" surface of the book. (pp. 24-5)

[The] twelve **"Swallows and Amazons"** books of Ransome provide a classic example of all these tendencies. The themes of growth and development through the sequences are not very profound, but they are reflected with great integrity up through incident and character to the surface. Where Ransome goes deeper, the prose becomes more impressive; where the theme is imposed or artificial, or less than honest, the structure and style follow suit. Not only is Ransome consistent in this way, but if we exclude the "fantasies" of **Peter Duck, Missee Lee,** and, in a slightly different sense, **Great Northern?** we find a coherent thematic development which the readers can *use.* At the end of the sequence, the patterns of *closure* appropriate to the developing child have changed; Ransome's use of the children's novel has been completed, and his readers, like his characters, may move on. (*Closure* is a term used by gestalt psychologists to describe the tendency to psychologically complete an incomplete pattern, or to see complete patterns more readily than incomplete ones.)

*Swallows and Amazons,* therefore, is striking in its circularity. It begins and ends on the same spot—the field outside Holly Howe—with the same character—Roger—and with the visible security reinforcement of family: "Hello, there's Mother and Vicky coming down the field." There is a restricted learning area, and codified games, and, as with many other children's books, the landscape acts as an encompassing and finite background.

We can see at once that some of the standard critical stances are not particularly significant (as Margery Fisher's observation that Nancy matures between *Swallows and Amazons* and *The Picts and the Martyrs*) or totally misleading. Marcus Crouch is a case in point:

> One might feel a theoretical regret that Ransome did not choose to show children and adults in partnership, and that, with the exception of Captain Flint and a few others, the adults are

hostile and barbarous, like the Hullabaloos, or tyrannous like Great Aunt Maria . . . [see excerpt above, 1972].

It would be difficult to be more perverse. Although he is criticising what has generally been seen as a virtue (". . . an incomplete society, one in which children lived apart from the adult world . . .") he contrives to name the *only* hostile adults in the whole sequence—and Great Aunt Maria, as her character is presented in *The Picts and the Martyrs,* should hardly be included. Crouch also accuses Ransome of being "reluctant to call adults by name," despite the fact that there are very few examples, and these occur in the weakest books.

Bob Dixon, in a far more gentle comment, is closer to the truth:

> Mother . . . along with other adults, is always on hand to help and advise about practicalities. Thus the children can combine adventure with security, which probably mainly accounts for the book's popularity.

Thus the children securely "live apart." In *Swallows and Amazons,* Mother plays a major role. She hands down permission, provisions the party, checks their arrival, and appears in almost every chapter. When she is not there to provide the *clozure* to an episode, there are the farmers, the charcoal burners, Captain Flint. (pp. 25-7)

The more dangerous the exploit, the firmer the adult presence. The night-sailing episode, for example, is framed by Mother's visit to Titty on the island, by her reported watching over the lake, by John's confessional. Only when the danger is more apparent than real—as with the storm on the island which brings out almost all the adults—can the children assert their limited superiority. "It's when they all get together," said Nancy. "They can't help themselves, poor things". . . . (p. 27)

*Swallows and Amazons* thus provides both immediately recognisable incidents and wish-fulfillment within quite a subtle framework of protected freedom. The author-child contract is quite clear, just as it is between adult and child within the book. We recognise the comparative weakness of the "stolen treasure" device for what it is—an untruth both in syntagmatic and paradigmatic terms.

The same generalisations hold for *Swallowdale,* where the real danger when *Swallow* sinks brings the immediate appearance of Captain Flint. Similarly, the move onwards from the island is backed up by some of Ransome's most vivid and affectionate creations, the Swainsons. This increased surface skill, it must be said, throws Ransome's tendency to sentimentality into higher relief, and emphasises the artificiality of the Great Aunt as a device. Nevertheless, Susan's final words as they return to the island (*not* to normal, non-holiday life)—"Isn't it a blessing to get home" . . .—emphasise that a step has been taken towards greater independence.

*Winter Holiday* and *Pigeon Post* follow similar patterns, although in the first of these the manipulation of incident by adults—the stressing that games are games—tends to weaken Ransome's increasing atmospheric (and thus purely surface) skills.

The quality and value of *The Picts and the Martyrs*—the real end of the sequence—can thus be seen in the integration of all these elements without artificiality. Nancy's belated realisation that she has a good deal in common with Aunt Maria is not

as significant for her syntagmatic development as a character as it is for the thematic transform. Caricature is only possible in the context of a game; here we have gone beyond make-believe. (pp. 27-8)

The children have grown up and out of "natural" games; the games that are to be played "offstage" are now artificially imposed by Nancy. With the readers, the children have started to leave childhood—and just as the characters have matured, so has the style and structure. As *Great Northern?* demonstrates, Ransome has both come to the limits of his craft *and* has exhausted the significant resources of gameplaying.

Although it would be unwise to place too much emphasis on the integrity of the sequence *qua* sequence, the fact that the Walkers are absent from *The Picts and the Martyrs* coheres with the fact that they have already experienced their maturing experience in the most important of the books, *We Didn't Mean to Go to Sea.* The style, as always, reflects in its assurance the greater resonance to significant levels of experience and growth, and character and incident rise to new levels of naturalism. The changes of pace from the sea voyage to Mother waiting (helplessly) at Pin Mill are of the same quality as the emergence of Susan and John from the game-oriented role-playing of the earlier books. Titty's character recedes; Roger's stabilises. (p. 29)

*We Didn't Mean to Go to Sea* sums up the point about adventure and security. Some readers have complained that the massive co-incidence of the children meeting their father just as they sail into the Dutch harbour undercuts the hard naturalism and authenticity of the voyage. Quite clearly, however, the greater the danger, the greater the reaffirmation of normality, and the ultimate dispenser of permission, Commander Walker, more than fills the role. He dwarfs the erratic Captain Flint (whose name is, of course, a significantly derivative transform) and the comparatively helpless mother figure [Susan], and the point is underlined. (p. 30)

The long and gentle coda to the book, as they sail peacefully home, reasserts adult control (and adult respect), and the integrity of the family. The very structure of *We Didn't Mean to Go to Sea* is a clearly perceptible growth-game pattern, and its coherence is demonstrable at all levels from theme to style.

In comparison, its sequel *Secret Water* is a much lesser book, returning, perhaps half-heartedly, to games in a well-mapped play-area, with strict time limits and mild dangers. Characters revert to type—except, perhaps, that John appears to be more solemn, and Nancy more tiresomely tomboyish—and there is a tidiness and inevitability about the book which again reflects accurately its relative shallowness. Unlike *The Picts and the Martyrs* it is a regression.

A word might be said about the two books set on the Norfolk Broads, *Coot Club* and *The Big Six.* Again, the adult framework is strong, with Mrs Barrable, the Doctor, the Lawyer, the Policeman, and sundry mothers, fathers, eelmen, and wherrymen at hand. *Coot Club* is noticeably broken-backed in structure, and the ambiguity of the plot surfaces in the cardboard villains, the contrived climax, and one of Ransome's uncharacteristic displays of venom:

> On came the *Margoletta,* sweeping up with the tide, and filling the quiet evening with a loud, treacly voice.
>
> "I want to be a darling, a doodle-um, a duckle-um, I want to be a ducky, doodle darling, yes I do."

"Indeed," muttered Port, with a good deal of bitterness. . . .

(p. 31)

*The Big Six,* rather like *Pigeon Post,* is a highly energetic and well-crafted piece, and it might fairly stand beside many a respected detective story. It does not attempt to reach any further than plot level, and there are moments both of ironic interplay between the play of Dorothea and the seriousness of Bill, Joe, and Pete, and over all a gentle autumnal atmosphere.

*Missee Lee,* if it succeeds, succeeds entirely on the level of the "good yarn"—that is transforming only a relatively shallow plot-level, rather than a theme-level—and touching only lightly any moral or realistic issues. The characters are scarcely more than names. *Peter Duck,* on the other hand, slips badly in its attempt to be a pirates-and-buried-treasure yarn. The characters of Peter Duck and Bill, the cabin boy, are too close to an unpleasant reality to sit comfortably with the shallow plotting. The gang of pirates on the *Viper* may be villainous, yet they are usually taken lightly. But not always:

> "I say, Uncle Jim," said Peggy. "If the *Viper* does catch us up, what can they really do?"
>
> "They can't do anything," said Captain Flint. "Not anything that matters."
>
> Bill opened his mouth and shut it again. Peter Duck looked oddly at Captain Flint. . . .

(pp. 31-2)

Such a false intrusion of an anomalous plot structure is rare in Ransome, possibly because the main sequence has a unity of progression outwards from secure games, secure settings, and secure family relationships.

It would be a neat thesis to observe that with the last book, *Great Northern?* we have moved to the point of open-endedness. The book begins and ends out in the Minches; there is no coda—merely an uncaptioned picture of *Sea Bear* sailing away. There is now no need of a home to return to; in terms of the sequence, the audience is free to go its own way; development is reflected in structure. There can be no ending, just as there can be no more Ransome children's books. Unfortunately, characters are once again caricatures, incidents contrived, villains villainous. The book has a *point:* true, it is a fashionable ecological one, but the subject matter should not disguise from us the fact that we are dealing with a very shallow piece indeed, and, as always, the surface signals this. For all its incidental skills, *Great Northern?* reads as an afterthought, Ransome dealing with the shells of characters who have, in reality, already left him.

When we talk about significant figures in children's books, of classics, and of good writers, it is important to see Ransome for what he is. In the majority of his books he is both a good craftsman, in that he deals honestly and consistently with the materials he sets himself, and an appropriate writer for children, in that his base themes are generally appropriate to children's developmental needs. On the rare occasions when his themes reflect deeper human motivations, this is reflected in an appropriately subtle and polished surface style, and a modulation of character. Further, the whole sequence can be read as a growth-game, even a growth-aid, moving at least as consistently as the surface features of his characters from childhood into adolescence. In this sense, then, the books are rich but limited, and that may be enough to assure him of his status. (p. 32)

*Peter Hunt, "Ransome Revisited: A Structural and Developmental Approach," in* Children's literature in education, *Vol. 12, No. 1 (Spring), 1981, pp. 24-33.*

## FRED INGLIS

[Arthur Ransome] wrote of the absolute safety of a Lake District (and Norfolk Broads) bounded by the absolute justice of the parental writ. Ransome mattered fundamentally because I saw him [when read as a schoolboy] also as a celebrant of the great world of home. The splendour and detail of his stories, taking place as they did in an unending and paradisal holiday, were woven from a love of the landscape. . . . [Ransome] gave voice for children to that extraordinary loyalty to place which the Romantics put into circulation (and found in Shakespeare), and did so quite without sentimentality or overblown patriotism.

I began with Ransome's sense of place. But . . . he has immeasurably more to give. He and Kipling, in their different world, took me past the cardboard figures who performed the events of the Biggles books, into the depths and meanings of character which are the subjects and objects of the English novel, and the foundation of the morality we call liberalism. Ransome was a far lesser artist, but a far plainer, less affected, more honest man, and his prose speaks out for these qualities. But both men set their books firmly in a believable reality, both loved their home landscape fiercely . . . , both gave their characters a racy, quick, idiosyncratic and attractive speech. (pp. 66-8)

In temper, style, and ethics Ransome belongs entirely to the best Edwardians. . . . There *is* after all something in Ransome which is stolid and unimaginative; it comes out in the *Autobiography* as well as in the children's novels. But this something is also equable, serene, brave, and all-competent. (p. 130)

[Ransome] is as unlike the present writers for children as he could be. Like them, he looks to the creation of free, autonomous spirits amongst the children about and for whom he writes. But the Swallows and Amazons have little of the polymorphous independence admired by the new class which writes for children. That is why Ransome, for all that he sustains continuity so easily, marks the end of a line of values. As a novelist, he too is an agent of the symbol-making industry. . . . Ransome envisions a way of life, a human order, and a set of values, which for all their beauty and vividness, can only find a rather ghostly harbour today. (pp. 130-31)

Even where Ransome is clearly recollecting his own best childhood memories, of the drought summer in *Pigeon Post* or the long, hard frost of *Winter Holiday,* and transposing them from the 1890s to the 1930s, he writes the plain, straight, rather practical, unreflective prose we would expect of the man he was.

It is his subject-matter which counts. . . . Ransome was lucky. He had his subject-matter in the activity which made him happiest, sailing. Consequently it doesn't really matter that the Swallows and the Amazons and the D's are only ever to be seen on holiday. . . . But the holidays for Ransome's children do not simply provide the leisure time in which to solve some detective problem. They are sailing-time, and since sailing is so many things at once—pastime, means of commerce, transport, means of warfare, the occasion of worship and of burial, the frail collusion of culture with the barely harnessable powers of Nature, or just a pleasant Sunday afternoon—since sailing is these many things, it can stand for much in adult life which

*Tom came sailing home. From* Coot Club, *written and illustrated by Arthur Ransome. Jonathan Cape, 1955. Reprinted by permission of Jonathan Cape Ltd, on behalf of the Literary Estate of Arthur Ransome.*

could otherwise only feature in a children's novel in a rather unreal way. . . .

By comparison [with Joseph Conrad], Ransome is a simple man. But these solid novels convey his commitment to the mysteries of sailing in terms which Conrad would have approved. The simplicity is a function both of those to whom Ransome speaks . . . and of the situation of the children in the fiction. They do not need to question what they are doing: it is its own reward. (pp. 132-33)

[The] mystery of sailing-boats gives [Ransome's] plain, technical writing its resonance. . . . Ransome's novels most exemplify beautiful absorption in activity for its own worthy sake. Sailing is such an excellent subject because it enables such absorption without seeming silly, as so many of the sports which attract a similar absorption can appear to be to an outsider. (pp. 134-35)

[Sailing] is a way of rejoining your history. . . . The games played by the children in *Swallows and Amazons* quote Queen Elizabeth and Francis Drake as well as Cortez and *Treasure Island*. They quote Nansen of the *Fram* and Scott of the Antarctic in *Winter Holiday*, Natty Bumppo and Mallory and Irving in *Swallowdale*, Klondyke gold-miners in *Pigeon Post*. The romantic wildness and solitude of the Lake District in the thirties gave Ransome a context in which children might re-invent that heroism. (p. 135)

It is Ransome's strength to hold freedom in balance against its moral counterweight, duty. (p. 136)

I mean that Ransome takes life seriously, unselfconsciously so; and that therefore the actions of his characters are important, not just for themselves, but because they are principled. . . . [These] children are free moral agents, and they live within a secure framework of a role and its duties. In this way they are unlike present-day children, these short thirty or forty years later. The Swallows' father is in the Royal Navy; the children each assign to themselves a naval rank: John is Captain, Susan First Mate, Titty Able-seaman, Roger Ship's Boy and, in perhaps the best of the novels, *We Didn't Mean to Go to Sea,* Engineer.

It is hard to pick one novel out for special attention amongst so many contenders. Ransome's writing is unusually full and expansive in the world of children's novels. Most contemporary novelists now write, no doubt rightly, for very much more short-winded readers. Other novels—*Great Northern?* or *Coot Club* for instance—embody much more richly Ransome's passion for natural life, and they communicate this, not in some spirit of dreadful brightness in order to tell children about birds, but as a full response to the experience of natural beauty, of sailing and walking amongst that beauty (in the Scottish Highlands), and of keeping alive a non-exploitative moral attitude towards the natural life which belongs there. Those novels I have already mentioned, which include the endearing and sometimes tiresome Nancy and Peggy as well as Dick and Dorothea, take in a wider range of experience and, though always carefully plotted with a studied regard for relevance and form, allow themselves a more discursive pattern of episodes: the visit to the charcoal-burners in *Winter Holiday,* the moment of discovery in *Secret Water.* (pp. 136-37)

Nancy throws into relief the difficulty of knowing how to live in terms of the life and values commended on and around the lake. . . . Ordinary life is not enough for her, and so she animates and directs the remorseless cartoon life which the others willingly adopt. (p. 137)

[Nancy], who stands farthest away from everyday life and relationships, is in the limiting sense entirely childish, and for all Uncle Jim-Captain Flint's believable benevolence, he connives far too much at her childishness. She is a convincing character who focusses Ransome's own over-indulgence; he never breathes a word of criticism towards her.

Nancy's absence from *We Didn't Mean to Go to Sea* points us to the nature of its success, in terms of both form and content. For in this novel the adventure is real and not fantasy, and it is entirely credible. Furthermore, the title catches the exact point of anguish in the book. . . . (p. 138)

[Right] through the book, Ransome's touch and pacing are faultless. We are a third of the way into the book before the awful moment at which they realize the *Goblin* is dragging her anchor. The calm and leisurely movement of the narrative has not been for a moment redundant, although a child would hardly be likely to notice the relevance and interconnectedness of all the detail. . . .

Ransome is as workmanlike with his art of novel-writing as he would have been with the art of sailing; and so, naturally and easily, he allowed the strapping, handsome undergraduate who has taken the children under his wing to tell them enough about his boat to make it possible for them to sail it, but never too much to bore the reader and make the novel into a sailing manual, nor to take the terror out of their ignorance when the catastrophe comes.

The tranquillity and pleasure of the first part of the novel are sharpened by the tension with which we wait for the adventure. The writing is plain and wholesome and firm; it is undecorated and its cadences fix only the scene and no special attitude towards it. (p. 140)

Ransome's matter-of-factness and his careful enumeration of technical detail have their limiting aspect, no doubt. There are plenty of people who are simply bored stiff at once by his subject-matter. . . . His matter-of-factness may seem flat to those with a taste for a rounder rhetoric, and some of his novels have their heavinesses and their long troughs. In this one, however, the length is never *longueur*. For all its 300 pages, it is economical. And his digressions are courteously adjusted to his audience. . . . Ransome pauses in the tale while he makes sure that his audience knows what he is talking about. He looks up, so to speak, explains what he means, and then goes on.

This attention to technical detail is the heart of the book. Not only is Ransome writing about what he knows and loves best in all the world, it is the subject-matter which brings together practice and morality in an absolute fusion. Ransome was not a reflective writer, nor even one, it seems, who busied himself with the expression of emotion at all. . . . The circumstances of *We Didn't Mean to Go to Sea* allow personal feeling to transpire straight from action and not reflection. Events from outside force right conduct on those with the knowledge to perform it. Right conduct brings right feeling—fulfilment and happiness. (pp. 141-42)

One admires the sheer vividness of the description [of the storm]. . . . Ransome's best effects are often his briefest:

> They looked astern, and could see grey water, white tops of waves, and a strip of pale sky under grey clouds. Of the land there was nothing to be seen at all. The *Goblin* was utterly alone, racing along, up and down, up and down. Fast as she was sailing, the seas moved faster still. Wave after wave swept up on her quarter, lifted her, and passed on. Wave after wave came rolling up, broke with the loud noise of churning water, and left a long mane of foam. . . .

Such prose is not in any way external to the action. This comes out in the touching pages which describe the rescue of the almost drowned kitten. The incident is attractively done in itself, as well as suggesting (as John and Susan think on our behalf) how the children might themselves have been struggling feebly on a spar in the empty sea. The kitten's rescue serves as emblem of return to warm, normal living. (p. 143)

The rest of the novel [after meeting the Flemish pilot] is largely a long, though stirring, coda. Indeed, the pleasure it gives is due to the excitement's being over, and our resting in the calmness of a beautiful safety. (p. 144)

They are restored to the harmony of a perfect social order. But they are restored while having added to it. They come home changed, and home to the new expectations of their parents, who love them and deal justly with them. . . . [One] of Ransome's many strengths is to suggest the continued need for such ideal parents as Commander Ted and Mrs Mary Walker, so un-Victorian but also so excellently authoritative. They are part of the ideal social order prefigured by this marvellous book. The children live out a brief version of the good life,

one in which the natural, abrupt dangers of life require exceptional courage, skill in understanding and handling an antique culture, warmth, natural sympathy, independence. They join culture and nature together again—the sailing-boat and the sea—and therefore quicken work into creative life. And having succeeded temporarily in doing these things for themselves, and finding both the intensity of existence and a form within which to contain and express it, they go back to the huge happiness of home. The novel shows its readers how to keep 'the promise of happiness'. (pp. 144-45)

*Fred Inglis, in his* The Promise of Happiness: Value and Meaning in Children's Fiction, *Cambridge University Press, 1981, 333 p.**

## NEIL PHILIP

Ransome initiated a new and healthy movement in children's literature, one that respected the child audience and took the real life of children as its starting point. The reader is never short-changed; but never, it must be admitted, surprised by riches.

I recently abridged two of Ransome's Norfolk novels (*Coot Club* and *The Big Six*) into one volume, *Swallows and Amazons for Ever!* to accompany a television serial. Ransome, I thought, was a prolix writer, there would be no trouble pruning; I was wrong. I am left with a great admiration for his craftsmanship: there is nothing redundant in his prose, nothing that does not directly affect his narrative. Though he is not a brief writer, he is a very tight one.

The main problem in cutting was the exactness of his time-scales: we know what his characters are doing all day, every day. This inclusiveness seems to me both Ransome's greatest virtue and his greatest flaw. His detailed descriptions capture the endless quality of time for the young, but his refusal to select leaves one moment much the same as another: he gives everything equal weight. He writes in uncritical acceptance of immediate experience rather than with the selective perception of memory. And because he leaves no holes, because everything is stated in full, he cannot imply, conceal, intrigue. He allows himself no sleight of hand. The result is a meticulous surface with nothing much working underneath: the books are all subject matter and no theme. Ransome's books offer a complete alternative world to replace the reader's own, rather than a partial counterpoint to replenish it.

Some readers are bored, of course, by the consequent stress on technicalities, but many, knowing nothing about sailing, are absorbed, as children often are, at the sight of someone doing a difficult job with thoroughness, authority and confidence. They are drawn in, too, by Ransome's lucid, direct prose, by his lively dialogue, and by the skill with which he sews his imagined fictions on to a real and intimately known and loved landscape.

Though Ransome was apt to grumble, 'Children?! I can't stand them', he knew precisely how to address them. (pp. 6-7)

*Neil Philip, "Arthur Ransome," in* British Book News, *Spring, 1984, pp. 6-7.*

## HUGH BROGAN

From the start of his career [Ransome] wanted to be a story-teller, as distinct from a novelist. He never seems to have aspired to make novels, although in the end he found himself writing them about children. When he produced a series of studies of fiction-writers he called it *A History of Story-Telling,* although among the authors discussed was, for example, Flaubert, who seems absurdly diminished by such a rubric. There might be various reasons for this limited ambition. The prestige of the story was high in that age of Stevenson, Kipling, Wells, Doyle, Conrad. In his youth Ransome lacked the knowledge of men and women that is necessary for serious novel-writing. It is unlikely that this influenced him. What he wanted to do was to equal the enchanters of his childhood as a teller of tales. He was willing to branch out: much of the imaginative work that survives from his youth is quite outside a child's range. But he had no doubt as to where his imagination worked most intensely, although he had as yet no idea of how best to exploit the fact. He was still fatally attracted by whimsy. He much admired the children's tales of E. Nesbit, which were coming out in rapid succession . . . , but he had no suspicion that he was to be her successor. Indeed he still had much to learn before such a succession was possible. (pp. 45-6)

[Both *The Souls of the Streets* and *The Stone Lady,* two early collections of essays,] were clearly the works of a writer: of someone who could handle language, tell a story, expound an idea. There was promise in them. That promise became much clearer in Arthur's next significant undertaking, a series of little nature books for children [*The Child's Book of the Seasons, The Things in Our Garden,* and *Pond and Stream,* all published in 1906. They were later collected into one volume, *The Imp and the Elf and the Ogre* (1910).]

Ransome was still at the stage of scribbling to order; a dangerous practice, but one which can sometimes have stimulating and surprising results, as with the new books. A small publisher commissioned five short volumes on, respectively, the garden; ponds and streams; the seasons; woods; fields and country lanes. Each was to have a few illustrations by some struggling artist, and a text by the equally struggling Arthur Ransome. The market they were aimed at was that of the unimaginative (always the largest): those parents, teachers and librarians who have no idea what children really like, and accept unquestioningly the current assumptions. In Edwardian England those assumptions were predominantly coy.

Had Ransome found himself, he could hardly have undertaken this commission as conscientiously as he did. The first book, on the garden, hit exactly the desired treacly note. . . . By the time we have been taken to visit the snails and slugs (lovable, even though they damage the lettuces) we are likely to have been put off nature study and children for life. Words like 'wee', 'fairy' and 'jolly' pepper the text. Maiden aunts must have loved this volume.

Ransome next tackled the book of the seasons. Someone who could take the sex out of pollination . . . should have had no difficulty in making spring and summer boring, but the writer's instinct began to assert itself, and any reader with knowledge of the mature Ransome can see odd signals in the text, like bubbles as a pot starts to boil. There begin to be symptoms of characterisation. Ransome abandons the description of the life of birds and animals, at which he was not very skilled, and tells instead about the things in which his touch never failed: the activities of humans, especially country humans (haymaking, sheep-shearing, ploughing); and, his especial genuis, how to do things—in this case, how to make a cowslip ball. The Imp shows traits of the kind that would later distinguish Roger in the *Swallow* books, wriggling through corn-shocks, and losing a blackberry race to his sister: 'The Imp is like me, and eats nearly as many as he picks. Blackberries are easier to carry

that way.' The Ogre remembers that when he was little he liked wriggling through corn-shocks himself.

He recalls himself strictly to business at the opening of the third book of the series, *Pond and Stream.* Tadpoles, newts and caddisflies fill the foreground; but in the background the new music becomes stronger and stronger. We may guess that Ransome could not spend so much time in the company of the Imp and the Elf, however loathsome their sobriquets, without getting interested in them, or at least without trying to make them interesting; and the only way he knew of doing that was to try and place them in the real world—in other words, in the only childhood he knew about at first hand, his own. Where else were 'the becks that trickle down the valley. You know what a beck is? The Imp and the Elf are north country children, and they would not understand you if you called the beck a stream.' His uncertain grasp of the children's reality is illustrated by the fact that a few pages later the Imp actually uses the word stream; but immediately afterwards he and his creator escape to the banks of a beck, and the magic begins. As Ransome was later to demonstrate so frequently, he had an acute sense of the individuality of streams and rivers, and the beck in this book, though schematically conceived (it was meant simply to illustrate the varieties of waterlife), suddenly acquires reality when it runs under a little bridge made of a slab of solid slate, which the Imp, still Rogerish, insists on wriggling below himself, under the scornful supervision of his sister. Then the party climbs the beck and meets a dipper, painstakingly described; but Ransome still had a lot to learn, and the passage has none of the charm of Titty's encounter with the same bird in *Swallows and Amazons.* Then, by one of those turns that seem accidental, or merely mechanical (after all, the children having inspected a duckpond and a beck, where else is there to go?) but are really determined by the deepest forces of an artist's nature, they get into a boat and row out upon the lake.

The lake comes from nowhere, suddenly, like Keats's perilous seas forlorn, but like them it is instantly recognised as enchanted. 'Half way down the lake there is a little rocky island.' Natural history is thrown to the winds, and Ransome describes a journey thither.

> We run the boat carefully aground in a pebbly inlet at one end of the island. We take the baskets ashore, and camp in the shadow of a little group of pines. There is no need to tell you what a picnic tea is like. You know quite well how jolly it is, and how the bun-loaf tastes better than the finest cake, and the sandwiches disappear as if by magic, and the tea seems to have vanished almost as soon as the cork is pulled from the bottle.
>
> As soon as tea is over we prowl over the rockinesses of the little island, and creep among the hazels and pines and tiny oaks and undergrowth. Do you know trees never look so beautiful as when you get glimpses of blue water between their fluttering leaves? When we have picked our way through to the other end, we climb upon a high rock with a flat top to it, and heather growing in its crevices; and here we lie, torpid after our tea, and pretend that we are viking-folk from the north who have forced our way here by land and sea, and are looking for the first time upon a lake that no one knew before us. The Imp tells us a story

of how he fought with a red-haired warrior, and how they both fell backwards into the sea, and how he killed the other man dead, and then came home to change his wet clothes, long, long ago in the white north. And the Elf, not to be beaten, has her story, too, how she rode on a dragon one night and saw the lake—this very lake—far away beneath her, like a shining shield with a blue island boss in the middle of it. And how the fiery dragon flapped down so that she could pick a scrap of heather from the island, and how here was the very heather that she picked. . . .

[This passage] contains, in suspension as it were, the essentials of the *Swallow* books. The narrative tone is still unsure, but for the rest we have the deep feeling for Peel Island and Coniston Water; the fantasising, which was to make the lake, for the Swallows, a vast unexplored ocean; the feeling for actuality which prevents the fantasies from boring or getting out of hand; and finally, in the relationship of the Ogre with his charges, the relationship of Captain Flint with his nieces. It does not matter (we are dealing with the imagination) that the Imp is a boy; what is described here, though at the time of writing Ransome did not know it, is an early expedition of the Amazons to Wild Cat Island.

Before the book ends the children are taught a little more natural history, but Ransome's real achievement has been to convey the magic of a day spent in the open air.

> As the two of them go off to bed, very happy and very, very tired, we can hear the long kr-r-r-r-r of the nightjar in the pinewoods up on the hills, and below us in the woods at the head of the lake two owls answering each other.

In these words Ransome almost achieved his true literary identity. (pp. 50-4)

No writing had ever made him so happy [as did that of *Swallows and Amazons*]. . . . He wrote the story continuously (which was not his later practice) until he reached what became chapter 24, carried along on the wave of creative gusto. At night he would take the manuscript to his bedroom, so that he could reach out his hand and touch its cover as it lay beside him in the dark (a piece of magic like dipping that same hand in Coniston). This urgency, this artistic certainty and delight, surprised the author, but need not surprise anyone else. By no blundering process of trial and error, but by the natural growth of his skill and spirit, he had evolved to the point where he could at last achieve the original form which he needed to fulfil his ambitions. He had wanted to write stories for children since his early youth. He had reflected endlessly on the art of narration. The years of journalism, little though he thanked them, had given his style lucidity, flexibility and strength. They had also cleared his mind on matters of value: had confirmed his commitment to the world of the imagination, not that of action. Finally, he had a vision, a burden of feeling and memory to discharge: for the deepest psychological reasons the world of childhood on the waters of Coniston and Windermere was full of significance. Writing about it would enable him to act out a profound personal drama, and thus be free. The process by which he came to write *Swallows and Amazons* was, in short, perfectly logical, though the accidental played its part. The materials had all been assembled, but they might have waited over-long for the detonating spark. It was most fortunate that

the Altounyans decided to make him a present of those slippers. (p. 304)

It is easy enough to find superficial reasons for Ransome's great success with *Swallows and Amazons* and its successors. There had been hundreds of school stories since *Tom Brown,* but no one had thought to write holiday stories. It was a gloriously obvious idea, once discovered, a fresh appeal to the half-innocent egoism of the young: they liked to see their schooldays dignified and romanticised in fiction, and were naturally responsive to the same treatment of their holidays. Any professional writer who hit on the formula—and Ransome was exactly that—was bound to succeed in such an undertaking, and a generation of writers, following in Ransome's steps, also profited. But their work never had the enormous popularity of the *Swallow* books, and now is almost wholly forgotten.

Ransome's strengths as a writer were not easily duplicated. They were too deeply involved with his personal history. Proust's dictum that the self which lives in time and the self which writes are not the same would not have appealed to Arthur Ransome, the stout admirer of Sainte-Beuve. But the self of his books is plainly cooler, shrewder, more intelligent, more patient, more good-humoured, more worldly wise, than the Arthur of life. Perhaps Proust did not go far enough. Perhaps he should have said that the self which writes is *better* than the self of time. At any rate it was so with Arthur. His happiness in writing *Swallows and Amazons* both relaxed and stimulated him, bringing into play powers he scarcely knew he had, and putting all disabling self-consciousness to sleep.

Why was he so happy? Perhaps it was because the invention of John enabled him to put his own young self into the tale. For the Walkers are not simply the Altounyans in light disguise, even in *Swallows and Amazons* where the fit is designedly closest. There are mysteries about them, of which their surname is the greatest: it was that of Arthur's first wife. Perhaps Arthur unconsciously hoped that there was some magic in using the name which would draw [his daughter] Tabitha, a half-Walker, back to him. But whatever the explanation, the choice can hardly have been accidental (Arthur nowhere attempts to explain it). Neither was the substitution of a boy for a girl as the eldest child. Arthur had been the eldest himself. Through the substitution he was able to depict himself as he must at times quite passionately have wanted to be: reliable, unimaginative, good-hearted, skilled in all practical matters, and on entirely harmonious terms with his parents. 'BETTER DROWNED THAN DUFFERS: IF NOT DUFFERS WON'T DROWN': John's father's telegram is famous. John's comment is enormously significant: 'Daddy knows we aren't duffers.' It was something that the boy Arthur could never have said to himself with any confidence; yet how much he had wanted to! Now, in fiction, all could be arranged.

So Arthur gave to himself, as well as to the Altounyans, the absolutely cloudless Lakeland childhood that he desired; and thus assured, his imagination was free to rampage. He knew just what the book ought to be. He did not live to encounter that marvellously self-serving critical doctrine according to which the only subject of art is art and even such works as *Emma* are concerned chiefly with their own writing; but his tale comes close to exemplifying it. As early as 1906 he had published an essay on books and children, in poor old *Temple Bar,* in which he had laid down what children's literature ought to be; and *Swallows and Amazons* perfectly illustrates his doctrine. The essence of the child, he held, is its imagination, the way in which, left to itself and not withered by obtuse or manipulative adults, 'it adopts any material at hand, and weaves for itself a web of imaginative life', building the world again into a splendid pageantry: and all without ever (or hardly ever) blurring its sense of the actual. Such a child is Titty, the most richly-conceived of all his characters. (pp. 312-14)

For Ransome, the glorious thing about *Swallows and Amazons* was that it liberated the child in himself. Utterly committed to what he was doing, he felt free, for example, to take liberties with the Furness geography: so that Peel Island of Coniston and Blake Holme of Windermere could merge to become Wild Cat Island; so that the Old Man of Coniston (Kanchenjunga) could look across the lake to Bowness-on-Windermere (Rio); so that Silver Holme (Cormorant Island) and Belle Isle (Long Island) and Allen Tarn (the Octopus Lagoon) and Bank Ground Farm (Holly Howe) could all, as it were, rub shoulders; and so that the old *Gondola*, which he had loved so much as a child, could be moored as houseboat in a bay of his composite lake, and be inhabited by a bald, fat man, busy writing a book, and hostile to children: Ransome's daytime self, the self he was escaping from; Captain Flint, the unrecognised *alter ego* of Captain John.

*Swallows and Amazons*, then, is full of symbolic meaning; its plot recapitulates several of the most important dramas of its author's life, and beautifully resolves them. Children do not bother their heads about such considerations. They find, instead, that someone is playing a fascinating game in the book's pages. . . . And once they are drawn into the game, they will perforce learn about many things: not just the joys of sailing and camping, and the particular skills which Ransome was so good at describing, but the charm of the human comedy—Ransome's humour is quieter than that of E. Nesbit, but just as firmly grounded on observation and a love of character—and increasingly, as they read and re-read all the books, a vision of nature and society which may colour their outlook for the rest of their lives. How it is done must remain, in the end, a secret between children and the author; but an adult may suggest that it could not have been done at all for a generation to which reading was less important than it was to the children of the 1930s and 1940s. Ransome is able to assume that children take their reading seriously and are not daunted by demands on their attention, intelligence and vocabulary. (pp. 314-15)

*Swallowdale* is the longest of Ransome's children's books. It is also, in one respect, the most audacious: it has almost nothing that can be described as a plot. The most dramatic incidents are the holing of *Swallow* and the spraining of Roger's ankle. Nowhere else was Ransome to escape so entirely all need for the suspension of disbelief (even *Swallows and Amazons* had featured a burglary). The author stakes everything on his ability to make the absolutely commonplace fascinating by his imagination and the imaginative use of language. Sometimes the imagination gets a little out of hand: Titty, in her agitation over her fancied murder of the Great-Aunt, seems at times in need of a strait-jacket. But on the whole the book succeeds as a sunny enchantment. The lake ceases to be the unknown ocean of the first story, instead taking on its true character as a mere among the English fells. The farm-folk, who were purely background figures in *Swallows*, now appear more solid. Even the Amazons gain credibility as figures at home in the Furness world. (p. 318)

*Peter Duck* deserved its success, but . . . Arthur had had [*Treasure Island*] with him in Aleppo, and its influence, with that of John Masefield, is all-pervasive; it was not really so original as its predecessors. But even if it worked within a well-estab-

lished tradition, the familiar Ransome virtues were amply in evidence. Even the waterspout, the most sensational episode in the story, was based on the one which Arthur, Genia and the Ancient Mariner had seen in the Gulf of Riga in 1923. This incident may even have been the germ of *Peter Duck*, for that grizzled mariner is of course the Ancient Mariner himself (sea-changed, rather like the Altounyans, into fiction, and made a Lowestoft man in the process) and the book is in a way the sequel to *Racundra's First Cruise*. As Arthur well knew, the contrast between the rash, enthusiastic, romantic Captain Flint, hankering for treasure, and the wise, unmercenary old sailor is the energising principle of the book: Mr Duck is never more impressive than in the glances of loathing he directs at the treasure-chest after it has been recovered, or in the rebuke he delivers to Captain Flint:

> "And now," said Captain Flint at breakfast, "the first thing to do is to get across the island, find Mr. Duck's tree, and bring the stuff aboard."
>
> "Begging your pardon, sir," said Peter Duck, "the first thing's the ship."

Peter Duck's own romanticism shows unforgettably when they see the Yankee clipper homeward bound. "'Rot screw steamers," he burst out fiercely, "driving vessels like her off the seas where they belong!"' The 1930s were the last decade of regular clipper trade, and both Arthur and Peter Duck knew it. But Ransome was just as concerned to show the greatness of the old *Thermopylae* hand as the beauty of sail, and nobly achieved both. (pp. 329-30)

*Winter Holiday* is the first of his books without a false note from beginning to end. The evocation of the snowbound fells and the icebound lake and all the delights of such a season is captivating. . . . With *Swallows and Amazons* and *We Didn't Mean to Go to Sea* it is also one of the key sections of the hidden, and perhaps unconscious, autobiography that Ransome put into his children's stories. Dick and Dorothea are delightful additions to his cast of characters, as he well knew ('if people don't like my little astronomer and scientifically minded Dick, I'll eat ten new hats at a sitting') and Dick has proved a most popular model for young readers. . . . The brother and sister appear to be projections of two sides of Ransome's own character. Dick is the young Rugbeian Arthur, bespectacled, with a strong scientific bent, deaf and blind to everything except the matter in hand. His triumph in the story is also a triumph of the author's wish-fulfilment. Dorothea, the future writer, has been denigrated for being Titty's inferior in intuition. Actually, Dorothea has plenty of insight into people and situations; but what sets her apart from all the others, including Titty, is her concern with language. She alone constantly tries to find the right phrase or word; and although the style she evolves for herself could hardly be worse . . . it is something to have any style at all at the age of eleven. There can be no doubt that Dorothea's vocation was a true one; and the skill with which Ransome displays it tells us much about his own. To clinch the identification, there is the fact that the Callums are academic brats: their father is a Professor of Archaeology. (pp. 332-33)

[In] spite of all the usual difficulties and more than the usual doubts . . . , Arthur somehow produced *Coot Club.* Such records of the struggle as have been preserved show with uncommon clarity how Arthur wrought himself up to creative pitch.

He truly believed that he had done with the Walkers, Blacketts and Callums, but like many writers he looked for inspiration, positive or negative, to themes and situations in the earlier work. Thus, Nancy and Peggy's prim and domineering Great-Aunt had been very unlike his own Great-Aunt Susan. Were not old people sometimes lively and children priggish? And then there had been the idea he had toyed with for **Winter Holiday**, a contrast between two sets of children, a town pair and a country pair, 'complete savages and contrast to the townies, but with less ingenuity in devising adventures, but greater practical power of carrying them out'. Suppose the two ideas were merged? The book could be called *Webfooted Grandmother*. 'Grandmother's relations to her two are precise opposite to those of the G.A. to the Amazons. That is, she regards them as too desperately proper and is doing her best to tone them up to the less civilised life of Tom, Port and Starboard and the Pirates.' The theme of the book, then, would be the conversion of the Propers to web-footedness. At the end of the book they could start to pull on gloves 'and then refrain on seeing the faces of Port and Starboard, the fear is expressed privately among the Coots that the Propers may "relapse"'. So far so good: but what was to happen between the beginning and the end?

It could be something of a cruise book. The children would have to travel all over the Broads, experiencing as much of the life of the region as possible. So, quite early, Ransome had the idea of Port and Starboard missing their ship and having to beg their passage on a wherry and a Thames barge. Tom Dudgeon was invented, so far as can be discovered, for the express purpose of casting off a motor-cruiser full of trippers. But it was a long time before Ransome saw the full significance of the Hullabaloos. It took him some time even to say, tentatively, 'I think perhaps the same motor cruiser with crowd of Hullabaloos should wander in and out from chapter to chapter, so that there is always a danger of Tom being recognised by them. This would give a sort of feeling of outlawry to Tom and in lesser degree to the three pirates.' (pp. 335-36)

He tried out names. What were the Propers to be called? Mary and Jane? (This unimaginative suggestion looks even worse in light of the fact that the same two names were originally those allotted to the Amazons.) Prudence and Grade? ('Prue' and 'Grue'). 'Genia [Ransome's second wife] suggests Dick and Dorothea.' It was of course a brilliantly right suggestion, but it struck no immediate sparks. (p. 336)

He accepted the idea that the Propers should be a boy and a girl ('Prudence and James') but resisted the Callum suggestion. For Dick and Dorothea were not figures who could be allotted minor parts in a moral scheme of the sort he had in mind. Besides, he was trying to make a new departure, to avoid exclusive identification with the Swallows and Amazons. 'Beginning. The Propers in the train from Norwich to Wroxham with in corner of carriage Tom with pot of paint?' In spite of himself, however, the seed began to germinate. He knew and loved the **Winter Holiday** children so well. He began to imagine how they would respond to the Norfolk experience, and how affect it: 'Dorothea enhances the outlawry of Tom for all of them.' (In the end, more subtly, her fantasy just makes Tom uncomfortable.) He jotted down scraps of things they would say: Dorothea, thinking about Tom, 'Nancy would have done just the same.' It dawned on him that the Callums would provide two admirable pairs of eyes for observing the Broads: new to the country, explorers (like the Walkers in *Swallows and Amazons*); and then, a much better theme than the de-civilising

of the Propers, something arising directly out of **Winter Holiday**, something so close to his heart as to set his imagination roaring forward,

Dick's stars      Dorothea
\            /
*Learning sailing*

Let it be Dick and Dorothea, on their way to visit Mrs Barrable (once the webfooted grandmother, now their mother's former teacher), who meet Tom in the train. Let them be desperate to learn to sail because of their exposure to the Swallows and Amazons. Let it be Mrs Barrable's yacht which Tom invades while fleeing from the Hullabaloos. Let the Coots undertake to teach the Callums in return for helping the outlaw. Everything fell into place.

The result was a worthy successor to **Winter Holiday.** If at times it touches greatness, it is for a reason barely to be glimpsed in Ransome's working notes. In the writing, the war between the bird-protector Tom and the motor-cruising Hullabaloos, with their gramophone, radio, yachting-caps and beach-pyjamas, became symbolic of the forces contesting the future of the Broads. The more Ransome detailed the society of the Bure, the Thurne and the Waveney the more clearly he showed that more was at stake than the future of a child-outlaw. The book gained greatly in force since Ransome scrupulously accepted the constraints of chronology and geography. The result was a wonderful picture of the Norfolk waters at a crucial moment of transition. The activities of the RSPB had brought back the bitterns, but the day of the wherry was almost over. The lorry, the radio (later, television), the motor-car, agrarian greed, government policy, sewage and artificial fertilisers were going to do more to undermine the social and natural life of the Broads than Ransome began to guess. In life, the Hullabaloos were going to win. That does not make their defeat in fiction less pleasing; it makes Ransome's scrupulous portrayal of the Broads in 1933 all the more valuable and interesting; and it reminds us that the issues he chose to write about were not trivial: especially not to him. As he had loved the old Russia and the traditional Lake District, so he loved the old Norfolk. *Coot Club* and certain passages of *The Big Six* are his vindication of that love. (pp. 336-38)

[The new book] was to be called **Pigeon Post,** or *The Grubbers,* or *Grubbers All.* (Later on he wanted to call it *High Topps,* but the publishers insisted on the first, best title.) . . . It was largely concerned with mining, and Arthur found that he had a lot to learn. Fortunately there was a friendly expert at hand, Oscar Gnosspelius. . . .

> He had spent much of his life as prospector, in Peru and Africa, and he gallantly threw himself into the business of my prospecting children, lecturing me on gosson, veins, reefs, pyrites and what not, demonstrating, with the tools he had himself used, the methods of panning and washing, and taking me up Weatherlam to make sure of the details of Slater Bob's activities and the ancient tunnels on the hill. . . . [Thanks] to Oscar Gnosspelius, I believe there are no mining errors in the book.

**Pigeon Post** was eventually dedicated to Gnosspelius. But meanwhile Arthur found it impossible to finish. . . . There was to be no Ransome for Christmas in 1935.

The move to Suffolk was immediately followed by what can only be described as an orgy of yachting. . . . It was delightful to be going to sea again, and his happiness gave him the first flash of pure inspiration he had had since beginning *Swallows and Amazons.*

> (*To G. Wren Howard, 15 January 1936*) Spirits here are rising again at last. During the last four days I have seen, grabbed, clutched and pinioned a really gorgeous idea for another book. Swallows only. No Nancy or Peggy or Captain Flint. But a GORGEOUS idea with a first class climax inevitable and handed out on a plate. Lovely new angle of technical approach and everything else I could wish. So I breathe again. I was really afraid I'd done for myself or rather for these stories by uprooting, but I haven't . . . And, here's something to sadden niggards in gold leaf (I name no names), there are EIGHT words in its entirely admirable memorable and inevitable title. . . . . . . EIGHT! Cheer up. Monosyllables only. But eight of the very best.

Actually, there are only seven words in the title of *We Didn't Mean to Go to Sea:* perhaps it was originally *Did Not.* Arthur was not wrong about the excellence of his notion. He made his usual thorough synopsis of the book, finished off the pictures for *Swallowdale,* and then resumed work on *Pigeon Post.* (pp. 344-46)

[*Pigeon Post*] is one of his richest achievements. It is full of lively individual characterisation and fascinating technical detail. It contains a vivid depiction of the impact of drought on the Lake District, to set beside the earlier portrayal of a hard winter. With many slow, small, skilful turns of the screw, it arrives at the terrible climax of fire on the fells. Ransome's hard work was well rewarded. (p. 347)

[The deepest theme of *We Didn't Mean to Go to Sea*] was the tensions that arise between even the nicest children and the most loving parents.

In *We Didn't Mean to Go to Sea* he at last settled accounts with Cyril Ransome. As his letter announcing its conception makes plain, the climax of the turbulent voyage was from the first to be the meeting with the children's father. And so it was carried out. John is very much the hero of the book, and gets his reward for his courage, initiative, steady nerves and good luck when his father, after listening to the tale of his adventures, squeezes his shoulder: '"You'll be a seaman yet, my son." And John, for one dreadful moment, felt that something was going wrong with his eyes. A sort of wetness, and hotness . . . Partly salt . . .' For one dreadful moment it seems that something is going wrong with the book; but the author quickly recovers his usual poise. He can be forgiven his lapse. For his daydream of at last earning and winning the approval that had been so rigidly withheld had at length given him the theme for a book of which Conrad would have been proud.

Ransome brought all his seasoned skill to the job of making his tale of childish heroism plausible: all his knowledge of the land and sea. But the chief instrument of his success is the character of Susan. In earlier books she had always been something of a propitiatory sacrifice: without at least one preternaturally good and domesticated child no one would have believed that the Walkers would have been allowed to become the Swallows, sailing off on adult-free adventures. But in *We Didn't Mean,* Susan, without for a moment ceasing to be herself, is fully human at last, and it is through her seasickness, her anxiety, her fear and tears that the dangers of the night sea

are brought home to the reader. The book belongs to her as much as to her brother, for she overcomes nearly disabling terrors and proves, at last, as reliable a Mate as ever. This was perhaps Ransome's greatest triumph of psychological portraiture; a triumph that as usual he makes seem quite effortless. (pp. 357-58)

*Secret Water,* set in empty Essex marshlands, is the quietest of all the *Swallow* books. It is dedicated to the Busk family, and their yacht *Lapwing* figures prominently in the story, which is largely a distillation of Arthur's happy voyages with them to Hamford Water. Perhaps the opening pages are too quiet: they are some of the most stiffly awkward that Ransome ever wrote. He did not find his form till he had got the Swallows safely marooned on Horsey Island. The technical challenge, even the business of handling a cast of eleven children (the largest number he ever tackled), was not particularly formidable. Considering how children's books are infested by twins (usually identical) it was witty of him to include two brothers, Dum and Dee: 'they're not twins, but everybody thinks they are.' The glory of the book, apart from the Swallows' fall from grace (even Susan ends up a savage, wallowing in the mud), is the character of Bridget. The book belongs to her even more entirely than *Winter Holiday* does to Dorothea. She has her own well-defined point of view, which throws a quite new light on, for example, the characters of Titty and Roger.

> "Don't forget to wash behind your ears," said Roger.
>
> "Used they to say that to you?" said Bridget earnestly, and wondered why Roger grinned a little sheepishly and Susan laughed. . . .

By the end of the book she has decisively established her own position in the family. She seems to have a stronger character than any of the others, except perhaps Susan. Yet she remains very much the young child: her relationship with the kitten Sinbad is particularly well-observed. . . . It is a pity that Ransome never put Bridget in a book again. (pp. 367-68)

[*The Big Six* was a] long-planned detective story, a sequel to *Coot Club.* . . . The book is a true sequel, in that it completes Ransome's picture of Norfolk life, especially in the chapters on night-fishing for eel and on catching a monster pike—the first parts of the book to be written (it also contains cautionary tales on how not to smoke eels and set light to Christmas puddings). The main theme of the book resembles that of *We Didn't Mean to Go to Sea,* for it too concerns the placing on young shoulders of a burden of anxiety and difficulty almost too heavy for them to bear; but the burden is imposed by an enemy, not a father; is shared between three—Joe, Bill and Pete—the whole Coot Club rallies to lift it, and by superior intelligence, devotion and energy, does so. The book is thus a celebration of solidarity, not of individual courage and resourcefulness. The screw of suspense is tightened relentlessly until the very last chapter (if we don't count the postscript on '**What Happened to the Fish**'), indeed almost to the last page. The plot of *The Big Six* is perhaps Ransome's most ingenious contrivance, and the book ought certainly to figure in any list of classics of detective fiction. It also refutes completely the canard that Ransome's stories are only for and about middle-class children. Joe, Bill and Pete, boatbuilders' sons, who speak and think in Norfolk dialect (Ransome's ear for regional speech was excellent), are the heroes of the book even though, unsurprisingly, it is Dorothea who organises the detection and Dick who brings about the villains' destruction with his camera.

They are treated with complete straightforwardness, subtly individualised, with no restraint of the author's characteristic
humour. Ransome grew increasingly fond of the Death-and-
Glories, and his last attempt at fiction for children would again
put them at centre stage. (pp. 377-78)

The secret of [*Missee Lee's*] appeal is Miss Lee herself, even
more than the vivid colours of the Chinese scene. Miss Lee,
every inch a pirate, yet hankering for Cambridge, examinations
and the degree of Bachelor of Arts, is at once a funny, sinister,
touching and, by the end, curiously impressive figure. Her
attempt to have the best of two worlds lands her in many comic
contradictions ('She gripped her Horace as if the book were a
pistol holster and she were about to pull a pistol from it') but
finally, though she makes her choice, of Chinese piracy rather
than Western learning, it is for reasons that the West, in the
persons of the children and Captain Flint, wholly respects, and
at a still deeper level she achieves, it seems, for a moment at
least, the vision of a noble synthesis.

> The old amah was laughing and crying at the
> same time. The counsellor had come slowly
> down from the poop. Running his fingers through
> his beard, he was saying something that sounded
> like a charm.
>
> "What's he saying?" asked Roger.
>
> Miss Lee hesitated a moment. "Vir pietate
> glavis," she said.
>
> "He quotes Confucius. He speaks of duty to a
> father. He is light. My place is here."

Ultimately Miss Lee's passion for both Horace and Confucius
is as enlightening, and as civilised, as Peter Duck's passion
for tall ships and his contempt for the treasure brought back,
at such risk, from Crab Island. He and she stand together as
Arthur Ransome's most thoroughly original, satisfying and
pleasurable human creations. Beside them the children and
Captain Flint seem a little pallid, a little lacking in the vigour
of life. (pp. 381-82)

*Missee Lee* was hardly published before Jonathan Cape began
to hound him for its successor. By Twelfth Night 1942 he was
hard at work, not altogether to his satisfaction.

> (*To Margaret Renold, 6 January*) I am pound-
> ing out the stuff for the new book in the worst
> possible manner, before I'm ready with the story.
> Absolutely damnable. The result will be awful.
> I wish I had a decent yarn in my head. But I
> haven't. . . .

He had announced his new theme to Margaret months before.
(p. 384)

> Subject: I think the Great Aunt of *Swallowdale.*
> Captain Flint takes Mrs Blackett off for a jaunt
> abroad, leaving Nancy and Peggy in charge of
> Beckfoot. Damned good for them. The G.A.,
> hearing this, writes a letter to them refraining
> from giving her opinion of their mother but
> making it very plain, and invites herself to
> Beckfoot to look after them. Now then: WHAT?
> Or have you an immense idea of your own?

When *The Picts and the Martyrs* was published Mrs Renold
wrote to say that although it was full of good things, 'the *reason*
for all the story is a poor one. Great Aunts of that kind must

have died out about 40 years ago. And you make Cook and
her children so convinced that Mrs Blackett is a spineless creature and they have to protect her—I ask you! I don't think
grown-ups are your strong point.' The observation about Great
Aunts is interesting but irrelevant. So far as readers of *Swallowdale* were concerned, Great-Aunt Maria already existed in
full rigour, and poor Mrs Blackett's character was beyond
saving. Arthur was simply exploiting material which he had
not yet used up; and the creator of Black Jake and Missee Lee
was not likely to let mere implausibility stand between him
and a literary project.

Ransome knew quite well what he was about when he planned
*Picts.* His child readers were clamouring for another book about
the lake; he had just returned there; it was good for business
to continue to spring surprises on his public. It seemed entirely
proper to follow up a thrillingly exotic tale with a story about
the quietest of domestic crises; and with Nancy Blackett on
hand, in her first leading role since *Pigeon Post,* there could
be no shortage of excitement. Indeed, although *The Picts and
the Martyrs* was planned as a mere farce, by the end of the
book it had developed a comic life of its own; Nancy, whose
character had come to seem so predictable, had developed new
and interesting traits; and the Great-Aunt herself had become,
for a moment, sympathetic. Her tribute to her niece was well-
earned ('Ruth showed that she possesses much of the tact that
was characteristic of your grandfather'), and so was Timothy's

*Wet and piebald in the doorway. From* The Picts and the
Martyrs: Or, Not Welcome at All, *written and illustrated
by Arthur Ransome. Jonathan Cape, 1959. Reprinted by
permission of Jonathan Cape Ltd, on behalf of the Literary
Estate of Arthur Ransome.*

comment ('I think your Great-Aunt is remarkably like her Great Niece'). Who would have thought that Nancy could ever display tact? The farmer's boy Jacky, another *revenant* from *Swallowdale,* is a delightful character; Dick and Dorothea are, as usual, admirable figures through whose eyes to observe and respond to the action. *The Picts and the Martyrs* is the shortest, and one of the simplest, of the stories; but it is also one of the most immediately enjoyable. (pp. 384-85)

*The Picts and the Martyrs* was finished by the beginning of August, and as usual Arthur decamped, leaving Genia to read the rough draft. . . . On his return to London he found a letter from Genia waiting for him, with her opinion. It was of course unfavourable—immensely so—she had never been ruder about one of his books. 'My dear darling: I am very sorry I am going to hurt you very much—but I don't believe in Fools Paradise or in beating about the bush.' The book was dead, repeating worn-out situations: 'pale imitations of something that happened many times before.' The adventures were spurius, dragged-in, unconvincing, farcical, grown-up affairs. After *Peter Duck, We Didn't Mean to Go to Sea* and *Missee Lee,* even faithful readers would find it dull. . . . Genia was entitled to have a poor opinion of *The Picts,* and entitled to stick to it however many people disagreed with her (though eventually, as with all Arthur's works, she came to think it a masterpiece and to defend it against all criticism). What she was not entitled to do was to try to impose her views on Arthur, not to mention his unlucky publishers.

She might at least have remembered the awful things she had said about *Peter Duck* while it was being written, and how dismissive she had been of *We Didn't Mean to Go to Sea,* and how she had praised *Missee Lee* with faint damns. But she never allowed the expression of her views to be tempered by judgment. She was incapable of understanding that although Arthur's art was a small one, it was genuine; and when an artist has settled upon a subject, has chosen, or been chosen by, an idea, there is no alternative for the wise critic to trusting the artist's instinct and trying to understand where it is leading him. Genia's arguments amounted to an assertion that *The Picts and the Martyrs* should never have been written. Yet today it is clear that, like its predecessors, it has an inevitability about it: it grows out of *Swallowdale* and *Pigeon Post* as naturally as *The Big Six* grew out of *Coot Club;* it is a corrective to *Missee Lee* as *Peter Duck* was a corrective to *Swallowdale.* Genia would have been wise to welcome it as evidence that her husband's talent was still growing and diversifying.

Instead she stopped him in his tracks. For Arthur, the composition of each of his stories was an act of desperate faith in himself; a faith which had been cruelly tested in the course of his life, most of all at its beginning, when his parents had so little belief in him. By taking their tone with him, by stressing his imprudence and incompetence and played-outness, by viewing with alarm, by wallowing in a truly Russian gloom about money and competitors ('Your rivals would be very happy and well justified in saying that you "missed the bus"'), Genia was cutting at the tap-root of his creativity. His anxiety was a light sleeper, even after years of success; it always woke and tormented him while he worked at a story; an attack like this one could only stir it up to raging activity. Besides, of late he had had to drive himself to work in a way that suggests he may have begun at last to tire even of his life-long commitment to writing stories for children. Genia did not have the insight to see that her letter might destroy, not *The Picts and the Martyrs* but its successor. How could Arthur set out to create another book if he had to face this sort of thing when it was finished?

Yet it was all done with such total unconsciousness that one cannot help warming to Genia. She was so obviously devoted to Arthur. 'My dear darling.' Sincerity is always winning. If only she had not been such an abominably bad critic. (pp. 386-88)

Nothing survives to explain [Ransome's] return to story-telling and the Swallows. Nearly two years had passed since the revision of *The Picts and the Martyrs,* more than one since the abandonment of *The River Comes First* [a work he never finished]. Presumably Genia had lifted her veto. Arthur did not yet think he was a spent force. He began again. (p. 402)

The subject [of *Great Northern?*], a fiendish egg-collector's designs on a pair of Great Northern Divers nesting in the Hebrides, verges on the melodramatic; the plot, which pits the Swallows, Amazons and Callums, cruising in the isles, against the egg-collector, seems to be an uneasy conflation of the mode of *Peter Duck* with that of *Coot Club;* and indeed the birds' eggs theme is too like that of *Coot Club* for comfort. Ransome has little or nothing new to say about the children's characters. But he knows his business, and by infinite attention to detail makes his commonplace tale solidly interesting and convincing. If the Hebridean scene does not wholly come to life (Ransome knew it so much less well than he knew the Lake District and East Anglia) the pictures are as good as any in the whole series. The last of all, '**Farewell to the Sea Bear**', showing a boy in a kilt standing on a headland and gazing out to sea, where a white sail slips into the distance, is curiously touching, showing nothing that is described in the text, but much that may be inferred, and symbolising, no doubt unconsciously, an author's farewell to his readers. (pp. 410-11)

> *Hugh Brogan, in his* The Life of Arthur Ransome, *Jonathan Cape, 1984, 456 p.*

---

***OLD PETER'S RUSSIAN TALES*** **(1916)**

### AUTHOR'S COMMENTARY

The stories in this book are those that Russian peasants tell to their children and each other. In Russia hardly anybody is too old for fairy stories, and I have even heard soldiers on their way to the war talking of very wise and very beautiful princesses as they drank their tea by the side of the road. I think there must be more fairy stories told in Russia than anywhere else in the world. In this book are a few of those I like best. I have taken my own way with them more or less, writing them mostly from memory. They, or versions of them, are to be found in the coloured chap-books, in Afanasiev's great collection, or in solemn, serious volumes of folklorists' writing for the learned. My book is not for the learned, or indeed for grown-up people at all. No people who really like fairy stories ever grow up altogether. ⟨p. 9⟩

> *Arthur Ransome, in a note to his* Old Peter's Russian Tales, *1916. Reprint by Puffin Books, 1974, pp. 9-10.*

---

Quite rightly for his purpose, Mr. Ransome does not worry about sources, and he tells his tales with the skill belonging to an experienced man of letters, writing far away in Russia in view of a forest where Old Peter sits at night and talks to his grandchildren. We like particularly **"The Cat Who Became Head-Forester"** and **"Little Master Misery",** who is not unknown in this country.

"Russian Tales," in The Saturday Review, London, Vol. 122, No. 3189, December 9, 1916, p. x.*

**"Old Peter's Russian Tales"** are of the same type as Mr. Donald Mackenzie's ["Stories of Russian Folk-Life"], but they are better told. Information regarding Russian life is given in a playful manner, the samovar is described, the smell of the smoke of peasants' tobacco is suggested. The tales, though they are second-rate literary matter, should read aloud well. The feeling is that the author is having a pleasant relaxation.

"Russian Legend and History," in The Times Literary Supplement, No. 778, December 14, 1916, p. 607.*

The stories have many counterparts in other folklore and are well told with humorous touches. They differ enough from familiar versions to give novelty to old plots and they have plots which are new to our children.

A review of "Old Peter's Russian Tales," in The Booklist, Vol. 14, No. 3, December, 1917, p. 101.

Right from the start, it seems that Arthur Ransome had no doubts as to how to write for children. . . .

[Old Peter] tells traditional fairy tales to entertain his two grandchildren. Vanya and Maroosia, Old Peter's "two pigeons", provide the reader with a link between the known world of childhood and the fantastic world of princes and princesses, of speaking animals and magic tablecloths. They can be relied upon to hurry Old Peter along, and to ask pertinent questions when a new character turns up. . . . (p. 58)

Like all good fairy stories, these tales have their share of gruesome happenings, wicked stepmothers, cruel brothers and sisters and wistful, downtrodden heroes. They veer abruptly from gaiety to sadness and back again. . . . Underlying the stories is another essential ingredient of a good folk tale: a powerful morality, based on the notion that God will help the meek and that a good heart is worth more than beauty or brains. (pp. 58-9)

Mary Anne Bonney, in a review of "Old Peter's Russian Tales," in Punch, Vol. 286, No. 7468, January 18, 1984, pp. 58-60.

### THE SOLDIER AND DEATH: A RUSSIAN FOLK TALE TOLD IN ENGLISH (1920)

On the wrapper we are informed that it is a "merry" Russian folk-tale. . . . [The] tale, though amusing, is lightly touched with grimness. An allegorical signification—a somewhat involved one—possibly lies beneath the plain narrative—that war is eternal, and so the man-at-arms can never pass away. The general characteristics of the healthy-minded European soldier are well delineated; he reminds the reviewer somewhat of Denis in *The Cloister and the Hearth*. But he commits unpardonable sins, one against Heaven and the other against Hell, and so he is obliged to stay upon the earth. The devil refuses him admittance to his underworld when he descends and tells him that he is "a sinful soul come to you to be stewed in the boiling pitch." . . . [To] find out exactly why he is refused admittance [to heaven] you must read this queer and admirable little book. It all comes of having once imprisoned Death in a magic sack so that for a short time nobody had been able to pass out of the world. The allegorical meaning will baffle many readers. Mr. Arthur Ransome . . . has done his work admirably.

A review of "The Soldier and Death: A Russian Folk-Tale," in New Statesman, Vol. XX, No. 514, February 17, 1923, p. 582.

Mr. Ransome has told with fine artistry a satirical Russian peasant folktale, preserving in the simplicity of his English the exotic native atmosphere. The story, ebullient and unsophisticated in its humor, is quite unrelated to what we conceive to be the prevailing mood of Russian literary expression. As simple and delightful as any of Andersen's fairy tales, this droll and merry story should have wide popularity among children and their elders.

A review of "The Soldier and Death," in The Outlook, Vol. 133, No. 15, April 11, 1923, p. 668.

[Parents] and relatives will probably buy [this little volume] in large numbers and so they should; and it should have a place in the primary school class library and the children's section anywhere. Dr. Ransome has resurrected a Russian story which came to his knowledge nearly forty years ago. . . . As the foreword points out, it is a slightly disturbing, not a pretty tale, and will thus provide something beyond entertainment for junior readers. It has tragic elements which raise it above the bed-time story-book level and it should be possible to read it again and again without getting tired of it. "A soldier served God and the Great Tzar for twenty-five years, earned three dry biscuits, and set off to walk his way home," is its opening sentence and it sets the right note of expectation for the experienced fairy-tale enthusiast, but he will find himself continually surprised at the turn of events, at the ending most of all. The whole has a depth of colour quite different from anything in the fairy stories we popularly perpetuate and degrade.

A review of "The Soldier and Death," in The Junior Bookshelf, Vol. 27, No. 1, January, 1963, p. 26.

**The Soldier and Death** is one of those universal tales of life and death which can only be re-written with real personal force. Ransome tells this Russian folk-tale in a style that is easy, direct and colloquial but with great dignity in its homeliness. The combination of the exotic grandeur of Tsarist Russia and the naïve simplicity of a humble soldier is given full measure in the text. . . . [This is] a fine piece of literature.

Margery Fisher, in a review of "The Soldier and Death," in her Growing Point, Vol. 1, No. 8, March, 1963, p. 120.

### SWALLOWS AND AMAZONS (1930)

#### AUTHOR'S COMMENTARY

1929 was for me the year of crisis, a hinge year as it were, joining and dividing two quite different lives. It was the year in which, at last, I felt myself released from the obligation to go on with the work that had come to me with the war. Feeling free from that obligation I seem to have run amuck with liberty. To refuse a career offered by the *Manchester Guardian* must have seemed to [editor] C. P. Scott something very like sacrilege. (p. 330)

C.P.S. told me that . . . I was to go to Berlin as resident correspondent. This was exactly what I wished to avoid. It was one thing to get a telegram asking for a leading article on some subject I was supposed to know something about. It would be quite another thing to be tied to a newspaper office. . . . I went home to share a decision that would affect my wife as much as myself, and we foresaw that if I were to accept that offer I should once again be hopelessly involved in controversial politics, which of all things I most loathed, and that, if I were again to become so involved, I should never be able to get out. By March 19 Evgenia and I had made up our minds and I gave three months' notice to the *Manchester Guardian.* . . . On March 24, after a couple of days' sailing, with a weight off my shoulders but with no prospects whatever, I began the writing of *Swallows and Amazons.*

I had for some time been growing intimate with a family of imaginary children. I had even sketched out the story of two boats in which my four (five including the baby) were to meet another two, Nancy and Peggy, who had sprung to life one day when, sailing on Coniston, I had seen two girls playing on the lake-shore. For once I had without difficulty shaped the tale into scenes and even found the chapter-headings. The whole book was clear in my head. I had only to write it, but dreaded the discovery that after all these years of writing discursively I was unable to write narrative. I well remember the pleasure I had in the first chapter, and my fear that it would also be the last. I could think of nothing else and grudged every moment that had to be given to other activities. I wrote on plain paper with holes along one edge, so that the sheets could be clipped into a loose-leaf quarto binding. Night after night I used to bring it in a small attaché case from my workroom in the old barn to the cottage, so that I could reach out and lay my hand on it in the dark beside my bed. When I had fifty pages in that loose cover I felt that I had gone so far with it that this time I should be able to write the whole story. (pp. 330-31)

I took the complete typescript to London. I hardly liked to let it out of my hands. I had a hope, just half a hope, that this time, at long last, I had stumbled on the way to write my sort of book. Fifteen years had passed since last I had written a story long enough to be called a book. Seven years had passed since *Racundra's First Cruise,* and that had been matter of fact and not fiction. *Rod and Line* had been a book about fishing. My books about Russia and China had been political, so that I never counted them as books at all. If I could not write stories now, I should never write them and must count myself a failure. *Swallows and Amazons* was to settle my fate. (pp. 334-35)

*Arthur Ransome, in his* The Autobiography of Arthur Ransome, *edited by Rupert Hart-Davis, Jonathan Cape, 1976, 368 p.*

———————

The novel-reader must cast off some of his days and be aged anything from ten to twelve years to get the most enjoyment out of *Swallows and Amazons.* The outward aspect of the book, with its attractive map-wrapper, will please the grown-up eye and may raise an expectation that the children in it are psychologically studied for adult reading. But the child-reader will be delighted to find nothing so uninteresting to him as child-psychology, and the things that do interest him treated on a real and serious plane. The ideal reader should certainly be not too old for make-believe about a miniature desert-island—well in reach of both the mainland and an understandingly nautical mother—but old enough to appreciate some practical advice to desert-islanders about boats, tents and camp-fire cooking.

*Proteus, in a review of "Swallows and Amazons," in* New Statesman, *Vol. XXXV, No. 907, August 2, 1930, p. 542.*

Mr. Ransome's book can be guaranteed to make any family long to imitate the adventures of the Walkers. . . . Yet, provided that the island can be found, there is no reason why any seaworthy child should not do as the Walkers did. One of the great charms of the book is its extreme reasonableness. Mr. Ransome is as thoughtful of detail as Defoe: he tells how tents were made, how pike (the sharks of those waters) were scaled, how meals were cooked, and leading lights set above the tiny harbour. The only thing that he does not give away is the whereabouts of Wild Cat Island. . . . His book, which has no particular plot, is simply the story of a long game of exploration and battle, played by the four Walkers with their invaders, Peggy and Nancy. . . . The chapter headings, **"A Peak in Darien," "The Arrow with the Green Feather," "The Battle in Houseboat Bay,"** and **"Skull and Crossbones,"** give some idea of the ingredients of the book, whose quality is excellent.

*Barbara Euphan Todd, "Parents Beware!" in* The Spectator, *Vol. 145, No. 5333, September 13, 1930, p. 358.**

So it seems that Able-Seaman Titty was right all the time about the treasure. . . . When they got the trunk open it held not exactly ingots; that was disappointing. But Captain Flint took it seriously enough—it was the manuscript of the book he had been writing all summer and the journals that he had kept for years and years.

Arthur Ransome has written a new kind of a book. . . .

[This] book, which tells a story not beyond the bounds of possibility, manages to get . . . the thrill and zest of romantic adventure.

Of course, I was skeptical at first. Could children handle a boat and be as levelheaded and as unquarrelsome as these? A friend who sailed a boat near the Cape as a little girl, assures me that it is perfectly possible for children to behave as these children do—in regard to their boat, that is. I should be inclined to put in at least three more barked shins and perhaps a mosquito bite or two. They are pretty nice children. I'm glad Uncle Arthur got back his manuscript and published the book.

*Genevieve Taggard, "Certainly Not Duffers," in* New York Herald Tribune Books, *March 15, 1931, p. 8.*

This is a most enjoyable tale. . . .

Nowhere does the story exceed the bounds of possibility. One of the most lifelike characters is an understanding mother, who . . . knows how to suggest and keep in touch, without interfering or breaking the spell of the game.

This is a book for almost any age. Boys and girls from 9 to 12 are absorbed in the story, while for adults it is like watching, from another room and unobserved, delightful and natural children at play.

*Anne T. Eaton, in a review of "Swallows and Amazons," in* The New York Times Book Review, *April 5, 1931, p. 18.*

It is easily imaginable that **"Swallows and Amazons"** attained its special quality of happiness in its author's mind when . . . he was living through the tragedies of the Front or exploring the chaos of revolutionary Russia. For here is everything that the Front was not and that Russia is not—peace, innocence, family life at its loveliest, laughter and security.

The story is plotted so slightly that the American boy, reared on "westerns," may turn up his nose at such a low-pitched tale. It will be his loss. . . .

Mr. Ransome has marshalled many aides. First, a reality of scene. As in Defoe, no detail is too insignificant to gloss over, yet the itemizing never grows wearisome, and a store of handy things to know about sailing is secreted in the pages. Second, a reality of characters. They are born alive and do not have to be described.

**"Swallows and Amazons"** will gain by being read aloud. The child who hears will live gaily, whether on Wild Cat Island or in Octopus Lagoon, while the parent who reads will remember idyllic hours. For this book is both silvery present and golden retrospect. All that is tedious and sullen and deceptive vanishes in its sunniness as clouds vanish in the tempered air of a summer day. The reader has only one dread—that some quarrel, some calamity may mar the course of things, inasmuch as they are so human. But the spell lasts. And we think that the book will last, too, from edition unto edition.

> *T. Morris Longstreth, in a review of "Swallows and Amazons," in* The Saturday Review of Literature, *Vol. VII, No. 42, May 9, 1931, p. 820.*

One of the most famous adventures in children's literature begins when John, Susan, Titty, and Roger Walker sail their borrowed boat, the *Swallow,* to an island in the English Lake District and camp there alone for the summer holidays. . . . In its first chapters the "Swallows" are introduced in swift, sure strokes. A little later Nancy and Peggy Blackett, the owners of the *Amazon,* are depicted with the same economy. . . .

Susan, Roger, and Peggy are lesser characters than John, Nancy, and Titty and serve as foils to the other three. . . .

The real heroine of *Swallows and Amazons* is Titty. (Her name, unfortunately a funny one to modern children, is probably short for Elizabeth.) Imaginative, sensitive, yet just as competent as the others, Titty is the one who brings along *Robinson Crusoe* because "'it tells you just what to do on an island.'" . . . In the whole series the times of greatest emotion center on her, as happens in this book when she blinks back tears, watching her mother leave the island. If moral John is the head of *Swallows and Amazons,* and active Nancy the hands, Titty is the heart. (p. 601)

Captain Flint's boyish enthusiasms, rotund figure, and adventurous sailing life as well as his writing profession obviously reflect Ransome himself. It is as if the author were physically present in the story, and this presence welds him all the more to the reader.

So pervasive is the Lake District landscape in *Swallows and Amazons* that it becomes a character as well. . . .

The landscape is also represented in the illustrations. Flat perspectives—calm bodies of water broken by the perpendicular masts of boats and the rounded presences of the fells—evoke the region perfectly. Early editions of the books were sometimes illustrated by other people, but the most suitable artist has always been the author himself. He excused the non-professionalism of his pictures by stating that they were done by Nancy Blackett. But, like Hugh Lofting's illustrations for the *Doctor Dolittle* books (Lippincott), the amateur quality of the drawings is appropriate to their directness and simplicity. (p. 602)

The label "holiday adventure" has stuck to the series so persistently that later critics have tended to ignore the complex imaginative structure underneath the realistic surface of the books. The greatest difference between Ransome and his many imitators is that in his books the children's freedom is not only physical but creative. In both cases it is a limited, and therefore cogent, freedom—physically very protected and imaginatively consisting not of irrelevant pretending but of mirroring adult roles. (p. 603)

The protected physical freedom is enriched by the characters' creative freedom. In the early books the children are always playing games. Some are private, such as Titty's pretending to be a cormorant, but the important ones involve everyone. The games are intrinsically connected to the action and form the theme of each book. Thus, in *Swallows and Amazons,* the children are neither playing at being sailors and explorers in an urban backyard nor simply sailing and camping in an outdoor setting. They are really sailing but, at the same time, pretending to be sailors.

In the first book transition to what the children call their real life is subtly achieved. As soon as the telegram arrives, the Walkers make up the "Ship's Articles" with John as the master, Susan the mate, Titty the able seaman, and Roger the ship's boy. For the rest of the series the children never waver from their established roles. It becomes so natural to hear someone refer to Captain John or to answer "Aye, aye, sir" that the reader forgets the children are playing a game. Significantly, after these roles are set, Ransome never again refers to his characters as the children. (p. 604)

*Swallows and Amazons* begins and ends in a leisurely manner. . . . The love that Ransome felt for the book—he describes in *Autobiography* . . . how he kept the manuscript by his bed so he could reach out and touch it in the dark [see excerpt above in the Author's Commentary for this title]—is evident in this lingering; but sometimes it becomes self-indulgent. After Titty's capture of the *Amazon,* finding the "treasure" seems anti-climactic, and there is a sense of the author not wanting the story to end.

Ransome has been criticized for always depicting middle-class children privileged enough to be able to have holidays and to sail their own boats. But surely the appeal of *Swallows and Amazons* lies in the fact that the reader is also offered this chance, however vicariously. In a time when it is unsafe for many children to walk to school alone, the characters' independence might be even more of an attraction. And it is unlikely that even in safer times many children could have experienced the liberty granted to the Walkers and the Blacketts, protected as it is. Perhaps Ransome's characters have always been idealized—because they are so civilized. Their resourcefulness, good humor, and self-reliance are shown so convincingly that these qualities become possibilities. Ransome depicts them behaving as other children would like to think they would behave, given the same freedom.

The endearing characteristics of *Swallows and Amazons* are not dated. Now there is an even stronger interest in the outdoor pursuits of which the author was such an advocate. And Ransome, an enthusiastic collector of folk tales, was a master of the elements of story. His straightforward prose and suspenseful plots still carry most of the books forward, despite their length.

Ransome devotees, both children and adults, share an incurable addiction; they recognize one another with a nostalgic look and an instant desire to talk about their favorite characters. Probably the series will never regain its former popularity. But for those children who experience the magic of *Swallows and Amazons,* it must be as exhilarating now as it was thirty years ago to discover that there are eleven more books waiting to be read. (pp. 604-05)

Kit Pearson, "A Second Look: 'Swallows and Amazons'," in The Horn Book Magazine, Vol. LIX, No. 5, October, 1983, pp. 601-05.

### SWALLOWDALE  (1931)

For the second time Mr. Arthur Ransome has opened a door for us, and we defy anyone not to be enchanted when he has slipped through into the world of the author's creating. . . . The story continues the adventures of John, Susan, Titty and Roger, nice ordinary children with an extraordinarily sensible mother. . . . The story is crowded with useful hints on sailing and camping; is exciting but not sensational, funny but never ludicrous; in fact it is a perfect book for children of all ages, and better reading for the rest of us than are most novels. Above all, the children talk as children do talk, and the plot is excellent.

"Magic Doorways," in The Spectator, Vol. 147, No. 5397, December 5, 1931, p. 788.*

"Swallowdale," like its predecessor, "Swallows and Amazons," meets the test of a good book for children, for it can be read with pleasure by adults as well as boys and girls. There is something entirely convincing and satisfying in the businesslike way in which the author sets to work to describe the second Summer that Captain John, Mate Susan, Able Seaman Titty and Ship's Boy Roger spend camping on Wild Cat Island. The book has the sincerity of natural, unspoiled children, playing in their own way and quite forgetful of the grown-up world. One guesses the author to be one of those rare adults who can meet children on their own ground without making them self-conscious. He knows boys and girls, and in his chronicle of the doings and sayings of the Swallows and the Amazons, whether they are pirates or sailors or explorers or, for a brief period, merely themselves, there are no false notes.

The book is full of adventure, not artificial excitement, but the kind that a child who has not been too much interfered with will find for himself anywhere, though, in this instance, an island for camping, a sail boat and a sympathetic and sensible mother furnish an ideal starting point for imaginative play. Another charm of the book is the background. Adults consciously, and children unconsciously, will feel the beauty of lake and waterfall, of the lovely hidden valley which is the Swallowdale of the story, of brook and moorland and distant hills, all of them forming part of the story, never serving as mere decorative details.

Anne T. Eaton, in a review of "Swallowdale," in The New York Times Book Review, February 14, 1932, p. 13.

There is something very appealing about the simple daily activities of a family of boys and girls, and when these are related with simplicity and a childlike heed to detail a book of enduring charm is sure to be the result. It is this quality that Mr. Ransome has succeeded in giving his two books . . . which relate the summer adventures of the Swallows and the Amazons. . . .

The description of camp routine, climbing Kanchenjunga, getting lost in the fog and finally, when Swallow is repaired, the race with Amazon makes up the book. But it is all so natural that after reading a few pages you find yourself transported to Wild Cat Island, and if you have never camped you are determined to do so at the first possible opportunity. The children give the most fascinating names to all of the important places on the island—and all of the places *are* important—and they never fail to call them by these names. This constantly keeping in character is half of the fascination of the book.

Any one over seven and under seventy who loves the real country will enjoy the book and it is an excellent read-aloud book for various ages.

Pauline Sutorius Aird, "Camping Out: 'Swallowdale'," in New York Herald Tribune Books, Vol. 8, No. 25, February 28, 1932, p. 8.

### PETER DUCK  (1932)

#### AUTHOR'S COMMENTARY

In *Peter Duck* the pictures were supposed to have been made by the children themselves to illustrate the story they had themselves invented, so the bad drawing did not matter very much, and at least one of the drawings, Roger's picture of a night scene, which was perfectly black all over, was quite easy. This was the beginning of what afterwards became a habit. I had much disliked the excellent drawings made by professional artists for the earlier books because, though very good drawings, they did not seem to me to illustrate the stories but were merely skilful exercises by accomplished technicians. After the *Peter Duck* experiment, Cape suggested that in future I should be my own illustrator. . . . I have been ever since, and my bad drawings have come to seem part of the books, as indeed they are. In the end I did pictures for the first two books as well, and must admit that I have had a great deal of pleasure out of doing so, though the actual process would have been much less painful if at an earlier age I had learnt how to draw. Of course I have always had Nancy Blackett to take some of the blame for my scratchy line and uncertain anatomy. (p. 344)

Arthur Ransome, in his The Autobiography of Arthur Ransome, edited by Rupert Hart-Davis, Jonathan Cape, 1976, 368 p.

Mr. Ransome's children have a wonderful adventure, but that is nothing because innumerable people engaged in the mass production of "literature" for the young are constantly imposing incredible adventures on incredible children. What matters is that the captains and mates who sailed away in the *Wild Cat* to the Carribees and were chased by Black Jake in his piratical *Viper* are ordinary, everyday, real children, yours and mine. Mr. Ransome does not give them surnames, or say who their parents are or where they live; he does not even trouble to describe them. But I have lived with them as they worked the schooner under Captain Flint and Peter Duck from Lowestoft to Crab Island and back. It all seemed natural enough, one thing just led to another as it does when one lives it. It was only by harking back to literature when the fun was over that I began to realise the rarity of Mr. Ransome's achievement. . . . Peter Duck should be good for many a Christmas. . . .

*Barrington Gates, in a review of "Peter Duck," in* The New Statesman & Nation, *n.s. Vol. IV, No. 94, December 10, 1932, p. 754.*

[The] effect which this book has on the reader [is that of] making us . . . wish to go a-sailing. It brings that nostalgia for deep water and wind and spray which drags so fiercely at the heartstrings. . . .

The story contains all the ingredients necessary to make it not only eminently readable, but also thrilling enough to satisfy the most exacting of tastes.

*"The Call of the Sea," in* The Saturday Review, *London, Vol. 154, No. 4027, December 31, 1932, p. 702.*

**"Peter Duck"** is the only third book in a series for children that is actually better than the first one. . . .

[The chase between Peter Duck and the bad man, Black Jake, is on] through fog and adventure, including earthquakes convincing as anything that happened on the comparatively placid northern lake. It is very moral adventure, and Black Jake's crew come to a satisfactory end, but even a grown-up is likely to keep reading till their fate is settled.

It would be hard to find more lovable examples of "escape literature" for children than these *Swallow* stories. It is possible to begin with any of them. These children of Mr. Ransome's series are in children's literature to stay. They live by virtue not only of what happens to them, but by the fair play and basal kind heartedness with which they meet whatever happens.

*May Lamberton Becker, in a review of "Peter Duck," in* New York Herald Tribune Books, *May 7, 1933, p. 7.*

Readers who enjoyed (as who did not?) the author's delightful **"Swallows and Amazons"** and **"Swallowdale"** will be quick to welcome a third volume dealing with the same boys and girls. . . . The adventures are very clearly those which the Amazons and Swallows had always hoped to have; as the author describes them they are completely convincing. Mr. Ransome is one of those rare authors who can write for children and about children at the same time. He has also accomplished the exceptional feat of writing three books about the same characters and keeping all three stories on the same high level of excellence.

Possibly boys and girls will prefer **"Peter Duck"** because the adventures will seem to them more grown up and more dangerous, though for adults **"Swallows and Amazons,"** with the imaginative Titty playing Robinson Crusoe when she is left alone on the island, and Roger, soberly tacking across the field like a sailboat, will still be the favorite volume. The author's fine prose style is a delight.

*Anne T. Eaton, in a review of "Peter Duck," in* The New York Times Book Review, *May 14, 1933, p. 10.*

What an incredible, hilarious voyage this is—six children, two adults and a young castaway aboard a trim schooner bound for a treasure island in the Caribbean. Alternate chills and chuckles accompany the reading of their mad adventure. . . . Peter Duck, being a seagoing man, maintains throughout a philosophic aloofness to treasures, but Captain Flint is so engrossed in treasure hunting and so oblivious to all danger that timorous, non-seagoing parents might question his guardianship of six

children. Yet having met these children before we know that they can cope successfully with all problems, from preparing pemmican to hoisting sail. Swallows and Amazons forever! We feel a tiny regret that in this third book of Swallows and Amazons the children are sometimes eclipsed by the adults, yet we can forgive Arthur Ransome anything for having put into a book one of our secret desires, a successful trip to treasure island!

*Eleanor Herrmann, in a review of "Peter Duck," in* Library Journal, *Vol. 58, No. 17, October 1, 1933, p. 804.*

---

***WINTER HOLIDAY*** (1933)

Those who read **"Peter Duck"** last year have been looking forward eagerly to Mr. Ransome's next story; and we can promise them that they will not be disappointed. . . . [**"Winter Holiday"**] differs from that enchanting story in one important particular. In last year's book the children had an adventure which every grown-up person would say could not have happened to them in present-day life. It is true that it was related with such convincing realism that only a grown-up who had never been a child could fail to be carried away by it when actually reading the book. . . . But no one can say that **"Winter Holiday"** is improbable. It is about some boys and girls who were spending a part of the Christmas holidays near one of the English lakes, and who were detained for an extra month by quarantine for mumps. Every parent of schoolchildren will recognize the severe realism of the details about health certificates. Yet it is full of a strange glamour which imaginative people of all ages will feel. In reading it we see the landscape and the events through the eyes of the characters in the book. Young readers will find themselves taking part in signalling to the Martians and going to the North Pole, and old readers will be carried back in their minds to those wonderful games of childhood when the whole world of everyday things was doubled with another more glorious world into which they could transport themselves at a moment's notice and in which they led a heroic life. Miss Nancy Blackett's charming illustrations contribute a great deal to the fascination of the book; she is herself one of the characters in the story, and makes us see how things looked to them. One could hardly have a better story about children.

*"Stories about Children," in* The Times Literary Supplement, *No. 1660, November 23, 1933, p. 834.\**

[The] two best books of children's fiction this year are as they were last, the new Lofting and the new Ransome. . . . Mr. Ransome's style is highly distinguished, his narrative hair-raising, credible, and amusing, and . . . his book is (as last year) far the best story produced for the Christmas pleasure of boys or girls in their teens.

*A review of "Winter Holiday," in* The Spectator, *Vol. 151, No. 5501, December 1, 1933, p. 818.*

[**"Winter Holiday"** affords] bracing entertainment for all who are or have been actively young.

The wonder is that these *Swallows and Amazons* books not only keep up so well but manage to convince their public that they get steadily better. . . .

[Readers of **"Winter Holiday"**] will have a sharp shock on the first page; happily it will be brief. There is not a sign of Swallows or Amazons. Instead, in the familiar countryside, now under snow, we meet two children nobody ever heard of before: Dick and Dorothea. To be sure, they are right; related, not too distantly, to the Bastables. Dick is an astronomer. He has a spyglass—I mean telescope—and a notebook. . . .

Dorothea is a novelist. Both take their life-works with the absorbed seriousness ten-years-old reserves for work it does not have to do—in other words, the right kind of play. Naturally they use their scientific equipment to signal Mars—or, as crass outsiders might call it, a house at some distance in the snow. To their delight, Mars responds. It is—ah, this is something like—it is inhabited by Captain John Walker, of the *Swallow,* Nancy Blackett, Mate of the *Amazon,* and the entire ship's company of either craft. Before the end of the holiday even Captain Flint has joined the party. Meanwhile, an igloo has been built and lived in, elaborate signal codes devised, a crag-fast sheep (polar bear) rescued, and the deep purpose of the season, an expedition to the North Pole, successfully brought off by heroic and sustained efforts.

There is something beautifully, satisfyingly lasting about all this. I shall not soon forget the moment in an earlier volume when a like enterprise had just been accomplished—the ascent of Kanchenjunga. People over fourteen might fall into the vulgar error of thinking this a lake country hill, but while there is the Everest expedition to read about and intrepid children to put it instantly into action, Kanchenjunga it is. . . .

I believe that if these books about Swallows and Amazons live—and I cannot imagine their not living a long time—it will be because they lay hold on the underlying continuity of imaginative play, the heartfelt constructive make-believe that carries childhood along from one generation to another. . . .

> *May Lamberton Becker, in a review of "Winter Holiday," in* New York Herald Tribune Books, *March 18, 1934, p. 9.*

["**Winter Holiday**"] seems to indicate that Mr. Ransome will be able to go on indefinitely keeping us informed of the doings of this enterprising group of young people. This is no sequel written for the sake of adding another volume to a series. It reads as though the author had further information to share with us about the adventures of these very real boys and girls, adventures which have such a sustained and consistent quality of imagination that the reader, like the children of the story, is all but convinced that the make-believe is real. . . .

In this as in his other stories Arthur Ransome has caught completely the spirit of imaginative play. His characters have the entire absorption in what they are doing, the complete lack of self-consciousness and the independence of intelligent, unspoiled children who are left alone to use their imagination and to exercise their ingenuity without too much supervision. Yet one feels that the adults in the story supply a background of genuine understanding that comes from a sense of humor and a lively recollection of their own youth. There is zest in the way Mr. Ransome tells a story and some excellent characterization in the portraits of the eight children. Dorothea and Dick, who have something of the engaging qualities of Titty and Roger, are worthy additions to the original half dozen.

"**Winter Holiday**," like its predecessors, is an outdoor story. It is full of the feeling of frosty air, snow-covered slopes with blue cloud shadows, of short Winter afternoons, stars at night, frozen brooks and snowy woods and clearings. The author shares with the reader his own enjoyment of well-known and well-loved country; in addition it is a rare pleasure to find a book written for children with real charm of style.

> *Anne T. Eaton, in a review of "Winter Holiday," in* The New York Times Book Review, *April 15, 1934, p. 12.*

---

## *COOT CLUB* (1934)

I was delighted to find the hero has the courage to cast off the moorings of a motor launch full of beastly people and to set it adrift. Unfortunately this wicked action is universally condoned, and worse still is prompted by a higher morality in the boy. He risks running the launch aground for the sake of a nest of hatching coots who have been disturbed by the B.B.C. programmes. However it is technically lawless and a good beginning. . . . Compared with the three earlier books (**Peter Duck** is in a class by itself), **Coot Club** is as flat and monotonous, yet almost as charming, as the country through which the Coots sail. . . . [In] spite of the hateful Hullabaloos hunting Tom Dudgeon through the book, there is an extraordinary peacefulness about the story. Mr. Ransome has described sluggish broads, the excitement of watching the crested grebes, dabchicks, and divers, of hearing the bittern and the grasshopper warbler, and the strangeness of seeing the distant sails tacking about, as it seems, across the land, as well as he described the feeling of Westmorland in **Swallowdale**. It is this feeling for country rather than the feeling for children which always makes me read each of Mr. Ransome's books before Christmas, although I know that I shall have to start reading it aloud on Boxing Day. Mr. Ransome plunges his readers into a dreamlike world, where all is better ordered, luckier and pleasanter than life. The world he describes has more in common with Mrs. Ewing's *Hector* than with Richard Jefferies' *Bevis.* Jefferies makes his boys quarrel and sulk. They are individuals whose characters develop as they grow up, and are powerful enough to influence us for the whole of our lives. The Swallows and the Amazons never change. I have always felt that their delightful adventures, perhaps the chief of which came from having Captain Flint as an uncle, were wasted on them. Thus I am glad that the whole crowd of them has gone. There were too many of them and they were not passionate enough. An admirable innovation in **Coot Club** is that village boys appear and at moments talk their own language. Perhaps in a future volume Mr. Ransome will describe the contact of the wild children of the Westmorland farms, clattering over the rocks in their clogs, and riding ponies bare-back, with some thoughtful little star-gazer like Dick.

> *David Garnett, in a review of "Coot Club," in* The New Statesman & Nation, *n.s. Vol. VIII, No. 198, December 8, 1934, p. 867.*

[Mr. Arthur Ransome develops] a tale which must have a catholic appeal to all young readers. He knows about every class of craft that sails the Broads. . . . [By the end of the book, Dick and Dorothea have] learnt a good deal about life in sail—and Mr. Ransome's readers will have done the same.

*Coot Club* . . . is as good as anything Mr. Ransome has done, and he gives full measure: 350 pages, with numerous sketches, as usual by himself. Perhaps his success as a writer for young people is due to the fact that he takes his readers more seriously than the authors of most "juveniles" do; for in reality he is a children's novelist, and has the peculiar quality of being able to reveal children to themselves.

*A review of "Coot Club," in* The Times Literary Supplement, *No. 1715, December 13, 1934, p. 894.*

In each of the Ransome stories some continuous enterprise carries the action, whether in climbing Kanchenjunga . . . or pushing an expedition to the Pole. **"Coot Club"** puts these adventures life-sized into the actual life of its children; this is its chief point of departure from the rest of the series.

*May Lamberton Becker, in a review of "Coot Club," in* New York Herald Tribune Books, *September 15, 1935, p. 8.*

Arthur Ransome's latest book is noteworthy for more than one reason. Like all the best books written for children it can be enjoyed by grown-ups. Indeed, it will probably be impossible for any adult interested in boys and girls, addicted to sailing, and fond of outdoor life, to lay down **"Coot Club."** . . . Not only is **"Coot Club"** as delightful a story as one could wish, it is also—and this, if we did not know what Mr. Ransome can do, would be perhaps the most surprising thing about it— the fifth of a group of books dealing with the same characters, and a fifth book that has all the freshness and spontaneity of the first one. In fact, in some respects, **"Coot Club"** is the best of the five. . . .

There is humor and fine characterization in the book, down to William the pug, who is a dog to be remembered. Mrs. Barrable, the artist hostess, is as convincingly real as she is delightful. In fact, with such sensible and understanding grownups for parents and friends one does not wonder that the young people in Mr. Ransome's books are a thoroughly satisfactory lot. The drawings by the author and Helene Carter are attractive and enlightening. A book that ten-to-twelve-year-olds should not miss.

*Anne T. Eaton, in a review of "Coot Club," in* The New York Times Book Review, *October 6, 1935, p. 10.*

---

### PIGEON POST (1936)

All the really good books specially written for boys and girls are variations on the theme of *Bevis* and the best and the most popular of such books being written now are those by Arthur Ransome. . . . *Pigeon Post* appeals to me far more than *Peter Duck* . . . or *Coot Club*. There is a certain loyalty in our hearts which makes us delighted to meet John and Susan and Titty and Roger once more. . . .

[The] children in Mr. Ransome's books are always perfectly well-behaved. They never quarrel or fight or take each other's things, or break any of the rules. Victorian children were always being naughty and on that account were frequently convincingly alive. Mr. Ransome no doubt hopes by describing such unnatural perfection to win as much liberty for his young readers as the Swallows and Amazons prove themselves worthy to enjoy; he is anxious to conciliate fussy parents, but there is a danger that he may encourage priggishness. Apart from this the chief criticism I have to make is that he has collected all his characters together in one big camp . . . and that it is difficult to keep track of what each of eight children is doing. The succession of adventures and of difficulties to be overcome is excellent. The chief features of *Pigeon Post* are the homing pigeons which keep Mrs. Blackett away from the camp—though I am sorry to say she does visit it—and which summon the aid of the fire-fighters when a great conflagration sweeps over the

fells, and the hunt for gold in all the old mine-workings with which the fells are honeycombed. There is an interlude of water-dowsing and the digging and building of a well which enables them to camp on the edge of High Topps instead of in the valley beneath; a fine description of charcoal burning and the construction of a blast furnace which the children keep going all night, working in relays at the bellows, with disastrous results. Mr. Ransome is unquestionably the best writer we have of books for children, because he has a genius for describing just how to do the things that children all want to do. This interest in external things is essential, but the extrovert author suffers from the severe limitations that he cannot provide any sort of philosophy of life which we find in *Bevis* and, speaking from dimming memories, I should say also in *Huckleberry Finn*. Bevis has one theory of life and Mark has another, and the rival philosophies conflict in everything they say and do and light up their characters. It comes out admirably when Bevis and Ted are picking up sides before the battle and Bevis insists on choosing his soldiers for their intelligence without worrying about their size, while Mark wants him to pick brawn, and reproaches him that he has already lost the battle. . . . Nothing so fundamentally important as this quarrel ever crops up in any of Mr. Ransome's books, in which there is a tacit assumption that there is only one common-sense code of behaviour which everyone does his best to follow: the philosophy of changing one's stockings when they are wet.

*David Garnett, in a review of "Pigeon Post," in* The New Statesman & Nation, *n.s. Vol. XII, No. 302, December 5, 1936, p. 896.*

This new book of Arthur Ransome's is uniform in production with his previous stories of the now famous group of boys and girls. The illustrations suffice, but are sometimes irritating because of the poor figure drawing. (p. 31)

As a story, *Pigeon Post* follows the lines of the other Ransome books, but prospecting for gold is the underlying theme, and a very good one. . . .

[The] reader will find a great deal of sensible, practical information here about the [carrier pigeons] and their ways.

One of the pleasant things about all Mr. Ransome's books is his serious and respectful attitude to the young reader. He does not baulk issues. If he finds himself embarked on a subject about which the reader is bound to ask questions, he forestalls these questions and is at pains to answer them as fully and clearly as possible, even with diagrams. It is that sort of fair play, I think, which endears his books to the hearts of so many young people to-day. (p. 33)

*Eleanor Graham, in a review of "Pigeon Post," in* The Junior Bookshelf, *Vol. 1, No. 2, February, 1937, pp. 31, 33.*

How the Ransome stories, close built as novels for adults might be and rarely are, can keep up their spontaneity and so continue to satisfy, is something that amazes any one who has had a sorry experience with series books. . . .

[Prospecting for gold in **"Pigeon Post"**] is taken rather more seriously than the earlier dramatic enterprises: after all, the children are two years older than when they climbed Kanchenjunga. But then, the charm and distinction of all these enterprises is that they are carried out—polar expeditions, Himalayan climbs, skirmishes with natives—with the passionate earnestness to which children dedicate such play—if they are intelligent and unsupervised. This intensity of belief in a world one has one's self created lights up the books like an inner lamp and warms them like a hidden fire. A tired grown-up whose childhood was imaginative and out-of-doors will come alive again under the influence of this light and fire.

These are unusual children, largely because they are largely let alone—for the period of the story, that is. . . . Ransome, choosing to look at life through the eyes of such children, often sees it with extraordinary lucidity. One of the episodes in the present story, which like all its episodes is not a detachable fragment but part of its structure, makes this clear. There has been a long drought on the fells, the brooks have gone dry: the little creatures of the woods are searching for springs. One of the boys has seen at school the operations of a "dowser" hunting underground water with a hazel branch, and the children in a general spirit of inquiry, make themselves a hazel wand and set about using it. Nothing happens till it gets into the hands of one little girl, then it unaccountably twists and turns. The child herself feels no pride but a distaste a grown-up might think out of all proportion to its cause. The very sight of a hazel wand makes her shudder. The other children respect her feelings, and give up the search. But—the little animals are thirsty. So Titty, with courage only a sensitive child can appreciate, nerves herself to go out alone—it would be too dreadful if the others were watching—and holds the wand, shivering, till it does turn. The others follow and dig; water at last begins to moisten the ground. Then only, all terror leaves Titty. . . .

The gold seeking, with the pigeon post keeping the children in touch with home, sends the story rushing rapidly ahead. If you think there will be disappointment at the close, do not stop with the next to the last chapter, for at the end you will not be disappointed. These books are already numbered among classics of childhood.

> *May Lamberton Becker, in a review of "Pigeon Post,"*
> *in* New York Herald Tribune Books, *September 26,*
> *1937, p. 8.*

[This] is not quite the equal of the author's earlier **"Swallowdale"** stories. . . . [The] simple, spontaneous charm of *Swallows and Amazons* is lacking. Even so, the story is still a better-than-average one for boys and girls from 8 to 12.

> *Letha M. Davidson, in a review of "Pigeon Post,"*
> *in* Library Journal, *Vol. 62, October 1, 1937, p. 745.*

A book (by no means the best) in the **'Swallows and Amazons'** series, displaying Ransome's characteristic attention to technical detail. . . . Written firmly from the children's point of view but lacking any real delineation of relationships between children and adults.

> *H. Keith Evans, in a review of "Pigeon Post," in*
> The School Librarian, *Vol. 14, No. 2, July, 1966, p.*
> *153.*

------

### WE DIDN'T MEAN TO GO TO SEA   (1937)

It is a test of the credibility and the freshness of Arthur Ransome's writing that I could find myself utterly absorbed in his *We Didn't Mean To Go To Sea*. . . . As a story I found it more convincing, as well as more exciting, than sailing with the same children over Lake Windermere. I also like Mr. Ransome's own illustrations. . . . Indeed, if I were awarding a prize book for vacation reading I would give it to *We Didn't Mean*

*To Go To Sea.* It puts one so completely in the mood of a real vacation.

> *Anne Carroll Moore, in a review of "We Didn't*
> *Mean to Go to Sea," in* The Horn Book Magazine,
> *Vol. XIV, No. 3, May, 1938, p. 174.*

Arthur Ransome upsets all our ideas about books in series, for John, Susan, Titty and Roger, who have already figured as principals in some four volumes, reappear in Mr. Ransome's latest book with the same freshness and reality that delighted us when we first made their acquaintance in **"Swallows and Amazons."** They are the same and yet different, for Mr. Ransome with rare skill has made these four young people grow older in a fashion entirely natural and consistent. Though 12-year-old readers may not consciously realize it, this author's fine power of characterization is one of the reasons why the adventures of the Swallowdale clan never lose their interest, and it explains, too, why an adult can read Mr. Ransome's books with genuine pleasure. . . .

Mrs. Walker agrees to let the delighted children spend two or three days in the Goblin [, a small cutter, with Jim Brading, a young skipper,] on condition that they do not go outside the harbor and that they are back in time to meet their father. . . . [No] one was more surprised than they when they found themselves on the high seas with Jim Brading left behind.

How they assumed the responsibility of getting themselves and Jim's boat back safely makes excellent reading.

There were qualms of conscience and also qualms of seasickness, and moments of sheer terror, for Mr. Ransome always sticks to reality. . . .

The author's drawings add to the vividness of the tale, and the end papers show with nautical exactness the course of the Goblin's unexpected voyage. **"We Didn't Mean to Go to Sea"** is a story no 10 to 14 year old should miss.

> *Anne T. Eaton, in a review of "We Didn't Mean to*
> *Go to Sea," in* The New York Times Book Review,
> *May 8, 1938, p. 12.*

Arthur Ransome is at his best in *We Didn't Mean To Go To Sea*. . . . [This is] a story that must have happened, so real it seems. It sweeps along as rapidly as the storm that carried the children out to sea and the children's reactions are so true to character and the sequence of events so right that it is almost as though the story told itself with no help from an author. The end leaves one feeling not only completely satisfied, but refreshed as though some of the sea spray had splashed the reader.

> *Ruth A. Hill, in a review of "We Didn't Mean to Go*
> *to Sea," in* Library Journal, *Vol. 63, No. 19, November 1, 1938, p. 821.*

The difference between a good story and a mere thriller may lie very simply in different treatment of the same material—in a substantial relation to real life in the former, and in distorted characterisation, exaggeration of circumstances and deliberate abandonment of real life values in the latter.

Possible effects of differing treatment on the same material are easily demonstrated in the case of such material as Arthur Ransome used in his *We didn't mean to go to sea,* with its plot about a boat at anchor with a group of children sleeping on board, with no grown-ups at hand to bear the burden of responsibility. In the night, the boat slipped her moorings and was carried out to sea on the tide. Waking to such a discovery would startle most people. If the children on board her proved to be ignorant of tides, channels or of how to manage a boat, catastrophe would be almost sure to follow. But if the author makes his children mischievous and destructive, the reader begins to suspect his intentions, and the outcome is anticipated with an extra quiver of excitement which does not arise wholly from concern for the fate of the characters. The responsible author, having chosen this type of character would continue— and with no loss of interest—to describe as nearly as he could, how events would have turned out in real life. The sensational writer, not caring about actuality but only concerned to get the utmost of drama and suspense out of his plot would deliberately prevent his characters from doing anything that might tend to relieve the tension or save the situation. He would, in fact, use them as mere puppets, to make bad worse as though by accident, and to raise the emotional tension in the reader. He would get thrills enough, of course, but the story would have no real value. It would not ring true and would suffer under any detached re-reading intended to see how it all came about.

The author may say, "Well, it was my story anyway. I invented characters and plot; and what I say, goes."

Yet, the curious fact is that, once characters and scene have been established the author is no longer master supreme. The characters he has invented have their own wills, rights and initiative; and unless these are respected, the whole run of the story becomes forced, faked.

Ransome's story, treated in another way, could easily be made into one of the awful warning stories so dear to Victorian parents, with moral values distorted and the characters, again treated as puppets with no initiative of their own, reacting to some morbid sense of guilt, and drifting helplessly, almost fatalistically, to their doom presented by the author as the just punishment of a frightful deity bearing no relation to the Christian God.

Ransome, of course, does none of these things. He gets the thrill of probability out of all he writes. Having chosen to set on his boat a group of ordinary, sensible, handy boys and girls, he lets them discover for themselves both the full horror of their predicament and the way out of it, each summoning to the aid of all, every scrap of previous experience or hear-say knowledge that might help, with that extra something of consciousness that seems to come in moments of real danger to everyone who can remain calm enough to be aware of it. His children had, naturally, their moments of sick fright, but the need for courage and action prevented panic.

Integrity, common sense and common knowledge make Ransome the master he is of this type of story, and have earned for him not only popularity but the trust of his readers who have tried him out, and proved that his directions and instructions work. (pp. 175-77)

> *Eleanor Graham, in a review of "We Didn't Mean to Go to Sea," in* The Junior Bookshelf, *Vol. 14, No. 5, November, 1950, pp. 175-77.*

---

## *SECRET WATER* (1939)

The Ransome books seem to me specially worth recommending just now when most children's lives are going on a little differently, for they inspire confidence, preach independence and demonstrate undeniably that boys and girls can be self-reliant, responsible and capable human beings.

The Swallows, in the first chapter, are preparing for a camping, sailing, exploring holiday with their parents when the blow falls. Commander Walker is recalled from leave by the Admiralty. The awful suspense which the reader endures while the young Walkers lugubriously tidy instead of opening up the *Goblin,* kindles a very real sympathy for them and also creates a good atmosphere for the rest of the story. Of course, the parents decide to let the children carry on except that the *Goblin* is replaced by a smaller sailing dinghy.

"You'll be marooned, fair and square," says their father. "You'll have to depend on yourselves alone. There'll be nobody coming along every day to see that you're all right."

In this breezy and reassuring style the author conveys the assurance that his characters can and will carry the thing through. Most young readers will feel the inferred compliment, their self-respect expanding in response, and since the whole long story justifies both promise and faith, they reach the end with an eagerness to try these things for themselves. And there again, Mr. Ransome scores, for his integrity is such that given the circumstances, many children could manage as well as the Swallows. (pp. 106-07)

> *Eleanor Graham, in a review of "Secret Water," in* The Junior Bookshelf, *Vol. 4, No. 2, December, 1939, pp. 106-07.*

Mr. Ransome's new **Secret Water** is, as usual, admirable, and will greatly please his immense child public. His ease and resource seem so spontaneous that they must be the result of unremitting toil. . . . This slips along like the flowing tides he describes so well. I wish he drew half as well as he writes.

> *Amabel Williams-Ellis, in a review of "Secret Water," in* The Spectator, *Vol. 163, No. 5815, December 8, 1939, p. 840.*

Horrid little goody-goodies as the Lockett children are [in M. E. Atkinson's *Smuggler's Gap*], they are almost surpassed by the brats in **Secret Water.** "They're the politest children I've ever met," says an adult who strays into the story. She is quite right; the little beasts are out of place in secular writing. The story . . . has all the flatness of a children's game "improved" by an adult. (p. 840)

> *Anthony West, "Coloured and Plain," in* The New Statesman & Nation, *n.s. Vol. XVIII, No. 459, December 9, 1939, pp. 838, 840.\**

The great charm of Arthur Ransome's books for children is that he never writes with an eye on the audience. His stories of boys and girls are told with the lack of self-consciousness and the integrity which are found in the undertakings and imaginative make-believe of natural, unspoiled children. Mr. Ransome's values are true, the adventures in his books are on a child's own level; never made unreal by manufactured thrills, they take place in the genuine world of childhood, not in an adult's romanticized idea of it.

Children will understand and adults will enjoy observing the way in which make-believe becomes real and exciting without ever ceasing to be make-believe; as, for instance, when Titty and Roger discover the mastodon's footprints. Like the author's other books, **"Secret Water"** is full of fascinating details of sailing, and here again are intriguing lists of supplies, camp time tables, descriptions of camp routine. . . .

[A] new group of children, known as the Eels, prove to be excellent co-adventurers and congenial spirits.

Boys and girls from 9 to 13 can have no better company than the young people of Mr. Ransome's books.

> *Anne T. Eaton, "Life at Sea," in* The New York Times Book Review, *May 5, 1940, p. 10.*

---

### THE BIG SIX  (1940)

The good writer for children sticks out a mile. He or she respects children, enjoys what they enjoy, is actively interested in the story, loves incidental detail, and never writes down. Mr. Arthur Ransome, our Children's Author No. 1, has all these qualities, and adds to them a vivid charm, and a mastery of the technique children love best. He has no scruples against giving instruction, but it is always a necessary part of the story, and he always assumes an active and enquiring intelligence in his readers.... A fish's funeral, an inn called 'The Roaring Donkey,' the escape of the boat [*Death and Glory*] from *force majeure,* the lore of birds and animals—do you know what happens if you show a nursing ferret your closed fist?—and clearly drawn characters, go to make up a small work of art. (pp. 616, 618)

> *L. A. G. Strong, in a review of "The Big Six," in* The Spectator, *Vol. 165, No. 5867, December 6, 1940, pp. 616, 618.*

[Here is] the prolific Mr. Ransome again, extraordinary writer, so original, so matter of fact, with his maps and his local place names and his almost grinding insistence on matters of technical proficiency. The setting is once more the Norfolk Broads, about which Mr. Ransome obviously knows everything that can be known. As usual every single detail of the boatman's art and craft is meticulously explored. As usual the style is clipped, pared-away, astringent, to my ear monotonous and, somehow, a bit suffocating. As usual the characters are flat, colourless, humourless, totally external: symbols of co-operative efficiency. I don't know why I always rather dislike them: I suppose it is because they are always so on the spot, up to the mark, and, somehow, sterilised. But that is beside the point. The point is that Mr. Ransome again equals or perhaps excels himself, and that every boy who enjoys him—and every boy does—will vote this detective story super.

> *Rosamond Lehmann, "A Flourishing Crop," in* The New Statesman & Nation, *Vol. XX, No. 511, December 7, 1940, p. 576.**

It is my reasoned opinion that this is Arthur Ransome's best book. Rally round, Ransome fans; this is a beauty.

It is not a bit like the synthetic thrillers in which a child stumps the experts; what these children do is what any bright twelve-year-old would [do]....

It is a story for any one, old or young, whose idea of rapture is "messing about in boats." Arthur Ransome, working between bombs—one destroyed his drawings and another the publisher's plates—has preserved a peaceful holiday imperturbability inexpressibly soothing to the nerves just now.

> *May Lamberton Becker, in a review of "The Big Six," in* New York Herald Tribune Books, *April 6, 1941, p. 8.*

[Out of war-torn England] comes a new Arthur Ransome story, as fresh in interest, as perceptive and as true in values as all his others.

The boys of "Coot Club" (Tom Dudgeon, the doctor's son, the village boys, Pete, Joe and Bill) and Dorothea and Dick of "Coot Club" and "Winter Holiday," reappear in "The Big Six." Almost at the start of the story the first four find themselves under suspicion, along the river, of setting boats adrift....

[The] six organize themselves into the "Big Six"—like the "Big Five" of Scotland Yard.... Then begins a chase that will delight a reader of almost any age....

These are real children, drawn by one who has observed boys and girls with wisdom, sympathy and humor, one who enjoys and understands them. The schemes of the Big Six for catching the wrongdoers have the same mixture of practical good sense and make-believe that is found in the doings of children in real life. Mr. Ransome has made satisfying drawings, including practical sketch maps that show the routes and distances the young detectives needed to know.

> *Anne T. Eaton, in a review of "The Big Six," in* The New York Times Book Review, *May 18, 1941, p. 10.*

---

### MISSEE LEE  (1941)

The most famous young folks in contemporary English literature . . . are far from Lake Windermere at the outset of the most ambitious and successful of the romances about them. They have sailed three parts round the world in the good ship "Wild Cat," whose two dinghies are named "Swallow" and "Amazon" to keep up the tradition of Titty, Roger, Peggy, John, Nancy and Susan, so popular with children on both sides of the sea.

They are not far from the coast of China, when their pet monkey drops a lighted cigar into the petrol tank, the "Wild Cat" burns, and the young folks, in two parties, take to the little boats. They have long been warned of the dire possibility of meeting "Missee Lee," mysterious female pirate.... One of the boatloads comes upon her camp on an island, precipitating one of the snappiest mystery-adventures children have in recent books. For Missee Lee so long remains a sinister mystery that actually finding her is a complete surprise....

It is good entertainment, written—as always with Arthur Ransome—with adult fiction technique used to develop a story from a young person's point of view. He knows both China and seamanship so well that he can make you believe anything about either. His drawings give the story added realism: they look like sketches made on the spot by a determined amateur who had to keep a record and couldn't use a camera.

> *May Lamberton Becker, in a review of "Missee Lee," in* New York Herald Tribune Books, *April 5, 1942, p. 8.*

[Arthur Ransome's books] now amount to a considerable library of fine stories that combine adventure, genuine characterization and good writing in a way found but rarely in books for boys and girls. Indeed, Arthur Ransome's books pass the supreme test; adults as well as children find them excellent reading. . . .

The adventures approach grimness at times and the account of the escape and Missee Lee's unexpected share in it, will be followed with breathless attention. Needless to say there is plenty about boats and sailing. . . .

It is all extraordinary and all entirely convincing. Mr. Ransome never violates the consistency of his characters; John and Susan, Titty and Roger, Nancy and Peggy, act and speak in perfect accord with all that we know of them, their standards are those of genuine, normal childhood. It is to be noted that though Gibber, Roger's monkey, is the cause of the fire, he is never blamed for the disaster, and in the midst of uncertainties Titty never forgets her parrot.

The drawings by the author have a lively, on-the-spot quality. It is almost impossible not to believe that it all really happened, with the author on hand to see just how it took place. One of the year's best books for boys and girls from 10 to 14.

> *Anne T. Eaton, in a review of "Missee Lee: Based on Information Supplied by the Swallows and Amazons," in* The New York Times Books Review, *April 5, 1942, p. 10.*

Another book by Arthur Ransome is greeted with joy. An exciting foreign setting for the exploits of the Swallows and Amazons sets the stage for high adventure, quite unlike anything they have experienced hitherto. . . . Through all [the] new and unforeseen events, the children are as real and consistent in character as ever. They are high hearted and resourceful, they are courageous under truly alarming conditions. We read of them again with undiminished pleasure and rejoice in their final safety. (pp. 179-80)

> *Alice M. Jordan, in a review of "Missee Lee," in* The Horn Book Magazine, *Vol. XVIII, No. 3, May, 1942, pp. 179-80.*

**Missee Lee,** like **Peter Duck,** is a by-product of the enormous energy of the Swallows and Amazons; they tell the story (Titty, mostly) in a rare moment of inaction. Arthur Ransome slyly allowed his characters to slip into this very tall story the kind of things children would naturally choose—pirates, gun-fights, sea chases; but he saw to it that he remained in control of the tale and its characters all through. Who but Ransome would have involved Captain Flint and his young friends . . . with a pirate innocent of eye-patches or wooden legs, a tiny Cambridge graduate with a passion for teaching the classics? Who but Ransome would have thought of an escape from Missee Lee's benevolent clutches . . . by making and manipulating a paper and cardboard beast in the Dragon Festival? In this jovial, crackling adventure story he had the best of two worlds; he played the story-teller in two generations, matching a child's inventive exhilaration to a skilled writer's tricks of the trade. **Missee Lee** should contribute usefully to the noticeable upward trend in Ransomes. (pp. 1708-09)

> *Margery Fisher, in a review of "Missee Lee," in her* Growing Point, *Vol. 9, No. 9, April, 1971, pp. 1708-09.*

**Missee Lee** has an exotic colour and a particular humour all of its own, and it is a sign of Ransome's skill as a storyteller, and grasp of the details which make his tales so convincing— the rigging and manoeuvring of a junk are described as accurately as those of more homely craft—that his heroes and heroines can escape execution by charming a ten-gong taicoon with their parrot and developing an unexpected passion for Latin lessons and leave the reader's credulity scarcely strained.

It is possible that the passage of time bolsters the plausibility of these tales, and even gives them an additional nostalgic charm, but like Ransome's simple line drawings, deliberately executed with childish naivete, they have a timeless strength which, along with Captain Nancy's irrepressible exclamations of "jibbooms and bobstays" and "barbecued billygoats" still rings true. (p. 60)

> *Mary Anne Bonney "Ransome Notes," in* Punch, *Vol. 286, No. 7468, January 18, 1984, pp. 56, 58-60.*

---

### THE PICTS AND THE MARTYRS; OR, NOT WELCOME AT ALL (1943)

[It] is a little difficult to swallow the main assumption of Mr. Ransome's latest story, that a Great Aunt can be something worse than the still centre of a cyclone. On this hangs the whole necessity of throwing Dick and Dorothea Callum out of Beckfoot, and making them lurk in the woods like Picts, while the Amazons martyr themselves, with white frocks, hair-ribbons, and duets on the piano. Perhaps I am prejudiced, well on the way to being a great-aunt myself, but I find it hard to believe in such a monster as Miss Turner. But even if the plot of this latest Ransome is a little strained, the texture is as dependable as ever, and (though there are no Swallows, no delightful Titty) stay-at-home children will find this the best substitute for a Lakes holiday. Mr. Ransome's books, indeed, owe half their charm to being the perfect realisation of favourite day-dreams—lovely food, no quarrels (not even with the maddeningly bossy Nancy), games of pirates and explorers that need never stop for meals or bed, and action of the kind that a child might conceivably hope to have on the really perfect summer holiday. (p. 42)

Mr. Ransome writes about children whose parents can afford to buy dinghies, rent a farm for the summer holidays, and give eight-and-sixpenny books as birthday presents. . . . I wonder whether Mr. Ransome's stories appeal to children who live entirely outside the world of nannies, cooks and private boat-houses? Or may the line between Ransome readers and non-readers be drawn between town and country-minded children, and have nothing to do with class and income? (pp. 42, 44)

> *Janet Adam Smith, in a review of "The Picts and the Martyrs; or, Not Welcome at All," in* The Spectator, *Vol. 171, No. 6002, July 9, 1943, pp. 42, 44.*

Howard Spring once wrote that Arthur Ransome's stories are in a class that "out-tops by head and shoulders and half a body the customary stuff." That is a statement which because of a noticeable raising of the general standard becomes less true year by year, but it is still not far from the truth.

I approached **The Picts and the Martyrs** with a very critical mind, looking for faults. I could not find any, nor did I expect to find them. I have heard librarians say that children do not like Ransome because the young people in his books live a sort of life that the vast majority of children do not understand. I have always suspected fallacious reasoning and insufficient observation and investigation to be the root of this attitude among librarians. My careful reading of this latest book confirms my suspicions. The essence of all the Ransome stories, or at any rate the **"Swallowdale"** series, is fundamentally this. Mr. Ransome has an almost uncanny ability to interpret that heaven-sent attribute of children, the capacity to give reality to the world of make-believe. Combine with this a facile pen, a flair for characterisation, and successful projection of the author into the minds of his characters, and the result is a unique story. For Ransome's stories are unique, as is proved by the less successful attempts of his many imitators.

The fact that the Swallows and Amazons have sailing boats and long holidays during which to enjoy them with the English Lakes as background is incidental. The same sort of story could be, and in reality is, enacted in tents in the back garden or on waste ground; in attics and in boxrooms. Mr. Ransome has an imagination and an attitude of mind that retains its youth. He is not an adult being youthful. When he is writing he becomes a young person again. That is his secret. A good writer must become one with his characters and this Ransome accomplishes to perfection. His grown-ups are less successfully drawn than the younger people and they occupy the stage less frequently. Each character, too, is individual, whether it be the dynamic Nancy, the studious Dick or the self-assured and accomplished Jacky from the farm. The Great Aunt is the skeleton in the cupboard.

It might be thought impossible that the Picts could be kept out of the way, "non-existent," for a whole week without straining our credulity, but it proves to be possible despite some very "near misses."

I feel that *The Picts and the Martyrs* is at least as good as its forerunners. (pp. 111-12)

> *A review of "The Picts and the Martyrs," in* The Junior Bookshelf, *Vol. 7, No. 3, November, 1943, pp. 111-12.*

Few authors have the satisfaction of knowing that their next book will be a classic, but the saga of **"Swallows and Amazons"** is so firmly established in children's literature that a new volume takes at once its place in the canon. . . .

The fun arising from [Dick and Dot hiding in the woods] never flags. Discovery is always at their heels: it is not easy to be non-existent. The G.A. leaves at last in a sortie that takes the most experienced reader by surprise. . . .

> *May Lamberton Becker, "Pictures and Stories with Power to Charm," in* New York Herald Tribune Weekly Book Review, *November 14, 1943, p. 6.\**

The Swallows don't appear in this volume, which some of Mr. Ransome's following may regret, and there is rather too much of the eldest Amazon, an overwhelmingly wholesome and resourceful English schoolgirl.

> *A review of "The Picts and the Martyrs," in* The New Yorker, *Vol. XIX, No. 42, December 4, 1943, p. 113.*

---

### GREAT NORTHERN?  (1947)

Mr. Ransome's new book has been eagerly looked for, and it lives up to the high standard we expect. He has the rare art of making everything seem alive from the first word, and in an effortless and masterly way he creates for us the world of the children in his stories.

We break new ground in this book, and follow the adventures of the Walker, Blackett and Callum children, on a voyage to the Outer Hebrides. (p. 133)

The story is as excellent as *The Coot Club,* one of the most enjoyable of Mr. Ransome's books, which also has bird-preservation as its theme.

In *Great Northern,* Dick Callum, the "Ship's naturalist," plays a central role; his efforts to photograph the birds and protect the eggs are a most thrilling part of the story, which grows in suspense until the last chapter. After this mounting excitement the end seems to come rather suddenly, but perhaps it is that one always wants another chapter or two in Mr. Ransome's books. This book need no recommendation. It will appeal to a wide circle of young readers, and many older ones as well. (pp. 133-34)

> *A review of "Great Northern," in* The Junior Bookshelf, *Vol. 11, No. 3, October, 1947, pp. 133-34.*

Suspense? It is maintained up to the very last page. You may have often held your breath over a book, but never one of this kind, a mystery unique in juvenile fiction. Indeed, by this time anything Swallows and Amazons do in Arthur Ransome's stories isn't fiction: Captain Flint, Nancy, Roger, Dick, Titty and the rest are live people, personal friends of young folk all over the world.

> *May Lamberton Becker, in a review of "Great Northern?" in* New York Herald Tribune Weekly Book Review, *June 13, 1948, p. 8.*

Even if you shouldn't happen to care very strongly about birds, you feel with Dick a desperate earnestness that the loons must be saved. It is this quality of intensity which the youngsters bring to both work and play, even more than the sense of outdoors, the fun and the vigor of the characters, that has made Arthur Ransome's books so well-beloved by a whole generation of readers.

> *Ellen Lewis Buell, in a review of "Great Northern?" in* The New York Times Book Review, *June 13, 1948, p. 23.*

When Arthur Ransome wrote *Swallows and Amazons* he originated a new kind of adventure story. The escape from the limited environment of the child's everyday, or even holiday life is obviously the writer's intention here, as it is in *Treasure Island.* But the adventure theme of *Swallows and Amazons* is woven into the fabric of the imaginative play of a child's mental world. Romance becomes not a distant unattainable prospect, but waits on the threshold of every child's imagination. Arthur Ransome, in all his writing, seems to be saying to his readers that one way to come alive and find life an exciting adventure is to open the door of imagination.

Whether Arthur Ransome writes of imaginative or actual adventure, his stories tell of boats and water-ways where he is entirely at home. His serious purpose in writing his books can be seen not only in their solid content but also in his themes. The theme of *Great Northern?* for instance, is developed with such skill and sympathy that it calls for serious study and analysis.

Arthur Ransome has a concern for the wild birds that nest in river sedge or on shores of lonely lakes near the sea. In more than one of his stories he makes this concern not his alone, but that of his imagined characters. Since children tend to identify themselves with the characters of their stories, the result is that concern for wild life is carried over and becomes as operative in the reading child as it is in the imagined characters. . . . (p. 138)

The idea at the back of *Great Northern?* is the protection of wild life, but this subject is an abstraction which the concrete minds of children find too diffuse to grasp in any broad sense.

So Arthur Ransome has given his idea a particular aspect. The emphasis falls on the identity of the diving bird that Dick, the "ship's naturalist" discovers nesting in the Hebrides. Is it or isn't it a Great Northern?

The importance of a discovery which proves all existing bird books inaccurate now takes precedence and governs the action of the story. The individual characters realize the necessity of subordinating their conflicting desires and plans under a common compulsion—their obligation to genuine scientific discovery. Dick must be enabled to photograph the birds because, in the words of the villain of the piece, "what's hit's history, what's missed mystery." In other words, there must be proof.

This, in the main, is the idea behind the story. That it has real significance for children is undeniable. Whether it will hold their attention depends on the construction of the story and the way it is told. Let us look first at the framework.

Arthur Ransome is not a writer who overlooks the points which make a story a good one in the minds of his readers. He creates characters of the kind to whom things happen and he is skilful in giving the "shove" that starts them happening. Birds have enemies, sometimes human enemies, and to "confound their knavish tricks" provides the action and interaction of the book. The construction, with this basis, makes an interesting study in the working out of a plot. In a preliminary excursion inland from the cove where their boat is anchored, some of the children in the story explore the heather-covered uplands while Dick with his passion for birds follows the shore line of two small lochs in the hope of adding to the list of birds seen on the voyage. Dick discovers the Great Northern Divers nesting on a small island and makes a quick sketch, uncertain of their identity. The others find their movements are being watched by unfriendly inhabitants—that they are, in fact, being stalked.

On their return to the ship Dick is puzzled to discover that while his drawing corresponds with the picture of the Great Northern in his bird guide, the book states clearly that these birds "nest abroad." Yet he had seen them nesting here. Their ship returns to the harbor and the cruise is over, or so they all think. But Dick finds a "bird man" whose ship is in the harbor and visits him to get his opinion on the identity of the Diver. To Dick's horror the bird man is in reality an enemy of birds who shoots and stuffs them and collects their eggs for his private collection. His interest in Dick's discovery convinces the others of its scientific importance.

The conviction that Dick's birds are in danger of extermination, the need to circumvent the bird man's cruel design, and the importance of photographing the discovery are now of paramount importance to the characters of the story. Their ship returns to the cove where the discovery was made. At this point the pattern of the story is woven of three threads: Dick stalks the birds, the natives stalk the children, and the villain stalks Dick. All three threads converge at the point where the original discovery was made; the climax is dramatic and the conclusion follows with dispatch.

We see that, so far, the story has significance and a well-constructed plot in which suspense is built up to a dramatic climax. But to suggest that in these lie the reason for the lasting pleasure Arthur Ransome's stories have for children would be to ignore the qualities which constitute his right to stand beside the other writers of permanent books of children's literature. The fusion of his storytelling genius with his art as a writer marks his stature as a creative writer. In *Great Northern?* we

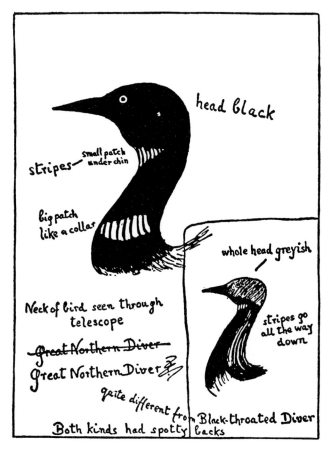

*Another page from Dick's notebook showing the two kinds of divers. From* Great Northern?, *written and illustrated by Arthur Ransome. The Macmillan Company, 1948. Copyright, 1947, by Arthur Ransome. All rights reserved. Reprinted with permission of Macmillan Publishing Company.*

can discern three distinct styles of writing, each appropriate to the matter in hand. Let us examine them.

Arthur Ransome is aware that most children are Robinson Crusoes at heart. They build rafts, construct all kinds of hiding places and explore underground as well as aboveground when they can. When he describes in careful detail how a ship is put on legs for "scrubbing," or the construction of a "pict-house," or the making of a "hide" behind which bird-watching may be carried on, Ransome is dealing with fundamental and universal interests of children and he writes about them with the precise minuteness and practical language of Defoe when he describes Robinson Crusoe's ingenious contrivances.

The dialogue, of which there is a great deal, is a device for advancing the story and realizing the characters. His style here is natural, lively, and unassuming. (pp. 138-40)

Easy and colloquial as the dialogue is, it nevertheless reveals the individuality of each speaker. We know not only what the characters of his stories are doing at the moment, we know how they will be likely to act in any given situation. They are so well realized that they take on the attribute of actuality. To their readers the characters created by Arthur Ransome are often more real than many of their companions in everyday life.

As well as these two styles of writing—the practical and the conversational—Arthur Ransome has another way of writing, a way that is so subtly a part of the story that it creates imperceptibly a picture of beauty and meaning. For it is the Hebrides themselves that Arthur Ransome has written into his story of *Great Northern?*—the rocky coasts where gulls whirl and scream, the narrow coves, the heather growing on the hillsides, the mist-filled valleys where deer are grazing, the reed-bordered lochs where Dick heard for the first time the long wavering note "like wild laughter"—the cry of the Great Northern Diver. (p. 141)

> *Lillian H. Smith, "Stories," in her* The Unreluctant Years: A Critical Approach to Children's Literature, *American Library Association, 1953, pp. 130-48.\**

*Great Northern?* summed up [Arthur Ransome's] work most admirably. At the same time, while he continued to refuse most resolutely to be the pioneer of a new kind of children's book, he foreshadowed some of the development to come. *Great Northern?* is a watershed-book between two differing concepts. (p. 142)

The first books had been about manufactured adventures. The children might be caught up in the realities of forest fire and sailing and climbing hazards, but basically they were making-believe. Halfway through the series in *We Didn't Mean to Go to Sea,* the adventures became real. In *Great Northern?,* although Dorothea still reads romance into the events of every day and the others continue to invent—sometimes tiresomely—their own derogatory names for the owners of the land on which they play, the essence of the story is not play at all but real earnest.

In 1947 the theme of *Great Northern?* was novel. To many readers it seemed strange that so much should be made of a piece of ornithological research. Today no one would be surprised that the Ship's Naturalist should go to extraordinary lengths to protect a rare breeding bird and that his friends should support him to their own discomfort and potential danger. Today however there would be no story. Dick, a responsible boy whatever one may think of the others, would call in the R.S.P.B. to maintain 24-hour watches and there would be no need for decoys and red herrings. The idea of the book, if not the execution, is very modern. (p. 143)

No one evokes better than Dr Ransome the ecstasy of being free in the open air in wild places. He does it without fuss. There are no detailed landscapes, no paintings of dawn and sunset. The children get on with what they are doing, and the reader shares their deep physical and spiritual satisfaction in their activity and its fulfilment. There is no 'fine writing,' only plain, exact words conveying concrete images. One knows precisely what is happening and how it comes about.

There were two valid criticisms of the earlier Ransome books. The more important was that the books showed an incomplete society, one in which children lived apart from the adult world and in which they were seen only on holiday. We know, it is true, what the Amazons were like at home when they became Martyrs, but the mind rejects the thought of them at school. *Great Northern?* does not really answer this criticism. Uncle Jim (Captain Flint) comes into the story more than he did in previous books, but he still has the habit of opting out of responsibility. The other adults are villainous like the Egg-Collector—it is characteristic of the author that he is reluctant to call adults by name—or obtuse like the Highland Chief. The other criticism, which may be an intrusion from the adult world, is that the children are too unbearably competent. One longs

for a little human fallibility. In *Great Northern?* Ransome allows them to be beaten at their own game. The Gaels literally run rings around them, giving them an unforgettable lesson in fieldcraft.

Because Ransome's children are so often engaged in serious practical business they may seem to be lacking in humour and normal high spirits. They rarely play the fool, but their enjoyment is always clear. They have a marvellous time and they know it. Their humour springs not from fantasy but from a practical acceptance of the real world. There is an admirable and typical passage in *Great Northern?* when the egg-collector, having failed to cozen Dick into helping him, tries to buy Captain Flint with his 'long narrow cheque-book'. When Captain Flint's fury threatens to choke him,

> "Spit in the water," said Nancy, "You'll feel better".

> (pp. 143-44)

> *Marcus Crouch, "Open Air," in his* Nesbit Tradition: The Children's Novel in England 1945-1970, *Ernest Benn Limited, 1972, pp. 142-60.\**

---

## *THE FOOL OF THE WORLD AND THE FLYING SHIP: A RUSSIAN TALE* (1968)

Arthur Ransome's **"Old Peter"** tales are not ideal for picture-book treatment. They are perfect for telling aloud, but the balanced phrases, which come so well off the tongue, hinder movement from picture to picture. So, although one may joyfully welcome a new edition of *The Fool of the World,* it makes admittedly an imperfect picture-book. This is a story which crops up in the folk-literature of almost all countries; here it has an unmistakable Russian character. . . .

> *A review of "The Fool of the World and the Flying Ship," in* The Junior Bookshelf, *Vol. 34, No. 6, December, 1970, p. 348.*

I find it very refreshing to come across a story cast in the traditional mould, and told very firmly in the traditional language. . . .

The language is both distinguished and uncondescending. . . . The story has all the essentials of repetition, rhythm and logical development, and the stylized language is beautifully matched by the bright formalized illustrations [by Uri Shulevitz].

> *Gabrielle Maunder, in a review of "The Fool of the World and the Flying Ship," in* The School Librarian, *Vol. 19, No. 2, June, 1971, p. 183.*

The late Mr. Ransome is one of the most admired and influential writers of works for children and *The Fool of the World* provides further evidence of the validity of our respect. . . . It is a fascinating story, presented by Ransome with dignity and humor; while designed to delight and entertain the young, *The Fool of the World,* to use a Lockean expression, may also "afford useful reflection to a grown man." . . . [The] Shulevitz illustrations never obscure or lessen the vitality of Ransome's text. . . . (p. 226)

> *Charity Chang, "Uri Shulevitz, Illustrator and Writer," in* Children's Literature: Annual of the Modern Language Association Seminar on Children's Literature and The Children's Literature Association, Vol. 3, *edited by Francelia Butler, Temple University Press, 1974, pp. 226-27.\**

# Margaret (Wright) Rau

## 1913-

**China-born American author of nonfiction and photographer.**

**Rau is recognized for creating distinctive information books about the life cycles of rare animals and authoritative works on present-day China for children from the middle grades through junior high. In her books on the Chinese panda, the Australian kangaroo, and the Japanese snow monkey, Rau accurately describes a particular animal that represents an unusual species while examining other botanical and zoological life in the environment. Acclaimed for her extensive research on the history, geography, sociology and, most importantly, the contemporary developments of China, she has also written about the land and people of Australia with characteristic knowledge and enthusiasm. Her biography of the blind educator who established schools for the visually handicapped throughout the Orient, *Dawn from the West: The Story of Genevieve Caulfield*, develops the themes of courageous determination, concern for another people, and commitment to the ideal that every individual has a worthy contribution to make. In order to create a precise and up-to-date picture for her youthful American readers, Rau illustrates many of her books with photographs she herself has taken.**

**Born of missionary parents in Swatow, Rau spoke Chinese before English. Her works underscore her love for the only land she knew until the age of twelve. While *The Giant Panda at Home* reveals her familiarity with the local terrain, both the Caulfield biography and *The Snow Monkey at Home* benefit from the authenticity she brings from first-hand knowledge of the Far East. Rau's use of primary sources attests to the accuracy and reliability of her facts. She employs current native zoological findings in *The Giant Panda* and utilizes both English and Japanese sources in the bibliography for *The Snow Monkey*. An extensive traveler, Rau has visited Europe and the Soviet Union, and made a ten-month trip across the Australian continent to write her travelogue, *Red Earth, Blue Sky*. Since 1974, she has been permitted to return repeatedly to China. This makes her uniquely qualified to tell American readers about modern China in terms of the nation's history and culture she knows so well.**

**As befits her subjects, Rau's writing for children is matter-of-fact, but critics also comment on her ability to move her readers. There are memorable moments of suspense in *The Gray Kangaroo at Home*, drama in *Musk Oxen: Bearded Ones of the Arctic*, and human interest in her geographical accounts. The photoessay *Jimmy of Cherry Valley* enables readers to experience vicariously the hard work and heartache that accompanies the growing of cherry trees. Reviewers compare Rau favorably with other recognized authorities and invariably recommend her works for both principal and supplementary reading. They generally extol the perspicuity with which Rau imparts her considerable knowledge and understanding of out-of-the-ordinary animals, people, professions, and places. Some critics complain that her prose is pedantic; others decry her detachment and ask for a more personal account in her books about China, expecting her to identify each individual she meets and analyze the conflict of ideologies she encounters. There are, however, many who appreciate her**

Photograph by Tomeo Hanami. Courtesy of Margaret Rau

ability to catch and maintain the interest of younger readers. These reviewers applaud Rau's lack of sentimentality and censure and are aware that she is writing basic introductory material. Rau's photographs come under attack more frequently than do her texts. Critics place partial blame on her editors for permitting poor placement and inappropriate captions. Despite the amateur quality of the illustrations, there are those who praise them for adding interest and realism. Rau holds a secure position among writers of juvenile nonfiction. Her books are considered superior representatives of their genre and have received regional and national recognition for their contribution to the study of science and the social studies.

(See also *Something about the Author*, Vol. 9; *Contemporary Authors New Revision Series*, Vol. 8; and *Contemporary Authors*, Vols. 61-64.)

---

## DAWN FROM THE WEST: THE STORY OF GENEVIEVE CAULFIELD (1964)

[*Dawn from the West*] relates the almost incredible activities of Genevieve Caulfield, a blind girl who earned a degree from Columbia University and immediately set about fulfilling her dream of going to the Orient to teach the blind. Girls 10 years and up should find action aplenty as well as inspirational appeal in this story of a courageous real-life American Catholic heroine.

*Ethna Sheehan, in a review of "Dawn from the West," in* America, *Vol. 110, No. 25, June 20, 1964, p. 850.*

Margaret Rau's own background in Eastern lore together with personal interviews have combined to produce an authentic biography. Unfortunately her prose is unexciting and she sometimes forgets to explain how Miss Caulfield managed difficult situations without sight.

*Catherine Owens Peare, in a review of "Dawn from the West: The Story of Genevieve Caulfield," in* The New York Times Book Review, *July 26, 1964, p. 26.*

In late 1963 President Johnson presented to Genevieve Caulfield the Medal of Freedom, the nation's highest civilian medal. Blind from infancy, Miss Caulfield has spent 40 years of service in the Far East establishing schools for the blind. On the whole, Margaret Rau has done an excellent job of showing in simple, stirring though somewhat romanticized narrative to what extent one can, through courage and determination, overcome a severe handicap and make an important contribution to society.

*Mary D. Ross, in a review of "Dawn from the West: The Story of Genevieve Caulfield," in* School Library Journal, *Vol. 22, No. 1, September, 1975, p. 110.*

### THE PENGUIN BOOK   (1968)

Mr. Popper would be pleased to meet Captain Cook's cousins in this precise catalogue: not only the Adelie but also the Emperor, King, Ringneck, Gentoo, Macaroni, Rockhopper, Magellanic and Blackfoot. Following a resume of general qualities, each has an individual characterization, including mating and nesting habits, movement on land and sea (and modifications since the arrival of man), and references to evolutionary history (e.g. adaptation of the wing to swimming). The one-a-chapter treatment emphasizes differences among penguins, making this a good companion to Darling's *Penguins* which emphasizes shared characteristics and limits information on variations.

*A review of "The Penguin Book," in* Kirkus Service, *Vol. XXXVI, No. 12, June 15, 1968, p. 648.*

At last we have a straightforward, factual, interesting book for children that introduces them, in separate chapters, to flightless birds in general with a little evolutionary background (the oversimplification of the explanation is excusable). . . . The book closes with an epilogue that provides some of the highlights of historic expeditions and research on Antarctic penguins. . . . [There's] a good index. Mrs. Rau's book on penguins should be acquired by all school and public libraries, for it is superior to any other children's book on these birds currently in print.

*A review of "The Penguin Book," in* Science Books, *Vol. 4, No. 2, September, 1968, p. 137.*

This is a very interesting book which packs a large amount of information into a few pages. True, the animals selected are particularly interesting in themselves, but the choice of topics and emphasis adds even more. Anyone short of an expert on penguins will find this book informative, pleasant reading. I highly recommend it.

*Fred Geis, Jr., in a review of "The Penguin Book," in* Appraisal: Children's Science Books, *Vol. 2, No. 2, Spring, 1969, p. 20.*

### THE YANGTZE RIVER   (1970)

The most heavily used river in Asia is tracked from its beginning in the Kokoshili Mountains of Tibet to where its silt rests in the Chu Shan Islands, in this clearly written book. . . . The cultures and various life styles of the 230 million people living in the Yangtze basin are described in an absorbing manner. Political commentary is held to a minimum; that given is basically fair. Interesting sidelights are provided on the historical smoking of opium, child slave labor, the Red Guard, etc. Photos from several sources reinforce the text, as do a pronunciation guide and an index. While not necessarily a replacement for Spencer's *Yangtze, China's River Highway* (Garrard, 1963), this is a good addition to material on the subject.

*Linda L. Clark, in a review of "The Yangtze River," in* School Library Journal, *an appendix to* Library Journal, *Vol. 17, No. 7, March, 1971, p. 130.*

Life along the Yangtze River is described, from its source to its mouth. Use of the river to unify the human activities of this vast area is highly effective, and the book as a whole is a useful overview. That the Yangtze is a major medium of transportation needs more emphasis. . . . The text reads well; a glossary aids in pronunciation of Chinese proper names. There are major deficiencies from the point of view of the geographer. Although there is one location map showing the river and naming places described; the book lacks relief maps. Explanation of livelihoods, city locations and physical phenomena is sometimes inadequate. There is no substantial discussion of the population size and its relationship to the large-scale use of labor, to the choice of animals raised (pigs, chickens, beasts of burden) and to the high use of carbohydrates in human diet. Shortcomings of the Communist regime often appear to be overlooked. Reorganization might, in many passages create better balance. For example, the Red Guards are discussed at one point without adverse criticism; it is only later that excesses committed by this group are mentioned.

*A review of "The Yangtze River," in* Science Books, *Vol. 6, No. 4, March, 1971, p. 342.*

### JIMMY OF CHERRY VALLEY   (1973)

City folk, who might think that tending an orchard is just a matter of putting seedlings in the ground and picking the fruit, will sweat along with fourteen-year-old Jimmy as he irrigates, fertilizes, sprays and prunes—only to lose his first crop to a late April frost. While the usual "day in the life" padding is kept to a bare minimum, Jimmy debates the fine points of cultivation with the valley's older farmers . . . and his disappointment—which Jimmy finally chalks up to experience—adds a note of documentary realism.

*A review of "Jimmy of Cherry Valley," in* Kirkus Reviews, *Vol. XLI, No. 18, September 15, 1973, p. 1041.*

Rau's photoessay reveals that at fourteen Jimmy Boyd is well on his way to becoming a professional orchard man, courtesy of his father who, after purchasing and planting 15 trees, strikes a bargain with Jimmy guaranteeing him one quarter of the anticipated profits in return for Jimmy's care and maintenance

*From* Jimmy of Cherry Valley, *written and illustrated by Margaret Rau. Julian Messner, 1973. Copyright © 1973 by Margaret Rau. All rights reserved. Reprinted by permission of Julian Messner, a division of Simon & Schuster, Inc.*

of the trees. Besides projecting the virtues of conscientious hard work, photos and text fill readers in on some uncommonly known details of orchard work and so provide a glimpse of an otherwise unseen world.

> *A review of "Jimmy of Cherry Valley," in* The Booklist, *Vol. 70, No. 6, November 15, 1973, p. 342.*

A dry but serviceable account of a boy's experiences caring for a small cherry orchard. . . . Black-and-white photographs generously illustrate the processes of pruning, irrigating, and grafting clearly described in the concise text. Virtually a cherry growers' manual, this will be useful for science units on farming or foods. However, the other facets of the boy's life—football, playing in the school band—are disappointingly portrayed in a manner that is neither exciting nor memorable.

> *Evelyn Stewart, in a review of "Jimmy of Cherry Valley," in* School Library Journal, *an appendix to* Library Journal, *Vol. 20, No. 5, January, 1974, p. 51.*

Commercial cherry orchards in California are attractively and accurately described in this reference/storybook. Children will find it easy to identify with Jimmy, the son of a real-life cherry orchard operator. . . . The yearly development of the trees is convincingly shown in a series of six photographs. An excellent index is included. There is no discussion of other cherry-growing areas. Further, a short paragraph giving scientific data

regarding the tree would have been a worthwhile addition; publishers should be encouraged to adopt such a practice in all such children's books.

> *A review of "Jimmy of Cherry Valley," in* Science Books, *Vol. X, No. 2, September, 1974, p. 173.*

---

### OUR WORLD: THE PEOPLE'S REPUBLIC OF CHINA   (1974)

Rau's condensed history reflects the new objectivity which has been made possible by the opening of relations with China; even questionable facts (particularly the explanation of the death of Lin Piao) are accepted at face value but the conflict between Mao and Chiang is dispassionately recalled. Readers at this age level will be most interested in the glimpses of China today which briefly, but quite effectively convey the popular interest in athletics and physical fitness, the dramatic but still incomplete drive for women's liberation, the greatly improved standard of living (still spartan by American standards), the democratic organization of the People's Liberation Army, innovations like the "barefoot doctors," the pervasive influence of the Party and even the revival of traditional handicrafts like ivory carving and puppetry. No one area of life is closely scrutinized, but Rau manages to capture small events—such as the verbal reprimanding of reckless cyclists by child traffic guards—which make a very unfamiliar society seem human rather than monolithic and forbidding.

> *A review of "The People's Republic of China," in* Kirkus Reviews, *Vol. XLII, No. 4, March 15, 1974, p. 306.*

In her overview of modern China Rau also covers the past, explaining the centuries of peasant repression that finally resulted in Mao's successful revolution. Her sympathetic account of those years of struggle . . . sets the stage for her description of the economic and cultural changes that followed the revolution. Though essentially factual, the presentation lacks depth in that often too little information is given to explain certain actions on the part of either the U.S. government or China; linked with this is a failure to acknowledge the highly charged emotional situation created by the difference in the two countries' ideologies. Nonetheless, the author's consideration of such familiar activities as sports, schooling, and one family's activities on a Sunday afternoon show common concerns between the two peoples.

> *A review of "Our World: The People's Republic of China," in* The Booklist, *Vol. 70, No. 19, June 1, 1974, p. 1107.*

Emphasizing life today in the **People's Republic of China**, Rau also recounts 19th- and 20th-Century history. Thoroughly discussed are the campaign for equal rights for women; family life (husbands and wives have been separated in order to work for the country's welfare); education ("Almost everything the children study has a political flavor . . ."); the fine arts (". . . almost all [entertainment] . . . is concerned with keeping the people from slipping back into the old ways."); etc. Though the Nationalist Chinese do not come out looking well, this is more objective than Sidel's *Revolutionary China: People, Politics, and Ping-Pong* (Delacorte, 1974); it is far more informative than *China—in Pictures* (Sterling, 1973) and more up-to-date than Buell's *World of Red China* (Dodd, 1967).

> *Elaine G. Mew, in a review of "Our World: The People's Republic of China," in* Library Journal, *Vol. 99, No. 12, June 15, 1974, p. 2670.*

A brisk and objective overview. . . . Rau deals competently with historical material and discusses internal politics and international relations lucidly. Such topics are covered in many other books about China, however; what is less usual is the coverage (at this reading level, particularly) of the contemporary scene. . . . An index is appended.

> *Zena Sutherland, in a review of "The People's Republic of China," in* Bulletin of the Center for Children's Books, *Vol. 27, No. 11, July-August, 1974, p. 184.*

Major portions of Rau's 1974 look at modern China remain the same, but there are significant revisions in reporting certain aspects of government function and in explaining the Cultural Revolution and some of its repercussions. Also, the final chapter has been completely rewritten to reflect China's problems with Vietnam, its internal unrest over civil rights, and its efforts to keep on a path of continuing modernization.

> *Denise M. Wilms, in a review of "Our World: The People's Republic of China," in* Booklist, *Vol. 78, No. 16, April 15, 1982, p. 1098.*

---

## MUSK OXEN: BEARDED ONES OF THE ARCTIC   (1976)

A handsome, intent look at the musk ox, the Arctic's largest land mammal, who happens to be more closely related to goats than to oxen and has no musk glands whatsoever. Where Peter Mathiessen's older, more intimate appreciation (*Oomingmak,* 1967) focused on efforts to transplant the animals back to Alaska and Canada where they had become extinct, Rau is best on the herds' life on the Greenland ice cap—where they close ranks to defend themselves against wolves but are vulnerable to freezing rainfall, now increasingly a danger in a land that has previously been a frozen desert. [Patricia] Collins' muted aquatint etchings . . . capture the sense of Arctic snow and silence, and echo Rau's well-informed, affectionate concern.

> *A review of "Musk Oxen: Bearded Ones of the Arctic," in* Kirkus Reviews, *Vol. XLIV, No. 20, October 15, 1976, p. 1142.*

Informative but plodding, this covers the physical and behavioral characteristics of the musk ox . . . plus the other animals and plants which share its ecological niche. . . . Information is current through 1975, mentioning the release of musk oxen in Siberia. However, although it's clear and even interesting at times (cows may occasionally defend the rest of the herd against wolves, for example), the style tends to be difficult and pompous.

> *Susan Sprague, in a review of "Musk Oxen: Bearded Ones of the Arctic," in* School Library Journal, *Vol. 23, No. 5, January, 1977, p. 96.*

A brief and interesting narrative on the return of a valuable Arctic inhabitant from near extinction. . . . How this animal is peculiarly adapted for survival in the open Arctic winter makes fascinating reading. Index.

> *Christina Carr Young, in a review of "Musk Oxen: Bearded Ones of the Arctic," in* Childhood Education, *Vol. 53, No. 5, (March, 1977), p. 262.*

This book is well researched and interestingly written. Rau covers the life cycle of the musk ox and clearly explains its activities throughout the year. The descriptions of the terrain,

weather conditions, plants and animals that share the habitat of the musk ox are vivid and helpful. The historical and economic factors that relate to the musk ox are presented well. There is considerable discussion of the interrelationships between different organisms—mostly animals, though some plants are mentioned. Although there is much information in this small book, the style of writing is far from encyclopedic. It is a fascinating, informative story. Especially good are the descriptions of the reproductive, maturation and protective behavior of these animals. The only detraction from the writing is the occasional use of the male pronoun "he" where "it" would be more accurate.

> *Joseph K. Hichar, in a review of "Musk Oxen: Bearded Ones of the Arctic," in* Science Books & Films, *Vol. XIII, No. 2, September, 1977, p. 98.*

---

## THE GIANT PANDA AT HOME   (1977)

This is a straightforward, unpretentious and eloquent account of the life of a panda in far western China. The author reveals in every description of the rocks, plants and small scurrying animals, that she has walked these mountains herself—a rare experience. Efforts are now being made by the People's Republic of China to preserve the rare wildlife of the Szechuan Province described here. Serious readers of all ages will see Ling-Ling and Hsing-Hsing with new eyes after reading this account. . . .

> *Brigitte Weeks, in a review of "The Giant Panda at Home," in* Book World—The Washington Post, *March 20, 1977, p. H4.*

Taken out of the zoo, the giant panda is much more than just a cute curiosity. It's a wild animal, remarkably well-adapted to its home in the harsh, mountainous region of western China. . . . [Rau's narrative is] clearly written, with an impressive bibliography, and the most mature treatment of the popular animal in the wild.

> *A review of "The Giant Panda at Home," in* Kirkus Reviews, *Vol. XLV, No. 7, April 1, 1977, p. 356.*

This narrative of a year in the life of a giant panda is set in the Szechuan Province Wanglang Preserve, located in the mountainous region of far-western China. Rau follows a female down, up, down, and up the mountains as she locates a male, mates, summers, gives birth to two cubs, mothers and raises them, loses one to wild dogs and the other to independence, and begins the cycle again. While other children's books on the giant panda have focused upon those in captivity, Rau has used accounts of recent Chinese zoological expeditions as well as natural history source material. Thus the complete environmental background (terrain, flora, fauna, climate) which surrounds the panda is provided, making its adaptations and behavior more comprehensible. . . . The prologue, epilogue, and bibliography document sources as well as Rau's concern for preservation of the panda's natural terrain.

> *M. J. A., in a review of "The Giant Panda at Home," in* Booklist, *Vol. 73, No. 21, July 1, 1977, p. 1655.*

A well-written and accurate picture of the life of the giant panda in its native habitat. . . . [The] author provides an engrossing narrative. . . . This fills a longstanding need for a solidly researched account for the middle grades of these rare, popular, sad-faced creatures.

*John D. Boniol, Jr., in a review of "The Giant Panda at Home," in* School Library Journal, *Vol. 24, No. 1, September, 1977, p. 136.*

[*The Giant Panda at Home*] is carefully researched, well written and should prove attractive to a larger audience than the juvenile group to which it is directed.... The illuminating writing style provides understanding of the integration of this giant animal with the ecosystems of the Wanglang Preserve in north-central Szechuan. I wish there were less speculation and projection about supposed "emotional responses" to changes in the environment by what the natives call the "bear-cat." Nevertheless, the text enables the reader to identify with the many creatures of the Szechuan Sanctuary which was established in 1965, increasing our understanding of a land few persons will be privileged to visit.... An excellent bibliography of more than 40 books and articles will guide the reader with more extended interests. This book is close to perfection for the intended audience and older readers as well.

*David G. Barry, in a review of "The Giant Panda at Home," in* Science Books & Films, *Vol. XIV, No. 1, May, 1978, p. 39.*

## THE GRAY KANGAROO AT HOME   (1978)

Similar in scope to her *Giant Panda at Home* ..., [this presents an eastern *Gray Kangaroo*] against a carefully researched background of appropriate flora and fauna. Rau begins with a detailed description of the Warrumbungle National Park in New South Wales, and goes on to describe fully a cycle of seasons in the life of a kangaroo doe. Accurate and well written, the coverage has depth, far outreaching Darling's *Kangaroos and Other Animals with Pockets* (Morrow, 1958) or Jenkin's *Kangaroos, Opossums and Other Marsupials* (Holiday, 1975).

*Patricia Manning, in a review of "The Gray Kangaroo at Home," in* School Library Journal, *Vol. 24, No. 8, April, 1978, p. 88.*

[Rau] happily makes no concession to the age of her readers and manages to convey information in a straightforward, informative style that is never dull. The account of how the 3/4-inch baby kangaroo makes the hazardous journey to its mother's pouch is high adventure.

*Brigitte Weeks, in a review of "The Gray Kangaroo at Home," in* Book World—The Washington Post, *April 9, 1978, p. E4.*

[Unlike] the usual semi-fictionalized animal life, this isn't limited to [the kangaroos's] experiences; nor does Rau call the young one Little Kangaroo or try to make a drama of its encounters. Incidents such as the doe's struggles with an eagle who threatens her joey and her flight with the other animals from a great fire are supplemented with more general information on marsupial evolution, the species' mating habits and development patterns, and its various forest neighbors. This more flexible approach makes her well-grounded report more informative than many and more readable as well.

*A review of "The Gray Kangaroo at Home," in* Kirkus Reviews, *Vol. XLVI, No. 8, April 15, 1978, p. 440.*

As she did last year in *The Giant Panda at Home,* Margaret Rau has given us a beautifully written nature book clearly depicting the life cycle of a single species of animal.... Read-

ers ten and over will be drawn into the excitement of the daily struggle for survival of the mother and "joey" kangaroo, and learn much about their unique and often harsh environment and the other animals who share it.... [A] thoroughly enjoyable volume which deserves a larger readership than it will probably get. An extensive bibliography and index complete a distinctive book.

*Diane Holzheimer, in a review of "The Gray Kangaroo at Home," in* Appraisal: Children's Science Books, *Vol. 12, No. 1, Winter, 1979, p. 32.*

Many children's books dealing with animals suffer from anthropomorphism and an overly sentimentalized view of nature that has come to be known as the "Bambi syndrome." It is therefore refreshing to read a book such as this which presents a carefully balanced view of the natural world.... The author manages to communicate a large amount of information about kangaroo biology and behavior (and to provide descriptions of other Australian wildlife) without resorting to asides that would break the rhythm of the narrative. The story ends with an epilogue that describes current efforts aimed at the conservation of Australian wildlife, and especially, the role that young people have played in these efforts. This last point may be used to start a discussion of what role young people can play in wildlife conservation in this country.

*Erik Paul Scully, in a review of "The Gray Kangaroo at Home," in* Science Books & Films, *Vol. XV, No. 2, September, 1979, p. 103.*

## THE PEOPLE OF NEW CHINA   (1978)

Rau often makes you feel that you're touring China with an official guide—as she repeatedly compares today's conditions to the deplorable ones in "the old China," points along the way to all the items, services, and pleasures that cost "just a few pennies," and populates each village, commune, and city en route with paragons of right thinking. "You are a lucky girl," Hsi-fan's grandparents remind her, while apprentice Ming-li and her friends "are proud of the great forests which clothe the hills, for they have helped plant them"—and teenage Pao-lang, touring the once-Forbidden City in Peking, "is grateful that in the new China no one starves while others live in luxury." But even an official tour has much to show us of Chinese life today, and Rau exposes us to the malls of small family shops (whose owners are not allowed to hire outside employees), the carefully layered system of medical care, the accounting procedures followed when the village rice harvest is sold, the leisure activities which revolve around participants' places of work, the primitive but efficiently managed sanitary facilities, the cultural provisions for children who adopt very early the overriding wish "to serve the people." And—far more than Hsi-fan and the other named young people whom we never really meet, even in Rau's numerous photos, her passing glances at a street-cleaning trio's 9 a.m. knitting break, or a child-created puppet show demonstrating the importance of cleanliness, give some very human interest to a once-forbidden culture. The travelogue twin to Rau's historically ordered *People's Republic of China* (1974), which covers much of the same socio-cultural ground.

*A review of "The People of New China," in* Kirkus Reviews, *Vol. XLVI, No. 12, July 1, 1978, p. 693.*

Vignettes of family interaction in villages and cities introduce readers to the variety of life in China from the South to the

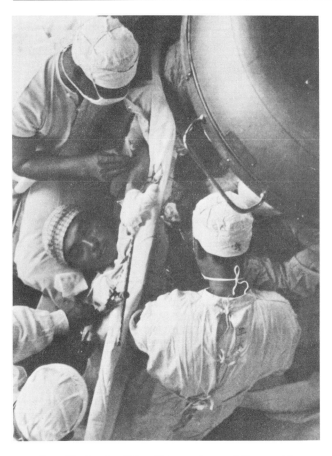

*From* The People of New China, *written and illustrated by Margaret Rau. Julian Messner, 1978. Copyright © 1978, 1979 by Margaret Rau. All rights reserved. Reprinted by permission of Julian Messner, a division of Simon & Schuster, Inc.*

North. . . . Natural-looking photographs appear on almost every page and greatly enhance the text. Like Rau's other books on the subject, this is a lively, readable account which neither over-praises nor over-condemns.

> *Dorothea Scott, in a review of "The People of New China," in* School Library Journal, *Vol. 25, No. 1, September, 1978, p. 146.*

There is, unfortunately, little of China visitor Rau herself in this sympathetic, generally informative view of Chinese life today. In fact, there is not really much on actual people either, title notwithstanding. What readers will find is lots of description focused nominally around the child named—but never actually introduced—at some point in each chapter. Information does flow plentifully . . . and chapters representatively cover contrasting country and city life in north and south China regions. Pieces of relevant history and occasional testimonial statements offer a modicum of context for the experience presented here, and the author's own photographs ably provide illustration. One only wishes the information came with more sense of involvement, as did Axelbank's *The China Challenge* . . . for slightly older readers.

> *Denise M. Wilms, in a review of "The People of New China," in* Booklist, *Vol. 75, No. 1, September 1, 1978, p. 52.*

This can serve as a companion volume to the author's *The People's Republic of China* . . . although it covers some of the same material. . . . The tone is not laudatory, but it is sympathetic; the writing style is direct and the material well-organized. A pronunciation guide and an index are appended.

> *Zena Sutherland, in a review of "The People of New China," in* Bulletin of the Center for Children's Books, *Vol. 32, No. 3, November, 1978, p. 51.*

---

## THE SNOW MONKEY AT HOME (1979)

[As she did in her *Giant Panda* and *Gray Kangaroo at Home*], Rau skillfully integrates information on the *Macaca fuscata* of the Japanese Alps with her reconstructed life of one male snow monkey. Though many fictionalized animal lives leave an impression of sameness between one species and the next, this sustains interest by highlighting specific behavior peculiar to the snow monkey. . . . Rau follows her featured monkey through his gradual growth toward independence and responsibility, his founding and leadership of a splinter troop (common in his northern territory where large groups are less able to survive the winters), and his unaccountable (but frequently observed) abandonment of the social group for a life of solitary wandering. Rau also observes the demise of the mother troop's old leader, and along the way she notes new habits (the washing of sprayed apples) and phenomena (deformed babies) which might be consequences of the invasion of the area by the monkeys' biggest enemy, man. Exemplary.

> *A review of "The Snow Monkey at Home," in* Kirkus Reviews, *Vol. XLVII, No. 23, December 1, 1979, p. 1378.*

Firsthand observation and extensive research provide the background for remarks on the physical characteristics, habits, behavior patterns, and wilderness companions of these monkeys that survive in a colder climate than any other species of monkey. Detailed descriptions of natural occurrences such as birthing, mating, grooming, courting, vocalizing, and care of the young are recorded in a careful, well-written style that underlines the author's interest in and enthusiasm for her subject. Most fascinating are the community organization and societal hierarchy that regulate these animals' lives. . . . Notes on current research and ecological status, along with a lengthy bibliography citing interviews, periodicals, and books (both in English and Japanese), are appended.

> *Barbara Elleman, in a review of "The Snow Monkey at Home," in* Booklist, *Vol. 76, No. 8, December 15, 1979, p. 617.*

The approach is scientific, particularly in descriptions of communicative aspects of behavior, physical appearance of the animal as it changes with seasons and age, and the complex social machinery of the macaque. Sentimentality is avoided; the graphic descriptions of birth and mating are detached and precise. The author's lively style, reminiscent of that of Jean George, enables her to engender and sustain interest in a minute examination of an obscure species.

> *Dora Jean Young, in a review of "The Snow Monkey at Home," in* School Library Journal, *Vol. 26, No. 5, January, 1980, p. 74.*

A quiet power marks Margaret Rau's writings for young people. In *The Snow Monkey at Home*, this author of earlier books on the musk ox, giant panda and gray kangaroo takes complex information from her observation and research and gives it the texture and flow of a compelling story. . . .

[A] well-crafted book in which even the bibliography, highly specialized, has class.

> *Peggy Thomson, "Born to Be Wild: Animals and Their Habitats," in* Book World—The Washington Post, *January 13, 1980, p. 10.\**

In this book there is sadness, joy, excitement, and suspense. The reader is brought into the world of the snow monkey and emerges, perhaps with new insights into his or her own behavior. . . . Included is an excellent bibliography and an index.

> *Ann F. Pratt, in a review of "The Snow Monkey at Home," in* Appraisal: Children's Science Books, *Vol. 13, No. 3, Fall, 1980, p. 56.*

Throughout the book the author's poetic feeling for and awareness of the beauty and wholeness of nature is evident. The text itself contains a wealth of information concerning the life, habits and behavior of the unusual snow monkeys of Japan. It is beautifully written. . . . Unfortunately, however, the word "shimmying" is used twice when "shinnying" is meant. Because of its size and format, the book appears at first glance to be designed for a child, but it is doubtful if the average pupil, even in intermediate grades, could handle easily such words as indigenous, surreptitiously, animosity or limned. Yet these, and others of similar nature, are common. A number of terms, such as hormonal changes, are introduced without further explanation. One wonders why, however, along with more or less technical terms such as genitals and buttocks, the babyish "belly button" is used instead of the more appropriate (in context) "navel." The bibliography, which is excellent, consists almost entirely of references for adult reading. An index is included, but no glossary. Were it not for the format which proclaims "for children," the book would merit the highest appraisal.

> *A review of "The Snow Monkey at Home," in* Science Books & Films, *Vol. XVI, No. 2, November-December, 1980, p. 78.*

---

### RED EARTH, BLUE SKY: THE AUSTRALIAN OUTBACK (1981)

#### AUTHOR'S COMMENTARY

In 1976 I was down under in Australia writing a book on the kangaroo. The book completed I embarked on a journey around the great continent to see as much as I could of it. I went by bus and train because only at ground level can the topography of an area be fully appreciated.

And so I came to Alice Springs in the Red Center of the Outback. I visited Ayers Rock but did not have much time to explore the surrounding country. However, going south to Adelaide over an unbelievably corrugated road in the dead of night, I was intrigued by the dark, flat wastes that spread away on all sides, lighted only by huge stars. Scarcely a light planted by man shone out in all that great platter of land.

Like many travelers before me I felt the mystery of endless space and time. I made up my mind to return one day and give more of my attention to this silent platter of seeming infinity.

So it was that in 1978 I came back to travel at leisure through that part of the Outback which stretches from Alice Springs in the center of Australia to the green coastal fringe in the south.

My way took me through two states—the Northern Territory and South Australia. I was fortunate to have arrived in September, the down-under spring, after rare drenching winter rains had brought up foliage that even old-timers had never seen before.

Under the mulga trees the wilderness was spangled with a riot of tiny desert flowers. They did not last, however, as week by week the sun grew hotter and spring slid into the down-under summer. Then I experienced relentless days of brassy heat, furious gales, thunderstorms when great forked bolts of lightning danced over the plains.

I met and talked to many Outback people, both Aborigine and white. They welcomed me into their homesteads, into the little settlement of Indulkina. They entertained me in their dugout homes in Coober Pedy. Warm, hospitable, proud, they lived in isolated islands in that great sea of land.

I have not space to name all the children with whom I became friends—laughing, independent, tough, yet surprisingly gentle. They showed me their treasures: hollow eggs of desert birds, tiny sand toads, mountain dragon lizards with their scoop of freshly laid eggs beside them. They drove me to their secret spots, following rough tracks in jeeps they were almost too small to handle. Yet handle them they did. They confided to me their dreams and their fears—dreams and fears that began and ended in the great whirl of Outback.

And so I came away to write their story. If I have not done them or their land justice, it is because the subject is too immense to enclose within the covers of a single book. (pp. v-vi)

> *Margaret Rau, in a foreword to her* Red Earth, Blue Sky: The Australian Outback, *Thomas Y. Crowell, 1981, pp. v-vi.*

---

Sprinkling her writing with the colorful lingo of the bush country, the author describes the desert wilderness: its many colors, searing heat, torrid winds, and exotic plant and animal life. She traces the coming of people to Australia and tells how the introduction of sheep and cattle to the Outback lured white settlers away from the green coast to the sacred ancestral land of the Aborigines. Depicting life on cattle and sheep stations, in mining and railroad towns, and in Aborigine settlements, the book—using real families as examples—shows how the hardy inhabitants work, go to school, withstand the elements, and entertain themselves. Problems created by the clash of the Aborigine and white cultures and the government's efforts to help the Aborigines preserve their traditions are objectively and thoroughly discussed, although the tragic aspects of a people in cultural limbo are only touched on. A final chapter assesses the ecological future of the Outback. Index.

> *Kate M. Flanagan, in a review of "Red Earth, Blue Sky: The Australian Outback," in* The Horn Book Magazine, *Vol. LVII, No. 3, June, 1981, p. 320.*

[Rau has] amassed a great deal of first-hand information about Outback life—especially for the children. Both white youngsters and Aboriginal kids, she makes plain, find boarding school a trial after the freedom of the School-of-the-Air courses (for the former) and local primary-school classrooms (for the latter); and we encounter both whites and Aboriginal children who drop out. Similarly, there are white as well as Aboriginal drifters. That sense of a common response to the remoteness and harshness and friendly informality sets her book apart from

*Two children walk on new railway tracks that seem to stretch on and on against the flat platter of plain.
From* Red Earth, Blue Sky: The Australian Outback, *written by Margaret Rau. Photographs by the
author. Thomas Y. Crowell Co., Inc., 1981. Copyright © 1981 by Margaret Rau. All rights reserved.
Reprinted by permission of Harper & Row, Publishers, Inc.*

those that tend to focus either on station or Aboriginal life; but
unfortunately it is also repetitive and somewhat uncertainly
organized—with quite small print and small, blurry photos.
But the child who once gets into it will meet individuals, learn
about camel-breeding as well as cattle-herding, descend into
Coober Pedy's underground homes, share in the annual get-
togethers of the School-of-the-Air children, and ponder, with
Rau, the future of that "great silent platter of land." It's very
well done; one can only regret that it isn't better presented.
(pp. 804-05)

> *A review of "Red Earth, Blue Sky: The Australian
> Outback," in* Kirkus Reviews, *Vol. XLIX, No. 13,
> July 1, 1981, pp. 804-05.*

Rau, who discerningly wrote about Australia's favorite animal
in *The Gray Kangaroo at Home,* describes the area and its
inhabitants (both aborigines and newer settlers) with warmth
and great insight, recounting the beauty of the country and the
joys of the people along with the problems and hardships.
Emphasis is placed on the children, with their comments on
the School of the Air and the Royal Flying Doctor Service, as
well as on everyday chores and special holidays. Unfortunately,
the author's photographs are small and often dark, shading the

graphic scenes so vividly rendered in the text. Fascinating
background reading for Patricia Wrightson's novels.

> *Barbara Elleman, in a review of "Red Earth, Blue
> Sky: The Australian Outback," in* Booklist, *Vol. 77,
> Nos. 22 & 23, July 15 & August, 1981, p. 1449.*

This travel book about contemporary life in the Australian
outback is distinguished by its focus on individuals and families
whom the author met. . . . There are a few overgeneralizations,
fuzzy facts and clichés, but overall, the text is both accurate
and interesting, and provides a more realistic description of
contemporary Aboriginal life than do most children's books
on the subject. It would benefit from the addition of a glossary
of Australian and English terms. Unfortunately, many of the
75 black-and-white photographs taken by the author are of poor
quality and lack inherent or human interest. (pp. 145-46)

> *Nancy J. Schmidt, in a review of "Red Earth, Blue
> Sky: The Australian Outback," in* School Library
> Journal, *Vol. 28, No. 2, October, 1981, pp. 145-46.*

***Red Earth, Blue Sky: The Australian Outback*** is fascinating. . . .
The impact of the Outback terrain and climate on its human
society is the main theme of this book. This theme is apparent
throughout the presentations of children's challenging lives in

locales such as cattle stations, sheep stations, opal mines, and scattered settlements. Each of the book's 14 chapters presents a distinctive topic in a compact but not overpowering fashion. Black-and-white photographs taken by the author are included generously, and they are quite helpful supplements to the textual information. Her photographs are especially convincing portrayals of the bleakness of the Outback's desert landscape. Many students will find this book to be as absorbing as a story with characters and a plot. On the other hand, students who are researching the Outback will find it an informative reference. (pp. 389-90)

> *David W. Moore, in a review of "Red Earth, Blue Sky: The Australian Outback," in* Journal of Reading, *Vol. 25, No. 4, January, 1982, pp. 389-90.*

---

### THE MINORITY PEOPLES OF CHINA   (1982)

There are fifty-six minority groups in China, varying in size, and organized into Autonomous Regions and Autonomous Districts. Prefaced by a section that gives background information about ethnic strains and political changes, the text discusses the lifestyles and customs of some of these minority groups. . . . Each chapter is built around a fictional child character, and gives some geographical and historical information but focuses on the lives of the inhabitants: what they wear and eat and learn, their patterns of worship and work and play, how they live. A colorful, varied, and informative book is written in a relaxed, informal style; an index gives access to the contents.

> *Zena Sutherland, in a review of "The Minority Peoples of China," in* Bulletin of the Center for Children's Books, *Vol. 36, No. 3, November, 1982, p. 52.*

The Chinese are *not* all alike as Rau amply demonstrates in this lively volume. . . . The final chapter discusses the role of the Institute of National Minorities, government-run centers which not only educate outstanding students but apparently foster pride in ethnic tradition as well. The black-and-white photos occasionally disappoint. Some are blurred, others are simply uninformative. Worse, there are no pictures of the youngsters featured in the book. Some confusions mar the text. The introduction lists five Autonomous Regions; later pages add two more. However, the book does bring together valuable information that is scattered across pages of valuable reference books. It would team up nicely with *The Magic Boat* (Vanguard, 1980), a collection of folk tales also containing material on the variety of people living in China today.

> *Ellen D. Warwick, in a review of "The Minority Peoples of China," in* School Library Journal, *Vol. 29, No. 4, December, 1982, p. 68.*

Readers get acquainted with [some 56 minority nationalities] in the author's chapter-length profiles, which focus on a young boy or girl and create scenes from everyday life that act as a springboard for description of each group's background and present status. Eleven-year-old Baima Lhamo, for example, is a young Tibetan girl whom readers will see rising at 6:30 to the tune of military music and who later on accompanies her grandmother to an ancient monastery to worship. In contrast is a Mongolian boy named Sodo, who leads a nomadic life as his family moves with the seasons. Each discussion unobtrusively incorporates information on living conditions (often harsh), common food, important social customs, and perhaps celebrations such as a wedding or special festival. Accompanying

*Two Tibetan girls gather brush for cooking fuel. They are wearing warm Han Chinese jackets and sneakers. From* Holding Up the Sky: Young People in China, *written and illustrated by Margaret Rau. Lodestar Books, 1983. Copyright © 1983 by Margaret Rau. All rights reserved. Reprinted by permission of the publisher, Lodestar Books, a Division of E. P. Dutton, Inc.*

photographs are of uneven quality, but the text is smoothly written and often vivid. An absorbing profile that could be an important source for units on China. (pp. 502-03)

> *Denise M. Wilms, in a review of "The Minority Peoples of China," in* Booklist, *Vol. 79, No. 7, December 1, 1982, pp. 502-03.*

Like [Catherine Edwards Sadler's] *Two Chinese Families*, this book provides insight into the daily lives of Chinese families. . . .

In addition to helping awaken upper elementary-aged students' interest in the minority groups of China, there is some potential for this volume to be used in a broader discussion of minority group treatment in different nations and societies. The index makes the book a useful general reference text as well as a good supplementary text for a unit devoted to China or Asia.

More extensive use of photographs to illustrate the text would make this volume more serviceable to those of us who have no visual images to which to relate the text. The characters presented in each of the essays have emotional depth and are representative of a way of life.

*Robert Ubbelohde, in a review of "The Minority Peoples of China," in* Curriculum Review, *Vol. 22, No. 4, October, 1983, p. 92.*

---

### HOLDING UP THE SKY: YOUNG PEOPLE IN CHINA   (1983)

A cross section of Chinese young people is introduced in this fascinating look at life in China. There is Gu Ernang, who lives in the isolated loessland section of China. His home is a crude hovel dug into a cliff where he lives with his brother, parents, and grandparents. He wants to leave his desolate life to join the army, but his grandparents object. On the other end of the spectrum is 24-year-old Meiling, who lives in bustling Shanghai. She and a friend are taking advantage of the government's loosening of regulations to start a small food stand in a park. They are also using a dating service to find themselves husbands. Intermingled with the life stories of a cross section of young adults is all sorts of historical, geographical, and sociological information. Rau does an excellent job of weaving this in unobtrusively; she also makes clear the role of the Communist government in the lives of both the Han and minority people. One minor puzzlement—in the author's note it states, ''My book is a composite picture of the people I met and with whom I talked,'' leaving open to speculation whether the various people profiled are in fact real individuals. That question aside, Rau shows remarkable writing skills, and the portraits she paints will be of great interest to American readers for the similarities as well as the differences they show.

*Ilene Cooper, in a review of "Holding Up the Sky: Young People in China," in* Booklist, *Vol. 79, No. 16, April 15, 1983, p. 1097.*

Rau's book describes in 12 short chapters the daily lives, work and aspirations of representative young Chinese (ages 18 to 29) in various regions of the People's Republic today. . . . Occasional dialogue and description of feelings enliven and personalize the factual material and further readers' understanding of changing attitudes toward women, minority groups and religion. An excellent vehicle for comparing United States and Chinese culture in areas American young people will find germane to their own lives.

*Marguerite M. Lambert, in a review of "Holding Up the Sky: Young People in China," in* School Library Journal, *Vol. 30, No. 2, October, 1983, p. 172.*

Rau presents a series of portraits of young people (some are adolescents still living with parents, some are students or young married workers) to show both the diversity of backgrounds and lifestyles in a vast country, and to show what life is like in contemporary China. The book succeeds in giving a great deal of information about concepts, creeds, educational practices, village life, etc. Unfortunately, it does not so successfully give a picture of youth in China, since most of the information is of a general nature. None of the young people who are the subjects of the separate chapters seems real, perhaps in part because there are no photographs of them; although the book is profusely illustrated by photographs, a chapter on **"Gu Ernang of Loessland,"** for example, has three pictures of outdoor scenes, and in the chapter, **"The Wedding"** there is a photograph of ''a peasant woman'' and ''a typical apartment kitchen.'' An index is included.

*Zena Sutherland, in a review of "Holding Up the Sky: Young People in China," in* Bulletin of the Center for Children's Books, *Vol. 37, No. 4, December, 1983, p. 76.*

# George Selden (Thompson)

## 1929-

American author of fiction and nonfiction, playwright, and screenwriter.

Selden holds a secure place among writers of animal fantasy for *The Cricket in Times Square*, which tells how a country cricket makes good in New York City with the help of a street-wise mouse, a cat, and a boy. Twenty years after the publication of *Cricket*, Selden wrote its sequel, *Tucker's Countryside*, in which the city animals come to the aid of their friend when his meadow is threatened by housing developers. Selden returns to the urban setting with which he is chiefly associated in *Harry Cat's Pet Puppy* and the picture book *Chester Cricket's Pigeon Ride*. In *Chester Cricket's New Home*, however, he narrates Chester's discovery of a permanent place to live through the kindness of his woodland friends. In all five books, Selden describes the animals's heartwarming anthropomorphic concerns—ranging from fundraising for the impoverished Bellini family and preserving natural resources to adopting an orphaned puppy—in an engaging style applauded for its witty New York dialogue, brisk pace, and subtle use of satire. Through his believable protagonists, Selden comments on animal habits and needs and provides insight into human problems and personalities. Often compared with Kenneth Grahame's *The Wind in the Willows* and E. B. White's *Charlotte's Web*, Selden's books share the mutual theme of loyalty among friends. Selden has created other imaginative stories besides the *Cricket* series, such as *The Garden under the Sea* and *The Genie of Sutton Place*. *Garden* (republished as *Oscar Lobster's Fair Exchange*) is about four aquatic creatures who decorate their ocean floor with such abandoned possessions as sunglasses and a lunch box. In *Genie*, young Tim magically resurrects the majestic Abdullah from an ancient rug. Selden has also written two biographies of famous archaeologists: *Heinrich Schliemann, Discoverer of Buried Treasure* and *Sir Arthur Evans, Discoverer of Knossos*.

A New York resident, Selden first conceived the idea for his best-known book when he heard a cricket one night in the subway. His creation of concert star Chester Cricket was natural for a music lover and devotee of opera who, like his character, comes from Connecticut. Selden's vivid settings are not limited to the inner city. His acquaintance with Long Island Sound adds realism to *The Garden under the Sea*, while in *Tucker's Countryside* he centers on the theme of conservation in a strictly rural setting. Selden has had a lifelong interest in archaeology; his uncommon knowledge of this discipline is apparent not only in his two social science biographies but in secondary characters in *Irma and Jerry* and *Genie* as well. Critics have high praise for *Cricket;* in particular, they cite the way Selden interweaves his love for music, Manhattan, and animals with the Bellini's financial plight, thus providing his most effective plot. Both *Tucker's Countryside* and *Harry Cat's Pet Puppy* win similar acclaim for structure and style. Reviewers find that Selden's other fantasies exhibit his facility with clever dialogue, his familiarity with the great metropolis, and his ability to touch with humor and compassion—but with less success. A few disappointed critics note weak plots, superficial characterization, and, most frequently, a cloying

Photograph by Marcia Johnston

sweetness. Those who enjoy the books, however, commend their whimsy and irresistible charm. Selden's knack for creating books of sheer entertainment by using inventive concepts—a sea garden made of human souvenirs, an unpredictable twentieth-century Genie, or a fast-talking urban team of animals and a boy—endears him to his readers. *Cricket* was a Newbery Honor Book in 1961 and won the Lewis Carroll Shelf Award in 1963. Miller-Brody Productions made a dramatized recording of *Cricket* in 1972 and ABC-TV televised the story in April, 1973.

(See also *Something about the Author*, Vol. 4 and *Contemporary Authors*, Vols. 5-8, rev. ed.)

---

## GENERAL COMMENTARY

### MAY HILL ARBUTHNOT AND ZENA SUTHERLAND

[In *The Cricket in Times Square*, the] The New York setting provides a solid base of realism, for the animal characters live in the Times Square subway station. Tucker is a tough, slangy city mouse, a pure Damon Runyon character, and his friend Harry the Cat is a sage creature. . . . The style is breezy, the dialogue entertaining, the whole situation fresh and imaginative.

Just as charming and cheerful is the sequel, ***Tucker's Countryside,*** which also has a painless message about conservation.... Like E. B. White, Selden brings his animal characters so vividly to life that they have unforgettable personalities, and both books pay tribute to the tenderness and loyalty of friendship.

> *May Hill Arbuthnot and Zena Sutherland, "Modern Fantasy: George Selden," in their* Children and Books, *fourth edition, Scott, Foresman and Company, 1972, p. 232.*

---

### THE DOG THAT COULD SWIM UNDER WATER: MEMOIRS OF A SPRINGER SPANIEL (1956)

Told in the first person, these adventures of Flossy Thompson, a likeable and fairly enterprising neighborhood dog, form a lightly humorous animal fantasy. Flossy is a friendly soul who loves to observe the life around her—springtime in the nearby meadow, the peculiarities of her various canine and feline friends. She was particularly delighted to discover one day that she could swim under water.... The consequences of this skill of Flossy's have amusing consequences, not the least of which helps a friend in a precarious predicament and the result is good local wit. (pp. 43-4)

> *A review of "The Dog That Could Swim under Water," in* Virginia Kirkus' Service, *Vol. XXIV, No. 2, January 15, 1956, pp. 43-4.*

A dog story that is different because the dog, confidingly, does all the talking and is naively most amusing....

The dogs are well characterized, and the detail of the story, a sort that will please children of eight to ten or thereabouts.

> *Olive Deane Hormel, "Widening Horizons," in* The Christian Science Monitor, *July 26, 1956, p. 11.*\*

The dogs think and act like human beings, even to the point of recognizing a doll as being dressed in a colonial costume, and the whole tone is too coy and precious to have much appeal.

> *A review of "The Dog That Could Swim under Water: Memoirs of a Springer Spaniel," in* Bulletin of the Children's Book Center, *Vol. X, No. 9, May, 1957, p. 121.*

---

### THE GARDEN UNDER THE SEA (1957; republished as *Oscar Lobster's Fair Exchange*)

An animal story in the tradition of *The Wind in the Willows* takes Long Island Sound for its quiet setting and the sea creatures around Turtle Rock for its lively and opinionated characters. Actually, not much happens. What counts is the way in which Peter Starfish, Oscar Lobster, Hector Crab, James Fish and the old periwinkle, their mentor and guide in all matters of importance, take their small action. We first hear of it when Peter meets Hector, and Oscar, who is whipping him up about the disgraceful collecting being done by the shore people. When the sea creatures decide to retaliate and make a garden of their own with human relics, the principle that is learned by everyone, including Janet and Howard, the children on shore, is that one must not salvage for loot alone. It's a long story with many episodes, during the course of which we become increasingly fascinated with Mr. Selden's knowledge of the sea, and his ear for a humorous, salty tale. (pp. 37-8)

> *A review of "Garden under the Sea," in* Virginia Kirkus' Service, *Vol. XXV, No. 2, January 15, 1957, pp. 37-8.*

This is a wonderfully written fantasy, so plausible that it just might have been the way the author says. The undersea characters must have been understood and loved, for how else could one picture the aquaplaning of Peter Starfish?

> *Rae Emerson Donlon, "Sea Facts and Fancies," in* The Christian Science Monitor, *May 9, 1957, p. 14.*\*

A rather forced attempt at animal fantasy that somewhat imitates but never compares with Hatch's The Lobster Books.... The four, a lobster, a crab, a starfish, and a cunner, have no reality as animals since they are endowed with complete knowledge of all things relating to human beings. The fantasy is labored and the humor too self-conscious to have much appeal.

> *Zena Sutherland, in a review of "The Garden under the Sea," in* Bulletin of the Children's Book Center, *Vol. XI, No. 8, April, 1958, p. 85.*

The idea has appeal and individual incidents are delightful. (Fishermen, especially, will chuckle at James Fish learning the techniques of eating bait without swallowing the hook.) However, too much time is spent on underwater sightseeing at the expense of plot development to sustain interest throughout. Additional purchase.

> *Barbara Bader, in a review of "Oscar Lobster's Fair Exchange," in* Library Journal, *Vol. 91, No. 13, July, 1966, p. 3538.*

George Selden's book has a salty flavor, and his swimming undersea world evokes a kind of nostalgia for a recently past summer, but one never really develops too much interest in his creatures, and their adventures are too drawn out to get very exciting. (p. 16)

> *Elinore Standard, "The Light Fantastic," in* Book Week—World Journal Tribune, *Fall Children's Issue, October 30, 1966, pp. 14, 16.*\*

---

### THE CRICKET IN TIMES SQUARE (1960)

[The] Times Square subway station seems like a matter-of-fact place. No cricket is observed ordinarily consorting there with a mouse named Tucker or a friendly calm cat called Harry. But subway crowds miss much that is going on at their feet and so did the Bellini family who ran a pathetic failure of a newsstand there. Young Mario Bellini did notice the cricket and wished to take him home as a pet....

Even trapped in a little cage with a bell and placed on the newsstand shelf Chester, aided and abetted by his friends during the almost deserted hours, brought trouble to the Bellini family and the increasing enmity of Mama Bellini, until Tucker, typical New Yorker, (good judge of character, excellent business brain, kindhearted and managing) had a brain wave.... [Chester Cricket's] success and what it did to the Bellini's business and to the traffic situation at that particular subway station ... makes as cheering reading as we have met in some time....

George Selden's first books, **"The Dog That Could Swim Under Water"** and **"The Garden Under the Sea,"** had the same excellent writing and original imaginative twist but they lacked the unified plot we have here. This is absolutely grand fun for anyone, a nine to ninety book.... As we finished this convincing fantasy on the late local express out of the Grand Central we would hardly have turned a hair if we had spotted Chester walking down the aisle at some Connecticut station....

*"A Connecticut Cricket," in* The New York Herald Tribune Book Review, *November 13, 1960, p. 5.*

This fantasy may well be the charmer of the fall season. And if its reviews sound more like a dust jacket blurb, it's because there is a good deal to praise. Mr. Selden capitalizes on the readers who accept caprice when tempered with logic. He's created a story they know didn't happen—but wouldn't it be wonderful if it did? . . .

A talent for images that delight children and special attention to particulars mark this book. Mama Bellini talks like a New Yorker, the settings are carefully and colorfully correct, the after-hours parties of Tucker, Harry and Chester hilarious.

*Mary Lee Krupka, "In the Heart of Town," in* The New York Times Book Review, *November 13, 1960, p. 50.*

Who ever would have dreamed that a solid and enduring friendship could exist between a mouse, a cat, and a cricket? But that's just what we find, and accept as the most natural thing in the world, in this captivating book, one which deserves shelf space with such congenial companions as "Stuart Little" and "Charlotte's Web." . . .

More engaging characters than Tucker, Harry, and Chester would be hard to find between book covers. Their adventures radiate warmth, humor, and loving kindness. . . .

*Polly Goodwin, in a review of "The Cricket in Times Square," in* Chicago Sunday Tribune Magazine of Books, *December 25, 1960, p. 6.*

[*The Cricket in Times Square*] is original in setting and in combinations of characters, including a human hero, which gives the book wider age appeal than that of most talking animal tales. The story is laid chiefly in the Times Square subway station where Tucker Mouse and Harry Cat share their home with a cricket from Connecticut, proving that New Yorkers can be friendly indeed. The book has spontaneity and is full of surprising events and convincing nonsense. (p. 470)

*Ruth Hill Viguers, "Golden Years and Time of Tumult, 1920-1967: Worlds without Boundaries, Literary Fairy Tales and Fantasy," in* A Critical History of Children's Literature *by Cornelia Meigs, Anne Thaxter Eaton, Elizabeth Nesbitt, and Ruth Hill Viguers, edited by Cornelia Meigs, revised edition, Macmillan Publishing Company, 1969, pp. 446-83.*

[In Hugh E. Wright's *The Interminable Trudge of Samuel the Snail,* there is animal clowning. Chester the Cricket in *The Cricket in Times Square*] has, in its way, more reality. There are no houses, shells, burrows or holes—their place is taken by the New York subway, a news-stand in the station at Times Square, and a drainpipe home of a mouse called Tucker who, unlike most fictional mice, is neither neat nor good at housekeeping. His hole is a magpie nest of oddments picked up from the subway station: lost jewellery, money, buttons, scraps and bits of food. Nearly all the action takes place underground, and in man-made surroundings.

Tucker meets a cricket from Connecticut who has jumped off a train, and they both become friends with a roving cat, Harry, a fugitive from the East Side who shares the drainpipe with the mouse. The drama and amusement of the story come from the three creatures' adventures with, and observation of, the Italian family who owns the news-stand. There is nothing unlikely in the scavenging animals living below ground and existing on scraps humans throw away, or the helpless insect's being carried there in a picnic sandwich. Fantasy only lies in their friendship, their ability to understand each other and talk and comment on the humans, and the rosy glow that this imparts to a reality that must have been hard and uncompromising. The unnatural nature of the cat/mouse friendship is, indeed, attributed to non-natural New York. (p. 144)

*Margaret Blount, "Dressed Animals and Others," in her* Animal Land: The Creatures of Children's Fiction, *William Morrow & Company, Inc., 1975, pp. 131-51.\**

[A] word for a classic of its kind, *The Cricket in Times Square.* . . . Once the juvenile is disabused of the idea that the Americans have finally taken to the noblest of all ball games, once they have grasped that this is another story of sapient animals, they will probably find George Selden's narrative touching, amusing and exciting. Narrowly sidestepping the pitfalls of whimsey, Selden invented that rare commodity, a children's book with subtle, vigorous and credible characterisations. It is seventeen years now since *The Cricket in Times Square* won its first award, and so far its charm is wearing well indeed. One small grumble; the Puffin blurb advertises the book as appealing to a wide range of ages, 'beginning at seven and ending at thirteen.' Too arbitrary; there is no reason why readers should not delight in Selden's Chester Cricket and his friends Harry the Cat and Tucker Mouse long after the thirteenth birthday has been left behind. (p. 27)

*Benny Green, "Child Labour," in* The Spectator, *Vol. 238, No. 7763, April 16, 1977, pp. 26-7.\**

---

***I SEE WHAT I SEE!*** (1962)

Six children and Jerry visit Central Park, take a subway and a ferry and arrive at Staten Island—all on a cloud of fantasy. The lion in the zoo is "stalking along through the tall dry grass in Africa". The subway is the "Confusing Cavern". The ferry is a "Both-Way-Boat". Only Jerry sees things realistically, for which he is castigated by his more imaginative companions. As Jerry shatters each illusion by a quiet statement of fact, the children become more and more furious. Finally they play a trick on Jerry, but prove nothing, and in the end, when Jerry compromises by "seeing" the New York skyline as a cobweb of lights", . . . he is still the outsider. In his attempt to stress the place of the imaginative child, was it necessary for the over-sympathetic author to make his precocious little group so mean in their brainwashing and ostracizing practices? This reader's sympathy was with Jerry—and the story seems lacking in appeal both from the literary and psychological viewpoints.

*A review of "I See What I See!" in* Virginia Kirkus' Service, *Vol. XXX, No. 15, August 1, 1962, p. 682.*

The conversation of the children is natural, and the theme of the story has appeal, but the book is weakened by the quick conversion: an unimaginative child is not likely (as Jerry is, it is implied) to think fancifully because of one incident. (p. 87)

*Zena Sutherland, in a review of "I See What I See!" in* Bulletin of the Center for Children's Books, *Vol. XVI, No. 5, January, 1963, pp. 86-7.*

---

### HEINRICH SCHLIEMANN, DISCOVERER OF BURIED TREASURE   (1964)

The power of Schliemann's compulsion to prove Homer's verses accurate is lost here and his years of business in Russia, as well as Gold Rush California, are only mentioned hastily. However, the techniques Schliemann developed for archeological digging are informative and his final triumphs and trophies are accurately described. . . . The effects of his finds on archaeological study are also put in context.

*A review of "Heinrich Schliemann: Discoverer of Buried Treasure," in* Virginia Kirkus' Service, *Vol. XXXII, No. 9, May 1, 1964, p. 454.*

The story of Schliemann could offer a challenge for [the 8 and up] age group, but the style is pedestrian, relying heavily on subject-predicate construction to achieve the simple reading effect. Nevertheless, it's passable.

*Dorothy Winch, in a review of "Heinrich Schliemann, Discoverer of Buried Treasure," in* Library Journal, *Vol. 89, No. 12, June 15, 1964, p. 2660.*

The life stories of great scientists can be exciting adventure to young children ready for the larger world. . . . ["**Heinrich Schliemann: Discoverer of Buried Treasure**," "Alexander the Great, Scientist-King," by Robert C. Scuggs, and "Sigmund Freud: Doctor of Secrets and Dreams," by John H. Mann] feature three men children rarely have opportunity to meet. Of the books that tell important incidents in each man's childhood and professional life and necessary scientific concepts, Heinrich Schliemann's story is the best. Consistently entertaining, it conveys the dedication of the 19th-century German archeologist who spent his fortune and later years in the search and eventual discovery of Troy and other Homeric States. Lorence Bjorklund's carefully drawn illustrations enhance the clear explanation of Schliemann's contribution. . . .

*Margaret F. O'Connell, in a review of "Heinrich Schliemann: Discoverer of Buried Treasure," in* The New York Times Book Review, *September 20, 1964, p. 26.*

---

### SIR ARTHUR EVANS, DISCOVERER OF KNOSSOS   (1964)

The wonderful story of the Minoan Civilization, its disappearance from the knowledge of man except in legend, then its dramatic discovery in recent times by Arthur Evans, can be enjoyed at various levels by everyone.

Here George Selden tells in a simple manner of the boyhood of Evans, of his abiding interest in archaeology, and of his eventual success in discovering Knossos and the palace of Minos. . . . [It] makes compulsive reading. Middle juniors will love this, and upper juniors will want to follow the story up in a more detailed account.

*S. W. Allen, in a review of "Sir Arthur Evans," in* The School Librarian and School Library Review, *Vol. 13, No. 2, July, 1965, p. 249.*

A brief sketch of the life and career of Arthur Evans. . . . The book does give the facts about Evans' meeting with Schliemann

and about his discoveries of Cretan treasures, but the writing style is so gushy that it masks the appeal of the subject.

*Zena Sutherland, in a review of "Sir Arthur Evans: Discoverer of Knossos," in* Bulletin of the Center for Children's Books, *Vol. 19, No. 3, November, 1965, p. 49.*

---

### SPARROW SOCKS   (1965)

[This] story is all about the undoubted power of word of mouth advertising. Angus McFee, the young night watchman of the small factory where the sock machine was housed, kindly set the machine for the tiniest of socks for the sparrows to wear. The birds wore them well and this brought them to the attention of cautious Scottish consumers who had been going elsewhere for their footgear. The intricate illustrations [by Peter Lippman] offer more fun than the fairly simple story of a small business going broke. (pp. 1035-36)

*A review of "Sparrow Socks," in* Virginia Kirkus' Service, *Vol. XXXIII, No. 19, October 1, 1965, pp. 1035-36.*

A few years ago Mr. Selden wrote a book called **"The Cricket in Times Square."** Ever since then we have waited for his next. **"Sparrow Socks"** is not a repeat performance. All the same there is a great charm in his tale. . . . Author and illustrator show a Scotland that is as genuine as any sock-wearing sparrow.

*Pamela Marsh, "The Excited Ant and the Warm Sparrow," in* The Christian Science Monitor, *November 4, 1965, p. B4.\**

[This] sad little drama when the sparrows return their socks to help the destitute businessmen will touch even a lean and hungry alley cat. The absurd is beautifully embellished with the ridiculous, to create a delightful fantasy. The absolute seriousness of the dour Scot proprietors is the perfect foil for the flighty antics of Angus and his friends.

The incongruity of the giant machine making "beauteous new, warm and woolly winter socks with the stripes and the bright red toe" for the towns' sparrows gives us a hilarious story that is guaranteed to cause many giggles.

This book is as good for the very young as the author's very fine *The Cricket in Times Square* is for older children. (pp. 10-11)

*Phyllis Cohen, in a review of "Sparrow Socks," in* Young Readers Review, *Vol. II, No. 4, December, 1965, pp. 10-11.*

Guess what, there really is something new under the sun, a new plot for a picture book. . . . The illustrations have a Rube Goldberg madness, with some lovely touches such as the McFee wall in which Whistler's mother and an American Gothic figure have in hand bright red socks. The text has the same kind of humor: the sparrows and humans don't converse together, but when the sparrows talk to each other, they use Scottish dialect.

*Zena Sutherland, in a review of "Sparrow Socks," in* Bulletin of the Center for Children's Books, *Vol. 19, No. 5, January, 1966, p. 89.*

---

## THE DUNKARD (1968)

Looking for "the most interesting grown-up that anyone had ever seen" to bring to Grown-Up Day at school, our hero finds a chubby, middle-aged, happy-looking gent singing "Oh, dunking is a joyous thing, / A genuine delight. / It makes you want to laugh and sing. / I dunk both day and night." An unabashed and unashamed, thoroughly dedicated dunkard, he teaches the boy (who forgets to introduce himself as George until the third chapter) to dunk anything. . . . George covers his perfect find in a sheet to prolong the surprise at school. . . . He worries through one secretary, a fireman, a dentist, a veterinarian, an acrobat, two doctors, a hairdresser and a skinny poet until his moment of triumph arrives; the reactions are somewhat subdued (Miss Brill is sure he has mispronounced the word) but the dry dipso-maniac steals the show-and-tell scene with his verses in defense of dunking, even gets proper Miss Brill to indulge. . . . [This] clever spoof speaks in the voice of children and the pose is maintained throughout with understated jocularity. It takes time to read but the whole family will listen.

> *A review of "The Dunkard," in* Kirkus Service, *Vol. XXXVI, No. 3, February 1, 1968, p. 112.*

George Selden's story starts off from an ordinary notion and leads into hilarious offbeat territory. . . . This book may require librarians to demonstrate with crullers and coffee. It will certainly set anyone to laughing who reads it. And it has the endorsement of the chairman of the board of Dunkin' Doughnuts. (pp. 46-7)

> *Jerome Beatty, Jr., in a review of "The Dunkard," in* The New York Times Book Review, *May 5, 1968, pp. 46-7.*

Dunking is one of those small private pleasures almost anyone can enjoy. So is this pleasantly silly book, which promotes the practice of dunking to a fine art. . . . This story, which nicely typifies Important School Days, will appeal to the obsession children have with peculiar eating habits in a way that adults won't find in the least offensive.

> *Elinor S. Cullen, in a review of "The Dunkard," in* Library Journal, *Vol. 93, No. 13, July, 1968, p. 2731.*

---

## TUCKER'S COUNTRYSIDE (1969)

The line between convincing charm and sugary sentimentality in animal stories is a fine one indeed. A wholesome touch of tartness and irony, as in Beatrix Potter's books or *The Wind in the Willows* or Maurice Sendak's *Higglety-Pigglety Pop!*, protects against the kind of unbelievable sweetness that ruins George Selden's *Tucker's Countryside*, a sequel to his *Cricket in Times Square*. The book is awash in embarrassing goodness and cuteness. The animals—Chester Cricket, Tucker Mouse, Harry Cat, and John Robin; the girl, Ellen, who saves a meadow; and the entire quasibucolic setting in a well-manicured Connecticut suburb are rendered in a coy style that should be abolished forthwith.

> *Michele Murray, "Life under the Rule of Dictators: A Pair of Differing Viewpoints," in* The National Observer, *June 9, 1969, p. 23.\**

Not to equivocate, this is whimsy at its sparkling best. It will be greeted with loud cheers by the admirers of *The Cricket in Times Square.* . . . The characters are a delight, the dialogue

is amusing, the action is satisfying, and the conservation theme is used to advantage. More, more.

> *Zena Sutherland, in a review of "Tucker's Countryside," in* Saturday Review, *Vol. LII, No. 26, June 28, 1969, p. 39.*

A delightful, breezy story and lively, humorous drawings [by Garth Williams] echo the success of text and pictures in the author's and illustrator's earlier *The Cricket in Times Square.* . . . The Old Meadow is in danger of becoming the site for apartment houses, and the local animals hope that the wily, big-city duo [Tucker Mouse and Harry Cat] can come up with a plan for saving the area. Tucker finally outwits the human Hedleyites. . . . The clever observations offered of different animal habits and human idiosyncracies, the individualized personalities of the animals, (pompous, petulant, excitable, clever Tucker; calm, teasing Harry; serious, conscientious Chester), the lively action of the story—all of these aspects spell success. . . .

> *Evelyn F. Newlands, in a review of "Tucker's Countryside," in* School Library Journal, *an appendix to* Library Journal, *Vol. 16, No. 1, September, 1969, p. 161.*

There are certain books which, by their distinction and originality form a measure for all others. Such a one was George Selden's *The Cricket in Times Square.* It possessed wit, humour and style, which marked it out among the animal-fantasy stories. Now we have an equally enchanting sequel. . . . [The] urban creatures find it hard to adapt to the countryside: 'Subways I can sleep through. Commuters I can sleep through. But that brook just goes on . . . and on . . . and on!'

The flavour of the book is apparent even in such a brief snatch—indubitably American, with shades of Damon Runyan in its dialogue. . . . [The] book is a joy to read aloud to all, from seven up.

> *Gabrielle Maunder, in a review of "Tucker's Countryside," in* Children's Book Review, *Vol. I, No. 3, June, 1971, p. 92.*

There is a lack of wit and clarity to this sequence to *The Cricket in Times Square.* Perhaps it is because the engaging characters of Chester cricket, Harry cat and Tucker the voluble mouse, are removed from the gritty brilliance of the Times Square subway station to the mellow greenery of Hedley's Old Meadow. Reviewers of the earlier book have made strong comparisons with *The Wind in the Willows*, but this is meaningless in Tucker's countryside for here the enemy is man, who threatens to lay waste the space and privacy of the Connecticut scene. Mole and Ratty would hardly have been satisfied by the solution in which the enemy is tamed and invited in to view pseudo-historic remains; why what next a nature trail? No, George Selden is much more at home in the brash noisy city where his chirpy characters fight for survival amongst the pounding feet of the homeward rushing commuters.

Moments of splendour are still to be found and the writing has a rich brilliance so promising in the earlier book. Tucker mouse organises the animal population "to build a discovery", in other words a mouse-made ancient monument, constructed with some chewing here, a quick removal there, and everywhere some "benign deception" as Tucker calls it. Here is the wit and the brilliance not in the conventional tribulations of the animals against the flood or the bulldozer.

*A review of "Tucker's Countryside," in* The Junior Bookshelf, *Vol. 35, No. 3, June, 1971, p. 187.*

This is the world the way it *ought* to be. The values it presents are those to which we give lip service. The book is humorous, wistful, and friendly. But what does it tell children about society the way it really is? What does it lead them to expect? Magic solutions? (p. 130)

> *Betty Bacon, "Realism and the Testing of Reality (I): From Now to 1984," in* The Cool Web: The Pattern of Children's Reading, *Margaret Meek, Aidan Warlow, and Criselda Barton, eds., The Bodley Head, 1977, pp. 129-33.\**

---

### THE GENIE OF SUTTON PLACE   (1973)

A tale of fantasy whose cast of characters include a 1000-year-old genie with an eye for the girls and a pet-shop owner who is himself an ex-dog must surely be characterized as promising. Yet the sum of this story's occasionally inspired parts leaves a disappointing hole in the reader's ultimate pleasure.

One difficulty is that author George Selden . . . successfully evokes the magic of the Arabian Nights, only to dissipate its venerable dazzle in the service of a rather pedestrian contemporary tale of Manhattan days. . . . [All] too soon, Abdullah exchanges his jeweled turban and exotic pantaloons for drab livery. . . . As for his awesome magical powers, they are put to no more exalted challenge than the rescue of Tim's pet dog Sam from a pound on West Houston Street.

True, Sam's deliverance entails his becoming a human being, but little is changed by this metamorphosis. As a dog, Sam had an inexplicable crush on Aunt Lucy (a thorough-going pill) and, as a man, his dogged devotion only deepens drearily. In fact, not since Puck dispensed his magical love potion in "A Midsummer Night's Dream" have more unlikely romances blossomed. . . .

Unfortunately, the book fails to convince the reader fully of its fictive reality. The element of make-believe somehow has more dimension than the flesh-and-blood characters. As a result, we are less tolerant of jarring elements than we might be in a tale of tighter weave. Why, for example, in a story that clearly takes place in New York City is the museum where the genie is found called the National rather than the Metropolitan? What makes the author reach so unerringly for the grating phrase—"my suspicions got nervous" . . . "it made my heart jiggle" . . . "There was a chuckle riding inside his voice"? And how come the book's copy editor allowed a careless inconsistency of plot to pass unnoticed? It is, in sum, a lightweight novel that reads easily but leaves no echoes to reverberate in an inquiring child's mind.

> *Selma Lanes, in a review of "The Genie of Sutton Place," in* The New York Times Book Review, *June 24, 1973, p. 8.*

[*The Genie of Sutton Place* is] a sophisticated but somewhat low-comedy story. . . . There's a good bit of wit in the writing, exaggeration of characters, overstimulated plot albeit original in concept. This hasn't the ingenuous charm of Selden's earlier books, but it's fun.

> *Zena Sutherland, in a review of "The Genie of Sutton Place," in* Bulletin of the Center for Children's Books, *Vol. 26, No. 11, July-August, 1973, p. 176.*

Children who remember the author, above all else, for his *The Cricket in Times Square* will find their faith justified and renewed by the new book set in New York—an altogether felicitous combination of wit and fantasy, hilarity and wisdom. Timothy Farr tells, most engagingly, the story of the "'wondrous summer'" when he turned thirteen. . . . Readers will long remember Sam as bungling hound and blundering man; Madame Sosostris, the would-be séance medium wearing a tie-dyed dishtowel as a turban; Dooley, the genie, as novice driver at the wheel of Aunt Lucy's Cadillac in New York traffic; and Tim, the only child in the story, but an enormously delightful one. (pp. 382-83)

> *Ethel L. Heins, in a review of "The Genie of Sutton Place," in* The Horn Book Magazine, *Vol. XLIX, No. 4, August, 1973, pp. 382-83.*

This is the finest genie a boy has ever owned; deep-voiced and dark, friendly, full of a sense of power and poetry that gives *The Genie of Sutton Place* . . . all its charm. . . .

Dooley is the troubleshooter every child (and adult) has dreamed about. He solves Tim's immediate problem by changing Sam into a man. Modern harassments—like traffic lights and locked doors and unpleasant people—are dismissed with a snap of the fingers or an elegantly turned verse. . . .

[George Selden] has written a delightful fantasy with a host of improbable characters. But without the presence of Dooley, it would be an unremarkable story. The genie towers above the tale, with his panache, wit, sumptuous poetic style, and the very human approach he takes to human predicaments.

> *Jennifer Farley Smith, "A Genie Named Dooley and Other Magic," in* The Christian Science Monitor, *October 3, 1973, p. 10.\**

A boy, his dog and his worlds of Greenwich village seances and plushy relatives, together with a marvelous up-from-the-rug genie, give this continuously moving story great appeal. The genie's magic enlivens the tale, waxing and waning like the mystic moon. Real people, real situations, real emotions and growth balance its fantasy with merry wit. Who would have guessed such excitement from an archaeologist and a museum?

> *O. Robert Brown, Jr., in a review of "The Genie of Sutton Place," in* Childhood Education, *Vol. 50, No. 5 (March, 1974), p. 294.*

---

### HARRY CAT'S PET PUPPY   (1974)

Those old buddies, big-time operator Harry the Cat and scrounger Tucker Mouse, are keeping house again in their Times Square drainpipe, and have grown domestic enough to become sentimental over a homeless dishrag of a pup whom they name Huppy. As Tucker himself is the first to admit, there still seems something ludicrous about a cat and a mouse making such good roommates, but Huppy's pet-as-surrogate-child role is easy enough to fathom. . . . Selden pokes gentle fun at the animals' New York accents and at their behavior—half grown-up wise guy, half squabbling kid. But most of the fun still lies in their elaborate attempts to live up to human standards, with the details of Tucker's aspirations to drainpipe elegance the most fascinating. Big as he is, Huppy is a more manageable problem than the two tackled in their last, rural adventure, and [illustrator] Garth Williams shows just how every improbable encounter actually looked. It's good to see the old guys back home again where they belong.

*A review of "Harry the Cat's Pet Puppy," in* Kirkus Reviews, *Vol. XLII, No. 24, December 15, 1974, p. 1305.*

Hooray! The characters who delighted readers in *The Cricket in Times Square* are back—not Chester Cricket, who's still in his rural retreat, but Harry Cat and Tucker Mouse.... Everything about the book is appealing: the humor, the dialogue, the characterization, the yeasty style, the setting and the beguiling illustrations.

*Zena Sutherland, in a review of "Harry Cat's Pet Puppy," in* Bulletin of the Center for Children's Books, *Vol. 28, No. 8, April, 1975, p. 137.*

As adoptive parents of a homeless puppy, [Harry Cat and Tucker Mouse's] unique solutions to the difficulties encountered in rearing their waif and unearthing a suitable permanent residence for him are wrought with warmth and hilarity. Their protective and genuine concern for the development and future of their helpless, lovable charge results in a rash of excitingly witty episodes. Both the situations and the dialogue are causes for mirth as one peruses the adventures of the human-like mice, cats, birds, and dogs.... This is a wonderful book for reading aloud so that everyone may laugh and relish it together.

*Lynne List, in a review of "Harry Cat's Pet Puppy," in* The Reading Teacher, *Vol. 29, No. 5, February, 1976, p. 511.*

George Selden's third tale about the Times Square friends, *Harry Cat's Pet Puppy,* has a tight construction and a consistently witty development of the paradox by which Harry Cat adopts a stray puppy and tackles the resulting problems with the crusty co-operation of Tucker Mouse.... Each of the animal characters has a given personality and a consistent role in the story which is warm-hearted without being sentimental and full of a zippy dialogue which aligns these intelligent animals with humanity as easily as the plausible details of their American housewifery.

*Margery Fisher, in a review of "Harry Cat's Pet Puppy," in her* Growing Point, *Vol. 16, No. 9, April, 1978, p. 3291.*

[The] gutters and alleys of convincing urban squalor overflow with compensatory schmaltz. Huppy lisps baby-talk, peeps meltingly out from under floppy ears, tugs at our heart-strings with his fluffy paws, until, in a culminating piece of chutzpah, he becomes a symbol of manhood. The pianist is derided for his sentimental fondness for his cat. "Yich! Sick-making! That's one guy who really needs a dog."

*Marion Glastonbury, "Animal Land," in* The Times Educational Supplement, *No. 3284, June 16, 1978, p. 45.**

As usual, George Selden writes with aplomb, wit and a touch of mild irony; his dialogue is snappy and robust, each character individualised by speech as well as by behaviour. The hard-boiled floozie-pigeon, Lulu, contrasts neatly with the prissy haughtiness of Miss Catherine, an aristocrat to her claw-tips. The situations that tax the patience and ingenuity of Harry and Tucker are disarmingly human but carefully chosen details are a constant reminder that this is a world of animals, realised with a sympathy and confidence that are rare.

*A review of "Harry Cat's Pet Puppy," in* The Junior Bookshelf, *Vol. 42, No. 4, August, 1978, p. 195.*

## CHESTER CRICKET'S PIGEON RIDE   (1981)

*The Cricket in Times Square* began a series that might have been spared this sequel, *Chester Cricket's Pigeon Ride.* There is less than half a story here. Even readers of earlier installments will not feel keyed in to the cricket's unlikely world and curious friends. Little care is spent on supporting the motives or feelings of the cricket, his old friends in the subway, or his new friends, a coy, liberated hen-pigeon named Lulu whooo speaks in a pecuoooliar pigeon patois. The rationale for the story seems to be the aerial ride, a pleasant idea unfulfilled by George Selden's words or by Garth Williams' illustrations, like efforts pushed for a short, mercantile deadline. These words and pictures do not carry the interesting matchbox world of a cricket-person or the vertigo of a pigeon ride among skyscrapers. It will take brighter tools to coax forth more sympathy for a Times Square cricket than for a New York cockroach.

*Jan Adkins, in a review of "Chester Cricket's Pigeon Ride," in* Book World—The Washington Post, *August 9, 1981, p. 9.*

In an 8½" x 10½" format that suits the slighter content, Selden's *Cricket in Times Square* begins to miss the countryside and soon finds himself following a sycamore-tree smell to nearby Bryant Park. There, after a hairy crossing of 42nd St. that takes five pages to complete, he chirps blissfully and attracts, with his music, an admiring pigeon. Lulu, the pigeon, then takes him for a spin that affords some lofty full-page views of Manhattan as well as another thrill when he falls from atop the Empire State Building, dropping several flights before she catches him. All this provides some idle diversion at the tourist level, but it's old-hat picture-book fare and not up to Chester's debut performance.

*A review of "Chester Cricket's Pigeon Ride," in* Kirkus Reviews, *Vol. XLIX, No. 18, September 15, 1981, p. 1161.*

[Mr. Selden] seems, at times, almost disinterested in his material. He has always been a literate and sweetly humorous writer for children and he does conjure up some amusing and quite lyrical moments but they are left to sparkle from a rather routine travelogue. This is a pleasant, not unusual book by an unusually talented author and artist. It is their own fault that we know just how much better they are able to do.

*Karla Kuskin, in a review of "Chester Cricket's Pigeon Ride," in* The New York Times Book Review, *September 20, 1981, p. 30.*

## IRMA AND JERRY   (1982)

Jerry is a naive cocker spaniel recently transplanted from academia to Greenwich Village, where Irma, a tough cat with a heart of gold, involves him in the lives and fortunes of a cross section of New Yorkers—a lonely archeologist, a tough cop, struggling actors and May the bag lady.... Jerry is unbearably coy, and the tone veers from highly sentimental (the death of the bag lady) to farcical (Jerry's appearance in an off-off-Broadway play). The episodic plot and myriad characters allow Selden to explore stereotypes to the full, but many of his references ("realizing my potential") will be understood only by older readers, while the idea of talking animals in this context may turn them off.

*Caroline S. Parr, in a review of "Irma and Jerry," in* School Library Journal, *Vol. 29, No. 3, November, 1982, p. 104.*

Irma is a streetwise city cat. Jerry is an overprivileged dog. They meet in Manhattan, and thereby hangs a tale—told by the dog. It could work. But after I had slogged my way through the jumbled plot and a dizzying array of puns, exclamation points and things designated ''[swearword],'' I knew it hadn't. In fact, I was thoroughly baffled.

Whom is this book for? It's laced with adult references, yet most of the ''humor'' is straight from the Saturday morning tube. Something is out of whack here, unless . . . I finally hit on a possible explanation. This book is not only by but for a dog. To test this theory, I read it to my pooch.

Pooch: First of all, the dog is a turkey. One minute he's acting like a puppy, the next minute he's spouting Aristotle.

Me: Maybe it was a literary device. You know, the canine philosopher.

Pooch: If I may quote Jerry, ''To [swearword] with all that philosophy!''

Me: What about the cat?

Pooch: I admit to prejudice there. But I certainly can't relate to a feline that sounds like Shirley MacLaine playing Irma la Douce. And while we're talking character development, let me tell you I *loathed* that canary. You know, the one that says things like ''youz can loin!'' Grrr!

Me *(tactfully changing subject)*: Any comment on the plot?

Pooch: It almost gave me distemper. Drunken animals, kleptomaniac scientist, senile bag lady—I ask you, what is this book supposed to be saying to young dogs?

Me: Sure you're not losing your sense of humor?

Pooch: Yes. Matter of fact, that fellow the dog collaborated with, George Selden, has written some very funny books. I liked **''Tucker's Countryside.''**

Me: So did I. But can't you find something positive to say about **''Irma and Jerry''**?

Pooch: The descriptions of Greenwich Village are nice.

Me: That's it?

Pooch: That's it.

I had to agree.

*Barbara Brenner, in a review of "Irma and Jerry," in* The New York Times Book Review, *March 13, 1983, p. 29.*

Employing a number of well-known literary conventions, the author develops a lively first-person narrative . . . and tells a story in which human beings play second fiddle to anthropomorphic animal characters. . . . Sheer entertainment as to action and dialogue, the story captures the atmosphere of the metropolis that O. Henry called ''Bagdad-on-the-Subway.'' (pp. 167-68)

*Paul Heins, in a review of "Irma and Jerry," in* The Horn Book Magazine, *Vol. LIX, No. 2, April, 1983, pp. 167-68.*

## CHESTER CRICKET'S NEW HOME   (1983)

Chester Cricket made his debut 20 and some years ago in a funny, touching and improbable story, **''The Cricket in Times Square.''** More adventures were told in **''Tucker's Countryside,''** and in a scenic picture book, **''Chester Cricket's Pigeon Ride.''** These three books delighted readers with their action, feeling, wisdom and charm. Unfortunately, the same cannot be said for the latest one.

In this slight tale, Chester is left homeless when two stout humans crush his house in a tree stump by sitting on it. Although his friends offer shelter, none of the invitations works out. . . . Desperate, Chester is driven to end it all when—surprise!—a perfect new home is created for him by Simon Turtle and Walter Water Snake inside an old log in the turtle's pond.

Besides providing a good story, George Selden usually can be counted on for rewarding glimpses into animal (read human) ways. There are flashes of this—when Chester visits his ruined stump house by moonlight and finds it transformed into a ragged thing of beauty, and when Donald Dragonfly offers sincerely to share his branch. But **''Chester Cricket's New Home''** is thin, shapeless and slow. The dialogue, through which most of the action is reported (instead of being played out), seems endless. Many young readers will find the book tough going.

*Ellen Rudin, in a review of "Chester Cricket's New Home," in* The New York Times Book Review, *January 22, 1984, p. 24.*

In a sequel to the stories about Chester that began in 1960 with *A Cricket in Times Square,* both author and illustrator [Garth Williams] adhere to the standards of excellence and the appealing qualities that attracted earlier readers. . . . It's the lively style, the strong characterization, and the humorous dialogue that give the book substance and sparkle.

*Zena Sutherland, in a review of "Chester Cricket's New Home," in* Bulletin of the Center for Children's Books, *Vol. 37, No. 6, February, 1984, p. 118.*

By means of gentle satire the author laughs at the foibles, mannerisms and weaknesses of human beings, disguised here as animals and birds. The unlucky hero, insect though he may be, has, like most human beings, a longing for affection and the comfort and security of a home of his own. The story is a shrewd appraisal of human conduct and is very funny at times. The author's habit of giving incongruous names to the animals and birds—Dorothy Robin, Lady Beatrice Pheasant, Henry and Emily Chipmunk—will irritate some readers.

*A review of "Chester-Cricket's New Home," in* The Junior Bookshelf, *Vol. 48, No. 1, February, 1984, p. 29.*

George Selden's buoyant humour carries him through the difficulties which are bound to occur when the home life of a cricket, water-snake, chipmunk and pheasant are represented in part natural and part human terms and when these animals are shown in closer relations than they would naturally enjoy in a real American landscape. This new look at lively Chester lacks the firm structure of that inimitable first tale *A Cricket in Times Square,* but there is much to enjoy in the account of how Chester's friends, when his log home is wrecked . . . , set to work to find him another. No doubt Simon Turtle could have gnawed out a suitable hole in a log, with the help of Walter Water-snake: we believe in the enterprise because of the engaging chat of these improbable allies. Meanwhile Chester tries to accommodate to several unsuitable temporary homes— tossed by wind on the dragonfly's perch, uneasy in the grass clumps offered by the snobbish pheasants and miserable in the home of the obsessively tidy chipmunks. In each case the comparison with human types is as neat as it is entertaining. . . . Though we may regret the absence of Harry Cat and Tucker Mouse, we must allow that Chester plays admirably in this new frolic.

> *Margery Fisher, in a review of "Chester Cricket's New Home," in her* Growing Point, *Vol. 22, No. 6, March, 1984, p. 4213.*

# Elizabeth George Speare

## 1908-

**American author of fiction and nonfiction and journalist.**

Speare's books reflect her pervading interest in history and her belief in the inner strength of human nature. Her four works of historical fiction—*Calico Captive*, *The Witch of Blackbird Pond*, *The Bronze Bow*, and *The Sign of the Beaver*—focus on resourceful characters who struggle to survive and adjust to an often harsh environment. With the exception of *The Sign of the Beaver*, Speare writes for upper-grade readers and incorporates romantic interest to lighten the stories. A lifelong resident of New England, Speare feels a special kinship with the early settlers and has chosen pre-Revolutionary America as the setting of most of her books, including her one nonfiction title, *Life in Colonial America*. Recognized as a skilled weaver of fact and fiction, she is commended for her lively characterizations and exciting plots.

Speare performs meticulous research, even using primary sources as the basis of some of her works. In *Calico Captive*, for example, she expands upon the actual 1807 diary of Susanna Johnson, who was captured with her family and sent by the Indians on a forced march to Canada. A happy personal life coupled with a strong religious faith have helped mold Speare's confidence in a person's ability to face adversity courageously, a conviction which is demonstrated in the lives of her protagonists. Kit Tyler in *The Witch of Blackbird Pond*, Speare's most popular novel, exhibits irrepressible gaiety and independence despite often intense social pressure from the dour inhabitants of seventeenth-century Wethersfield, Connecticut, Speare's home for twenty years. Daniel, a Palestinian youth living in the time of Christ, expresses similar strength of character when he lets love supplant his hatred of the Romans in *The Bronze Bow*. Readers welcomed *The Sign of the Beaver* after Speare's twenty-year absence from writing fiction. The story examines self-reliance on a younger level: twelve-year-old Matt is forced to spend several months alone in a forest cabin where he is befriended by the Indian boy, Attean, and his tribe.

Speare's five books have won two Newbery Medals and one Newbery Honor Book award, a fact which underscores the excellence of her writing. Critics praise her for creating characters who are well-developed and fully human, though occasional reviewers note that the problems she presents are resolved too easily. Speare's settings inspire consistent acclaim and critics credit her with depicting vivid historical backgrounds which influence the plots but do not overwhelm them. Her talent for making history come alive through gripping narratives gives Speare a secure place among fiction writers of the last three decades. *The Witch of Blackbird Pond* received the Newbery Medal in 1959 and was added to the International Board on Books for Young People (IBBY) Honour List in 1960; *The Bronze Bow* won the Newbery Medal in 1962 and was nominated to the IBBY Honour List in 1964; and *The Sign of the Beaver* was the first recipient of the Scott O'Dell Award for Historical Fiction in 1983 and was a Newbery Honor Book in 1984.

*Courtesy of Elizabeth George Speare*

(See also *Something about the Author*, Volume 5 and *Contemporary Authors*, Vols. 1-4, rev. ed.)

---

### GENERAL COMMENTARY

#### ELIZABETH H. GROSS

Elizabeth Speare in [*The Bronze Bow*] and in *The Witch of Blackbird Pond* has written compellingly of a boy, Daniel, and a girl, Kit, who change and mature through circumstances and the influence of the goodness and evil of people. Daniel, brooding and taciturn, consumed with hatred for the Romans . . . ; and Kit, lively and thoughtless, raised to luxury and beauty but cast into Puritan Connecticut . . .—both learn that love, justice, freedom and dignity are forces as powerful in Biblical Palestine as in Puritan New England. Although in both books the adult characters exert considerable influence on the outcome of the story, it is the young friends of Kit and Daniel who, by their faith, courage and steadfast loyalty, enable them to work out their problems to a satisfying conclusion. (p. 5)

*Elizabeth H. Gross, "Twenty Medal Books: In Perspective," in* Newbery and Caldecott Medal Books: 1956-1965, *edited by Lee Kingman, The Horn Book, Incorporated, 1965, pp. 3-10.**

## CALICO CAPTIVE (1957)

Vital and vivid, this short novel based on the actual captivity of a pre-Revolutionary girl of Charlestown, Vermont presents American history with force and verve. The author graces veracity with a selective eye and ear for incident and dialogue. The heroine, Miriam Willard, with her family a captive of Indians, undertook a forced march north to Canada.... Bartered by the Indians to French captors, Miriam finds herself in the sumptuous elegance of the Du Quesne family.... With the additional excitement of the French-English conflict this is a sterling calibre for teen-aged girls.

>           *A review of "Calico Captive," in* Virginia Kirkus'
>           Service, *Vol. XXV, No. 18, September 15, 1957, p. 693.*

[This] is superior historical fiction.... The writing is so vivid that the reader shares with [the Willard family] their experiences on the long trek to Canada and in Montreal.... They live in different households there and so one gets a picture of several phases of life in the city. Realistically, not everything ends happily but the book closes with Miriam feeling sure which of her two suitors she wants to marry and free at last to go to him. It will be a favorite with older girls.

>           *Jennie D. Lindquist, in a review of "Calico Captive," in* The Horn Book Magazine, *Vol. XXXIII, No. 5, October, 1957, p. 406.*

[This is] a splendid story.... The author wisely adds many perfectly possible experiences—Miriam's problem with the boldly staring young Indian, Mehkoa, her troubles with the coquettish and jealous French girl and the courtship of the dashing Pierre. The whole story is excellent. It is that rarity in historical novels, one that does not seem to be written to provide "background" but to tell a good story, in which the setting is important both because it affects the characters and plot and because it is vividly recreated by the author.

>           *Margaret Sherwood Libby, in a review of "Calico Captive," in* New York Herald Tribune Book Review, *November 17, 1957, p. 32.*

The author has drawn her characters with a deft touch and paints a vivid picture of the danger and difficulty of such an experience without ever resorting to sensationalism or melodrama. An exceptionally mature story that should have wide appeal.

>           *A review of "Calico Captive," in* Bulletin of the Children's Book Center, *Vol. 11, No. 4, December, 1957, p. 48.*

The account of the journey through the wilderness, harrowing enough in all conscience, is mercifully cut short before it becomes tedious but enough is said to emphasise the fortitude of Susanna, newly delivered of a child, in the face of the rigours of the journey. Skilfully drawn is the background of enmity and prejudice between French and English which was soon to break out in open war. The author takes great pains, even with her Indian characters, so that one is aware of a constant conflict, in the literary sense, between individuals rather than vague blocs. This helps to lend conviction to a story which must be among the most impressive of forgotten epics of everyday heroism.

>           *A review of "Calico Captive," in* The Junior Bookshelf, *Vol. 27, No. 5, November, 1963, p. 304.*

On the whole, **Calico Captive** is good reading. For the most part it maintains its lightness convincingly by presenting the story through the point of view of its heroine Miriam. She is inclined to overlook the larger horror, to concentrate instead on trivialities that affect her vanity. The meanness of the moment, not the threat of tragedy in the future, affects Miriam, as when the kidnappers steal her best dress: "There in the wilderness, surrounded by savage enemies, bound for a fate she dared not imagine, she wept her heart out for a flowered dress she would never wear again." Epic-minded fiction writers who present their settlers gazing nobly into the future, as if only a bit of cement were needed to turn them into monuments for the park or the city hall, ought to examine Speare's theme: that concerns of the moment and persistent self-interest are also a part of the pioneer spirit.

>           *Sam Leaton Sebesta and William J. Iverson, "Realistic Fiction: 'Calico Captive',"* in their Literature for Thursday's Child, *Science Research Associates, Inc., 1975, p. 292.*

---

## THE WITCH OF BLACKBIRD POND (1958)

### AUTHOR'S COMMENTARY

[In a sense, the] occupation of writing can never be lonely because the solitude is so richly peopled.... I am sure it must be true of all writers, that in the months in which they live closely with the people they have created, these fictitious lives become entangled with their own, and on looking back they find that the imagined experiences have merged with the actual past and that the past is infinitely richer because of them.

Where these imaginary people come from is one of the intriguing mysteries of this solitary profession.... One of the most common questions asked any writer is, "How do you begin your stories? Do they start with an idea, or an incident, or a character?" Looking back, I can answer that for me they begin with people.

The main characters in ... [*Calico Captive*] came to me full-grown from the pages of an actual narrative published in 1807. As I thought about Susanna Johnson and her husband and children and her younger sister Miriam, and as I followed their adventures, filling in from my own imaginings the events about which the narrative itself is silent, other people emerged from nowhere to join them, and in the end these people of my own creating were no less real than the characters I had adopted.

When I began to think about a second novel, I had every intention of following the same pattern. I turned this time to Connecticut, my adopted state, and I found its history both dramatic and inspiring. But after months of reading I had not found a single incident that seemed to spark a story or a plot of ground on which I could stake a claim. Then gradually I became aware that some people were waiting, not in the pages of history but in my own mind. There was a girl, lonely and insecure, a child who needed friendship, a gentle and wise old woman, and two young men, one shy and uncertain, the other self-confident and merry. Behind them, shadowy, indistinct, other people waited. Each of these people began to take on sharper outlines, individual dimensions, and they were already moving and talking and reaching out in relationship to each other, long before I had found a place for them to live or a time in which they could be born. Finally I was compelled to find a home for them.

I chose Wethersfield, the town in which my husband and I have lived for twenty years, because it is one of the oldest towns in New England, one of the first of the Connecticut settlements; because it was once a bustling river port with all the romance and color of the old sailing ships; and because the girl I could now see quite clearly seemed in some way not yet known to me to be at home in the quiet and lovely Wethersfield meadows that still lie for undisturbed stretches along the Connecticut River. I chose the year 1687 arbitrarily because the story of the Connecticut Charter was irresistible, a perfect little vignette, revealing in miniature all of the powerful forces which, nearly one hundred years before the Revolution, were moving America irrevocably toward independence.

Once time and place had been established, the most delightful part of the work began. The usual term for this procedure is historical research, but I should hesitate to dignify by such a scholarly term the haphazard, indiscriminate, greedy forage in which I indulged. History, geography, town records, genealogies, novels set in the same period—I gulped all these down with, at first, little thought of anything but my own enjoyment. There were fascinating bypaths from which I had to drag myself back—Quakerism for one, and the early development of education in New England. The astonishing thing is that I do not remember anywhere in my long-distant schooling a fondness for history. It seems that only now that my imaginary people have lured me back into the past it has become absorbing, and it has taken me more than half a lifetime to discover for myself what Elizabeth Gray Vining said in her Newbery acceptance speech, that "History is people."

Gradually, as I steeped myself in the past, the terrain began to appear familiar and natural. It is a very exciting thing to use the magical magnifying glass that is called historical research—a glass with the added perspective of Time. I can move this glass over a map of the world and focus it on a chosen spot—Wethersfield, for example, in 1687—and what was only a black dot on the map leaps into focus and becomes a town, with grassy lanes shaded by ancient elms, with square rough-timbered houses, a spacious green and a small, turreted church. As the glass moves closer I can see the new bell in the turret, and the bloody head of a wolf nailed to the church door. I can peer inside the houses and see the wooden and pewter dishes on the long board, and the Indian corn pudding on the dishes, and the rough flax waiting to be spun, even the words in the letters hidden in an old chest. Just beyond the town the shining ribbon of the Connecticut River is alive with sailing ships, and the glass moves closer to reveal the rigging on the ships and the cargo they carry. Most exciting of all, the people who move in and out of those houses and ships are exactly the same as the people I know there today—people who are kind and quarrelsome, ambitious and anxious, well-intentioned and blundering, fighting and loving each other, like the people in my own family and on my own street.

Within the framework of the magnifying glass these people begin to act out their story. Part of this is involuntary on the part of the author. I had always been sceptical of writers who claimed that a story wrote itself, but I understand now exactly what they meant. However, there are deliberate elements as well. Much as one hopes to conceal the machinery, no story can be constructed without it. One can only hope to camouflage the engines and to muffle their chugging.

Once the focus is established, the rim of the magnifying glass becomes a fixed frame, beyond which one cannot move. Now, to switch similes in midstream, constructing the historical story becomes much like putting together a Chinese puzzle, in which there are a number of brightly colored and oddly shaped fragments which may be fitted into an infinite number of designs, all within the one determined frame.

In the forming of this design there are certain rules. I did not discover these rules, but by trial and error proved their truth for myself. One of these rules, for example, is that, once the pattern is determined, some of the pieces, lovely and intriguing as they appear, must be discarded, and this can be just as difficult and heart-rending as having to leave one child at home from a picnic. Not only must every piece that is chosen be shaped to fit the final design, but to be most effective it must also be colored to blend with every other piece. No matter how tempting a fragment of history, a quaint local custom or a curious recipe, no matter how fascinating it is in itself, it must also have a chameleon quality. It must blend with the piece beside it. The fragment of history must take on a new color because it is seen through the eyes of a person and tinged with his emotion, or it must lend some of its own color to the character and be itself reflected in his thoughts and actions. Anyone who has ever constructed a Chinese puzzle knows how baffling and exasperating these stubborn fragments can be, but he also knows the feeling of triumphant glee when a cherished piece finally drops snugly and beautifully into a carefully prepared spot.

All this is like having my own personal Berkeley Square into which I can step every morning. For the duration of a novel I can lead two lives, the imaginary life becoming more and more engrossing and real, so that now, looking back upon those days, the life that I led in Wethersfield in 1687 is woven deeply into the fabric of my actual life, and is truly a part of my experience. (pp. 266-69)

[I] believe very strongly that one of the greatest gifts we can give [our children] is the opportunity sometimes to escape from our urgency—an opportunity to be somebody altogether different from themselves, to live in another time and another place, to swing out on a vast arc of experience into a realm of pure adventure.

Children need textbooks for the heart as well as for the mind. The enduring values of life—courage, devotion, compassion, forgiveness—none of these can be absorbed entirely by the mind but must instead be received into the heart. These values are the raw material of fiction. When a story stirs us deeply, for a moment at least we realize these qualities in ourselves, we possess them in our hearts. In a very real way they become part of our experience and we can never altogether lose them. In our anxiety to prepare our children for a Space Age, we must make very sure that they do not miss those imaginary adventures which can so greatly illumine and enrich their lives. (pp. 269-70)

*Elizabeth George Speare, in a Newbery Award Acceptance Speech, given at the meeting of the American Library Association, Washington, D.C. on June 23, 1959, in* The Horn Book Magazine, *Vol. XXXV, No. 4, August, 1959, pp. 265-70.*

---

One of the best books of 1957, an excellent historical tale with an American setting, was **"Calico Captive,"** by Elizabeth Speare. Her new book is even better. From the moment when Kit Tyler sees the bleak line of the shore of Saybrook . . . , every moment of her life in the Connecticut of 1687 is of absorbing interest.

Rarely has a book taken us back into seventeenth-century life as this does. The secret perhaps is that Kit is a fully realized character and so are her two cousins and the three young men who play important parts in the story. We want to know if this gay, impulsive girl, brought up in luxury, . . . will adjust to the dour Puritan town of Wethersfield, where she hopes to live. . . . Even before the Dolphin sails up the river to Wethersfield Kit is the object of suspicion. There are mutterings about witchcraft. At the time she treats them lightly, but before she is in America a year such suspicions threaten her very life and the life of a strange old Quaker woman living like a hermit by Blackbird Pond. The emphasis of this story is on romance and danger but these are both bound up in Kit's case with events of importance to the colony, especially the struggle to keep the charter from Governor Andros.

> *Margaret Sherwood Libby, in a review of "The Witch of Blackbird Pond," in* New York Herald Tribune Book Review, *November 2, 1958, p. 20.*

**The Witch of Blackbird Pond** reveals not only the wisdom, the beliefs and feelings of Elizabeth George Speare, but her imaginative, creative talents and her superb writing abilities. . . .

With her natural bent for research and her ever-inquiring mind, Elizabeth George Speare dug into the files of Puritanical New England, including the actual courthouse records on which she based the testimony and evidence read at Kit's trial for witchcraft. In telling Kit's story, she wisely chose to dramatize the life and customs of the times by contrast. What could be more scandalizing to the dour New Englander of 1687 than a gay, impulsive girl who had grown up on a "heathen" island, running free as the wind in a world filled with sunshine? And to such a girl, what could be more disheartening than the gray, barren shores of Wethersfield at that time? (p. 1291)

The setting is stern and as uncompromising as the strong-willed but fair-minded Puritans in their struggle to preserve their charter. Yet, in spite of Kit's unconventional behavior and her rebellion against bigotry, there is a happy buoyancy, too. People did have fun in those days. (p. 1292)

> *Mary Silva Cosgrave, "Elizabeth George Speare— Newbery Award Winner," in* Library *Journal, Vol. 84, No. 8, April 15, 1959, pp. 1291-92.*

It is [the] pervading spirit of undimmed faith in the essential goodness of things which gives **The Witch of Blackbird Pond** both its charm and its meaning. (p. 273)

Here is a book, meant for the young reader, which is far from delicate; it manages to grapple with evil while still sustaining faith in man's yearning for the stars. Under the shadow of the twentieth century's nameless fears, thank heaven for a book which encourages compassion. Set in the seventeenth century it may be, but the values of **The Witch** are timeless. . . .

**The Witch of Blackbird Pond** is transcending its original intention. Time may decide to ignore age limits and label Elizabeth George Speare's new book an enduring part of America's artistic heritage. (p. 274)

> *Helen Reeder Cross, "Elizabeth George Speare," in* The Horn Book Magazine, *Vol. XXXV, No. 4, August, 1959, pp. 271-74.*

The Cop-Out Book is often the most insidious. At its worst, it promises much and delivers nothing. But the better ones are the most infuriating, for often they are only a step away from being the exact kind of literature we'd like to see for girls *and* boys *about* girls. The actual cop-out may be only a crucial line, a paragraph, the last chapter. But somewhere a sexist compromise is made, somewhere the book adjusts to the stereotyped role of woman, often for the sake of social pressure and conformity. The compromise brings with it a change, and this change is not only disturbing, but often distorts the logical development of the character herself. Suddenly her development is redirected—or, rather, stunted. (p. 21)

Sometimes it is the focus of a book that makes it a cop-out. When we read . . . **[The Witch of Blackbird Pond]** . . . , we praised Kit's independent spirit, her rejection of bigoted values, and her truly striking courage at a time when women were burned for witchcraft. From a feminist standpoint, the book is marred only by the plot's revolving around the standard question: "Whom shall Kit marry?" In too many books we find the male character worrying about *what* shall he be—while the female character worries about *who* shall he be. (p. 22)

> *The Feminists on Children's Literature, "A Feminist Look at Children's Books," in* School Library Journal, *an appendix to* Library Journal, *Vol. 17, No. 5, January, 1971, pp. 19-24.\**

[It] can be a dangerous practice, this business of categorizing books, of looking for certain things in books. . . . I rather enjoyed reading an extract from a paper given at a conference on sexism in children's books in the United States. I quote: "Cop-out books are those which start out right, but compromise somewhere, such as the tomboy who becomes a lady etc. Even such an excellent character as Kit in **Witch of Blackbird Pond** has as her main worry who 'he' will be." For those of you who know **Witch of Blackbird Pond**, an enjoyable and readable historical novel set in seventeenth-century Connecticut—what a ludicrous comment! What could an enterprising girl do at that time and in that place except look for her man! (pp. 111-12)

> *Janet Hill, "Accepting the Eleanor Farjeon Award," in* Signal, *No. 9, September, 1972, pp. 109-14.\**

[Kit's Connecticut] family is puritanical, and the harsh, repressive atmosphere contrasts strongly with her former carefree life. Mercy, Kit's lame younger cousin, is a model of patience and humility who works without complaint, even when desperately sick, and readily accepts her situation. Kit befriends Hannah Tupper, an old Quaker woman widely regarded as a witch. After a devastating illness hits the community, the townspeople hysterically conclude that Hannah Tupper is to blame. Kit rescues the old woman, but is arrested herself on charges of witchcraft. The young sailor who originally delivered Kit to her new home brings a young child to Kit's trial who provides evidence of her innocence. As is typical of such books, all problems are resolved: The child, long abused, is reunited with a now more appreciative family; Hannah is safe from further persecution; all marriageable females, including even Mercy, are betrothed; and Kit and her uncle have accommodated their differences in a flood of mutual respect.

Mercy's characterization is simultaneously highly idealized and taken for granted. She is not considered marriageable and her family makes no provision for a dowry for her. Being both female and crippled, her qualities of forbearance, self-effacement, and unassertiveness are thereby multiplied. Where others are shown having a spectrum of personality attributes, Mercy is shown in extremes—it is she who becomes the most ill from the epidemic; it is she who is "good enough" for the minister.

The setting of colonial America adds some mild interest to this typical adolescent historical romance. (pp. 304-05)

*Barbara H. Baskin and Karen H. Harris, "An Annotated Guide to Juvenile Fiction Portraying the Handicapped, 1940-1975: 'The Witch of Blackbird Pond'," in their* Notes from a Different Drummer: A Guide to Juvenile Fiction Portraying the Handicapped, *R. R. Bowker Company, 1977, pp. 304-05.*

---

## THE BRONZE BOW (1961)

### AUTHOR'S COMMENTARY

**The Bronze Bow,** which was my third book, was quite different from the first two, both in the purpose and in the making. It was not so much an adventure as a challenge, and at the book's completion I knew that I had recorded no more than the first steps of a lifelong search that can never be fulfilled. (p. 337)

Even now I wonder how I had the rashness to venture upon ground which is not only hallowed but salted as well with traps for the well-meaning trespasser. For many years there had been in my mind the urge to write something about the land of the New Testament. . . . True, I did not rush in, but never for one moment did I walk serenely. I approached with uncertainty, and I was beset every step of the way by doubt and discouragement.

When I stood in just this spot before you in June of 1959, I was already committed to this quest. I had completed a year of research, but my characters and story existed only in the shadowy glimpses I tried then to describe to you. One scene only was very clear to me. . . . (pp. 337-38)

On a Friday afternoon the preceding March, in Mr. Melcher's office in New York, the unbelievable moment had come when the Newbery medal for **The Witch of Blackbird Pond** was placed in my hand. . . . On Sunday morning my husband and I ended this improbable Queen-for-a-day week end with a service at Riverside Church. In my overstimulated state the trumpeting organ prelude was a final intoxicant. I did not hear a word of the service, because, in response to the music, the climax and final chapter of my new story began to play itself out in my mind so compellingly that I was aware of nothing else. From that moment I knew where I was going, and in all the changes and about-faces that were continually to alter my course, that final chapter, though it was many times rewritten, remained essentially intact, just as I first saw it that morning.

I told you that June that my stories began with people. Yet I made the mistake of trying to begin this story with a theme. I knew what I wanted to do. I was teaching a Sunday School class at the time, and I longed to lift the personality of Jesus off the flat and lifeless pages of our textbook. I wanted to give my pupils, and others like them, a glimpse of the divided and turbulent society of Palestine, an occupied country with many parallels in our own day. And I wanted to stir in them some personal sharing of what must have been the response of boys and girls who actually saw and heard the carpenter from Nazareth.

I think the initial theme of the book rose out of a discussion our class had one Sunday morning on the great heroes of history, and on what qualities a hero must possess. I longed to have them see that the preacher who walked the hills of Galilee was not a mythical figure, but a compelling and dynamic leader, a hero to whom a boy in any age would gladly offer all his loyalty.

I had no illusions that this would be easy. But I did not foresee the almost insurmountable difficulties that would block my way for the next three years. The research itself was never a barrier. I plunged eagerly into Jewish history, into the accounts of travelers who spread before me the land, the people, and the ways of Palestine, and into the rich and complex treasury of Bible scholarship. Finally I knew that I must pull myself from the absorbing joy of reading and begin the task of writing.

And here I came up against the truth I stated to you. There was no story to write, because there were no people. I had an outline, and some shadowy figures. But no real and living people.

There was a girl, of course. I had written two stories about girls, and I assumed that was my natural province. So I forced myself to begin Chapter One. I gave my girl a brother and sent them off on a lighthearted picnic on a mountaintop in Galilee, bright with spring flowers. In Chapter Two my heroine, hidden behind a rock, witnessed some lively action. But Chapter Three brought me to a dead end. I suddenly saw that a girl hidden behind a rock would never be a heroine. Palestine was an eastern country in which women stayed submissively at home. Even the remarkably emancipated female my heroine was going to be would need the most ridiculous contriving to be on stage at the right moments. And a girl's-eye view of Palestine would be a narrow and limited view.

Suppose I were to write from the brother's point of view instead? I rewrote the three chapters, and this time my boy and his sister met a young outlaw on the mountain. Daniel was not a new invention; he was the hero I had had in mind all along. He was to be the romantic and bold young leader of a band of Zealots. But the boy I saw on the mountain was quite different from the confident leader I had planned. This boy was unsure and defiant and bitterly unhappy. All at once he began to move and to talk and to think with a fierce urgency that left no room for doubt. I had a person at last, a real person, and to my dismay he was a wild and difficult one. But the story had to be his. As I began the first chapter for the third time, the girl and her brother leaped to life beside Daniel, and I knew that I was on the right road.

But the lightheartedness and the spring flowers were gone. This was an altogether unfamiliar path. From the first it took a direction I had never planned. Sudden turns opened up vistas I had never anticipated. There were blind alleys from which I had to patiently retrace my steps. Events I had moved toward with confidence turned out to be mirages as I approached, and worthless. Moreover, I saw that this road must lead to violence, and all my life I have been a timid mouse, shrinking from the least hint of violence.

And the most serious stumbling block of all loomed constantly ahead. I wanted my young people to meet Jesus. But how could I portray Jesus, when many years of searching to understand his life and his teachings left me still facing a mystery? I read countless versions of the life of Jesus, most of them written with reverence and deep faith, some with skepticism, a few even with venom, each one differing from the others. The personality of the Man from Nazareth has been at the mercy of hundreds of interpreters. There is no definitive biography. The quest for the historical Jesus has never yielded the surety for which the scholars hoped. The incontestable facts of history barely establish his having lived at all. Yet he stands like a mountain peak, which, however high we climb, looms forever higher, rising into the mist, its full dimension hidden from our sight.

In the end I realized that in this case research was defeating my purpose and only clouding my vision. The sum of my search is contained in one line which I put into the mouth of Simon the disciple, "We are forced to choose, not knowing." In my portrait of Jesus I failed. I know that failure was intrinsic in the attempt, but I wish that I could have climbed higher. I knew before I had gone far on this road that I was not big enough to do what I had hoped. But I set myself to do, to the best of my ability, one small thing. I would show the change wrought in just one boy who came to know the teacher in Galilee. This is the story of *The Bronze Bow*. (pp. 338-41)

There are many needful ways of equipping young people for the future. We have chosen to place books in their hands, books that will serve not only as companions and teachers but as guardians. For the world into which our children are about to step is filled with peril. And perhaps of all the dangers that lie in wait, the most terrifying is that they may settle for a world without meaning. . . .

Young people do not want to accept meaninglessness. They look urgently to the adult world for evidence that we have proved our values to be enduring. Yet perhaps never before have they looked so clearly, so despairingly, at the evidence we offer. They demand an honest answer. Those of us who have found Love and Honor and Duty to be a sure foundation must somehow find words which have the ring of truth. (p. 341)

> *Elizabeth George Speare, in a Newbery Award Acceptance Speech given at the meeting of the American Library Association, Miami Beach on June 19, 1962 in* The Horn Book Magazine, *Vol. XXXVIII, No. 4, August, 1962, pp. 336-41.*

---

Daniel of Galilee joins the powerful Rosh in the mountains and participates in the underground vowed to bend the bronze bow of Rome. Sent to Capernaum to dispatch information, Daniel by chance observes the healing power of Jesus and is profoundly fascinated. . . . Daniel's hatred is steeled by the constant reminder of his parents' crucifixion and the deadening effect it had on his younger sister Leah who sits in silence day after day. As Rosh's methods become more cruel, he is renounced by the brave mountain band and Daniel appeals to Jesus to fill the now empty leadership role. How puzzled he is when the great prophet preaches love as the best antidote to the bronze bow of Rome, and how miraculous when he finds his own heart thawing. . . . The author succeeds admirably in re-entering the era and filling it with entirely human characters. Intentionally Jesus remains a shadowy figure, for it is his effect on Daniel that is essential to the boy's development. Alive and colorful biblical fare in the well modulated manner of Elizabeth Speare.

> *A review of "The Bronze Bow," in* Virginia Kirkus' Service, *Vol. XXIX, No. 14, July 15, 1961, p. 615.*

The book is remarkable in its integration of setting and reality of characters—especially Daniel and Leah, in the strength of the message without preaching, and in the holding power of the plot. . . .

[This is an] exciting, deeply moving story. . . .

Mrs. Speare writes with compassion and restraint. The small flaws are lost in the over-all power of the story. Stubborn

Daniel had to fight, had to see his idol fall and all his hopes crash before he could really hear the lines of the Song of David,

> He trains my hands for war,
> So that my arms can bend a bow of bronze,

and understand the only strength that can do what physical strength cannot. . . .

Here is a book that is so thrilling it is bound to have many readers—readers whose attitudes are being formed, whose prejudices are not yet frozen. And because the reader lives through every word of the story he feels the conviction that is at the heart of it: the only power great enough to accomplish what might cannot is the power of love.

> *Ruth Hill Viguers, in a review of "The Bronze Bow," in* The Horn Book Magazine, *Vol. XXXVII, No. 5, October, 1961, p. 432.*

Superbly written, **"The Bronze Bow"** is alive, adventurous, and respectful of historical fact and spirit. It offers a refined understanding of the common man's contemporary reaction to Jesus.

This the author sees as delicate and complicated, influenced by the supernatural, and always above retrospective simplification. In Daniel's ultimate acceptance, there is both cost and joy, and these are beautifully balanced and then convincingly welded in a strong and moving final scene.

> *Mary Louise Hector, "In the Time of Jesus," in* The New York Times Book Review, *November 12, 1961, p. 20.*

If this had been a book for adults Daniel would have, perhaps, clung to his hate. The solution is conventional and contrived, as the problem is not. There is a flaw in the book, good as it is in many ways. The story is well told, but it lacks suspense and atmosphere. The characters, too, although neatly drawn, do not possess any inner life; they exist for the purpose of the story.

On the whole, and with regret, therefore, this is a less than excellent book. I doubt if an English jury would have thought it of medal-winning standard.

> *A review of "The Bronze Bow," in* The Junior Bookshelf, *Vol. 26, No. 5, November, 1962, p. 269.*

[*The Bronze Bow*] is thickly pious and its factitious historical setting is presented in language so drab and abstract and even, occasionally, illiterate, that it is impossible to adjust one's ear to it ("Prodded on by weary drivers, the camels swayed slowly." "The morsels of food had not begun to whet his hunger.") But the trouble is less with the book's prose or even with its fake historical and religious paraphernalia than with the smugness of its doctrine. (p. 115)

What is wrong with prize-winners like **The Bronze Bow** . . . is that they are deficient in reality, so deficient indeed that it requires an entire educational bureaucracy to talk the children into accepting them. One is encouraged by the extent to which the children are able to resist such persuasion and reject such products; but it is sad that the experts have given so little advice concerning alternatives, especially since so many parents and teachers must themselves be at a loss. (p. 116)

> *Jason Epstein, "'Good Bunnies Always Obey': Books for American Children," in* Commentary, *Vol. 35, No. 2, February, 1963, pp. 112-22.\**

True to historical fact, this stunning story . . . is powerful and breathtakingly real. Anger and revenge dominate a story where the gentle theme of love over hate develops slowly but surely, though with great subtlety. The issues of the period are made clear as well-drawn characters give expression to the impact that historical events had upon those who lived through such times as those of Roman conquerors.

The portrait of Jesus, particularly, is superbly developed. Great skill is shown in bestowing the gentle teacher with characteristics that are neither sentimental nor weak. Instead, Jesus of Nazareth's character reflects strength, conviction, and persuasive leadership in accordance with the existing evidence about him rather than with the conceptions expressed by some artists. (p. 323)

> *Constantine Georgiou, "History in Children's Literature," in his* Children and Their Literature, *Prentice-Hall, Inc., 1969, pp. 303-58.**

---

### LIFE IN COLONIAL AMERICA   (1963)

[Speare] has captured the spirit of life in early America by making worthwhile use of diaries, letters, travelers' tales, etc. Her extensive research is evidenced by the careful details, selectivity, and clear organization. . . . [The] author presents the material with unusual enthusiasm. . . . [It] will make excellent supplementary reading for beginning students of American history.

> *A review of "Life in Colonial America," in* Virginia Kirkus' Service, *Vol. XXXI, No. 20, October 15, 1963, p. 1009.*

The fresh and interesting text covers life in the southern, central and New England Colonies—the homes, the army, schools, trades and crafts, travel and pleasure. . . . It is amazing how [Mrs. Speare's] selection of material conveys the essence of the 17th and 18th-century life.

> *Margaret Sherwood Libby, "Our Past in Present Tense," in* Book Week—The Sunday Herald Tribune, *Fall Children's Issue, November 10, 1963, p. 20.**

Anyone of any age who shares an affection for this period will open this fine, tempting-looking book with great expectation. And when he starts reading his hopes will be more than fulfilled, unless he has noticed that the author also wrote those two absorbing Newbery Award winning stories. . . . Then the use of words, the skillful presentation of facts so that they glow with interest will come as no surprise.

> *A review of "Life in Colonial America," in* The Christian Science Monitor, *November 14, 1963, p. 9B.*

Despite the inevitable comparison with Edwin Tunis's *Colonial Living* (World), this book deserves a place in most libraries. More a panorama of life in the early American colonies and rather less about the implements and appurtenances of everyday living, it makes a good companion to the Tunis volume. . . . However, the scope of the material is rather limited and it is somewhat thin in historical content. For example, none of the New England colonies is entered by name in the index, and only in passing do some appear in the body of the text.

> *Esther M. Swift, in a review of "Life in Colonial America," in* Library Journal, *Vol. 88, No. 20, November 15, 1963, p. 4489.*

While the appeal of material relics is universal, it is nowhere more enthusiastically recognized than in America. . . . The roots of our history are short but grow straight and deep and, in such a period of ordeal as today, they influence the citizens of our hybrid, heterogeneous population toward an inseparable unity, a brotherhood that encompasses human beings of all racial and national backgrounds.

Elizabeth George Speare . . . has very wisely chosen to play upon these truths in **"Life in Colonial America."** Old prints, the drawings of Charles Walker, and photographs of items now displayed in our historical museums illustrate her simple and direct prose. Her book is a happily literary presentation of materials culled from our past with taste and telling effect.

> *Carl Carmer, in a review of "Life in Colonial America," in* The New York Times Book Review, *November 24, 1963, p. 50.*

Organized into broad areas such as **"The Dutch and the Quakers"** or **"Tradesmen and Craftsmen,"** the text covers, in subtopics within the areas, innumerable aspects of colonial life. The writing style is good, but the material is not as well organized as that of Tunis (*Colonial Living*, World, 1957). . . .

> *Zena Sutherland, in a review of "Life in Colonial America," in* Bulletin of the Center for Children's Books, *Vol. XVII, No. 4, December, 1963, p. 65.*

---

### THE SIGN OF THE BEAVER   (1983)

With a marvelous sense of setting and two memorable characters, Speare weaves a tale of survival and values in America after the French and Indian War. Matt, almost 13, is left in the new cabin in Maine while his father returns to collect the rest of the family. . . . [Matt, trying to get honey,] is attacked by bees and saved by an Indian, Saknis, and his grandson, Attean. From this point on the story follows the two boys as Matt tries to teach Attean to read but finds that he is being taught the Indian ways. As Matt reads parts of *Robinson Crusoe* to Attean he begins to question the white man's values and to see that the white man is not necessarily better. Matt begins to respect the Indian ways, always knowing that Attean has become the teacher and sometimes resenting this. It is not until he refuses to leave with the Indians but decides to wait for his very late-arriving family that he gains Attean's respect and the name "Brother." Speare describes the forest in poetic terms, the crack of a beaver's tail, the colors of fall leaves, and one can almost feel the solitude. Both the bare settler's cabin and the colors and bustle of the Indian village are described in enough detail to bring them alive. In the end, Matt knows sadly that the life he and the Indians are living will disappear as more settlers come and also realizes that his family will never fully understand what his summer has been like. Matt joins other memorable characters, *Kit* [in **The Witch of Blackbird Pond,** *Julie* in Jean Craighead George's *Julie of the Wolves*, and *Karana* in Scott O'Dell's *Island of the Blue Dolphin*], in finding his inner strength and values in a changing world in this well-written and fast reading story. While written for grades five and up, it would be an excellent read-aloud in lower grades. (pp. 118-19)

*Margaret C. Howell, in a review of "The Sign of the Beaver," in* School Library Journal, *Vol. 29, No. 8, April, 1983, pp. 118-19.*

[The precarious friendship between Matt and Attean serves] as an apt vehicle for Speare's exciting plot line. Subtly she shores her story with thought-provoking themes, and readers will find themselves caught up in Attean's teachings on forest survival, the celebrations and daily life of the Beaver people, Matt's simple life-style on the frontier, and, most importantly, the question of white man's encroachment on Indian land. At times the dialogue becomes stereotypical—"Him my dog. Him come," "Me go with you"—but all the characters forcefully emerge as living, breathing humans and as such have striking staying power.... [This] is a top recommendation for a read-aloud in which story compels attention and theme motivates discussion.

*Barbara Elleman, in a review of "The Sign of the Beaver," in* Booklist, *Vol. 79, No. 16, April 15, 1983, p. 1098.*

It is an event when someone as respected and well read as Elizabeth Speare writes a new book after more than 20 years of silence. She occupies a unique place in children's literature, for she established her reputation with just three books.... Her new book of historical fiction is distinguished in style and compelling in narrative force....

Although it is no surprise that the family is long delayed and Matt is faced with unexpected difficulties, the reader becomes deeply involved with Matt's character and the intimate details of his daily struggle....

As usual in Mrs. Speare's novels, each word rings true.

*Jean Fritz, in a review of "The Sign of the Beaver," in* The New York Times Book Review, *May 8, 1983, p. 37.*

A sturdy, never faltering story.... There's nothing original about the message, but Speare uses the *Robinson Crusoe* turnabout to good advantage, makes the boys' changing relationship natural and affecting, and effectively evokes the forest setting and the textures of wilderness living.

*A review of "The Sign of the Beaver," in* Kirkus Reviews, *Vol. LI, No. 10, May 15, 1983, p. 580.*

The author's clever paralleling of [Matt's and Attean's] book adventures with their real-life situation is intriguing. Attean asking questions and Matt reflecting about the stories is a major means of the author's skillful character portrayals.

Readers will be able to relate to more than just the story. Through the actions of Matt the author gives many suggestions that would help them survive in any wilderness.

*Ronald A. Jobe, in a review of "The Sign of the Beaver," in* Language Arts, *Vol. 60, No. 8, November-December, 1983, p. 1023.*

[Of Elizabeth George Speare's] four books two have won Newbery Medals, and who is to say that this one will not be as successful? It is certainly just the kind of story our American cousins like, being concerned with the pioneering past and with the exploration of character. If we are disposed to approach it with a greater degree of detachment, there is still a great deal here for our delight and admiration....

It is difficult to maintain the impetus of a novel in which there is, for much of the action, only a single character, but Miss Speare is successful in drawing in the wilderness as an actor in her drama. The vulnerable Matt is well drawn, but most young readers are likely to side with Attean, the young would-be hunter, with his pride, his skills, his carefully concealed humanity. It is a nice touch to make Matt teach Attean to read and write through the medium of *Robinson Crusoe,* and to show how, in these circumstances, roles are reversed: Attean, who ought to identify with Man Friday, becomes the teacher, while Matt, a Crusoe with no skills adapted to survival, becomes the reluctant learner.

While not of the quality of her earlier work, Miss Speare's novel is a fine one, full of wisdom and practical good sense as well as understanding of human behaviour under stress. It is an astonishing achievement for a writer of seventy-five.

*A review of "The Sign of the Beaver," in* The Junior Bookshelf, *Vol. 43, No. 3, June, 1984, p. 145.*

# Ianthe Thomas

## 1951-

**Black American author of picture books.**

Thomas focuses on personal relationships which are warm, positive, and endearing. She avoids the often-stereotypical portrayals of blacks in picture books by depicting loving and lovable fathers as well as friendships which cross the boundaries of generation, race, and divorce. Although Thomas is a New Yorker, she does not limit herself to the urban scene of *My Street's a Morning Cool Street* or the jazz musician's night world of *Willie Blows a Mean Horn*. She appears equally convincing when writing about the rural South; books such as *Lordy, Aunt Hattie* and *Hi, Mrs. Mallory!* are praised for providing an accurate, appealing picture of this region and satisfying child-adult relationships. Her works are also memorable for such captivating protagonists as big sister Nina, persuading her little brother home with joyous make-believe in *Walk Home Tired, Billy Jenkins*, and bright, tender-hearted L'il Bits, grieving over the death of old Mrs. Mallory.

Thomas has had a varied career outside literature. Her experiences in teaching nursery school, working in children's theater, and developing educational curriculum have given her a rare understanding of childhood. Thomas studied sculpture at the Universidad de Coimbra in Portugal and has exhibited her wrought-iron and mild steel pieces in one-woman shows. Her books reflect her perception as a visual artist; she consistently stimulates the imagination by appealing to all the senses. Thomas shows a special ability to modulate the moods she creates and to touch upon feelings important to a child. Her stories subtly radiate her affirmative view of life. Critics consider Thomas's writing remarkable for its disarming simplicity, and they appreciate her poetic prose and rhythmic sense. Although some critics view her use of black dialect as a drawback for beginning readers, others claim it adds richness and realism, especially when read aloud. Reviewers complain that Thomas's plots lack substance and narrative flow but also point out that *My Street's a Morning Cool Street* should inspire other exercises in observation, that *Hi, Mrs. Mallory!* could open discussions on life, death, friendship, love, poverty, and old age, and that *Walk Home Tired* might lead to classroom plays. Thomas centers on the universal values of love and caring that bridge differences, survive death and divorce, and enrich the experience of living. Her books encourage creativity while simultaneously reassuring children of the comfort found in family and friends.

---

### LORDY, AUNT HATTIE (1973)

It's evident that Jeppa Lee and her Aunt Hattie are playing a game here, for what little girl wouldn't know that summer vacation had begun, and what grownup would answer a straight question ("What day is today, Aunt Hattie?") with "A day so hot that the cotton snakes done slithered down under the cotton-bulb shade"? Even so Aunt Hattie seems curiously unconcerned about the accuracy of her pretty imagery ("Sun done shined and whistled to the crocuses"—in summer?), but never mind: if her loving evocation of juicy huckleberries and jumping catfish and cool, sweet lemonade is as fuzzy as [illustrator

*Photograph by Hillary Hodge*

Thomas] di Grazia's sunbathed, soft focus scenes of milk jugs and willow trees and brown Jeppa Lee in a green and yellow field, Thomas' and di Grazia's game here is not so much recreation of a Southern summer day as undifferentiated nostalgia for a black childhood—and they are sure to have an impressive gallery of grownup takers.

> *A review of "Lordy, Aunt Hattie," in* Kirkus Reviews, *Vol. XLI, No. 9, May 1, 1973, p. 512.*

[The] mood of high summer, hot and lazy and bucolic, . . . is celebrated in the story of a black child's day. . . . [The] day passes, full of the good things of summer, full of the love between Aunt Hattie and Jeppa Lee. The story isn't substantial, but it has appeal in its rhythmic pattern of events and its catalog of pleasant pursuits and, above all, its atmosphere of rural peace and abundance. . . .

> *Zena Sutherland, in a review of "Lordy, Aunt Hattie," in* Bulletin of the Center for Children's Books, *Vol. 27, No. 1, September, 1973, p. 19.*

[In **"Lordy, Aunt Hattie,"** the story] remains incomplete, which is a shame because Ianthe Thomas, in whatever she does give to us, seems to be a distinctive, and captivating writer. But, too often, you have to grip with: "'No, baby, it's time for the dust to rise so high and thick every time Mr. Jim takes that horse to market,' said Aunt Hattie.'' That what happens? Where were the editors? Just a minute more, and this could have been a wonderful invention. . . .

> *June Jordan, in a review of "Lordy, Aunt Hattie,"
> in* The New York Times Book Review, *November
> 4, 1973, p. 27.*

---

### WALK HOME TIRED, BILLY JENKINS (1974)

This is all in the words of older Nina, who talks tired Billy Jenkins home from the playground by pretending to take him in a silver sailboat, a smooth-riding plane, and a train, . . . all shined up proud. . . . Modestly affirmative, though Nina's verbal pictures of the imaginary vehicles aren't particularly evocative.

> *A review of "Walk Home Tired, Billy Jenkins," in*
> Kirkus Reviews, *Vol. XLII, No. 21, November 1,
> 1974, p. 1147.*

Warmth and wonder emanate from the melodious verse spoken by a lanky black girl about 10 years old. Designing the greatest ways to travel, self-assured Nina plays Pied Piper for Billy Jenkins. . . . A brief, gratifying journey through one beguiling girl's imagination.

> *A review of "Walk Home Tired, Billy Jenkins," in*
> The Booklist, *Vol. 71, No. 8, December 15, 1974, p.
> 427.*

[Small, weary Billy Jenkins resists big sister Nina's attempts to coax him to walk home.] The relationship, the simplicity of the story, and the appeal of imaginative play may be dimmed for some readers because of the lack of action.

> *Zena Sutherland, in a review of "Walk Home Tired,
> Billy Jenkins," in* Bulletin of the Center for Children's Books, *Vol. 28, No. 10, June, 1975, p. 169.*

Little Billy Jenkins says he's too tired to walk home, so Nina creates images of their travelling . . . through the city streets to distract him. The older Black child's genuine concern for Billy is a model for positive sibling relationships. This story is ideal for dramatization.

> *A review of "Walk Home Tired, Billy Jenkins," in*
> Interracial Books for Children, *Vol. 6, Nos. 5 & 6,
> 1975, p. 10.*

**Walk Home Tired, Billy Jenkins** is a fun mixture of fantasy and reality. . . .

The fantasy is not escapist; it's just fun. Nina's buoyancy and strength are shown in the text as well as in the illustrations [of Thomas di Grazia]. The fondness the two children have for each other is also clear. **Walk Home Tired, Billy Jenkins** is a delightful story for younger children despite its less-than-delightful inner-city setting. The book's characters shine with life and energy in an environment designed to take their shine away.

> *Lydia Bassett, in a review of "Walk Home Tired,
> Billy Jenkins," in* Interracial Books for Children,
> *Vol. 6, Nos. 5 & 6, 1975, p. 14.*

---

### MY STREET'S A MORNING COOL STREET (1976)

A warm, positive, and poetic description of a city street as seen through the eyes of a young black boy makes this picturebook a welcomed relief from the many blunt and bland

books on this subject. Its young narrator takes you on a sensory excursion, allowing you to experience the sights, sounds, moods, action, and people around him. The text is as imagery-filled and captivating as the colorfully detailed blue-yellow-grey ink illustrations [by Emily A. McCully]. . . . Here's a rich reading and visual experience for the young.

> *Patricia A. Spence, in a review of "My Street's a
> Morning Cool Street," in* Children's Book Review
> Service, *Vol. 4, No. 11, June, 1976, p. 91.*

A morning cool street where people move slow and say, "Go back to sleep, morning. / I ain't ready for your early sun," where "You got to wipe the sleep out of your eyes / and feel your coat flap when the cars go by," where the meat man and the fruit man with his cloud of flies all walk—the slow-motion sights and sounds that wait for time gradually to energize them are ticked off by a young boy who makes his way to school. Thomas' verbal portrait isn't quite so musically rhythmic as either **Lordy, Aunt Hattie** . . . or **Walk Home Tired, Billy Jenkins** . . . , but never mind; that drowsy early morning ambience still shines through.

> *Denise M. Wilms, in a review of "My Street's a
> Morning Cool Street," in* Booklist, *Vol. 73, No. 1,
> September 1, 1976, p. 43.*

This picturebook details the awakening of a street in an urban Black neighborhood. The illustrations have a fresh early morning busyness. However, the narrative (written in Black English) seems merely a rebroadcast of the type of stories found in readers and workbooks.

> *Karel Rose, in a review of "My Street's a Morning
> Cool Street," in* School Library Journal, *Vol. 23,
> No. 6, February, 1977, p. 58.*

[The use of Black dialect is] unrestrained. . . . Strictly speaking [it] is not poetry, but it employs (and quite well) many poetic devices, the first of which is the implied metaphor of its title. The text works as a detailed extension as an unnamed boy walks down his street on the way to school, noticing the many ordinary scenes in a most unordinary fashion. "Fruit man coming. Them flies follow him like a black umbrella. They don't hide the sun though." His saunter ends with an over-the-shoulder smile at his "morning cool street" as he enters P.S. 3. . . . The book should be an effective springboard for noticing exercises along other streets.

> *Mary Agnes Taylor, in a review of "My Street's a
> Morning Cool Street," in* The Reading Teacher,
> *Vol. 30, No. 8, May, 1977, p. 947.*

---

### ELIZA'S DADDY (1976)

Eliza's parents are divorced; every Saturday afternoon her father comes to take her wherever she wants to go. Fearing that her father's new daughter is beautiful, smart, can ride a horse, and that "Everyone in the world called her Wonderful Angel Daughter," Eliza finally asks if she can visit her father's new home. Greeted by Mandy, Eliza is relieved to discover that her stepsister does *not* know how to ride a horse, and all ends well. . . . All is not sweetness and light: Thomas also shows the thorny side of Eliza's situation, (Eliza's parents barely speak to each other; her father does not even enter the house when he picks her up). . . . [A] difficult but familiar situation is realistically, humorously, and sensitively portrayed through the Black middle class families. . . .

*Melinda Schroeder, in a review of "Eliza's Daddy," in* School Library Journal, *Vol. 23, No. 6, February, 1977, p. 58.*

---

## HI, MRS. MALLORY! (1979)

A quiet, short, and unadorned story of friendship and death told by a young Black girl about her elderly white neighbor and their lives in a farm community. Li'l Bits brings her education and companionship to Mrs. Mallory who gives soup, laughter, and a zest for life in return. The sadness of the sudden death of the old lady and the void it leaves in Li'l Bits' life is mitigated when Mrs. Mallory's dog, Lazlo, moves in with Li'l Bits—a poignant reminder, or a legacy, of a relationship built on the sharing of selves that Li'l Bits can never forget nor negate.... It *looks* easy enough for reluctant readers, but Li'l Bits' narrative is in a vernacular that may confuse, though most children will not be hampered by it. It's fine for reading aloud and an excellent opener to talk about love, death, poverty, friendship, and age.

*Marjorie Lewis, in a review of "Hi, Mrs. Mallory!" in* School Library Journal, *Vol. 25, No. 9, May, 1979, p. 68.*

Written in Black English, this short, easy-to-read book touches many areas: the friendship of an elderly, unconventional white woman with a young Black girl; an elderly person without any nearby family; animal affections for people; and a young child's grief at the death of a friend. Children sensitive to some of these ideas and emotions will understand the special relationship between these two people.

*Annette C. Blank, in a review of "Hi, Mrs. Mallory!" in* Children's Book Review Service, *Vol. 7, No. 11, June, 1979, p. 105.*

This pleasant, rather sweet reminiscence of a little girl about her friendship with an elderly woman who dies suddenly has no real plot—it is simply a series of memories of a house, meals together, and bits of conversation.... A warmly affectionate tone and a simplicity of narration keep the story from becoming overly sentimental.

*Marilyn Kaye, in a review of "Hi, Mrs. Mallory!" in* Booklist, *Vol. 75, No. 22, July 15, 1979, p. 1631.*

It's nice to have a story of friendship between generations, nice to have a story about a black child whose problems aren't ethnic, but as a story this isn't substantial: there's little direction, and the adjustment to death is handled in slight fashion, for the child cries when told, then adopts one of Mrs. Mallory's dogs.

*Zena Sutherland, in a review of "Hi, Mrs. Mallory!" in* Bulletin of the Center for Children's Books, *Vol. 32, No. 11, July-August, 1979, p. 203.*

This is a book about love—a love and caring and sharing which surmount traditional boundaries and extend beyond death. (p. 16)

The fact that Mrs. Mallory is white and Li'l Bits Black is incidental to the story. The touching message of this delightful book is that age, race or economics need not necessarily prevent relating to one another in caring, supportive, joyous ways. It's a message this world needs. (p. 17)

*Jane Pennington, in a review of "Hi, Mrs. Mallory!" in* Interracial Books for Children Bulletin, *Vol. 11, No. 6, 1980, pp. 16-17.*

## WILLIE BLOWS A MEAN HORN (1981)

The love between father and son is clearly depicted in this jazz story. However, it fails to appeal to today's child (e.g., why a Coleman Hawkins poster, rather than a Miles Davis?) and that means that it will not achieve much readership. A good idea that simply doesn't make it.

*James S. Haskins, in a review of "Willie Blows a Mean Horn," in* Children's Book Review Service, *Vol. 9, No. 7, February, 1981, p. 55.*

Music is the tie that binds father and son in this sensitive story of a young boy's devotion to his jazz musician father. The first-person narrative is well suited to [this] intimate view.... This is a book to be read not for its action but for its reassuring theme of love. The prose is natural and musical throughout.... The book is too small to use in storytelling sessions but is well suited for reading aloud to small groups. (pp. 118-19)

*Joan Weller, in a review of "Willie Blows a Mean Horn," in* School Library Journal, *Vol. 27, No. 8, April, 1981, pp. 118-19.*

The same flavor that permeates Isadora's *Ben's Trumpet* ... infuses this warm story of a young black boy's enthusiasm for jazz.... Thomas captures the mood with a dreamy pace that unfolds as if in slow motion, giving time to reflect on the generated feelings as well as the beat of the music.

*Barbara Elleman, in a review of "Willie Blows a Mean Horn," in* Booklist, *Vol. 77, No. 15, April 1, 1981, p. 1109.*

Like Isadora's *Jesse and Abe*, this has a backstage setting and is told by a child who is at a performance. The plot is nebulous.... This has less evocation of atmosphere than the Isadora book, with more focus on the family relationships; there is less structure in the story line.

*Zena Sutherland, in a review of "Willie Blows a Mean Horn," in* Bulletin of the Center for Children's Books, *Vol. 34, No. 11, July-August, 1981, p. 221.*

Ianthe Thomas often writes about how older childen and adults take care of young children. This theme was used beautifully in **Walk Home Tired, Billy Jenkins** and is central to **Willie Blows a Mean Horn**. This story is also anchored in the importance of jazz, that significant African American art form. (p. 26)

The text is lovely. The book has a nice rhythm—a late-night, sleep-time, love-my-Daddy, like-to-see-my-Daddy-play-late-at-night rhythm. The story focuses on the details of the father-son relationship and the special things about that relationship that would thrill a child: waiting for the end of the performance, wiping the sweat from his Daddy's face, getting carried home after falling asleep, learning the care of the horn....

[One gets a] sense of history and culture ... from the text. (p. 27)

*Geraldine L. Wilson, in a review of "Willie Blows a Mean Horn," in* Interracial Books for Children Bulletin, *Vol. 13, Nos. 4 & 5, 1982, pp. 26-7.*

# Shigeo Watanabe

## 1928-

Japanese author of fiction and nonfiction, critic, and translator.

**Watanabe helps young children master simple tasks in his picture book series, "I Can Do It All by Myself." Containing short, direct texts and bright, simple illustrations by Yasuo Ohtomo, these books treat such personal and social skills as eating with the proper utensils, dressing oneself, playing alone, and learning the functions of certain toys. Watanabe centers attention on the slow-witted but always optimistic Little Bear. This character's silly attempts to be independent leave listeners and readers feeling amused and superior, while the bear's final success in sometimes unexpected ways teaches them to persevere.**

**Watanabe has had vast and varied experiences with children and books. On a personal level, his eleven siblings and three sons have given him understanding which lends itself to his subjects with humor and sensitivity. Professionally, he has worked as a children's librarian and storyteller in the United States and Japan, as well as a professor of library science with expertise in school media. Watanabe continues to write scholarly articles, give lectures on children's literature and library services to various international groups, and translate classic children's books from English to Japanese. Author of many books for the young in Japanese, relatively few of Watanabe's works have been translated. Generally, critics find the economically worded texts, subject matter, and presentation to be precisely geared toward the preschooler's attention and skill levels. Watanabe was chosen as the May Hill Arbuthnot Honor Lecturer by the American Library Association in 1977.**

**(See also *Something about the Author*, Vol. 32 and *Contemporary Authors*, Vol. 112.)**

---

## GENERAL COMMENTARY

### GABRIELLE MAUNDER

One of my most favourite books last year was Watanabe and Ohtomo's *How do I put it on?* The endearing young bear having terrible problems over dressing was a delightful conceit, and I am overjoyed with these two companion volumes [*How do I Eat It?* and *Hallo! How are You?*]. The first follows the clothes book very closely, and the absurdity of trying to eat a slice of bread and butter with a spoon, and to pour runny strawberry jam from a jar is hilarious. The final solution is suitably catastrophic and the children with whom I shared this book rolled around with laughter, as I did. What is so enchanting about these books is the eternal optimism of the small bear—this time it *must* be right!

That optimism is the central theme of the second book, where he tries a newly-learned greeting on a variety of inappropriate objects, with no effect, until he meets his father who responds just in time and makes it all right.

These books are not only entrancing in themselves, but they are ideal books for the young learner, their vocabulary and

*Courtesy of Shigeo Watanabe*

sequential pattern exactly designed to help the child in his mastery of text.

*Gabrielle Maunder, in a review of "How Do I Eat It?" and "Hallo! How Are You?" in* The School Librarian, *Vol. 29, No. 1, March, 1981, p. 23.*

### KICKI MOXON BROWNE

There are already several excellent books in this series about a small bear grappling with the world around him. . . . [In *I'm the King of the Castle!* and *I can do it!*], the bear digs in the sand with great vim and concentration, and struggles with various wheeled vehicles: "I can roller-skate" (crash) "Well, nearly." The text consists of one short sentence for each picture. Only direct speech is used, and this gives the books a light touch, involving the reader more readily.

*Kicki Moxon Browne, "On the Right Wavelength," in* The Times Literary Supplement, *No. 4121, March 26, 1982, p. 346.\**

### BEVERLY WOODS

[The text in *I Can Ride It* and *I'm the King of the Castle*] is simple enough for beginning readers to decipher and for very, very young children to attend to. The theme of "I can do it" is great—I just wish the author had not "hit us over the head" with it by spelling it out so directly on the title pages. It is enough that this is a delightful series. One can do without the inscribed morals: setting goals, playing alone, etc.

> *Beverly Woods, in a review of "I Can Ride It" and "I'm the King of the Castle," in* Children's Book Review Service, *Vol. 10, No. 14, August, 1982, p. 134.*

## CLARISSA ERWIN

*"Playing Alone"* and *"Setting Goals"* of the upbeat series, *I Can Do It All By Myself,* really encourage the very young to "go for it!" with bright vocabulary, illustration and concept. . . . These lovely books [*I'm the King of the Castle!* and *I Can Ride It!*] are true boosters for preschool confidence, self-concept and beginning reading skills. A perfect choice for preschool story times.

> *Clarissa Erwin, in a review of "I Can Ride It!" and "I'm the King of the Castle!" in* School Library Journal, *Vol. 29, No. 4, December, 1982, p. 61.*

## NANCY CHAMBERS

None of its successors has quite matched *How Do I Put It On?,* which introduced the dauntless bear and his humorous encounters with various tasks and situations. That first idea of getting mixed up about what piece of clothing goes where has the simple inevitability about it that characterizes many first-rate books for this age, while the ideas for later titles have a more got-up feel to them. Too, the first book used the kind of repetition in the text that meant children could read it straightaway, a pattern that hasn't always been followed since. Nonetheless, the books continue to delight young children, and each new one reinforces their firm position in the read-to-bits category.

> *Nancy Chambers, "Board Books: 'How Do I Eat It?', 'I Can Do It!' and 'I'm the King of the Castle!'," in* The Signal Review 1: A Selective Guide to Children's Books 1982, *edited by Nancy Chambers, The Thimble Press, 1983, p. 5.*

---

### *HOW DO I PUT IT ON? GETTING DRESSED*   (1977)

[The 'child' in this very simple picture book] is confused as to how to put on his clothes. 'Do I put it on like this?' followed by pictures of the correct way.

Young children will think it fun to see the bear putting on his clothes in the wrong way—'What a silly bear! *I* know better'.

A simple story like this can become a treasured book for a very young child who will demand it again and again.

> *Eileen Colwell, in a review of "How Do I Put It On?" in* The Junior Bookshelf, *Vol. 43, No. 5, October, 1979, p. 267.*

[This] is very brief, very simple, and nicely gauged for the young child. . . . There is one sentence per page, and the text doesn't get into problems of front vs. back or left shoe vs. right shoe, but relates each garment to its location. . . . The lap audience should . . . enjoy the exploration of one of the big problems—and accomplishments—in their lives.

> *Zena Sutherland, in a review of "How Do I Put It On?" in* Bulletin of the Center for Children's Books, *Vol. 33, No. 7, March, 1980, p. 143.*

The single-mindedness of this most elementary of how-to's, and its ingenuous protagonist, combine to appeal to the very

youngest of book lovers. . . . [The bear] shows us his efforts with shirt, pants, cap, and shoes while asking, "Do I put it on like this?" Children will chime in with the bear's answers; soon second-guessing the bruin becomes a rewarding game during inevitably requested rereadings.

> *Judith Goldberger, in a review of "How Do I Put It On?" in* Booklist, *Vol. 76, No. 14, March 15, 1980, p. 1065.*

One line of bold print on each page presents everyday vocabulary with limited repetition. However, the content is confusing. Only a very young child would try to put a hat on his foot or shoes on his ears. . . . Children 2-7 will see humor in the mistakes the bear makes and it reinforces beginning reading skills. For children who do require very introductory skill and concept books, this may fill a gap.

> *Brenda Watson, in a review of "How Do I Put It On?" in* The World of Children's Books, *Vol. VI, 1981, p. 39.*

---

### *WHAT A GOOD LUNCH! EATING*   (1979; British edition as *How Do I Eat It?*)

[The author] turns his attention to the table as his very young bear attempts the not-as-easy-as-it-looks task of lunching. . . . The youngest of audiences can take satisfaction, both from knowing more than bear and from seeing their own eating plights realized in a noncastigating light. As with the previous title, Watanabe strikes sympathetic chords within children of an age in which acquiring social skills is a frustrating preoccupation.

> *Judith Goldberger, in a review of "What a Good Lunch!" in* Booklist, *Vol. 76, No. 20, June 15, 1980, p. 1541.*

[If] the young listener (or the reader-aloud) expects a lesson on table implements or manners, he or she will have a surprise. The cub pours everything into one dish, eats it with his paws, and beams, "What a good lunch! I ate it all by myself!" It's enough to warm the heart of any messy beginning eater.

> *Zena Sutherland, in a review of "What a Good Lunch!" in* Bulletin of the Center for Children's Books, *Vol. 34, No. 1, September, 1980, p. 24.*

---

### *GET SET! GO! OVERCOMING OBSTACLES*   (1980; British edition as *Ready, Steady, Go!*)

Watanabe and Ohtomo present #3 in their tender, funny *I Can Do It All By Myself* books.

Here Bear, the star player, has grown a bit and enters an obstacle race with Giraffe, Rabbit and other peers. . . . [The text consists of] a few words on each page as Bear essays the balance beam ("Ow!"), swings around the bar ("Thump!"), wriggles through the tunnel ("Oops!") and meets other challenges. Does he win? Readers may or may not agree. They do know nothing has stopped Bear. There he is at the finish line, having persevered in spite of all the mishaps.

> *A review of "Get Set! Go!" in* Publishers Weekly, *Vol. 219, No. 14, April 3, 1981, p. 74.*

Bear is having difficulties, but he approaches each new obstacle with enthusiasm and optimism. . . . This amiable animal's antics are amusing and should encourage that child whose fear of failure keeps her or him from trying new things.

> *Maxine Kamin, in a review of "Get Set! Go!" in*
> Children's Book Review Service, *Vol. 9, No. 11,*
> *June, 1981, p. 93.*

---

### *I'M THE KING OF THE CASTLE! PLAYING ALONE* (1982)

Watanabe's clear, simple text is related by Bear, who goes out to play in the sandbox all by himself. It's a treat for children his age to listen and see as Bear creates all kinds of terrific things with his pail and shovel and discovers that being alone doesn't have to mean being lonely or bored.

> *A review of "I'm the King of the Castle!" in* Pub-
> lishers Weekly, *Vol. 222, No. 2, July 9, 1982, p.*
> *48.*

---

### *I CAN RIDE IT! SETTING GOALS* (1982; British edition as *I Can Do It!*)

Although the short sentences and large print make this suitable for beginning independent reading, the concept of setting a goal and achieving manual proficiency are more appropriate for the pre-school child, and some young children will be able to read the text. . . . [The small learner] masters the intricacies of riding a toy bus, using a skateboard and roller-skates, and moving from a tricycle to a two-wheeler with training wheels. . . . Very nice indeed.

> *Zena Sutherland, in a review of "I Can Ride It!" in*
> Bulletin of the Center for Children's Books, *Vol. 36,*
> *No. 2, October, 1982, p. 38.*

---

### *WHERE'S MY DADDY?* (1982)

[Bear] is trying to find his father. But the birds haven't seen Daddy. Neither has the milkman nor the mailman. And even Mommy, who has a big kiss for the little one, doesn't know where he is. When his father is finally found, Bear is pleased to have located him without anyone's help. The idea is a familiar one, but it is treated in a fresh, appealing way. Printed in large, clear type, the text is simple and direct. . . .

> *Nancy Sheridan, in a review of "Where's My Daddy?"*
> *in* The Horn Book Magazine, *Vol. LIX, No. 1, Feb-*
> *ruary, 1983, p. 42.*

[This] examines the rewards of perseverance in a slightly different manner than the author presented in *I Can Ride It!*. . . . It is, of course, difficult for young children to pursue a goal in the face of adult indifference, and this story successfully captures the great satisfaction attained in following a question to its conclusion—a valuable lesson for children getting ready for school or just learning to make their way in the world. . . . [This is a] good choice for preschoolers.

> *Clarissa Erwin, in a review of "Where's My Daddy?"*
> *in* School Library Journal, *Vol. 29, No. 9, May,*
> *1983, p. 67.*

---

### *I CAN BUILD A HOUSE!* (1983)

The dauntless hero of the previous picture stories, Bear, is a bigger "boy" now and just as eager to learn by doing as he has proved himself so far. Ohtomo's brightly colored paintings and Watanabe's brisk text combine to amuse little ones and, finally, to applaud Bear. Building a house of his own, he discovers, is harder than learning to dress and feed himself. He piles blocks together, but they don't provide a big enough *pied-à-terre*. A house of pillows collapses. A good-sized carton is promising, but requires some figuring out by Bear to turn it into the classy structure we see him enjoying at last. . . .

> *A review of "I Can Build a House!" in* Publishers
> Weekly, *Vol. 223, No. 15, April 15, 1983, p. 51.*

While this series wears thin as children's attention spans lengthen, it still serves young ones who are trying to get themselves coordinated—and maintain independence. . . . The simple text can be elaborated into narrative by adults, who will find themselves pressed immediately into the service of finding a suitable box for similar home or nursery-school projects.

> *Betsy Hearne, in a review of "I Can Build a House!"*
> *in* Booklist, *Vol. 79, No. 20, June 15, 1983, p. 1342.*

Another cheerful book in Watanabe's engaging and encouraging series. . . . This has no didactic tone, but it says a great deal about accepting small defeats with equanimity.

> *Zena Sutherland, in a review of "I Can Build a*
> *House!" in* Bulletin of the Center for Children's Books,
> *Vol. 37, No. 2, October, 1983, p. 38.*

---

### *I CAN TAKE A WALK!* (1984)

Another of Watanabe's successful **"I can do it all by myself"** books. In this one, little Bear takes his first walk alone and does so with daring and imagination. . . . Young children who may be a little hesitant about their own first excursions will be inspired by Bear's confidence. . . . A nice meld of concept and execution.

> *Ilene Cooper, in a review of "I Can Take a Walk!"*
> *in* Booklist, *Vol. 80, No. 15, April 1, 1984, p. 1122.*

Like earlier Watanabe books, this stresses the achievement of a new skill in a child's repertoire of accomplishments that lead to independence. Unlike the earlier books, this focuses less on a physical skill than on self-reliance. . . . The read-aloud audience can share the satisfaction of the bear's final comment, "What a good walk!"

> *Zena Sutherland, in a review of "I Can Take a Walk!"*
> *in* Bulletin of the Center for Children's Books, *Vol.*
> *37, No. 9, May, 1984, p. 177.*

This is the eighth learning and amusing book in the notable **"I Can Do It All by Myself"** line. . . . Bear goes for a walk by himself, pretending he's climbing a mountain (a tiny rise), crossing a high bridge (a little bench), scaring flying monsters (pigeons) and, finally, picking his way along the edge of a towering cliff. As it happens, this cliff (a stone wall) is a challenge. Bear has managed to get up onto the wall, but he loses his cool when it's time to get down. Luckily, Daddy comes along and lends a hand. . . . So ends another milestone in the episodes that Watanabe tells with economy and spirit.

> *A review of "I Can Take a Walk!" in* Publishers
> Weekly, *Vol. 225, No. 8, February 24, 1984, p.*
> *140.*

# Jay Williams

## 1914-1978

American author of fiction and nonfiction, reteller, poet, and playwright.

Proficient in several genres, Williams utilized authentic backgrounds, imaginative plots, and pleasing wit in his more than sixty books for children. He claimed he was always either thinking of a story or writing it down. Seeing himself as a teller of tales rather than as a moralist or teacher, Williams sought to ask rather than answer questions about life. His most popular books appear to be the science fiction/fantasy series about Danny Dunn, an inquisitive youngster whose penchant for adventure and trouble is told in works that combine exciting plots with scientific facts. Williams's earliest books were written for boys, and consist of several volumes of mysteries *(The Roman Moon Mystery)*, historical fiction *(The Sword and the Scythe)*, realistic fiction *(The Magic Gate)*, and history *(The Battle for the Atlantic)*. His scholarly knowledge of the Roman era and the Middle Ages impressed critics and historians and led to his authorship of several American Heritage volumes. The latter half of Williams's career was devoted largely to fantasy, both for older children *(The People of the Ax)* and younger ones *(The Cookie Tree)*. His picture books often feature original, turn-about fairy tales in which the princess rescues the prince or is otherwise superior to the male—this in the days before questioning traditional gender roles became fashionable. He also wrote modern dialogue for his historical fiction and fairy tales to make the stories more relevant for today's readers.

Following work as a comic and master of ceremonies in vaudeville shows and night clubs, Williams became a press agent and theatrical actor before turning to writing full time. For the early *Danny Dunn* books, he regularly collaborated with Raymond Abrashkin, a science teacher and journalist who wrote the screenplay for the English film "Little Fugitive" in which Williams played the featured role. Until his death after the fifth book, Abrashkin conceived most of the ideas, while Williams did the writing; Abrashkin continued to receive coauthor credit for the remainder of the series. Williams also created many books for adults, including six detective stories under the pseudonym Michael Delving.

Williams's critical reception is largely favorable. He is commended for his ability to explain complex ideas in a simple way and for infusing lively humor into his usually well-conceived plots. Reviewers applaud the thorough research evident in his histories, historical novels, and works of science fiction. They acclaim the *Danny Dunn* books for their unique blend of fact and fiction, their ability to entertain, and their scientific veracity, while faulting them for having one-dimensional, stereotyped characters. Though most critics praise Williams's fairy-tale spoofs for their depiction of heroic females, some point out that the books go too far in reverse sexism. The consensus, however, is that Williams produced an entertaining and often informative body of literature for all ages, a contribution for which he will be warmly remembered. Among the honors conferred upon Williams were the Lewis Carroll Shelf Award in 1973 for *The Hawkstone*, the Irma Simonton Black Award in 1977 for *Everyone Knows What a Dragon Looks*

*Photograph by William F. Joli; courtesy of Barbara Williams*

*Like,* and several child-selected awards. *Danny Dunn and the Homework Machine* has been adapted into film.

(See also *Something about the Author*, Vols. 3, 24 [obituary]; *Contemporary Authors New Revision Series*, Vol. 2; and *Contemporary Authors*, Vols. 1-4, rev. ed., Vols. 81-84, [obituary].)

---

## AUTHOR'S COMMENTARY

It is no longer a foregone conclusion that series books will be ill-contrived or sloppily written. Far from it! A great many quite respectable authors have discovered that there are delights for them as well as for their readers in carrying the same set of characters through a series of adventures. . . . Many of us whose serious concern is writing for children have found unexpected satisfactions in repeating the same characters, or using the same framework, or at least the same imaginary country, in one book after another.

Part of it lies, I guess, in parental love. After all, once we have invented characters who please us, they are our children: we set them moving through their worlds, which we have equally created, and then cast them adrift in the real world. Somehow, they lose their reality for us once we have finished that one book which tells about a certain specific set of happenings. So, if we can write about them again, and then again, they can remain alive for us—they continue their existences and by doing so prolong for us the initial joy of knowing them.

For our readers, the pleasure is much the same. It is the pleasure of the familiar—one more tale about those brave Swallows and Amazons! Will there be another story about the Borrowers? It is like the anticipation of Christmas presents to hope that there may be. (p. 113)

There are dangers, of course, for the author of a series. There is the temptation to scamp your work—after all, *you* know these characters so well, and surely everyone else knows them by now, so isn't it easier, when your desk is piled high with work, to meet the clamor for "one more story about those same people" by rapidly writing *just* the story and forgetting about the people? The author who falls into such a trap discovers it soon enough when he re-reads his book and discovers to his horror that the very thing which gave his work its life is absent—the story is there, but the characters have gone to lunch, leaving only cardboard cut-outs behind them. . . . It is one of the basic challenges in a series: to keep the people really alive, to make each new adventure seem fresh and believable and full of fun.

It all depends, I suppose, on one's approach to one's work. Why write for children in the first place? I think most serious authors do it because it is such fun to try to get into touch with the minds of children, to recover the sense of excitement and surprise which is so much a part of childhood and is so easy to lose when you grow up. And they are the most appreciative of audiences, too; their letters show it. When a child sits down and writes a long two-page letter, showing in every line how much of a strain the writing is, just to tell an author that "this book is the best book I ever read," you do not have to take the praise too seriously but you know what a burst of ecstasy made that letter necessary to be written.

I think a book which is fun for a child is a kind of voyage into a new land of wonder. Does this sound old-fashioned nowadays, when it is more customary to talk about books introducing children to reality, or making them good citizens, or preparing them for adulthood by providing them with the psychological tools of adjustment . . . and so on? I'm afraid it is old-fashioned. I cannot think of books as devices for improving the child's mind or elevating the soul. I think that for most children the test of a book is whether it is exciting or not. If it can be funny as well, that's all to the good. If it can make you feel—as my daughter put it when she was eight and had read "Charlotte's Web"—"a little sad in a good way," that's also a bonus. But excitement, that special sense of joy which comes from knowing you are in a country where *anything* may suddenly happen, that is the province of a book which children can take to their hearts. . . . The voyage into the unknown is the most intriguing of all lures. This, I think, is the author's major responsibility: to unroll the map on which even the most familiar and everyday scene is marked Terra Incognita.

But shouldn't children's books have a moral? Shouldn't they deliver the sugar-coated pill of wisdom, delicately cloaked as entertainment? Shouldn't they, at the least, teach the child something about the real world?

I think that a book written honestly out of the author's need to write, out of his personal urgency to create worlds for himself and people them with his own figures, will always carry a serious message. It won't be a message thought out beforehand and then wrapped up in a tailored garment—no, I'm convinced

that children have enough sense and good taste to leave such predigested pap alone. The message I'm talking about is less concrete, harder to put your finger on. It is, in general, the summation of all the writer knows and thinks and feels, which, if he is honest, appears in his work and will convey his deepest beliefs about right and wrong, about the nature of life and how it ought to be lived. The author is neither a teacher nor a sage; he has no hard and fast rules, not even about the way in which he writes, nor any answers to burning issues. He has only himself, a human being with some experience of living, a mind that makes up stories about people, and an imagination which can use words to convey these things. . . . Children do not turn away from books because they aren't "literature" or because they are not well-written, or because they don't teach anything. They will turn away from books when the books cease to offer any surprises. But when an author opens the magic box of his imagination, freely, happily, and without reservations, the child can seize the bird of pleasure with both hands, as it flutters out. (pp. 114-15)

*Jay Williams, in a letter read at the Yakima PNLA Conference on August 29, 1963, in* PNLA Quarterly, *Vol. 28, No. 2, January, 1964, pp. 110-15.*

---

## GENERAL COMMENTARY

### MARGERY FISHER

Jay Williams and Raymond Abrashkin take the idea of absurd scientific invention as far as possible in two light-hearted stories, **Danny Dunn and the Anti-Gravity Paint** and **The Homework Machine**. Simple and entertaining though they are, these stories are not merely farce. The children who so much enjoy feeding their school problems to a computer, in the second story, are very well drawn, and this makes their difficulties credible and amusing. Besides, there is an implied comment on the dangerous side of automation that gives the book ballast. Their chief purpose, all the same, is to promote fun and laughter over ordinary things going wrong. (p. 158)

*Margery Fisher, "Climates of Humour," in her* Intent Upon Reading: A Critical Appraisal of Modern Fiction for Children, *1961. Reprint by Franklin Watts, Inc., 1962, pp. 153-69.\**

### MARGERY FISHER

Experimenting with a miniature computer, a mechanical probe and a time-machine, Danny displays equally the logic and the unreason in his nature. His friends Joe Pearson, a melancholy boy with a talent for instant rhyming, and Irene Miller, the lively daughter of an astronomer, make sure that Danny is reminded often enough of his failures to make it impossible for him to boast of his successes. This natural, independent and enterprising trio are excellent mouthpieces for the author. Because of their university environment, they are casual and knowledgeable about advanced science and technology, and through them many experimental concepts have been easily and clearly presented to young readers. But the **"Danny Dunn"** stories are not textbooks in disguise. If they emphasize that the sciences are an essential part of everybody's life, they do this with a blithe and alert humour for which Danny himself is largely responsible. (p. 80)

*Margery Fisher, "Who's Who in Children's Books: Danny Dunn," in her* Who's Who in Children's Books: A Treasury of the Familiar Characters of Childhood, *Holt, Rinehart and Winston, 1975, Weidenfeld and Nicolson, 1975, pp. 79-80.*

## MASHA KABAKOW RUDMAN

Some writers feel so strongly about the heretofore unbalanced treatment of women in fairy tales that they have gone to the other extreme and made the men victims. Jay Williams, in the admittedly humorous and charmingly illustrated book, *The Practical Princess,* has Princess Bedelia performing all kinds of clever acts. After brilliantly outwitting a snobbish and vicious dragon, she rescues the sleeping prince. Unfortunately, all of the males in the book are simpletons; further, they permit themselves to be ordered about and humiliated by her. The happy ending, for example, occurs when the prince agrees to shave his beard and cut his hair to please Princess Bedelia. Williams's later fairy tale, *Petronella,* is far more equitable in its treatment of males and females, although the prince is the clown character in the story; in fact, the hero is the sorcerer. The prince is depicted as foolish simply in order to overturn the myth of the perfect prince, not as discrimination against males. (p. 303)

> *Masha Kabakow Rudman, "The Female: 'The Practical Princess',"* in her Children's Literature: An Issues Approach, *D. C. Heath and Company, 1976, pp. 290-357.*\*

## AIDAN CHAMBERS

[*Chambers, a respected British author and critic, gives a critical assessment of Williams's place in children's literature, recounts a conversation they had, and ends with some general comments on writing.*]

I suppose, if one asked the critics, they'd say that, as an author for children, Jay Williams is simply a popular writer. They would probably have Danny Dunn in mind and remember the humor of the picture books, though they'd probably uneasily exclude the ones illustrated by Friso Henstra . . . Usually they forget the fantasies like *The Hawkstone* and *The People of the Axe* . . . but even these have a deceptive directness of style. I said as much to Jay. And it was that remark which sparked him off, and for the first time he talked freely to me about what he thinks of his own work. . . . Jay began:

I enjoy telling stories. I start out with a story; in the course of writing, it begins to tell me what I think of life. All kinds of questions arise which the story forces me to answer.

*Is that so in everything you write?*

I think so. And the theme that seems to run through every story I've ever written is this: the mystery of what lies beneath the surfaces of things. The stories are all about appearances of things. In my books everyone is asking questions.

*I've never seen anyone—any reviewer—picking that up and commenting on it.*

Maybe that's because I'm a pretty good storyteller.

*You mean the ease of your writing makes your books seem simpler than they really are?*

Maybe. In the **"Danny Dunn"** books, for example, the stories look as though they are pretty simple—about a kid who gets mixed up in scientific adventures—but they really deal with the necessity of thinking for yourself, of asking certain key questions about the universe, of trying all the time to get at the truth. *Everyone Knows What a Dragon Looks Like* is precisely like that. The dragon in that story is a bald, fat little man with an amiable grin. He's not at all what he seems. I got the image from a Chinese and Japanese painting, and in

Chinese art dragons are often associated with water spirits. The picture that started me off was of a little man, the form assumed by the dragon that was the Spirit of the Southern Star. I simply used that idea to say again: Truth takes many forms. You don't always recognize it. Don't judge by appearances, look beneath the surfaces of things. (pp. 93-4)

How appallingly easy it is to pass over something and never to find its true quality! And isn't that why we need writers, and writers for the young especially, who can show us the magic of the masks and what lies behind them? Thank heaven, then, for the Jay Williamses of the world. (p. 96)

> *Aidan Chambers, in an interview with Jay Williams, in* The Horn Book Magazine, *Vol. LIII, No. 1, February, 1977, pp. 92-6.*\*

## ENID DAVIS

Delighted with the non-sexist (and attractive) world of Jay Williams's *The Practical Princess,* I decided to investigate his other picture books. I wanted to know if humanism was inherent in his imagination or merely suggested by his publishers.

Jay Williams is the author of some seventeen picture books and early readers, as well as numerous other fiction and nonfiction titles on other reading levels. In his picture books he almost always creates a modern fairy tale, using contemporary language and attitudes to supply much of the humor.

In my review of eleven of these titles I have discovered heroines as liberated as Bedelia the Practical and some disappointing relapses into stereotyped characters and attitudes. Except for Prudence in *The Silver Whistle,* all of Williams's heroines are beautiful, in addition to being wise and kind. In fact, one of his princes says this about his love: "And if she is brave, sensible, energetic, and wise, she is also very beautiful." (*The Good For Nothing Prince*) Is she all right in spite of the former qualities because she is also pretty? Williams also has the irritating habit of calling his adult heroines "girls," but his heroes "young men." On the whole, however, Williams should be knighted for his attempts to individualize his young women and still keep to a traditional fairy tale structure—trouble, rescue, marriage.

[Davis proceeds to describe eight books which she regards as "golden books": *The Silver Whistle, The Question Box, Petronella, The Practical Princess, Stupid Marco, The Youngest Captain, Forgetful Fred,* and *The Good For Nothing Prince.*] (p. 14)

In [*The King With Six Friends, School for Sillies* and *A Box Full of Infinity,* three works which the critic considers "books of lead,"] the hero overcomes all obstacles without the help of the princess. In the first book the princess never speaks. "The princess is yours," says the king, as the "princess was brought" to meet her mate. The female servant in the inn visited by the king and his six white male friends was "a pretty girl who served them." And for her help and service the king "paid the girl, and gave her a kiss of thanks."

In the second title, Kit, a cheerful and kind scholar, finds a princess weeping from loneliness in the palace garden. He makes it all better by promising her a wedding and proceeds to teach her arrogant father a lesson. She then disappears from the plot and the only other woman mentioned has just finished mopping a floor.

In the third book, Ben, a poor prince, rescues a princess from a wizard who stole her because "he likes to be able to tell his friends that he has a princess doing his housework." "I don't mind the work," reveals the princess, "but I am so sick and tired of this wizard." (pp. 17-18)

The scales tip in Jay Williams's favor, of course. His golden books outweigh those of lead. . . . [*People Of the Ax*] is a fantasy about how our civilization will be looked upon in horror someday by creatures far better than ourselves and is a fine example of anti-sexist writing. (And a fairly exciting tale.) . . .

I believe Jay Williams is sincere and comfortable creating brave and intelligent heroines. No publisher could force such an apparent lack of prejudice. I'm with Sylvia [of *Stupid Marco*]. Jay does rescue princesses from boredom! (p. 18)

> *Enid Davis, "Maidens with Spunk: Books by Jay Williams," in her* The Liberty Cap: A Catalogue of Non-Sexist Materials for Children, *Academy Press Limited, 1977, pp. 14-18.*

---

## THE STOLEN ORACLE   (1943)

An exciting mystery story of the Roman Empire in the days of Caesar Augustus. It concerns the theft of the Sibylline books from the Temple of Apollo, for which two Roman boys are wrongfully accused. In the following fortnight, as the boys search for the real culprit, Horace, Maecenas and other characters from history enter the picture. The setting for the story and the persons who play a part are vividly and accurately drawn.

> *Alice M. Jordan, in a review of "The Stolen Oracle," in* The Horn Book Magazine, *Vol. XX, No. 1, January, 1944, p. 42.*

Rome in the time of Emperor Augustus becomes vividly alive in [*The Stolen Oracle*]. . . . Authentic background, peopled with charioteers, gladiators and even the poet, Horace, make it a valuable addition to school and public libraries.

> *Margaret Miller, in a review of "The Stolen Oracle," in* Library Journal, *Vol. 69, No. 3, February 1, 1944, p. 120.*

[Every] tale for boys touching Roman times is an object of interest to schools; this story is well above the average in combining liveliness with accuracy. The latter is buttressed by an introductory note explaining just where and why the story takes minor liberties, and the former maintained by a strenuous search [for the stolen books]. . . . [The boys's search] leads them into so many tight spots that interest keeps sharp, and as the Romans are permitted to talk much as we do and not in the peculiar speech once thought proper to give them in high school novels, a sense of nearness is maintained.

> *May Lamberton Becker, in a review of "The Stolen Oracle," in* New York Herald Tribune Weekly Book Review, *February 6, 1944, p. 5.*

---

## THE COUNTERFEIT AFRICAN   (1944)

Here is a swift-moving story involving what mystery fans call "a good clean murder" and shrewd detection. . . . The distinctive feature is that its hero is Marius, the Roman general whose military career just preceded that of Julius Caesar, and the campaign during which it goes on is that against Jugurtha. That its effect is of taking place at this day and hour is partly due to up-to-date speech—from which, as this is after all a

boy's book, profanity has been left out—but more largely to the realization that human nature being what it is, a general in the army will be likely to think, act and even talk much the same way in any epoch if—and this is the point—if he is that sort of general. . . .

Against Marius the distrust of upper-class military men for one risen from the plebs has reached the point of dangerous plots in Rome. . . . [There] are plotters in the camp itself and when Marius learns of them he summons Felix, a young officer. He is to carry under his armor a curiously wrapped buckskin package and guard it with his life. The youth returns to his tent where Gaius, whose watch he has taken, lay ill; he now lies dead, with a sword in his spine. Felix, accused, takes to flight, while proof is being collected: the way in which it is proved that no soldier made that cut shows real detective methods. The wanderings of Felix, crackling with narrow escapes, and surprises concerned with the package keep action jumping, and the style is that of a natural writer.

> *May Lamberton Becker, "From Rome and Poland," in* New York Herald Tribune Weekly Book Review, *November 12, 1944, p. 28.\**

How the plot is defeated and a murder mystery solved makes exciting reading, but author fails to give a convincing picture of the period. Recommended for limited purchase.

> *Dorothy Lawson, in a review of "The Counterfeit African," in* Library Journal, *Vol. 69, No. 21, December 1, 1944, p. 1052.*

---

## THE SWORD AND THE SCYTHE   (1946)

The emotional and political development of a 14th century German peasant in the time of the earliest peasant revolts is the stirring material of this excellent background action book. . . . The series of adventures of which [Martin] is a part takes the reader through the great peasant "war", to the bitter end of failure and points the way to the still unfinished business of making all men free. . . . Good school and library material.

> *A review of "The Sword and the Scythe," in* Virginia Kirkus' Bookshop Service, *Vol. XIV, No. 23, December 1, 1946, p. 594.*

Into a tale of the Peasants' War in 14th century Germany are woven plots and counterplots, magic and mystery aplenty. . . . True to the basic course of the war and supported by excellent sources, the exciting adventures of Martin Beimler take on a close relationship to the fight of the Common Man in World War II.

> *Alice M. Jordan, in a review of "The Sword and the Scythe," in* The Horn Book Magazine, *Vol. XXIII, No. 1, January-February, 1947, p. 37.*

---

## THE ROMAN MOON MYSTERY   (1948)

Jay Williams has a remarkable talent for tearing away the romantic glamour of remote historical periods and getting down to the bedrock human emotions and motives that change very little over the centuries. In **"The Sword and the Scythe"** he mercilessly debunked the myth of chivalry, to show us the oppressed peasants and artisans making their first brave stand against the rapacious knights. His new work does an equally effective job with the glories of imperial Rome. The medium is a fast-paced detective story involving two murders and several incidental killings. . . . Influential politicians, including the Emperor Nero, bring pressure to throw the blame on a group accused of subversive activities, a handful of humble people who call themselves Nazarenes. . . . Some older critics may object to modern slang in the mouths of Roman G.I.'s. But boys and girls from 12 up will find the natural-sounding dialogue a help in understanding that the men of olden times were *people*, and very like ourselves.

> *Nina Brown Baker, in a review of "The Roman Moon Mystery," in* The New York Times Book Review, *April 4, 1948, p. 29.*

A most unusual mystery this is. It takes place in Rome in the time of Nero, yet runs along with the lively pace of a modern story. This is due to the style in general, but most particularly because the conversations of the characters are full of American colloquialisms. Mr. Williams in his brief foreword says he wrote the story that way because the counterpart of our modern slang "may be found in any of the works of popular Latin authors of the Augustan age—Horace or Petronius, for example." People of that age did not talk in formal language any more than we do today. His point is well taken, and the result is entertaining. . . .

[How Justus and Marcia] solve the mystery of who committed the crime, though not in time to save Capito, and how Justus begins to turn toward Christianity himself makes interesting reading.

> *Irmengarde Eberle, in a review of "The Roman Moon Mystery," in* New York Herald Tribune Weekly Book Review, *July 25, 1948, p. 8.*

[This is a] swift-moving tale. . . . The details of Roman manners have been carefully studied. . . . In his desire to make his characters real, the author uses modern colloquial speech and the slang of the period as found in certain Latin writers, which prove effective. [This is a] well-sustained mystery. . . . An exciting book, sympathetic to the Christians. (pp. 377-78)

> *Alice M. Jordan, in a review of "The Roman Moon Mystery," in* The Horn Book Magazine, *Vol. XXIV, No. 5, September-October, 1948, pp. 377-78.*

### THE MAGIC GATE   (1949)

The same lively wit and knowledge of boys that Mr. Williams hitherto has applied to tales of old Rome and the Middle Ages he now employs in a modern story. The themes are serious: helping a boy of eleven to see that money isn't so very important—that friendship, loyalty, courage may be more important and cannot be bought. Also, he shows the value of imaginative play, and of doing things well with one's hands. By the time Steve is a full member of the gang, he has made his own wooden sword, also a dagger (paper cutter), and helped to build a log cabin. For all these, explicit instructions are given at the back.

One is inclined to believe Mr. Williams's boys, and to be cheered by a group that knows books so well that they refer casually to several classic hero tales. We hope the action and excitement will lure many eleven-year-olds to demand access to more tools and more work with wood.

> *Louise S. Bechtel, in a review of "The Magic Gate," in* New York Herald Tribune Book Review, *January 15, 1950, p. 6.*

A lonely boy in a new home finds summer companionship with a neighborhood gang of his own age, who are playing an elaborate game of knighthood. . . . Mr. Williams gives directions and diagrams for the handwork and brings a true sense of values into a lively story. For younger boys than those who read his historical mystery tales.

> *Alice M. Jordan, in a review of "The Magic Gate," in* The Horn Book Magazine, *Vol. XXVI, No. 2, March-April, 1950, p. 105.*

### DANNY DUNN AND THE ANTI-GRAVITY PAINT   (with Raymond Abrashkin, 1956)

Fanciful science fiction, though not as good as Ellen Mac-Gregor's efforts in that direction, nevertheless makes entertaining reading that may set more young geniuses to hanging up their own signs. Vastly more interesting to Danny Dunn than school work is the project of Professor Bullfinch, the inventor his mother housekeeps for. It all comes to a climax one day when Danny upsets the container of anti-gravity paint which makes objects rise to the ceiling and forecasts the solution to the problem of space travel. (p. 574)

> *A review of "Danny Dunn and the Anti-Gravity Paint," in* Virginia Kirkus' Service, *Vol. XXIV, No. 16, August 15, 1956, pp. 574-75.*

[This is] an exciting and hilarious adventure in outer space for young science fiction fans. Besides having fun they'll learn a lot about the solar system and the effects of gravity—and the lack of it.

> *M.M.R., "Adventures Here and There: 'Danny Dunn and the Anti-Gravity Paint'," in* Chicago Tribune, *Part 4, Section 2, November 11, 1956, p. 20.*

["**Danny Dunn and the Anti-Gravity Paint**"] has little scientific plausibility, but hardly pretends to be more than a comic fairy-tale with space-trimmings. . . . [A] quiet sense of the absurd should evoke many young chuckles.

> *H. H. Holmes, "Journeys into Outer Space," in* New York Herald Tribune Book Review *(© I.H.T. Corporation; reprinted by permission), November 18, 1956, p. 34.\**

Any young science fiction fan will find a kinship with Danny Dunn, who whiles away his time in the classroom dreaming of trips into space. They will appreciate, even envy, his clumsiness—which leads Professor Bullfinch to discover the anti-gravity paint that makes space travel a reality. Certainly, they will admire Danny's courage after he accidentally sends the space ship zooming upward with himself and three others aboard. . . .

A scientifically instructive book, this is full of fun and suspense.

> *Marjorie Burger, "Space-Boy," in* The New York Times Book Review, *November 18, 1956, p. 45.*

An amusing bit of science fantasy. . . . [The adventures of Danny, Professor Bullfinch, Joe, and Dr. Grimes] are improbable, even for science fiction, but are told with a verve and humor that makes them fun to read.

> *A review of "Danny Dunn and the Anti-Gravity Paint," in* Bulletin of the Children's Book Center, *Vol. 10, No. 5, January, 1957, p. 71.*

### DANNY DUNN ON A DESERT ISLAND (with Raymond Abrashkin, 1957)

Another story of Danny Dunn and his friends. . . . This time [Professor Bullfinch and Dr. Grimes] are embroiled in an argument as to which is the more practical. They decide to put the matter to a test by spending a month on a desert island. . . . The book does not have quite the spontaneous humor of the first story, the two adults seeming especially unrealistic in their childish bickering. It will, however, have appeal for the details of how the group provided the necessary food, clothing and shelter by reproducing some of the tools used by primitive man.

> *A review of "Danny Dunn on a Desert Island," in* Bulletin of the Children's Book Center, *Vol. 11, No. 2, October, 1957, p. 32.*

Readers who first met Danny and his three friends, Joe, Professor Bullfinch and Dr. Grimes, in **"Danny Dunn and the Anti-Gravity Paint"** will expect high adventure and excitement in this sequel. They will not be disappointed. . . . Danny has a knack for getting his friends into difficulties, but he is equally capable of getting them out again—and into new ones. Perhaps the most suspenseful moment is when Joe is rescued just as island natives are holding him over a boiling pot. As a matter of fact, there isn't a quiet moment in this wildly funny story.

> *Marjorie Burger, "Stranded in the Stone Age," in* The New York Times Book Review, *November 24, 1957, p. 36.*

A very light but entertaining story. . . . [The] account of the castaways' improvisations makes amusing reading, even if not quite up to Jules Verne's standards. Happily free of some of the wilder fantasies of earlier books in the series, and likely to be enjoyed by boys of eight to twelve.

> *R. W. Doust, in a review of "Danny Dunn on a Desert Island," in* Children's Book News, *Vol. 3, No. 4, July-August, 1968, p. 204.*

---

### DANNY DUNN AND THE HOMEWORK MACHINE (with Raymond Abrashkin, 1958; British edition as *The Homework Machine*)

Danny Dunn, whose previous adventures have won him many friends, once again embarks on an ambitious scientific venture. . . . Besides being confounded by the moral overtones of [having a computing machine do his homework], Danny is also faced with the temperamental ups and downs of the calculator. A satisfactory resolution for all concerned follows in the track of much hilarious confusion and considerable good sense.

> *A review of "Danny Dunn and the Homework Machine," in* Virginia Kirkus' Service, *Vol. XXVI, No. 12, June 15, 1958, p. 416.*

Danny, the impetuous, inventive boy of ***Danny Dunn and the antigravity paint*** . . . , and two companions find themselves in some amusing and uncomfortable predicaments. . . . Besides being highly entertained by Danny's latest doings, readers will learn something about automatic computers. Not essential but fun.

> *A review of "Danny Dunn and the Homework Machine," in* The Booklist and Subscription Books Bulletin, *Vol. 55, No. 2, September 15, 1958, p. 54.*

Comic situations, believable characters, and a minor scientific slant should make this slight story popular with the 8-10-year-olds. Should have more appeal than **"Danny Dunn and the Anti-Gravity Paint"** or **"Danny Dunn on a Desert Island."**

> *Mabel Berry, in a review of "Danny Dunn and the Homework Machine," in* Junior Libraries, *an appendix to* Library Journal, *Vol. 5, No. 1, September, 1958, p. 52.*

---

### THE BATTLE FOR THE ATLANTIC (1959)

The gradual development of the United States from [Britain's] lend-lease friend to an active ally evolved naturally as more and more of our convoy ships became the target of enemy attack. An excellent review of the actual progress of the Atlantic campaign, this book . . . makes an informative and uniquely logical analysis of a valiant struggle fought at sea. Much specific data of men and ships gives color to the lucid text, which also tries to explain his own century to the student of contemporary history.

> *A review of "The Battle for the Atlantic," in* Virginia Kirkus' Service, *Vol. XXVII, No. 13, July 1, 1959, p. 456.*

[A "Landmark Book"] useful not only for younger boys, but also for older boys in slow-learning groups. Straight-forward style, large print, simple language, accurate drama of history. Boys will love the courage and heroism of these fighting men of World War II. Maps, photographs, index give reference value. . . . Recommended.

> *Ruth C. Buell, in a review of "The Battle for the Atlantic," in* Junior Libraries, *an appendix to* Library Journal, *Vol. 6, No. 3, November, 1959, p. 49.*

[This account] will give youngsters a feeling for the enormity of the battle and for its importance in history. The book helps to develop an understanding of war years that are now shadows to the children of the men who fought during them. Maps, photographs, and index complement the well-written text.

> *Jane Ann Flynn, in a review of "The Battle for the Atlantic," in* Social Education, *Vol. XXIV, No. 8, December, 1960, p. 394.*

---

### DANNY DUNN AND THE WEATHER MACHINE (with Raymond Abrashkin, 1959)

[Written] with fantastic events, realistic details, and deft humor. This time the indefatigable boy decides to build his own weather station. . . . Danny and his two fellow meteorologists find that they can make rain. In a hilarious sequence of improbable events, they end the local drought when the transmitter gets caught up accidentally by a plane and emits rain-making rays. An entertaining story with some interesting facts incorporated in casual fashion.

> *Zena Sutherland, in a review of "Danny Dunn and the Weather Machine," in* Bulletin of the Center for Children's Books, *Vol. 13, No. 1, September, 1959, p. 24.*

By the end of this fourth book about the impetuous, tampering boy adults may wonder why the professor does not remove his laboratory and inventions from Danny's vicinity but this thought is not likely to occur to the reader who is searching for funny stories.

> *A review of "Danny Dunn and the Weather Machine," in* The Booklist and Subscription Books Bulletin, *Vol. 56, No. 2, September 15, 1959, p. 58.*

Curiosity may have killed the cat, but the agility with which young Danny Dunn's curiosity gets him into and out of fantastic situations should make him last through some several more intriguing books. . . . [Once] again Danny and his friends, Joe, Irene and Professor Bullfinch romp through an exciting and informative adventure.

> *Marjorie Burger, "The Rain Makers," in* The New York Times Book Review, *October 4, 1959, p. 40.*

The professor's tolerance of children experimenting in his laboratory during his absence is rather unconvincing, and his warning that scientists need to practice discipline has little effect upon Danny. Lively conversation, some humorous incidents scarcely compensate for a plot with many extraneous incidents, stereotyped characters, and dubious ethical implications. Not recommended.

> *Helen M. Robinson, in a review of "Danny Dunn and the Weather Machine," in* Junior Libraries, *an appendix to* Library Journal, *Vol. 6, No. 3, November, 1959, p. 43.*

There is no attempt here at real characterisation or depth of feeling and atmosphere, but the humour is good and strong and Danny is the perpetrator of this humour. With his friends he could probably awaken further interest in science in readers of books about him. The author writes fluently and light-heartedly, and produces a group of youngsters who are animated for a brief spell by their swift and spirited actions.

> *Eva Astbury, in a review of "Danny Dunn and the Weather Machine," in* The Junior Bookshelf, *Vol. 39, No. 5, October, 1975, p. 323.*

---

### THE TOURNAMENT OF THE LIONS  (1960)

A tale within a tale. Two young squires, Phillipe and Robert, are in attendance at a tournament at Saumur in 1448. . . . During the course of their stay, they are told the story of Roland and Oliver by Sir Bertrand, Master of the Squires. This famous story is extremely well told in this version, and the matrix material is equally well written. The action moves along at a good pace, the language is consistently appropriate, and there is an enormous amount of information about knighthood and the feudal system incorporated with skill.

> *Zena Sutherland, in a review of "The Tournament of the Lions," in* Bulletin of the Center for Children's Books, *Vol. 13, No. 8, April, 1960, p. 140.*

Not a substitute for the "Song of Roland," but an enjoyable and well-written novel with no outstanding characteristics. Accuracy in detail and good characterization. This will make good additional reading for large collections needing material on the Middle Ages.

> *Carol Whitney, in a review of "The Tournament of the Lions," in* Junior Libraries, *an appendix to* Library Journal, *Vol. 6, No. 9, May, 1960, p. 65.*

Fleurs-de-lis, trumpets, ladies, chivalrous knights, all the sights and sounds of medieval battles and pageants—Mr. Williams has chosen a magnificent setting, magnificently evoked, for his story of Roland and Oliver from the Chanson de Roland. A knight retells the story to two young high-spirited squires . . . and makes their story as absorbing as the story-within-the-story. . . . [Williams's] language retains a hint of the [splendor of the story of Roland] yet ten-year-olds can understand it, teen-agers enjoy it.

> *Pamela Marsh, in a review of "The Tournament of the Lions," in* The Christian Science Monitor, *May 12, 1960, p. 3B.*

---

### DANNY DUNN ON THE OCEAN FLOOR   (with Raymond Abrashkin, 1960)

Once again Danny Dunn goes beyond the limits usually binding his contemporaries. . . . The usual blend of zany humor and scientific possibility surround Danny Dunn in this new adventure which will be welcomed by his fans and, among new readers, will win him new friends.

> *A review of "Danny Dunn on the Ocean Floor," in* Virginia Kirkus' Service, *Vol. XXVIII, No. 14, July 15, 1960, p. 560.*

Readers who have survived the suspense in the earlier stories about Danny Dunn and company . . . will know just about what to expect when they pick up this latest installment of their scientific adventures. Wherever Danny Dunn is, there is sure to be excitement, adventure, hilarity and trouble.

All these are present indeed, plus an authentic picture of deep-sea exploration. . . .

> *Marjorie Burger, "Deep Trouble," in* The New York Times Book Review, *February 12, 1961, p. 38.*

Another science fantasy tale about the ever-busy Danny, whose adventures combine mishaps and prowess in equal proportions. . . . The style is light and quickly paced, with enough humor to mitigate the improbabilities of the plot. The book is weakened slightly by the tendency to exaggerate the idiosyncrasies of some of the adult characters. There is a good bit of information about marine life painlessly incorporated into the story.

> *Zena Sutherland, in a review of "Danny Dunn on the Ocean Floor," in* Bulletin of the Center for Children's Books, *Vol. 15, No. 3, November, 1961, p. 52.*

In **Danny Dunn and the Ocean Floor** this wise-cracking American schoolboy plays Stubbins to the Professor's Dr. Dolittle, for a newly invented underwater vessel enables the two of them to study the language of sea-creatures in the wild, as it were—with startling results. Most startling of all, and comic in a slapstick way, is the contrivance by which Danny extricates the submarine from a deep and tortuous cave. These adventures depend on a nonsensical extension of scientific truth and keep up with modern inventions very nicely.

*Margery Fisher, in a review of "Danny Dunn on the Ocean Floor," in her* Growing Point, *Vol. 5, No. 3, September, 1966, p. 754.*

---

### *DANNY DUNN AND THE FOSSIL CAVE* (with Raymond Abrashkin, 1961)

There are tunnels and caves, underground streams and stalactites all mixed up together in a story so full of pace that it never falters. There is science and realism, humour and drama, making a book which would appeal to even the most determined non-reader. Well up to the standard of previous books in the series, if not better, Danny Dunn might well be hailed as the character to persuade any child from the T.V. screen to a book.

*G. L. Hughes, in a review of "Danny Dunn and the Fossil Cave," in* The Junior Bookshelf, *Vol. 35, No. 3, June, 1971, p. 173.*

'Facts are fun,' [*Danny Dunn and the Fossil Cave*] says in the blurb, and there you have it, really: plenty of solid information about pot-holing and geology and laughter along the way. ('This is most interesting,' Dr Tresselt said thoughtfully. 'We appear to be standing on a mass of loose rubble. I have the feeling that our combined weights are unsettling it.') This is the sort of dead-pan joke that made me roar when I was young; it raised a ghostly giggle, even now. (p. 780)

*Nina Bawden, "Real Enough," in* New Statesman, *Vol. 81, No. 2098, June 4, 1971, pp. 779-80.**

[If] Dr Tresselt sometimes sounds like a walking textbook, there is plenty of fun, too, as the Bullfinch-Tresselt Underground Expedition gets into difficulties. There is nothing infantile about the book and it is that rare thing, so often sought by teachers: a junior novel which could be offered to a slow-reading 13 year-old, without offence.

*A review of "Danny Dunn and the Fossil Cave," in* The Times Literary Supplement, *No. 3618, July 2, 1971, p. 775.*

---

### *DANNY DUNN AND THE HEAT RAY* (with Raymond Abrashkin, 1962)

Danny Dunn's adventures in science—usually on the fringe of fantasy, with more than a modicum of fact behind them, are sure favorites with the 9-12 year olds. . . . This time he has a new adventure that uses up to the minute scientific data—as he decides to try [a laser for himself]. . . . Science-minded youngsters of today love this series, and even this unscientific minded adult found this entertaining reading. Checked for scientific accuracy—as are others of Danny's experiments.

*A review of "Danny Dunn and the Heat Ray," in* Virginia Kirkus' Service, *Vol. XXX, No. 14, July 15, 1962, p. 627.*

There is clearly an appeal in these stories, since this is the eighth book in the series. In this volume, Danny Dunn becomes involved in the world of modern technology, with much dialogue involving laser beams. . . . For myself, I could wish that the characters were a bit more probable and less like composites from *Dr. Who* and *Norman and Henry Bones, Boy Detectives*. For scientifically minded eight and nine year olds, however, this should provide another adventure in a popular junior SF series.

*Gabrielle Maunder, in a review of "Danny Dunn and the Heat Ray," in* Children's Book Review, *Vol. III, No. 3, June, 1973, p. 79.*

---

### *KNIGHTS OF THE CRUSADES* (1962)

"Knights of the Crusades" opens with the Battle of Hastings and covers the succeeding three hundred years, telling not only the running story of the Crusades, but also the breadth of their social and cultural and economic impact on Europe. The research is sound and solid, but never slows down the pace of the narrative, and the occasional quotes from contemporary sources actually manage to advance the story—an exceptional phenomenon.

*Gerald Raftery, in a review of "Knights of the Crusades," in* The New York Times Book Review, *September 30, 1962, p. 28.*

[The text] does very well in making a complex subject intelligible for those meeting it for the first time. The book list here too is notable, including contemporary sources like Villehardouin, good historical novels, and fine adult reading on the subject. . . .

*A review of "Knights of the Crusades," in* Books, *November 11, 1962, p. 35.*

This volume is an exciting and welcome surprise [compared to the usual series book]. . . . The text itself is a superior piece of historical writing, not the mere padding which so often serves only to keep the pictures from running into each other. (p. 614)

*Margaret Warren Brown, in a review of "Knights of the Crusades," in* The Horn Book Magazine, *Vol. XXXVIII, No. 6, December, 1962, pp. 614-15.*

[The text] is a competent and straightforward attempt to put the crusaders into some historical and social perspective. But the book is really an excuse for the hundred and fifty or so pictures. . . . Any child fortunate enough to be given it will look at it again and again. But—and it is a big but—I am distinctly uneasy about the book's scholarly pretensions. The reading list at the end shows a fine disregard for the difference between fact and fiction. . . . All the same, this is a book one would be glad to possess.

*Gillian Lewis, in a review of "Knights of the Crusades," in* Growing Point, *Vol. 2, No. 6, December, 1963, p. 247.*

---

### *JOAN OF ARC* (1963)

The tragically beautiful tale of the Maid of Orleans is skillfully retold. . . . Through a well-paced text the reader leads with the heroine the armies of France, faces condemnation by clerics and laymen, and stands at the stake. Detailed attention is given to social customs of the 15th century. A final chapter presents a 20th-century view of the legends surrounding St. Joan. (pp. 3363-64)

*Glenn E. Estes, in a review of "Joan of Arc," in* Library Journal, *Vol. 88, No. 16, September 15, 1963, pp. 3363-64.*

The best-written of the four [latest titles in the Horizon Caravel series] is Jay Williams's "Joan of Arc." Straightforward, literate, touched with style, the book is a good, balanced introduction to the Maid, accepting the mysteries of her extraordinary achievements without attempting easy rationalizations to take away the miraculous quality. It is a satisfying narrative unfolded against an exciting historical background.

> Edmund Fuller, in a review of "Joan of Arc," in The New York Times Book Review, September 15, 1963, p. 30.

[This] account places Joan in clear historical perspective; though the customs and condition of French life in the Middle Ages, the forces of church and state, and the methods of warfare are realistically presented, the spirit of the legend of Joan is preserved. A note on Joan in modern art and an excellent list of books for further reading are appended.

> "Biography: 'Joan of Arc'," in Books for Children: 1960-1965, American Library Association, 1966, p. 242.

---

### DANNY DUNN, TIME TRAVELER   (with Raymond Abrashkin, 1963; British edition as Danny Dunn—Time Traveller)

Danny Dunn has a following in America, but book-reading children here may find him insufficiently rounded for interest. He seems to belong to the two-dimensional world of the strip-cartoon. In **Danny Dunn—Time Traveller** he and his friends and a caricature of a professor operate a "chronocycle", making rather unenterprising trips. . . .

> "News from Space," in The Times Literary Supplement, No. 3303, June 17, 1965, p. 504.*

Writers of science fiction raise their towers of improbability on a variety of foundations, but for one reason or another humour is seldom one of them, although it is surely hard not to believe in characters and situations that make you laugh. The tales of Danny Dunn certainly push doubt aside most adequately. His exploits as a time traveller have a logic part mathematical part historical. Professor Bullfinch's Time Machine is so complex that even he is not sure where it will lead him or how it happens that friend Joe, caught up in the first experiment, is somehow duplicated by a Joe in the future who tags along with the party. This is not only a fine comic episode but the solution of where and how the second Joe materialised is one to intrigue anyone with a mathematical turn of mind. The logic of history is seen in the second and backward journey, when the Professor [and] the children find themselves in 1750, at which time their own house, newly built by Jonathan Turner, is being visited by Benjamin Franklin. This is useful when the electrical part of the machine fails; Franklin and his friend, another ardent experimenter with the sciences, are able to help with a Leyden Jar. Slangy, fast, spontaneously funny, these stories are one of America's best exports.

> Margery Fisher, in a review of "Danny Dunn Time Traveller," in her Growing Point, Vol. 4, No. 2, July, 1965, p. 541.

---

### THE QUESTION BOX   (1965)

[Villette's Great Clock] has a special warning device that mysteriously appeared whenever an attempt was made on the village. With two exceptions, nobody knew how the clock worked. There was Maria, a little girl who always asked questions and who spent hours sneaking into the clock-works to watch the

cog wheels, and there was a spy from the enemy, who checked out a book from the library. The story is nicely silly, with a convincing Old World aura, and children should appreciate the moral—that adults should always answer questions.

> A review of "The Question Box," in Virginia Kirkus' Service, Vol. XXXIII, No. 4, February 15, 1965, p. 171.

A quaint Old World village with a famous clock atop a high tower, an inquisitive little girl and a scheming count's plan to capture the village are the well-blended ingredients in Jay Williams's new tale. . . . How 8-year-old Maria solves the mystery of the clock and foils the wicked count's plot makes a lively climax to this well-told, amusing tale. There are elements of wisdom and good sense along with the excitement, and the author arranges his incidents with a refreshing childlike logic and directness that scorns mere adult plausibility.

> Marjorie Burger, in a review of "The Question Box," in The New York Times Book Review, April 18, 1965, p. 16.

---

### LEONARDO DA VINCI   (1965)

The "Horizon" format is well suited to a panoramic view of Leonardo the artist, engineer, and thinker. . . . [Text] is straightforward and succinct. Leonardo's innovations as a painter are covered in less breadth and depth than in the recent Cooper study, but sufficiently to indicate his originality. No attempt is made to reconstruct the details of his life, but this stands alone as a comprehensive study of his work.

> Barbara Bader, in a review of "Leonardo da Vinci," in School Library Journal, an appendix to Library Journal, Vol. 12, No. 2, October, 1965, p. 91.

A wonderful choice to read before, after, along with "Frank Lloyd Wright," for this fine biography (which keeps pace with other fine biographies in this series) tells the story of a genius who lived five centuries ago with such immediacy that he seems to be as contemporary as Wright. . . . **"Leonardo da Vinci"** is a magnificent book about a magnificent man.

> A review of "Leonardo da Vinci," in Publishers Weekly, Vol. 188, No. 21, November 22, 1965, p. 66.

Of the several recently published works about Leonardo da Vinci, this one reflects most accurately the spirit of the man and his times. It is well written. The distinction between fact and speculation is marked, the use of quotations judicious, and although much is incorporated about his contemporaries, Leonardo da Vinci always dominates the picture. The significance and the magnitude of his imagination become clearly evident to the reader after seeing him at work as an apprentice, artist, engineer, inventor, and scientist. . . . Enjoyable as reading and indispensable for reference, the book concludes with a carefully selected bibliography, an index, and a note on United States museums with collections of Renaissance art.

> Priscilla L. Moulton, in a review of "Leonardo da Vinci," in The Horn Book Magazine, Vol. XLI, No. 6, December, 1965, p. 643.

---

*DANNY DUNN AND THE AUTOMATIC HOUSE* (with Raymond Abrashkin, 1965)

["**Danny Dunn and the Automatic House**"] is fictionalized science of a rather dry sort. . . . [Danny Dunn is] a kind of jet-age Tom Swift. In this book Danny is involved in a futuristic house, a nightmare of automation that opens itself, shuts itself, vacuums itself and cooks. The authors's dialogue has the spontaneity of a press conference at the Kremlin, but they are successful in delivering a simple science lesson on the robot "brain."

> *Ellen Goodman, in a review of "Danny Dunn and the Automatic House," in* The New York Times Book Review, *November 7, 1965, p. 46.*

The new "**Danny Dunn**" adventure will appeal chiefly to small boys of mechanical bent precocious enough to reach out to the somewhat egg-headed and distinctly American humour of Danny and his friend Irene. . . . These slapstick tales flatter children who like to explain to parents how lasers and voders work (and the slapstick is very good too).

> *Margery Fisher, in a review of "Danny Dunn and the Automatic House," in her* Growing Point, *Vol. 6, No. 3, September, 1967, p. 954.*

This is my introduction to Danny Dunn. . . . It is primary school science fiction and on that level is fairly good. But every character is so dull and stereotyped. There is Professor Bullfinch and his young friend Danny, a budding scientist. Mum is tucked away in her kitchen baking endless cookies and producing coffee. The whole American university campus background, with its emphasis on proving itself to the world, is very alien to the English reader. Perhaps I am taking it all too seriously; I suspect that an eight-year-old boy will be amused by the professor's automatic house and intrigued by Danny's escapades in it. If it gives him a taste for science fiction which can be channelled on to John Wyndham at a later date then all is well. But please let us never forget that these are our most important readers and only writing of the very highest quality should be offered to them.

> *Joan M. Murphy, in a review of "Danny Dunn and the Automatic House," in* The School Librarian and School Library Review, *Vol. 15, No. 3, December, 1967, p. 369.*

---

*PHILBERT THE FEARFUL* (1966)

[When I read the beginning of "**Philbert the Fearful**,"] I had a strong hunch this book was going to be great fun. After I had laughed my way through its antic story, . . . I knew my hunch was right. (Why not? It was written by a co-author of the "**Danny Dunn**" books, which are great fun too.) But that Philbert! Guinevere can keep Sir Lancelot. Sir Philbert's the knight for me.

> *A review of "Philbert the Fearful," in* Publishers Weekly, *Vol. 189, No. 6, February 7, 1966, p. 90.*

A funny story about Sir Philbert, an appealing character but cowardly and overly concerned with his health. The doctor ordered the reluctant knight to help rescue the emperor's daughter. . . . He won the princess' hand and his health improved, too. Children will enjoy the moral—brains are of more use than bravado.

> *E. Louise Davis, in a review of "Philbert the Fearful," in* School Library Journal, *an appendix to* Library Journal, *Vol. 13, No. 7, March, 1966, p. 245.*

[Along with Guido Rocca's "Gaetano the Pheasant," "**Philbert the Fearful**"] is one of the new books for 6 to 8 year olds] I found above the general ruck of inbetweenness. . . . Mr. Williams manages his tongue-in-cheek fable without condescension or cuteness and leaves us with a lasting, likable hero after an entertaining series of adventures.

> *Al Hine, in a review of "Philbert the Fearful," in* The New York Times Book Review, *Part II, May 8, 1966, p. 39.*

---

*WHAT CAN YOU DO WITH A WORD?* (1966)

Fred worked for a witch who one day made a word machine that turned out words with the physical characteristics of their meanings. (A rather sophisticated idea for beginning readers.) . . . Contrived, unconvincing fantasy. Though called "a beginning reader" by the publisher, this is not first-grade reading.

> *Hope H. McGrady, in a review of "What Can You Do with a Word?" in* Library Journal, *Vol. 91, No. 13, July, 1966, p. 3530.*

Probably the most appealing of [the Collier "Beginning Readers" which include Conrad Aiken's *Tom, Sue and the Clock*, Pearl S. Buck's *The Little Fox in the Middle*, Erskine Caldwell's *The Deer at Our House*, and Gladys Schmitt's *Boris the Lopsided Bear*], from the beginning reader's point of view, is Jay Williams' **What Can You Do With a Word?**, its title notwithstanding. Thoroughly used to writing juveniles is Mr. Williams, and past experience tells. His tale is the only one with real narrative flair; even his repetition seems intentional. A witch invents a word machine which produces words of wondrous usefulness at the turn of a crank. ZIGZAG has angles sharp enough to fell a tree; and SPANG proves sufficiently stretchable to catapult the hero, Fred, into the middle of next week where he encounters high adventure. Words, of course, are the real heroes of Mr. Williams' simple fairy tale—a bit of propaganda that is quite to the point. (pp. 18-19)

> *Selma G. Lanes, in a review of "What Can You Do with a Word?" in* Book Week—The Washington Post, *July 10, 1966, pp. 18-19.*

A brief fanciful story that doesn't quite come off. . . . The book hasn't quite enough humor to be an amusing story, not enough action to be an adventure story, and not enough consistency in the way the words (from the word machine) are used to be meaningful.

> *Zena Sutherland, in a review of "What Can You Do with a Word?" in* Bulletin of the Center for Children's Books, *Vol. 20, No. 8, April, 1967, p. 131.*

---

*LIFE IN THE MIDDLE AGES* (1966)

A general survey of the Middle Ages organized into chapters on such subjects as the village, castle, camp of war, church, etc. . . . Unfortunately, the text stresses the melodramatic side of every aspect of medieval life, treating the reader to an unlimited series of extremes that are calculated to explain the many crudities of life (e.g., "Sometimes lords of the Church were as greedy as knights—they came, after all, from the same noble background. The Bishop of Auxerre crucified one of his foresters for selling some of the lord's pigeons for his own profit'', p. 81). Examples such as this and tales of gullibility, along with a lot of useless generalizations and odd facts (e.g., travellers to Jerusalem were called "palmers" because they brought back palm leaves from the Holy Land), all make the book appear superficial to the adult reader and will encourage the young reader to continue in his usual thought pattern of exciting but romantic misjudgments of the medieval world. The index is useful, but there are no additional reading lists. . . . [The] text is not among the best available, readable as it is. (pp. 5257-58)

> *Lee Ash, in a review of "Life in the Middle Ages,"* in Library Journal, *Vol. 91, No. 18, October 15, 1966, pp. 5257-58.*

What a marvelous libretto to have nearby when you are reading a novel with a medieval setting. But then, look who wrote it. . . . "Mr. Williams," wrote Orville Prescott, "probably knows more about the Middle Ages than any other novelist writing today." He writes better about it for young people than anybody this reviewer knows of—he makes any historical time, any historical character seem as alive and topical as if he were a reporter on a daily paper. (Stipulated, a reporter with a drawerful of Pulitzer prizes.)

> *A review of "Life in the Middle Ages,"* in Publishers Weekly, *Vol. 190, No. 16, October 17, 1966, p. 63.*

*Life in the Middle Ages* runs rapidly and expertly over familiar ground. In spite of the mandatory simplifications of such a survey of medieval society, Jay Williams manages to avoid gross distortions. . . . The charm of this book lies in the anecdotes that balance the generalizations, and in the homely examples: the number of eggs, chickens, and geese served at a royal dinner party, the mechanical crucifixes with which priests of the Auvergue provided their own miracles. . . . [This is a] well-written introduction to medieval social history.

> *Richard Winston, "Flourishes and Trumpets," in* Book Week—World Journal Tribune, *October 30, 1966, p. 32.*

[*Life in the Middle Ages* has] a highly readable text. . . . The author maintains that the alarums and excursions of kings and barons represented only a small fraction of what went on. . . . [He shows] the daily life of the bulk of medieval society—the peasants and villagers, the guildsmen, scholars, squires, monks. Of course, the "ordinances of chivalry" are also presented, for no picture of the Middle Ages would be complete without a description of castle life and the ceremonies and traditions of knighthood. Altogether, this is one of the best of the many background studies of medieval Europe geared to a teen-age audience.

> *Marion West Stoer, "Making Vivid the Past," in* The Christian Science Monitor, *November 3, 1966, p. B9.*

The same insouciance [that characterizes the pictorial reproductions] marks the text. Mr. Williams does not define his chosen period. This is perhaps allowable, since in some respects one can accurately say "at this time" of the centuries of the feudal period, because the structure of society and agricultural life altered little from William to the Wars of the Roses. In subjects such as armour and weapons and foreign trade Mr. Williams shows the chronological development over the whole period, occasionally with dates, more often by "later" and "in time". This gives a reasonable historical view.

More frequently, however, he makes inadmissible generalizations about life over five centuries, like "There was no sugar". He describes the Guild situation or the state of the Church in the fifteenth century as though this were the picture throughout the period, whereas he deals almost entirely with the earliest conditions in the universities. He jumps back and forth within his subjects from one century to another.

Nevertheless, the book is packed with valuable details and the many well-chosen examples are drawn from the whole period and from the whole of western Christendom, while excellent use is made of contemporary writings.

> *"Pictures Are Not Enough," in* The Times Literary Supplement, *No. 3431, November 30, 1967, p. 1159.*

---

### *THE SPANISH ARMADA* (1966)

This is a naïve, melodramatic presentation of the defeat of the Spanish Armada and consequent weakening of Spanish power. The author sees England as the angel of God making war upon Spain, the scourge of mankind, as the serpent in the garden. Top-heavy and one-sided with the exploits of Hawkins and Drake, the book also renders an almost childish presentation of the problems of the times. The author does a fine job in describing the ships pitted against one another and the actual defeat of the Spaniards. But then he hastens back to his beloved Elizabeth and her crew.

> *A review of "The Spanish Armada," in* Best Sellers, *Vol. 26, No. 19, January 1, 1967, p. 371.*

[There are] intriguing anecdotes among the vast array of facts [Mr. Williams] has researched for this comprehensive account of the events leading up to that exciting, decisive sea battle. Mr. Williams fills in the background of mounting hostility between English and Spanish sailors—both groups exploring, plundering, greedy for rewards.

> *Patience M. Daltry, in a review of "The Spanish Armada," in* The Christian Science Monitor, *February 2, 1967, p. 7.*

Many maps, drawings and paintings make a most attractive volume. . . . The text is a good match for the illustrations. There are some vivid pen portraits: Mary Queen of Scots sending letters out from prison in the bung of a beer barrel; Drake climbing a tree in Panama to become the first Englishman to see the Pacific Ocean. Boys should relish this book that abounds in the excitement and hardships of a seaman's life in the 16th century.

> *Kate McQuade, in a review of "The Spanish Armada," in* The New York Times Book Review, *February 5, 1967, p. 32.*

Jay Williams's absorbing and lively Caravel book, *The Armada*, describes fully the only plot against England after 1066 to come within sight of success. Using the recent researches of Mattingly and others, he brings out well the excitement of the successive days' engagements in the final confrontation. . . . The mixed motives of both Catholics and Protestants and their attitudes towards each other are well revealed. A useful selection sketches the development of naval warfare, with technical details of Hawkins's reformed design for the English warships.

> *"Plots and Plans," in* The Times Literary Supplement, *No. 3458, June 6, 1968, p. 592.**

---

### THE COOKIE TREE   (1967)

[One] morning a strange tree appears in the middle of the village. It has silvery bark and under each golden leaf is a chocolate cookie. . . .

Debate rages. Is the tree a bad omen? Should it be watched, destroyed, or given to the king as a gift? . . .

Fortunately, the children have taken matters into their own capable hands. To them it is obvious that the tree and its cookies must be the gift of a kind magician and so they eat during the elders' debate. . . .

Though the story is good the main charm of the book is the style of the storyteller and the uncluttered, solid pictures [by Blake Hampton]. Williams' tale has a flavor as appealing as the fruit of his tree. . . .

This is very different from the author's many other books. He is quite versatile and rarely keeps to a pattern. This book, like most of his others, shows a pleasant irreverence for established, expected, behavior patterns. If there is a common thread, it is that his books show people who act sensible despite the demands of tradition.

> *Phyllis Cohen, in a review of "The Cookie Tree," in* Young Readers Review, *Vol. III, No. 9, May, 1967, p. 6.*

---

### DANNY DUNN AND THE VOICE FROM SPACE   (with Raymond Abrashkin, 1967)

[After Danny nets Hubert Badger tramping across the countryside, the "tramp" reappears on the doorstep of Professor Bullfinch] and is introduced as a famous astronomer. *(Surprise!)* Seems he's come to enlist the Professor's help in an attempt to monitor sounds from distant planets; seems the Professor has just developed (and perfects, with Danny's accidental assistance) the very tool that will make the attempt practical . . . and Danny Dunn-ites can tell it from there. There's the usual medley of pure scientific and parascientific information leading to a pseudoscientific conclusion and a thinner than usual veneer of Joe Miller jokes—and as usual, the great discovery depends on Danny's just-informed intuition.

> *A review of "Danny Dunn and the Voice from Space," in* Kirkus Service, *Vol. XXXV, No. 12, June 15, 1967, p. 695.*

In many respects, this is a thoroughly enjoyable book. The authors have woven interesting science and a well-paced story together nicely. The ending is beautifully underplayed. The only possible complaint is that Danny's world is too sugar-coated to be believable. There are only happy people in this world. Sir Edward gets angry, but it's only a "plant" to keep the plot going. This book doesn't provide much conflict or suspense, but it does have humor, good science (despite occasional lectures to the reader), some excitement, and a briskness which keeps the story moving well.

> *Ben W. Bova, in a review of "Danny Dunn and the Voice from Space," in* Appraisal: Children's Science Books, *Vol. 1, No. 3, Fall, 1968, p. 29.*

The idea of messages from space which denote an intelligent origin is not new, but its embodying in a readable SF story for top juniors is not so common. Since it is a book by, and about, Americans, most of which takes place in Britain, with a little simple science and astronomy thrown in too, it is quite worth buying.

> *Norman Culpan, in a review of "Danny Dunn and the Voice from Space," in* The School Librarian, *Vol. 17, No. 4, December, 1969, p. 421.*

---

### THE SWORD OF KING ARTHUR   (1968)

Nobody, but nobody, not even Jay Williams, can sway me from my loyalty to Howard Pyle's magnificent stories of King Arthur and his court (all from *Scribners*). But nobody who has ever worked in a bookstore can deny that Pyle's prose is hard going for younger readers. Jay Williams is the man to introduce them to Arthur and his valiant knights.

> *A review of "The Sword of King Arthur," in* Publishers Weekly, *Vol. 193, No. 17, April 22, 1968, p. 52.*

[This] simplified and modernized version of Arthur's long life and of his knights and their adventures recounts many dramatic episodes with an abundance of heroic action but without precise delineation of character. (p. 1289)

> *A review of "The Sword of King Arthur," in* The Booklist and Subscription Books Bulletin, *Vol. 64, No. 22, July 15, 1968, pp. 1288-89.*

Based on Malory, this presents the more important legends of King Arthur simply and clearly for younger readers. . . . Although this lacks Pyle's graceful literary style, it is a fast-moving, straightforward adaptation which retains a medieval quality while omitting the archaic phraseology found in the more comprehensive and more difficult versions by Pyle, Lannier, and Picard. A good introduction to the more advanced versions, this will also be useful for slow or reluctant older readers.

> *Anna Binicos, in a review of "The Sword of King Arthur," in* School Library Journal, *an appendix to* Library Journal, *Vol. 15, No. 1, September, 1968, p. 142.*

---

### THE HORN OF ROLAND   (1968)

Not simply the *Chanson* celebrating Roncesvalles but the legend of Roland as assembled from many sources, as previously available to children in James Baldwin's *The Story of Roland.* This differs in sequence and in substance; it is also more compact; most important, it is far, far more fluent and vigorous. And, as narrowed to focus on the human drama—the clashing pride of Roland and Charlemagne, the competition between Roland and Ganelon, particularly the complementary personalities of Roland and Oliver—it makes a fascinating story. . . . Mr. Williams explains his use of sources, does not explain, unfortunately, that there was no such nephew of Charlemagne and that what passes for history here mirrors neither the events nor the spirit of his time. Maybe the omission seems to matter because the story is so convincing.

A review of "The Horn of Roland," in Kirkus Service, Vol. XXXVI, No. 19, October 1, 1968, p. 1120.

This satisfactory retelling of Roland's adventures may be especially useful with older but slower readers, since it is clearly written and uses a simple vocabulary. Teachers could easily use these stories in the study of the Middle Ages, and children reading them may be sufficiently inspired to attempt Baldwin's *Story of Roland* (Scribners, 1930).

*Marcelee Gralapp, in a review of "The Horn of Roland," in* School Library Journal, *an appendix to* Library Journal, *Vol. 15, No. 5, January, 1969, p. 77.*

A vigorous and colorful retelling of the most familiar adventures of the French epic hero—a chronological account that begins with the boyhood of Roland and ends with his death at Roncesvalles. The emphasis in this version is on heroic action, the brave exploits of Roland in battle. The long descriptive passages and romantic embellishments characteristic of James Baldwin's *The Story of Roland* (Scribners) are sacrificed to a fast-paced adventure, which may attract more readers. Nuances of character—Roland's brashness and the motivation for Ganelon's treachery—are presented with more depth in *The Song of Roland* by Robert and Marguerite Goldston (Bobbs) for older readers. But the author succeeds in providing a younger audience with a lively introduction to Roland in vivid language strong in its simplicity and medieval in flavor. (pp. 167-68)

*Diane Farrell, in a review of "The Horn of Roland," in* The Horn Book Magazine, *Vol. XLV, No. 2, April, 1969, pp. 167-68.*

### THE PRACTICAL PRINCESS (1969)

Jay Williams' clever, iconoclastic text and Friso Henstra's Pop-née-Victorian, elaborately stylized illustrations, combine to make a very appealing spoof of a fairy tale. Princess Bedelia, besides being the usual things a princess should be, . . . is blessed with a rather suspect virtue for royalty—common sense. She psychs out the snobbery of a fire-breathing dragon with an appetite for princesses, and appeases his undiscerning eye with an offering of the gaudiest royal trappings—stuffed with straw and gunpowder which blows up the dragon on contact with his breath. . . . Though some words in the text may require explanation for the youngest audience (snob, geographical, salamander, boundary), this delightful story is an excellent choice for read-alouds and story hour programs. Today's children will relish the exploits of the gutsy, independent, and practical Bedelia, and find this spoof uncommonly good. (pp. 106, 109)

*Margherite Girard, in a review of "The Practical Princess," in* School Library Journal, *an appendix to* Library Journal, *Vol. 15, No. 8, April, 1969, pp. 106, 109.*

A turnabout fairy tale: Princess Bedelia is intelligent, brave, active, kills a dragon, and rescues an enchanted prince from a wicked sorcerer. All the men in this story are incompetent and ignorant. This is a sexist story because it humiliates and downgrades men.

*Masha Kabakow Rudman, "The Female: 'The Practical Princess'," in her* Children's Literature: An Issues Approach, *D. C. Heath and Company, 1976, p. 354.*

### SCHOOL FOR SILLIES (1969)

It's hardly news that the biggest fool is he who thinks himself all-wise, but in showing up King Kilian and winning his daughter's hand wandering scholar Kit produces some tricky surprises. . . . [Told] with the same stylish dispatch as *The Practical Princess,* and smartly comical.

*A review of "School for Sillies," in* Kirkus Reviews, *Vol. XXXVII, No. 21, November 1, 1969, p. 1146.*

Jay Williams is writing grand fables—grand, original fables. He adds his own special brand of lemon extract to keep them from ever getting too soggy-solemn.

*A review of "School for Sillies," in* Publishers Weekly, *Vol. 196, No. 25, December 29, 1969, p. 67.*

[The creators of *The Practical Princess*] are back, but not with the same success. . . . The wisdom—that we are not as smart as we may think we are—may be lost on some small children, but all will be charmed by the simple story and large pictures.

*Kathlyn K. Lundgren, in a review of "School for Sillies," in* School Library Journal, *an appendix to* Library Journal, *Vol. 16, No. 7, March, 1970, p. 1192.*

### THE GOOD-FOR-NOTHING PRINCE (1969)

The author has a graceful, witty way of telling a story. This one is about an extremely lazy prince whose father's wizard accidentally makes the prince disappear into a strange country where he has to exert himself greatly to rescue a beautiful princess. Any fairy-tale fancier will be pleased.

*Hazel Wilson, in a review of "The Good-for-Nothing Prince," in* Parent's Magazine & Better Family Living, *Vol. XLV, No. 6, June, 1970, p. 23.*

Ola is prepared for rescue; ropes, food, etc. are in her suitcase. Yet she waits for the prince before making her move. You cannot portray a person as energetic and resourceful and then keep her waiting for a poor excuse of a man to help her get out of her prison. (p. 17)

*Enid Davis, "Maidens with Spunk: Books by Jay Williams," in her* The Liberty Cap: A Catalogue of Non-Sexist Materials for Children, *Academy Press Limited, 1977, pp. 14-17.*

### DANNY DUNN AND THE SMALLIFYING MACHINE (with Raymond Abrashkin, 1969)

[Welcome] to another instalment of that robust, untendentious, cheerful saga of young curiosity, the **"Danny Dunn"** series. *Danny Dunn and the smallifying machine* is neatly planned round a simple assumption—that a machine could be invented to diminish anyone or anything placed on its platform. If we accept this, all else follows, for we know by now that if there is a switch to press Danny Dunn will press it. There remains the ingenuity of the working out—the lively descriptions of Professor Bullfinch and his young friends wandering in a world where a dragonfly is a nightmare and a stone a mountain. . . . [The smallified friends return to normal] by a device so exquisitely simple that I will only say that you don't need even O Level Physics to work it out. Why is there no medal for

Humour? The **"Danny Dunn"** books get my personal medal, for what it's worth.

> *Margery Fisher, in a review of "Danny Dunn and the Smallifying Machine," in her* Growing Point, *Vol. 9, No. 2, July, 1970, p. 1558.*

Stories have been published in which children lived with bees or ants and became the same size but never before have they shrunk, with an adult, and become so small that gravity loses most of its meaning. . . . [More happens] too, with the result that a really exciting book emerges. Exciting because it is not just an adventure story, but the reader also learns some of the basic facts of science in a simple easy-to-read fashion. A book all children should enjoy.

> *A review of "Danny Dunn and the Smallifying Machine," in* The Junior Bookshelf, *Vol. 34, No. 4, August, 1970, p. 214.*

[The world as seen from the height of one quarter of an inch] is a fascinating world and full of unexpected scientific twists. It is also exciting, funny and full of adventure. The authors know well how to combine these elements to keep their readers entertained and informed. Apart from being a 'good read', this could provide the starting point for a number of stimulating personal investigations in the junior school.

> *C.E.J. Smith, in a review of "Danny Dunn and the Smallifying Machine," in* The School Librarian, *Vol. 18, No. 3, September, 1970, p. 368.*

There is a great deal of 'scientific' information imparted (butterflies' wings are scaly; short things hit the ground faster than tall things when they fall from an upright position; very light things rise in updrafts of warm air), and at times the action seems contrived for the express purpose of transmitting these facts.

In fact, the whole book seems too contrived. The ending comes with a sort of omigosh-I'm-running-out-of-paper rush, and leaves the reader with a feeling of wha-happened? This is perhaps a problem which arises from being one more book in a series, or perhaps it is just the product of a somewhat uncoordinated collaboration, but I have read lots of books that were better than **"Danny Dunn and the Smallifying Machine,"** and I imagine most kids have too.

> *Charlotte Moslander, in a review of "Danny Dunn and the Smallifying Machine," in* Luna Monthly, *No. 22, March, 1971, p. 22.*

---

### *A BOX FULL OF INFINITY*   (1970)

So slight is the story of the pauperish prince who, with the help of a golden pretzel, hoodwinks a wizard to rescue a princess and win a fortune, that little lapses loom large: the so-called pretzel is certainly a symbol of infinity—but something less than a pretzel—and something less than infinite insofar as its links are broken. Moreover, the trick that the talking pretzel plays on the wizard . . . could have been pulled off by anyone or anything capable of adding "And one more." Needs a little smartening up all round.

> *A review of "A Box Full of Infinity," in* Kirkus Reviews, *Vol. XXXVIII, No. 22, November 15, 1970, p. 1247.*

This might have been just another story of a poor king who sends his son out to seek his fortune. However, it has both charm and originality deriving from its straightforward, humorous language and the clever use of the pretzel . . . as a key plot element. . . . In lighthearted fashion the author gives readers an unsophisticated yet apt insight into the concept of infinity. . . . A good read-aloud for second and third graders, this will also be enjoyed by fourth graders reading it themselves.

> *Eleanor Glaser, in a review of "A Box Full of Infinity," in* School Library Journal, *an appendix to* Library Journal, *Vol. 17, No. 6, February, 1971, p. 52.*

---

### *THE SILVER WHISTLE*   (1971)

We've said it before, will say it again we hope, that Jay Williams writes the most delightful, the wittiest fairy tales you can ask for. . . . [His collaboration with Friso Henstra] here is no exception: their combined writing and illustrating of the story of a girl as homely as the day is long, and a mind to stay that way, makes a story book that is "a nice change" indeed.

> *A review of "The Silver Whistle," in* Publishers Weekly, *Vol. 199, No. 21, May 24, 1971, p. 69.*

Prudence, Jay Williams' latest pragmatic heroine (similar to Bedelia, *The Practical Princess* . . .), receives a magic whistle as a legacy from her mother and is hired by a nasty old witch who wants her to obtain the magical mirror of Morna. Anyone who looks in the mirror becomes beautiful, and the witch hopes to use this subterfuge to marry the prince. . . . The prince, who prefers freckles and good sense to beauty, chooses Prudence as his wife. The author has become expert at this kind of neo-folktale with its contemporary attitudes and modern-sounding dialogue.

> *Dorothy Gunzenhauser, in a review of "The Silver Whistle," in* School Library Journal, *an appendix to* Library Journal, *Vol. 18, No. 1, September, 1971, p. 111.*

A folk-like tale. . . . The writing style is brisk, humorous, and deceptively simple, the story a refreshing variant of the poverty-to-royal-marriage-via-magic-device theme. . . .

> *Zena Sutherland, in a review of "The Silver Whistle," in* Bulletin of the Center for Children's Books, *Vol. 25, No. 2, October, 1971, p. 36.*

---

### *THE HAWKSTONE*   (1971)

Efforts to keep his ancestors' land in Connecticut take Colin from the everyday world of family small talk and neighborly visits to a mystical, timeless one after he acquires the magic hawkstone. Colin finds the stone, which derives its power from its wearer's "love of the land," at a time when high taxes threaten to drive his family from their farm. . . . [Six spirits who had once possessed both the land and the stone] lead Colin at last to a buried treasure that will more than pay the taxes, become a bit thick toward the end as they crowd around directing his every move; in the other dimension, the flip conversations are awkwardly forced from the start ("Up to bed, Buster"—"Oh poop, I forgot"—"Well, well, if it isn't the other half of Damon and Pythias"). Boys might breeze through this as easily as Colin moves through the centuries, but it has neither the dispatch of Williams' **"Danny Dunn"** books nor the resonance of compelling fantasy.

> A review of "The Hawkstone," in Kirkus Reviews, Vol. XXXIX, No. 19, October 1, 1971, p. 1073.

[*The Hawkstone*] uses many well-worn themes—the child who saves the family fortunes, the hero winning a contest against the odds, buried treasure, the talisman that connects to the past and makes of them something moving and something new. . . . [One] of the pleasures of the book is the skill and richness with which a small town community is portrayed; and the past . . . is the past of the Red Indian as well as of the early settler, the War of Independence volunteer and others. . . . And it is not one of those amoral tales in which luck and magic do the trick; a stiff contribution of courage is exacted from Colin too. Particularly admirable is the description of the trance-like skill with which, wearing the Hawkstone, Colin finds he can draw a bow, and the slowly accumulating sense of the history of the place.

> A review of "The Hawkstone," in The Times Literary Supplement, No. 3687, November 3, 1972, p. 1331.

There is no change of mood, no tingling of the spine, when Colin discovers the stone, nor when he is 'possessed'. It is difficult to be concerned about people and a place which the writer does not lead us to comprehend imaginatively. I wonder how many readers will get far enough into this competent, but unhumorous and not quite convincing, story to enjoy Colin gradually winning the shooting match, and removing a copperhead snake from its hole, before finding the treasure which saves his home?

> R. Walker, in a review of "The Hawkstone," in Children's Book Review, Vol. II, No. 6, December, 1972, p. 186.

It sounds trite in summary, but this novel is written with such sensitivity and affection for its subject, that the story never becomes maudlin or melodramatic. . . . The courage of one 'spirit,' the shrewdness of another, the tenacity of still another, added to Colin's overcoming his own fears, combine to produce the happy ending.

One senses throughout *The Hawkstone* an almost mystical feeling for the land and those who have made their livelihood from it. Colin's efforts to help his family pay the extra taxes are portrayed as simply another in a long line of almost heroic acts by people who felt that this little piece of the North American continent was worth anything that might be required to keep it theirs.

> Charlotte Moslander, in a review of "The Hawkstone," in Luna Monthly, No. 44, January, 1973, p. 17.

The transitions from age to age, person to person, are engineered smoothly; glimpses of the past and of individual men and women build up a picture of life on Hyatt land through two centuries—an enjoyable, well-plotted story.

> George Bott, in a review of "The Hawkstone," in The Junior Bookshelf, Vol. 37, No. 1, February, 1973, p. 62.

---

*DANNY DUNN AND THE SWAMP MONSTER* (with Raymond Abrashkin, 1971)

A sure winner for that difficult "middle" age group, especially boys and those less able readers. . . .

The **"Danny Dunn"** books have that particular humor and sophisticated wit to be found in the **"Dr. Seuss"** books for younger readers; it has such a special appeal because it is the type of humour that the children use amongst themselves. Add to this the suspense of a modern scientific thriller, plus an authorship which includes Jay Williams, and you have a guaranteed success story. (p. 234)

Fact and fiction blend superbly, the old and the new, from the primitive tribespeople to the ultra modern scientific equipment, but strangest of all is their very plausible discovery in the swamp which does solve all the many mysteries surrounding the creature. (pp. 234-35)

> Jean Russell, in a review of "Danny Dunn and the Swamp Monster," in The Junior Bookshelf, Vol. 36, No. 4, August, 1972, pp. 234-35.

The Monster of the new **"Danny Dunn"** adventure is a [survivor], but in reading terms a perfectly possible one. The humour in the **"Danny Dunn"** books is subtle as well as open. Science is never distorted though it is often exaggerated; a situation may be absurd but it will emanate from simple truth. So although we don't have to believe that there actually is a swamp in the Upper Nile region where a catfish has grown so huge that it has supplied its own electrical barrier round itself and its habitat, it seems perfectly reasonable to suggest that such a creature could exist. Feeling comfortable, then, about the central assumption, we can settle down to enjoy the reactions of the characters—the energetic enjoyment of Danny, Professor Bullfinch's learned enthusiasm, the superstitious terror of the local tribesmen and the cunning greed of the zoo-collector who is defeated just because Danny's quick mind sees how they can wire up the natural power generated in the "monster's" skin. This lively, practical tale adds a nice comic gloss to nature. (pp. 2017-18)

> Margery Fisher, in a review of "Danny Dunn and the Swamp Monster," in her Growing Point, Vol. 11, No. 4, October, 1972, pp. 2017-18.

The **"Danny Dunn"** series is obviously intended for small boys who like adventure, science, and light reading. The style is readable, the vocabulary simple (except for the scientific terms, all of which are carefully explained), the characters are stereotypes, but not vicious ones (the absent-minded genius, the stay-at-home housekeeper mother), and the adventures never put anyone into really grave danger. None of the volumes is great literature, but look how many generations have enjoyed the exploits of Nancy Drew and the Hardy Boys. . . .

The book will find an enthusiastic welcome among Danny Dunn fans. Everyone else may as well forget it.

> Charlotte Moslander, "Lilliputia: 'Danny Dunn and the Swamp Monster'," in Luna Monthly, No. 48, Fall, 1973, p. 22.

---

*THE HERO FROM OTHERWHERE* (1972)

Fantasy is like Pegasus: You can soar on his back. But you must hold the golden bridle, given by Minerva, and that gift is artistry. . . .

["**The Hero from Otherwhere**"] actually has two heroes: poetic Jesse and scientific Rich, junior-high-school enemies. They get whisked away to Gwyliath (another world whose fate is somehow linked with ours) to find the three lost strands—courage, knowledge, pity—of the cord that used to bind Fenris, Wolf of Fear, so he may be bound again.

The region he is plaguing is called Hyperborea. Change one letter of that and you have "hyperbored," which I was, for the first 10 chapters—where moral intentions stick out like sign posts, and allegorical meanings are insistently driven home.

So Pegasus galoomphs along, but in Chapter 11 belatedly takes wing. A truly funny character, Professor Ilbird, is introduced. Things liven up. And the end—Jesse and Rich choosing friendship over material rewards—for all its predictability and didacticism, still manages to be touching.

> Doris Orgel, "Galoomphing Along on the Wings of Pegasus," in The New York Times Book Review, November 5, 1972, p. 12.*

This book should have been longer by at least five paragraphs for sometimes the author introduces a plot twist with no background and the reader is left wondering. Other than that, it's a very good fantasy. . . . The writing is evocative and the story is very worthwhile. Especially recommended for those with some sensitivity.

> A review of "The Hero from Otherwhere," in Children's Book Review Service, Vol. 1, No. 5, January, 1973, p. 32.

The realistic and the fanciful elements are not always smoothly blended, but both the conception of the intricacies and magic of the adventure, and the gradual changing of Jesse's and Rich's attitudes toward each other and their learning to compromise and complement, are soundly developed.

> Zena Sutherland, in a review of "The Hero from Otherwhere," in Bulletin of the Center for Children's Books, Vol. 26, No. 6, February, 1973, p. 99.

Jay Williams successfully puts across the theme of friendship but fails to draw well-rounded, believable characters. However, junior high readers will enjoy the improbable adventures and imaginative descriptions.

> Glenda Heaberlin, in a review of "The Hero from Otherwhere," in School Library Journal, an appendix to Library Journal, Vol. 19, No. 8, April, 1973, p. 79.

---

**PETRONELLA** (1973)

Another fairy tale with the tired theme of matching up princesses and princes to live happily ever after. However, there is a switch. As in . . . [*The Practical Princess* and *The Silver Whistle*], it is the princess who must accomplish the traditional three tasks. Although courage and talent play a part, the princess's exploits are not of the aggressive variety often carried out by princes. Instead, Petronella passes her tests by using typical "feminine" qualities—kindness, consideration and empathy. Petronella ends up the one chosen instead of the one who chooses, and she is always referred to as a girl (whereas the prince and the enchanter are referred to as men). Nevertheless, she is depicted as being active and is valued for admirable human qualities, rather than solely for her looks.

> Melinda Schroeder, in a review of "Petronella," in School Library Journal, an appendix to Library Journal, Vol. 20, No. 1, September, 1973, p. 64.

---

**FORGETFUL FRED** (1974)

["**Forgetful Fred**"] is about the young servant of Bumberdumble Pott, the world's richest man. Intent on finding the Bitter Fruit of Satisfaction . . . , Pott sends Fred questing. His adventures are related with the traditional language and devices of fairy tales. It is all quite familiar. . . . Though the art is more inventive than the tale neither writer (Jay Williams) nor illustrator (Friso Henstra) seems attuned to a young audience. . . . [How] does one explain to a 6-year-old just what the Bitter Fruit of Satisfaction is?

> Karla Kuskin, in a review of "Forgetful Fred," in The New York Times Book Review, May 5, 1974, p. 47.

A mediocre story. . . . Stories like this are a glut on the market—they contribute nothing to the literature for children. The 4 to 8 group will not grasp the meaning of the "bitter fruit of satisfaction," nor will they suffer through the stilted pedestrian prose [and] shopworn plot. . . .

> Janice P. Patterson, in a review of "Forgetful Fred," in Children's Book Review Service, Vol. 2, No. 10, June, 1974, p. 84.

An original fairy tale. . . . There's a pleasant note of mild irreverence as foil for the standard pattern, and a brisk, no-nonsense writing style for the fanciful plot.

> Zena Sutherland, in a review of "Forgetful Fred," in Bulletin of the Center for Children's Books, Vol. 28, No. 1, September, 1974, p. 20.

---

**DANNY DUNN, INVISIBLE BOY** (with Raymond Abrashkin, 1974)

[In *Danny Dunn, Invisible Boy*, science] is cleverly and responsibly exploited. Professor Bullfinch invents ISIT, a kind of visual bugging device. . . . This can be fun when used for trial runs, and useful for exposing the school bully and cheat. The story takes a more sober turn when the Pentagon steps in, seeing ISIT as a valuable tactical weapon and also, more important, as an aid for Big Brother. The children act quickly to destroy this threat to democracy, and Bullfinch wins a breathing space to enable mankind to grow up to its scientific technology. Not so funny after all. The story moves briskly, but the actors creak a little on their wooden joints.

> "Sheriff of Medicine Creek," in The Times Literary Supplement, No. 3774, July 5, 1974, p. 714.*

The new "**Danny Dunn**" story is as funny, fascinating and fantastic as those which have gone before. Danny's adventures in the *Invisible Boy* may not be quite so outlandish as those in earlier books in the series, but who would not wish that he could simulate invisibility. . . . Danny Dunn and his friends [outwit the American Army] and much more, providing a chuckle a page and, on the serious side, making one see that the ability to be invisible, or for other people to become invisible, may have as many disadvantages as advantages.

*G. L. Hughes, in a review of "Danny Dunn Invisible Boy," in* The Junior Bookshelf, *Vol. 38, No. 4, August, 1974, p. 240.*

The hardware in *Danny Dunn invisible boy* is up to the standard of the Smallifying and Homework machines. . . . The description of Danny's experiments with the probe are fascinating in technological terms and lead naturally to the point of the story, the discovery of deceit. . . . Fearing its misuse (not without reason) Danny finds a way to destroy the Professor's notes by remote control before engineering the destruction of the machine, so that he becomes not only the invisible voice of conscience but also the instrument of peace. The important theme of the book is enforced naturally and easily at the end of one of the swiftest and most ingenious stories in this splendid series, in which humour and science are expertly blended.

*Margery Fisher, in a review of "Danny Dunn Invisible Boy," in her* Growing Point, *Vol. 13, No. 4, October, 1974, p. 2474.*

---

### THE PEOPLE OF THE AX   (1974; British edition as *People of the Axe*)

Humans are battling semi-human beings, called Crom. The Crom have apparently discovered iron, and 15-year-old Arne goes with a female companion to relate this news to a Wise Woman. The journey and its aftermath change Arne and the world. *People of the Axe* utilizes many familiar sci-fi plot elements, such as a primitive post-atomic civilization, ESP, and so on. However the book is well-written, with a gripping plot and especially good characterization.

*John Smothers, in a review of "The People of the Axe," in* Children's Book Review Service, *Vol. 3, No. 7, February, 1975, p. 56.*

Plain, direct and impressive, too, *People of the Axe* has [the theme] of youth seeking a new sphere of life, but the plot is complex and the book gains a particular emotional force from its basic ambiguity. Are we in the past or the future? Why is Arne dissatisfied with the tribal organisation in which fighting is by token only? . . . What if the brutish Crom who had captured him, and whose race was historically deemed to be lower than his own, was in fact also human? What if Arne, the potential Seer, had in him also the seeds of aggression, as the Crom might have the rudiments of a Soul? Behind the obvious political moral lies a straight look at the deepest attributes of Man. Exciting, firmly handled, the plot is properly integrated with the underlying thought in this stirring tale. (pp. 2821-22)

*Margery Fisher, in a review of "People of the Axe," in her* Growing Point, *Vol. 14, No. 8, March, 1976, pp. 2821-22.*

An intriguing story which at first sight is just yet another epic of a boy growing to manhood in the Dark Ages. Adult life is greeted with an initiation ceremony in which all receive an axe and, more importantly, a soul. Thus might is matched with compassion. . . .

In a final encounter with the Crom, Arne uses the power within him to impart a soul to the creature, and one sees a new era of true civilisation ahead. This is an exciting story, and at the same time an indictment of the lack of humanity in our own time.

*M. R. Hewitt, in a review of "People of the Axe," in* The Junior Bookshelf, *Vol. 40, No. 2, April, 1976, p. 115.*

Similar in general theme but superior to [H. M.] Hoover's books is Jay Williams' *The People Of The Ax*. . . . Though reminiscent of LeGuin and Boule, Williams' simple but powerful style and deft handling of plot enhance the thought-provoking examination of man's inhumanity to man. (p. 218)

*Margaret P. Esmonde, "After Armageddon: The Post Cataclysmic Novel for Young Readers," in* Children's Literature: Annual of the Modern Language Association Seminar on Children's Literature and The Children's Literature Association, *Vol. 6, edited by Francelia Butler, Temple University Press, 1977, pp. 211-20.**

This is in some ways an ambitious book that makes certain demands on the young reader; but Jay Williams does not altogether avoid cliché, naivety and echoes of Earthsea. He describes rather than creates the experiences of his characters.

*Graham Hammond, "Death Duties," in* The Times Literary Supplement, *No. 3864, April 2, 1983, p. 383.**

---

### DANNY DUNN, SCIENTIFIC DETECTIVE   (with Raymond Abrashkin, 1975)

As a boy detective Danny Dunn has lots of competition but the young scientist performs creditably here. Amateur sleuths are unlikely to lose any sleep over the crime or its solution: What could be a more obvious setup than an uncrackable safe? And who could be a more likely suspect than the store manager, Mr. Anguish, who asked Professor Bullfinch to design it? Yet the gadgetry Danny improvises would be the envy of any junior Sherlock. . . . With help from his pal Irene, occasional poetic encouragement from his non-scientist buddy Joe, and with fatherly, black Detective Ellison to keep their investigations in line, Danny keeps up a brisk pace. And young investigators will want to track down the pedigree of the Professor's chemical bloodhound.

*A review of "Danny Dunn: Scientific Detective," in* Kirkus Reviews, *Vol. XLIII, No. 24, December 15, 1975, p. 1380.*

The "Danny Dunn" books are funny in a very unobtrusive and delightful way. It is partly a matter of improbable situations being shown to be probable, partly a matter of style, of a certain laconic wit and a deft manipulation of dialogue. *Danny Dunn Scientific Detective* follows pretty closely the formula of the other books in the series, being built round two scientific points. . . . [By] the usual combination of luck, coincidence and sharp observation, [Danny] identifies and catches the villain. Amusing and fast-moving, the tale demonstrates in an agreeably light manner the use of reason and deduction.

*Margery Fisher, in a review of "Danny Dunn Scientific Detective," in her* Growing Point, *Vol. 14, No. 9, April, 1976, p. 2852.*

Danny Dunn in his 14th adventure aids the local police detective in solving an innocuous crime by using the "scientific method" in his deductions. The story is trite, characters one-dimensional. Danny should be permanently retired.

Alibeth Howell, in a review of "Danny Dunn, Scientific Detective," in School Library Journal, Vol. 22, No. 8, April, 1976, p. 80.

## EVERYONE KNOWS WHAT A DRAGON LOOKS LIKE (1976)

The latest of Williams' fairy tale pastiches is set in the village of Wu on the edge of China, where wild horsemen are about to invade and a fat old man appears in answer to the elders' prayers to the Great Cloud Dragon. Officially rejected, as the Mandarin and each of his councilors casts the mythical dragon in his own image, the old man is fed and befriended by Wu's poor little gate-keeper, and for him he saves the city. It's a slick enough blend of traditional elements, but without the enlivening turnabout of Williams' *Practical Princess* or *Petronella*.

A review of "Everyone Knows What a Dragon Looks Like," in Kirkus Reviews, Vol. XLIV, No. 14, July 15, 1976, p. 791.

[When a small, fat] man appeared, claiming to be the Great Cloud Dragon that was going to save the city from the Wild Horsemen, all the people laughed at him. That is, all except the young gatekeeper, Han. . . . This is an imaginative and beautifully written fairy tale filled with colorful description. . . . [It] is a thoroughly enchanting story for reading aloud, acting out, or enjoying individually. . . .

Barbara Dill, in a review of "Everyone Knows What a Dragon Looks Like," in Wilson Library Bulletin, Vol. 51, No. 1, September, 1976, p. 79.

## THE BURGLAR NEXT DOOR (1976; British edition as *Daylight Robbery*)

Writing "at" spoils Jay Williams's *Daylight Robbery* entirely. Its banal metaphor of "building bridges" between people and its turgid insistence on the theme of "folks are not what they seem" could well have been dispensed with in favour of a sharpening up of plot and characterization. . . . [This detective story] breaks the first rule of the genre: don't hold back essential clues from the reader—even, or especially, the child reader.

Rosamund Faith, "Classroom Lore," in The Times Literary Supplement, No. 3915, March 25, 1977, p. 361.*

Penny Bloom, central character of *Daylight Robbery,* is a far more believable twelve-year-old [than Claire of Meta Mayne Reid's *The Noguls and the Horse*], both in her attitudes and in her degree of worldly knowledge. When her friend Amos Tutt is accused of theft she sets to work to prove his innocence in a very youthful way. . . . However, by the time she has realised who the thief was and what Amos was doing in the empty house, she has learned to be more wary in her judgment of people. Set in a small American town, the story moves smoothly and swiftly from street to street and house to house, establishing the characters briskly and firmly in their particular circumstances and taking a shrewd but sympathetic look at the difficulties inherent in youth. (pp. 3087-88)

Margery Fisher, in a review of "Daylight Robbery," in her Growing Point, Vol. 15, No. 9, April, 1977, pp. 3087-88.

[*Daylight Robbery* is] constructed in the classic style [of the detective story]. . . .

The attraction of the story is considerably increased by the attention given to the characterisation of Penny. She comes very much alive with her doubts and soul-searchings, her hopes, her day-dreams and her exploration of her friendship with Amos. Girl readers will find it easy to identify with Penny as she plots her way across what a psychologist has called the uncharted seas of adolescence.

Donald Young, in a review of "Daylight Robbery," in The Junior Bookshelf, Vol. 41, No. 3, June, 1977, p. 187.

## THE REWARD WORTH HAVING (1977)

Another letdown. Jay Williams has a flair for made up fairy tales with a contemporary twist. This time round, however, he has neglected to add the twist. Here, to tell it baldly, three soldiers do a good deed for a "little man no bigger than a rabbit" and each is rewarded with his choice of three caged birds. . . . [Mercer Mayer's illustrations] compensate for the spontaneity the printed word fails to deliver. But this remains a wan pastiche in a deceptively dressy-looking format.

Joyce Milton, in a review of "The Reward Worth Having," in The New York Times Book Review, June 19, 1977, p. 28.

Fans of the Williams/Mercer combination are in for another *tour de force*. . . . In his fictional comment on human foibles, the author reminds us that "Life calls to Life." With its themes and exquisite descriptive details, the story is comparable to one by H. C. Andersen.

Ruth M. Stein, in a review of "The Reward Worth Having," in Language Arts, Vol. 54, No. 6, September, 1977, p. 686.

## THE TIME OF THE KRAKEN (1977)

A tale of high adventure in the tradition of Norse mythology which, at the end, turns out to be a space fantasy. Thorgeir Redhair, one of the Vollings (remarkably like the Vikings), sets out to save the world from the destructive force of the legendary Kraken. Joined by the huntress Ylga who is his equal and plays a major role in the venture, Thorgeir's quest for a powerful weapon to use against the monstrous Kraken leads him through many adventures to the temple of the goddess Arveid. . . . The message (a bit preachy) that a religion of peace may, through differences of doctrine and interpretation, be fanned into warlike intolerance is integrated into a well-written scifi fantasy that is one of the few examples of the genre in which equality of the sexes reigns. (pp. 150-51)

Shirley Wilton, in a review of "The Time of Kraken," in School Library Journal, Vol. 24, No. 1, September, 1977, pp. 150-51.

After a long, slow start, this science-fiction future Nordic myth is absorbing, exciting and almost nonsexist. There are visions, villains and talking beasts on this distant (in space and time) planet peopled by Icelandic descendants. . . . There is a hero, a heroine, a quest and gory deeds, but it will need pushing.

*Lenore Rosenthal, in a review of "Time of Kraken,"
in* Children's Book Review Service, *Vol. 6, No. 3,
November, 1977, p. 30.*

When it comes to the sober creation of new myth, I don't know
anybody much better than Jay Williams. Well—new myth?
*The Time of the Kraken* starts very much like an old one. The
atmosphere is that of the Icelandic saga, except that there are
theological oddities that don't quite fit. . . . The tale's awfully
thrilling, given those oddities; one thinks—nice, strong management of traditional tensions: and then. . . . Well, Arveid,
it turns out, was a certain Professor Morton Arveid: and the
planet on which it's all occurring is not the Earth. There are
one or two quite stinging reversals of expectation, and a down-
beat ending; but my goodness, it *does* work, quite reverber-
antly.

*Edward Blishen, "Other Times, Other Worlds," in*
The Times Educational Supplement, *No. 3269, February 3, 1978, p. 40.\**

A threat to the world and a dangerous quest to counter it are
not unusual themes in science fiction. Jay Williams builds his
dramatic tale on these familiar girders and succeeds in manipulating legend and fantasy into a sparkling original adventure. . . .

Conflict knits this unorthodox saga together. . . . Quiet heroism keeps the story moving; imaginative insight gives it coherence.

*George Bott, in a review of "The Time of the Kraken,"
in* The Junior Bookshelf, *Vol. 42, No. 3, June, 1978,
p. 164.*

Jay Williams's book is a skilful linking of an epic-type story
with SF. . . . Pace, until near the end, is moderate; but the plea
for tolerance and co-operation, and the ingenious resolution of
hostile creeds, is embodied in the protagonist and the action,
not preached.

*Norman Culpan, in a review of "The Time of the
Kraken," in* The School Librarian, *Vol. 26, No. 2,
June, 1978, p. 169.*

---

### DANNY DUNN AND THE UNIVERSAL GLUE   (with Raymond Abrashkin, 1977)

In their latest adventure, Danny, Joe, and Irene discover a
mysterious factory pollutant which is seeping into the town's
reservoir and causing deterioration of the dam. . . . [Professor
Bullfinch's] amazing new universal glue can even repair concrete dams. Characterization is minimal, the plot leans heavily
on coincidence, and it all degenerates into an unsatisfying ecological tract. Useful only where Danny Dunn has an avid and
indiscriminate following.

*Julia E. Davis, in a review of "Danny Dunn and the
Universal Glue," in* School Library Journal, *Vol.
24, No. 5, January, 1978, p. 92.*

[This] latest addition to a well-established series is more convincing as adventure than as comedy. . . .

The adults in this story are wholly credible; they have their
own everyday problems and the relationships between the grown
ups and the children are convincing with reasonable demands
being made and met on both sides. This is a fast moving tale

successfully written from a child's view of things and it should
hold its readers' attention.

*Lesley Lancaster, "One Hit, Two Misses," in* The
Times Educational Supplement, *No. 3293, August
11, 1978, p. 18.\**

---

### THE WICKED TRICKS OF TYL UILENSPIEGEL   (1978)

Tyl Uilenspiegel, the trickster-hero of Holland, is a good choice
for [ages six through eight]. Many of his "merry pranks" turn
on semantic interpretation (or misinterpretation): remember when
he sold tickets to those who wanted to see a horse with his
head where his tail should be? Of course, when the buyers got
inside the barn, they saw a plain horse turned wrong way round
in his stall. Now, that is a level of verbal humor likely to strike
a six-, seven- or eight-year old as the height of wit.

Jay Williams has chosen four of Tyl's escapades to make a
52-page book that is just this side of a picture book. In each
of the stories, Tyl is cheerful and basically good-hearted, more
clever than wicked, in spite of the title. He tricks an avaricious
merchant out of a few of his possessions, he cures a greedy
governor of his piggishness, and he fools the Spanish enemy
into providing food for the hungry Dutch townspeople they are
besieging—nothing to unsettle a seven-year-old's strict moral
sense. Williams presents the stories in a straightforward way,
though with no particular flair. Still clarity is probably most
important here, and the tales are funny if the telling isn't.

*Anne Scott MacLeod, "Dutch Treats and Irish
Laughter," in* Book World—The Washington Post,
*May 14, 1978, p. G4.\**

Here and there the prose is stiff, but for the most part Williams
is simple and direct in his writing style, and he does communicate the zest and merriness that have made the Tyl Uilenspiegel stories popular for several centuries.

*Zena Sutherland, in a review of "The Wicked Tricks
of Tyl Uilenspiegel," in* Bulletin of the Center for
Children's Books, *Vol. 31, No. 10, June, 1978, p.
168.*

---

### THE PRACTICAL PRINCESS AND OTHER LIBERATING FAIRY TALES   (1978)

Five of the six inverted tales in this book have been previously
published in picture book format. Thus, the ever practical Bedelia and adventurous Petronella may already be old friends.
However, the sly humor of the inversions and the sophisticated
approach of these stories has appeal for older children, who
will find the present format more acceptable. . . . This is a
good collection of original stories and offers promise of fun
for story hours.

*Ellen Loughran, in a review of "The Practical Prin-
cess and Other Liberating Fairy Tales," in* Children's Book Review Service, *Vol. 7, No. 9, April,
1979, p. 85.*

An entertaining fairy tale book with a difference, easy to read
and amusing to both boys and girls. For once princesses take
over the leading role from princes; but the heroes are by no
means spineless.

*A review of "The Practical Princess and Other Lib-
erating Fairy Tales," in* Books for Your Children,
*Vol. 14, No. 3, Summer, 1979.*

Supporters of "Women's Lib" theories will love this collection of six highly original fairy tales, with their unheroic heroes, and their bold, resourceful energetic heroines. . . .

An amusing book, very well presented, it will make an ideal present from an aunt to a favourite niece, especially one plagued by an older brother!

> *Alice Thatcher, in a review of "The Practical Princess," in* The Junior Bookshelf, *Vol. 43, No. 4, August, 1979, p. 213.*

Williams' princes and other males are stupid and inept, altogether unsuitable partners for his princesses charming. They are not even the lucky simpletons of traditional folk stories, and their unredeemed lack of spunk makes their liberated mates and would-be mates look, pardon the expression, overbearing. While the style is certainly adequate both to reading aloud and to independent reading, no child (nor feminist) should be satisfied with stories that elevate women at the expense of men. The sexes do not need any further reasons for alienation.

> *Ruth K. MacDonald, in a review of "The Practical Princess and Other Liberating Fairy Tales," in* School Library Journal, *Vol. 26, No. 1, September, 1979, p. 124.*

The princesses of Jay Williams still defeat the dragon, accomplish three impossible tasks, rescue the prince, or accompany an incompetent one on a quest, but they usually want to have it both ways. They want to be independent, but they also want to be kept. And it turns out that it is not enough to be liberated: the standard forms of princessly beauty are still essential to the good life. The reader may fear that in a collection of tales about practical and liberated princesses, no stone is going to be left unturned to see what chauvinist pigs might be lurking underneath. He can rest assured—though not totally assured. Anyone who wishes to write spoof fairy tales, for whatever reason, even if to de-mythologise princesses, had better read James Thurber's *The thirteen clocks* to see how it is done. The only way to make a parody of a fairy tale is to write a proper fairy tale.

> *Ralph Lavender, in a review of "The Practical Princess and Other Liberating Fairy Tales," in* The School Librarian, *Vol. 28, No. 3, September, 1980, p. 271.*

[**The Practical Princess and Other Liberating Fairy Tales**] is an attempt to write new tales of clever women who outsmart dragons, wizards, and the general stupidity of the world. The trouble is that there are not heroes worthy of the heroines in the fictional worlds that Williams creates. Take for example the names of the heroes of the tales: Stupid Marco, Forgetful Fred, and Philbert the Fearful. Each of these men finds a heroine to cherish him, not because he is a man of manly or even otherwise noteworthy virtues, but rather because he is likable or accidentally lucky enough to stumble onto her rescue. The heroines may be clever, practical, and courageous, but one wonders about their judgement if they consistently marry such nice but otherwise unexceptional men. Certainly amiability is a virtue to be affirmed, but if women are to be the equals of men in fairy tales, then there must be men in the tales equal to the best and brightest of the women. (p. 18)

> *Ruth MacDonald, "The Tale Retold: Feminist Fairy Tales," in* Children's Literature Association Quarterly, *Vol. 7, No. 2, Summer, 1982, pp. 18-20.\**

## THE MAGIC GRANDFATHER (1979)

Presenting magic as an alternative to the evils of TV addiction may seem to be a didactic approach to a light-hearted fantasy, but the author carries it off with his own logic and conviction. Sam is an amiable, somewhat phlegmatic boy whose two great loves are television and his grandfather. . . . [Sam] frequently visits Grandpa in his fascinating cluttered apartment and one night stumbles upon the realization that his wise and loving relative leads a secret life as an enchanter. . . . [When a spell accidentally misfires,] the old man plunges out of the world of reality into another universe, and the burden of restoring him falls squarely upon Sam. A posthumously published story showing some resemblance to the author's well-loved *Danny Dunn* books. . . . (pp. 418-19)

> *Ethel L. Heins, in a review of "The Magic Grandfather," in* The Horn Book Magazine, *Vol. LV, No. 4, August, 1979, pp. 418-19.*

The slow, wordy start could deter some children, but in the last chapters the action moves swiftly and crisply to a very exciting climax. While I am doubtful whether this type of magic should be expounded in such detail in a book for children, the author can be congratulated on an original and imaginative idea and a great deal of research. (p. 213)

> *Alice Thatcher, in a review of "The Magic Grandfather," in* The Junior Bookshelf, *Vol. 43, No. 4, August, 1979, pp. 212-13.*

The rather lame ending is not up to the rest of the book's high standard of excitement and humour. Grandfather's return is rather clumsily contrived, but the book ends happily on a forward-looking note. Could it be that Sam is a magician too, and Sarah a witch? Look out for the next in the series.

> *R. B. Southern, in a review of "The Magic Grandfather," in* The School Librarian, *Vol. 27, No. 3, September, 1979, p. 254.*

Two fine books [**The Magic Grandfather** and *When Grandfather Journeys into Winter* by Craig Kee Strete] can lead to discussions of relationships with the elderly. **The Magic Grandfather** is certain to keep the reader or listener thoroughly involved and may lead to debates of the power of the mind, or the watching of television versus the use of imagination and concentration.

> *A review of "The Magic Grandfather," in* The Reading Teacher, *Vol. 33, No. 4, January, 1980, p. 481.*

## ONE BIG WISH (1980)

Another posthumous story is a reminder of Williams's inimitable gifts to children, more than 80 wonderful adventures. Exemplifying the author's waggish humor, the tale of farmer Fred Butterspoon begins when Fred kindly frees an old woman from a bramble bush on his farm. She grants him wish fulfillment, in gratitude, then vanishes. The farmer figures he might as well wish for a million dollars and there it is, a pile too big to carry. Further wishes merely complicate his problems. . . . Finally, the beleagured farmer wishes he had never started "the whole thing!" In a flash, he's back where he started, about to free an old woman from a bramble bush, and then the story segues into an unpredictable, mirthful resolution.

> *A review of "One Big Wish," in* Publishers Weekly, *Vol. 217, No. 3, January 25, 1980, p. 340.*

[This is] a nonsensical tall tale in the folk tradition. . . . It's the sort of disaster humor small children enjoy, in a nicely told story, and the let-not-your-reach-exceed-your-grasp message is given with a light touch.

*Zena Sutherland, in a review of "One Big Wish,"
in* Bulletin of the Center for Children's Books, *Vol.
33, No. 8, April, 1980, p. 163.*

---

### THE WATER OF LIFE  (1980)

This is a fantasy about a helpful fisherman named Pilchard who is searching for the "water of life" (youth) for the king. . . . The fisherman finds he can "give a hand" to those he meets along his journey and thereby enrich his own life. This allegorical tale shows that the real values of life are elusive and ordinary (the water of life is found to be the stream running outside the king's window) and that simple rewards may be satisfying. . . . A rich tale for a perceptive reader or listener.

*Ruth W. Bauer, in a review of "The Water of Life,"
in* Children's Book Review Service, *Vol. 9, No. 1,
September, 1980, p. 5.*

This pixieish, modern fairy tale is among those unpublished by Williams before his death and a reminder of his singular contribution to children's literature. . . . [What happens after Pilchard gives his magic safeguards to needy folk] is a jubilant moment that readers won't forget.

*A review of "The Water of Life," in* Publishers
Weekly, *Vol. 218, No. 16, October 17, 1980, p. 66.*

Williams has utilized a variety of folk motifs in this literary tale. . . . Traditional versions of such motif combinations including the Grimm tale of identical title stand far above this lecture on goodness. The tale lacks a heart or any true conflict.

*George Shannon, in a review of "The Water of Life,"
in* School Library Journal, *Vol. 27, No. 3, November,
1980, p. 68.*

# APPENDIX

The following is a listing of all sources used in Volume 8 of *Children's Literature Review*. Included in this list are all copyright and reprint rights and acknowledgments for those essays for which permission was obtained. Every effort has been made to trace copyright, but if omissions have been made, please let us know.

**THE EXCERPTS IN CLR, VOLUME 8, WERE REPRINTED FROM THE FOLLOWING PERIODICALS:**

*America*, v. 110, June 20, 1964. © 1964. All rights reserved. Reprinted with permission of America Press, Inc.

*Appraisal: Children's Science Books*, v. 1, Fall, 1968; v. 2, Spring, 1969; v. 12, Winter, 1979; v. 13, Spring, 1980; v. 13, Fall, 1980. Copyright © 1968, 1969, 1979, 1980 by the Children's Science Book Review Committee. All reprinted by permission.

*Appraisal: Science Books for Young People*, v. 14, Spring, 1981; v. 16, Winter, 1983. Copyright © 1981, 1983 by the Children's Science Book Review Committee. All reprinted by permission.

*The Athenaeum*, n. 3418, July 30, 1910. Reprinted by permission.

*The Atlantic Bookshelf*, a section of *The Atlantic Monthly*, October, 1935 for a review of "The Coot Club" by Anne Carroll Moore. Copyright © 1935 Anne Carroll Moore. Reprinted with permission.

*The Atlantic Monthly*, v. CVI, December, 1910 for "Lying Like Truth" by Margaret Sherwood; v. 192, December, 1953 for a review of "Otis Spofford" by Margaret Ford Kiernan; v. 214, December, 1964 for a review of "Ribsy" by Charlotte Jackson. Copyright © 1910, 1953, 1964 by the respective authors. All reprinted with permission.

*The Babbling Bookworm*, v. 5, October, 1977. Copyright 1977 The Babbling Bookworm Newsletter. Reprinted by permission.

*Best Sellers*, v. 26, January 1, 1967. Copyright 1967, by the University of Scranton. Reprinted by permission.

*Book Week—New York Herald Tribune*, December 5, 1965. © 1965, *The Washington Post*. Reprinted by permission.

*Book Week—The Sunday Herald Tribune*, November 10, 1963. © 1963, *The Washington Post*. Reprinted by permission.

*Book Week—The Washington Post*, November 22, 1964; July 10, 1966. © 1964, 1966, *The Washington Post*. Reprinted by permission.

*Book Week—World Journal Tribune*, October 30, 1966. © 1966, *The Washington Post*. Reprinted by permission.

*Book Window*, v. 7, Spring, 1980 for a review of "The Missing Maple Syrup Sap Mystery" by Margaret Walker; v. 8, Spring, 1981 for a review of "Henry and Beezus" by S. McD. © 1980, 1981 S.C.B.A. and the respective contributors. Both reprinted by permission.

*Book World—The Washington Post,* July 8, 1973. Copyright © 1973 The Washington Post Company. Reprinted by permission./ March 20, 1977; October 9, 1977; April 9, 1978; May 14, 1978; January 13, 1980; July 12, 1981; August 9, 1981; September 12, 1982; August 14, 1983; October 9, 1983; September 9, 1984. © 1977, 1978, 1980, 1981, 1982, 1983, 1984, *The Washington Post.* All reprinted by permission.

*Bookbird,* v. VI, September 15, 1968. Reprinted by permission.

*Booklist,* v. 73, September 1, 1976; v. 73, July 1, 1977; v. 74, October 1, 1977; v. 75, September 1, 1978; v. 75, May 1, 1979; v. 75, July 15, 1979; v. 76, November 1, 1979; v. 76, December 15, 1979; v. 76, March 15, 1980; v. 76, June 15, 1980; v. 76, July 15, 1980; v. 77, September 15, 1980; v. 77; March 15, 1981; v. 77, April 1, 1981, v. 77, July & August, 1981, v. 78, September 1, 1981; v. 78, October 15, 1981; v. 78, April 15, 1982; v. 79, September 1, 1982; v. 79, October 1, 1982; v. 79, December 1, 1982; v. 79, April 1, 1983; v. 79, April 15, 1983; v. 79, June 1, 1983; v. 79, June 15, 1983; v. 80, September 1, 1983; v. 80, September 15, 1983; v. 80, October 15, 1983; v. 80, January 1, 1984; v. 80, April 1, 1984; v. 80, April 15, 1984; v. 80, July 1984; v. 81, September 1, 1984; v. 81, October 1, 1984. Copyright © 1976, 1977, 1978, 1979, 1980, 1981, 1982, 1983, 1984 by the American Library Association. All reprinted by permission.

*The Booklist,* v. 14, December, 1917; v. 50, September 1, 1953; v. 51, September 1, 1954; v. 70, November 15, 1973; v. 70, December 1, 1973; v. 70, February 15, 1974; v. 70, March 1, 1974; v. 70, June 1, 1974; v. 71, December 15, 1974; v. 72, October 1, 1975; v. 72, December 15, 1975; v. 72, March 15, 1976; v. 72, June 1, 1976; v. 72, July 15, 1976. Copyright © 1917, 1953, 1954, 1973, 1974, 1975, 1976 by The American Library Association. All reprinted by permission.

*The Booklist and Subscription Books Bulletin,* v. 53, September 1, 1956; v. 55, September 15, 1958; v. 56, September 15, 1959; v. 58, June 15, 1962; v. 64, June 15, 1968. Copyright © 1956, 1958, 1959, 1962, 1968 by the American Library Association. All reprinted by permission.

*The Bookman,* New York, v. XXX, October, 1909.

*Books,* November 11, 1962. © I.H.T. Corporation. Reprinted by permission.

*Books for Your Children,* v. 11, Summer, 1976; v. 14, Summer, 1979. © *Books for Your Children* 1976, 1979. Both reprinted by permission.

*British Book News,* Children's Books, Spring, 1984. © The British Council, 1984. Courtesy of *British Book News.*

*Bulletin of the Center for Children's Books,* v. 13, September, 1959; v. 13, April, 1960; v. XV, September, 1961; v. 15, November, 1961; v. XV, April, 1962; v. 16, December, 1962, v. XVI, January, 1963; v. XVII, October, 1963; v. XVII, December, 1963; v. XVIII, December, 1964; v. XVIII, February, 1965; v. 25, October, 1971; v. 25, March, 1972; v. 26, February, 1973; v. 26, July-August, 1973; v. 27, September, 1973; v. 27, July-August, 1974; v. 28, September, 1974; v. 28, February, 1975; v. 28, April, 1975; v. 28, June, 1975; v. 28, July-August, 1975; v. 31, October, 1977; v. 31, December, 1977; v. 31, June, 1978; v. 32, November, 1978; v. 32, June, 1979; v. 32, July-August, 1979; v. 33, March, 1980; v. 33, April, 1980; v. 34, September, 1980; v. 34, July-August, 1981; v. 35, November, 1981; v. 36, September, 1982; v. 36, October, 1982; v. 36, November, 1982; v. 36, February, 1983; v. 37, October, 1983; v. 37, December, 1983; v. 37, January, 1984; v. 37, February, 1984; v. 37, May, 1984; v. 38, September, 1984; v. 38, October, 1984. © 1959, 1960, 1961, 1962, 1963, 1964, 1965, 1971, 1972, 1973, 1974, 1975, 1977, 1978, 1979, 1980, 1981, 1982, 1983, 1984 by The University of Chicago. All reprinted by permission of The University of Chicago Press.

*Bulletin of the Children's Book Center,* v. 3, September, 1950; v. 6, September, 1952; v. 10, January, 1957; v. 11, October, 1957; v. 11, December, 1957; v. X, May, 1957; v. XI, April, 1958. All reprinted by permission of The University of Chicago Press.

*Canadian Author & Bookman,* v. 44, Spring, 1969 for an extract from a letter to L. M. Montgomery in 1908 from Bliss Carman. © 1969 by *Canadian Author & Bookman.* Reprinted by permission of Canadian Authors Assoc.

*Canadian Children's Literature: A Journal of Criticism and Review,* n. 30, 1983. Box 335, Guelph, Ontario, Canada N1H 6K5. Reprinted by permission.

*Catholic Library World,* v. 51, February, 1980; v. 52, July-August, 1981. Both reprinted by permission.

*Catholic World,* v. XCVI, October, 1912.

*Chicago Sunday Tribune Magazine of Books,* December 25, 1960. Reprinted by permission of *Chicago Tribune.*

*Chicago Tribune,* p. 4, November 11, 1956. © 1956 Chicago Tribune. Reprinted by permission.

*Childhood Education,* v. 50, March, 1974; v. 53, March, 1977; v. 59, March, 1983. Copyright © 1974, 1977, 1983 by the Association for Childhood Education International, 11141 Georgia Ave. 200, Wheaton, MD 20902. All reprinted by permission of the Association.

*Children's Book News,* v. 3, July-August, 1968. Copyright © 1968 by Baker Book Services Ltd. Reprinted by permission.

*Children's Book Review,* v. I, June, 1971; v. II, October, 1972; v. II, December, 1972; v. III, June, 1973; v. V, Spring, 1975. © 1971, 1972, 1973, 1975 Five Owls Press Ltd. All rights reserved. All reprinted by permission.

*Children's Book Review Service,* v. 1, January, 1973; v. 2, September, 1973; v. 2, June, 1974; v. 3, February, 1975; v. 3, April, 1975; v. 4, June, 1976; v. 6, October, 1977; v. 6, November, 1977; v. 6, June, 1978; v. 7, April, 1979; v. 7, June, 1979; v. 9, September, 1980; v. 9, February, 1981; v. 9, June, 1981; v. 10, Winter, 1982; v. 10, August, 1982; v. 11, September, 1982; v. 12, October, 1983; v. 12, May, 1984; v. 12, Spring, 1984; v. 13, September, 1984. Copyright © 1973, 1974, 1975, 1976, 1977, 1978, 1979, 1980, 1981, 1982, 1983, 1984 Children's Book Review Service, Inc. All reprinted by permission.

*Children's Literature Association Quarterly,* v. 7, Summer, 1982. Reprinted by permission.

*Children's literature in education,* n. 7, March, 1972; v. 17, Summer, 1975; v. 12, Spring, 1981; v. 14, Autumn, 1983. © 1972, 1975, 1981, 1983, Agathon Press, Inc. All reprinted by permission of the publisher.

*The Christian Science Monitor,* September 6, 1951; July 26, 1956; May 9, 1957; November 27, 1957; May 12, 1960; April 5, 1962; November 15, 1962; November 14, 1963; November 4, 1965; November 3, 1966; February 2, 1967; November 6, 1969; October 3, 1973; May 7, 1975; October 15, 1979; May 14, 1982. © 1951, 1956, 1957, 1960, 1962, 1963, 1965, 1966, 1967, 1969, 1973, 1975, 1979, 1982 The Christian Science Publishing Society. All rights reserved. All reprinted by permission from *The Christian Science Monitor.*

*Commentary,* v. 35, February, 1963 for " 'Good Bunnies Always Obey': Books for American Children" by Jason Epstein. All rights reserved. Reprinted by permission of the publisher and the author.

*Curriculum Review,* v. 22, October, 1983. © 1983 Curriculum Advisory Service. Reprinted by permission of the Curriculum Advisory Service, Chicago, IL.

*The Dalhousie Review,* v. 24, April, 1944; v. 56, Summer, 1976. Both reprinted by permission of the publisher.

*Early Years,* v. 13, August-September, 1982. © copyright 1982 by Alan Raymond Inc. Reprinted with permission of the publisher, Darien, CT 06820.

*Elementary English,* v. XLIV, November, 1967 for "Beverly Cleary: Wonderful World of Humor" by Paul C. Burns and Ruth Hines; v. 51, September, 1974 for "Penelope Farmer: The Development of an Author" by Margaret K. McElderry. Copyright © 1967, 1974 by the National Council of Teachers of English. Both reprinted by permission of the publisher and the respective authors.

*Growing Point,* v. 1, March, 1963; v. 2, December, 1963; v. 4, July 1965; v. 4, September, 1965; v. 5, September, 1966; v. 5, November, 1966; v. 6 September, 1967; v. 8, November, 1969; v. 9, July 1970; v. 9, April, 1971; v. 10, December, 1971; v. 11, September, 1972; v. 11, October, 1972; v. 11, January, 1973; v. 13, October, 1974; v. 13, January, 1975; v. 14, October, 1975; v. 14, March, 1976; v. 14, April, 1976; v. 15, May, 1976; v. 15, April, 1977; v. 16, October, 1977; v. 16, January, 1978; v. 16, April, 1978; v. 19, July, 1980; v. 21, January, 1983; v. 22, May, 1983; v. 22, March, 1984. All reprinted by permission.

*The Guardian Weekly,* v. 104, June 5, 1971. Copyright © 1971 by Guardian Publications Ltd. Reprinted by permission.

*The Horn Book Magazine,* v. LX, August, 1984 for "Newbery Medal" award acceptance speech given at the meeting of the American Library Association in Dallas on June 24, 1984 by Beverly Cleary. Copyright © 1984 by Beverly Cleary. Reprinted by permission./ v. XIV, May, 1938; v. XVIII, May, 1942; v. XX, January, 1944; v. XXIII, January, 1947; v. XXIV, September-October, 1948; v. XXVI, March-April, 1950; v. XXVII, December, 1951; v. XXXIII, June, 1957; v. XXXIII, October, 1957; v. XXXV, August, 1959; v. XXXV, December, 1959; v. XXXVII, October, 1961; v. XXXVIII, April, 1962; v. XXXVIII, August, 1962; v. XXXVIII, October, 1962; v. XXXVIII, December, 1962; v. XXXIX, October, 1963; v. XL, December, 1964; v. XLI, February, 1965; v. XLI, December, 1965; v. XLV, April 1969; v. XLV, December, 1969; v. XLVI, August, 1970; v. XLIX, August, 1973; v. L, April, 1974; v. L, October, 1974; v. L, December, 1974; v. LI, August, 1975; v. LII, April, 1976; v. LII, August, 1976; v. LII, October, 1976; v. LIII, February, 1977; v. LIII, December, 1977; v. LV, August, 1979; v. LV, December, 1979; v. LVI, December, 1980; v. LVII, June, 1981; v. LVIII, April, 1982; v. LVIII, October, 1982; v. LVIII, December, 1982; v. LIX, February, 1983; v. LIX, April, 1983; v. LIX, August, 1983; v. LIX, August, 1983; v. LIX, October, 1983; v. LIX, December, 1983; v. LX, June, 1984; v. LX, September-October, 1984. Copyright © 1938, 1942, 1944, 1947, 1948, 1950, 1951, 1957, 1959, 1961, 1962, 1963, 1964, 1965, 1969, 1970, 1973, 1974, 1975, 1976, 1977, 1979, 1980, 1981, 1982, 1983, 1984 by The Horn Book, Inc., Boston. All reprinted by permission.

*In Review: Canadian Books for Children,* v. 9, Winter, 1975; v. 11, Summer, 1977. Both reprinted by permission.

*The Independent,* v. LXVII, December 16, 1909; v. LXIX, August 18, 1910.

*Instructor,* v. LXXXVIII, April, 1978. Copyright © 1978 by The Instructor Publications, Inc. Used by permission.

*Interracial Books for Children,* v. 6, 1975. Both reprinted by permission of *The Bulletin—Interracial Books for Children,* 1841 Broadway, New York, NY 10023.

*Interracial Books for Children Bulletin,* v. 11, 1980; v. 13, 1982. All reprinted by permission of *Interracial Books for Children Bulletin,* 1841 Broadway, New York, NY 10023.

*Journal of Reading,* v. 25, January, 1982 for a review of "Red Earth, Blue Sky: The Australian Outback" by David W. Moore. Copyright 1982 by the International Reading Association, Inc. Reprinted with permission of the International Reading Association and the author.

*The Junior Bookshelf,* v. 1, November, 1936; v. 1, February, 1937; v. 1, July, 1937; v. 4, December, 1939; v. 7, November, 1943; v. 8, July, 1944; v. 11, October, 1947; v. 14, November, 1950; v. 26, November, 1962; v. 26, December, 1962; v. 27, January, 1963; v. 27, November, 1963; v. 28, January, 1964; v. 29, August, 1965; v. 31, April, 1967; v. 31, August, 1967; v. 33, December, 1969; v. 34, August, 1970; v. 34, December, 1970; v. 35, June, 1971; v. 35, August, 1971; v. 36, August, 1972; v. 37, February, 1973; v. 38, December, 1974; v. 38, August, 1974; v. 39, February, 1975; v. 39, April, 1975; v. 39, October, 1975; v. 40, February, 1976; v. 40, April, 1976; v. 41, June, 1977; v. 42, June, 1978; v. 42, August, 1978; v. 43, February, 1979; v. 43, June, 1979; v. 43, August, 1979; v. 43, October, 1979; v. 44, December, 1980; v. 45, October, 1981; v. 48, February, 1984; v. 43, June, 1984. All reprinted by permission.

*Junior Libraries,* an appendix to *Library Journal,* v. 2, September, 1955; v. 5, September, 1958; v. 6, October, 1959; v. 6, November, 1959; v. 6, May, 1960. Copyright © 1955, 1958, 1959, 1960. All reprinted from *Junior Libraries,* published by R. R. Bowker Co./A Xerox Corporation, by permission.

*Kirkus Reviews,* v. XXXVII, May 15, 1969; v. XXXVII, November 1, 1969; v. XXXVIII, November 15, 1970; v. XXXIX, April 15, 1971; v. XXXIX, October 1, 1971; v. XLI, May 1, 1973; v. XLI, September 15, 1973; v. XLI, October 1, 1973; v. XLI, November 1, 1973; v. XLI, November 15, 1973; v. XLII, March 15, 1974; v. XLII, November 1, 1974; v. XLII, December 15, 1974; v. XLIII, March 15, 1975; v. XLIII, September 15, 1975; v. XLIII, November 15, 1975; v. XLIII, December 15, 1975; v. XLIV, February 1, 1976; v. XLIV, April 15, 1976; v. XLIV, July 15, 1976; v. XLIV, October 15, 1976; v. XLV, April 1, 1977; v. XLV, May 15, 1977; v. XLVI, April 15, 1978; v. XLVI, July 1, 1978; v. XLVII, August 1, 1979; v. XLVII, December 1, 1979; v. XLVIII, February 1, 1980; v. XLVIII, October 1, 1980; v. XLIX, March 15, 1981; v. XLIX, July 1, 1981; v. XLIX, September 15, 1981; v. XLIX, October 15, 1981; v. L, July 1, 1982; v. LI, March 15, 1983; v. LI, May 1, 1983; v. LI, May 15, 1983. Copyright © 1969, 1970, 1971, 1973, 1974, 1975, 1976, 1977, 1978, 1979, 1980, 1981, 1982, 1983 The Kirkus Service, Inc. All reprinted by permission.

*Kirkus Reviews,* Juvenile Issue, v. LI, September 1, 1983; v. LII, March 1, 1984; v. LII, September 1, 1984. Copyright © 1983, 1984 The Kirkus Service, Inc. All reprinted by permission.

*Kirkus Service,* v. XXXV, February 1, 1967; v. XXXV, June 15, 1967; v. XXXVI, February 1, 1968; v. XXXVI, June 15, 1968; v. XXXVI, October 1, 1968. Copyright © 1967, 1968 The Kirkus Service, Inc. All reprinted by permission.

*Kliatt Young Adult Paperback Book Guide,* v. XIV, September, 1980; v. XV, September, 1981. Copyright © by Kliatt Paperback Book Guide. Both reprinted by permission.

*Language Arts,* v. 54, September, 1977 for a review of "The Reward Worth Having" by Ruth M. Stein; v. 55, February, 1978 for a review of "The Buried Moon and Other Stories" by Ruth M. Stein; v. 56, January, 1979 for "Profile: Beverly Cleary—The Children's Force at Work" by Mary June Roggenbuck; v. 60, November-December, 1983 for a review of "New Road!" by Ronald A. Jobe; v. 60, November-December, 1983 for a review of "The Sign of the Beaver" by Ronald A. Jobe. Copyright © 1977, 1978, 1979, 1983 by the National Council of Teachers of English. All reprinted by permission of the publisher and the respective authors.

*The Library Association Record,* v. 39, May, 1937. Reprinted by permission.

*Library Journal,* v. 58, October 1, 1933; v. 62, October 1, 1937; v. 63, November 1, 1938; v. 69, February 1, 1944; v. 69, December 1, 1944; v. 75, September 15, 1950; v. 77, October 15, 1952; v. 82, September 15, 1957; v. 84, April 15, 1959; v. 87, September 15, 1962; v. 88, September 15, 1963; v. 88, November 15, 1963; v. 89, June 15, 1964; v. 91, July, 1966; v. 91, October 15, 1966; v. 91, November 15, 1966; v. 93, July, 1968; v. 99, June 15, 1974. Copyright © 1933, 1937, 1938, 1944, 1950, 1952, 1957, 1959, 1962, 1963, 1964, 1966, 1968, 1974 by Xerox Corporation. All reprinted from *Library Journal,* published by R. R. Bowker Co. (a Xerox company), by permission.

*Literary Digest,* v. XLVII, October 18, 1913.

*Luna Monthly,* n. 22, March, 1971; n. 44, January, 1973; n. 48, Fall, 1973. All reprinted by permission.

*The Nation,* v. LXXXIX, September 2, 1909; v. XC, June 9, 1910; v. XCIII, August 10, 1911; v. XCV, August 22, 1912; v. CI, August 26, 1915.

*The National Observer,* June 9, 1969; November 3, 1969. © Dow Jones & Company, Inc. 1969. All rights reserved. Both reprinted by permission of *The National Observer.*

*New Statesman,* v. XX, February 17, 1923; v. XXXV, August 2, 1930; v. LXXXI, June 4, 1971; v. 84, November 10, 1972. © 1923, 1930, 1971, 1972 The Statesman & Nation Publishing Co. Ltd. All reprinted by permission.

*The New Statesman & Nation,* v. XI, December 5, 1931; n.s. v. IV, December 10, 1932; n.s. v. VIII, December 8, 1934; n.s. v. XII,

December 5, 1936; n.s. v. XVIII, December 9, 1939; v. XX, December 7, 1940. © 1931, 1932, 1934, 1936, 1939, 1940 The Statesman & Nation Publishing Co. Ltd. All reprinted by permission.

*New York Herald Tribune*, May 12, 1957. © 1957 I.H.T. Corporation. Reprinted by permission.

*New York Herald Tribune Book Review*, January 15, 1950; October 14, 1951; October 12, 1952; September 27, 1953; November 6, 1955; November 18, 1956; November 17, 1957; November 2, 1958; November 1, 1959; November 13, 1960. © 1950, 1951, 1952, 1953, 1955, 1956, 1957, 1958, 1959, 1960 I.H.T. Corporation. All reprinted by permission.

*New York Herald Tribune Books*, March 15, 1931; February 28, 1932; May 7, 1933; March 18, 1934; September 15, 1935; September 13, 1936; September 26, 1937; May 1, 1938; April 6, 1941; April 5, 1942. © 1931, 1932, 1933, 1934, 1935, 1936, 1937, 1938, 1941, 1942 I.H.T. Corporation. All reprinted by permission.

*New York Herald Tribune Weekly Book Review*, November 14, 1943; February 6, 1944; November 12, 1944; June 13, 1948; July 25, 1948. © 1943, 1944, 1948 I.H.T. Corporation. All reprinted by permission.

*The New York Times Book Review*, July 18, 1908./ September 21, 1919; September 11, 1921; August 26, 1923; April 5, 1931; February 14, 1932; May 14, 1933; April 15, 1934; October 6, 1935; September 13, 1936; May 8, 1938; July 30, 1939; May 5, 1940; May 18, 1941; April 5, 1942; April 4, 1948; June 13, 1948; September 14, 1952; October 4, 1953; September 26, 1954; September 16, 1956; November 18, 1956; June 23, 1957; November 24, 1957; October 4, 1959; October 9, 1960; November 13, 1960; February 12, 1961; November 12, 1961; April 1, 1962; September 30, 1962; September 15, 1963; November 24, 1963; July 26, 1964; September 20, 1964; April 18, 1965; November 7, 1965; December 26, 1965; May 1, 1966; p. II, May 8, 1966; August 21, 1966; February 5, 1967; May 5, 1968; July 20, 1969; November 9, 1969; May 2, 1971; August 27, 1972; January 21, 1973; March 11, 1973; June 24, 1973; November 4, 1973; January 13, 1974; May 5, 1974; May 4, 1975; October 5, 1975; September 19, 1976; June 19, 1977; October 14, 1979; November 18, 1979; April 27, 1980; September 20, 1981; November 1, 1981; September 26, 1982; February 13, 1983; March 13, 1983; May 8, 1983; October 23, 1983; January 22, 1984; November 11, 1984. Copyright © 1919, 1921, 1923, 1931, 1932, 1933, 1934, 1935, 1936, 1938, 1939, 1940, 1941, 1942, 1948, 1952, 1953, 1954, 1956, 1957, 1959, 1960, 1961, 1962, 1963, 1964, 1965, 1966, 1967, 1968, 1969, 1970, 1971, 1972, 1973, 1974, 1975, 1976, 1977, 1979, 1980, 1981, 1982, 1983, 1984 by The New York Times Company. All reprinted by permission.

*The New Yorker*, v. XIX, December 4, 1943. © 1943 by The New Yorker Magazine, Inc. Reprinted by permission.

*Oklahoma Librarian*, v. 21, July, 1971 for "How Long Does It Take to Write a Book?" by Beverly Cleary. © 1971 by Beverly Cleary. Reprinted by permission.

*The Outlook*, v. 89, August 22, 1908; v. XCII, October 2, 1909; v. 99, September 2, 1911; v. 101, June 29, 1912; v. 105, October 4, 1913; v. 110, August 25, 1915; v. 123, September 17, 1919; v. 133, April 11, 1923.

*Parent's Magazine & Better Family Living*, v. XLV, June, 1970. Copyright © 1970 Parent's Magazine Enterprises. Reprinted from *Parent's* by permission.

*PNLA Quarterly*, v. 28, January, 1964. Reprinted by permission.

*Publishers Weekly*, v. LXXXVIII, September 18, 1915; v. XCVI, August 16, 1919; v. 160, August 4, 1951; v. 164, August 15, 1953; v. 166, July 10, 1954; v. 168, August 13, 1955; v. 180, September 11, 1961; v. 188, November 22, 1965; v. 189, February 7, 1966; v. 190, October 17, 1966; v. 191, April 3, 1967. Copyright © 1915, 1919, 1951, 1953, 1954, 1955, 1961, 1965, 1966, 1967 by R. R. Bowker Company. All reprinted from *Publishers Weekly*, published by R. R. Bowker Company, by permission./ v. 193, April 15, 1968; v. 193, April 22, 1968; v. 195, April 14, 1969; v. 196, December 29, 1969; v. 197, May 14, 1970; v. 199, May 24, 1971; v. 203, April 23, 1973; v. 204, August 27, 1973; v. 204, October 15, 1973; v. 205, March 11, 1974; v. 206, August 26, 1974; v. 207, March 24, 1975; v. 207, March 31, 1975; v. 208, August 11, 1975; v. 212, August 29, 1977; v. 216, July 30, 1979; v. 216, December 24, 1979; v. 217, January 25, 1980; v. 218, August 1, 1980; v. 218, October 17, 1980; v. 219, April 3, 1981; v. 220, July 10, 1981; v. 222, July 9, 1982; v. 222, October 22, 1982; v. 223, February 18, 1983; v. 223, March 11, 1983; v. 223, April 15, 1983; v. 224, September 2, 1983; v. 225, February 24, 1984; v. 225, March 2, 1984; v. 225, May 18, 1984. Copyright © 1968, 1969, 1970, 1971, 1973, 1974, 1975, 1977, 1979, 1980, 1981, 1982, 1983, 1984 by Xerox Corporation. All reprinted from *Publishers Weekly*, published by R. R. Bowker Company, a Xerox company, by permission.

*Punch*, v. 285, August 17, 1983; v. 286, January 18, 1984. © 1983, 1984 by Punch Publications Ltd. All rights reserved. None may be reprinted without permission.

*The Reading Teacher*, v. 29, February, 1976; v. 30, May, 1977; v. 33, January, 1980. Copyright 1976, 1977, 1980 by the International Reading Association, Inc. All reprinted with permission of the International Reading Association.

*Saturday Review*, v. XLIV, October 28, 1961; v. XLIX, April 16, 1966; v. L, March 18, 1967; v. LII, June 28, 1969; v. LIII, May 9, 1970. © 1961, 1966, 1967, 1969, 1970 *Saturday Review* magazine. All reprinted by permission.

*The Saturday Review,* New York, v. XXXIX, November 17, 1956. © 1956 *Saturday Review* magazine. Reprinted by permission.

*The Saturday Review of Literature,* v. VII, May 9, 1931; v. XXXIII, November 11, 1950; v. XXXIV, November 10, 1951. © 1931, 1950, 1951 *Saturday Review* magazine. All reprinted by permission.

*The Saturday Review,* London, v. 122, December 9, 1916; v. 154, December 31, 1932.

*The School Librarian,* v. 14, July, 1966; v. 17, September, 1969; v. 17, December, 1969; v. 18, September, 1970; v. 19, June, 1971; v. 20, June, 1972; v. 22, June, 1974; v. 26, June, 1978; v. 26, September, 1978; v. 27, September, 1979; v. 28, September, 1980; v. 29, March, 1981; v. 29, June, 1981; v. 31, December, 1983; v. 32, June, 1984. All reprinted by permission.

*The School Librarian and School Library Review,* v. 4, March, 1949; v. 13, July, 1965; v. 15, December, 1967. All reprinted by permission.

*School Library Journal,* an appendix to *Library Journal,* v. 8, November, 1961; v. 8, May, 1962; v. 12, October, 1965; v. 12, March, 1966; v. 12, May, 1966; v. 15, September, 1968; v. 15, January, 1969; v. 15, April 1969; v. 16, September, 1969; v. 16, December, 1969; v. 16, March, 1970; v. 17, January, 1971; v. 17, February, 1971; v. 17, March, 1971; v. 18, September, 1971; v. 19, September, 1972; v. 19, April, 1973; v. 20, September, 1973; v. 20, January, 1974; v. 22, April, 1976; v. 24, September, 1977. Copyright © 1961, 1962, 1965, 1966, 1968, 1969, 1970, 1971, 1972, 1973, 1974, 1976, 1977. All reprinted from *School Library Journal,* published by R. R. Bowker/A Xerox Corporation, by permission.

*School Library Journal,* v. 22, September, 1975; v. 22, December, 1975; v. 22, January, 1976; v. 22, May, 1976; v. 23, September, 1976; v. 23, January, 1977; v. 23, February, 1977; v. 24, September, 1977; v. 24, January, 1978; v. 24, February, 1978; v. 24, April, 1978; v. 25, September, 1978; v. 25, November, 1978; v. 25, May, 1979; v. 26, September, 1979; v. 26, January, 1980; v. 26, February, 1980; v. 27, September, 1980; v. 27, October, 1980; v. 27, November, 1980; v. 27, April, 1981; v. 27, May, 1981; v. 27, August, 1981; v. 28, October, 1981; v. 28, November, 1981; v. 28, December, 1981; v. 28, May, 1982; v. 28, August, 1982; v. 29, October, 1982; v. 29, November, 1982; v. 29, December, 1982; v. 29, April, 1983; v. 29, May, 1983; v. 30, September, 1983; v. 30, October, 1983; v. 30, December, 1983; v. 30, January, 1984; v. 30, August, 1984; v. 31, September, 1984; v. 31, November, 1984. Copyright © 1975, 1976, 1977, 1978, 1979, 1980, 1981, 1982, 1983, 1984. All reprinted from *School Library Journal,* published by R. R. Bowker Co./A Xerox Corporation, by permission.

*Science Books,* v. 18, January-February, 1983 for a review of "Tool Book" by Richard J. Merrill. Copyright 1983 by the American Association for the Advancement of Science. Reprinted by permission of the publisher and the author./ v. 4, September, 1968; v. 6, March, 1971; v. X, September, 1974. Copyright 1968, 1971, 1974 by the American Association for the Advancement of Science. All reprinted by permission.

*Science Books & Films,* v. XIII, September, 1977 for "Musk Oxen: Bearded Ones of the Arctic" by Joseph K. Hichar; v. XIV, May, 1978 for a review of "The Giant Panda at Home" by David G. Barry; v. XV, September, 1979 for a review of "The Gray Kangaroo at Home" by Erik Paul Scully. Copyright 1977, 1978, 1979, by the AAAS. All reprinted by permission of the publisher and the respective authors./ v. XVI, November-December, 1980. Copyright 1980 by the AAAS. Reprinted by permission of the publisher.

*Signal,* n. 9, September, 1972 for "Accepting the Eleanor Farjeon Award" by Janet Hill; n. 17, May, 1975 for "Penelope Farmer's Novels" by Hugh Crago; n. 23, May, 1977 for "The Reader in the Book: Notes from Work in Progress" by Aidan Chambers. Copyright © 1972, 1975, 1977, 1981 the respective authors. All reprinted by permission of the respective authors and The Thimble Press, Lockwood Station Road, South Woodchester, Glos. GL5 5EQ, England./ n. 34, January, 1981. Copyright © 1981 The Thimble Press. Reprinted by permission of The Thimble Press, Lockwood Station Road, South Woodchester, Glos. GL5 5EQ, England.

*Social Education,* v. XXIV, December, 1960; v. 43, October, 1979. Copyright, 1960, 1979, by the National Council for the Social Studies. Both reprinted with permission of the National Council for the Social Studies.

*The Southeastern Librarian,* v. XVIII, Fall, 1968. Reprinted by permission.

*Southerly,* v. 12, 1951. Reprinted by permission of the publisher and the author.

*The Spectator,* v. 145, September 13, 1930; v. 147, December 5, 1931; v. 151, December 1, 1933; v. 159, December 3, 1937; v. 163, December 8, 1939; v. 165, December 6, 1940; v. 171, July 9, 1943; v. 238, April 16, 1977. © 1930, 1931, 1933, 1937, 1939, 1940, 1943, 1966, 1977 by *The Spectator.* All reprinted by permission of *The Spectator.*

*The Times Educational Supplement,* n. 3269, February 3, 1978; n. 3284, June 16, 1978; n. 3293, August 11, 1978; n. 3349, August 22, 1980; n. 3360, November 14, 1980. © Times Newspapers Ltd 1978, 1980. (London). All reproduced from *The Times Educational Supplement* by permission.

*The Times Literary Supplement,* n. 3303, June 17, 1965; n. 3431, November 30, 1967; n. 3458, June 6, 1968; n. 3618, July 2, 1971; n. 3687, November 3, 1972; n. 3774, July 5, 1974; n. 3915, March 25, 1977; n. 4121, March 26, 1982; n. 3864, April 2, 1983. © Times

Newspapers Ltd. (London) 1965, 1967, 1968, 1971, 1972, 1974, 1977, 1982, 1983. All reproduced from *The Times Literary Supplement* by permission.

*Virginia Kirkus' Bookshop Service,* v. XIV, December 1, 1946; v. XVIII, July 15, 1950; v. XIX, July 1, 1951; v. XXI, July 1, 1953. All reprinted by permission.

*Virginia Kirkus' Service,* v. XXIV, January 15, 1956; v. XXIV, August 15, 1956; v. XXV, January 15, 1957; v. XXV, July 1, 1957; v. XXV, September 15, 1957; v. XXVI, June 15, 1958; v. XXVIII, July 1, 1959; v. XXVIII, July 1, 1960; v. XXVIII, July 15, 1960; v. XXIX, February 1, 1961; v. XXIX, July 15, 1961; v. XXX, July 15, 1962; v. XXX, August 1, 1962; v. XXXI, October 15, 1963; v. XXXII, May 1, 1964; v. XXXII, August 15, 1964; v. XXXIII, February 15, 1965; v. XXXIII, October 1, 1965; v. XXXIV, January 1, 1966; v. XXXIV, March 15, 1966; v. XXXIV, August 15, 1966. All reprinted by permission.

*Wilson Library Bulletin,* v. 36, October, 1961; v. 45, October, 1970; v. 51, September, 1976; v. 55, October, 1980. Copyright © 1961, 1970, 1976, 1980 by the H. W. Wilson Company. All reprinted by permission.

*The World of Children's Books,* v. VI, 1981. © 1981 Jon C. Stott. Reprinted by permission.

*Young Readers Review,* v. II, November, 1965; v. II, December, 1965; v. II, February, 1966; v. III, May, 1967; v. IV, May, 1968. Copyright © 1965, 1966, 1967, 1968 *Young Readers Review*. All reprinted by permission.

**THE EXCERPTS IN CLR, VOLUME 8, WERE REPRINTED FROM THE FOLLOWING BOOKS:**

Arbuthnot, May Hill. From *Children and Books*. Scott, Foresman, 1947. Copyright, 1947, Scott, Foresman and Company. Reprinted by permission.

Arbuthnot, May Hill and Zena Sutherland. From *Children and Books*. Fourth edition. Scott, Foresman, 1972. Copyright © 1972, 1964, 1957, 1947 by Scott, Foresman and Company. Reprinted by permission.

Arbuthnot, May Hill, Zena Sutherland, and Dianne L. Monson. From *Children and Books*. Sixth edition. Scott, Foresman, 1981. Copyright © 1981, 1977, 1972, 1964, 1957, 1947 by Scott, Foresman and Company. All rights reserved. Reprinted by permission.

Baskin, Barbara H. and Karen H. Harris. From *Books for the Gifted Child*. Bowker, 1980. Copyright © 1980 by Xerox Corporation. All rights reserved. Reprinted with permission of the R. R. Bowker Company.

Baskin, Barbara H. and Karen H. Harris. From *Notes from a Different Drummer: A Guide to Juvenile Fiction Portraying the Handicapped*. Bowker, 1977. Copyright © 1977 by Barbara H. Baskin and Karen H. Harris. All rights reserved. Reprinted with permission of the R. R. Bowker Company.

Blount, Margaret. From *Animal Land: The Creatures of Children's Fiction*. William Morrow & Company, Inc., 1975. Copyright © 1975 by Margaret Ingle-Finch. All rights reserved. Abridged by permission of the author.

Bolger, Francis W. P. From *The Years Before "Anne."* Prince Edward Island Heritage Foundation, 1974. Copyright Canada, 1974 by The Prince Edward Island Heritage Foundation. All rights reserved. Reprinted by permission.

*Books for Children: 1960-1965*. American Library Association, 1966. Copyright © 1960, 1961, 1962, 1963, 1964, 1965 by the American Library Association. Reprinted by permission.

Brogan, Hugh. From *The Life of Arthur Ransome*. Jonathan Cape, 1984. Copyright Hugh Brogan © 1984. Reprinted by permission of Mark Paterson on behalf of Hugh Brogan. In Canada by Jonathan Cape Ltd.

Cadogan, Mary and Patricia Craig. From *You're a Brick, Angela! A New Look at Girls' Fiction from 1839 to 1975*. Victor Gollancz Ltd., 1976. © Mary Cadogan and Patricia Craig 1976. Reprinted by permission of the authors.

Chambers, Nancy. From "Board Books: 'How Do I Eat It?', 'I Can Do It!' and 'I'm the King of the Castle!'," in *The Signal Review 1: A Selective Guide to Children's Books 1982*. Edited by Nancy Chambers. Thimble Press, 1983. Copyright © 1983 The Thimble Press. Reprinted by permission of The Thimble Press, Lockwood Station Road, South Woodchester, Glos. GL5 5EQ, England.

Chang, Charity. From "Uri Shulevitz, Illustrator and Writer," in *Children's Literature: Annual of the Modern Language Association Seminar on Children's Literature and The Children's Literature Association, Vol. 3*. Edited by Francelia Butler. Temple University Press, 1974. © 1974 by Francelia Butler. All rights reserved. Reprinted by permission of Francelia Butler.

Cianciolo, Patricia Jean. From *Picture Books for Children*. Revised edition. American Library Association, 1981. Copyright © 1981 by the American Library Association. All rights reserved. Reprinted by permission.

Cowan, Ann S. From "Canadian Writers: Lucy Maud & Emily Byrd," in *L. M. Montgomery: An Assessment*. Edited by John Robert Sorfleet. Canadian Children's Press, 1976. Copyright © The authors and Canadian Children's Press, 1976. Reprinted by permission.

Crouch, Marcus. From *The Nesbit Tradition: The Children's Novel in England 1945-1970*. Ernest Benn Limited, 1972. © Marcus Crouch 1972. Reprinted by permission of the author.

Cullinan, Bernice E. with Mary K. Karrer and Arlene M. Pillar. From *Literature and the Child*. Harcourt Brace Jovanovich, 1981. Copyright © 1981 by Harcourt Brace Jovanovich, Inc. All rights reserved. Reprinted by permission of the publisher.

Davis, Enid. From *The Liberty Cap: A Catalogue of Non-Sexist Materials for Children*. Academy Chicago Publishers, 1977. Copyright © 1977 by Academy Chicago Publishers. All rights reserved. Reprinted by permission.

Dreyer, Sharon Spredemann. From *The Bookfinder: A Guide to Children's Literature about the Needs and Problems of Youth Aged 2-15, Vol. 1*. American Guidance Service, Inc., 1977. © 1977 American Guidance Service, Inc. All rights reserved. Reprinted by permission.

Egoff, Sheila. From *The Republic of Childhood: A Critical Guide to Canadian Children's Literature in English*. Second edition. © Oxford University Press, Canadian Branch, 1975. Reprinted by permission.

Egoff, Sheila A. From *Thursday's Child: Trends and Patterns in Contemporary Children's Literature*. American Library Association, 1981. Copyright © 1981 by The American Library Association. All rights reserved. Reprinted by permission.

Esmonde, Margaret P. From ''After Armageddon: The Post Cataclysmic Novel for Young Readers,'' in *Children's Literature: Annual of the Modern Language Association Seminar on Children's Literature and The Children's Literature Association, Vol. 6.* Edited by Francelia Butler. Temple University Press, 1977. © 1977 by Francelia Butler. All rights reserved. Reprinted by permission of Francelia Butler.

Eyre, Frank. From *British Children's Books in the Twentieth Century.* Revised edition. Longman Books, 1971. Dutton, 1973. Copyright © 1971 by Frank Eyre. All rights reserved. Reprinted by permission of the publisher, E. P. Dutton, Inc. In Canada by Penguin Books Ltd.

Fisher, Margery. From *Intent Upon Reading: A Critical Appraisal of Modern Fiction for Children.* Hodder & Stoughton Children's Books (formerly Brockhampton Press), 1961. Copyright © 1961 by Margery Fisher. Reprinted by permission.

Fisher, Margery. From *Who's Who in Children's Books: A Treasury of the Familiar Characters of Childhood.* Holt, Rinehart and Winston, 1975, Weidenfeld and Nicolson, 1975. Copyright © 1975 by Margery Fisher. All rights reserved. Reprinted by permission.

Fredeman, Jane Cowan. From ''The Land of Lost Content: The Use of Fantasy in L. M. Montgomery's Novels,'' in *L. M. Montgomery: An Assessment.* Edited by John Robert Sorfleet. Canadian Children's Press, 1976. Copyright © The authors and Canadian Children's Press, 1976. Reprinted by permission.

Georgiou, Constantine. From *Children and Their Literature.* Prentice-Hall, Inc., 1969. © 1969 by Prentice-Hall, Inc. All rights reserved. Reprinted by permission of the author.

Gillen, Mollie. From *The Wheel of Things: A Biography of L. M. Montgomery, Author of ''Anne of Green Gables.''* Fitzhenry & Whiteside, 1975. © 1975 Fitzhenry & Whiteside Limited, 195 Allstate Pkwy., Markham, Ontario L3R 4T8. All rights reserved. Reprinted by permission.

From a review of ''The Mouse and the Motorcycle,'' in *Good Books for Children: A Selection of Outstanding Children's Books Published, 1950-65.* Edited by Mary K. Eakin. Third edition. University of Chicago Press, 1966. © 1959, 1962, and 1966 by The University of Chicago. All rights reserved. Reprinted by permission of The University of Chicago Press.

Green, H. M. From *A History of Australian Literature, Pure and Applied: 1923-1950, Vol. II.* Angus & Robertson, 1961. Reprinted with the permission of Angus & Robertson (UK) Ltd.

Green, Roger Lancelyn. From *Tellers of Tales.* Revised edition. Franklin Watts, Inc., 1965, Kaye and Ward, 1969. Copyright 1946, 1953, 1956, © 1965 by Edmund Ward (Publishers) Ltd. Reprinted by permission of William Heinemann Limited.

Gross, Elizabeth. From ''Twenty Medal Books: In Perspective,'' in *Newbery and Caldecott Medal Books: 1956-1965.* Edited by Lee Kingman. Horn Book, 1965. Copyright © 1965 by The Horn Book, Inc. All rights reserved. Reprinted by permission.

Hart-Davis, Rupert. From a prologue to *The Autobiography of Arthur Ransome.* By Arthur Ransome, edited by Rupert Hart-Davis. Jonathan Cape, 1976. Prologue and epilogue © 1976 by Rupert Hart-Davis. Reprinted by permission of Jonathan Cape Ltd. on behalf of the Arthur Ransome Estate and the Editor.

Hetherington, John. From *Norman Lindsay.* Third edition. Oxford University Press, Melbourne, 1969. Reprinted by permission of Oxford University Press, Inc.

Hildick, Wallace. From *Children and Fiction: A Critical Study of the Artistic and Psychological Factors Involved in Writing Fiction for and about Children.* World Publishing Company, 1971. Copyright © 1970 by E. W. Hildick. All rights reserved. Reprinted by permission of the author.

Huck, Charlotte S. and Doris Young Kuhn. From *Children's Literature in the Elementary School.* Second edition. Holt, Rinehart and Winston, 1968. Copyright © 1961, 1968 by Holt, Rinehart and Winston, Inc. All rights reserved. Reprinted by permission of Holt, Rinehart and Winston, Publishers, CBS College Publishing.

From ''The Analyses: 'Ramona the Brave','' in *Human—and Anti-Human—Values in Children's Books: A Content Rating Instrument for Educators and Concerned Parents.* Edited by Council on Interracial Books for Children, Inc. Racism and Sexism Resource Center for Educators, 1976. Copyright © 1976 by the Council on Interracial Books for Children, Inc. All rights reserved. Reprinted by permission.

Inglis, Fred. From *The Promise of Happiness: Value and Meaning in Children's Fiction.* Cambridge University Press, 1981. © Cambridge University Press 1981. Reprinted by permission.

Lindsay, Norman. From an extract from ''Children's Authors: Norman Lindsay,'' in *The Singing Roads: A Guide to Australian Children's Authors and Illustrators, Part I.* Edited by Hugh Anderson. Fourth edition. Wentworth Books, 1972. Reprinted by permission of Hugh Anderson.

Little, Jean. From ''But What about Jane?'' in *L. M. Montgomery: An Assessment.* Edited by John Robert Sorfleet. Canadian Children's Press, 1976. Copyright © The authors and Canadian Children's Press, 1976. Reprinted by permission.

MacMechan, Archibald. From an extract from "Fans and Critics," in *The Wheel of Things: A Biography of L. M. Montgomery, Author of "Anne of Green Gables."* By Mollie Gillen. Fitzhenry & Whiteside, 1975. © 1975 Fitzhenry & Whiteside Limited, 195 Allstate Pkwy., Markham, Ontario L3R 4T8. All rights reserved. Reprinted by permission.

Montgomery, L. M. From *The Alpine Path: The Story of My Career*. Fitzhenry & Whiteside, 1974. © 1974 Fitzhenry & Whiteside Limited, 195 Allstate Pkwy., Markham, Ontario L3R 4T8. All rights reserved. Reprinted by permission.

Moss, Elaine. From "Fiction I, Stories for 5-8 Year Olds: 'Ramona the Pest'," and "Fiction 2, Stories for 8-11 Year Olds: 'William and Mary'," in *Children's Books of the Year: 1974*. Edited by Elaine Moss. Hamish Hamilton, 1975. © Elaine Moss 1975. All rights reserved. Reprinted by permission.

Peterson, Linda Kauffman, and Marilyn Leathers Solt. From *Newbery and Caldecott Medal and Honor Books: An Annotated Bibliography*. G. K. Hall & Co., 1982. Copyright © 1982 by Marilyn Solt and Linda Peterson. Reprinted by permission.

Phelps, Arthur L. From *Canadian Writers*. McClelland and Stewart, 1951. Copyright in Canada, 1951 McClelland and Stewart Limited, Toronto.

Ransome, Arthur. From *The Autobiography of Arthur Ransome*. Edited by Rupert Hart-Davis. Jonathan Cape, 1976. Text © 1976 The Arthur Ransome Estate. Reprinted by permission of Jonathan Cape Ltd. on behalf of the Arthur Ransome Estate and the Editor.

Ransome, Arthur. From a note to *Old Peter's Russian Tales*. By Arthur Ransome. Jonathan Cape, 1984. Reprinted by permission of Jonathan Cape Ltd. on behalf of the Arthur Ransome Estate.

Rau, Margaret. From a foreword to *Red Earth, Blue Sky: The Australian Outback*. Thomas Y. Crowell Co., Inc., 1981. Copyright © 1981 by Margaret Rau. All rights reserved. Reprinted by permission of Harper & Row, Publishers, Inc.

Rees, David. From *The Marble in the Water: Essays on Contemporary Writers of Fiction for Children and Young Adults*. The Horn Book, Inc., 1980. Copyright © 1979, 1980 by David Rees. All rights reserved. Reprinted by permission.

Roderick, Colin. From *20 Australian Novelists*. Angus & Robertson, 1947. Reprinted with the permission of Angus & Robertson (UK) Ltd.

Rubio, Mary. From "Satire, Realism & Imagination in 'Anne of Green Gables'," in *L. M. Montgomery: An Assessment*. Edited by John Robert Sorfleet. Canadian Children's Press, 1976. Copyright © The authors and Canadian Children's Press, 1976. Reprinted by permission.

Rudman, Masha Kabakow. From *Children's Literature: An Issues Approach*. Heath, 1976. Copyright © 1976 by D. C. Heath and Company. All rights reserved. Reprinted by permission.

Sadker, Myra Pollack, and David Miller Sadker. From *Now Upon a Time: A Contemporary View of Children's Literature*. Harper & Row, 1977. Copyright © 1977 by Myra Pollack Sadker and David Miller Sadker. All rights reserved. Reprinted by permission of Harper & Row, Publishers, Inc.

Saxby, H. M. From *A History of Australian Children's Literature, 1841-1941*. Wentworth Books, 1969. © H. M. Saxby. Reprinted by permission of the author.

Sebesta, Sam Leaton, and William J. Iverson. From *Literature for Thursday's Child*. Science Research Associates, 1975. © 1975, Science Research Associates, Inc. All rights reserved. Reprinted by permission of the publisher.

Shelley, Hugh. From *Arthur Ransome*. Bodley Head, 1960. © The Bodley Head Ltd., 1960. Reprinted by permission of The Bodley Head Ltd.

Smith, Janet Adam. From *Children's Illustrated Books*. Collins, 1948. Reprinted by permission of the author.

Smith, Lillian. From *The Unreluctant Years: A Critical Approach to Children's Literature*. American Library Association, 1953. Copyright © 1953, 1981 by the American Library Association. All rights reserved. Reprinted by permission.

Spirt, Diana L. From *Introducing More Books: A Guide for the Middle Grades*. R. R. Bowker Company, 1978. Copyright © 1978 by Diana L. Spirt. All rights reserved. Reprinted by permission of the author.

Steele, Mary. From "Fiction: 'Ralph S. Mouse'," in *The Signal Review 1: A Selective Guide to Children's Books, 1982*. Edited by Nancy Chambers. Thimble Press, 1983. Copyright © 1983 by The Thimble Press. Reprinted by permission.

Thomas, Gillian. From "The Decline of Anne: Matron vs. Child," in *L. M. Montgomery: An Assessment*. Edited by John Robert Sorfleet. Canadian Children's Press, 1976. Copyright © The authors and Canadian Children's Press, 1976. Reprinted by permission.

Townsend, John Rowe. From *Written for Children: An Outline of English-Language Children's Literature*. Revised edition. J. B. Lippincott Co., 1983. Kestrel Books, 1983. Copyright © 1965, 1974, 1983 by John Rowe Townsend. All rights reserved. Reprinted by permission of Harper & Row, Publishers, Inc. In Canada by Penguin Books Ltd.

Trease, Geoffrey. From *Tales Out of School*. Heinemann, 1948. Reprinted by permission of William Heinemann Limited.

Viguers, Ruth Hill. From "Experiences to Share," in *A Critical History of Children's Literature*. By Cornelia Meigs, Anne Thaxter Eaton, Elizabeth Nesbitt, and Ruth Hill Viguers, edited by Cornelia Meigs. Macmillan, 1953. Copyright, 1953, by The Macmillan Company. All rights reserved. Reprinted with permission of Macmillan Publishing Company.

Viguers, Ruth Hill. From "Golden Years and Time of Tumult, 1920-1967," in *A Critical History of Children's Literature*. By Cornelia Meigs, Anne Thaxter Eaton, Elizabeth Nesbitt, and Ruth Hill Viguers, edited by Cornelia Meigs. Revised edition. Macmillan, 1969. Copyright © 1953, 1969 by Macmillan Publishing Company. Reprinted with permission of Macmillan Publishing Company.

Waterston, Elizabeth. From "Lucy Maud Montgomery," in *The Clear Spirit: Twenty Canadian Women and Their Times*. Edited by Mary Quayle Innis. University of Toronto Press, 1966. © University of Toronto Press 1966. Reprinted by permission.

Whitaker, Muriel A. From "'Queer Children': L. M. Montgomery's Heroines," in *L. M. Montgomery: An Assessment*. Edited by John Robert Sorfleet. Canadian Children's Press, 1976. Copyright © The authors and Canadian Children's Press, 1976. Reprinted by permission.

White, Dorothy Neal. From *About Books for Children*. New Zealand Library Association, 1946. Reprinted by permission.

# CUMULATIVE INDEX TO AUTHORS

This index lists all author entries in *Children's Literature Review* and includes cross-references to them in other Gale sources. References in the index are identified as follows:

**AITN:** *Authors in the News,* Volumes 1-2
**CA:** *Contemporary Authors* (original series), Volumes 1-112
**CANR:** *Contemporary Authors New Revision Series,* Volumes 1-13
**CAP:** *Contemporary Authors Permanent Series,* Volumes 1-2
**CA-R:** *Contemporary Authors* (revised editions), Volumes 1-44
**CLC:** *Contemporary Literary Criticism,* Volumes 1-32
**CLR:** *Children's Literature Review,* Volumes 1-8
**DLB:** *Dictionary of Literary Biography,* Volumes 1-33
**DLB-DS:** *Dictionary of Literary Biography Documentary Series,* Volumes 1-4
**DLB-Y:** *Dictionary of Literary Biography Yearbook,* Volumes 1980-1983
**NCLC:** *Nineteenth-Century Literature Criticism,* Volumes 1-8
**SATA:** *Something about the Author,* Volumes 1-38
**TCLC:** *Twentieth-Century Literary Criticism,* Volumes 1-16
**YABC:** *Yesterday's Authors of Books for Children,* Volumes 1-2

Author Index

Author Index

# CUMULATIVE INDEX TO NATIONALITIES

# CUMULATIVE INDEX TO TITLES

Title Index

Title Index

Title Index

**Title Index**

Title Index